# CAVES AND RITUAL IN MEDIEVAL EUROPE, AD 500–1500

*Edited by*

Knut Andreas Bergsvik and Marion Dowd

OXBOW | books
Oxford & Philadelphia

First published in 2018. Reprinted in 2022 in the United Kingdom by
OXBOW BOOKS
The Old Music Hall, 106–108 Cowley Road, Oxford OX4 1JE

and in the United States by
OXBOW BOOKS
1950 Lawrence Road, Havertown, PA 19083



Paperback Edition: ISBN 978-1-78925-807-3
Digital Edition: ISBN 978-1-78570-833-6 (epub)

A CIP record for this book is available from the British Library

Library of Congress Control Number: 2017956891



Printed in the United Kingdom by Short Run Press, Exeter

For a complete list of Oxbow titles, please contact:

UNITED KINGDOM
Oxbow Books
Telephone (01865) 241249, Fax (01865) 794449
Email: oxbow@oxbowbooks.com
www.oxbowbooks.com

UNITED STATES OF AMERICA
Oxbow Books
Telephone (610) 853-9131, Fax (610) 853-9146
Email: queries@casemateacademic.com
www.casemateacademic.com/oxbow

Oxbow Books is part of the Casemate Group

*Front cover, top: Predjama cave and castle, Slovenia (photo: S. Sykora); bottom: a Sámi grave in a cave on the island of Spildra, Norway (photo: A. Svestad).*
*Back cover: Bracken's Cave on the coast of Rathlin Island, Co. Antrim, Ireland (photo: A. McInroy).*

# Contents

# Preface

It is no small irony that this book has been edited by two prehistorians. In the course of our separate researches into the prehistoric archaeology of caves and rockshelters in Norway and Ireland respectively, we became aware that these natural landscape features contained rich medieval assemblages that represented a wide range of human activities. This data, with few exceptions, had been almost entirely neglected by medieval historians and archaeologists. We soon discovered that the situation was typical of most other countries in Europe. This realisation became the impetus for a session at the 19th Annual Meeting of the European Association of Archaeologists (EAA) in Pilsen, in the Czech Republic, in September 2013 titled, 'The use and perception of caves and rockshelters in early medieval Europe (AD 400–1200)'.

As we had hoped, the session attracted much interest and enthusiasm. A wide range of questions were raised that reflected the poorly understood role of caves in medieval Europe up to that point. For instance, how were caves and rockshelters used and perceived by people during these centuries? Did they serve different functions across different parts of Europe? Were there differences between how local populations versus immigrants engaged with caves? To what extent did local geology influence usage? Were artificial rock-cut caverns used in similar ways to natural caves, and did deep caves function differently to rockshelters? What can be said of those who utilised caves in terms of social status, ethnicity, or gender? Was there a correlation between cave morphology or location and specific ritual or secular activities? Were there differences between Christian and Muslim cave use? How did the conversion to Christianity affect caves that were ritually significant in earlier pagan times? Were caves still used for burial after the conversion to Christianity? How did popular religious practises in caves differ from formal official Christian activities? How did cave churches relate to wider Christian landscapes? What emotions did caves evoke? Methodological questions were also raised: How can we distinguish, archeologically, between ritual and secular functions of caves? How do we deal with legacy data from antiquarian cave investigations? What is the relationship between medieval cave archaeology and how these places are referred to in medieval texts? How can early literary sources be better integrated with the archaeological data? How should folkloristic accounts of caves be used, if at all? Can placenames be useful in understanding medieval cave archaeology?

The discussion that emerged from the 2013 EAA session in Pilsen resulted in a decision to bring together a unique publication on medieval uses and perceptions of caves and rockshelters. The religious and ritual role of caves triggered the greatest interest at the conference and therefore we decided to hone in on this topic in the current volume. This aspect of cave usage cannot be clearly identified in all parts of Europe, however, and thus some of the papers contained herein deal with the evidence for secular rather than ritual activities. We have attempted to include studies from disparate regions across Europe by inviting contributors who were not part of the original conference, thus the studies range geographically from Norway to Malta, and from Ireland to Crimea. The start and end dates of the medieval period, or Middle Ages, across this vast region vary widely and thus we adopted a date range of AD 500–1500 as the most inclusive chronological framework. Together, these papers establish the deeply embedded ritual significance of caves and rockshelters in medieval Europe, sometimes central to religious landscapes and ritual practices, and at other times on the periphery. This book also touches upon a wide variety of themes, and we believe *Caves and Ritual in Medieval Europe, AD 500–1500* will be of interest and relevance to medieval archaeologists and historians, specialists in medieval religious history, as well as to cave archaeologists.

We would like to warmly thank all 22 authors for their willingness to contribute to this volume and for many insightful discussions on the topic of cave use in medieval Europe. The scientific committee of the EAA Annual Meeting in Pilsen is to be thanked for including our session at the conference. We are most grateful to the Department of

Archaeology, History, Cultural Studies and Religion, and the University Museum, at the University of Bergen (Norway); and to CERIS and the School of Science at the Institute of Technology Sligo (Ireland), for generously providing funding towards publication costs. Our sincere thanks are due to Dr. Rory Sherlock for copy-editing the manuscript and Per Viggo Bergsvik who helped with the images. At Oxbow we are grateful to Julie Gardiner and Katie Allen for their help and advice throughout the publication process.

Knut Andreas Bergsvik and Marion Dowd
Bergen and Sligo, August 2017

# List of contributors


*Kristján Ahronsson*
Department of History and Archaeology
Bangor University
Bangor, Gwynedd
LL57 2DG
Wales
k.ahronson@bangor.ac.uk

*Pablo Arias*
Instituto Internacional de Investigaciones Prehistóricas de Cantabria (Universidad de Cantabria-Gobierno de Cantabria-Banco Santander)
Universidad de Cantabria
Av. de los Castros, 52
39005 Santander
Spain
pablo.arias@unican.es

*Ian Armit*
School of Archaeological and Forensic Sciences
University of Bradford
BD7 1DP
United Kingdom
i.armit@bradford.ac.uk

*Knut Andreas Bergsvik*
University Museum
University of Bergen
Haakon Sheteligs plass 10
5007 Bergen
Norway
knut.bergsvik@uib.no

*Keith Buhagiar*
Department of Classics and Archaeology
Faculty of Arts
University of Malta
Msida
Malta
keith.buhagiar@um.edu.mt

*Mario Buhagiar*
Department of History of Art
Faculty of Arts
University of Malta
Msida
Malta
mario.buhagiar@um.edu.mt

*Lindsey Büster*
School of Archaeological and Forensic Sciences
University of Bradford
University of Bradford
BD7 1DP
United Kingdom
l.s.buster1@bradford.ac.uk

*Enrique Gutiérrez Cuenca*
Proyecto Mauranus
Eulogio Fernández Barros, 7-3º A
39600 Maliaño
Spain
egcuenca@gmail.com

*Paolo de Vingo*
Università di Torino
Dipartimento di Studi Storici
Palazzo Venturi
via G. Verdi 25
10124 Torino
Italy
paolo.devingo@unito.it

*Nicolas Dneprovsky*
Izdatel'stvo 'Nevskaya Lavra'
Alexandro-Nevskaya Lavra
Naberezhnaya reki Monastyrki, 1
191167 St. Petersburg
Russian Federation
engarejeli@yandex.ru

*Marion Dowd*
Centre for Environmental Research Innovation and Sustainability (CERIS)
School of Science
Institute of Technology Sligo, Sligo
Ireland
dowd.marion@itsligo.ie

*Francisco Etxeberria*
Facultad de Medicina
Universidad del País Vasco
2014 San Sebastián
Spain
paco.etxeberria@ehu.eus

*Manel Feijoó*
Arqueología-Ciencias de la Antigüedad
Universidad de Zaragoza
Pedro Cerbuna 12
50009 Zaragoza
Spain
txemifeijoo@gmail.com

*José Ángel Hierro Gárate*
Proyecto Mauranus/SCOPE
Grupo Tetuán-Las Canteras 1, 1º B
39004 Santander, Spain
jahierrogarate@gmail.com

*Martin Golec*
Department of History
Faculty of Arts
Palacký University
tř. Svobody 8
Olomouc, 779 00
Czech Republic
golec@seznam.cz

*Lourdes Herrasti*
Sociedad de Ciencias Aranzadi
Alto de Zorroaga s/n
20014 San Sebastián
Spain
lourdes.herrasti@gmail.com

*Alf Tore Hommedal*
University Museum
University of Bergen
Haakon Sheteligs plass 10
5007 Bergen
Norway
alf.tore.hommedal@uib.no

*Roberto Ontañón*
Instituto Internacional de Investigaciones Prehistóricas de Cantabria
Museo de Prehistoria y Arqueología y Cuevas Prehistóricas de Cantabria
Ruiz de Alda, 19
39009 Santander
Spain
ontanon_r@cantabria.es

*Vladimír Peša*
Regional museum and gallery at Česká Lípa
Department of Archaeology
Náměstí Osvobození 297
470 34 Česká Lípa
Czech Republic
pesa@muzeumcl.cz
archvla@centrum.cz

*Agni Prijatelj*
Durham University
Department of Archaeology
South Road
Durham
DH1 3LE
United Kingdom
agni.prijatelj@durham.ac.uk

*Mechthild Schulze-Dörrlamm*
Römisch-Germanisches Zentralmuseum
Leibniz-Forschungsinstitut für Archäologie
Ernst-Ludwig-Pl. 2
55116 Mainz
Germany
schulzedoerrlamm@rgzm.de

*Asgeir Svestad*
Department of Archaeology, History, Religious Studies and Theology
UiT The Arctic University of Norway
P.O. Box 6050 Langnes
9037 Tromsø
Norway
asgeir.svestad@uit.no

*Paloma Uzquiano*
UNED
C/Mediodía Grande 17
28005 Madrid
Spain
p_uzquiano@hotmail.com

*Michał Wojenka*
Institute of Archaeology
Jagiellonian University
Ul. Gołębia 11
31-007 Kraków
Poland
michal.wojenka@uj.edu.pl

# Chapter 1

# Caves and rockshelters in medieval Europe: religious and secular use

*Knut Andreas Bergsvik and Marion Dowd*

Caves have fascinated humans from the earliest times. Though natural geological features, caves can feel supernatural, unpredictable, animated, dangerous but also inviting. From the birth of the discipline of archaeology in the mid-1800s, caves have attracted the attention of antiquarians and archaeologists. Traditionally, caves were targeted in the search for Palaeolithic deposits, not least because the stable underground environment favours the preservation and survival of organic material. The most important early hominid and Palaeolithic finds from around the world, for instance, have come from caves and the subterranean world continues to produce the most scientifically ground-breaking archaeological discoveries (e.g. the Sterkfontein and Rising Star caves of the so-called Cradle of Humankind in South Africa). Not surprisingly, therefore, cave archaeology has become synonymous with the Palaeolithic. Caves and rockshelters, however, are multi-period sites but because of their long use-histories, many Palaeolithic cave excavations involved digging through (and frequently discarding) deep cultural layers from later prehistoric and historic periods. When archaeological material of later date was retrieved from early excavations, it was usually a by-product of Palaeolithic research.

Things have started to change in recent years and younger stratigraphy from caves has begun to attract greater attention. The number of archaeological excavations focussed on later periods of cave activities is increasing, as is the publication of such assemblages and sites (e.g. Dowd 2015, and contributions in edited volumes such as Branigan and Dearne 1992; Tolan-Smith and Bonsall 1997; Kornfeld *et al.* 2007; Bergsvik and Skeates 2012; Moyes 2012; Mavridis and Jensen 2013; Dowd 2016). Overall, studies from across Europe demonstrate a remarkable variation in terms of how caves and rockshelters were used in all archaeological periods, from the Palaeolithic through to recent centuries. The evidence can vary from sites utilised briefly during hunting and fishing expeditions, to caves that were greatly modified and intensively used for ritual activities – and in both instances examples can be found from every archaeological period. Such diversity is also found during the Middle Ages in Europe.

Of all archaeological periods, it could be argued that the medieval usage of caves has been the most overlooked. There are at least two reasons that can partially explain this neglect. Firstly, stratigraphically, the upper layers in cave sediments are more vulnerable to natural or cultural formation processes, disturbance and destruction than deeper, older strata. Frequently antiquarians and archaeologists were to blame for the removal, destruction and/or disposal of medieval cultural layers without any analysis, as de Vingo notes for Italy and southern France (chapter 10). The situation in Poland and the Czech Republic is similar where publications on Palaeolithic material might refer to the discovery of medieval artefacts in caves, but these never made their way into museum collections; at some Polish sites, organic material from upper historic strata was even used for the production of guano (see Wojenka, chapter 14; Peša, chapter 15; and Golec, chapter 16). Prijatelj reports that the medieval use of caves has been almost totally overlooked in Slovenian scholarship (chapter 17), and Hommedal discusses the consequences of the less than ideal excavations of the Selja caves that took place in the mid-1800s (chapter 4). There are also problems with artificial rock-cut 'caves'. As Schulze-Dörrlamm (chapter 13) highlights, the subsequent use of medieval cave churches and monasteries left little for archaeologists to study apart from architectural details, inscriptions and wall paintings.

The second reason which partially explains the scholarly neglect of medieval cave use is that medieval archaeology has had a particular research history distinct from that of earlier periods. The above-ground register of medieval monuments and buildings meant that antiquarian scholars focussed primarily on architecture and art history. Modern scholarship has inherited the antiquarian bias towards medieval monuments erected by the political and clerical élite. When medieval archaeology began to develop as a discipline in the 1950s and 1960s, caves once again fell outside of mainstream research in favour of medieval towns and the extensive cultural layers and excellent preservation often encountered in urban environments (e.g. Graham-Campbell and Valor 2007; Carver and Klápště 2011). Although the focus gradually shifted towards the archaeology of the 'ordinary people' of the Middle Ages and their material culture, it tended to be populations who lived in urban rather than rural areas. Rural communities and the areas where most caves and rockshelters are situated were rarely if ever studied. In later years, contract/commercial (or 'rescue') archaeology did involve archaeological excavations in rural districts across Europe, but caves and rockshelters again passed under the radar as most large-scale projects involved the construction of infrastructure or industries in open agricultural landscapes where caves and rockshelters did not exist as they are a largely karst phenomenon. In summary, up to the present day, caves have scarcely ever featured in medieval research and they play a minor role in overviews and reference works devoted to the period. A quick search for the words 'cave' or 'rockshelter' in the indices of texts on medieval history and archaeology demonstrate this point.

The aim of this collection, then, is to cast some light on what has been an entirely neglected field of research. With contributions from different parts of Europe, the broad range of religious, ritual and secular roles that caves and rockshelters assumed in the lives of medieval people soon becomes apparent. Below we touch upon some of the main themes explored by the various authors, but in the first instance it is necessary to discuss some issues of terminology.

## The difference between a cave, rockshelter and artificial 'cave'

For the purposes of this book, and in line with most cave archaeology research, a cave can be defined as any natural underground cavity in rock that is formed by the solvent and erosive action of surface water as it slowly travels downwards through joints, bedding planes and fissures (Coleman 1965, 84; Fogg and Fogg 2001, 149). Caves occur in permeable and soluble rock types with poor porosity – which in Europe consist primarily of limestone. Composed chiefly of calcite, limestone is dissolved by the slightly acidic carbon dioxide contained in surface water, particularly rainwater and tannic acid from upland bogs. Over millennia, the continuous flow of erosive water combined with gradual chemical erosion cause underground fissures and joints to slowly enlarge, eventually developing into cave chambers and passages (Mitchell and Ryan 2001, 14–15). Caves vary enormously in size and, technically, can include passages just a few metres to many kilometres in length. One of the defining characteristics is the level of natural light. Small caves and the outer parts of large systems are bathed in sunlight by day, giving rise to the term 'daylight zone'. Artificial light is optional for most activities in the daylight zone of caves, hence their attractiveness to humans over millennia for habitation, shelter and craft activities. The 'twilight zone' of a cave occurs deeper inside large cave systems – an area where low light dominates and the levels change (often imperceptibly) according to the time of day or season. The 'dark zone' only occurs in very deep caves where absolutely no natural daylight penetrates. These spaces are permanently shrouded in impenetrable darkness, yet have also attracted human activities – primarily of a ritual nature but also as hideaways. The dark zone is not conducive to habitation because of the need for artificial lightning, low temperatures and dampness. Despite the modern pervasive cliché of prehistoric (and sometimes historic) 'cave-men', archaeology provides little evidence – from any period – that people actually lived in the deepest, darkest extremities of caves. Traces of dwelling and settlement activities (when identified) are typically found in the daylight zone at cave entrances or within rockshelters.

Caves can also develop in coastal areas that are exposed to relentless wave action which, together with large stones, serves to erode and enlarge natural rock fissures and clefts. Sea caves are usually shallower than karst caves, but some are deep and can have twilight zones and occasionally even dark zones (e.g. Bjerck 2012). Rockshelters, as the name suggests, comprise spaces that receive protection from overhanging rock, generally a consequence of the natural erosion of a soft rock face leaving a harder 'lip' of rock jutting out overhead. Yet another site type is the boulder chamber, occurring in isolation or in scree. These natural tumbles of boulders sometimes enclose chambers or shelters. Rockshelters and boulder chambers tend to be fully or partially exposed to daylight but afford some shelter from the elements, and thus have long been utilised for short-term occupation, as animal shelters and occasionally for rituals. Artificial 'caves' include artificially rock-cut subterranean chambers that share similar features to natural caves. Such sites typically occur in regions where natural caves are absent or in hot countries where there is an abundance of soft rock that can be easily dug out. Some artificial caves may originally have been natural caverns that were modified and enlarged beyond recognition, such as certain cave churches or catacombs. Artificial 'caves' also include chambers that were constructed of stone or similar building materials with the intention of mimicking a natural cave.

It has been convincingly argued that caves and rockshelters should not be considered a single category in terms of understanding ritual activities. In Mesoamerican archaeology, for instance, the distinction between caves and rockshelters is based on the presence or absence of a dark zone which significantly influences the nature of ritual activities and also determines whether a site is suitable for ritual or secular purposes (Clottes 2012; Moyes and Brady 2012). The dark zones of caves are particularly well-suited to ritual because of the affordances of seclusion and privacy, and the frequent perception of the subterranean as an otherworldly and timeless environment (see articles in Dowd and Hensey 2016). In this book, Arias *et al.* (chapter 8) deal with funerary rites that took place in the darkness of La Garma cave in northern Spain, and Prijatelj (chapter 17) discusses several examples of sites in Slovenia where darkness played an important role in Late Antique funerary customs.

As darkness is a central requirement for rituals at many cave sites, it is essential to distinguish between caves with a dark zone and sites which at best provide semi-dark environments, such as shallow caves, rockshelters, boulder chambers and some variants of rock-cut 'caves'. Unfortunately, the quality and quantity of light is seldom specified in site reports and publications (Taçon *et al.* 2012, 136), and rarely in this publication – which means that further work is required of archaeologists in considering this vital aspect of caves. Darkness is, however, not the only element of the subterranean that enhances or accommodates ritual activity. Factors such the stable and unchanging character of sites, the protection offered by caves and rockshelters, and occasionally restricted accessibility are considered important by many scholars (e.g. Bradley 2000; Dowd 2015). Numerous studies from around the world illustrate that rituals have taken place in the daylight zones of caves and rockshelters (e.g. Lewis-Williams and Dowson 1990; Layton 1992; Baird *et al.* 2011; Prufer and Prufer 2012), and this book provides even more examples, particularly from northern Europe.

## Chronology and the Middle Ages

Depending on different regional circumstances, there is great variety as to when the Middle Ages began depending on historic events and processes across Europe (Høiris and Ingesman 2010). Similarly, the end of the Middle Ages has been set as early as the mid-thirteenth century and as late as the early sixteenth century (Hoyt 1966, 1). This book covers various cultural regions in Europe where different date ranges are relevant. In Crimea many scholars argue for a commencement date in the 5th century. In Ireland, for instance, the 'early medieval' period commences with the introduction of Christianity about AD 400 and ends with the Anglo-Normal invasion of 1169, while in much of southern, western and central Europe the collapse of the Western Roman Empire in AD 476 is regarded as a key event in defining the origins of the Middle Ages. In some of the countries discussed in this book – such as Spain, Italy, France, Germany, the Czech Republic and Poland – AD 500 is conveniently set as a start date for the Middle Ages, while *c.* AD 600 is relevant to Malta, Great Britain and Slovenia. Further north, the conversion to Christianity is again considered a defining milestone and approximately AD 1000 marks the beginning of the Middle Ages in Norway and Iceland.

Because the medieval period is thus considered by archaeologists and historians to begin and end at different times in different countries, in this book we have adopted the most inclusive chronological timeframe possible of AD 500–1500. We have sought *not* to standardise the terms used for this chronological period, thus in some countries the timeframe in question incorporates both the 'early medieval' and 'high medieval' periods (e.g. Ireland), while elsewhere scholars would use the term 'Middle Ages' (e.g. Czech Republic). The majority of the papers here consider activities at caves and rockshelters within the timeframe of AD 500–1500 (often more restricted than this broad timeframe); however, some chapters also expand into preceding and succeeding periods as some of the patterns that occur during the Middle Ages originated before this period or extended beyond it. Thus, de Vingo (chapter 10), M. Buhagiar (chapter 11) and Prijatelj (chapter 17) all consider Antique (Roman) use of caves in Italy/France, Malta and Slovenia respectively, while Prijatelj (chapter 17) and Dowd (chapter 7) explore aspects of post-medieval cave use. Svestad adopts a long durée approach covering the period *c.* 900 BC–AD 1700.

One of our primary aims has been to demonstrate the widespread and persistent phenomenon of religious/ritual cave use in medieval times across widely disparate regions of Europe, addressing Christian activities but also how caves and rockshelters were perceived and used by people from other religious backgrounds. Thus, this volume includes articles on Sámi and Norse rituals from Norway (Svestad, chapter 2; Bergsvik, chapter 3), a Pictish site in Scotland (Büster and Armit, chapter 5), and Muslim sites in Iberia (Feijó, chapter 9).

## Non-ritual use of caves and rockshelters

Though caves have long been associated with religious and ritual usage from earliest prehistory, far more prevalent is the use of caves to fulfil a wide range of secular and practical functions such as domestic occupation, shelter, animal pens, storage, workshops and hideouts – leading Straus (1997) to coin the phrase 'convenient cavities'. In addressing the full range of activities in caves in Roman Britain (Branigan and Dearne 1992), in Ireland in historic times (Dowd 2015), and in the Czech Republic in modern times (Peša 2013), it is clear that ritual activities are but a minor component of a much wider range of predominantly practical functions.

Secular cave usage was also common during the medieval period, and several of the contributions in this volume concentrate either entirely or partially on this aspect – typically because there is a dearth of evidence for any ritual or religious activities in caves in these regions. In his contribution on caves in the Ligurian-Piedmontese region of Italy, de Vingo (chapter 10) discusses cave sites that were occupied after the collapse of the Western Roman Empire, from the fifth to the seventh centuries. He argues that defence at these cave dwellings was probably an important 'adjustment' to new political realities after the security of Rome had vanished. The rich pottery assemblages from these caves indicate they were not occupied sporadically as hideouts, but rather on a more long-term basis. The sites were located centrally to international trading routes and were also conveniently positioned for the economic exploitation of resources located within the surrounding hills and highlands. The economic importance of caves and rockshelters is also underlined by Prijatelj (chapter 17) who argues that some of the Late Antique and medieval caves – even if used episodically – may have been integrated into transhumance networks in the eastern Adriatic, and were initially facilitated by the Romans to resolve regional conflicts of interest. The use of caves in the southern part of Poland during the thirteenth and fourteenth centuries can also be linked primarily to an unstable political background – identified by Wojenka (chapter 14) in the form of a 'military horizon' in some caves. He associates the discovery of military artefacts with the struggle for control over the territory around Kraków and the use of caves as ready-made places of refuge by soldiers. Evidence for counterfeiting and smithing in caves also occurs in this region, sometimes in association with medieval castles. In the Czech Republic, Peša (chapter 15) demonstrates the association between caves and fortified settlements in the early Middle Ages, and in Slovenia Prijatelj (chapter 17) illustrates the relationship between caves and castles in late medieval times. Peša presents evidence of tar production and a counterfeiter's workshop within caves. Similar practices are documented from medieval phases of the famous Bull Rock Cave in the Moravian Karst (Golec, chapter 16). Workshop activities are also apparent in Norwegian caves that were located some distance from contemporary settlements, often in relation to hunting and fishing expeditions (Bergsvik, chapter 3).

The majority of the sites mentioned above are natural caves or rockshelters, some of which were partially modified, but K. Buhagiar's contribution (chapter 12) deals specifically with artificial caves and the medieval Maltese phenomenon of fertile agricultural *giardini* where rock-cut settlements were located in cliff faces overlooking water galleries. The galleries themselves were also artificially excavated to ensure a regular supply of water for gardens and fields. Many caves utilised between the fifth and twelfth centuries in Iberia were also rock-cut (Feijó, chapter 9). These were situated along major river valleys and were used for a number of different purposes, such as occupation, barns, cellars, and for defence. Communities, both Christian and Muslim, employed caves to fulfil a multitude of purposes, including as hermitages.

A problem discussed explicitly by Feijó is that it is sometimes difficult to determine whether caves were occupied for religious/ritual reasons or served as domestic dwellings. Here he touches upon a theme that is clearly relevant for many of the other chapters in this volume. It is often difficult to disentangle and recognise artefacts that represent ritual deposits if they occur within caves that also contain evidence of residential and/or craft/industrial activities, not least when dealing with data from old excavations where stratigraphic and contextual details are poor. Other material from such sites – for instance, faunal remains and pottery – that may be contemporary with potential votive deposits often casts doubt on any ritual interpretation thereby typically resulting in a secular interpretation. Of course, secular and ritual activities are not necessarily mutually exclusive, as many scholars have discussed: the dichotomy between sacred and profane is a modern (mis)conception and archaeologists would serve the data better by allowing for a greater integration of ritual with other aspects of life (e.g. Brück 1999; Bradley 2005). Bradley (2005, 34) points out that ritual is a process 'by which certain actions gain an added emphasis through particular kinds of performance'. The problem is to identify actions as rituals, particularly if they took place within a domestic sphere or industrial site (caves or otherwise), because not all repeated actions and performances at such places were necessarily ritual in character.

## Non-Christian rituals

At some of the cave and rockshelter sites discussed in this volume, evidence for non-Christian ritual practices and deposition is quite clear. In his contribution on the funerary sites of the Sámi – the indigenous population of Fenno-Scandinavia, Svestad (chapter 2) contends that burials are seldom found in caves but rather in scree under large stones, sites that could be considered boulder chambers. This burial tradition can be dated from *c.* 800 BC until the Sámi were Christianised around AD 1700. The custom is closely related to the Sámi concept that the world of the dead is situated beneath the world of the living. The bear held a special position in Sámi religion and many were buried in a similar fashion to humans. By hibernating in caves, the bear regularly moves between the two realms and, according to Svestad, these metaphorical qualities strengthen the understanding of the relationship between life and death amongst the Sámi. In western Norway, shallow caves and rockshelters were used for rituals by local Norse populations from *c.* AD 550 onwards (Bergsvik, chapter 3). The evidence consists of a small number of burials, but primarily sites where special artefacts (e.g. combs, fibulae, weapons) were deliberately deposited. Such rituals probably reflect beliefs in caves and rockshelters as dwellings for supernatural beings, including giants, land spirits and dwarfs. These beliefs are well-documented in medieval Norse mythology and seem to have discouraged human occupation, not only during the non-Christian Viking period but also throughout the Middle Ages. In Germany, several caves contain non-Christian burials and occasionally deposits of 'special' artefacts. Keys – possibly worn as amulets – have been found in two different caves and can probably be regarded as votive deposits (Schulze-Dörrlamm, chapter 13). Büster and Armit (chapter 5) discuss the Scottish Pictish site of Sculptor's Cave which was used for mortuary rituals between the Late Bronze Age and the Roman Age. The entrance walls were later carved with Pictish symbols from the sixth to ninth centuries, with engravings of fish, flowers, crescents, horseshoes, ovals and geometric designs. No other traces of human occupation can be linked to this period of activity in Sculptor's Cave, and the authors argue that the symbols may have been carved to mark, or perhaps even seal, an important passage to the underworld, a place that for a long time had been connected to the dead and the ancestors.

## The co-existence of non-Christian and Christian cave rituals

In some regions of Europe, 'pagan' or non-Christian rituals continued in tandem with Christian rites long after the conversion to Christianity. For example, Estonia was only Christianised in 1208–1227 and pre-Christian traditions continued there until the nineteenth century including offerings to sacred natural places such as groves, trees, hills, stones and springs (Valk 2003) (see Ersgård (2002) for similar traditions in southern Sweden). In Germany, non-Christian cultic activities prevailed long after Christianity was made the official religion (Schulze-Dörrlamm, chapter 13). According to Peša (chapter 15), intact but empty vessels from the late Middle Ages have been found in several caves and rockshelters in the Czech Republic, possibly representing votive offerings. Golec (chapter 16) draws attention to Czech documentary accounts of Slavic gods – perhaps the Perun/Svantovit – that were worshipped in the eleventh and twelfth centuries. Prijatelj (chapter 17) presents similar evidence from caves in Slovenia where folkloric accounts claim that supernatural forces associated with fertility and death – personified by the female counterparts *vile* and *babe* – were worshipped in Christianised areas. In Irish folklore, caves were one location where supernatural females tempted and challenged mortal males (Dowd 2015, 208 ff), while in Norway popular belief in 'underground people' and beautiful female temptresses was common in rural areas up to the nineteenth century (Holm 1999).

Non-Christian beliefs and practices were often tolerated by the church (e.g. Thunmark-Nylén 1989), but not always. According to Norwegian and Icelandic medieval literary sources, the Church viewed the continuity of non-Christian beliefs and practices as problematic and took measures to oppress them (Bergsvik, chapter 3). This seems to have been the case during the fourth century in many parts of the late Roman provinces where cave cults of Mithras, in particular, were targeted (Clauss 2000). According to Prijatelj (chapter 17), Christian intolerance to non-Christian rituals sometimes led to the blocking of caves. As suggested by Büster and Armit (chapter 5), the late Pictish crosses in Sculptor's Cave may have served to Christianise this non-Christian mortuary cave. Besides the destruction of sites and/or prohibiting their usage, another strategy employed by early Christians was to take over non-Christian ritual sites and transform them into Christian sacred places. This 'continuity of cult' theme is common to many parts of Europe and a prominent example is the second century artificial cave of Mithreaum in Rome, which was integrated into the early medieval basilica of San Clemente (Schulze-Dörrlamm 2008). Another is the church and memorial stone at Jelling, Denmark, both of which were erected by King Harald Bluetooth in close proximity to his father's and mother's pagan burial monuments. This took place during the conversion to Christianity in the mid-900s AD (Jensen 2004, 371–381). In Malta, M. Buhagiar (chapter 11) illustrates how Late Antique sanctuaries continued as burial sites into Christian times, while in western Norway, Hommedal (chapter 4) suggests that the cave of St Sunnifa may have been established over a much older Norse ritual site. Often, however, the archaeological evidence for continuity of cult activity is weak. In Germany, the Christian site of Externsteine was believed to have been a pre-Christian ritual site but Schulze-Dörrlamm (chapter 13) finds little evidence to verify this. Similarly, Dowd (chapter 7) challenges the popular assumption that holy wells revered as part of popular Catholic religious practises were originally non-Christian sacred wells as there is effectively no material remains to support this contention.

## Christianity and caves

In spite of Church efforts to prohibit non-Christian cave cults, caves and rockshelters were frequently appropriated for Christian rituals – as demonstrated by the majority of papers in this volume. The question of why caves were used in this fashion, and what the underlying theological foundations were, are worth considering. In the first instance, caves were directly associated with the life of Jesus. The Gospels of Luke and Matthew refer to the birth of Jesus occurring in a stable and house respectively, but some third century sources contend he was born in a cave. The Gospels of Matthew, Mark and Luke mention that, following his death, the body of Jesus was placed in a rock-cut grave. These cave-related events are monumentalised by the basilica in Bethlehem and the Holy Sepulchre in Jerusalem (Feijó, chapter 9; Schulze-Dörrlamm 2008, 545). John the Apostle is supposed to have received visions for the Book of Revelation in a cave on the island of Patmos, Greece (Boxall 2010, 23). Caves were also closely connected to early Christian eremitic monasticism. The Egyptian St Anthony the Great, considered one of the first Christian hermits, retreated for a time to a cave while fighting the demons that plagued him, and caves in remote areas were later considered important sites for spiritual retreat (e.g. Endsjø 2008). Finally, there is the prevalent idea that evil forces (often dragons) reside deep inside caves – a concept found in non-Christian myths (e.g. Ogden 2013); and in Christianity, figures such as St George and St Michael slay dragons that in some legends emerge from caves. The role of the Archangel Michael was to lead God's army against Satan and to guard the boundary between good and evil. According to legend, Michael appeared to the Bishop of Sipontum close to a cave at Monte Gargano, Italy in AD 492. The site subsequently became a major religious focus (Arnold 2000).

Many churches dedicated to the Archangel Michael were cave churches or churches containing crypts that represented caves (e.g. Steinsland 1997). This reflected theological concerns about the topographic location of hell. In the latter part of the Middle Ages the underworld was specifically associated with hell – an idea that Dante Alighieri coherently developed in his book *Divina Comedia* of 1320. The medieval Christian relationship to caves was complex and ambiguous. On the one hand, crucial events in the New Testament took place in caves, which made them powerful reference points or symbols in the belief system. However, caves were also considered entrances to the underworld: places linked to dragons, to the devil and to hell. The symbolic significance of this particular boundary was equally great, because caves could then be used to mobilise warriors – such as St Michael – to the cause of Christianity.

Artificial rock-cut churches and monasteries are a specific category of Christian site. This phenomenon characterises early (mainly Coptic and Byzantine) Christianity in many regions, and famous examples outside Europe include Lalibela in Ethiopia, Petra in Jordan, and Cappadocia in Turkey. Several rock-cut churches are discussed in the present volume. Dneprovskij (chapter 18) deals exclusively with three churches cut into limestone formations close to the town of Eski-Kermen in Crimea during the Byzantine period. He provides a detailed analysis of the liturgical arrangement as well as the inscriptions and frescoes in the 'Cave of the Three Horsemen'. According to Dneprovskij, the three warriors symbolised salvation of the soul of a deceased prominent inhabitant of Eski-Kermen. M. Buhagiar (chapter 11) similarly explores rock-cut cave sanctuaries in Malta, a country more famous for its Bronze Age rock-cut hypogea (e.g. Skeates 2010), but a variety of rock-cut tombs and miniature catacombs were also common from late Roman times through to the Christian Middle Ages and until the Muslim conquest of AD 870. M. Buhagiar explores the architecture, decorative features and practices such as funerary feasting at the Maltese sites and relates these to various cultural influences from other parts of the Mediterranean. In another paper dedicated to Malta, K. Buhagiar (chapter 12) considers the period after the Norman conquest of AD 1127, and how the layout and decorative elements of cave churches reflect cultural influences and interaction with the neighbouring island of Sicily. Both urban and rural cave churches are known and, as he posits, 'cave churches must have been a landmark within the late medieval Maltese landscape'. Most of these rural churches were parish churches and K. Buhagiar finds no support for the theory that some had been part of Greek monastic establishments, as is the case in other parts of the Mediterranean region.

In western and northern Europe, caves and cave churches were often associated with hermits, monasteries and saints during the Middle Ages. Feijó (chapter 9) argues that several artificial caves in the Iberian Peninsula were Christian hermitages – though it is sometimes difficult to distinguish between domestic cave dwellings and caves that were cut and occupied for religious purposes. In this context, it is also worth noting that a primary symbol for the *reconquista* of the Iberian Peninsula is Cueva Santa, a cave in Asturias, northern Spain (Schulze-Dörrlamm 2008). Feijó also discusses rock-cut caves that were used by Muslims in Islamic Iberia. Similar to the Christian evidence, many caves served a secular function but some related to Muslim eremitism. Caves were central to Islamic beliefs primarily because the first revelation to the Prophet Muhammad occurred in a cave, and because he reputedly hid in a cave on his flight from Mecca to Medina (Feijó, chapter 9). In

Germany, tradition records that hermits and missionaries occupied caves in the early Middle Ages from around AD 600, but there is little corresponding archaeological evidence (Schulze-Dörrlamm, chapter 13). Stronger evidence for cave eremites is found from the eleventh to fifteenth centuries when some rock-cut caves were developed into monasteries (e.g. the Felseneremitage in Bad Kreuznach) and churches (e.g. the Steinkirche in the Harz Mountains). Similarly, there are folkloric accounts referring to hermits and saints occupying caves in Poland, the Czech Republic and Slovenia (chapters 14, 15 and 17 respectively), but again, the archaeological evidence is regrettably weak. In the case of the Czech Republic and Slovakia, folklore and documentary sources indicate that Christian hermits (later to become saints) drawn from society's élite occupied caves as early as the ninth century. Peša (chapter 15) explains that these caves were later incorporated into monastic foundations and became cultic centres during the High Middle Ages. In Ireland, many small caves located close to, or within, early medieval or high medieval ecclesiastical complexes are also associated with saints in folklore, and occasionally in medieval manuscripts. However, as with other parts of Europe, there is no concrete archaeological evidence to indicate that holy men ever occupied caves, but equally, none of the pertinent sites have been archaeologically excavated (Dowd, chapter 7).

A core element of early Christian eremitism and monasticism is the idea of spiritual retreat and voluntary isolation from society. It appears from the continental evidence, however, that isolation may not always have been important or viable. The problem of isolation is specifically dealt with by Ahronsson in his contribution on early Christian cave sites in Scotland and Iceland (chapter 6). Rather than being removed from society, Ahronsson argues that Scottish hermits and saints were only temporarily separated from the wider population. He compares Scottish natural caves that were inscribed with crosses, probably during the 6th to 9th centuries, with artificial rock-cut caves that boast similar engravings in southern Iceland. He argues that the latter sites relate to early Christian communities – either Scottish or Irish, thus pre-dating the Norse colonisation of Iceland that occurred around AD 870. If this is the case, it could be argued that these early Christians were indeed greatly isolated from their places of origin. Another Irish connection is found in western Norway (Hommedal, chapter 4). According to Norwegian legend, the Irish Christian princess Sunnifa fled from her heathen husband-to-be and landed on the island of Selja. She hid from the local population in a natural cave but was subsequently killed when the cave collapsed. The legend continues that King Olaf Tryggvason discovered her bones at the cave in the late 900s, which led to the sanctification of Sunnifa and the establishment of a cave sanctuary – including significant modification of the natural cave – as part of the initial Christianisation of Norway. Churches and a monastery were also erected on this remote island and it became an important pilgrimage site and even an Episcopal seat until the seat and St Sunnifa's relics were moved to the town of Bergen on the mainland sometime around the late eleventh century.

Though antiquarians and archaeologists traditionally assumed that burials found in caves date to prehistoric times, there is now growing evidence for the continued use of caves as burial spaces across medieval Europe. This may simply reflect the fact that caves were 'convenient cavities' and places to hastily dispose of diseased corpses or those who died by violent means. However, it may also reveal the continuation of non-Christian practises, even in Christianised regions; or the religious importance of a cave which gave it elevated status as a burial site; or specific beliefs systems and superstitions that precluded burial in a typical Christian manner (e.g. chapters 2, 3, 4, 11, 17). Such 'deviant' burials in caves are an aspect of some Christianised regions. Arias and colleagues (chapter 8) discuss the skeletons of five individuals found deep inside the dark cave of La Garma close to Santander in northern Spain, deposited there in the seventh-eighth centuries. Skulls had been deliberately smashed and other unusual features distinguished the burial rites as non-normative. A belt buckle of Visigothic type indicate that these were local Christians, but for some reason they had been given burials that deviated from the norm. The nature or circumstances of their lives or deaths may have been relevant, and the authors suggest the cave was used for interment because of a fear that the dead would return to disturb the living.

## Final thoughts

The primary impetus for the compilation of this volume was to begin a consideration of the role of caves as religious and ritual foci in medieval landscapes across Europe. The broad spread of papers testifies that this was not a regional phenomenon, nor was it associated only with the dominant religious tradition of Christianity. An assumption that caves were used only by low status or liminal individuals in medieval times ties in with popular and misleading perceptions of 'cavemen', but the archaeological and documentary evidence illustrates that caves were used by individuals of widely different social ranking. For instance, the continental data suggest that cave-dwelling Christian hermits and saints were often high-status individuals who would have been regarded with reverence by lay populations. The counterfeiting materials found in certain other caves imply use by skilled craftworkers closely linked to adjacent castles and the élite. Nonetheless, across Europe ordinary domestic occupation of caves was probably usually associated with low status individuals, the dispossessed or poor farmers. However, we have also seen evidence for military and religious occupation of caves and thus each instance of medieval cave occupation needs to be assessed on an individual basis. Close examination of the artefacts, ecofacts, wall engravings and modifications to cave interiors plays an important role in disentangling the nature of cave occupation and cave occupants. In terms of gender and age biases, there is evidence that some caves were used specifically by adult males, for example, in the aforementioned eremitic and military contexts. So far, however, we have little evidence from the papers contained in this book of caves associated specifically with women or with children. In many instances, of course, caves were occupied and used by whole families and all members of the community.

It is abundantly clear that the subterranean world continued to have agency and significance in the period AD 500–1500. If this book serves to begin a conversation about the role of caves and rockshelters in medieval Europe, and specifically in a religious, funerary and ritual context, then it will have fulfilled our origin aim.

## References


Arnold, J.C., 2000. Arcadia becomes Jerusalem: angelic caverns and shrine conversion at Monte Gargano. *Speculum* 75(3), 567–588.

Baird, D., Carruthers, D., Fairbairn, A. and Pearson, J., 2011. Ritual in the landscape: Evidence from Pınarbaşı in the seventh-millennium cal BC Konya Plain. *Antiquity* 85(328), 380–394.

Bergsvik, K.A. and Skeates, R., eds., 2012. *Caves in Context. The Cultural Significance of Caves and Rockshelters in Europe*. Oxford: Oxbow Books.

Bjerck, H.B., 2012. On the outer fringe of the human world: phenomenological perspectives on anthropomorphic cave paintings in Norway. *In*: K.A. Bergsvik and R. Skeates, eds. *Caves in Context. The Cultural Significance of Caves and Rockshelters in Europe*. Oxford: Oxbow Books, 48–64.

Boxall, I., 2010. Reading the Apocalypse on the island of Patmos. *Scripture Bulletin* XL(1), 22–33.

Bradley, R., 2000. *An Archaeology of Natural Places*. London: Routledge.

Bradley, R., 2005. *Ritual and Domestic Life in Prehistoric Europe*. London: Routledge.

Branigan, K. and Dearne, M.J., eds., 1992. *Romano-British Cavemen. Cave Use in Roman Britain*. Oxbow Monograph 19. Oxford: Oxbow Books.

Brück, J., 1999. Ritual and rationality: some problems of interpretation in European archaeology. *European Journal of Archaeology* 2(3), 313–343.

Carver, M. and Klápště, J., eds., 2011. *The Archaeology of Medieval Europe. Vol. 2. Twelfth to Sixteenth Centuries AD*. Aarhus: Aarhus University Press.

Clauss, M., 2000. *The Roman Cult of Mithras: The God and his Mysteries*. Edinburgh: Edinburgh University Press.

Clottes, J., 2012. Ritual cave use in European Paleolithic sites. *In*: H. Moyes, ed. *Sacred Darkness. A Global Perspective on the Ritual Use of Caves*. Boulder, CO: University Press of Colorado, 15–26.

Coleman, J.C., 1965. *The Caves of Ireland*. Tralee: Anvil Books.

Dowd, M., 2015. *The Archaeology of Caves in Ireland*. Oxford: Oxbow Books.

Dowd, M., ed., 2016. *Underground Archaeology. Studies on Human Bones and Artefacts from Ireland's Caves*. Oxford: Oxbow Books.

Dowd, M. and Hensey, R., eds., 2016. *The Archaeology of Darkness*. Oxford: Oxbow Books.

Endsjø, D.Ø., 2008. *Primordial Landcapes, Incorruptible Bodies. Desert Ascetism and the Christian Appropriation of Greek Ideas on Geography, Bodies and Immortality*. New York: Peter Lang.

Ersgård, L., 2002. Vässtannortjörn. *In*: K. Jennbert, A. Andrén, and C. Raudevere, eds. *Plats och praxis. Studier av nordisk förkriten ritual*. Lund: Nordic Academic Press, 287–297.

Fogg, P. and Fogg, T., 2001. *Beneath Our Feet: The Caves and Limestone Scenery of the North of Ireland*. Belfast: Environment and Heritage Service.

Graham-Campbell, J. and Valor, M., eds., 2007. *The Archaeology of Medieval Europe. Vol. 1. Eighth to Twelfth centuries AD*. Aarhus: Aarhus University Press.

Holm, I., 1999. Clearence cairns: the farmers' and the archaeologists' views. *In*: A. Gazin-Schwartz and C.J. Holtorf, eds. *Archaeology and Folklore*. London and New York: Routledge, 214–227.

Hoyt, R.S., 1966. *Europe in the Middle Ages*. 2nd ed. New York: Harcourt, Brace & World.

Høiris, O. and Ingesman, P., 2010. Indledning. *In*: O. Høiris and P. Ingesman, eds. *Middelalderens verden. Verdensbilledet, tænkningen, rummet og religionen*. Aarhus: Aarhus Universitetsforlag, 11–27.

Jensen, J., 2004. *Danmarks Oldtid. Yngre jernalder og vikingetid 400–1050 e.Kr*. Copenhagen: Gyldendal.

Kornfeld, M., Vasil'ev, S., and Miotti, L., eds., 2007. *On Shelter's Ledge: Histories, Theories and Methods of Rockshelter Research*. BAR International Series 1655. Oxford: British Archaeological Reports.

Layton, R., 1992. *Australian Rock Art. A New Synthesis*. Cambridge: Cambridge University Press.

Lewis-Williams, J.D. and Dowson, T., 1990. Through the veil: San rock paintings and the rock face. *South African Archaeological Bulletin* 45, 5–16.

Mavridis, F. and Jensen, J.T., eds., 2013. *Stable Places and Changing Perceptions: Cave Archaeology in Greece*. BAR International Series 2558. Oxford: Archaeopress.

Mitchell, F. and Ryan, M., 2001. *Reading the Irish Landscape*. Dublin: Town House and Country House.

Moyes, H., ed., 2012. *Sacred Darkness. A Global Perspective on the Ritual Use of Caves*. Boulder, CO: University Press of Colorado.

Moyes, H. and Brady, J.E., 2012. Caves as sacred spaces in Mesoamerica. *In*: H. Moyes, ed. *Sacred Darkness. A Global Perspective on the Ritual Use of Caves*. Boulder, CO: University Press of Colorado, 151–170.

Ogden, D., 2013. *Dragons, Serpents, and Slayers in the Classical and Early Christian Worlds*. Oxford: Oxford University Press.

Peša, V., 2013. Der neuzeitliche Mensch in der Höhle: Die Speläoantropologie als archäologische Quelle. *Památky Archeologické* 104, 231–316.

Prufer, O.H. and Prufer, K.M., 2012. Ceremonial use of caves and rockshelters in Ohio. *In*: H. Moyes, ed. *Sacred Darkness.*

*A Global Perspective on the Ritual Use of Caves*. Boulder, CO: University Press of Colorado, 225–235.

Schulze-Dörrlamm, M., 2008. Zur Nutzung von Höhlen in der christlichen Welt des frühen Mittelalters (7.–10. Jahrhundert) *Jahrbuch des Römisch-Germanischen Zentramuseums Mainz* 55, 529–675.

Skeates, R., 2010. *An Archaeology of the Senses. Prehistoric Malta*. Oxford: Oxford University Press.

Steinsland, G., 1997. Hulehelligdommen på Selja. På leiting etter førkristne spor - en vandring i myter, makter og tegn. *In*: M. Rindal, ed. *Selja – heilag stad i 1000 år*. Oslo: Universitetsforlaget, 11–33.

Straus, L. G., 1997. Convenient Cavities: Some Human Uses of Caves and Rockshelters. *In*: C. Bonsall and C. Tolan-Smith, eds. *The Human Use of Caves*. Oxford: Arcaheopress, 1–8.

Taçon, P.S.C., Brennan, W., Kelleher, M. and Pross, D., 2012. Differential Australian cave and rockshelter use during the Peistocene and Holocene. *In*: H. Moyes ed. *Sacred Darkness. A Global Perspective on the Ritual Use of Caves*. Boulder, CO: University Press of Colorado, 135–148.

Thunmark-Nylén, L., 1989. Samfund och tro på religionsskiftets Gotland. *In*: A. Andrén, ed. *Medeltidens födelse*. Lund: Gyllenstjernska Krapperupstiftelsen, 213–232.

Tolan-Smith, C. and Bonsall, C., 1997. The human use of caves. *In*: C. Bonsall and C. Tolan-Smith, eds. *The Human Use of Caves*. Oxford: Archaeopress, 217–218.

Valk, H., 2003. Christianization in Estonia: a process of dual faith and syncretism. *In*: M. Carver, ed. *The Cross Goes North. Process of Conversion in Northern Europe, AD 300–1300*. Woodbridge: York Medieval Press, 571–579.

# Part I
# Northwestern Europe

# Chapter 2

# Entering other realms: Sámi burials in natural rock cavities and caves in northern Fenno-Scandinavia between 900 BC and AD 1700

*Asgeir Svestad*

*In the northernmost areas of Fenno-Scandinavia, cavities in the landscape have been utilised for various purposes, including ritual activities, since the Mesolithic (Bjerck 2012). In the first millennium AD, these environments served as burial places for the Sámi, the indigenous population of Fenno-Scandinavia. The location and deposition of burials in cavities demonstrate an intimate relation with Sámi religious concepts and practices documented from the seventeenth and eighteenth centuries. Burials in cavities seem to offer particular prerequisites with regard to entering other realms. Furthermore, they demonstrate intimate relations with another kind of burial, namely, bear graves. The bear was considered the most sacred animal of the Sámi. There is reason to believe that the sacredness of the bear affected Sámi concepts of the dead and mortuary rituals in the distant past. This is particularly evident with regard to burials and rituals associated with cavities.*

## Introduction

Sámi burials in cavities or crevices in rock occur in graves most commonly known as 'scree and rock graves' (Schanche 2000; Hansen and Olsen 2014). These graves most typically appear in the Varanger area in Finnmark, northern Norway as constructed chambers covered with stone slabs on rocky beaches; they demonstrate a heterogeneous morphology, which include graves in natural cavities and other contexts. In general, scree and rock graves date from 900 BC to AD 1700, which includes the Late Bronze Age (1100–500 BC) or late Early Metal Age (1000/900 BC–BC/AD), the Iron Age (500 BC–AD 1000), the medieval period (*c.* AD 1000–1520), and early modern period (*c.* AD 1520–1870), all according to Nordic chronology (Helle 2003; see also Edgren and Törnblom 1993; Baudou 1995; Solberg 2000; Hansen and Olsen 2014). This makes the Sámi pre-Christian burial customs one of the longest surviving burial traditions in Europe spanning almost three millennia. During this vast period, major changes took place in Fenno-Scandinavia, of which Sámi graves comprise a major source of knowledge regarding the history, religion, and religious practice of the Sámi.

While Christianisation took place between *c.* AD 1000 and 1250 in most of Fenno-Scandinavia, it did not occur until later amongst the Sámi, that is, AD 1550–1750. However, pre-Christian Sámi practices and beliefs continued to exist well into the twentieth century, constituting a unique historical and cultural situation regarding the investigation of Sámi religion and religious practices (see, for example, Manker 1961; Storå 1971; Svestad 2011). The existence of numerous written accounts from the final stages of Sámi religion permits a long-term investigation of continuity and change in Sámi religion and religious practices, albeit not without certain limitations, as discussed later in this chapter.

Burial in natural cavities has not been given particular attention in the investigation of Sámi graves and burial customs. Cavities with burials are mostly found under 'loose' blocks or boulders (often in scree), occasionally under bedrock and rockshelters, or in natural caves. In general, these graves seem to conform to general features, ritual practices, and religious concepts (Schanche 2000). An investigation in 2014 of a grave of this kind in Skjellesvik in northern Norway (see below) altered the chronology and knowledge of Sámi graves. Hence, graves in cavities demonstrate particular features that in a conspicuous way illuminate Sámi concepts and rituals concerning death and the dead. These features become further evident when compared with bear graves, another unique Fenno-Scandinavian Sámi grave type, which dates from *c.* AD 200 to 1700/1800.

The bear was a significant animal to Arctic peoples in prehistoric times, as can be seen from the many Fenno-Scandinavian rock carvings, such as the famous examples at Alta in Finnmark that include numerous scenes of humans hunting bears in dens (e.g. Gjerde 2010; Helskog 2012, 2014) (Fig. 2.1). The ethnic affiliation of these carvings is unclear, although it is very likely that they were made by the ancestors of those later known as Sámi. Further, the bear is the second most portrayed animal on Sámi shaman drums after the reindeer (Kjellström and Rydving 1988, 26). Bear ceremonies – or the bear cult that relates to bear graves – are not only known from the Sámi but exist among Finns and other northern peoples further east on the Eurasian continent and elsewhere in the circumpolar region (e.g. Hallowell 1924; Holmberg 1926; Itkonen 1946; Edsman 1994). Sámi bear graves are not identical to Sámi human graves, but the former demonstrate a heterogeneous morphological similarity to the latter. Bear graves also reflect crucial aspects of Sámi burial customs and, it seems, burials in cavities in particular.

This chapter will examine Sámi graves in cavities and the affiliated rituals in comparison with bear graves, within the time span covered by volume. The chapter begins with a brief presentation of Sámi religion and religious practices as reflected in written accounts, with particular attention to concepts of the dead, the afterlife, and the bear cult. Following this, I will outline the general features of Sámi burial customs, before turning to graves in cavities in particular. Finally, the discussion will attempt to synthesise the different aspects touched upon in this chapter.

*Figure 2.1: Rock carving of bear hunt scene (approximately 25cm long) at Kåfjord in Alta, north Norway. Photo: K. Tansem, World Heritage Rock Art Centre – Alta Museum © 2004.*

## Sámi cosmology, religious concepts and rituals in the written accounts

Evidence concerning Sámi pre-Christian religious practices has survived from written accounts recorded by missionaries and priests who sought to convert the Sámi during the seventeenth and eighteenth centuries. These accounts have been the subject of comprehensive studies on Sámi religion within the history of religion and affiliated disciplines (e.g. Fritzner 1877; Itkonen 1946; Pettersson 1957; Mebius 1968, 1972; Storå 1971; Bäckman 1975; Bäckman and Hultkrantz 1978; Rydving 1995; Pentikäinen 1997; Hansen and Olsen 2014). Their accuracy has been rightfully criticised for several reasons, in particular with regard to the clouded subjectivity of the compilers who attempted to convert the Sámi to Christianity (e.g. Storå 1971; Bäckman 1975; Rydving 1995; Hansen and Olsen 2014). It appears that Sámi religion varied between regions, but there is scholarly agreement that it had a common structure (Bäckman and Hultkranz 1985, 9; Rydving 1995, 22; Hansen and Olsen 2014, 315–318). This religion demonstrates similarities with the religious practices and concepts of other peoples to the north-east on the Eurasian continent regarding, for instance, shamanism, the world of the dead, sacrifice, and the bear cult (e.g. Holmberg 1987 [1915]; Pettersson 1957; Storå 1971; Bäckman and Hultkrantz 1985). Norse mythology also influenced Sámi religion, but the influence was probably more mutual than previously recognised according to recent scholarship (e.g. Mundal 2000; Price 2002; Solli 2002; Hansen and Olsen 2014).

Sámi religion may be characterised as a religion of practice with animistic and shamanistic elements (Bäckman and Hultkrantz 1985, 9; Rydving 1995, 19–23; Pentikäinen 1997, 324–326; Hansen and Olsen 2014, 314–315). It had no fixed liturgy, 'scripture', or priesthood, but consisted of rituals that were exercised through actions, myths, narratives and material manifestations. The Sámi shaman – *noaidi* in North Sámi – played an important role as a conductor of rituals and a mediator between worlds, but did not monopolise rituals and sacrifices. Thus, Sámi religion was a dynamic one that was open to individual interpretations, sometimes including the adoption of customs and rituals from other religions, namely Norse mythology, pre-Christian Finno-Ugric religions, and Christianity. Crucifixes and other Christian symbols as recorded in Sámi graves from the medieval period are prime examples of this (Schanche 2000).

The material surroundings or mythical landscape were crucial parts of the Sámi worldview in which their religion unfolded and developed (Mebius 1968; Mulk 1995, 17–20, 2009; Schanche 1995, 43; Rydving 1995,

96–103; Pentikäinen 1997, 102–104; Hansen and Olsen 2014, 218–219). According to written accounts, the Sámi universe was divided into three spheres: the world of divinity that lay above the terrestrial world of the living, which in turn lay above the world of the dead. This cosmology may represent a projection of missionaries' own Christian ideology (Hansen and Olsen 2014, 338). Nevertheless, a tripartite universe is presented on some Sámi shaman drums, which are generally perceived as a microcosm of the Sámi universe. This idea of the universe helped to form a very specific attitude towards the physical reality, one in which the landscape was made alive by a vast number of forces and powers, as well as the spirits of ancestors. In this way, the landscape constituted a sacred space where relations to gods, powers, and ancestors were maintained. The religious engagement with landscape was carried out through both collective and individual religious rituals and practices, in which sacrifices to gods, powers, ancestors, and animals played a crucial role in the enactment of the religion. Thus, there were individual or family based sacrificial places as well as communal sacrificial places (Rydving 1995, 96–103; Hansen and Olsen 2014, 314).

The material remnants of Sámi religion are of crucial importance. The sacred places and sanctuaries, referred to as *sieidi* in North Sámi, were scattered throughout the landscape, in the form of holy mountains and forests, and idols of rock and wood (Qvigstad 1926; Manker 1957; Vorren and Eriksen 1993; Sveen 2003; Äikäs *et al.* 2009). In some cases, *sieidi* only refers to wooden or stone objects. These sanctuaries are generally characterised by their distinctiveness in the surrounding environment, either being naturally formed (e.g. anthropomorphic or zoomorphic) or partially humanly made, such as wooden idols. The sanctuaries and idols not only seem to represent a god, power, or spirit, but also their physical presence seems to be a material manifestation of that entity.

### *The world of the dead and concepts of the departed*

According to Schanche (2000, 317), the rise of a distinct Sámi burial custom demonstrates the establishment of a collective autonomous underworld of the Sámi that separated mortuary rituals from the home or living space. The concept of the underworld in Sámi religion is complex and somewhat obscure, but generally seems attached to *Jápmiidáibmu* (in North Sámi) – the World of the Dead – an underworld located beneath the earth (Storå 1971, 195; Hansen and Olsen 2014, 111). According to written accounts, death did not imply an end to or annihilation of the Sámi, but a continuation in another existence among ancestors in the world(s) of the dead (Bäckman 1975, 84). An indication is given by the suffix *-áibmu*, which actually means 'air' in several Sámi dialects and may translate to 'spirit' or 'state of mind' (Bäckman 1975, 85; Svestad 2011, 46). These meanings indicate significant aspects of the realm of the dead compared with Sámi concepts of the departed and afterlife. The written accounts designate several realms of the dead, which are occasionally linked to particular places (not always beneath the earth), individuals and forces (Storå 1971; Bäckman 1975; Hansen and Olsen 2014). *Saajvoe* (or *Saajveaajmoe* in South Sámi), for instance, is linked to sacred mountains and sacred lakes, and referred to a kind of paradise for shamans and other distinguished or god-fearing persons. Another abode of the dead is *Ruohttaáibmu* (in North Sámi), the kingdom of the death demon *Rouhtta*, where the damned or persons who disobeyed the gods remained. This realm was possibly located deep down into the earth, underneath the regular realm of the dead where most people resided. Hence, the pre-Christian Sámi religious beliefs indicate a differentiated life after death depending on one's life among the living, which is a common concept among northern Eurasian peoples (Pettersson 1987).

Perception of the departed in Sámi religion is controversial, similar to ideas of the realm of the dead (e.g. Storå 1971; Bäckman 1975; Rydving 1995; Hansen and Olsen 2014). As pointed out by Rydving (1995, 142), the interplay between the living and the dead caused major problems for missionaries during conversion. This obstacle probably affected their recording of Sámi relations with their ancestors and may have caused simplifications, misconceptions, and confusion with Christian notions. Nevertheless, missionaries describe the Sámi concept of the departed in connection to the concept of a dual soul, more precisely a *free* or *shadow soul* and a *corporeal soul*. The concept of a soul seems misleading since it is so closely related to the Christian idea of a soul and life after death. Hence, the German concept of *Geist* (spirit) seems more adequate since it is supported by the Sámi term for the world of the dead: áibmu (Itkonen 1946, 161–162). However, scholars agree that after death, the free soul gradually released itself from the body for a new existence in the world of the dead, *Jápmiidáibmu*. The corporeal soul remained in the grave attached to the physical remains, and perhaps the skeleton in particular. From there, the soul could make trips as an apparition or ghost, frightening individuals who encountered it, even causing death. On the other hand, the spirit of the dead could also be useful in everyday life, for instance during reindeer herding (Bäckman and Hultkrantz 1978, 46; Rydving 1995, 141). This usefulness was dependent upon the enactment of correct sacrifices and mortuary rituals, such as the sacrifice of a reindeer and the correct handling of its bones (Pettersson 1957, 51, 107–109, 117–119; see also Mebius 1968, 55; Storå 1971, 189–193; Schanche 2000, 260–267). Further, according to the written sources, it was important to conduct individual sacrificial ceremonies or a remembrance feast for three days and annually for three years subsequent to burial (e.g. Pettersson 1957, 74; Mebius 1968, 55; Storå 1971, 183, 244). This could include the sacrifice of a reindeer and burial of the whole animal, particular parts, or its bones in the ground, but could also include other animals, such as cockerels, as well as objects. Following the sacrifice, people partook in a remembrance feast. According to Hans Mebius (1968, 55), information on the burial of sacrifices is so abundant in the sources that it appears as a characteristic feature of Sámi religion. The significance of the correct handling of bones seems related to perceptions of the deceased's skeleton, which was considered crucial for a new bodily existence of the dead in the afterlife. An indication of this is given in one of the sources, which refers to the funeral feast as *tacte juckam* (in antiquated Sámi orthography) or 'bone drink' (Schefferus 1956 [1673], 345).

### *Animal sacrifice and the bear cult*

The perception that death was as an extension of life in another existence also pertained to animals and other living creatures in Sámi religion. Hence, the correct handling of a sacrificed animal in relation to burial secured regeneration of the animal in the world of the dead, and thus prevented death and ensured good relations with ancestors (Schanche 2000, 266). Concern for the knucklebones, and particularly the skull and large bones of sacrificed animals, is a central theme in the religions of northern Eurasian peoples. This concern was probably not only important in mortuary ceremonies and rituals regarding the realm of the dead, but also regarding successful hunting and the regeneration of animals in the realm of the living (Schanche 2000, 266). This perception partly explains the many Sámi bone deposits and sacrificial places, which include heaps of animal bones and antlers, particularly of reindeer (e.g. Manker 1957).

The significance of knucklebones is particularly evident in rituals concerning the bear. The bear was the foremost beast and sacred animal to the Sámi and was named *Guds hund* ('God's dog'), according to the Norwegian missionary Johan Randulf (1723 cited by Qvigstad 1904, 27; cf. Bäckman and Hultkrantz 1978, 83). The Sámi considered the bear all-knowing and all-seeing, and able to understand human language. Accordingly, the Sámi did not refer to the bear by its rightful name, *guovža* (bear in North Sámi), particularly during a hunt, but with a vast number of indicative allusions (here mostly in antiquated Sámi orthography) such as *puoldekats* ('rock being'), *puolde pådnje* ('greybeard in the rock'), *pouldaja* ('grandfather in the rock'), *meacche-áddja* ('grandfather in the forest'), *moedda-aigja* ('grandfather with the skin dress'), and *sjele-kallo* ('that which has silver leaf on its forehead'), according to the Swedish priest Pehr Fjellström ([1755] 1981, 10–11), the Norwegian missionary Knud Leem ([1767] 1975, 502), and the ethnographer Sigrid Drake ([1918] 1979, 327–329; see also Hansen and Olsen 2014, 121). The perception of the bear as an extraordinary animal in Sámi language, myth, and religion is related to its human-like attributes, including its sitting and upright stances, cleverness, masturbation practices, and skeleton, amongst other things (Edsman 1994, 19–20, cf. Hallowell 1924). Adding to these qualities was the bear's particular ability to hibernate and survive without eating in dens in the ground, and apparently to rise again from the 'dead' in the spring (Broadbent 2010, 177; cf. Fjellström [1755] 1981).

The most detailed description of the Sámi bear hunt and bear cult is given in the account of Fjellström, as presented in an abridged version below (Fjellström [1755] 1981, 16–31; e.g. Randulf 1723 cited by Qvigstad 1904, 27–28). Fjellström characterises the bear hunt as a sacred act that had to be carried out according to certain rules and rituals that varied between Sámi regions, as did the subsequent handling and consuming of the slaughtered bear. In general, only men could participate in a bear hunt and the subsequent slaughter. The hunt was initiated in the autumn after the bear had entered the den, which could then be encircled or marked before the actual hunt took place in late winter/early spring. Singing of songs to honour the bear took place at different stages before and after the hunt. A particular spear or lance with a brass ring fastened to it was used for killing. Subsequent to the hunt, a feast was prepared at the settlement. Women were not allowed to stare at the hunters except through a brass ring while the meat was brought to the settlement and then inside the dwelling through the sacred *boassjo*-door (in Lule Sámi) or back door of the dwelling. Additionally, women decorated the hunters with brass chains and rings, but were not allowed to sleep or stay with the men while the bear was skinned, cooked, and consumed. Tools used for skinning were also decorated with brass chains and women had to put the first piece of meat through a brass ring. At the end of the feast the tail of the bear was brought to the women who ate as much as they could before decorating the remains of the tail with brass and returning it to the men, who buried it together with the bones of the bear. The bones were arranged in a particular grave in their proper order, either horizontally or vertically, with the skull on top. Fjellström ([1755] 1981, 28–29) describes the bear grave as either an oblong or deep ditch in the ground, depending on the arrangement of the bones. Different information, however, is given by the late seventeenth-century Norwegian priest and poet Petter Dass in his tributary poem to Nordland (County) in which the Sámi buried bears in caves (Dass [1739] 1967, 62).

## Sámi burial customs

The origin of Sámi burial customs seems to coincide with the emergence of Sámi ethnicity in the first millennium BC, but the details of the origin, chronology, distribution, and development of these customs has yet to be investigated, particularly outside the Varanger area in Finnmark in northern Norway (Schanche 2000, 315–317; Hansen and Olsen 2014, 107–113). A similar situation exists regarding the origin and development of Sámi ethnicity, which may have been significantly altered since the time of its emergence. Accordingly, Sámi graves have been thoroughly investigated only in some parts of northern Fenno-Scandinavia (Manker 1961; Schanche 2000), but they occur in most parts of this vast region as well as in the Kola Peninsula. Knowledge of Sámi graves and Sámi burial customs rely mainly on the work of Swedish ethnographer Ernst Manker (1961) and, more significantly, the work of the Norwegian archaeologist Audhild Schanche (2000). In addition, there are several minor works in which chronological, regional, morphological, and other aspects have been explored (e.g. Mulk 1995; Zachrisson *et al.* 1997; Taavitsainen 2003; Bergstøl 2008; Svestad 2010, 2011). The documentation of Sámi graves is insufficient in the majority of instances due to many accidental finds as well as anthropological collecting of human remains from Sámi graves between *c.* 1850 and 1940, during which finds and construction details were secondary or merely incidental (Schanche 2000, 192–193). A similar lack of documentation exists for the majority of bear graves, and for those referred to in the significant works of Inger Zachrisson and Elisabeth Iregren (1974), and Ragnhild Myrstad (1996), of which the latter is the most comprehensive with regard to the investigation of bear graves. Below, the general characteristics of Sámi burial customs as represented by human and bear graves are outlined, with emphasis on graves in cavities (Fig. 2.2).

### General features

As indicated above, Sámi graves are strongly associated with the so-called scree and rock graves (900 BC–AD 1700). Until recently, all graves dated to before *c.* AD 900 were located in the Varanger area which Schanche (2000, 322, 328–329, see also discussion below) believes to reflect the origin of the Sámi burial custom in this area, from where it dispersed to other Sámi areas in Fenno-Scandinavia during the late Viking Age (AD 900–1000) and early medieval period (AD 1000–1200). 'Scree' graves of the Varangian type, more correctly described as graves constructed from slab-shaped beach rocks (Fig. 2.3), are the best-known features, but Sámi graves appear in various contexts and include stone piles, cairns, and inhumations as well as graves in cavities beneath blocks of rock or large boulders or in caves. Furthermore, Sámi graves mostly appear as individual graves, both in isolation and in cemeteries. Collective burials are known in some instances, however, and may contain up to five individuals including both adults and children (Schanche 2000, 224). In addition, it is important to note that Sámi graves and cemeteries are often located in close proximity to Sámi sanctuaries and sacrificial places (Manker 1957; Vorren and Eriksen 1993; Schanche 2000).

With regard to constructed graves, the general impression is that they were designed with apertures and gaps, and were built to create dry conditions for the departed. Inhumation burials were shallow even though some graves were dug more than one metre deep into the ground, which is relatively shallow compared to the Christian burial custom of six feet (two metres) (Manker 1961; Schanche 2000; Svestad 2007, 2011). There is, however, a significant variation with regard to placement on or in the ground and other construction details. Sámi graves have a broader distribution than was previously believed, and a greater variation in form, including hybrids, has also been noted, particularly in areas bordering 'Germanised' regions or in coastal areas and southern and eastern Fenno-Scandinavia (Leppäaho 1937; Sjövold 1962, 1974; Kopisto 1971; Binns 1988; Zachrisson *et al.* 1997; Martynov 2002; Taavitsainen 2003; Ruohonen 2005; Bruun 2007; Bergstøl 2008; Broadbent 2010; Svestad 2011). Given the geographical distribution and variation in form, the very term 'scree and rock graves' is somewhat of a constraint on our understanding of Sámi burials. Thus, 'Sámi graves' as applied in this context is more appropriate to the various graves in question, except for hybrid Norse-Sámi graves (Bruun 2007; Svestad 2007).

The shrouding or wrapping of the corpse in birch bark appears as one of the most unique features of Sámi burial custom, as well as the placement of the corpse in a *pulka* (a reindeer sledge). While shrouding was prevalent throughout the whole period in most of the area – and from the Middle Ages, also in cloth or clothing – it is not clear when *pulkas* began to be used as containers, although *c.* AD 900 is the earliest determined date at present (Schanche 2000, 197; see also Shumkin *et al.* 2006; Svestad 2011). Both features occasionally occur together and from the earliest until *c.* AD 1000, birch-bark shrouding sown with reindeer sinew seems to dominate. Accordingly, shrouding customs changed through time as did the use of birch bark, which in the medieval period started to be employed as merely a cover or layer above or underneath a *pulka*, a hollowed tree trunk, or a wooden coffin. Inhumation burials, burials in coffins, and the replacement of birch-bark shrouding with cloth/clothing have been interpreted as Christian influences (Schanche 2000, 336; see also Ovsiannikov 1993). However, these features may also reflect influences from Norse ('Germanised'), Finnish, Karelian, and Baltic settlements during the Nordic Iron Age (500 BC–AD 1050) (Pettersson 1957). All the above features are more or less similar regardless of sex and age, although graves of children are in the minority compared to those of adults (Schanche 2000, 219).

Generally, the affiliation between birch bark and the religious practices of the Sámi is scant and almost non-existent in the written sources, particularly regarding birch-bark shrouding. However, the missionary Hans Skanke ([1728–1730] 1945, 200) mentions a sacrifice called *Damengare* (in Sámi), in which different parts of an animal's flesh and skeleton were placed in a sort of coffin made of birch bark that was subsequently buried in the

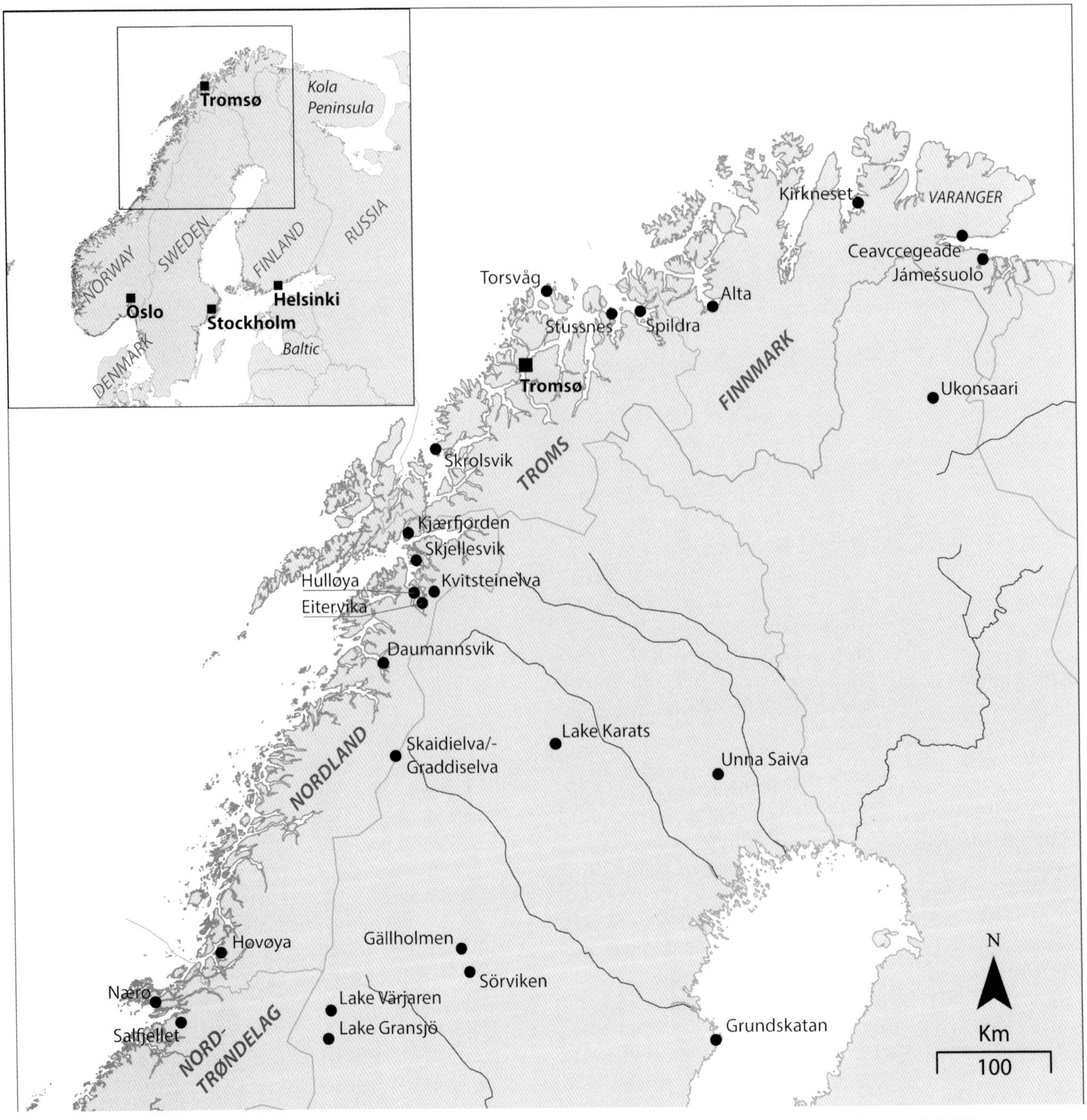


*Figure 2.2: Map including burial and sacrificial sites discussed in the text. Illustration: J.E. Arntzen © 2015.*

ground. According to Schanche (2000, 268), birch bark had a practical significance as protection against moisture and weather in addition to providing magico-religious protection. The representation of the birch and birch bark as significant or sacred among the Sámi in the written sources may support this perception (Schanche 2000, 267–268).

With regard to grave furnishings, the most typical finds consist of various animal bones, particularly bird, fish, and marrow-split reindeer bones. Animal bones seem to appear throughout the whole period (900 BC–AD 1700) (Schanche 2000, 315). Furthermore, various shells and objects such as sherds of asbestos-tempered ceramics of the Kjelmøy type (*c.* 900 BC–AD 300), and stone, bone, and sometimes also iron, implements, occur in graves from the late Early Metal Age to the Early Iron Age (900 BC–AD 300). Iron Age graves from AD 300–800 contain few objects, which include a small number of brooches and beads of western Norse origin that indicate external relations. Objects in graves from the Viking Age to the high medieval period (AD 800–1300) are much more abundant and include brooches, jewellery and pendants of bronze, brass and silver of Finnish and/or eastern Baltic origin. Graves from the medieval period onwards (AD 1000–1700) also contain various domestic and personal objects, as well as crucifixes and other Christian symbols from *c.* AD 1200 (Schanche 2000, 192–226, 336). There are some differences regarding the age and sex of individuals. Imported jewellery and chains, for instance, mostly occur in female graves, while rings and iron knives occur in graves of both sexes (Schanche 2000, 219). However, as Schanche noted (2000, 223), numerous finds deviate from what is usually classified as 'male' or 'female' in comparison to the actual sex determination of skeletons (e.g. Manker 1961; Zachrisson 1986; Sundström 1988). For instance, arrowheads are documented in two female graves from the late Early Metal Age (one also containing fragments of skis), while bronze needles, a spindle whorl, and glass beads are documented in a male grave from the Early Iron Age (Schanche 2000, 223, 322). Although this issue has not been further explored, these finds may indicate that the Sámi did not always distinguish between what were traditionally conceived as male and female activities.

Though the graves themselves come in a number of different forms, they contain a coherent and roughly unified material repertoire. This does not necessarily mean that Sámi society was homogeneous in prehistoric and early historic times, as seems to be the traditional view (for further discussion, see Hansen and Olsen 2014), but there appears to be some common structures or 'family resemblance' (Wittgenstein 1989, 31–32) within this heterogeneity. Hence, there is no single feature common to all graves, but they demonstrate a criss-crossing network of specific features. These include certain morphological characteristics: dry and airy conditions, the organisation of the surface of the grave, the use of *pulka* (or coffins, hollowed tree trunks or no container), shrouding or wrapping of the body in birch bark (or other matter), and possibly the north–south orientation of graves. Added to these features are numerous graves from the Christianisation period (*c.* AD 1550–1750) until the mid-twentieth century, which demonstrate similar as well as transitional features (Manker 1961; Schanche 2000; Svestad 2010, 2011).

## Graves in cavities

Graves in natural cavities are scattered across most of northern Fenno-Scandinavia. More than 130 are known in Norway with significantly fewer in Sweden, Finland and Russia, but only a small number have been scientifically investigated (Manker 1961; Schanche 2000). Generally, these graves are located in cavities beneath blocks of rock or clusters of various sized boulders, or in rockshelters, rather than in caves. In some cavities, it is hardly possible to kneel, let alone stand upright, but others are quite spacious. These graves generally appear without any associated construction features and are often uncovered, or are quite openly arranged towards the outer space in contrast to typical beach rock graves that have a constructed and covered chamber (Fig. 2.4, cf. Fig. 2.3). When construction features are present, they mostly appear in the form of covers of wooden logs, planks or stone slabs either on top of a burial or in the opening of the cavity, but small cairns or stone chambers covered with stone slabs in the cavity itself (mostly in the Varanger area) are also known. Apart from this, graves in cavities demonstrate most features of Sámi burial customs such as shrouding or wrapping of the corpse in birch bark, use of *pulka*, deposition of animal bones, etc. With regard to finds, the situation is similar.

Graves in cavities are particularly abundant along the coast of Troms and northern Nordland, especially in the Tysfjord and Salten regions (in Nordland) where they are often located in steep and large boulder scree

*Figure 2.3: Emptied Sámi beach rock grave at* Ceavccegeađgi, *Varanger, Finnmark County. Photo: A. Svestad © 2006.*

*Figure 2.4: Partly preserved Sámi grave (undated) in a small cave at Skaga at the Island of Spildra in Kvænangen, Troms County. Note the remains of birch bark wrapping in front and (barely visible) behind the cranium (centre left and centre right). Photo: A. Svestad © 2015.*

deposits near the sea shore. Here, a description is given of particular examples that display general features, as well as the well-known Skjellesvik burial, which provides a more detailed picture. The earliest dated grave of this kind is from Kvitsteinelva in the inner part of the Tysfjord municipality in Nordland County, where two alleged human bone fragments and an almost complete (but broken) vessel of Kjelmøy asbestos pottery were recorded in a cavity (Gjessing 1942, 273, plate IV; Schanche 2000, 401). The remains indicate a possible grave dated from the late Early Metal period or Roman Iron Age according to the dating of the pottery (900 BC–AD 300). Unfortunately, information is scarce yet typical for graves of this kind where there was a lack of scientific investigation and documentation. Compared to other Sámi graves, a large portion of graves in cavities have been dated (mostly typologically) to AD 600–1200 (Schanche 2000, 192; Gjessing 1928). In one of these graves, from a cavity under rock at Sandfjord in Torsvåg on the Vannøy Island in Troms County, a male corpse was shrouded in birch bark and placed in a *pulka*. The deceased wore a bronze ring dated to AD 1040–1250 (Andreassen 1990; Bratrein 1989, 191; Schanche 2000, 399). At another location in Eitervika in Tysfjord, a female grave was recorded in a cave underneath a large boulder in a major scree deposit. The grave dates to AD 1000–1100 based on finds of a horseshoe-shaped annular bronze brooch with faceted end knots and a bronze ring, both of Finnish or eastern Baltic origin, and both providing clear evidence of a significant Sámi connection in the Viking Age and early medieval period (Schanche 2000, 401; Schreiner 1927; Gjessing 1928; Serning 1956). In several instances, scree deposits contain almost entire cemeteries such as at Eitervika where graves are scattered throughout (Schreiner 1935, 5). These screes often comprise fairly stable fields of large boulders and stones, in which natural cavities beneath or between boulders stand out as favourable places for burial.

## The Skjellesvik burial

In 2014, an archaeological investigation was carried out on a previously known but undocumented grave in Uran (the Screes) in Skjellesvik in the inner part of Skrovkjosen, a minor fjord in Tysfjord's estuary. The inner part of Skrovkjosen has several cemeteries that include numerous recorded Sámi graves in cavities underneath rocks and erratics (Spa 2009). Above Uran lies Stálotjåhkkå Mountain, which represents *Stállo* (in Lule Sámi), the evil force in Sámi mythology, and adds to the religious nature of the area. The grave in question is located near the sea shore in a deep and fairly spacious cavity that includes several chambers beneath a cluster of large boulders (Figenschau 2014, 14) (Fig. 2.5). According to the excavation report, the largest chamber was about 3m deep, ranged in width from 1.5–4m, and reached a maximum height of 2.6m. Two minor side chambers extend from the

*Figure 2.5: The Skjellesvik cavity and grave (lower right) in Uran. The Stálotjåhkkå Mountain above (upper centre-left). Photo: A. Svestad © 2014.*

major chamber; one approximately 4.3m in a northerly direction and the other 5.5m in an easterly direction. *In situ* remains of the grave were documented in the central part of the main chamber, but it is evident that the burial had been severely disturbed in modern times. A cranium and numerous other human bones and bone fragments were collected and deposited at Tromsø Museum before excavation. A bone sample from the rib yielded a radiocarbon date to the early Merovingian period, AD 640–680 (1270 ± 30 BP, Beta-372864), which at the time of excavation was the earliest definite date from a Sámi grave outside the Varanger area. The *in situ* finds consisted of post-cranial human bones, fragments of birch bark, fragments of wood, wooden logs, a piece of wooden board with hewn ends (possibly from a *pulka*), a wooden pole with a carved notch, bag fittings typical of female graves, an unidentifiable worked bone object (tool?), a bird cranium, and shells. The wooden logs may represent remains of the grave's cover, which is documented from other Sámi graves in Tysfjord, elsewhere in Nordland as well as in other regions; for instance, in a grave in a cave in Sandvåg in the Skjervøy municipality further north in Troms County where the burial was covered with stone slabs and wooden logs (Schanche 2000, 398, see also 401–403). Some human bones appeared to have been wound in birch bark, but there were no traces of a grave. One wood and two birch-bark samples have recently been radiocarbon dated, yielding the following results: AD 425–600 (1530 ± 30 BP, Beta-404078), AD 1040–1220 (890 ± 30 BP, Beta-404079), and AD 1160–1265 (830 ± 30 BP, Beta-404080). The earliest date may correspond to the burial, while the two younger dates may indicate birch-bark shrouding related to a secondary burial. Notwithstanding, the date from the skeleton proves an earlier dating of Sámi graves significantly further south than the Varanger area, which implies that Sámi burial customs extended to larger parts of Fenno-Scandinavia at an earlier stage than was hitherto believed (Schanche 2000, 188, see more on this topic below). The date also strengthens the argument that the finds from Kvitsteinelva also represent a grave. Osteological analysis of the skeletal remains from the Skjellesvik grave concludes that they belong to a female of approximately 30 years of age, although determination of sex, age, and number of individuals is disputable (Sjøvold 2017). Shell finds that generally occur in Sámi graves from the early Iron Age or earlier also indicate a date in the early Iron Age, though their context in the Skjellesvik grave is questionable.

Two separate deposits of shells and animal bones and teeth from various species were also documented in the inner part of the eastern chamber of the cavity in Skjellesvik. Some shells were recorded in cracks between boulders in the wall of the cavity (Fig. 2.6). Analysis of the material has yet to be conducted, but the general impression is that bones came from livestock, birds, and fish (Figenschau 2014, 20–22). Bird and fish bones are common in Sámi graves, but bones of livestock are almost non-existent prior to the medieval period (see Schanche 2000, 197–204). It is difficult to determine whether these deposits were made by humans or animals, since the innermost or narrowest parts of similar cavities are extensively used by wild animals for shelter and food storage. However, the fact that the deposits are limited to particular zones of the flat area in only one of the side chambers may indicate ritual activity and sacrifice. This impression is strengthened by the deposition of shells in cracks, which, as pointed out by Figenschau (2014, 17–18), were most likely brought there by humans. Sacrifices of animal bones and antlers, particularly of reindeer, in cracks, joints, and cavities in rocky or mountain contexts are typical of Sámi religious practices, both separately and in relation to graves and cemeteries. The question of whether the bone and shell deposits in the grave at Skjellesvik belong to the grave or are separate events is currently impossible to answer. However, several other animal bone and antler deposits have been documented (but not analysed) between graves in the Uran scree, which support the suggestion of separate sacrifices, although some or all deposits cannot be fully excluded as remains of animal activity (cf. Spa 2009). These deposits may be later sacrifices, similar to what is known from other Sámi burial sites, such as a 200-years-later sacrifice of reindeer bones at the late medieval grave at Lake Gransjö in Jämtland County in northern Sweden (Sundström 1988; Boëthius 2010 and Hedlund 2011; see also Schanche 2000). A few other similar sacrificial places (bone or antler deposits) have been investigated, of which five in Varanger have been dated to AD 1000–1700 (Schanche 2000, 273).

*Figure 2.6: Interior of Skjellesvik cavity with shell deposit. Photo: S. Sivertsvik/Tromsø Museum © 2014.*

## Collective burial

One of the interesting aspects of Sámi graves in cavities is the presence of collective burials. At most, four individuals have been documented in the same grave, such as on Hulløya Island, but also in Tysfjord where remains of three males and one individual of undetermined sex were documented in a cavity underneath large boulders in scree. Some or all of the individuals were originally shrouded in birch bark and, additionally, one in a *pulka* (Schanche 2000, 402; Schreiner 1935, 5). Unfortunately, there is no dating of this grave but the birch bark shrouding may indicate the early medieval period or earlier.

At another mainland location in the allusive Daumannsvik ('Dead Man's Bay') in Sørfold, somewhat north in Nordland, four individuals covered by four wooden planks were recorded in a cave (Schanche 2000, 403; Schreiner 1931). Skeletal analysis identified one male and one female. The grave is not dated, but the cover of wooden planks is similar to the grave in Skjellesvik and other finds of wooden logs or similar in graves in cavities. Further north at Stussnes, on Skjervøy Island in Troms County, a similar grave has been recorded in a small cave, which included two individuals covered with stone slabs (Schanche 2000, 398).

The fact that these cavities are quite spacious points to one of their most important physical prerequisites. The question thus arises regarding the collective character of the burials: do they represent reuse or are corpses contemporaneous? In general, we must await further analysis to better address this question. Notwithstanding, single graves or cavities that include several individuals may represent cemeteries in their own right, as indicated by Schanche (2000, 224).

## Bear graves

Brown bear (*Ursus arctos arctos*) graves comprise a unique phenomenon in Fenno-Scandinavia, which clearly relates to Sámi religious ideology and practices. Altogether, 45 or 46 bear burial sites are known in northern Norway and northern Sweden (Zachrisson and Iregren 1974; Mulk and Iregren 1995; Myrstad 1996; Broadbent and Storå 2003; Dunfjell-Aagård 2005; Solbakk 2008), but the number may be higher based on the definition of bear graves (compare Zachrisson and Iregren 1974 with Myrstad 1996). The earliest definitively dated bear grave is located in a cave in Kjærfjorden on Tjeldøy Island in the northernmost part of Nordland County (Myrstad 1996, 39). This grave dates to the late Roman period, more precisely to AD 220–325. However, there are indications from other locations in Nordland of earlier bear graves corresponding to the emergence of Sámi burial customs, such as the bear skull from a cave on the island of Hovøya in Bindal dated to 1260–1075 BC (2960 ± 45 BP, TUa-5026) (Dunfjeld-Aagård 2005, 95–97, Myrstad 1996, 10). The majority of bear graves date from the late Viking Age and early medieval period (AD 900–1300), but a large proportion date from the seventeenth and eighteenth centuries, which marks the end of the bear-grave tradition in Fenno-Scandinavia (Myrstad 1996, see also Zachrisson and Iregren 1974; Mulk and Iregren 1995; Broadbent 2010; Oppvang and Kjellman 2016).

In general, bear burials occur in much the same contexts and manner as Sámi human burials. They have been recorded on islands and in proximity to human graves (Petersen 1940, 160; Zachrisson and Iregren 1974, 15–33; Mulk and Iregren 1995; Myrstad 1996, 30ff). The majority of bear graves are found in natural cavities beneath rocks or large boulders where skeletal remains are placed directly on the ground surface (Myrstad 1996, 48). This accounts for most bear graves along the coast of Nordland and Troms counties in northern Norway, and the northernmost interior of northern Norway and northern Sweden. The northern part of Nordland County and the Kvænangen region in Troms County stand out, with ten and six bear burials respectively. Some of the graves contain constructed elements such as cairns, stone slab covers or stone blocking at the entrance of the cavity, and other features (Myrstad 1996, 48–49). The Salfjellet grave in Nord-Trøndelag County (the southernmost bear grave in Norway) is a typical example of a cavity burial in which the bear cranium was deposited in a pit in the ground and covered with stone slabs, in a cavity under a large boulder (Petersen 1940, 15). This burial resembles the above-mentioned burial tradition described by Dass (1967 [1739]) and the latter of the two burial practices described by Fjellström (1981 [1755]).

Another type of bear grave is documented in the South Sámi forested areas of Sweden, which consist almost exclusively of inhumations displaying regional differences within the Sámi bear-grave tradition (Zachrisson and Iregren 1974). The Sörviken inhumation burial near Lake Storuman in northern Sweden, for instance, comprised skeletal remains of a bear covered with birch bark, wooden logs and a thick layer of moss (Zachrisson and Iregren 1974, 21). The dating indicates that this grave belongs to the final period of the bear grave tradition and corresponds with the first burial practice described by Fjellström (1981 [1755]).

Traces of birch bark have been documented in several Viking Age or early medieval period graves in addition to the Sörviken grave, both in the Swedish South Sámi area and in northern Norway (Zachrisson and Iregren 1974; Mulk and Iregren 1995; Myrstad 1996). One noteworthy instance is the grave beneath a rockshelter in Skaitielva/Graddiselva in Saltdal in Nordland County, which consisted of an undated post-cranial skeleton wrapped in birch bark (Myrstad 1996, 29). Another interesting find relates to an inhumation grave on Vägvisar islet in Lake Karats in the parish of Jokkmokk in northern Sweden (Mulk 1994; Mulk and Iregren 1995) where remains of a bear skeleton were placed on a layer of birch bark. This grave is dated to the ninth or tenth centuries.

In the majority of bear graves, only the skull has been recorded (Zachrisson and Iregren 1974; Myrstad 1996), whereas in other graves only post-cranial bones are present. Both features may represent intentional acts, but alternatively may be the result of disturbance, later removal and/or insufficient investigation and documentation, which is evident at numerous bear graves. Inhumation graves in which the majority of a bear skeleton is preserved may provide a more accurate picture. In some graves bones are carefully arranged and almost imitate the anatomy or body of the bear. The Sörviken burial and the adjacent Gällholmen burial (also at Lake Storuman) are well-known examples in which shoulder blades (*scapulae*) were deposited in approximate anatomical positions to the skull, and the remaining bones imitated the correct anatomical position of the bear (Zachrisson and Iregren 1974, 17, 22). In these graves, the majority of bones were clearly broken or split for marrow extraction, which is a common feature of most bear graves irrespective of age and regional affiliation as noted by Myrstad (1996, 50, cf. Zachrisson and Iregren 1974, 84; Mulk and Iregren 1995, 21; Broadbent 2010, 180). This aspect clearly proves that bears were exploited for food, and simultaneously contradicts information given of the bear cult in some written accounts, such as by Fjellström, that the bones were not to be broken (Fjellström [1755] 1981, 22, 28).

Only a few artefacts are documented from bear graves, such as in the Sörviken grave where a leaf-shaped pendant from a seventeenth- or eighteenth-century Sámi silver brooch was recovered during excavation (Zachrisson and Iregren 1974, 20). In the Salfjellet grave, a chain dated to the medieval period or later was fastened to the cheekbone (zygoma) of the bear's cranium (Petersen 1940) (Fig. 2.7). An identical find is noted from a bear grave at Lake Värjaren in Jämtland, just across the border in Sweden (Zachrisson and Iregren 1974, 33).

## Human graves and bear graves in proximity

Spildra is a fairly large island in the Kvænangen fjord in the northern part of Troms County. Similar to, for example, Varanger and Tysfjord, the Kvænangen fjord constitutes a significant region in Sámi history (e.g. Bjørklund 1985;

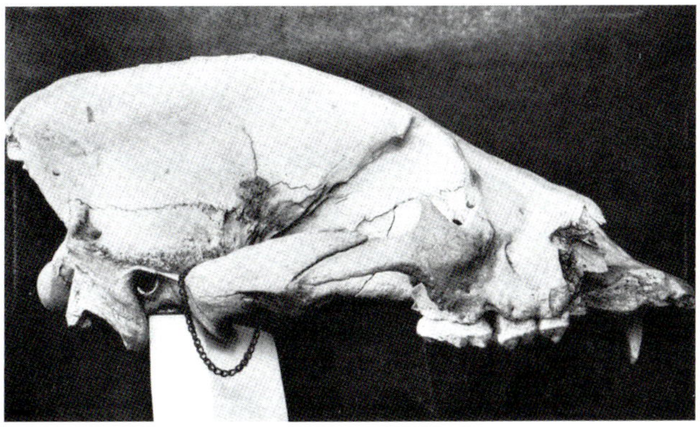

*Figure 2.7: Bear cranium of the Salsfjellet burial. Note the brass chain fastened to the cheekbone. Photo: Th. Petersen/NTNU © 1944.*

Grydeland 2001). Schanche (2000, 114) notes that traces of early Sámi presence are abundant and varied on this island, and several Sámi human graves and bear graves are recorded. Among the various traces are several sacrificial places, such as a six-metre high naturally-shaped column of rock named Árahávdi, which may be translated as 'The Fire Grave' (for a different translation, see Sveen 2003, 73). Another sacrificial stone is called *Báhppageađi* ('The Priest's Stone').

Six human graves, which mostly date to the early and high medieval period (AD 1000–1350), have been excavated at Spildra (Schanche 2000, 146–150). Most graves are located in small caves and cavities under rock. At Skaga, on the south-western part of the island of Spildra, human remains have been documented, along with large fragments of birch-bark shrouding, in a partly disturbed grave (grave 1 in Schanche 2000) in a cramped cavity beneath a flat rock. The grave did not have any constructed features but Schanche observed two minor stones, one of which was a *sieidi* (Sámi idol), a wind-eroded zoomorphic sandstone in the outer part of the cavity (Schanche 2000, 147–148; Fig. 2.8). The second was a small, round and smooth water-rolled stone, possibly another idol. Zoomorphic or anthropomorphic *sieidis* are documented on numerous Sámi sacrificial sites in Fenno-Scandinavia (e.g. Manker 1957; Vorren and Eriksen 1993; Sveen 2003), but are rare in grave contexts, as pointed out by Schanche (2000, 148). This grave is dated to AD 1030–1220.

Another grave worth mentioning is from Silkeberget further east on the southern part of the island. In a cavity that measures 3m in depth, 4.5m in width and approximately 0.7m in height, Schanche (2000, 144–146) documented a partly disturbed grave that contained remains of a child and an adult male that were shrouded in birch bark and placed in *pulka(s)*. The grave consisted of a rectangular chamber constructed from partially upright stone slabs. Finds consisted of a stone strike-a-light, an unidentifiable wooden object, a toe-joint of a young bear, and a wing bone

*Figure 2.8: Human cranium and (to the left) zoomorphic* sieidi *(not* in situ*) at the entrance of Skaga grave 1. Photo: T. Mikalsen © 2015.*

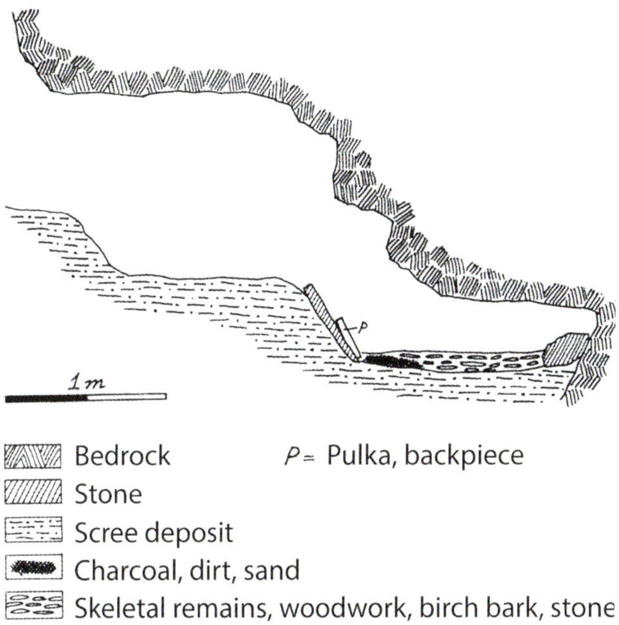


*Figure 2.9: Profile of grave 1 at Silkeberget, Spildra Island. Illustration: after Schanche © 2000, 146.*

of a herring gull (*Larus argentatus*). Radiocarbon dating places the grave at AD 1165–1410 (see Schanche 2000, 146; Fig. 2.9).

This quite rare find of a bear bone in a grave is perhaps symptomatic of a unique aspect of the Kvænangen region with regard to ritual and religious practices. So far, five or probably six bear graves have been documented in the area, all on the island of Spildra. This constitutes the largest known concentration of bear graves in Fenno-Scandinavia, and three have been radiocarbon dated to AD 1030–1220 (T-11214), AD 1170–1285 (T-11213), and

AD 1230–1300 (T-11215) respectively (Myrstad 1996, 32–34; Schanche 2000, 151–152). Four of the bear graves are located in Skagevågen or Skagedalen in proximity to the aforementioned sacrificial stone *Báhppageađi* and the human graves at Skaga. All the bear graves on the island are exposed in cavities beneath rock, similar to the majority of human graves on Spildra (Fig. 2.10). One of the bear graves (grave 1, Myrstad 1996, 32) contained a large piece of birch bark, emphasising the significance of this material in Sámi mortuary practices whether related to humans or bears (Schanche 2000, 397; see Fig. 2.11). The birch bark piece was recorded from the innermost and narrowest part of the cavity, but the bear's skull is missing and it appears the grave was disturbed in later times (probably on several occasions), which suggests that the whole skeleton was originally covered with birch bark.

*Figure 2.10: Bear grave 3 (undated) in Skagevågen on the Island of Spildra in Kvænangen, Troms County. The cranium is placed on top of post-cranial bones (just visible) with cut and split marks. Photo: A. Svestad © 2015.*

*Figure 2.11: Bear grave 1 (AD 1030–1220) in Skagevågen on the Island of Spildra in Kvænangen, Troms County. Several bones have cut and split marks. Note the large flake of birch bark at the back of the cavity (centre left). Photo: A. Svestad © 2015.*

Close proximity between human and bear graves is not only known from Spildra, but also further south in Troms and Nordland counties and in other parts of northern Fenno-Scandinavia, and possibly also at Salfjellet (Petersen 1940, 159; see also Myrstad 1996, 36).

## Discussion

### *The origin and distribution of Sámi burial customs*

Questions surrounding the origin and distribution of Sámi burial customs have been central to the investigation of Sámi graves. Based on the abundance of scree and rock graves in the Varanger area and their dating to the first millennium BC, Schanche (2000, 328–329) argued that Sámi burial customs first originated in this area and later dispersed into other regions of Fenno-Scandinavia from *c.* AD 900 onwards. The date(s) from the Skjellesvik grave, however, confirms the existence of Sámi burial customs by AD 600 in the Tysfjord region, which is quite a distance from Varanger. The earliest bear grave at Kjærfjorden, somewhat north of Tysfjord, was dated to AD 220–325 and points to an even earlier date for Sámi burial customs in this area. Both the human- and bear-grave dates indicate Sámi burial customs were present in Nordland prior to the diffusion hypothesis put forward by Schanche. Whether Sámi graves in Nordland and elsewhere outside the Varanger area reflect the origin of Sámi burial customs at the beginning of the first millennium BC has not been established. The possible human grave at Kvitsteinelva dated to 900 BC–AD 300, and a possible bear grave at Hovøya dated to 1260–1075 BC, provide clues to this question.

According to Schanche, the bear grave in Kjærfjorden indicates that Sámi burial customs were first established through bear burials in Nordland, and thereafter transferred to human burials. As stated earlier, bear graves occur in much the same contexts and exhibit similar features to human graves, but bear graves appear to have a more limited set of features. Thus, bear graves might appear to reflect or imitate human graves, indicating that human burials in general preceded the practice of burying bears. However, according to one of the main arguments in this chapter, which is elaborated below, human graves and bear graves demonstrate intimate relations on several levels possibly indicating a complex, interconnected and more or less contemporary origin. Accordingly, the development of Sámi burial customs does not have to originate in one place or area, such as Varanger, but different processes may have occurred in various regions amongst the hunter-gatherers of the Early Metal period in which Sámi burial customs began to develop. In fact, Schanche's argument that bear burial preceded the tradition of human burial in Nordland may support this idea. Furthermore, hunter-gatherer perceptions and experiences of bears as, for instance, expressed on various Fenno-Scandinavian rock carvings from the Younger

Stone Age, may have been a formative influence on Sámi burial customs in general.

### *Landscape affordances and ritual landscapes*

Perceptions in the written accounts related to the departed and the world of the dead demonstrate an intimate link with the construction of graves: the apertures, gaps and occasionally uncovered arrangements permitted souls to move in and out between the world of the living and the world of the dead. There is reason to believe that these perceptions and the graves themselves were mutually constitutive. The same process is probably also reflected in the placement of graves or cemeteries on islands or islets, such as *Jámešsuolo* ('The Ghost Islet'), in Bugøyfjord in eastern Finnmark, as a means of trying to avoid conflict with ghosts, or in cavity graves within separate scree deposits or under a rock. However, judging from the variety in Sámi graves, it appears that pre-Christian Sámi ideas and practices regarding the departed were significantly more complex than descriptions in the written accounts permit. The relationship between the written accounts of Sámi religion and pre-Christian cosmology, and the actual religious practices and rituals, is also controversial. For instance, the missionaries who recorded Sámi religion often copied one another thereby creating an idea of a homogenous religion. These accounts were also recorded many years after the Sámi religion ceased to exist in its so-called original form (Rydving 1995; Hansen and Olsen 2014). However, compared to the variety of graves and grave finds, Sámi religious ideas and practices were most likely altered, flexible, varying, and even inconsistent – between regions as well as individuals (Schanche 2000, 259).

The emergence of Sámi burial customs in the first millennium BC confirms that a Sámi religion existed for more than two-and-a-half millennia, even if that religion changed significantly over the centuries. There is a striking coherence between different kinds of Sámi graves and the type of landscape or landscape affordances that are evident in Sámi burial customs. Sámi graves thus manifest a material inertia with regard to location, morphology, and construction. This does not imply that religious concepts, rituals, and mortuary practices remained unchanged; rather, it suggests that the world of the dead was physically more or less the same through time.

From a phenomenological perspective, burial cavities seem to epitomise the qualities and affordances of Sámi landscapes in that they provide shelter, preservation or protection, and dwelling spaces for the dead (Svestad 2013, 212; Heidegger 1993). I think these affordances played a crucial role in the origin of Sámi burial customs as well as the religious concepts related to the existence of the world of the dead and life after death. The distinctive spaces within cavities literally stand out as entrances into other realms – gradually getting darker and narrower until fading into the earth, to the deepest, darkest, and most liminal areas. Hence, in a practical–physical as well as metaphoric manner, cavities distanced themselves from the outer world or world of the living in correspondence with a world underneath or beyond the visible earth (Schanche 2000, 284). These spaces also invited ritual and deposition in association with the dead. Cavities emphasised how the landscape itself and its physical characteristics impose divisions and offer possibilities with regard to mortuary practices, rituals, and religious ideas.

The Skjellesvik cavity reflects these characteristics and affordances in a visible way. The burial was carefully arranged against the wall of the major chamber of the cavity. From there the dead were provided with easy passage to the outer space among the living, as well as the world of the dead in the darkest and deepest part of the cavity. The possible ritual deposits or sacrifices of animal bones beyond the grave, in the innermost liminal zone, may signify a ritual to secure a good relationship with the spirits of dead, as reflected in the written accounts regarding perceptions of the departed and their souls. So too with the deposits of shells in the cracks between the boulders; these most likely represent intentional human deposits and sacrifices placed in the most tangible route to the world of the dead – the innermost cracks of the cavity. It is evidence of a link between mortuary practice in the Migration and/or Merovingian period, and religious concepts and rituals as described in the written accounts of Sámi religion thousands of years later. These finds also correspond with Schanche's (2000, 264; cf. Eliade 1964) view that Sámi mortuary rituals place an emphasis on the liminal phase of rites of passage.

As noted earlier, several deposits of animal bones have been recorded between graves in the Uran scree, which indicates multiple sacrificial practices or votive deposits at this cemetery. One must be cautious, however, as these deposits are not yet dated. Individual and collective ritual activity or sacrifice may have taken place later than the

*Figure 2.12: The scared Bear Stone at* Čiesti, *Varanger, Finnmark County. Photo: A. Svestad © 2015.*

burials as indicated in the written records of subsequent sacrificial ceremonies. This is also suggested by the medieval burial and offering at Lake Gransjö in northern Sweden made some 200 years later. Thus, communal remembrance feasts or sacrificial ceremonies may have taken place significantly later than an actual burial. At Uran, it is possible that the bone deposits represent both individual and communal sacrifices related to the general protection and nursing of the spirits of the dead.

### *Human–bear entanglements*

Sámi graves in cavities emphasise how landscape affordances, humans, and animals bring each other into being through burial, sacrifice, and ritual. As discussed by Myrstad (1996, 66–67), bear graves seem to resemble bear dens. It is well known that the brown bear prefers to place its den in steep and rugged terrain in scree deposits of large boulders, or in joints, or underneath erratic blocks in mountainous areas, but also in cavities of large tree roots or by digging out holes in the ground (Elgmork 1999). These variations are more or less analogous with the varied morphology of recorded bear graves, as presented above. Bear graves seem to reflect the quality of landscape or landscape affordances in a similar way to Sámi human graves and sanctuaries, and are altered according to a bear's preference in the surrounding environment (Svestad 2011, 44–45). Thus, it is probably no coincidence that most bear graves are located in cavities that resemble typical dens. Furthermore, that the bear was regarded almost equal to humans, and in particular was respected for its ability to survive in dens during winter without eating and then 'rise from the dead' in spring, emphasises the bear's unique ability to alternate between the world of the living and the world of the dead. The burial of a bear in dry, airy and shallow conditions may thus have been important for its resurrection as well as permitting the bear's spirit to move in and out of the grave in a manner similar to a human burial. The bear's natural affiliation with cavities may have emphasised these spaces as favourable entrances into other realms, both in a physical and metaphoric sense. Furthermore, it appears that the intimate relations between bears and humans were most significant with regard to death and rituals concerning the dead.

This relationship is apparent at the large cemetery of *Ceavccegeađge* ('The Greasy Stone') in Varanger where graves, and a sacred Bear Stone are located at the most prominent spot – the top of a small mountain known as Čiesti ('The Birds Rock', Fig. 2.12), which the cemetery encompasses. Other prominent locations that illustrate these links even further are the aforementioned Skaga and Skagadalen burial sites on the island of Spildra where human graves, bear graves, and a sacrificial stone are located in proximity. Even though human graves and bear graves are spatially separated, the association is evident through their mutual burial in cavities and the sacrificial stone uniting the various elements in the landscape. Spildra is not the only location where human graves and bear graves occur in proximity. At the pre-Christian Sámi cemetery at Kirkeneset in Lebesby, eastern Finnmark, a bear grave (with marrow-split bones but without the skull) was documented amongst human graves of identical morphology (Myrstad 1996, 30; Schanche 2000, 394). In one of the human graves two bear teeth were documented. At Skrolsvik, on the island of Senja in southern Troms, bears and humans appear to have been buried in the same grave and cavity, even though the accuracy of these finds is questionable (Myrstad 1996, 36–37). None of these graves have been dated, but those at Kirkeneset point to the medieval period or earlier.

The relationship between cavities and the world of the dead is interestingly illustrated in a drawing by the missionary Thomas von Westen of the now-lost Sámi shaman drum from the so-called Nærø manuscript (which exists only in transcripts) of the aforementioned Randulf (Fig. 2.13). It is noteworthy that the Salsfjellet bear grave is close to Nærøy where Randulf was a parish priest and later dean of the wider area of Namdalen in the county of Nord-Trøndelag. Depictions on Sámi shaman drums probably represented a microcosm of the Sámi universe, but they seem

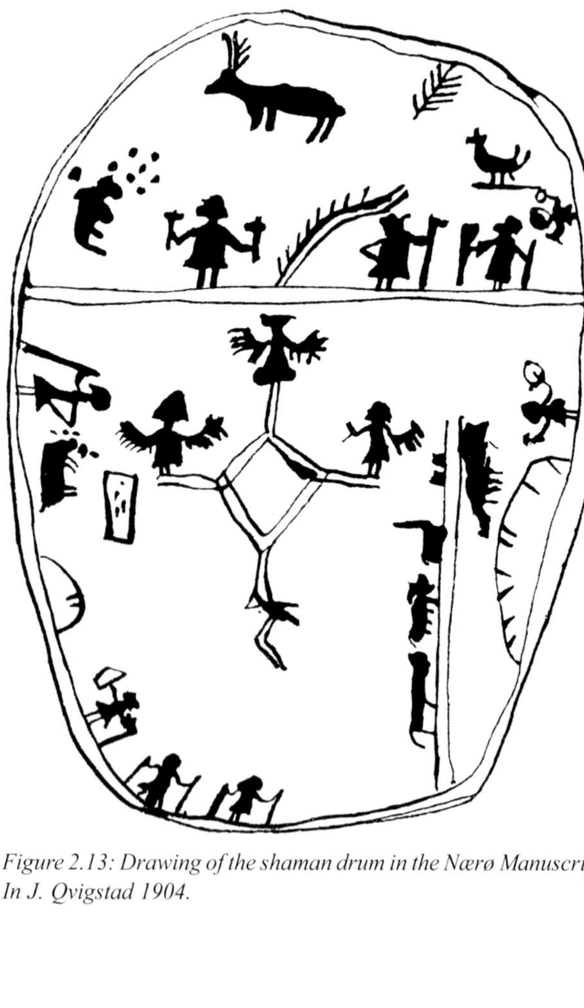

*Figure 2.13: Drawing of the shaman drum in the Nærø Manuscript. In J. Qvigstad 1904.*

to vary between regions with regard to figures, patterns, and divisions, which may reflect individual or regional interpretations of the different realms, gods and powers reigning therein (Hansen and Olsen 2014, 223). The kingdom of death, *Japmiidáibmu*, is generally depicted as a separate sphere, such as in the Nærø manuscript where the world of the dead constitutes a half-open space forming a sort of cave in the lower right area of the drum, similar to depictions of this realm on other Sámi drums (Manker 1961, 16). The world of the dead, *Jamicutsche*, in Randulf's (1723, cited in Qvigstad 1904, 18–19) designation and orthography, is represented by a semi-circular motif designated *Jamicutsche Palches* ('the road to the world of the dead'). This motif may be interpreted as a burial mound but is more likely a gap, aperture, or cavity indicated by the very name and shortened lines that indicate a constricted space.

The relation between humans and bears appears to have been significant, intimate, and complex in Sámi pre-Christian society and cosmology. This is further indicated by the bear grave at Skagadalen in which a large piece of birch bark was documented. It is not possible to establish whether or not this was a fragment of shrouding, but finds of birch bark from several other bear graves both in Norway and Sweden hint at this possibility, particularly the contemporaneous Viking Age bear grave from Karats in which the skeletal remains were placed on a layer of birch bark. Schanche (2000, 289) evades this feature in her comparison of human and bear graves stating that the latter demonstrate a significant minor morphological variation of the former. However, given the arguments in this chapter, and the significant lack of investigation and documentation of bear graves, a slight modification of Schanche's view now seems appropriate. Although the morphological variation appears limited, bear graves demonstrate what could be perceived as some of the most significant characteristics of Sámi graves: namely, their location in cavities, which are entrances to the realm of the dead, and the use of birch bark – two of the longest-lasting features of Sámi burial customs.

Further human–bear entanglements are indicated through finds of brass chains and a leaf-shaped pendant from a silver brooch in bear graves, which correspond, respectively, to the significance of brass in the bear cult in the written accounts and *sjele-kallo* ('that which has a silver leaf on its forehead') – one of the names for the bear. Brass and other metals were linked to a magic and protective force in Sámi pre-Christian ideology and particularly a ring and chain in relation to the bear hunt and cult (Petersen 1940, 157). Chains and other brass objects are recorded from numerous human graves. However, based on the scant archaeological evidence and information in written accounts, the ritual importance of brass in the bear cult (or burial) seems to be a late occurrence and not representative of religious practice prior to the high medieval period.

Finally, the grave at Silkeberget on the island of Spildra, where a toe-joint of a bear was documented beside a wing bone of a herring gull, artefacts, and the skeletal remains of two humans, indicates intricate relations between humans and bears. This find also challenges our understanding of burial and sacrifice in Sámi religious practices in the Late Iron Age and early medieval period.

### *Burial, sacrifice, worship*

Myrstad (1996, 53) notes that bones or antlers from other animals are documented on several sites with bear skulls. At Unna Saiva in northern Sweden, dated to AD 1000–1200, nine bear skulls were documented together with animal bones, antlers, jewellery and coins (Mulk and Iregren 1995, 12; Serning 1956). Another site with a similar find is the sacred Ukon Island in Lake Inari, northern Finland, in which a cave contained numerous bones of reindeer, bear, wolf, wolverine and birds, and a Permian silver ring dated to the eleventh or twelfth century AD (Nordman 1922, 4; Zachrisson 1984, 18). These sites have mostly been defined as ritual deposits or sacrificial sites (Zachrisson and Iregren 1974, 34–37), but this definition may rest upon a narrow 'Western' concept of what constitutes a grave, as argued by Myrstad (1996, 53). The argument finds further support in the north-east with regard to finds of bear skulls and skulls of other animals at sacrificial places of the Nenets (Jurak-Samoyeds), as well as in their tradition of placing the sacrifice of a reindeer calf in a bear burial to thank the bear for not killing the hunter, as referred to by Mebius (1968, 91). As noted by Theodor Petersen (1940, 162) the skull often represents the whole body in magic and cult as *pars pro toto*, which may imply a similar representation in instances where only the skull or other bones of the bear exist, such as the toe-joint in the Silkeberget grave. Petersen (1940, 160) also remarks that the boundary between bear graves and bear sacrifice may be in flux. This aspect is indicated by the only possible bear grave documented in a dwelling: the tenth-century AD Grundskatan bear burial at Bjurö Island in the Skellefteå municipality in Västerbotten County, north Sweden. In one of the corners of a rectangular dwelling (hut 4), a bear grave was ritually deposited in a cairn (Broadbent and Storå 2003; Broadbent 2010, 79–82, 180). A total of 66 bones of bear were documented, which most likely originated from the same adult individual. The bones were organised in three separate and partly structured piles; several bones exhibited marks of being chopped or broken for marrow extraction. The phalanges and claws were missing, indicating that the skin had been retained. Noel Broadbent (2010, 180–183) observed that the way the burial cairn and bones were organised signifies a deposit of ritual significance. Although the *in-situ* nature of this grave is contested (see Liedgren and Ramqvist 2012), Broadbent (2010, 180) points out that missing phalanges and claws reveal that the skin of the bear was retained with these bones attached to it, thus demonstrating consistency with the written sources of Sámi bear hunting and cult.

Sacrifices and burials are generally considered separate events, but the division between human and animal burial and sacrifice is not always apparent, as indicated in several of the aforementioned graves and through finds of shells and animal bones in Sámi graves. Thus, the distinction between animal sacrifice as part of mortuary rituals and the deposition of animal bones in graves appears complex. Written accounts are scarce with regard to information on animal bones in graves. Schanche (2000, 266; Pettersson 1957, 53) refers to the Vogul tradition in Siberia of placing the bones of a sacrificed animal in a grave. A similar tradition may have been present among the Sámi in the late Iron Age and early medieval period. However, Schanche (2000, 199) also refers to some interesting observations by the seminal archaeologist of Sámi graves, Andreas Georg Nordvi. In a letter to zoologist Japetus Steenstrup in Copenhagen in 1854, Nordvi noted that in an unopened Sámi grave in Varanger, he did not see any human skeletal remains but observed the largest collection of animal bones that he had ever encountered in a grave. According to Nordvi he made numerous similar observations (but with fewer animal bones), which are interesting in relation to the entanglements of humans and bears discussed in a ritual context.

As noted by Schanche (2000, 271), both the archaeological and written records demonstrate that rocky terrains were preferred by the Sámi for offerings or deposits of animal bones – particularly caves, rockshelters and cavities. When recorded, these sites are often associated with topographical formations that are distinctive within their surrounding environments, similar to *sieidis* and sanctuaries. Thus, sacrificial animal bones in cracks, fissures and cavities in the rock or in the ground demonstrate a characteristic feature of burial in cavities: both are located at openings or entrances to the underworld or other worlds. Schanche (2000, 273) also remarked that the relationship between bone deposits and sacrificial bone was complex and subtle in Sámi pre-Christian religion, but there is reason to believe that the relationship between sacrifice, worship and burial was equally complex and subtle, at least in some instances. A possible statement of this complexity is reflected at Skaga grave 1 with the remarkable find of one or possibly two *sieidi* in the grave itself. The distinctions between human graves, bear graves, worship and sacrifice occasionally seem blurred, which may reflect an inconsistency in Sámi religious concepts and practices in the late Iron Age and early medieval period. These aspects appear particularly noticeable with regard to rituals and religious practices associated with cavities.

## Conclusion

Although the archaeological record concerning Sámi graves and rituals in cavities is scant and lacks sufficient analyses and dating, recent research on the grave in Skjellesvik, and the comparison between human graves and bear graves, question Schanche's diffusion theory of the origin and dispersal of Sámi burial customs. There is no question that the Varanger area is significant in this regard but, as argued here, it is now necessary to modify our understanding of the emergence and development of Sámi burial customs. The intimate relationship between human graves and bear graves, new dates, and the re-evaluation of previous finds, point to the existence of Sámi burial customs outside the Varanger area at an earlier period than was hitherto recognised – probably in the first millennium BC – but it is not possible to provide a conclusive answer at this time. Future investigations will surely unearth fresh evidence and shed new light on this issue.

The fragmentary nature of the archaeological record does not allow for further reliable inferences regarding Sámi burials in natural cavities, although collective burial and wooden planking as part of constructed graves are more frequent in these funerary contexts than in others. It is difficult to conclude whether Sámi graves in such environments represent burials of particular or prominent individuals, or a certain custom within the Sámi burial tradition. However, the construction of graves in 'cavities' is apparent elsewhere, such as with the typical graves in Varanger, for instance. These graves are constructed from slab-shaped beach rocks, literally beneath the earth and thus in the world of the dead – *Jápmiidáibmu*. Thus, cavities, either natural or constructed, may be perceived as the most common and longest lasting feature of Sámi burial customs. Moreover, it is likely that burials in natural cavities demonstrate strong regional and local affiliations dependent on the quality of the landscape or surrounding environment. These burials are most abundant along the mountainous coast of Nordland and Troms where scree deposits or, more precisely, slab-shaped beach rocks typical of the Varanger area, are absent, and screes of various sized boulders are more common. However, natural caves or cavities seem to constitute spaces that, in a very clear manner, accentuate the relationship between the world of the living and the world of the dead through their distinct physical and metaphoric characteristics. Their similarity to bear dens and bear graves seems to further strengthen the relations, which appear to be no coincidence. The unique qualities of the bear towards life and death seem to have been influential. Additionally, looking at the archaeological record of graves in cavities in comparison to bear graves, the distinction between burial and sacrifice is not always apparent, at least not in the late Iron Age and early medieval period. This may represent a feature of Sámi religion that was altered or transformed into the known division in the late medieval period and/or early modern period in conjunction with increasing external religious influence.

It appears that landscape affordances had a crucial impact on the religious concepts and burial practices of the Sámi, and the way that they came into being and were constantly reinterpreted and modified. The nature of the surrounding environment thus appears to have had a formative influence on rituals, practices and religious beliefs regarding the departed (whether humans or bears) and the afterlife in the world(s) of the dead and amongst the living, as it did for the location and construction of burials and sacred places in cavities.

## References


Andreassen, R.L., 1990. *Ei urgrav på Vannøy fra tidlig middelalder*. Tromura. Kulturhistorie 17. Tromsø: University of Tromsø.

Äikäs, T., Puputti, A.-K., Núñez, M., Aspi, J. and Okkonen, J., 2009. Sacred and profane livelihood: animal bones from sieidi sites in Northern Finland. *Norwegian Archaeological Review* 42(2), 109–122.

Baudou, E., 1995. *Norrland forntid – ett historiskt perspektiv*. Umeå: CEWE-förlaget.

Bergstøl, J., 2008. *Samer i Østerdalen? En studie av etnisitet i jernalderen og middelalderen i det nordøstre Hedmark*. Acta Humaniora 325. Oslo: University of Oslo.

Binns, K.S., 1988. En flatmarksgrav fra Austein I Troms. En diskusjon om alder og kulturell tilhørighet. *Studia Historica Septentrionalia* 14(1), 120–139.

Bjerck, H., 2012. On the outer fringe of the human world: phenomenological perspectives on anthropomorphic cave paintings in Norway. *In*: K.A. Bergsvik and R. Skeates, eds. *Caves in Context: The Cultural Significance of Caves and Rockshelters in Europe*. Oxford: Oxbow Books, 48–64.

Bjørklund, I., 1985. *Fjordfolket i Kvænangen – Fra samisk samfunn til norsk utkant 1550–1980*. Oslo: Universitetsforlaget.

Boëthius, A., 2010. *Osteologisk analys av redeponeringen vid Gransjön, Frosvikens socken, Jämtlands län*. Reports in Osteology 11, University of Lund. Available from: http://lup.lub.lu.se/luur/download?func=downloadFileandrecordOId=2338622andfileOId=2338625 [accessed 9 January 2015].

Bratrein, H.D., 1989. *Karlsøy og Helgøy bygdebok. Vol. 1. Fra Steinalder til år 1700*. Hansnes: Karlsøy kommune.

Broadbent, N.D., 2010. *Lapps and Labyrinths: Saami Prehistory, Colonization and Cultural Resilience*. Washington D.C.: Arctic Studies Center/Smithsonian Institution Scholarly Press.

Broadbent, N.D. and Storå, J., 2003. En björngrav i Grundskatan. *Populär Arkeologi*, 1, 3–6.

Bruun, I.M., 2007. *Blandede Graver – Blandende Kulturerer? En Tolkning av Gravskikk og Etniske Forhold i Nord-Norge Gjennom Jernalder og Tidlig Middelalder*. Thesis (MA), University of Tromsø.

Bäckman, L., 1975. *Sájva. Föreställningar om hjälp- och skyddsväsen i heliga fjäll bland samerna*. Acta Universitatis Stockholmensis, Stockholm Studies in Comparative Religion 13. Stockholm: Almqvist and Wiksell.

Bäckman, L. and Hultkrantz, Å., 1978. *Studies in Lapp Shamanism*. Acta Universitatis Stockholmiensis, Stockholm Studies in Comparative Religion 16. Stockholm: Almqvist and Wiksell.

Bäckman, L. and Hultkrantz, Å. eds. 1985. *Saami Pre-Christian Religion: Studies on the Oldest Traces of Religion Among the Saamis*. Acta Universitatis Stockholmensis. Stockholm Studies in Comparative Religion 25. Stockholm: Almqvist and Wiksell.

Dass, P., 1967 [1739]. *Nordlands trompet, den nordske dale-viise*. Edition D.A. Seip. Oslo: Gyldendal Norsk Forlag.

Drake, S., 1918. *Västerbottenslapparna under förra hälften av 1800-talet: etnografiska studier*. Lapparne och deras land 7. Uppsala: Almqvist & Wiksell.

Denham, S.D., 2015. *Osteological Analysis of Human Remains from Skjellesvik, Tysfjord k., Nordland*. Oppdragsrapport 20. Stavanger: Universitetet i Stavanger/Arkeologisk museum.

Dunfjeld-Aagård, L., 2005. Sørsamiske kystområder: Tolking av fortidig samisk tilstedeværelse i Ytre Namdal. Thesis (MA), University of Tromsø.

Edgren, T. and Törnblom, L., 1993. *Finlands historia*, 1. Esbo: Schildts.

Edsman, C.-M., 1994. *Jägaren och makterna: samiska och finska björnceremonier*. Skrifter Serie C, Lapskt språk och lapsk kultur 6. Uppsala: Dialekt- och folkminnesarkivet i Uppsala.

Elgmork, K., 1999. *Bjørnens liv*. Hønefoss: Kolltopp.

Eliade, M., 1964. *Shamanism: Archaic Techniques of Ecstasy*. Transl. W.R. Trask. London: Routledge and Kegan Paul.

Figenschau, I., 2014. *Skjellesvik, Tysfjord. Arkeologisk nødutgraving*. Unpublished excavation report, Tromsø University Museum, Norway.

Fjellström, P., 1981 [1775]. *Kort berättelse om lapparnas björna-fänga, samt deras der wid brukade wiskeppelser*. Norrländska skrifter 5. Umeå: Två förleggare.

Fritzner, J., 1877. Lappernes hedenskab og trolldomskunst sammenholdt med andre folks, især normændenes, tro og overtro. *Historisk Tidsskrift* 1(4), 136–217.

Gjerde, J.M., 2010. Rock Art and Landscapes: Studies of Stone Age Rock Art from Northern Fennoscandia. Thesis (PhD), University of Tromsø, Norway.

Gjessing, G., 1928. Finsk-ugriske vikingetidssmykker i Norge. *Universitetets Oldsaksamlings Årbok* 1927, 23–41.

Gjessing, G., 1942. *Yngre steinalder i Nord-Norge*. Instituttet for sammenliknende kulturforskning. Serie B, Skrifter XXXIX. Oslo: Aschehoug (W. Nygaard).

Grydeland, S.E., 2001. *De sjøsamiske siida-samfunn: En studie med utgangspunkt i Kvænangen, Nord-Troms*. Nord-Troms Museums Skrifter. Sørkjosen: Nord-Troms Museum.

Hallowell, A.I., 1924. Bear ceremonialism in the northern hemisphere. *American Anthropologist*, 28:1, 1–175.

Hansen, L.I. and Olsen, B., 2014. *Hunters in Transition: an Outline of Early Sámi History*. The Northern World – North Europe and the Baltic *c*. 400–1700 AD. Peoples, Economies and Cultures, vol. 63. Leiden and Boston: Brill.

Heidegger, M., 1993. *Basic Writings*. London: Routledge.

Hedlund, T., 2011. *Osteologisk undersökning av samisk skelett (JLM 280 18) från Gransjö vid Ohredahke sameby, Frostviken socken, Jämtland*. Reports in Osteology 5, University of Lund. Available from: http://lup.lub.lu.se/luur/download?func=downloadFileandrecordOId=2338663andfileOId=2338675 [accessed 9 January 2015].

Helle, K., 2003. Introduction. *In*: K. Helle, ed. *The Cambridge History of Scandinavia – Volume 1: Prehistory to 1520*. Cambridge: Cambridge University Press.

Helskog, K., 2012. Bears and meanings among hunter-fisher-gatherers in northern Fennoscandia 9000–5000 BC. *Cambridge Archaeological Journal* 22(2), 209–236.

Helskog, K., 2014. *Communicating with the World of Beings: The World Heritage Rock Art sites in Alta, Arctic Norway*. Transl. T. Challman. Oxford: Oxbow Books.

Holmberg, U., 1926. *Die Religion der Tscheremissen*. FF Comunications 61. Helsinki: Suomalainen tiedeakatemia.

Holmberg, U., 1987 [1915]. *Lapparnas Religion (Lappalaisten uskonto)*. Uppsala multiethnic papers 10. Uppsala: Uppsala University, Centre for Mulitiethnic Research.

Itkonen, T.I., 1946. *Heidnische Religion und späterer Aberglaube bei den finnischen Lappen*. Suomalaais-Ugrilaisen Seuran Toimituksia LXXXVII. Helsinki: Suomalais-Ugrilainen Seura.

Kjellström, R. and Rydving, H., 1988. *Den samiska trumman*. Stockholm: Nordiska Museet.

Kopisto, A., 1971. Kuusamon lappalaishauta. *Suomen Museo* 78, 64–72.

Leem, K., 1975 [1767]. *Beskrivelse over Finnmarkens lapper*. Copenhagen: Rosenkilde and Bagger.

Leppäaho, J., 1937. Savokosken mukkalan lappalaiskalmisto. *Kotiseutu* 3/4, 134–144.

Liedgren, L. and Ramqvist, P.H., 2012. Noel Broadbents lappar och labyrinter. *Fornvännen* 107, 213–217.

Manker, E., 1957. *Lapparnas heliga ställen*. Acta Lapponica XIII. Uppsala: Gebers.

Manker, E., 1961. *Lappmarksgravar*. Acta Lapponica XVII. Stockholm: Almqvist and Wiksell.

Martynov, A., 2002. Archaeological past of the Solovetskii archipelago (Stone and early Metal Ages). *In*: E. Ieshko and N. Mikhailova, eds. *Natural and Cultural Heritage of the White Sea Island*. The Nordic Council of Ministers/The Barents Euro-Arctic Region. Petrozavodsk: Paconi, 31–39.

Mebius, H., 1968. *Värrõ: Studier i samernas förkristna offerriter*. Skrifter utgivna av religionshistoriska institutionen i Uppsala 5. Uppsala: Almqvist and Wiksell.

Mebius, H., 1972. Sjiele. Samiska traditioner om offer. *Saga och Sed* 1971, 55–120.

Mulk, I.M., 1994. Sacrificial places and their meaning in Saami society. *In*: D.L. Carmichael, J. Hubert, B. Reeves, and A. Schanche, eds. *Sacred Sites, Sacred Places*. One World Archaeology 23. London: Routledge, 121–131.

Mulk, I.M., 1995. *Sirkas – ett samiskt fångstsamhälle i förändring Kr.f.-1600 e.Kr.* Studia Archaeologica Universitatis Umensis 6. Umeå: University of Umeå.

Mulk, I.M., 2009. Conflicts over the repatriation of Sámi cultural heritage in Sweden. *Acta Borealia* 26(2), 194–215.

Mulk, I.M. and Iregren, E., 1995. *Björngraven i Karats*. Duoddaris 9. Jokkmokk: Ajtte.

Mundal, E., 2000. Coexistence of Saami and Norse culture – reflected in and interpreted by Old Norse myths. *In*: G. Barnes and M. Clunies Ross, eds. *Old Norse Myths, Literature and Society. Proceedings of the 11th International Saga Conference*. Sydney: Centre of Medieval Studies, University of Sydney, 346–355.

Myrstad, R., 1996. Bjørnegraver i Nord-Norge. Spor etter den samiske bjørnekulten. Thesis (MA), University of Tromsø.

Nordman, C.A., 1922. Silfverringen från Ukonsaari i Enare. *Finskt museum*, 29, 1–10.

Oppvang, J. and Kjellman, E., 2016. Ånesteinen, Sortland k. Innhenting av beinmateriale. Sikringsprosjekt 18.–21. mai 2016. Unpublished archaeological report. Tromsø: Tromsø Museum – Universitetsmuseet.

Ovsiannokov, O.V., 1993. The Arctic Russia in the Middle Ages: Recent Archaeological Discoveries and the Ancient Trade Route along the Arctic Coast. Thesis, University of Tromsø.

Pentikäinen, J., 1997. *Die Mytologie der Saamen*. Ethnologische Beiträge zur Circumpolarforschung, Band 3. Berlin: Reinhold Scheltzer.

Petersen, Th., 1940. En bjørnegrav. Trekk av lappisk folketro. *Viking* IV, 153–166.

Pettersson, O., 1957. *Jabmek and Jabmeaimo. A Comparative Study of the Dead and the Realm of the Dead in Lappish Religion*. Acta Universitatis Lundensis, Nova series 52(6). Lund: C.W.K. Gleerup.

Pettersson, O., 1987. Old Nordic and Christian elements in Saami ideas about the realm of the dead. *In*: T. Ahlback, ed. *Saami Religion*. Scripta Instituti Donneriani Aboensis 12. Åbo: The Donner institute for Research in Religious and Cultural History, 69–80.

Price, N.S., 2002. *The Viking Way. Religion and War in Late Iron Age Scandinavia*. Aun 31. Uppsala: Department of Archaeology and Ancient History, University of Uppsala.

Qvigstad, J., 1904. Kildeskrifter til den lappiske mythologi. *Det Kongelige Norske Videnskabers Selskabs Skrifter* 1903(1), 1–90.

Qvigstad, J., 1926. *Lappische Opfersteine unde heilige Berge in Norwegen*. Zur Sprach- und Volkskunde der Norwegischen Lappen. Oslo Etnografiske Museums skrifter 5(b1). Oslo: Etnografisk Museum.

Ruohonen, J., 2005. Rauha eläville, lepo kuolleille. Kirkkomaan ulkopuoliset hautapaikat arkeoogisen aineiston, hitoriallisten lähteiden, paikannismistön ja perimätiedon kuvaamana. Thesis (MA), University of Turku.

Rydving, H., 1995. *The End of Drum-time. Religious Change among the Lule Saami, 1670s–1740s*. Acta Universitatis Upsalensis, Historia Religionum 12 (2nd edn). Uppsala: University of Uppsala.

Schanche, A., 1995. Det symbolske landskapet – landskap og identitet i samisk kultur. *Ottar* 207, 38–47.

Schanche, A., 2000. *Graver i ur og berg – Samisk gravskikk og religion fra forhistorisk til nyere tid*. Karasjok: Davvi Girji.

Schefferus, J., 1956 [1673]. *Lappland*. Transl. H. Sundin, ed. E. Manker. Acta Lapponica VIII. Uppsala: Gebers.

Schreiner, K.E., 1927. *Menneskeknoklene fra Osebergskibet*. Offprint of Osebergfundet, vol. 5. Oslo: Universitetets Anatomiske Institutt.

Schreiner, K.E., 1931. *Zur Osteologie der Lappen*, 2. Serie B, Skrifter. Oslo: Instituttet for sammenlignende kulturforskning.

Schreiner, K.E., 1935. *Zur Osteologie der Lappen*, 1. Serie B, Skrifter. Oslo: Instituttet for sammenlignende kulturforskning.

Serning, I., 1956. *Lapska offerplatsfynd från järnålder och medeltid i de svenska lappmarkerna*. Acta Lapponica XI. Stockholm: Hugo Gebers Förlag.

Shumkin, V., Kolpakov, E.M., and Murashkin, A.I., 2006. *Oleneostrovskiy mogil'nik Barentseva morya*. Kol'skaya arkheologicheskaya ekspeditsiya, Rossiyskaya Akademiya Nauk. Available from: http://kae.rekvizit.ru/olen/olhist.htm [accessed 1 September 2015].

Sjövold, T., 1962. *The Iron Age Settlement of Arctic Norway I*. Tromsø Museums Skrifter, X (1). Tromsø and Oslo: Norwegian University Press.

Sjövold, T., 1974. *The Iron Age Settlement of Arctic Norway II*. Tromsø Museums Skrifter, X (2). Tromsø, Oslo and Bergen: Norwegian University Press.

Sjøvold, T. 2017. Skjelettdeler fra samisk urgrav fra Skjellesvik, Skrovkjosen, Tysfjord kommune. Unpublished osteological report. Stockholm: University of Stockholm.

Skanke, H., 1945 [1728–1730]. Epitomes Historiæ Missionis Lapponicæ Pars Prima. Anlangende de Nordske Lappers hedendom og superstitioner. Med utdrag av pars tertia samt anhang 3. og 4. *In*: O. Solberg, ed. *Nordlands og Troms finner i eldre håndskrifter*. Nordnorske Samlinger V(2). Oslo: Etnografisk Museum, 175–256.

Solbakk, A., 2008. *Hva vi tror på: Noaidevuohta – en innføring i nordsamenes religion*. Kárášjohka-Karasjok: ČálliidLágádus.

Solberg, B., 2000. *Jernalderen i Norge: 500 før Kristus til 1030 etter Kristus*. Oslo: Cappelen Akademisk Forlag.

Solli, B., 2002. *Seid. Myter, sjamanisme og kjønn i vikingenes tid*. Oslo: Pax.

Spa, L. von der, 2009. Skjøtselsplan for kulturminnelokalitetene i Skrovkjosen. Unpublished management plan. Karasjok: Samediggi-Sametinget.

Storå, N., 1971. *Burial Customs of the Skolt Lapps*. Folklore Fellows Communications LXXXIX 2, No. 210. Helsinki: Adademia Scientiarum Fennica.

Sundström, J., 1988. Graven vid Gransjön i Frostviken. *Åarjelsaemieh* 3, 136–144.

Sveen, A., 2003. *Mytisk landskap – Ved dansende skog og susende fjell*. Stamsund: Orkana.

Svestad, A., 2007. 'Folk er vanligvis ikke særlig villig til å snakke om de døde' – Synspunkter på materialitet og samisk gravskikk. *Arkeologi i Norr* 10, 41–76.

Svestad, A., 2010. De døde skjuler mange ting. Arkeologiske undersøkelser på Gullholmen kirkegård. *Tana-årboka/Deanu jahkegirji*, 77–91.

Svestad, A., 2011. The impact of materiality on Sámi burial customs and religious concepts. *Fennoscandia Archaeologica* XXVII, 39–56.

Svestad, A., 2013. What happened in Neiden? On the question of reburial ethics. *Norwegian Archaeological Review* 46(2), 194–222.

Taavitsainen, J.-P., 2003. Lapp cairns as a source on Metal Period settlement in the Inland Regions of Finland. *Acta Borealia* 20(1), 21–47.

Vorren, Ø. and Eriksen, H.K., 1993. *Samiske offerplasser i Varanger*. Stonglandseidet: Nordkalottforlaget.

Wittgenstein, L., 1989. *Philosophical Investigations*. 3rd edn. Oxford: Basil Blackwell.

Zachrisson, I., 1984. *De samiska metalldepåerna år 1000–1350: i ljuset av fyndet från Mörtträsket, Lappland*. Archaeology and Environment 3. Umeå: University of Umeå.

Zachrisson, I., 1986. *Lapps and Scandinavians*. Early Norrland 10. Stockholm: Almqvist & Wiksell.

Zachrisson, I., Alexandersen, V. and Gollwitzer, M., 1997. *Möten i gränsland – samer och germaner i Mellanskandinavien*. Monographs 4. Stockholm: Statens historiska museum.

Zachrisson, I. and Iregren, E., 1974. *Lappish Bear Graves in Northern Sweden*. Early Norrland 5. Stockholm: Almqvist & Wiksell.

# Chapter 3

# The perception and use of caves and rockshelters in Late Iron Age and medieval western Norway, *c.* AD 550–1550

*Knut Andreas Bergsvik*

*Archaeological data from 32 surveyed and excavated caves and rockshelters in western Norway show that dwelling was uncommon at these sites; they were more often used for placed (ritual) deposits, burials, and as workshops for metal smiths and stone masons. An extensive study of medieval Icelandic saga texts, Eddic poetry and other written sources reveals that caves were often scenes of negative activities and incidents for humans. They are also portrayed as homes for giants and other supernatural beings and powers in Norse mythology. It is argued here that people in western Norway associated caves with these beings during the Late Iron Age and that these perceptions continued well into the Christian Middle Ages. This resulted in a general avoidance of caves and rockshelters for dwelling purposes. On the other hand, they were important sites for worship and rituals.*

## Introduction

During the Stone Age, Bronze Age and Early Iron Age, caves and rockshelters were frequently used in Norway. Research on these sites has provided important data on subsistence and settlement patterns as well as on social relations and ritual practice. However, when entering into the early historic periods – the Late Iron Age and the Middle Ages – caves have largely been ignored by archaeologists. Similar to many other regions in Europe, medieval materials from caves and rockshelters are only briefly mentioned in excavation reports, and they are seldom published in their own right. Attention has nearly always been on the older data.

But the medieval material is there and it has great potential, particularly for the study of religion and rituals. In this chapter, the goal is to systematise the archaeological data, to present it, and to discuss it with a main focus on the religious use and perceptions of these sites in the early historic periods in western Norway, between *c.* AD 550–1550. This is a period which saw major changes in Norwegian society and politics. The most important changes were the process of early state formation, which made a fundamental breakthrough during the late 800s, and the conversion to Christianity and establishment of the Catholic Church around 1000. How the use of – and beliefs in – caves and rockshelters was affected by these major changes is an important issue.

This goal cannot be achieved without considering the written sources. Researchers studying the medieval period in Norway have access to a large body of texts that were written down from the thirteenth to the fifteenth century, mainly in Iceland. In these texts, caves and rockshelters are mentioned surprisingly often in connection to mythology, as well as for practical purposes. These extraordinary written sources, which are discussed below, allow for deep and nuanced analyses of how caves and rockshelters were perceived and used, and are a strong partner for archaeology. This is not to say that the function of archaeology is reduced to merely illustrating the information generated by the written sources. Instead, these two source types should be seen as complementary in terms of their interpretative potential and, clearly, neither is perfect. As will be evident from the following discussions, the written sources refer to certain types of activities and perceptions, which only to some degree overlap with the activities and functions that are documented through archaeological survey and excavation. This probably means that the two source types represent different aspects of reality. Over the last few years, major efforts have been made to bridge the gap between archaeology, religion, and literary studies on Norse mythology (e.g. Price 2002; Andrén 1989; Andrén *et al.* 2004, 2006; Lund 2009). As is pointed out by John Hines, the mythology as it is presented to us in the written sources 'provides an explicit expression of the significance of phenomena present in the archaeological record' (2003, 37). In line with this, the challenge of the following contribution is to merge the data provided by archaeology and written sources into a holistic or *thicker* understanding of the significance of caves and rockshelters for medieval people.

## Sources and basic methodological considerations

Caves and rockshelters are abundant in western Norway. Although no karstic or volcanic caves are present, there are several sea caves along the coast which have been formed by sea wave action. Rockshelters occur much more frequently. They have been shaped by geological processes such as rock-fall, or erosion in fault zones or fissures. A variant of the shelter category is the boulder rockshelter, typically found in screes or under large free-standing blocks. Caves and rockshelters have been subject to archaeological investigations for the last 150 years, with reports and material archived and stored at the university museums. A total of around 350 caves and rockshelters with traces of human use have been identified in western Norway, which includes the counties of Møre og Romsdal, Sogn og Fjordane, Hordaland, and Rogaland. As part of the present project, reports and material from rockshelters in these counties were surveyed in order to single out sites that have layers or archaeological material securely dated to the Late Iron Age and medieval period. Caves and rockshelters that have been created artificially as a result of quarrying during the Middle Ages (e.g. Baug 2015) are not considered. This museum survey was augmented by my own excavations (Bergsvik *et al.* 2014). A total of 32 sites form part of the analysis (see Fig. 3.1, Table 3.1).

There are major differences in the excavation methods that have been applied, as well as the locations of excavated areas in the rockshelters. There are also differences regarding the dating evidence. Typology may provide narrow frames of dating, but sometimes it may only provide broad dates covering the entire period in question. In other cases, only radiocarbon dates of cultural layers/features reveal activity. Sometimes, the rather broad ranges supplied by radiocarbon dates and artefact typology can be combined to provide more precise dates (Table 3.2). Broad dating frameworks are applied here, and these are divided into: the Merovingian period (*c.* 550–800), the Viking period (*c.* 800–1000), and the early (*c.* 1000–1150), high (*c.* 1150–1350) and late medieval (*c.* 1350–1536) periods. These period definitions will be used throughout this chapter. In addition, the terms Late Iron Age and Middle Ages will refer to the periods before and after *c.* 1000 AD.

The written sources have been surveyed for passages where caves and rockshelters are mentioned (denoted by the Norse word *hellir* [pl. *hellar*], which covers both cave and rockshelter). These mainly consist of the Old Norse written sources which include the Eddic poetry (anonymous Old Norse poems), *Snorri's Edda*, *Sturlunga saga*, *Íslendingabók*, *Landnámabók*, the sagas and tales of the Icelanders, and the sagas of the Norwegian kings and earls. *Saxo Gramaticus* and the legendary sagas are not included. To some extent, other written sources are also used, such as Adam of Bremen's *Gesta Hammaburgensis ecclesiæ pontificum*, and Icelandic and Norwegian medieval laws. Some critical consideration needs to be given to how these sources are evaluated and understood.

First, in research history, there have been major scholarly debates on the value of the Eddic poetry, *Snorri's Edda*, and the saga literature, particularly on their relevance as sources to the study of Norse mythology (e.g. Steinsland 2005, 35ff.; Thorvaldsen 2013). Although they originated as oral tradition during the Late Iron Age, they were first recorded in a Christian society during the Middle Ages. A main theme, therefore, has been the degree to which they have been influenced by Christian religious thought. Today, there seems to be a general agreement that skaldic poetry is the least affected by Christian thinking, whereas it is more uncertain to what extent the Eddic poetry has changed – or has even been invented – after the conversion (e.g. Schjødt 2008, 85ff.; Lund 2009, 17). It has been argued that some of the themes in the Eddic poems are of pre-Christian origin because of their presence in the iconography on Late Iron Age picture stones (e.g. the death of Sigurðr Fáfnisbani and Þórr's fishing trip) and possibly on gold bracteates from the fifth century AD (Andrén 1989; Axboe 2004). Although *Snorri's Edda* is also considered to be an important source, it needs to be used more carefully than the poems because of more evident Christian influences (Schjødt 2008, 97ff.; Løkka 2010, 52). This is truer still for the information on mythology contained within the sagas (Meulengracht Sørensen 1977, 54).

Secondly, concerning the saga texts, historians today are critical of their value as sources of historic events (e.g. Helle 2011). In our case, this means that we cannot be sure if the caves and rockshelters, and the people that used them, really existed as described in the sagas. In this context, however, historical accuracy is neither of major importance nor the main contribution of these texts. We here delimit ourselves to an anthropological approach (Meulengracht Sørensen 1995; Bagge 2014), which means that our primary interest is connected to how human use of the caves and rockshelters is described and how they are perceived by medieval writers. Related to this issue is the relevancy of the saga texts as sources for activities and incidents during the Late Iron

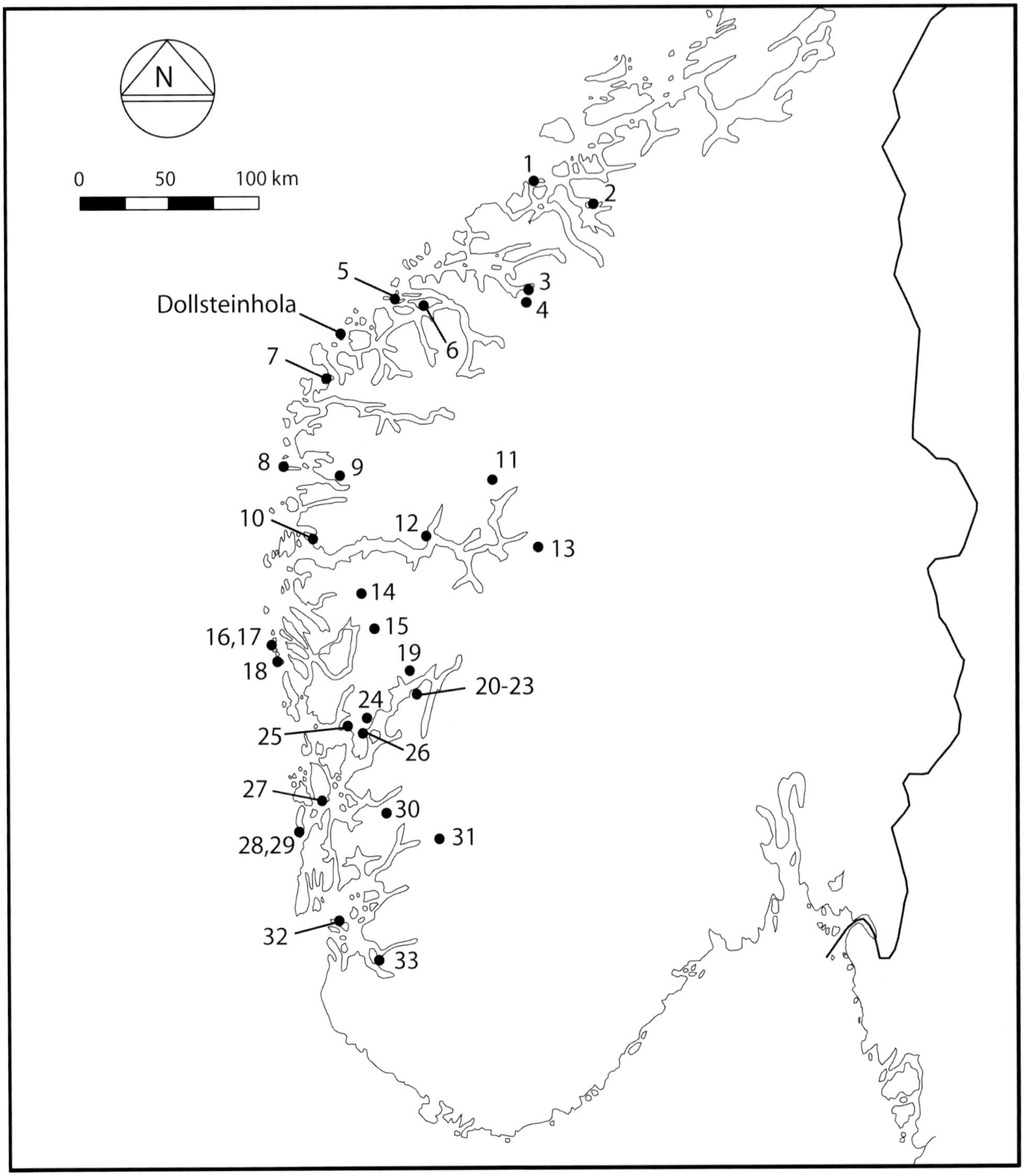


*Figure 3.1: Caves and rockshelters from the Late Iron Age and medieval period in western Norway (counties Rogaland, Hordaland, Sogn og Fjordane and Møre og Romsdal).*

Age. The problem is that even though many of the sagas describe the Viking period, the texts were mainly written down during the High Middle Ages. It is reasonable to assume that accounts of contemporary medieval incidents or perceptions are more reliable than those covering much earlier periods. However, it is generally argued that the sagas also present a relatively sensible picture of Late Iron Age culture and society (Steinsland and Meulengracht Sørensen 1994, 25–26; Price 2002; Lund 2009, 24).

Thirdly, most of the texts were written down in Iceland, and it could be argued that references to caves and rockshelters are relevant only for Iceland, and not for

*Table 3.1: Basic data from the Late Iron Age and medieval caves and rockshelters in Western Norway*

| *No.* | *Name* | *Museum no.* | *Farm, municipality, county* | *C/R/BR* | *M.a.s.l.* | *Metres to nearest agricultural settlement* | *Previous occupations*[1] | *Size of exc. area (m²)* | *Excavated year* | *C. size of the shelter (m²)* | *Dating* | *Function* | *Reference* |
|---|---|---|---|---|---|---|---|---|---|---|---|---|---|
| 1 | Kvernberghula | T24971 | Gløsvåg, Kristiansund, M. og Romsd. | C | 65 | 500 | STA | test-pits | 2006 | 45 | MP | Farm-related | Stafset 2006 |
| 2 | Årneshula | T18308 | Årnes, Surnadal, Møre og Romsdal | C | 140 | 500 | none | surface | 1961 | - | VP | Ritual site | Lie 2007 |
| 3 | Neshelleren | T18194 | Nes, Rauma, Møre og Romsdal | R | 40 | 25 | none | surface | *c.* 1980 | 50 | VP | Burial site | Museum number report (*tilvekst*) |
| 4 | Smiehelleren | T23210 | Monge, Rauma, Romsdal | R | 75 | 400 | BA, EIA, LIA | 24 | 2005 | 24 | MP/VP | Ritual site | Sauvage 2005; Haug 2012 |
| 5 | Lok. 23 Skjong | B14412 | Skjong, Giske, Møre og Romsdal | R | 25 | 350 | BA | 13.5 | 1986–87 | 15 | MVP | Farm-related site | Randers and Höglin 1988 |
| 6 | Skylehammeren | B8358, B14197 | Emblemsvåg, Ålesund, M. og Romsd. | R | 9.5 | 300 | BA, EIA | 10 | 1929, 1983 | 20 | LIA/MA | Farm-related site | Bøe 1923; Resi 1983; Barndon 2010 |
| 7 | Sunnivahelleren | B15273, BRM378 | Bø, Selje, Sogn og Fjordane | C | 40 | 950 | EIA | 1990–1992: *c.* 45 | 1866–1868, 1935–1940, 1990–1992 | 100 | LIA/MA | Ritual site | Hommedal 1997 |
| 8 | Pleta | B16164 | Tansøy, Flora, Sogn og Fjordane | R | 15 | 800 | STA | test-pits | 2004 | 35 | VP | Hunting-fishing station | Skrede 2005 |
| 9 | Jonstadhelleren | B13284 | Jonstad, Naustdal, Sogn og Fjordane | R | 100 | 250 | none | surface | 1979 | - | LIA/MA | Farm-related site | Museum number report (*tilvekst*) |
| 10 | Rønsethelleren | BRM 654 | Rønset, Hyllestad, Sogn og Fjordand | R | 67 | 250 | none | test-pits | 2008 | 70 | EM/HM | Workshop for quarring | Baug 2015 |
| 11 | Mannurdi | no number | Mo, Luster, Sogn og Fjordane | BR | 100 | 650 | none | surface | 1982–84 | 6 | VP | Burial site | Randers and Kvamme 1992 |
| 12 | Storreina | B8025 | Tjugum, Balestrand, Sogn og Fjordane | R | 270 | 1050 | none | surface | 1928 | 15 | VP | Burial site | Museum number report (*tilvekst*) |
| 13 | Skrivarhelleren | B14186 | Årdal, Sogn og Fjordane | R | 790 | 5500 | STA, BA, EIA | 10 | 1987–89 | 250 | VP/EM/HM | Hunting-fishing station | Prescott 1991 |
| 14 | Storsetehilleren | B6729, B6755, B13948 | Store Matre, Masfjorden, Hordaland | BR | 70 | 2400 | EIA | 1914:9, 1985:4 | 1985 | 54 | HM/LM | Shieling | Bjørn 1915; Ringstad 1985 |
| 15 | Skipshelleren | B8600 | Straume, Vaksdal, Hordaland | R | 20 | 230 | STA, BA, EIA | 94 | 1930–31 | 300 | MP/VP | Hunting-fishing station | Bøe 1934 |
| 16 | Hidlaren | B14629 | Breivik, Øygarden, Hordaland | C | 22 | 1800 | STA, BA | 13.6 | 1986, 92 | 20 | VP | Hunting-fishing station | Nærøy 1994; Hufthammer 1994 |
| 17 | Kollsøyhelleren | B11664 | Sele, Øygarden, Hordaland | R | 8m | 1800 | none | test-pits | 1970 | 15 | VP | Hunting-fishing station | Museum number report (*tilvekst*) |
| 18 | Kjerringholet | B8134 | Blom, Øygarden, Hordaland | C | 5m | 650 | EIA | 30 | 1930 | 17 | LIA/MA | Hunting-fishing station | Østebø 2008 |

(*Continued on next page*)

*Table 3.1: Basic data from the Late Iron Age and medieval caves and rockshelters in Western Norway* (Contined)

| *No.* | *Name* | *Museum no.* | *Farm, municipality, county* | *C/R/ BR* | *M.a.s.l.* | *Metres to nearest agricultural settlement* | *Previous occupations*[1] | *Size of exc. area (m²)* | *Excavated year* | *C. size of the shelter (m²)* | *Dating* | *Function* | *Reference* |
|---|---|---|---|---|---|---|---|---|---|---|---|---|---|
| 19 | Karaldevatn | | Indre Ålvik, Voss, Hordaland | R | 890 | 4800 | none | test-pits | 2001 | 15 | EM/HM | Hunting-fishing station | Valvik 2001 |
| 20 | Sævarhelleren | B16283 | Sævarhagen, Jondal, Hordaland | R | 37 | 200 | STA, BA, EIA | 25 | 2005–06 | 110 | HM | Farm-related site | Bergsvik *et al.* 2014 |
| 21 | Vasselhelleren | B16377 | Vassel, Jondal, Hordaland | R | 100 | 200 | BA, EIA | 3.5 | 2005 | 250 | LIA/MA | Farm-related site | Bergsvik *et al.* 2014 |
| 22 | Hallgrimshelleren | BRM 678 | Sævarhagen, Jondal, Hordaland | R | 13.5 | 100 | BA, EIA | 3 | 2005–06 | 70–80 | EM/HM | Metal workshop | Bergsvik *et al.* 2014 |
| 23 | Storaberghelleren | BRM 679 | Bakke, Jondal, Hordaland | R | 90 | 200 | STA | test-pits | 2006 | 25 | LM | Metal workshop | Bergsvik 2014 |
| 24 | Kvitafjellshelleren | BRM 652 | Fugleberg, Kvinnherad, Hordaland | R | 110 | 1750 | none | test-pits | 2006 | 60 | EM/HM | Workshop for quarring | Weber 1984; Baug 2015 |
| 25 | Holmefjordshelleren | B14234 | Søre Holmefjord, Fusa, Hordaland | R | 40 | 250 | BA, EIA | 4 | 1984 | 51 | MA | Metal workshop | Bjerck 1986 |
| 26 | Øv. Dåvatræhelleren | B15424 | Samnøy, Fusa, Hordaland | R | 25 | 100 | STA, BA, EIA | 6 | 1995–96 | 6 | LIA/MA | Farm-related site | Lødøen 1997 |
| 27 | Kobbehammerskleiva | B15176 | Spissøy, Bømlo, Hordaland | R | 4.5 | 1200 | BA, EIA, LIA | 21.5 | 1995–96 | 24 | EM/HM | Hunt.-fish. st. /Metal w. | Anfinset 1995, 1996; Bommen 2009 |
| 28 | Setrehelleren | B8350II | Vespestad, Bømlo, Hordaland | R | 9.5 | 100 | STA, EIA | 15 | 1932 | 75 | MP | Ritual site | Olsen and Shetelig 1933; Østebø 2008; Bommen 2009 |
| 29 | Jurhilleren | B16242 | Eide, Bømlo, Hordaland | R | 10 | 1000 | BA | test-pits | 2004 | 150 | MP | Hunting-fishing station | Valvik 2004 |
| 30 | Vinjakvelven | | Stordalsvassdraget, Etne, Hordaland | R | 820 | 5000 | none | test-pits | 1983 | - | MP | Shieling | Martinussen & Myhre 1985 |
| 31 | Juvvikshelleren | S6437a-e | Gauttun, Suldal, Rogaland | R | 100 | 60 | none | collected | 1936 | - | MA | Farm-related site | Storvik 2011 |
| 32 | Lok. 44 Rockshelter 1 | S10390b-1 | Ertenstein, Rennesøy, Rogaland | R | 20–22 | 420 | STA, BA | 15 | 1989–90 | 5 | EM/HM | Workshop for quarring | Høgestøl 1995 |
| 33 | Brasehidleren | S7863a-g | Meling, Forsand, Rogaland | R | 200 | 2500 | none | test -pits | 1952 | - | HM | Shieling | Storvik 2011 |

[1]Previous occupations: STA: Stone Age, BA: bronze Age, EIA: Early Iron Age, LIA: Late Iron Age, C: Cave, R: Rockshelter, BR: Boulder shelter

*Table 3.2: Radiocarbon determinations from late Iron Age and Medieval rockshelters in Western Norway. All calibrations have been performed with Oxcal 4.2 (Bronk Ramsey 2014)*

| *Site* | *Lab. No.* | *Excavated unit and layer* | *Method* | *Sample Material* | *$^{14}C$ Age BP* | *Cal. AD Age Range 2s* | *Reference* |
|---|---|---|---|---|---|---|---|
| 1. Kvernberghula | Tua-6472 | Test-pit 10, layer B1 | Standard | Charcoal coryllus, betula | 1435 ± 35 | 563–659 | NTNU C14-lab |
| 4. Smiehelleren | T-18218 | Hearth in house 100005 | Standard | Charcoal different species | 465 ± 45 | 1327–1617 | Sauvage 2005 |
| 4. Smiehelleren | T-18220 | Cooking pit 100039, top | Standard | Charcoal coryllus, betula, pinus | 1055 ± 65 | 777–1154 | Sauvage 2005 |
| 5. Lok. 23. Skjong | T-6969 | Layer 2, underneath turf | Standard | Charcoal coryllus, betula | 1450 ± 90 | 407–766 | Randers and Höglin 1988 |
| 7. Sunnivahelleren | T-9320 | Sunniva church ruin, area 2 | Standard | Charcoal pinus | 1210 ± 155 | 548–1155 | Hommedal this volume |
| 7. Sunnivahelleren | T-9321 | Sunniva church ruin, area 2 | Standard | Charcoal pinus | 1175 ± 75 | 682–993 | Hommedal this volume |
| 7. Sunnivahelleren | T-100052 | Sunniva church ruin, area 3 | Standard | Charcoal pinus | 1070 ± 85 | 769–1158 | Hommedal this volume |
| 7. Sunnivahelleren | T-100053 | Sunniva church ruin, area 3 | Standard | Charcoal pinus | 1160 ± 85 | 686–1017 | Hommedal this volume |
| 11. Mannurdi | T-5942 | Bones on the surface | Standard | Human bone | 1000 ± 70 | 891–1204 | Randers and Kvamme 1992 |
| 13. Skrivarhelleren | T-8530 | Upper unit, section H5, layer 2 | Standard | Charcoal betula, pinus | 1220 ± 40 | 684–892 | Prescott 1991 |
| 10. Rønset rockshelter | Tra-785 | Test-pit 1, layer 1 | AMS | Charcoal betula | 810 ± 35 | 1176–1272 | Baug 2013 |
| 10. Rønset rockshelter | Tra-784 | Test-pit 1, layer 5 | AMS | Charcoal betula | 990 ± 30 | 989–1153 | Baug 2013 |
| 10. Rønset rockshelter | Tra-786 | Test-pit 2, layer 3 | AMS | Charcoal pinus | 940 ± 30 | 1025–1160 | Baug 2013 |
| 14. Storsetehilleren | T-6947 | Square E, 40 cm below the surface | Standard | Charcoal betula | 780 ± 110 | 1026–1397 | Ringstad 1985 |
| 14. Storsetehilleren | T-6951 | Square F, 30 cm below the surface | Standard | Charcoal coryllus | 340 ± 140 | 1393–1891 | Ringstad 1985 |
| 16. Hidlaren | Ua-2459 | Hearth | AMS | Charcoal betula | 1170 ± 50 | 713–986 | Nærøy 1994 |
| 19. Karaldevatn | T-14903 | Test-pit 1, layer 2 | Standard | Charcoal different species | 840 ± 45 | 1046–1273 | Valvik 2001 |
| 20. Sævarhelleren | Poz-19348 | Section 4, Layer L2 | AMS | Charcoal | 750 ± 30 | 1222–1287 | Bergsvik et al. 2014 |
| 22. Hallgrimshelleren | Poz-15418 | 11x/29y, layer E | AMS | Charcoal | 860 ± 30 | 1049–1256 | Bergsvik et al. 2014 |
| 22. Hallgrimshelleren | Poz-15420 | Test-pit 2, layer 5 | AMS | Charcoal | 315 ± 30 | 1484–1648 | Bergsvik et al. 2014 |
| 22. Hallgrimshelleren | Poz-15422 | Test-pit 2, layer 7 | AMS | Charcoal | 320 ± 30 | 1483–1646 | Bergsvik et al. 2014 |
| 23. Storaberghelleren | Poz-19349 | Test-pit 2, layer 3 | AMS | Charcoal | 315 ± 30 | 1484–1648 | Bergsvik et al. 2014 |
| 24. Kvitafjell rockshelter | Tua-6702 | Test-pit 1, layer 2 | AMS | Charcoal pinus | 875 ± 35 | 1041–1246 | Baug 2013 |
| 24. Kvitafjell rockshelter | Tua-6703 | Test-pit 1, layer 4 | AMS | Charcoal betula | 845 ± 35 | 1050–1265 | Baug 2013 |
| 24. Kvitafjell rockshelter | Tua-6704 | Test-pit 1, layer 4 | AMS | Charcoal pinus | 950 ± 35 | 1021–1161 | Baug 2013 |
| 24. Kvitafjell rockshelter | Tua-6705 | Test-pit 1, layer 4 | AMS | Charcoal pinus | 840 ± 35 | 1052–1267 | Baug 2013 |
| 27. Kobbehammerskleiva | Beta-88559 | 94x/198y, SV, feature A, layer 3 | AMS | Charocal coryllus (shell) | 890 ± 60 | 1027–1251 | Anfinset 1996 |
| 27. Kobbehammerskleiva | Tua-7000 | 93x/199y, SV, layer 4 | AMS | Bone, terrestrial mammal | 890 ± 40 | 1034–1220 | Bommen 2009 |
| 27. Kobbehammerskleiva | Beta-88560 | 94x/198y, SV, feature A, layer 5 | AMS | Charocal coryllus (shell) | 870 ± 50 | 1040–1257 | Anfinset 1996 |
| 27. Kobbehammerskleiva | Beta-88562 | 93x/199y, SØ, layer 15 | AMS | Charocal coryllus (shell) | 920 ± 50 | 1023–1214 | Anfinset 1996 |
| 28. Setrehelleren | Tua-6923 | E6, layer 1 | AMS | Bone, terrestrial mammal | 1250 ± 30 | 676–870 | Bommen 2009 |
| 29. Jurhilleren | T-17215 | Test-pit 1, layer 2 | Standard | Charcoal | 1430 ± 80 | 426–765 | Valvik 2004 |
| 30. Vinjakvelven | T-5510 | Test pit 1, 15 cm deep | Standard | Charcoal | 280 ± 90 | 1440–1880 | Martinussen & Myhre 1985 |
| 32. Lok. 44 Ertenstein 1 | T-9067 | 100x/100y, layer 4 | Standard | Charcoal | 830 ± 95 | 1016–1384 | Høgestøl 1995 |

western Norway. However, these texts also mention several caves in Norway, as well as caves on Greenland and the Orkneys. Furthermore, the medieval inhabitants of Iceland had strong relationships to and knowledge of western Norway, and the populations shared much of the same culture in terms of history, language, subsistence and religion (Sigurðsson 1999; Schjødt 2008, 95). The fact that caves in Iceland and Norway have partly been shaped by different geological processes may have played a role in how they were used and perceived in these two areas, but this is unlikely to have occurred to the extent that the Icelandic sources are no longer relevant for interpreting the Norwegian archaeological data.

## The archaeological data

The range of artefacts and biofacts found at the 32 caves and rockshelters are presented in the following sections and are classified according to interpretations of their main functions. In brief, a relatively broad variety of activities took place in several of the rockshelters. Here, a distinction is made between what may be termed the primary or main function of a site (e.g. as a ritual site or a hunting-fishing station) and the secondary activities that took place during occupation related to these primary functions (such as making offerings, spinning, or smoking). This distinction is based upon an evaluation of the archaeological material available and the topographical locations of the individual sites. The main rockshelter functions are presented in the following sub-sections. It will be argued that although several sites were used for secular activities and are classified as hunting–fishing stations and shielings (summer farms), surprisingly many were used as workshops, burial sites and other ritual sites. For more detailed descriptions, dating, and discussions of the medieval rockshelters, see Bergsvik and Hansen (2015). The basic data is presented in Tables 3.1 and 3.2. A summary of the main functions of the caves and rockshelters is provided in Table 3.3. Note that most of the site names have the suffixes *-helleren*, *-hidlaren*, or *-hilleren*, which are all different Norwegian dialectical expressions for 'the rockshelter'. Similarly, the suffixes *-hula* and *-hola* mean 'the cave'.

### *Hunting–fishing stations*

Some of the sites can primarily be characterised as hunting – fishing stations. This is indicated partly by the archaeological data from these sites and partly by the site locations. Except for the site at Karaldevatn (19), these sites lie close to the shoreline of the coastal archipelago. Here, availability of fish resources and marine mammals are high.

At one of the recently excavated sites, Kobbehammer-skleiva (27), four radiocarbon date-spans indicate that the upper layers of the site were deposited in the early or High Middle Ages (Anfinset 1995; Anfinset 1996; Bommen 2009). A possible iron key and a bone needle were retrieved. Slag was also present at the site as well as flint – probably for striking fire. The faunal data consisted of a variety of wild as well as domesticated mammals, marine birds and different fish species. The artefact material shows that various work and craft activities took place. Several pieces of slag have a glossy surface that may stem from the addition of fluxing material while forging artefacts. Other slag pieces may perhaps be the result of raw iron refinement (primary forging). If this interpretation is correct, then both raw-iron cleansing and object forging may have taken place here. The rockshelter's location and faunal data indicate that the site was focussed on the procurement of marine resources in the Bømlo archipelagos, and that the occupants stayed there long enough to have brought food to last for a period of time. Although the main function of the site cannot be determined, it may have been a smithy where the smith partly procured his own food through fishing. Alternatively, the site may have been used as a hunting–fishing station independent of the smith's activities (Bergsvik and Hansen 2015).

Kjerringholet (18) (Fig. 3.2) is a relatively small and shallow cave site. Although most of this midden had accumulated in earlier periods, there were also layers that are dated broadly to the Late Iron Age/Middle Ages based on the presence of fragments of soapstone vessels (Skjølsvold 1961, Vangstad 2017) and bakestones (flat stones for baking bread) (Baug 2015; Fig. 3.3.1). According to the site report (Lindøe 1930), the midden inside and outside the shelter was extensive. However, it is not possible to say anything precise about the activities and the function of this site because of the crude excavation methods that were applied. Based on the presence of a cultural layer and the aforementioned artefacts, which indicate the production and consumption of food, Kjerringholet was probably a hunting–fishing station that was either used for a period of time or for several repeated occupations. Another excavated site can be found in a shallow cave at Hidlaren (16) (Fig. 3.4). Although no artefacts from the relevant periods were recovered, a hearth was radiocarbon-dated to the Viking Age (Nærøy 1994, 77–81). Related to the hearth were bones of different species of fish (mainly herring), seal and sheep or goat (Hufthammer 1994). The size of the site and the character of the material indicate that there were few and relatively short phases of occupation. Jurhilleren (29) has a similar location on the coast and is radiocarbon dated to the Merovingian period. A test-pit investigation of this site produced faunal material and shells, indicating consumption of food.

The mountain site of Karaldevatn (19) also belongs to this category. It has been radiocarbon dated to the early or high medieval periods. A test-pit was opened at the site but no artefacts were found (Valvik 2001). According to the excavator's assessment, which is supported here, the local

*Table 3.3: Classification of the function of the caves and rockshelters in Late Iron Age and medieval Western Norway based on an evaluation of the artefacts and site locations*

| | | *Hunting–fishing station* | | | | | *Shieling-shelter* | | | | | *Workshop quarrying/ metal smith's workshop* | | | | | *Farm-related shelter* | | | | | *Burial site/other ritual site* | | | | |
|---|---|---|---|---|---|---|---|---|---|---|---|---|---|---|---|---|---|---|---|---|---|---|---|---|---|---|
| **No.** | **Site name** | **MP** | **VP** | **EM** | **HM** | **LM** | **MP** | **VP** | **EM** | **HM** | **LM** | **MP** | **VP** | **EM** | **HM** | **LM** | **MP** | **VP** | **EM** | **HM** | **LM** | **MP** | **VP** | **EM** | **HM** | **LM** |
| 29 | Jurhilleren | | | | | | | | | | | | | | | | | | | | | | | | | |
| 16 | Hidlaren | | | | | | | | | | | | | | | | | | | | | | | | | |
| 19 | Karaldevatn | | | | | | | | | | | | | | | | | | | | | | | | | |
| 27 | Kobbehammerskleiva | | | | | | | | | | | | | | | | | | | | | | | | | |
| 18 | Kjerringholet | | | | | | | | | | | | | | | | | | | | | | | | | |
| 14 | Storsetehilleren | | | | | | | | | | | | | | | | | | | | | | | | | |
| 33 | Brasehilleren | | | | | | | | | | | | | | | | | | | | | | | | | |
| 30 | Vinjakvelven | | | | | | | | | | | | | | | | | | | | | | | | | |
| 10 | Rønsethelleren | | | | | | | | | | | | | | | | | | | | | | | | | |
| 24 | Kvitafjellshelleren | | | | | | | | | | | | | | | | | | | | | | | | | |
| 32 | Lok 44 Ertenstein | | | | | | | | | | | | | | | | | | | | | | | | | |
| 22 | Hallgrimshelleren | | | | | | | | | | | | | | | | | | | | | | | | | |
| 25 | Holmefjordhelleren | | | | | | | | | | | | | | | | | | | | | | | | | |
| 6 | Skylehammeren | | | | | | | | | | | | | | | | | | | | | | | | | |
| 23 | Storabergshelleren | | | | | | | | | | | | | | | | | | | | | | | | | |
| 1 | Kvernberghula | | | | | | | | | | | | | | | | | | | | | | | | | |
| 5 | Lok 23 Skjong | | | | | | | | | | | | | | | | | | | | | | | | | |
| 20 | Sævarhelleren | | | | | | | | | | | | | | | | | | | | | | | | | |
| 21 | Vasselhelleren | | | | | | | | | | | | | | | | | | | | | | | | | |
| 26 | Øvre Dåvatræhelleren | | | | | | | | | | | | | | | | | | | | | | | | | |
| 9 | Naustdalshelleren | | | | | | | | | | | | | | | | | | | | | | | | | |
| 31 | Juvvikshelleren | | | | | | | | | | | | | | | | | | | | | | | | | |
| 28 | Setrehelleren | ? | | | | | | | | | | | | | | | | | | | | | | | | |
| 15 | Skipshelleren | ? | | | | | | | | | | | | | | | | | | | | | | | | |
| 4 | Smihelleren | | | | | | | | | | | | | | | | | | | | | | | | | |
| 13 | Skrivarhelleren | | ? | | | | | | | | | | | | | | | | | | | | | | | |
| 8 | Pleta | | ? | | | | | | | | | | | | | | | | | | | | | | | |
| 17 | Kollsøyhelleren | | ? | | | | | | | | | | | | | | | | | | | | | | | |
| 11 | Mannurdi | | | | | | | | | | | | | | | | | | | | | | | | | |
| 3 | Neshelleren | | | | | | | | | | | | | | | | | | | | | | | | | |
| 12 | Storreina | | | | | | | | | | | | | | | | | | | | | | | | | |
| 2 | Årneshula | | | | | | | | | | | | | | | | | | | | | | | | | |

Black signature: precise date/function. Grey signature: broad date/uncertain function

area around the site is unsuitable for the location of a shieling and he suggests that the shelter functioned as a station for hunting/fishing in the mountain areas and was related to communication across the mountains to the Voss area.

*Figure 3.2: Kjerringholet (18) rockshelter during excavations in 1930. Photo: K. Lindøe. University Museum of Bergen.*

### *Shielings*

Three sites were probably used as shielings or were connected to such activities. In one of these sites, Storsetehilleren (14), two radiocarbon dates indicate that activities took place during the High Middle Ages and during the late Middle Ages/early modern period. The artefacts that can be dated by typology confirm this date: two spindle whorls of dark green serpentine/diabase (dating from the twelfth to the fourteenth century), and three sherds of a stoneware beaker, most likely of Raeren ware. In addition to these items, artefacts from the shelter comprise one or two pairs of scissors, knife fragments, honestones, bronze and iron fragments, pottery, and a soapstone vessel, as well as personal accessories such as buttons (one of leather, one in copper alloy), a silver fitting and a belt buckle in copper alloy (Bergsvik and Hansen 2015, 59–61). Analysis of the bone remains show that the dominant mammal bones were from domesticated animals (mainly sheep/goat), although red deer and a few fur-bearing animals were also found. The site occupants had also consumed freshwater fish (salmon and trout), presumably from the nearby river, as well as a number of marine species (seal, cod, haddock, redfish, and

*Figure 3.3: Artefacts from residential occupation/crafting in the rockshelters. 1. A fragment of a baking-stone from Kjerringholet (2). 2. Two crucibles from Skylehammeren (6). 3. A fragment of a soapstone-vessel from Vasselhelleren (21). 4. A spindle whorl from Jonstadhelleren (9). Photos: S. Skare. University Museum of Bergen.*

*Figure 3.4: Hidlaren (16) rockshelter. Photo: A. J. Nærøy. University Museum of Bergen.*

*Figure 3.5: Rønsethelleren (10) rockshelter. From Baug 2015: fig. 5.19. Photo: I. Baug.*

*Figure 3.6: Vasselhelleren (21) rockshelter during excavations in 2005. Photo: K.A. Bergsvik. University Museum of Bergen.*

saithe) (Brinkmann in Bjørn 1915 and Lathipariä in Ringstad 1985). The inventory shows that miscellaneous production activities took place at Storsetehidleren and they indicate that the rockshelter dwellers stayed at the site for longer periods than just a one-day visit. The shelter is interpreted as a short-term dwelling, probably a shieling connected to a local farm, from which tending of sheep/goats and cattle was carried out and hunting and fishing expeditions were organised.

A test-pit was also opened at Vinjakvelven (30). A charcoal layer was radiocarbon dated to the late medieval or the early modern period. No artefacts were found. The area generally has shielings that belonged to farms in Etne in recent history (Martinussen and Myhre 1985, 31). It is suggested here that the main function of the rockshelter was in connection with hunting/fishing trips, which were related to the occupation of the nearby shielings.

The rockshelter at Brasehidleren (33) is typologically dated to the high medieval period on the basis of a double composite antler or type D3 bone comb. In addition to the comb, a square bronze fitting, a spindle whorl, and a whetstone were found. The spindle whorl shows that spinning took place in the shelter, while the honestone points towards miscellaneous production or maintenance of tools (Bergsvik and Hansen 2015, 58). The objects indicate that the users of the shelter had organised themselves for a stay of some duration. Spindle whorls and honestones are common at excavated (surface) shieling sites from the Viking Age as well as from later periods (Bjørgo *et al.* 1992, 305). Considering that the site is situated in pasture (*c.* 2.5km from the nearest farm) it is suggested that it mainly functioned as a short-term seasonally used dwelling, possibly a shieling where secondary activities such as spinning and tending to tools took place alongside tending the animals.

### *Workshops for quarrying and metal smith's workshops*

A group of sites were used workshops for quarrying. Rønsethelleren (10) (Fig. 3.5) is situated in the middle of an area with large quarries associated with quern-stone manufacture. It has been test-pitted and three radiocarbon samples broadly date activity to the early and High Middle Ages. The archaeological deposits consisted of quern-stone production waste, layers of charcoal, and slag from forging. It is interpreted as a workshop for the quarry site, primarily for forging and re-sharpening iron tools, although small-scale quern-stone production was also carried out (Baug 2015, 44–49). Kvitafjellhelleren (24) lies close to bakestone quarries and it has been investigated twice by test-pitting. Four radiocarbon determinations date activities to the early and High Middle Ages (Baug 2015, 95). Unfinished bakestones were found on the surface of the shelter, as well as in the excavated trenches and test-pits. The deposits also contained large amounts of chlorite schist flakes from bakestone production (thinning). Furthermore, a tuyère and *c.* 20kg of slag have been found at the site (Weber 1984). The site was clearly a workshop for thinning bakestones, although forging and sharpening of iron tools also took place (Baug 2015, 93). Rockshelter Lok. 44 Ertenstein 1 (32) is located *c.* 50m from a stone quarry for building material and also for bakestones. The radiocarbon samples date activity broadly to the Early/High Middle Ages (Høgestøl 1995, 203–206; Baug 2015, 4). One of the medieval deposits outside the shelter is described as a *soapstone* (most likely green chlorite schist flakes) layer with charcoal and a thickness of up to 10cm. Fragments of unfinished bakestones were also found as well as a possible tuyère, slag, and a possible grinding stone. On this basis, the site can be classified as a workshop for quarrying.

Other sites in the workshop category were places for iron forging and/or working with non-ferrous metals. Two of these lie in the fjord village of Herand and they have been excavated by the present author. Hallgrimshelleren (22) lies *c.* 100m from the existing houses of Sævarhagen farm, which was also occupied during the medieval period (Losnegård 2006, 100). An occupational layer was radiocarbon-dated to the Early/High Middle Ages. This layer is characterised by much charcoal, slag and bone. Pieces of iron slag with a glossy surface were found as well as scrap iron: one iron nail and a few iron fragments. The glossy slag may represent forging involving the use of flux. Together with the bead-shaped hammerscales, this indicates that artefact production had taken place (cf. Narmo 1997, 153). The shelter was, therefore, used as a smithy. Given the location of the shelter in an infield area of the medieval settlement, the workshop is interpreted as being connected to Sævarhagen farm. Storaberghelleren (23) lies around 200m from the existing houses of Bakke farm, which was also occupied during the medieval period (Losnegård 2006). Three test-pits were excavated (Bergsvik 2014). The relevant layer was radiocarbon dated to the late medieval/early modern period. Pieces of slag were found as well as burned clay, bronze/copper sheet metal and a hone. In addition, several of the slag pieces are glossy and may stem from the use of flux during forging. It is, therefore, likely that the artefacts were forged. The copper alloy fragments may be the remains of copper alloy working, but this is not well substantiated. The hone reflects miscellaneous maintenance of tools. The site is classified as primarily a smithy that was somehow connected to the nearby agrarian settlement at Bakke.

Holmefjordhelleren (25) is situated no more than 250m from farmhouses that were occupied during the medieval period. No radiocarbon dates are available; however, bakestones are indicative of the Middle Ages and they date activities broadly to this period. Significant quantities of slag were found in addition to iron rivets, hones, bronze/copper sheet metal and bakestones. The excavator suggests that the shelter was a combined *eldhús* (multi-purpose workshop where fire related activities are carried out) and smithy for the local agrarian community (Bjerck 1986). Based on the predominance of metalworking related finds, it is possible to characterise the shelter as primarily a smithy where secondary activities such as baking or heating of foodstuffs took place. Finally, the site at Skylehammeren (6) is broadly dated to the Late Iron Age/Middle Ages based on the presence of a sherd from a soapstone vessel and also on two crucibles (Fig. 3.3.2) (see Pedersen 2010 on crucibles). Shells and faunal material were collected during early excavations at the site (Bøe 1923), though these cannot be positively related to the relevant phase as the rockshelter was also occupied in earlier periods. It is situated close to the contemporary shoreline and is in relatively close proximity to contemporary farms. The two crucibles indicate that the site was primarily a non-ferrous metal smith's workshop and that the consumption of food had also taken place.

### *Farm-related rockshelters*

Another small group of rockshelters are situated relatively close to farms. Lok. 23. Skjong (5) is radiocarbon dated to the Merovingian period. Sævarhelleren (20) has radiocarbon dates from the High Middle Ages. At Vasselhelleren (21) (Fig. 3.6), one sherd of a soapstone Viking Age/medieval vessel has been found (Fig. 3.3, 3). Sherds of this type of vessel were also found at Øvre Dåvatræhelleren (26). This is the only evidence for Late Iron Age/medieval use of these sites, despite extensive excavations. The lack of evidence implies that the function of these sites cannot be securely established. One may, however, suggest that they were integrated into the activities of nearby farms, perhaps as protected working spaces, places for tending animals, resting places for herders, or as storage facilities.

A few rockshelters are situated some distance from contemporary farms and their functions are even more difficult to establish, primarily because of a lack of good archaeological data. For example, Jonstadhelleren (9) can be broadly typologically dated to the Late Iron Age/Middle Ages on the basis of a soapstone spindle whorl (Fig. 3.3, 4). The whorl's base is flat and it is curved conically towards the top, which is similar to Hofseth's type IA/IIG:B (Late Iron Age) (Hofseth 1985) and Øye's type A (Øye 1988) (medieval). The artefact was collected from the surface of the site and no further archaeological investigations have been carried out. The site lies on a hillside just above the settlement and it may have been used as a shelter for watching over animals, while spinning was a secondary activity. Alternatively, the spindle whorl may have been an offering at the site or it stems from a burial. Similarly, Juvvikhelleren (31) is located close to agricultural settlements, though the terrain above the settlement is rather steep and rugged. The rockshelter was found by non-professionals who noted a hearth with burned bones that were not collected. Close to the hearth, they recovered a soapstone ladle, fragments of two leather shoes, a hone and a spindle whorl. Typologically, the ladle and shoes can be broadly dated to the Middle Ages based on parallels from medieval Bergen (Bergsvik and Hansen 2015). Based on the very sparse data, the main function of this shelter is interpreted more broadly as a farm-related shelter where occupation of unknown durations took place. The last cave in this category is located at Kvernberghula (1) and has been radiocarbon dated to the Merovingian period. Although faunal material was present in the cultural layer, this may be related to earlier occupation of the cave. Kvernberghula is situated in a cliff just above a plain that has an agricultural history stretching back to at least the Early Iron Age. The cave is difficult to access (involves light climbing) and it is not likely that it had any day-to-day practical function in the lives of the inhabitants of the farms below. Instead, it may have been a hiding place for the local population.

### *Burial and ritual sites*

A relatively large proportion of the caves and rockshelters in this overview are ritual sites and some are specifically burial sites. The most obvious of the latter category is Mannurdi (10), which is a boulder chamber in the middle of a rock talus slope (Fig. 3.7). It is too small for human occupation. Bones found there derive from an adult male, and were lying close together in a disarticulated state, indicating a secondary deposit. According to local folklore, the body of an executed person was placed there in the seventeenth century. However, a radiocarbon date places the skeleton firmly in the latter part of the Viking period (Randers and Kvamme 1992, 46). Another likely burial site is Neshelleren (3). Material from this shelter included two swords, two axes, a shield boss, a spearhead, two hammers, a borer, a soapstone bowl and a whetstone (Fig. 3.8). This combination of artefacts is a typical example of the grave goods of a relatively high status male from the Viking period (Solberg 2003, 268). The material was collected by amateurs but no skeletal material was recovered. A third probable burial site is located at Storreina (11). The material, which was collected by the local landowner, was found beneath a large stone slab inside a small cave. It consisted of a

*Figure 3.7: Mannurdi (1) boulder-rockshelter. Photo: K. Randers. University Museum of Bergen.*

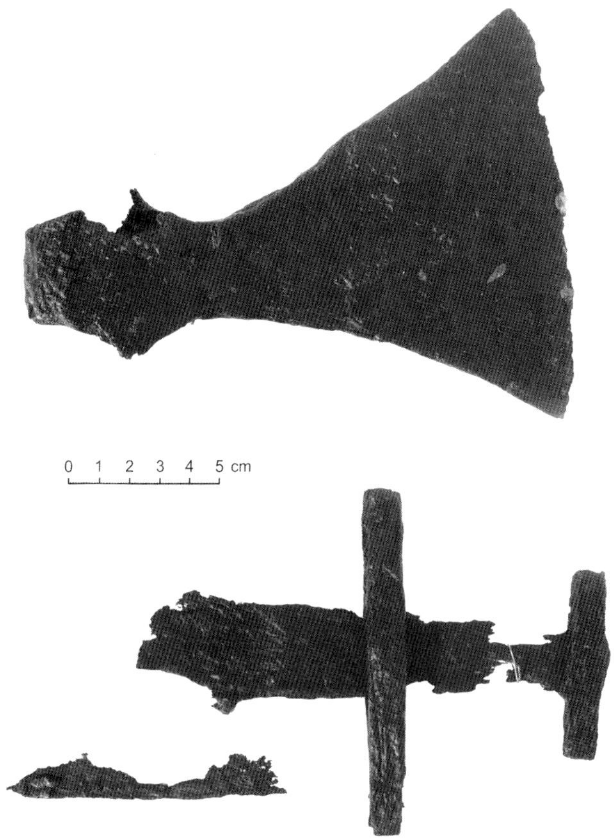


*Figure 3.8: Viking period grave goods from Neshelleren (3): an iron axe-head a sword-handle. Photo: O.B. Pedersen. NTNU Vitenskapsmuseet.*

textile-smoothener (*sømglatter*) of glass and a clay crucible. Jan Petersen interpreted the find as an intentional deposit (Petersen 1951, 329), though these artefacts could equally be considered to be the grave goods of a Viking-period burial. Until now, no medieval cave burial site has been uncovered in the area of analysis.

Rituals other than burials have taken place in some sites. A number of artefacts are probably offerings or *placed deposits* (Hamerow 2012, 130), which can be considered as such because of the context (e.g. a site that is difficult to access) and/or because of the value of the artefact itself – a valuable tool or jewellery, items that were not likely to have been lost or discarded.

A bone ferrule was found in a cave at Årneshula (2) (Fig. 3.9, 1). The piece was decorated with a carving in the (late) Viking-period Mammen style (Lie 2007, 114). Wood/charcoal and faunal material was present in the cave; the bones came from fish, birds, and both wild and domesticated mammals. None of the faunal remains were directly dated and they may not be contemporary with the bone ferrule. The cave is hard to find and difficult to access. Unless it was a hiding place, the site was probably not used for dwelling. Considering that the ferrule is also a rare specimen of high craftsmanship, it is perhaps likely that this artefact was deposited in the cave. To date, no medieval placed deposits in caves or rockshelters have yet been identified, although two 'two-handed' swords from the fifteenth century, which had been inserted between stones in scree at Remmen, Romsdal, might be considered as such (Lie 2008, 19).

A likely ritual site can be found in the boulder shelter at Smihelleren (4). This site also had earlier occupational layers and had been used as a burial site during the Bronze Age (Haug 2012). Several cooking pits were excavated immediately outside the shelter, two of which were dated to the Merovingian and Viking periods (Table 3.2). Despite total excavation of this site, no artefacts or occupation layers

*Figure 3.9: Artefacts (placed deposits?) from the rockshelters. 1. A bone ferrule decorated with Viking period animal style from Årneshula (2). 2. An iron projectile point from Skrivarhelleren (13). A Viking period bronze pin (fastener for a brooch) from Skrivarhelleren. 4. A silver circular brooch from Kollsøyhelleren (17). Photos: P. Fredriksen, NTNU Vitenskapsmuseet (1), and A.M. Olsen (2,3) and S. Skare (4), University Museum of Bergen.*

were identified from these periods (Sauvage 2005). Over the last few years, cooking pits have been found in large numbers close to burial monuments or hall buildings in Norway. This has led to the interpretation that these pits were used for preparing food for ritual consumption (funerary rituals/feasting) (e.g. Narmo 1996). Such an interpretation may also be valid in this case as Smihelleren was a Bronze Age burial site.

Several of the sites with placed deposits may also have been used very briefly as hunting stations. The rockshelter Setrehelleren (28) has extensive occupational layers dated to the Early Iron Age (Bommen 2009). A composite antler or bone comb was uncovered – together with an Early Iron Age bronze fibulae – in the upper zone the early Iron Age layers. The comb was 14.6 cm long and it had runic inscriptions on both sides (Fig. 3.10). The comb type itself and the inscriptions date it to the early part of the Merovingian period (Olsen and Shetelig 1933). A single radiocarbon date of bone may indicate that the site was used very briefly later (than the typological date of the comb) during the late Iron Age (Table 3.2). The context of the find and the quality of the artefact indicates that it was not lost during residential occupation. A likely interpretation is, therefore, that the bone comb (possibly together with the older fibulae), was intentionally deposited. Another similar example is the site Skrivarhelleren (13) (Prescott 1991). During excavations a bronze pin from a ring fibulae dated to the Viking period was found beneath a stone close to the wall of the shelter and was clearly a placed deposit (Fig. 3.9.3). This may also have been the case with a complete iron projectile point that was typologically dated to the same period and which was found in the top layer (III) at the site, although this may have been a lost item (Fig. 3.9.2). Layer III also contained finds from the Early Iron Age as well as the modern period. A test-excavation *c.* 15m from the main excavated area in this rockshelter provided a radiocarbon date from the Merovingian period. It should also be noted that some house remains immediately outside the shelter were radiocarbon dated to the High Middle Ages. The Late Iron Age evidence indicates very brief occupation of this site connected to hunting and herding in the highlands, or as an intermediate camp on the route across the mountains between eastern and western Norway. At Skipshelleren (15), a complete iron projectile point was also found, this time dated to the Merovingian period (Bøe 1934, 44). This site has been almost totally excavated (*c.* 100m sq) and it has extensive layers spanning the Stone Age to the Early Iron Age, containing large quantities of material. However, only the above point was found from the periods relevant to this chapter. The object may alternatively have been deposited in the shelter. The sites at Pleta (8) and Kollsøy (17) are only investigated by test-pits, and relatively little information is available. A Viking Age silver ring fibulae was found at Kollsøy (Fig. 3.9.4), and at Pleta, a blue glass pearl was dated to the same period. The special character of these artefacts indicates that they were not lost at the sites and, therefore, are interpreted as placed deposits. A few other artefacts and/or faunal remains were found at these two sites, possibly indicating contemporary residential activities. However, this material cannot be securely related to the Viking period.

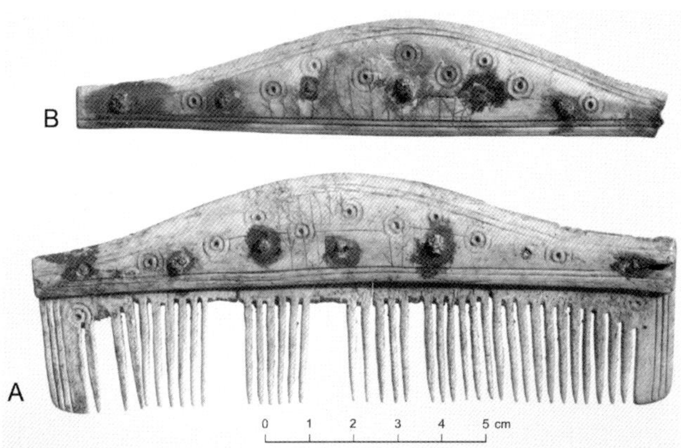


*Figure 3.10: A bone comb found in Setrehelleren rockshelter. The composite bone comb has runic inscriptions on both sides (A and B). The inscription reads (A):* **hAl mAz mAunA**, *and (B):* **Alu naA (A)lu nanA**. *In Norse this is interpreted as:* hǫll mær má una, ǫllu náa, ǫllu nenna, *which is translated by Grønvik as 'leaning maiden may be happy, achieve everything, be pleased with everything' (Grønvik 1987). Photo: A.M. Olsen, University Museum of Bergen.*

The cave at Sunnivahelleren (7) is situated on the small island of Selja on the coast and it also belongs to this category of site (see Hommedal, this volume). This site was a medieval Christian sanctuary, which, according to the radiocarbon dates, may already have been established during the Late Viking Age. During the early Middle Ages the cave and the area immediately outside were heavily modified, involving the construction of a stone church and a terrace. A Benedictine monastery was built just below these cave-related monuments. It is also possible that the cave at Bornihelleren on the island of Kinn, *c.* 60km further to the south, was related to an early medieval Christian cult, although this needs to be confirmed archaeologically.

## *The use of caves and rockshelters: AD 550–1550*

The functions of caves and rockshelters are displayed in Table 3.3; the following chronological tendencies can be observed. Few of the sites were used for dwelling. Not more than two from the early Iron Age and three sites from the medieval period can safely be characterised as hunting–fishing stations. Two of the medieval rockshelters have marked cultural deposits, whereas Late Iron Age sites seem to have been occupied only for brief episodes. Three medieval sites were shelter-shielings or rockshelters connected to shielings.

During the medieval period, several rockshelters were used as workshops for quarrying or smith's workshops. This seems to be a new way of using these places because the Iron Age sites – possibly with the exception of Skylehammeren – were not used in this fashion. An interesting aspect is that several of the workshops are situated relatively close to contemporary farms, which indicates that they were somehow related to activities at the farms. As is also clear from above, there seems to have been more farm-related rockshelters during the medieval period than in the Late Iron Age, although this is not entirely clear. Here we touch upon a problem of representation concerning the different rockshelter functions, particularly between the hunter–fisher rockshelters and the workshop/farm rockshelters. It is quite possible that the Late Iron Age and medieval hunter–fisher rockshelters – even if they are few in number – are over-represented in this overview compared to the number of workshop/farm rockshelters. As pointed out in the introduction, around 350 caves and rockshelters with traces of human occupation are documented in the relevant area. The large majority of these caves and rockshelters are situated in the *outfields* (agriculturally marginal environments, such as forests, hills, mountains or barren stretches along the coast) at relatively long distances from the fenced and cultivated *infields*, of farms, and these can mainly be connected to outfield hunting, fishing and herding. It could be argued that this pattern of distribution is largely the result of different goals, priorities, and methods during cultural heritage surveys in the outfield compared to surveys in the infield, i.e. that infield workshop/farm rockshelters are seldom surveyed. If this is the case, then the frequency of the phases dated to both the Late Iron Age and the Middle Ages is most likely to be representative of the (lack of) importance of the outfield caves and rockshelters in these periods. Since the infield has received much less attention in surveys and previous research, one might argue that the true representation is not as good. Results from 'The Rockshelter Project in Western Norway' conducted by the author is indicative of how important infield rockshelters were in these periods. During fieldwork in 2005 and 2006 in the village of Herand in Hardanger, a total of eight rockshelters were identified and investigated, and as many as four of these sites (those numbered 20–23 in this chapter) had traces of human occupation that dated to the Late Iron Age and medieval periods – although two were only very brief episodes (Bergsvik *et al*. 2014). This could imply that during these periods farm-related caves and rockshelters, and also shelter workshops, were more common than previously thought and they were characteristic features of farm organisation (see the discussion in Bergsvik and Hansen 2015). In contrast, the importance of caves and rockshelters as outfield hunting stations was already low during the Late Iron Age and it did not increase during the transition to the Middle Ages.

Only Late Iron Age caves and rockshelters were used as burial/ritual sites. On the other hand, these are relatively frequent compared to the other functions. Although for most of these sites it seems that the burials/placed deposits were the only activities that have taken place in the rockshelters, other sites may also have been used for other, additional activities. Even if rituals have not been identified in the medieval rockshelters, this does not mean that such activities did not take place. However, if rituals were performed, then they would have been integrated with other (primary) activities that more clearly define the rockshelter's functions, thus making them difficult to isolate. As will be discussed in more detail in the following sections, this change was probably connected to the conversion to Christianity, leading to a general halt – or at least a marked reduction – in the use of caves and rockshelters as burial sites, and perhaps also as places for offerings. In summary, we can see a change in the use of the caves and rockshelters from mainly being used as ritual sites and, to some extent, as hunting/fishing stations during the Late Iron Age to workshop sites and other activities taking place closer to the farms during the Middle Ages.

## Caves and rockshelters in the written sources

Caves and rockshelters are mentioned in several of the Icelandic medieval written sources. In many of these sources, they are connected to different kinds of occupation and use by humans. In others, they are related to gods and supernatural beings. Sometimes they are also places where humans and such beings interact. This section will describe and classify the written sources and the different aspects of medieval cave use will be critically discussed. When relevant, screes, clefts, cliffs, and sometimes specific mountains, are also included in addition to caves and rockshelters. The *mountain-zone* as a topographical category is, however, not included. The medieval written sources covering the Christian site at Sunnivahelleren (7) are discussed at length by Hommedal (this volume) and are not included here. In the following, when referring the written sources, the relevant chapter number is used unless indicated otherwise.

### Human occupation and use

Some of the literary sources mention that ordinary people reside in caves and rockshelters. In his short description of Iceland in *Adam von Bremen* IV.35, Adam states that:

> *Est autem insula permaxima, ita ut populos infra se multos contineat, qui solo pecorum fetu vivunt eorumque vellere teguntur; nullae ibi fruges, minima lignorum copia. Propterea in subterraneis habitant speluncis, communi tecto et strato gaudentes cum pecoribus suis. Itaque in simplicitate sancta vitam peragentes, cum nihil amplius quaerant, quam natura concedit.*

> This island, however, is so very large that it has on it many peoples, who make a living only by raising cattle and who

> clothe themselves with their pelts. No crops are grown there; the supply of food is very meagre. On this account the people dwell in underground caves, glad to have roof and food and bed in common with their cattle. Passing their lives is thus in holy simplicity, because they seek nothing more than what nature affords. (Translation from *Adam of Bremen* IV.35)

This source is, however, somewhat problematic. To the best of our knowledge, Adam never went to Iceland and instead he relied on secondary accounts. Furthermore, since he mastered Latin and was well-educated, he had a good knowledge of the classical anthropological and historical literature. In this literature, cave living is mentioned as a characteristic trait of primitive peoples, who live happy and simple lives (e.g. *Herodotus. The Histories* 4.183; *Strabo. The Geography* I.5.7, XXII.6.5 and XVI.4.13; *Jordanes. The Gothic History* 3). Although the above quote contains observations that are historically correct, it fits relatively well into this discourse. It is quite possible that Adam simply transferred the classic trope or cliché of cave use onto the Nordic context in order to construct a primitive image of Icelanders.

On the other hand, caves occur frequently in Iceland and some were clearly used by people for dwelling in the Late Iron Age (Ólafsson *et al.* 2009). Cave dwelling is also mentioned in a few of the sagas, which were written by people who lived in Iceland and who were probably also familiar with Norway. An indication of cave dwelling is given by a formula for the guarantee of peace (*griðamál*) which is referred to in *Grettis saga Ásmundarsonar* 72. For example, the following is said about a truce-breaker (*níðingr*): '*Hann skal firraz kirkjur ok kristna menn, heiðna hǫlða, hús ok hella, heim hvern, nema helvíti*' / 'He shall be barred from churches and the company of Christian men, heathens, houses and caves, from every world except Hell' (translation from *The saga of Grettir the Strong* 72).

Only a few of the sagas refer to caves and rockshelters as residential sites for ordinary people. Again, in *Grettis saga* 57, it appears that Hallmundr and his daughter live in a cave close to Balljökul in Iceland and were visited by the fugitive Grettir. In a somewhat similar story in the *Brandkrossa þáttr* 2, Grímr and Þorsteinn visit Geitir and his daughters, who live in a cave in Trøndelag, Norway. A problem with these two particular texts is that they contain significant supernatural elements. As will be discussed in more detail later, in several of the sagas a cave dwelling is connected to male and female giants (*jǫtnar*), and are visited by young high status men. It is possible, therefore, that the meetings with Hallmundr, Geitir, and their daughters should be seen as literary constructions or motifs of encounters between young warriors and giants, not as written evidence of people living permanently in caves and rockshelters.

Short-term human occupation is, on the other hand, mentioned in a number of sagas. In *Fljótsdœla saga* 17, at Njarðvík, Iceland, Þorkell, Gunnsteinn and Þorbjǫrn take refuge in a cave under a waterfall at Gönguskarð. This cave, the saga adds, '*er þér eruð vanir at hafa náttból om haustum, þa er þér gangið á fjall*' / 'where you often stay overnight in the autumn when you go to the mountain' (translation from *The Saga of the People of Fljotsdal* 17). Although this information is mentioned only in passing, it is important because it could indicate that caves were commonly used as transitory sites in early medieval Iceland. In more recent periods, such caves and rockshelters are well-known in Norway as places for staying overnight on the way between farms and summer farms, or on the way to hunting grounds in the mountains (Reinton 1957, 253; Hageland 2008). More central to the plot of the *Fljótsdœla saga* is the use of the cave as a place for hiding or refuge. This particular function is also mentioned in many of the sagas. Sometimes thieves seek to hide in caves, as in *Vatnsdœla saga* 41, and sometimes warriors on the run go there during feuds, as in *Harðar saga ok Hólmverja* 33. Here, Þorgeirr gyrðilskeggi gathered his men in a rockshelter at Arnarvatnsheiði, western Iceland, and they stayed there until they were attacked and had to flee to another location. Most often, the fugitives are on the run because they have killed someone and/or they have been proclaimed outlaws. This happens to Aron in *Sturlunga saga* (pg. 376) and *Arons saga* 10 (where *Aronshellir* is mentioned), Grettir in *Bjarnar saga Hitdœlakappa* 19, Gunnar and Helgi in *Gunnars saga Keldugnúpsfífls* 2, 3, and Grímr and his men in *Droplaugarsona saga* 14.

In *Kjalnesninga saga* 4, Búi kills Þorsteinn and hides for quite some time in a rockshelter at Kjalarnes, in south-west Iceland. Food and clothes are in the shelter, and there are hot springs nearby. Þorkell's hiding place was probably less comfortable – it was later called 'The Crawler's Cave' (*Kröfluhellir*) – by the river at Vatnadalur, northern Iceland, which is mentioned in *Vatnsdœla saga* 44, and the cave close to Þorkell Turrafrost's father in Trøndelag, Middle Norway, which is reported in *Fœreyínga saga* 16. For Óspakr, in the *Bandamanna saga med Oddsþattr* 12, the stay was fatal. After killing Már, he took refuge under a rockshelter in the Miðfjörður area of north-west Iceland and was later found dead.

In this context, it is interesting to note that the protagonists in the sagas sometimes express negative attitudes towards staying in the rockshelter or cave. In the *Fóstbrœðra saga* 23 (*Hauksbók* version), the rockshelter, later to be called *Þormóðr's cave (Þormóðshellir)*, at Eiriksfjörður, Greenland, was the hiding place for Þormóðr. He quickly becomes bored and gives himself away, with fatal consequences. In *Eyrbyggja saga* 40, Bjǫrn Breiðvíkingakappi takes refuge for three days in a rockshelter after being surprised by bad weather (produced by sorcery) on a journey to Snæfellsnes, western Iceland. Bjǫrn composes a poem where he complains about conditions in the shelter. Negative associations towards the cave are also expressed by Þorleifr in a poem in *Svarfdœla saga* 18 (verse 11):

*Hér sitk ok hvet hvassan*
*hlymbrand jǫru randar,*
*meðan óvinir órir*
*oss leiða matreiður.*
*Eigum bernskligt báðir*
*ból, þat er litt nýtr sólar,*
*oss hlælgir þat eigi,*
*út um hellisskúta*

Here I sit and sharpen
sly rim-fire for battle,
while ever-factious foes
fail to grant us food.
Denizens of dark caves,
denied the sun by day,
we while away our time,
where tedium has no end.
(Translation from *The Saga of the People from Svarfadardal*)

This could indicate that people of some social standing found it humiliating to seek refuge in rockshelters. Nevertheless, the aristocracy also occasionally hid in them. In *Orkneyinga Saga* 95, a rockshelter close to the sea at Hellisey, Orkney Islands, is used as a hideout for Haraldr jarl, his crew, and even his ship. In *Heimskringla* (*Óláfs saga Tryggvasonar* 48) by Snorri Sturluson, a rockshelter in Gauldal, Trøndelag, Norway is used as a hiding place by Hákon jarl and his thrall (slave) Karkr. Also in *Heimskringla* (*Magnúss saga Blinda ok Haralds Gilla* 14), the pretender to the throne, Sigurðr slembidjákn, hides in a small cleft in Bergen, Norway, and in *Haraldssona saga* 6 in *Heimskringla* the saga tells us that the same Sigurðr spent the entire winter in a cave in Gljuvrafjord at Hinnøy, northern Norway, with more than 20 of his men while on the run from the king. Finally, also in *Heimskringla* (*Saga Óláfs helga* 179), Óláfr rested in a rockshelter in inner Sunnmøre during his travels across the mountains to Sweden. In these texts, Sigurðr gets help from Sámi people to build boats, and Óláfr is miraculously able to clear the road through a large scree of stones.

A few sources briefly mention rockshelters and boulders as places for hiding or for storing goods. In *Eyrbyggja saga* 57 we are told that Snorri goði's wreckage is taken care of by Alfr under the cliff of Guðlaugshöfði in Bitra in northwest Iceland. When Sveinn Ásleifarson raided Suðreyiar (the Hebrides) in *Orkneyinga saga* 106, people hid their personal property in screes and under boulders.

In summary, with few exceptions, the sources do not refer to ordinary long-term residential occupation. Their most common function was as hiding places for fugitives and outlaws – sometimes those of the highest social status – and they evoke negative or at least ambivalent associations. The hiding-place theme is clearly a recurring one and leads us to suspect that it is a literary construction or motive amongst the saga writers. If this was the case, one could then ask: what was the background for this literary construction? What purpose did it serve? To provide a better understanding of this motive, we need to look at other aspects of caves and rockshelters in the sagas.

## *Murder, death and burial*

In the heroic Eddic poem *Atlamál in grœnlenzku* 56, Guðrún accuses Atli of starving her female relative to death in a cave. This theme of the killing of humans in caves and rockshelters is also found in the sagas. In *Finnboga saga Ramma* 13, Finnbogi kills Álfr in a cave close to Sandøy in Hålogaland, Norway, and in *Sturlunga saga* (page 485), Órækja is mutilated and castrated by Sturla in the cave of Surtshellir, Iceland. Some sources also refer to executions and burials taking place under cliffs or in clefts and these are considered relevant in this context. In *Bjarnar saga Hitdœlakappa* 22, at Snæfellsnes, northwest Iceland, Bjǫrn kills two outlaws (*skóggangsmenn*) and buries them at the base of a cliff under a pile of stones. In the *Eyrbyggja saga* 43, also at Snæfellsnes, the thrall Egill from Alptafjörður was taken up to a cleft and murdered there. The place was later called 'Egill's cleft' (*Egilsskarð*). This saga also tells about several thralls who fell off a cliff (chapter 18) and others who were hung close to a cliff (chapter 31). Similarly, in the *Vatnsdœla saga* 46, which takes place around Vatnadalur, northern Iceland, two *berserks* called Haukr were killed and taken up to a cleft, which was later called 'Hauk's cleft' (*Haukagil*) (see also *Þorvalds þáttr Viðfǫrla I* 4). In *Vatnsdœla saga* 16, a man was also believed to have sacrificed humans in front of a cliff. Also relevant here is the *Grœnlendinga þáttr* 2 from western Greenland, where Steinþórr loses his mind and commits suicide in a cleft. Some of the sagas also mention screes as places for killing and subsequent burial, for example *Svarfdœla saga* 19, *Orkneyinga saga* 74 and *Grettis saga Ásmundarsonar* 19. A prominent example comes from *Heimskringla* (*Haraldssona saga* 12), which describes how Sigurðr slembidjákn, after a battle in Holmengrå, Sweden, is executed and his body disposed of in a scree. Only in *Finnboga saga* 9 does there seem to be a burial under respectful circumstances. Finnbogi is buried under a stone at Ljósavatn, northern Iceland. Since *finr* usually denotes a Sámi person in these texts, and the saga mentions that a Sámi man participated in the funeral, this might be considered a Sámi burial (see below and Svestad this volume).

From the above sources, it seems that death and burial related to caves, cliffs, clefts and screes was often violent and sudden, and murders make up a significant share. In most cases, this happened to outlaws or thralls, but sometimes also to aristocratic men. There seem to be significant elements of humiliation, disrespect and negative associations involved. With few exceptions, the burials in such circumstances do not seem to be proper burials but merely places for disposal of the body or bones of the dead (although the incidents were, in some cases, significant enough to give names to the sites). It is possible that the places themselves were randomly chosen by the saga writers and that the violent incidents could have happened in any type of natural terrain. However, it was hardly coincidental. According to Folke Ström, the bodies of outlaws in Iceland could be disposed of in screes (Ström 1961, 47).

On the one hand, it could be argued that, for ordinary free people, caves, rockshelters, clefts and screes were connected to dishonour and were not regarded as places fit for burial. On the other hand, this might be too simple a conclusion. In the *Eyrbyggja saga* 11 there is a much-referenced story about a man called Þorsteinn þorskabítr. The day before he drowned on a fishing trip his wife had a vision of Þorsteinn's dead father welcoming him to a feast inside Helgafell mountain. This saga (Chapter 4) also refers to the common belief that people go to this mountain after death. As has been pointed out by many others (e.g. Steinsland 2005, 349), this might mean that some mountains were perceived to be domains of the dead, which could imply that some people received a *rocky* burial even if they were not thralls or outlaws. Therefore, the sagas display a somewhat mixed picture of death and burial in the mountains. The question is what the background for this uncertainty was, something that will be explored by looking more closely at the role of caves and rockshelters in Norse mythology as it is presented to us in the Eddic poetry and Snorri's Edda.

*Figure 3.11: The god Loki is tied up in a rockshelter. His wife Sigyn helps him by collecting venom from a snake. Xylography: Gunnar V. Forsell.*

## *Caves and rockshelters in Norse mythology: giants, dwarfs, and land spirits*

Caves are the scene of some of the most important events in Norse mythology. In *Edda. Snorri Sturluson* (Gylfaginning 48, 49), we are told that after Baldr's death, delegates were sent out of Ásgarðr (home of the æsir [gods]) to ask all beings and things to weep for Baldr to return him from Hel (the domain of the dead ruled over by the god/giantess Hel). After accomplishing this task, on their way back they pass a rockshelter where a giant woman presents herself as Þǫkk. The delegates ask her to weep for Baldr but she refuses and, therefore, Baldr remains in Hel. Þǫkk is believed to be no other than Loki, and for this deed he is captured by the other *æsir*, brought to a rockshelter, tied up and punished until Ragnarǫk (the end of the world) (Fig. 3.11). When tortured by having snake venom drip onto his face, his body trembles, causing earthquakes. A cave also plays a role at Ragnarǫk itself. In the Eddic poem *Vǫluspá*, the following is repeated in five different stanzas: '*Geyr nú Garmr miǫk / fyr Gnipahelli / festr mun slitna / en freki renna*' / 'Now Garm bays loud / before Looming cave / the fetter will break / and the ravener run free' (translation by U. Dronke).

These events are indeed decisive and may indicate that caves and rockshelters were in some way associated with death, catastrophe, and major changes in the world order. As has been argued at length by others (e.g. Steinsland 1991; Schjødt 2008; Heide 2014b), gods, heroes, and humans who go through transitions and initiations, and who gain access to knowledge in caves and rockshelters, are common themes in many texts. In these processes, giants (*jǫtnar*) are often central to the plot (the treacherous Loki is himself considered half god, half giant). In an Eddic poem related to death, *Helreið Brynhildar* 1, the dead Brynhildr is on her way to Hel, and is stopped by an angry giant woman who tells her: '*Skaltu í gǫgnum / gagni eigi grjóti studda / garða mína*' / 'You shall not journey through / my homestead set with stone …' (translation from *Brynhild's Ride to Hell*). Brynhildr replies by calling her a 'lady who lives in the rock' (*brúðr ór steini*). Another example of a transitional plot can be found in the Eddic poem *Hyndluljóð*. Here, prince Óttarr together with the goddess Freyja seek out the giant woman Hyndla who lives in a rockshelter (Fig. 3.12). Hyndla is visited because she possesses information on Óttarr's genealogy and access to this is important to legitimise his claim to the throne. The god Óðinn is a third example. According to *Heimskringla* (*Ynglinga saga* 5), Óðinn knew songs that could open stones and mountains. Cunningly, and in disguise, he gains access to the skaldic mead of the giant

*Figure 3.12: Freyja meets the giant woman Hyndla in a rockshelter. Drawning: L. Frölich (Gjellerup 1895).*

Suttungr (*Hávamál* 103–111 and *Edda Snorra Stulusonar, Skáldskaparmál* 1). The mead, which enables the drinker to create poetry, is kept inside a mountain and is guarded by Suttungr's daughter Gunnlǫð. After entering the mountain through a hole, Óðinn sleeps with Gunnlǫð for three nights and each night he drinks of the mead. Then he betrays her and carries the mead back to Ásgarðr. Considering Óðinn's relationship with Gunnlǫð, it is interesting that in Snorri's prologue to *Grímnismál*, Óðinn mocks Frigg about her foster son Agnarr conceiving children with a giant woman in a cave.

In Norse mythology giants are often outwitted by the gods, who are generally seen as positive and dominating beings (Clunies Ross 1994, 49). This antagonism between the gods and giants seen in *Snorri's Edda* is probably somewhat coloured by the Christian view of good and evil (Mundal 2012 [1995], 275). It is also possible that aspects of Latin or Anglo-Saxon giant myths influenced medieval writers (e.g. Clunies Ross 1983, 66; Nordvig 2013, 175). Nevertheless, as Gro Steinsland has convincingly argued, giants were an original and central element of Norse mythology (Steinsland 1991, 324). Even if giants are sometimes negative and dangerous in these myths, they are also portrayed as wise and cunning, and in many ways they represent a necessary counterpart to the gods (e.g. Mundal 2012 [1990], 174–176; Steinsland 2005, 254). This more balanced view of giants also seems to be reflected in several sagas where they have important roles and where they usually live in caves. Members of the aristocracy are even connected to giants in caves. In some sagas, such as *Orms þáttr Stórólfssonar* and *Bárðar saga Snæfellsáss*, the first Norwegian king, Haraldr hárfagra, is called Haraldr Dofrafostri, and in *Flateyjarbók* (I) 453–455, the reason for this particular name is given. Here, we are told that the young Haraldr was raised in a cave in the Dovre Mountains in eastern Norway, where the giant Dofri acted as his foster father. After five years in the cave, Dofri informs Haraldr that his father Hálfdan is dead and that he should now take over his father's reign. He also offers to help him in his struggle for rulership of the rest of Norway (Steinsland 2014, 167ff.). Dofrí also occurs in *Kjalnesinga saga* 12–15, where the young Icelandic hero Búi stays for some time in a cave on an assignment from King Haraldr to retrieve a board game. During his stay in the cave, Búi has a sexual relationship with Dofrí's daughter, Friðr. This combination of humans gaining access to knowledge/goods and/or having relationships with giant women is found in other texts, such as *Landnámabók* 175, and in *Bárðar saga Snæfellsáss* 1, *Gunnars saga Keldugnúpsfífls* 5–6, *Jökuls þáttr Búasonar* 2–3, and *Bergbúa þáttr*.

In some texts, the hero also kills a giant. Fighting with giants is important in some of the *íslendigasǫgur* and *þættir*, where the giants' qualities as containers of wisdom and knowledge are considerably downplayed. In these texts, where they are sometimes also called *troll* and *risar*, giants are mainly portrayed as stupid, dangerous and vicious, and sometimes they guard treasures or daughters of kings. In *Fljótsdœla saga* 5, Þorvaldr liberates the earl's daughter Droplaug from a giant in a cave. Another example is *Grettis saga Ásmundarsonar* 66 where Grettir slays a giant in a cave close to Eyardalsá, northern Iceland. Also in *Orms þattr Stórólfssonar*, the fierce giant Brusi lives in a cave and terrorises the local community at Sauøy, Sunnmøre, Norway (possibly meaning the cave of Dollsteinhola at Sandøy). Brusi is killed by Ormr after the giant has killed Ormr's friend Asbjǫrn. Interestingly, then, in the more realistic saga *Orkneyinga saga* 61, the young Kali Kolsson (later to become earl of the Orkneys) also visits Dollsteinhola cave (Fig. 3.13) to retrieve treasure but does not find it (and the *draugr* guarding it is also gone). Related to these tales is *Gull-Þóris saga* 3–4, although here the treasure is hidden by dragons, not giants. Relevant in this respect is *Adam von Bremen*, 40, 41, who refers to men of high social status from Friesland who visited the island of the Cyclopes to the north-east of Norway. Here they found gold and precious metals in front of some caves and they were pursued by the Cyclopes after stealing the treasure. In these stories, the goal of the young men or heroes is not so much to access knowledge, as it is to steal from, or fight and slay, the giants in order to gain personal honour, prestige, and wealth. Most likely, this different view of the giants – which is even more prominent in the legendary tales (*fornaldersǫgur*) (e.g. Mitchell 1991, 61–63) – can partly be considered a Christian demonising of the Old Norse gods. It is also possible that the one-dimensional characteristic of giants/dragons is the result of literary influences of classical giant myths on the Norse saga writers. Nevertheless, as Heide (2014a) notes, these more one-dimensional, and negative versions were clearly part of the perception of giants in medieval Nordic countries, and these need to be considered alongside the more positive view previously mentioned.

Although giants lived outside the world of the gods, in the mythology it is often somewhat unclear about where exactly their dwellings were. Sometimes they are to the east, sometimes at sea, sometimes in the underworld (Clunies Ross 1994, 50ff.; Heide 2014b). Based on the Eddic poetry, Løkka has recently argued that the homes of giants are only minimally related to mountains, rocks and stones (Løkka 2010, 239). Instead, the homes of the giants (*jǫtunheimar*) are often rich farms – apparently situated in the open landscape. However, the material in the current chapter, which includes a much wider array of written sources than those considered by Løkka, shows that giants are in fact very often connected to mountains and caves (see also Heide 2014a, 174; Heide 2014b). Since this theme is regularly repeated, it is likely that this connection was perceived as important.

In Norse mythology, *dvergar* (dwarfs) belong to the same sphere as giants and elves (Simek 1993). They are not explicitly connected to caves and rockshelters in the Eddic poems and sagas, but they clearly belong to mountains, boulders and the underworld. For example, in *Vǫluspá (Konungsbók)* 50 they are called *veggbergs vísir* (the wise in the mountains) and in the poem *Alvíssmál* 3 the dwarf Alvíss states that he lives underground and that his home is under a rock. In *Edda Snorra Sturlusonar* (*Skáldskaparmál* 39 – Otter's ransom) a dwarf called Andvari is forced by Loki to give up the gold that he keeps in the mountain. In the introduction to *Sörla þattr* in *Flateyarbók (I)* 228, dwarfs are said to live in stones, and in *Heimskringla* (*Ynglinga saga* 12), a dwarf is spotted under a stone. He lures the drunken king Sveigðir into the rock, which closes behind them. Dwarfs are considered to be expert craftsmen and particularly clever smiths. They extract valuables from the mountain and do it in deep secrecy. Suttungr's mead was made by dwarves from Kvasir's blood, and dwarfs were especially helpful to the gods as smiths by making famous artefacts such as Freya's necklace *Brísningamen*, Óðinn's spear *Gugnir* and Þorr's hammer *Mjǫllnir*. In some of the sources, the weapons that are made by dwarfs are cursed and some of the dwarfs have magical and transformative skills, such as the smith Vǫlund in the *Vǫlsunga saga* (Barndon 2005, 68).

The third type of beings in Norse mythology relevant to this discussion are land spirits (*landvættir*). In Iceland, they were seen as the original inhabitants of the land and they lived in nature, including in caves and stones (Solheim 1965). As threatening forces, they could be driven away (by fire) by the colonisers, but they could also be helpful if approached in a friendlier manner. In *Landnámabók* S329 (pg. 330), the farmer Hafr-Bjǫrn thrives as a result of help from a mountain dweller (*bergbúi*), and clairvoyant people can see land spirits who follow them around. In western Norway, in *Egills saga Skalla-Grímssonar* 57, Egil urges the land spirits to drive his enemies away from his claimed properties in Sogn, western Norway. The distinction between giants and land spirits is sometimes blurred in the sources (Mundal 1997, 37), and occasionally they appear together. For example, in a story in *Heimskringla* (Ólafs *saga Tryggvasonar* 33), the Danish king Haraldr asks a man with knowledge of sorcery to go to Iceland to see what he could find. The man reported back that he had seen dragons, land spirits as well as giants, and a giant (*bergrisi*) that was higher than the mountain. The term *bergbúi* is used many times in the sources, indicating a belief that the mountains were inhabited by supernatural beings. Examples of such unidentified beings are to be found in *Brennu-Njáls saga* 133, where *Flosi* had a dream about Járngrímr coming out of a mountain with an iron stick and prophesising battle and death, and also the somewhat less spectacular incidents recorded in *Þáttr Þorsteins forvitna in Flateyarbók III* 69.1 and *Þorvalds þáttr Viðförla* I 3 where Þorstein and Koðrán, respectively, receive prophesies from eremites living in stones.

### *Summary: caves and rockshelters according to the historical sources*

As one might expect, the Old Norse sources are relatively varied and complex concerning the human use of caves and rockshelters, as well as their place in pre-Christian religion. In the sagas, in terms of human use they are often referred to as hiding places for thieves, villains and outcasts. They were also sometimes used by the aristocracy in this fashion. Several of the sagas also connect the rockshelters and caves (and cliffs and screes) to death, punishment and burial for thralls and outcasts, clearly indicating that such locations were degrading. However, there are occasionally

*Figure 3.13: The entrance to Dollsteinhola cave, Sandøy, western Norway. Photo: K.A. Bergsvik.*

more positive associations and more respectful handling of the dead. In Norse mythology caves and rockshelters are connected to significant incidents and major transitions, such as *Ragnarǫk*. These places are also clearly connected to giants, dwarfs and land spirits. These beings are sometimes portrayed in a negative fashion. In Norse mythology, however, they can also be positive figures who are necessary for maintaining world order and human well-being. On this basis, one word characterises the perceptions of caves and rockshelters in the Norse written sources: ambivalence. On the one hand, they are connected to negative human experiences and to threatening and dangerous beings and situations. On the other hand, they are places of great achievements and the acquisition of knowledge and power. The next section will discuss whether this ambivalence is expressed in the archaeological record.

## Discussion

It is relatively clear that the archaeological and historical sources only briefly overlap in terms of how caves and rockshelters were used. While archaeology shows a relatively broad range of activities taking place in caves and rockshelters (even if the frequency is low), the historical sources only refer to a narrow range of uses – they were mainly hiding places and burial sites. On the other hand, the written sources provide rich accounts of religious beliefs. It is, therefore, important to ask: what was the relationship between beliefs and perceptions, and the practical and ritual use of these natural places?

### *Perception and practical use*

A relevant explanation of the lack of practical human usage in the historical sources is that they do not reflect how the caves and rockshelters were used in reality. This is clearly the case for other contemporary sites and activities. For example, in recent years archaeological excavations in Norway have uncovered extensive traces of Late Iron Age and medieval quarrying and iron production. These activities clearly represent major investments and income for large numbers of people, but they are hardly mentioned in the historical sources (e.g. Larsen 2009; Baug 2015). The reason for this is probably that the saga texts were points of view of the élite, and they mainly deal with the lives and (extraordinary) activities of the aristocracy. Ordinary farmers or thralls only appear as literary types (Meulengracht Sørensen 1977, 41). Similarly, the daily work on farms or in forests, such as crafting and subsistence activities, is not dealt with unless they serve a literary function (Birgisson 2013, 111). This may mean that, even if caves and rockshelters had crucial roles in the day-to-day subsistence and economy of Iceland and Norway, we cannot expect them to be mentioned unless they played important roles in the plots of the sagas.

Sometimes, however, ordinary subsistence activities are mentioned in passing. An example that is relevant for us is found in the *Fljótsdœla saga* 17, where a cave is used as a temporary shelter on the way between the lowlands and the mountains. Some artificial caves were used in this manner in Iceland (e.g. Hjartarson *et al.* 1991) and such sites from western Norway have been well-documented in recent history, where rockshelters were frequently used by hunters and herders of animals (e.g. Bang-Andersen 1955; Hageland 2008). One might, therefore, expect that this particular saga reference is the tip of the iceberg – in other words, that such short-term dwelling sites were much more common in reality than what is generally reflected in the written sources. Still, the archaeological material does not seem to confirm this expectation. As pointed out previously, relatively few such sites are dated to the Late Iron Age and there are also few from the medieval period. This could indicate *ex silentio* that the lack of reference in the written sources actually reflects the real usage.

This leads us to the question of why caves and rockshelters were so little used as residential sites during these periods. They were certainly available for use in the lowlands as well as in upland areas. In comparison, if we look at the latter part of the Early Iron Age in western Norway (*c.* 0–AD 550), they were frequently used for such purposes. Altogether, 49 Early Iron Age sites are known from this region, and 45 of these are temporary residential sites used during hunting, fishing or herding (Bergsvik 2017). As pointed out above, in our period – which is almost twice as long – only five sites have been clearly identified as hunting–fishing stations. This difference is important, considering that there were many similarities in the basic rural economy during these two main periods, which would imply similar needs for shelter sites. It is possible that people increasingly used cabins and built shelters in the outfields during the Late Iron Age and Middle Ages; however, this does not fully answer why so many rockshelters were left unoccupied.

One possible explanation is that caves and rockshelters were used by thralls or freed thralls during the Late Iron Age and the Middle Ages (e.g. Øye 2002, 391), and that they were considered unfit for – and therefore avoided by – the majority of the population. This could possibly be indicated by some of the saga texts referred to previously, where the literary characters express negative associations about staying in caves. Such a hypothesis is, however, not confirmed by the archaeological data. Admittedly, poor people are hard to identify archaeologically, which means that their presence in caves and rockshelters cannot be excluded. However, based on the artefact material, it is possible to argue for the presence of people of middle and high social ranking in the rockshelters during the Early Iron Age (Bergsvik 2017). Artefacts dated to the Late Iron Age in this study do not indicate that the users of rockshelters were of limited means. Furthermore, a discussion of the social identities of the Middle Age users of rockshelters in western Norway concludes that they had access to mainstream material culture (Bergsvik and Hansen 2015). In other words, there seems to be no clear association between shelter use and low social standing in Late Iron Age and medieval western Norway.

### *Perceptions and avoidance*

Another explanation for the relatively low frequency of residential occupation may be the negative and ambivalent position that caves and rockshelters had in Norse mythology. This would have been particularly relevant for the Late Iron Age; however, as will be argued later, it was probably just as relevant in the Middle Ages.

Recently, Julie Lund (2009, 161) has touched upon this problem in her discussion of the roles of mountains in the Norse written sources. She argues that because they were homes of giants and other beings, the alpine zone was perceived as dangerous and did not invite longer occupation. This argument could also be valid for the caves and rockshelters in these areas because they are openings into the mountains and such places are frequently mentioned in the written sources as dwellings of giants. The theory of avoidance of the alpine zone is, however, largely contradicted by the archaeological data, which shows that people used the highland valleys and mountain plateaus extensively in southern Norway for herding, hunting, and dwelling during the Iron Age and Middle Ages (e.g. Bjørgo *et al.* 1992; Øye 2002).

It is open to question whether references to mountain beings such as *bergbúi*, *bergrisí*, and *fjall-kona* (mountain woman) in these sources only relate to those that lived in the high mountains far away. They may equally refer to beings in smaller mountains, rocks, cliffs, and hills that also frequently occur in the lowland areas over all of western Norway. Again, we have to consider the problem of where the giants were thought to reside. It is, of course, possible that people thought that they lived far away in the east or in some abstract *Útgarðr* or *Jǫtunheimar* (the homes of the giants in the Norse mythology) (Clunies Ross 1994, 50ff.). This would probably have reduced their threatening potential in the every-day lives of people. Their dwellings (certainly the dwellings of *landvættir*) may, however, have been perceived to be much closer to people (Heide 2014b). Others have argued that society's élite reconstructed the homes of the gods (*æsir*) right at their doorstep, such as at Gudme at Funen, Denmark (Hedeager 2011, 137ff.). It could be argued that similar processes were at play concerning giants. If this was the case, and if Lund's basic idea is correct, then the danger – and also the source of wisdom, power and help – represented by giants, and probably also by the dwarfs and the land spirits (*landvættir*), could be found relatively close to agricultural settlements. This would mean that people dealt with supernatural powers whether they were found in mountain plateaus, or in cliffs, or in caves closer to farms.

Many of the characters in the sagas are reluctant or negative about living in caves and rockshelters, and they use them largely as a last resort. Although the background of these negative associations is not entirely clear from the texts, as indicated above, it may have to do with the fear associated with these places, which would have been widely recognised (Heide 2014a). Most likely, when the sagas were presented at medieval social gatherings it was unnecessary to bring up dangers (and their mythological background) – the audience knew what was lurking inside these places and people immediately identified with the unease of the human cave dwellers.

It is possible that only specific caves and rockshelters in local settings were connected to such dangers, for example, based on specific experiences or beliefs. As is pointed out by Stefan Brink and others, it is not possible to live and work in a landscape where every site is sacred all of the time (Brink 2001, 82; see also Schjødt 2008, 18). It could also be argued that, since the saga texts mainly deal with the activities of high status free men and the aristocracy, such fears would only be relevant to them. The implication is that relatively few sites were affected, in practice, by such sentiments. However, the current relative absence of archaeological data speaks against such interpretations: remarkably few caves and rockshelters have been used for ordinary residential occupation, even if they were numerous and available for use. This probably indicates that not only specific sites, but caves and rockshelters as a site category, were avoided as dwelling places during the Late Iron Age and medieval periods. Furthermore, the lack of use indicates that attitudes towards caves and rockshelters amongst society's élite as reflected in the sagas must have rubbed off on ordinary farmers and others, leading them to largely act similarly in terms of cave and rockshelter usage.

### Perceptions and rituals

Danger was, however, only one aspect of the beings that inhabited caves and rockshelters. As is touched upon in several of the sagas, giants or other beings who resided therein also possessed wisdom and powers that could be helpful to people. The literary motif of people hiding in caves and rockshelters could possibly be interpreted as a way of approaching these powers and, bearing in mind the young Kale from the *Orkneyinga saga*, it is easy to imagine that young men visited some caves in order to gain prestige. Communication with these beings and powers would have been triggered by a need for help, or to avoid future dangers. If we turn again to the written sources, several of the sagas of the earliest Christian kings mention that such heathen behaviour took place, to the extent that it had to be confronted. For example, in the *Saga Óláfs Tryggasonar af Oddr Snorrason Munk* 40 (page 156) it is stated that:

> *Oc huaruetna i fiarrlægiom bygþum oc iuðum fiollum um allan Noreg. oc ia dolum eða utnesiom. þa blotuðu margir leyniliga scurðguð oc treystuz þo eigi at lata þa heima vera ihusum sinum. oc truðu a scoga oc biorg. eða tiernir.*
>
> Everywhere in the remote settlements and widespread mountains throughout Norway and in the isolated valleys and outer promontories, many people sacrificed in secret to their idols, though they did not dare to keep them at home in their houses. They believed in woods and mountains and ponds. (*The Saga of Olaf Tryggvason by Oddr Snorrason Munk*, 52, page 102)

Furthermore, in a *þattr* about Óláfr in this saga, which is extended in Óláfs *saga Tryggvasonar* in *Flateyarbók (I)*, some of Óláfr's men overheard a conversation between giants in a cave in Trøndelag, Norway. Óláfr was told about this, and it is says in *Flateyarbók (I)* 321:

> *Eftir þat for Olafr konungr a land med allt hit bezsta lid sitt ok vm allar nalægar bygdir med krossum ok helgum domum og dreifdu uigdu uatnne um biorg ok hamra dali ok hola ok hreisnade med helgum bænum og guds fulltinge allt þar er þeir foru af öllum uęttum uhriæinum öndum ok freisti sou allt folk.*
>
> After that King Olaf went ashore with all of his best people in all of the villages in the vicinity, with crosses and relics and sprinkled holy water on rocks and cliffs, clefts and caves, and cleansed, with holy prayers, and God's help, everything where they went, for land spirits and unclean spirits, and saved in this way all of the people. (My translation after *Flatøybok. Bind II*, 321)

Famous passages on Christian (often more violent) cleansing of heathen places of worship are found in the sagas of later Christian kings. According to *Húngrvaka* III, one of the *Biskupa Sögur*, Christian sanctification of many different natural places – presumably pagan sacred sites – also happened during the process of conversion in Iceland (Lund 2009, 269).

These passages in the sagas on heathen beliefs and offerings and Christian sanctification could possibly be rejected as later constructions on the part of Christian scribes. However, as has recently been discussed (Lund 2009), Late Iron Age ritual depositions have been identified at natural places all over Scandinavia. This also took place by possible Norse occupants in Ireland, where Viking artefacts such as silver coins, arm-ring fragments and ingots were placed in caves (Dowd 2015, 201–207). In the archaeological data presented here, such deposits are also securely identified in a number of the Late Iron Age caves and rockshelters. In many cases, it seems that deposits were the only activities that occurred, indicating that they were targeted towards the sites themselves and/or the beings within them. Although the exact nature of these rituals or identities of the individuals who carried them out will not be expanded upon here, it can probably be argued that they were performed in order to deal with the places themselves (e.g. Lund 2010) and/or to communicate with beings that dwelled in the mountains. Furthermore, given that transformations and the changing status of gods and heroes are recurrent themes in several of the Norse myths and sagas (e.g. Steinsland 2005; Schjødt 2008), it is also likely that some of the caves and rockshelters served as stages for rituals of transition or initiation, possibly the worship of giants (Steinsland 1986). Such rituals may also have resulted in the deposition of artefacts. As Lund has pointed out, they may also have been carried out to establish and maintain a relationship between the living and the dead (Lund 2009, 261, 269). The latter point is supported by the burials from caves and rockshelters.

The archaeological data on burials is admittedly sparse, but there are interesting parallels in the historical sources and the archaeological data. This is particularly true in the case of the burial site at Mannurdi (11). Reference in the sagas to screes and clefts as places for the disposal of bodies clearly resembles the context of the bones found in this boulder shelter, particularly because no grave goods were identified.

It is possible, therefore, that the man found in Mannurdi was a murdered thrall or outlaw. The name *Mannurdi* (the man-scree) may relate to this particular incident, and even here there are parallels in the sagas (e.g. 'Egills cleft') or 'Hauk's cleft' (*Haukagil*) above. Storreina (12) and Neshelleren (3), on the other hand, appear to be graves with grave goods and should thus be interpreted as proper burials of individuals of some social status. It is possible that these two – perhaps also the example in Mannurdi – were related to a belief in mountains as domains of the dead, as was expressed in *Eyrbyggja saga*, and as such, they should be seen as an addition to the already relatively varied funerary rituals of Late Iron Age Norway (Solberg 2003, 186–188, 222–223). On the basis of the character of the grave goods, it can be argued that these burials are Norse; however, in this context one could also relate them to Sámi burial customs, which are characterised by placement of the dead in rockshelters or under large stones (see Svestad this volume). Although no Sámi cave burials have yet been identified in southern Norway (Schanche 2000, 161), there is broad agreement today that Sámi people lived in this region alongside the Norse during the Late Iron Age and medieval period, and that there were many different connections between them (e.g. Mundal 2012 [1996]; Bergstøl 2008). Furthermore, several scholars have pointed to parallels between Norse mythology and Sámi religion (e.g. Price 2002; Solli 2002), and to similarities in the ritual practices of the Sámi and the Norse (Lund 2015). The current data may indicate that there were also parallels in terms of burials in caves and rockshelters.

### *Development of myths on caves in Norway and Iceland*

Sámi/Norse relations may also have been important with regard to Late Iron Age perceptions of caves and rockshelters in the mythology because the Sámi are associated with giants. Steinsland (1991) has argued that the kings and earls of Norway traced their origins back, not only to the gods, but to a marriage or sexual relationship between a god and a giant woman. An important aspect of this is that giants are, in many of the sources, seen as equivalent to the Sámi (Mundal 2012 [1995], 273; see also Pálsson 1997). According to Else Mundal, this means that the Sámi people may sometimes take the place of giants, leaving the literary motif of the counterpart god – giant woman, to be replaced by the counterpart Norse man – Sámi woman, as exemplified by the marriage of Haraldr hárfagrí with the Sámi girl Snæfriðr. This indicates that giant/Sámi genealogy may have been important for legitimising the right to the throne in Norway and that continued alliances with the Sámi were central to achieving the right. What is interesting for us is that caves and rockshelters play central roles in several of these myths because the giants were encountered at such sites – many of the sexual relationships between gods/humans and giant women took place in caves. As pointed out previously, the young Haraldr hárfagrí spent five years with the giant Dofri in a cave in the Dovre Mountains, and it can be argued that Dofri himself was a Sámi (Mundal 2012 [1995], 273, 279). This myth of Dofri can be considered a core origin myth of Norway, which was important to medieval Norwegian kings (Steinsland 2014, 163ff.). This certainly adds a dimension to the perception of caves as places where wisdom and power could be achieved.

It is somewhat uncertain when the combination of giants/Sámi/caves entered Norse mythology. One possibility is that it happened sometime after Haraldr hárfagrí came to power (Mundal 2012 [1995], 273, 283). If this is correct, it is all the more interesting that caves were also central in some of the myths that may have been conceived as a direct result of Haraldr's harsh rulership of Norway – the emigration to Iceland from the late 800s onwards. In a recent contribution, Mathias Nordvig (2013) points out that the first settlers in Iceland experienced a completely new geology in terms of volcanic eruptions and lava flows, and that they integrated these phenomena into their mythology as eco-myths. Accordingly, there are several mythic motives connected to caves (lava tubes in particular) and volcanic activity in the Eddic poetry, Snorri's Edda, and other texts, such as noise and movement during volcanic eruptions. For instance, in *Vǫluspá*, giants rumble underground, dwarfs scream in front of mountain doors, and the dog Garmr barks in front of Gnipahellir cave. He also argues that Odin's theft of Suttungr's mead in *Skáldskaparmál* should be interpreted as a myth where lava is equivalent to mead, and should be seen as a response to the frequent volcanic eruptions, which made the skaldic skills of memory and knowledge of how to behave when the ground rumbles necessary in order to survive (Nordvig 2013, 171, 185).

These examples of Sámi alliances and Icelandic experiences show that the importance of caves and rockshelters in Norse mythology – as sources of extreme danger, and of wisdom and power – may stretch back to at least around AD 900. The question is if it is even older. The phenomenon is clearly timeless and global – caves have played and continue to play central roles in religious rituals all over the world (e.g. Bradley 2000; Lewis-Williams 2002; Moyes 2012). The results of such rituals are also found in several caves and rockshelters in Norway that have been dated to periods before AD 550 (Johansen 1997; Todnem 1999; Dommasnes 2009). One could argue that the perceptions and rituals documented above had old roots and that they were connected to a basic human attraction towards caves as ritual arenas. They may also, however, be the result of specific historical processes. According to this study, the character and frequency of the use of caves and rockshelters in western Norway changed significantly during the transition to the Merovingian period around AD 550. It is important to note that this transition was also characterised by several other major changes in society, which included subsistence, funerary customs, language, and technology (e.g. Solberg 2003, 202–203). Most likely, these fundamental changes were interrelated and, although cave rituals had been there before, new and more negative perceptions of caves and rockshelters may have emerged during these turbulent times. This problem clearly needs more research. However, it is quite possible that from around AD 550, giants and other mythological creatures were increasingly connected to caves, and this happened at the expense of human residential occupation.

### *Medieval use and perceptions*

Until now, the discussion has largely considered the Late Iron Age. As demonstrated above, however, there appear to be some changes in the archaeological data during the transition to the medieval period, particularly the introduction of workshops. The elements that do not change are just as interesting. For example, one could perhaps expect – because of the conversion and purification of pagan natural places – that caves were no longer avoided, and were again used as hunter–fishing stations or as other types of dwelling site, but this does not seem to have happened. The number of such sites are again few during the medieval period.

It is debateable if pagan beliefs in natural places – and the beings related to them – rapidly disappeared after AD 1000. There might, of course, have been a general attitude amongst the political and clerical élite during the early Middle Ages that such beings did not exist. Such a view is expressed by Snorri in his prologue to the Prose Edda, and in the late twelfth century by the author of the Latin *Historia Norwegie III*, who refers to the story about King Sveigde (who disappeared into a stone) and characterises it as, '*pro certo fabulum creditur*' / 'plainly a fairytale' One might also wonder if the terms *lygisaga* or *skrǫksaga* (lying tales) (see Meulengracht Sørensen 1995, 42ff.) partly refer to a lack of belief in the old myths. Nevertheless, runic inscriptions with Eddic verses and magic songs involving heathen gods and giants have been found during excavations of medieval settlement layers in the town of Bergen, Norway (Liestøl 1964, 35ff.). It must also be remembered that Norse mythology was recorded by Snorri as late as the thirteenth century. As pointed out by several authors (e.g. Hines 2003, 36; Nordvig 2013, 56), this probably indicates that people had knowledge of the mythology well into the Middle Ages, and not only as entertaining stories from the old days. In Scandinavia, a general belief in land spirits (*landvættir*) seems to have been common during the Middle Ages (e.g. von Sydow 1933), and it appears that caves and rockshelters were still places where they were thought to reside. A strong indication of this can be seen in a passage in *Hauksbók* (page 167) (*Heimslysing ok helgifrœði c. 9.*), where it is stated that:

> *Sumar konur ero sua vit lausar ok blíndar um þurft sína at þer taka mat sín oc fera a rœysar oc vt eða undir hella. oc signa land vettum oc eta siðan. til þess at land vettir skili þeim þa holler vera. oc til þess at þer skili þa eiga betra bu en aðr.*
>
> Some women are so foolish and blind about their interest that they carry their food up to screes or caves, dedicate it to the *landvætte*, and eat it afterwards, so that the *landvætte* will be friendly to them and that they will have better fortune with the herd than before. (My translation after Mundal 1997)

*Landvættir* were seen as evil forces by the church and their worship was prohibited in medieval laws (Solheim 1965; Mundal 1997). Furthermore, several early medieval laws also prohibited beliefs in, and offerings to, natural places such as mounds, groves, stones and trees (Brink 2001, 89; Lund 2009, 162). Such prohibitions are, for example, stated in the section on Christian law (chapter 29) in the old Norwegian law of the Gulathing (*Gulatingslovi*, 44), which is relevant for the geographical area in question here (see also Lund 2009, 162, 269 for Iceland). The fact that these beliefs and activities were regulated by law indicates that they were common all over Scandinavia and may have contributed to a continuing avoidance of caves and rockshelters for dwelling purposes. It is possible that the lack of human use was itself scary for many people. In any case, it seems clear from the archaeological data that the practice of deposition in caves and rockshelters came to an end around AD 1000, which may indicate that the prohibitions actually worked, even if beliefs lingered.

Another important change during the transition to the Middle Ages was the increased use of rockshelters as metal workshops and workshops for quarrying. Considering the information given previously, one might ask why smiths and stonemasons would want to seek out caves and rockshelters in order to work stone and metals. In the case of workshops for quarrying, they are situated conveniently close to quarries and this may be considered a sufficient reason to use them. However, an aspect of the activities at these locations could also be connected to Norse mythology and supernatural beings in the mountains. In these workshops, quern-stones and bakestones were made, and the blanks had been taken from the rock itself. The very act of quarrying may have been seen as a dangerous activity because of associated interference with the underworld beings. Furthermore, based on the presence of quern-stones in contexts of offering, Torun Zachrisson (1998) has pointed to the cosmic significance of quern rotation, such as in the Eddic poem *Grottasǫngr* where giant women are involved. The transformation of grain into bread and beer by means of the querns and bakestones also has strong mythological connotations, particularly concerning fertility (Zachrisson 1998, 361ff.). The shelter workshops involved not only the hewing of stone blanks but also the forging of tools that were used for this activity (Baug 2015).

For the medieval metal-smith's workshops, a number of practical and utilitarian arguments can also be put forward, such as protection from rain, control of light and heat, and the fact that they are often situated at a safe (fireproof) distance from the wooden buildings on farms (Bergsvik and Hansen 2015). Such explanations do not, however, cover all aspects of the use of these sites – there are also connections to the Norse mythology. In recent contributions, Randi Barndon (e.g. Barndon 2005 and 2009) has argued that the traces of forging found in several Iron Age caves and rockshelters may have been associated with dwarfs. Although none of the Late Iron Age rockshelters in this study have clear traces of metalworking (although Skylehammeren may possibly have been used for this purpose), based on the above argument on continuing beliefs, this theory may also be relevant for caves and rockshelters during the succeeding Middle Ages where such traces are found in several sites. A strong indication that belief in the power of the dwarfs continued into the Middle Ages can be seen in the woodcarvings on the portals of several medieval stave churches in Norway, where the dwarf Regin (from the *Vǫlsunga saga)* is depicted (Barndon 2005, 69). According to mythology, dwarfs were specialist smiths and were connected to stones, caves and the underground. Barndon (2005) points to the secret and transformative character of the dwarf activities and to caves, which also have transformative properties as they may have been seen as boundary zones between this world and the underworld. It is possible, therefore, that part of the reason for choosing rockshelters for workshops for quarrying was triggered by their potential for accessing the transformative powers and skills of dwarfs.

Finally, during the transition to the early Middle Ages, some caves became Christian sanctuaries. Hommedal (this volume) argues that Sunnivahelleren at Selja (7) became one of the most important sites for the establishment of Christianity in Norway, and the small and remote island of Selja was the episcopal seat until the late eleventh century. Considering the strong Christian prohibitions and persecutions connected to pagan worship in caves and other natural places during this early period, it is somewhat paradoxical that caves played such a crucial role in the Christianisation process. One explanation may be that this had to do with a continuity of the use of certain pre-Christian cultic sites, or with a degree of religious continuity – meaning that some of the Christian saints took over the roles of earlier cave-related giants (Steinsland 1997). However, the most important reason is probably found within the new Christian belief system itself – a system that was already well-established when introduced into Norway during the late tenth and early eleventh centuries. In this system, caves were locations of important biblical incidents, most importantly the birth of Christ (see Feijó this volume). The conception of caves as liminal spaces and entrances to hell also includes Christian elements (e.g. Semple 2013, 71). The appearance of St Michael near a cave in Monte Gargano, Italy in AD 492 was a particularly important incident and it led to the establishment of a large number of churches dedicated to him across medieval Europe (28 in Norway), amongst them the one at Selja (Steinsland 1997; Hommedal this volume). It is quite possible that the importance and strength of St Michael as a Christian figure – as a guardian of the boundary between heaven and hell and a slayer of dragons – contributed to a new perception of caves during the early medieval period in Norway, which had few connections to pre-Christian ritual sites and beliefs, and which operated relatively independently of these.

## Conclusions

In recent years, significant progress has been made in cross-disciplinary studies on Old Norse religion and rituals in northern Europe. Many researchers have discussed peoples' relationship to particular natural features in the landscape. Caves and rockshelters are often mentioned, but until now they have not received the attention that they deserve in relation to their importance in Norse mythology.

In this contribution, an effort has been made to explore the significance of these sites in western Norway during the Late Iron Age and Middle Ages. To achieve this, data from archaeological sites have been compiled and classified. A large body of medieval texts, which were mainly written down in Iceland, has also been examined in order to locate passages where caves and rockshelters are mentioned. The survey of the saga texts uncovered a marked ambivalence concerning these places. They are, on the one hand, portrayed as scenes of negative actions and incidents, and are associated with dangerous and threatening beings and powers. On the other hand, when people communicate with these beings, caves and rockshelters are places where wisdom, wealth and status can be accessed. The archaeological data shows that caves and rockshelters were used for several purposes. Despite their easy access and practical value, visits to caves and rockshelters were neither long lasting nor particularly frequent. Some of the sites were burial places and many were used for ritual deposition of special artefacts and valuables, while they were only used as hunting-fishing stations to a limited extent.

It is not yet clear when caves and rockshelters became so strongly related to supernatural beings but these perceptions were relevant during the latter part of the Late Iron Age. Parallel to Christian cave sanctuaries – which added new elements to the religious usage – these pre-Christian cave rituals continued after the conversion and well into the Middle Ages, although archaeologically this is mainly indicated by stone and metal crafting.

On the basis of these observations, it is argued here that caves and rockshelters as a site type were probably connected to supernatural beings in Norse mythology, such as giants, land spirits, and dwarfs during the Late Iron Age and medieval period. The ambivalence associated with these beings led to a general avoidance of caves and rockshelters for dwelling purposes, and to a preference for using these places as arenas for worship and ritual. This avoidance would have made perfect sense to them. From a modern perspective, it is easy to discard beliefs in caves and rockshelters as irrational superstitions. But for the Late Iron Age and medieval people, the beings in caves were real. Giants and land spirits lived there, and had to be attended to. Sometimes avoidance was the best strategy. At other times they required offerings, and other times again – when people needed something from the rock – they were approached in caves and rockshelters.

## Acknowledgements

I would like to thank Marion Dowd, Eldar Heide, Julie Lund and Else Mundal for valuable comments on the manuscript. Else Mundal also corrected Norse names and expressions, for which I am very grateful. I have benefited from discussions with my colleagues at the University Museum in Bergen: Gitte Hansen, Alf Tore Hommedal and Justin Kroesen.

## References

*Adam of Bremen. History of the Archbishops of Hamburg-Bremen.* 1959. Transl. F.J. Tschan. New York: Colombia University Press.

*Adam von Bremen. Hamburgische Kirchengeschicte.* 1917. Gesta Hammaburgensis ecclesiæ pontificum, ed. B. Schmeidler. Hannover und Leipzig: Hansche Buchhandlung.

Andrén, A., 1989. Dörrar til förgångna myter. En tolkning av de gotländska bildstenarna. *In*: A. Andrén, ed. *Medeltidens fødelse.* Lund: Symposier på Krapperups borg, 287–319.

Andrén, A., Jennbert, K., and Raudevere, C., eds., 2004. *Ordning mot kaos. Studier av förkristen kosmologi.* Lund: Nordic Academic Press.

Andrén, A., Jennbert, K., and Raudevere, C., eds., 2006. *Old Norse Religion in Long-Term Perspectives. Origins, Changes, and Interactions.* Lund: Nordic Academic Press.

Anfinset, N., 1995. Trekantsambandet. Funnrapport B-15176, Kobbehammerskleiva, Lok. 4. Spissøy, Gnr. 26., Bnr. 3. Bømlo k., Hordaland. Unpublished report on file at the topographical archive, University Museum of Bergen.

Anfinset, N., 1996. Trekantsambandet. Funnrapport B-15176, Kobbehammerskleiva, Lok. 4. Spissøy, Gnr. 26., Bnr. 3. Bømlo k., Hordaland. Unpublished report on file at the topographical archive, University Museum of Bergen.

*Alvíssmál.* 2014. *In*: J. Kristjánsson and V. Ólasson, eds. *Eddukvæði I. Goðakvæði. Íslenzk fornrit 36:1.* Reykjavík: Hið íslenzka fornritafélag, 438–443.

*Arons saga. 10. Aron fann móður sína* [online]. Available from: http://heimskringla.no/wiki/Arons_saga [accessed 8 July 2016].

*Atlamál in grœnlenzku.* 2014. *In*: J. Kristjánsson and V. Ólasson, eds. *Eddukvæði II. Hetjukvæði. Íslenzk fornrit* 36:2. Reykjavík: Hið íslenzka fornritafélag, 281–307.

Axboe, M., 2004. *Die Goldbrakteaten der Völkerwanderungzeit. Herstellungsprobleme und Chronologie.* Ergänzungsbände zum Realleksikon der germanischen Altertumskunde, vol. 38. Berlin: Walter de Gruyter.

Bagge, S., 2014. 'När sägen och dikt sopas bort…' Den Weibullske kildekritikk etter 100 år. *Historisk Tidsskrift* 93(4), 565–595.

*Bandamanna saga med Odds þattr.* 1933. Publ. F. Jónsson. Copenhagen: Samfund til udgivelse af gammel nordisk litteratur.

Bang-Andersen, A. 1955. Hidlere og læger i fjellet. *Stavanger Turistforenings Årbok* 1954, 25–73.

*Bárðar saga Snæfellsás.* 1991. *In*: Þ. Vilmundarson and B. Vilhjálmsson, eds. *Íslenzk fornrit. XIII Bindi. Harðar saga.* Reykjavík: Hið íslenzka fornritafélag, 99–172.

Barndon, R., 2005. Metall og myter – magi og transformasjon. *Primitive Tider* 8, 61–74.

Barndon, R., 2009. Caves and rockshelters. Sacred crafts and smith's graves in a long-term perspective. *In*: I. Holm, K. Stene and E. Svensson, eds. *Liminal Landscapes. Beyond the Concepts of 'Marginality' and 'Periphery'.* OAS 11. Oslo: Unipub, 47–65.

Baug, I., 2015. *Quarrying in Western Norway. An Archaeological Study of Production and Distribution in the Viking Period and Middle Ages.* Oxford: Archaeopress Archaeology.

*Bergbúa þáttr.* 1991. *In*: Þ. Vilmundarson and B. Vilhjálmsson, eds. *Íslenzk fornrit. XIII Bindi. Harðar saga.* Reykjavík: Hið íslenzka fornritafélag, 439–450.

Bergstøl, J. 2008. Samer i Østerdalen? En studie av etnisitet i jernalderen og middelalderen i det nordøstre Hedmark. Thesis (Dr. Art.), Univsersity of Oslo.

Bergsvik, K.A., 2014. Report from the survey of Storaberghelleren at Bakke, Herand, Jondal k., Hordaland. Unpublished report on file at the topographical archive, University Museum of Bergen.

Bergsvik, K.A. 2017. Caves and rockshelters in Iron Age coastal Norway: At the margins of society? *In*: S. Semple and C. Orsini, ed. *Life on the Edge.* Neue Studien zur Sachsenforschung. Hannover: Hannover Museum Press, 317–334.

Bergsvik, K.A., Bommen, C., and Waraas, T. A., 2014. Reports from the Excavations of Sævarhelleren, Hallgrimshelleren, and Vasselhelleren, Herand. Hordaland. Unpublished report on file at the topographical archive, University Museum of Bergen.

Bergsvik, K.A. and Hansen, G., 2015. Medieval Rockshelters in Western Norway: activities, functions and social identities. *In*: I. Baug, J. Larsen and S.S. Mygland, eds. *Nordic Middle Ages. Artefacts, Landscapes and Society. Essays in Honour of Ingvild Øye on her 70th birthday.* UBAS 8. Bergen: University of Bergen, 49–76.

Birgisson, B., 2013. *Den svarte vikingen.* Oslo: Spartacus.

*Bjarnar saga Hítdœlakappa.* 1893. Publ. R.C. Boer. Halle: Max Niemeyer.

Bjerck, H.B. 1986. Holmefjordmannen var 4000 år gammel!!! *Frå Fjon til Fusa* 1986, 7–14.

Bjørgo, T., Kristoffersen, S. and Prescott, C., 1992. *Arkeologiske undersøkelser i Nyset-Steggjevassdragene 1981–87.* Arkeologiske rapporter 16. Bergen: University of Bergen.

Bjørn, A. 1915. Et nyt hulefund paa Vestlandet. *Bergens Museums Aarbok* 1914/1915, 1–5.

Bommen, C., 2009. Bruken av hellarar i eldre jernalder i Sunnhordland. Thesis (MA), University of Bergen.

Bradley, R., 2000. *An Archaeology of Natural Places*. London: Routledge.

*Brandkrossa þattr*. 1950. *In*: J. Jóhannesson, ed. *Íslenzk fornrit. XI. Bindi. Austfirðinga sǫgur*. Reykjavík: Hið íslenzka fornritafélag, 181–191.

*Brennu-Njáls saga*. 1954. *In*: E.Ó. Sveinsson, ed. *Íslenzk fornrit XII. Brennu-Njáls saga*. Reykjavik: Hið islenzka fornritafélag, 1–464.

Brink, S., 2001. Mythologizing landscape. Place and space of cult and myth *In*: M. Stausberg, O. Sundqvist, A. van Nahl and A. Hultgård, eds. *Kontinuitäten und Brüche in der Religionsgeschichte. Festschrift für Anders Hultgård zu seinem 65. Geburtstag am 23.12.2001*. Ergänzungsbände zum Reallexikon der germanischen Altertumskunde. Berlin: Walter de Gruyter, 76–112.

Bronk Ramsey, C. 2014. OxCal version 4.2 [online]. Available from: http://c14.arch.ox.ac.uk/. [accessed 1 February 2015].

*Brynhild's ride to Hell*. 1996. Transl. C. Larrington. *In*: C. Larrington, ed. *The Poetic Edda*. Oxford: Oxford University Press, 192–194.

Bøe, J., 1923. Innberetning fra utgravningen av Skylehammeren. Unpublished report on file at the topographical archive, University Museum of Bergen.

Bøe, J., 1934. *Boplassen i Skipshelleren på Straume i Nordhordland*. Bergen: A.S. John Griegs Boktrykkeri.

Clunies Ross, M. 1983. Snorri Sturluson's use of the Norse origin-legend of the sons of Fornjotr in his *Edda*. *Arkiv för Nordisk Filologi* 98, 47–66.

Clunies Ross, M., 1994. *Prolonged Echoes. Old Norse Myths in Medieval Northern Society. Volume 1: The Myths*. Odense: Odense University Press.

Dommasnes, L.H., 2009. Graves, caves and liminal space in the Early Metal Age in Sunnmøre, North-Western Norway. *In*: I. Holm, K. Stene, and E. Svensson, eds. *Liminal Landscapes. Beyond the Concepts of 'Marginality' and 'Periphery'*. OAS 11. Oslo: Unipub, 29–46.

Dowd, M., 2015. *An Archaeology of Caves in Ireland*. Oxford: Oxbow Books.

*Droplaugarsona saga*. 1950. *In*: J. Jóhannesson, ed. *Íslenzk fornrit. XI. Bindi. Austfirðinga sǫgur*. Reykjavík: Hið íslenzka fornritafélag, 135–180.

*Edda Snorra Sturlusonar*. 1907. Publ. F. Jónsson. Reykjavík: Kostnaðarmaður: Sigurður Kristjánsson.

*Edda. Snorri Sturluson*. 1926. Publ. F. Jónsson. 2nd edn. Copenhagen: G.E.C. Gads forlag.

*Egils saga Skalla-Grimssonar*. 1932. *In*: S. Nordal, ed. *Íslenzk fornrit. II. Bindi. Egils saga Skalla-Grímssonar*. Reykjavík: Hið íslenzka fornritafélag, 1–300.

*Eyrbyggja saga*. 1935. *In*: E.Ó. Sveinsson and M. Þórðarson, ed. *Íslenzk fornrit. IV. Bindi. Eyrbyggja saga*. Reykjavík: Hið íslenzka fornritafélag, 1–184.

*Færeyínga saga*. 1832. Publ. C. Christian Rafn. Copenhagen: Jens Hostrup Schultz.

*Finnboga saga*. 1959. *In*: J. Halldórsson, ed. *Íslenzk fornrit. XIV. Bindi. Kjalnesinga saga*. Reykjavík: Hið íslenzka fornritafélag, 251–340.

*Flateyarbók (I)*. 1860. Förste bind. Publ. G. Vigfusson and C.R. Unger. Christiania: P.T. Mallings Forlagsboghandel.

*Flateyarbók (III)*. 1868. Tredie bind. Publ. G. Vigfusson and C.R. Unger. Christiania: P.T. Mallings Forlagsboghandel.

*Flatøybok. Bind II*. 2015. Transl. by E. Ekill, ed. T. Titlestad, E.A. Rowe and B. Birgisson. Stavanger: Saga Bok.

*Fljótsdæla saga*. 1950. *In*: J. Jóhannesson, ed. *Íslenzk fornrit. XI. Bindi. Austfirðinga sǫgur*. Reykjavík: Hið íslenzka fornritafélag, 213–296.

*Fóstbræðra saga*. 1892–96. *In*: *Hauksbók udgiven efter de Arnamanæanske håndskifter*. Copenhagen: Det kongelige norske oldtids-selskab, Thieles Bogtrykkeri.

Gjellerup, K., 1895. *Den Ældre Eddas gudesange*. Copenhagen: P.G. Philipsens forlag.

*Grettis saga Ásmundarsonar*. 1936. *In*: G. Jónsson, ed. *Íslenzk fornrit VII*. Reykjavik: Hið íslenzka fornritafélag.

*Grímnismál*. 2014. *In*: J. Kristjánsson and V. Ólasson, eds. *Eddukvæði I. Goðakvæði. Izlensk fornrit* 36(1). Reykjavík: Hið íslenzka fornritafélag, 367–379.

*Grottasǫngr*. 2014. *In*: J. Kristjánsson and V. Ólasson, eds. *Eddukvæði II. Hetjukvæði. Íslenzk Fornrit* 36(2). Reykjavík: Hið íslenzka fornritafélag, 431–436.

*Grœnlendinga þáttr*. 1935. *In*: E.Ó. Sveinsson and M. Þórðarson, ed. *Íslenzk fornrit. IV. Bindi. Eyrbyggja saga*. Reykjavík: Hið íslenzka fornritafélag, 270–292.

Grønvik, O., 1987. *Fra Ågedal til Setre. Sentrale runeinskrifter fra det 6. århundre*. Oslo: Universitetsforlaget.

*Gulatingslovi*. 1981. Transl. K. Robberstad. Oslo: Det Norske Samlaget.

*Gull-Þóris saga*. 1987. *In*: B. Halldórsson, J. Torfason, S. Tómason and Ö. Thorsson, eds. *Íslendinga sögur*. Reykjavík: Svárt á hvítu, 1120–1143.

*Gunnars saga Keldugnúpsfífls*. 1959. *In*: J. Halldórsson, ed. *Íslenzk fornrit. XIV. Bindi. Kjalnesinga saga*. Reykjavík: Hið íslenzka fornritafélag, 341–379.

Hageland, T., 2008. *Den store hellerboka for Agder og Rogaland*. Kristiansand: Vest-Agder fylkeskommune.

Hamerow, H., 2012. *Rural Settlements and Society in Anglo-Saxon England*. Oxford: Oxford University Press.

*Harðar saga ok Hólmverja*. 1908. Ed. Þ. Jónsson. Reykjavík: Sigurður Kristjánsson.

Haug, A., 2012. Rockshelters in central Norway: long-term changes in use, social organization and production. *In*: K.A. Bergsvik and R. Skeates, eds. *Caves in Context. The Cultural Significance of Caves and Rockshelters in Europe*. Oxford: Oxbow Books, 39–47.

*Hauksbók*. 1892–1896. Udgiven efter de Arnamagnæanske håndskrifter 1. Hæfte. Copenhagen: Det Kongelige Nordiske Oldskrift-Selskab. Thieles Bogtryggeri.

*Hávamál*. 2014. *In*: J. Kristjánsson and V. Ólasson, eds. *Eddukvæði I. Goðakvæði. Izlensk Fornrit* 36(1). Reykjavík: Hið íslenzka fornritafélag, 322–355.

Hedeager, L., 2011. *Iron Age Myth and Materiality. An Archaeology of Scandinavia AD 40–1000*. London and New York: Routledge.

Heide, E., 2014a. Barðar saga as a scource for reconstruction of Pre-Christian religion? *In*: D. Sävborg and K. Bek-Pedersen, eds. *Folklore in Old Norse: Old Norse in Folklore*. Tartu: University of Tartu Press, 170–180.

Heide, E. 2014b. Contradictory cosmology in Old Norse myth and religion – but still a system? *Maal og Minne* 1(2014), 102–143.

*Heimskringla I-III. Snorri Sturluson*. 1941–1951. Ed. B. Aðalbjarnarson. *Íslenzk fornrit* 26–28. Reykjavik: Hið íslenzka fornritafélag.

Helle, K. 2011. Hvor står den historiske kildekritikken i dag? *Collegium Medievale* 24, 50–86.

*Helreið Brynhildar*. 2014. *In*: J. Kristjánsson and V. Ólasson, eds. *Eddukvæði II. Hetjukvæði. Izlensk fornrit* 36(2). Reykjavík: Hið íslenzka fornritafélag, 349–351.

*Herodotus. The Histories*. 2013. Transl. T. Holland. London: Penguin.

Hines, J., 2003. Myth and reality: the contribution of archaeology. *In*: M. Clunies Ross, ed. *Old Norse Myths, Literature and Society*. Odense: University Press of Southern Denmark, 19–39.

*Historia Norwegie*. 2003. Transl. P. Fisher, ed. I. Ekrem and L.B. Mortensen. Copenhagen: Museum Tusculanum Press.

Hjartarson, Á., Guðmundsson, G. J., and Gísladóttir, H., 1991. *Manngerðir hellar á Íslandi*. Reykjavík: Bókaútgáfa Menningarsjóðs.

Hommedal, A.T., 1997. Bakgrunnen for helgenanlegget på Selja og staden si rolle i den tidlege kristninga av Vest-Noreg. *In*: M. Rindal, ed. *Selja – heilag stad i 1000 år*. Oslo: Universitetsforlaget, 43–76.

Hofseth, E.H., 1985. Det går i spinn. *In*: J.R. Næss, ed. *Artikkelsamling I*. AmS Skrifter 11. Stavanger: Arkeologisk museum i Stavanger, 33–61.

Hufthammer, A.K., 1994. Beinmaterialet fra Hidlaren på Kollsnes. *In*: A.J. Nærøy, ed. *Troll-prosjektet. Arkeologiske undersøkelser på Kollsnes, Øygarden k., Hordaland, 1989–1992*. Arkeologiske rapporter 19. Bergen: University of Bergen, 275–278.

*Húngrvaka*. 2002. *In*: Á. Egilsdóttir, ed. *Biskupa Sögur II. XVI. Bindi. Íslenzk fornrit*. Reykjavík: Hið íslenzka fornritafélag, 1–43.

*Hyndluljoð*. 2014. *In*: J. Kristjánsson and V. Ólasson, eds. *Eddukvæði I. Goðakvæði. Izlensk fornrit*, 36:1. Reykjavík: Hið íslenzka fornritafélag, 460–469.

Høgestøl, M., 1995. *Arkeologiske undersøkelser i Rennesøy kommune, Rogaland, Sørvest-Norge*. AmS-Varia 23. Stavanger: Arkeologisk Museum i Stavanger.

Johansen, B., 1997. *Ormalur. Aspekter av tillvaro och landskap*. Stockholm: Arkeologiska institutionen, Stockholms Universitet.

*Jordanes. The Gothic History*. 1915. Transl. C.C. Mierow. Princeton, NJ: Princeton University Press.

*Jökuls þattr Búasonar*. 1959. *In*: J. Halldórsson, ed. *Íslenzk fornrit* 14. *Bindi. Kjalnesinga saga*. Reykjavík: Hið íslenzka fornritafélag, 45–59.

*Kjalnesinga saga*. 1959. *In*: J. Halldórsson, ed. *Íslenzk fornrit. 14. Bindi. Kjalnesinga saga*. Reykjavík: Hið íslenzka fornritafélag, 1–44.

*Landnámabók*. 1968. *In*: J. Benediktsson, ed. *Íslenzk fornrit. I Bindi. Íslendingabók, Landnámabók*. Reykjavík: Hið íslenzka fornritafélag, 29–397.

Larsen, J.H., 2009. *Jernvinneundersøkelser. Faglig program. Bind 2*. Varia 78. Oslo: University of Oslo.

Lewis-Williams, D., 2002. *The Mind in the Cave. Conciousness amd the Origins of Art*. London: Thames & Hudson.

Lie, R.O. 2007. Huler og hellere på Nordmøre. Del 1. *Årbok for Nordmøre*, 2007, 95–131.

Lie, R.O. 2008. Huler og hellere på Nordmøre. Del 2. *Årbok for Nordmøre*, 2008, 5–25.

Liestøl, A. 1964. Runer fra Bryggen. *Viking* 27, 5–53.

Lindøe, K., 1930. Innberetning fra utgravningen av Kjerringholet. Unpublished report on file at the topographical archive, University Museum of Bergen.

Losnegård, G., 2006. *Jondal kommune. Frå øksehogg til tastetrykk. Bind III. Allmensoge*. Jondal: Jondal kommune.

Lund, J., 2009. *Åsted og vadested. Deponeringer, gjenstandsbiografier og rumlig strukturering som kilde til vikingtidens kognitive landskaper*. Acta Humaniora 389. Oslo: Unipub.

Lund, J., 2010. At the Water's Edge. *In*: M. Carver, A. Sanmark and S. Semple, eds. *Signals of Belief in Early England. Anglo-Saxon Paganism Revisited*. Oxford: Oxbow Books, 49–66.

Lund, J. 2015. Living places or animated objects? Sámi sacrificial places with metal objects and their South Scandinavian parallels. *Acta Borealia* 32(1), 29–39.

Lødøen, T., 1997. Arkeologiske undersøkelser i Øvste Dåvatræhelleren. Unpublished report on file in the topographical archive, University Museum of Bergen.

Løkka, N., 2010. Steder og landskap i norrøn mytologi. En analyse av topografi og kosmologi i gudediktene av Den eldre Edda. Thesis (PhD), University of Oslo.

Martinussen, A.O. and Myhre, B., 1985. *Kulturminner i Etnefjella. Konsekvensutredning for utbygging i Etnevassdraget*. Arkeologiske rapporter 8. Bergen: Historisk museum, Universitetet i Bergen.

Meulengracht Sørensen, P., 1977. *Saga og samfund. En indføring i oldislandsk litteratur*. København: Berlingske Forlag.

Meulengracht Sørensen, P., 1995. *Fortælling og ære. Studier i islendingesagaene*. Oslo: Universitetsforlaget.

Mitchell, S.A., 1991. *Heroic Sagas and Ballads*. London: Ithaca.

Moyes, H., ed., 2012. *Sacred Darkness. A Global Perspective on the Ritual Use of Caves*. Boulder, CO: University Press of Colorado.

Mundal, E., 1997. Heiden kult som kan knytast til holer og hellarar. *In*: M. Rindal, ed. *Selja – heilag stad i 1000 år*. Oslo: Universitetsforlaget, 35–42.

Mundal, E., 2012 [1990]. Forholdet mellom gudar og jotnar i norrøn mytologi i lys av det mytologiske namnematerialet. *In*: O.E. Haugen, B.Ø. Thorvaldsen, and J. Wellendorf, eds. *Fjǫld veit hon fræða*. Oslo: Novus forlag, 173–189.

Mundal, E., 2012 [1995]. Kong Harald Hårfagre og samejenta Snøfrid. Samefolket sin plass i den norske rikssamlingsmyten. *In*: O.E. Haugen, B.Ø. Thorvaldsen, and J. Wellendorf, eds. *Fjǫld veit hon fræða*. Oslo: Novus forlag, 271–284.

Mundal, E., 2012 [1996]. The perception of the Saamis and their religion in Old Norse sources. *In*: O.E. Haugen, B.Ø. Thorvaldsen and J. Wellendorf, eds. *Fjǫld veit hon fræða. Utvalde arbeid av Else Mundal*. Oslo: Novus forlag, 233–254.

Narmo, L.E. 1996. 'Kokekameratene på Leikvin'. Kult og kokegroper. *Viking*, LIX, 79–100.

Narmo, L.E., 1997. *Jernvinne, smie og kullproduksjon i Østerdalen*. Varia 43. Oslo: University of Oslo.

Nordvig, A.M.V., 2013. On Fire and Water. The Old Norse Mythical Worldview in an Eco-Mythological Perspective. Thesis (PhD). Aarhus University.

Nærøy, A.J., 1994. *Troll-prosjektet. Arkeologiske undersøkelser på Kollsnes, Øygarden k., Hordaland, 1989–1992*. Arkeologiske rapporter 19. Bergen: University of Bergen.

Ólafsson, G., Smith, K.P., and McGovern, T.H., 2009. Surtshellir: a fortified outlaw cave in West Iceland. *In*: J. Sheehan, D. ÓCorráin, and S. Lewis-Simpson, eds. *The Viking Age. Ireland and the West. Papers from the Proceedings of the Fifteenth Viking Congress, Cork, 18–27 August 2005*. Dublin: Four Courts Press, 283–297.

Olsen, M. and Shetelig, H. 1933. Runekammen fra Setre. *Bergens Museums Aarbok 1933. Historisk-antikvarisk rekke*, nr. 2, 1–92.

*Orkneyinga saga*. 1965. *In*: F. Guðmundsson, ed. *Íslenzk fornrit* 34. Reykjavik: Hið íslenzka fornritafélag.

*Orms þáttr Stórófssonar*. 1991. *In*: Þ. Vilmundarson and B. Vilhjálmsson, eds. *Íslenzk fornrit. XIII Bindi. Harðar saga*. Reykjavík: Hið íslenzka fornritafélag, 395–421.

Østebø, K., 2008. *Hellerbruk i vestnorsk Eldre Jernalder belyst ved lokalisering*. Thesis (MA), University of Bergen.

Øye, I., 1988. *Textile Equipment and its Working Environment, Bryggen in Bergen, c. 1150–1500*. The Bryggen Papers 2. Oslo: Norwegian University Press.

Øye, I., 2002. Landbruk under press 800–1350. *In*: B. Myhre and I. Øye, eds. *Norges Landbrukshistorie I. Jorda blir levevei: 4000 f.Kr.-1350 e.Kr*. Oslo: Samlaget, 215–414.

Pálsson, H., 1997. *Úr landnorðri: Samar og ystu rætur íslenskrar menningar*. Reykjavík: Bókmenntafræðistofnun Háskóla Íslands.

Pedersen, U. 2010. I smeltedigelen. Finsmedene i vikingtidsbyen Kaupang. Thesis (PhD), University of Oslo.

Petersen, J., 1951. *Vikingetidens redskaper*. Oslo: Dybwad.

Prescott, C., 1991. *Kulturhistoriske undersøkelser i Skrivarhellaren*. Arkeologiske rapporter 14. Bergen: University of Bergen.

Price, N., 2002. *The Viking way. Religion and war in Late Iron Age Scandinavia*. Uppsala: Uppsala University.

Randers, K. and Höglin, S., 1988. *Valderøya Vest 1986–1987*. Arkeologiske rapporter 12. Bergen: University of Bergen.

Randers, K. and Kvamme, M., 1992. *Breheimenundersøkelsene 1982–1984 I: Stølsområdene*. Arkeologiske rapporter 15. Bergen: University of Bergen.

Reinton, L., 1957. *Sæterbruket i Noreg II. Anna arbeid på sætra. Sætra i haustingsbruket og i matnøytsla elles*. Oslo: Aschehoug.

Resi, H.G., 1983. Report from excavation of Skylehelleren, Emblemsvåg, Ålesund k. Sogn og Fjordane. Unpublished report on file in the topographical archive, University Museum of Bergen.

Ringstad, B., 1985. Foreløpig innberetning om 'Storsetehilleren' i Matre, Masfjorden. Unpublished report on file at the topographical archive, University museum of Bergen.

*Saga Óláfs Tryggasonar af Oddr Snorrason Munk*. 1932. Publ. F. Jónsson. Copenhagen: G.E.C. Gads Forlag.

Sauvage, R., 2005. Utgravning av Smiehelleren på Monge gnr/bnr 69/8 i Rauma, Møre og Romsdal, i forbindelse med reguleringsplan for ny E-136 strekningen Monge-Marstein. Unpublished report on file at the topographical archive, Vitenskapsmuseet in Trondheim.

Schanche, A., 2000. *Graver i ur og berg: Samisk gravskikk og religion 1000 f.Kr. til 1700 e.Kr*. Karasjok: Davvi girji.

Schjødt, J.P., 2008. *Initiation between Worlds. Structure and Symbolism in Pre-Christian Scandinavian Religion*. Odense: The University Press of Southern Denmark.

Semple, S., 2013. *Perceptions of the Prehistoric in Anglo-Saxon England. Religion, Ritual, and Rulership in the Landscape*. Oxford: Oxford University Press.

Sigurðsson, J.V., 1999. *Norsk historie 800–1300*. Oslo: Det Norske Samlaget.

Simek, R., 1993. *Dictionary of northern mythology*. Cambridge: D.S. Brewer.

Skjølsvold, A., 1961. *Klebersteinsindustrien i Vikingtiden*. Oslo: Universitetsforlaget.

Skrede, M.A., 2005. *Innberetning av helleren Pleta. Flora kommune - reguleringsplan for hyttefelt på GBNR. 45/2*. Unpublished report on file in the topographical archive, University Museum of Bergen.

Solberg, B., 2003. *Jernalderen i Norge: Ca. 500 f.Kr.-1030 e.Kr*. 3rd edn. Oslo: Cappelen.

Solheim, S., 1965. Landvette. *In*: F. Hødnbø, ed. *Kulturhistorisk Leksikon for Nordisk Middelalder*. Vol. X. Oslo: Gyldendal, 299–302.

Solli, B., 2002. *Seid. Myter, sjamanisme og kjønn i Vikingenes tid*. Oslo: Pax.

Stafseth, T., 2006. *Innberetning om befaring. Reguleringsplan for kommunal veiforbindelse mellom Kvernbergmyran og Gløsvåveien v. Dale*. Molde: Møre og Romsdal Fylkeskommune.

Steinsland, G., 1986. Giants as recipients of cult? *In*: G. Steinsland, ed. *Words and Objects. Towards a Dialogue between Archaeology and History of Religion*. Oslo: Instituttet for Sammenlignende Kulturforskning, 212–222.

Steinsland, G., 1991. *Det hellige bryllup og Norrøn kongeideologi*. Oslo: Solum Forlag.

Steinsland, G., 1997. Hulehelligdommen på Selja. På leiting etter førkristne spor – en vandring i myter, makter og tegn. *In*: M. Rindal, ed. *Selja – heilag stad i 1000 år*. Oslo: Universitetsforlaget, 11–33.

Steinsland, G., 2005. *Norrøn religion. Myter, riter og samfunn*. Oslo: Pax A/S.

Steinsland, G., 2014. *Dovrefjell i tusen år. Mytene, historien og diktningen*. Bergen: Vigmostad og Bjørke.

Steinsland, G. and Meulengracht Sørensen, P., 1994. *Menneske og makter i vikingenes verden*. Oslo: Universitetsforlaget.

Storvik, I., 2011. Huler og hellere i Rogaland. Thesis (MA), University of Bergen.

*Strabo. The Geography*. 1917–1932 (8 volumes). Transl. H.L. Jones. Harvard: Harvard University Press.

Ström, F., 1961. *Nordisk Hedendom*. Gothenburg: Akademiförlaget-Gumperts.

*Sturlunga saga*. 1906. Efter membranen Krókfjarðarbók. Første bind. København og Kristiania: Det Kongelige Nordiske Oldskrifts-Selskab i kommisjonen i Gyldendalske boghandel. Nordisk forlag.

*Svarfdæla saga*. 1956. *In*: J. Kristjánsson, ed. *Íslenzk fornrit. IX. Bindi. Eyfirðinga sǫgur*. Reykjavík: Hið íslenzka fornritafélag, 1–44.

*The Saga of Grettir the Strong*. 1997. Transl. B. Scudder. *In*: V. Hreinsson, ed. *The Complete Sagas of the Icelanders including 49 Tales* II. Reykjavik: Leifur Eriksson Publishing, 49–191.

*The Saga of Olaf Tryggvason by Oddr Snorrason Munk*. 2003. Transl. T.M. Andersson. Ithaca, NY: Cornell University Press.

*The Saga of the People of Fljotsdal*. 1997. Transl. J. Porter. *In*: V. Hreinsson, ed. *The Complete Sagas of the Icelanders including 49 Tales* IV. Reykjavik: Leifur Eriksson Publishing, 378–433.

*The Saga of the People of Svarfadardal*. 1997. Transl. F.J. Heinemann. *In*: V. Hreinsson, ed. *The Complete Sagas of the Icelanders including 49 Tales* IV. Reykjavik: Leifur Eriksson Publishing, 149–192.

Thorvaldsen, B.Ø., 2013. Mytologi. *In*: O.E. Haugen, ed. *Handbok i norrøn filologi*. 2nd edn. Bergen: Fagbokforlaget, 464–511.

Todnem, R., 1999. Holer og hellere, for de levende eller for de døde? *In*: I. Fuglestvedt, T. Gansum, and A. Opedal, eds. *Et hus med mange rom. Vennebok til Bjørn Myhre på 60-årsdagen*. Stavanger: Arkeologisk museum i Stavanger, 103–120.

*Þorvalds þáttr Viðförla I*. 2003. *In*: S. Steingrímsson, Ó. Halldórsson, and P. Foote, eds., *Íslenzk fornrit XV.2. Biskupa sögur*, I. Síðarihluti – sögutextar. Reykjavík: Hið íslenzka fornritafélag, 49–89.

Valvik, K.A., 2001. *Kulturhistoriske registreringar. Nye Bjølvo kraftverk. Bjølsegrøvassdraget, Kvam herad*. Bergen: Hordaland Fylkekommune.

Valvik, K.A., 2004. *Kulturhistoriske registreringar. Innleiande registrering Langevåg vindpark, Bømlo kommune*. Bergen: Hordaland Fylkekommune.

Vangstad, H., 2017. From numeric data to cultural history: A typological analysis of soapstone vessels from the medieval Bryggen wharf in Bergen, Norway. *In*: G. Hansen and P. Storemyr, eds. *Soapstone in the North – Quarries, Products and People 7000 BC–AD 1700*. UBAS 9. Bergen: University of Bergen, 35–54.

*Vatnsdœla saga*. 1939. *In*: E.Ó. Sveinsson, ed. *Íslenzk fornrit* VIII. Reykjavik: Hið íslenzka fornritafélag.

*Vǫlsunga saga ok Ragnars saga loðbrókar*. 1906–1908. Ed. M. Olsen. Copenhagen: S-L. Møllers Bogtrykkeri.

*Vǫluspá*. 1997. Transl. U. Dronke. *In*: U. Dronke, ed. *The Poetic Edda*. Clarendon Press: Oxford, 7–24.

*Vǫluspá (Konungsbók)*. 2014. *In*: J. Kristjánsson and V. Ólasson, eds. *Eddukvæði I. Goðakvæði. Íslenzk fornrit* 36(1). Reykjavík: Hið íslenzka fornritafélag, 281–307.

von Sydow, C.W., 1933. Övernaturliga väsen. *In*: E. Bull and S. Steen, eds. *Byer og Bebyggelse*. Nordisk Kultur XVIII. Stockholm: Bonnier.

Weber, B. 1984. 'I Hardanger er Quernberg og Helleberg ... og Hellerne, det er tyndhugne Steene, bruger man til at bage tynde Brød Flatbrød på'. *Viking* 47, 149–160.

Zachrisson, T., 1998. *Gård, gräns, gravfält. Sammanhang kring ädelmetalldepåer och runstenar från vikingatid och tidig medeltid i Uppland och Gästrikland*. Stockholm: Stockholms Universitet.

# Chapter 4

# A holy cave and womb: the sanctuary on the island of Selja and the birth of the first Norwegian saints

*Alf Tore Hommedal*

*The island of Selja, on the west coast of Norway, played an important role in establishing Christianity in Norway in the eleventh and twelfth centuries. The sanctuary on Selja, with its rockshelter associated with the martyrdom of St Sunnifa and her entourage in the tenth century, is central in establishing this legendary Irish virgin queen refugee as the patron saint of western Norway and the town of Bergen. The sanctuary faces the sea and consists of three elements: a rockshelter with caves, a stone church, and a large stone terrace in front of the church. This chapter surveys the archaeological and written evidence for the sanctuary and its development up to its completion before AD 1170, when the relic of St Sunnifa was transferred to Bergen leaving her entourage, the Seljumenn, behind. The relationship between the development of the legend and the sanctuary is discussed. This study concludes that the sanctuary, with its massive stone terrace, was given its final form as part of the creation of the identity and memory of the probably fictional St Sunnifa and the Seljumenn.*

## The island of *Felicitas* and its pious virgin queen

According to the Norse sagas, King Olaf (Óláfr) II Haraldsson, who later became the national saint of Norway, reached the shores of Norway at the small island of Selja in AD 1015 (Figs. 4.1 and 4.2). He came from England with two goals in mind: to conquer and unify the kingdom, and to Christianise the country. The king and his men perceived it as a lucky omen to arrive on this island of *Sela* ('the blessedness') – in Latin referred to as *Felicitas*, which means luck, happiness, progress and fertility (Hommedal 2015). Why was it such a stroke of luck for the king to arrive on the shores of Selja? It was not uncommon for ships to reach this island on the far western coast of Norway when travelling across the sea from the west. Of course, the name of the island was, in itself, enough to create hope and optimism, but for the king and his men, or at least for the historians writing the king's history in the late twelfth and early thirteenth centuries, it must also have been important to connect the future holy king to Norway's first Christian sanctuary. According to the Church's official legend, *Acta sanctorum in Selio* from *c.* AD 1170, the sanctuary at Selja was established in AD 996, nearly two decades before the king is supposed to have reached this island of *felicitas*.

The story of King Óláfr's arrival leads us thus to Selja's holy rockshelter with its caves where the Irish queen, Sunnifa (Fig. 4.3), and her entourage of men, women and children – the *Seljumenn* – had, according to legend, been martyred some decades earlier at the time of the German emperor Otto I (AD 936-973). These Christian refugees had also been driven towards the shores of Selja where they lived peacefully in the caves, surviving on fish from the sea and serving the Lord in poverty and chastity. When the 'heathen Norsemen' came to attack the Christians, falsely accusing them of stealing sheep the Norsemen had grazing on the island, the pious Irish, according to legend, fled to the caves and prayed to God that he would give their souls eternal peace and provide a tomb for their bodies. At that point, rocks tumbled down and martyrised them all. Some decades later, in AD 996, the Norwegian Christian king Óláfr I Tryggvason and his men found amongst the rocks the sweet-smelling bones of the martyred Irish. On the orders of the bishop, and with the approval of the king, a church

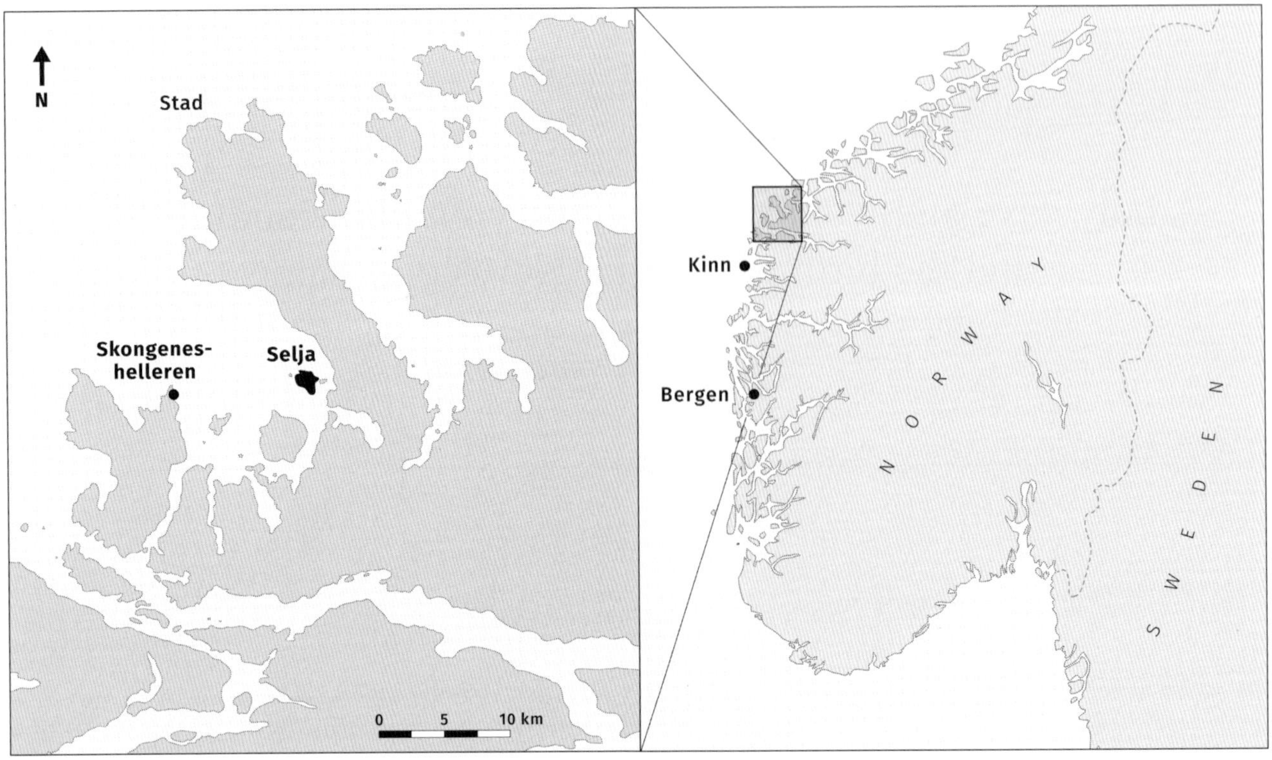


*Figure 4.1: Southern part of Norway with Selja and Bergen, the two maincult centres connected to St Sunnifa and the Seljumenn. The third cult centre, Kinn, is also marked. To the left is a more detailed location of Selja facing the open Atlantic Ocean, to the south of Stad. The cave Skongeneshelleren is marked. Illustration: P. Bækken.*

was built 'where God provides signs and miracles through the merits of his saints until this day' (Rindal 1997c, 309; Ommundsen 2011, 34).

The legend then continues with what appears to be an afterthought, recounting that when the bones were gathered up, the body of the blessed virgin and martyr, Sunnifa, was also found perfectly preserved, apparently in the cave. With great veneration, her body was moved and placed in a shrine; apparently in the church that was constructed on the island. After a period of time, the additional text says, the relics of St Sunnifa were transferred (a *translatio*) from Selja to the town of Bergen in AD 1170, and enshrined in the cathedral there (Fig. 4.1). This summary of *Acta sanctorum in Selio*, the oldest version of the legend of St Sunnifa and the Seljumenn, was written as the Church's official *acta* after the *translatio*. It is further summarised and discussed by, for example, church historian Stephan Borgehammar (1997a, b) and Latinist Åslaug Ommundsen (2010, 82–84; 2011, 32).

## The caves and sanctuary at Selja: an introduction and questions

This legend, with the holy rockshelter at its core, meant that in the eleventh and twelfth centuries, i.e. the first period of Christianity in Norway, Selja developed as an ecclesiastical centre comprising not only the saint's shrine but also, from the 1090s at the latest, a Benedictine monastery and, for a short period in the eleventh century, the first episcopal seat of western Norway. The pilgrimage site probably existed until the Lutheran Reformation in 1536–1537 and in secret even longer (Hommedal 1997b, 190–195; *in press*). The remnants of this centre today comprise one of the most spectacular cultural heritage sites in Norway, and the rockshelter with its two caves forms the most sacred and prestigious of the surviving physical remains (Figs. 4.2 and 4.5).

In what follows, the background and development of the sanctuary at Selja will be discussed – a rockshelter with caves that was once described by the preacher Arne Bakken as the 'womb that gave birth to the Church in Norway' (Hommedal 1995, 143). What information do we have about the caves as the origin of the cult of St Sunnifa and the Seljumenn? How did the rockshelter, serving as a chapel in its own right, function liturgically as a place of pilgrimage and veneration in the centuries following the establishment of the sanctuary? This chapter also considers whether the Christian cult connected to the medieval legend may have been preceded by a pagan cult at the caves. From years of research into the legend, there now seems to be a general agreement that the cardinal figure, St Sunnifa, is a secondary addition to an original legend that referred only to the Seljumenn. Scholars have suggested different interpretations for when the main figure appeared in the legend, but the

*Figure 4.2: Selja. The sanctuary during excavation in 1991 (in front) and the Benedictine monastery (with the tower), seen towards the west with Stad and the Atlantic Ocean. The plastic tent in the sanctuary marks the archaeological excavation site. Photo: K.A. Bergsvik.*

*Figure 4.3: St Sunnifa from Karlsøy church, Troms. The wooden sculpture (1.14m high) was probably carved in Lübeck* c. *AD 1520 and is now at the Museum of Cultural History, Oslo. St Sunnifa balances a block of rock in her hand as her attribute, referring to the way she was martyred. Photo: A.T. Hommedal.*

most widely-accepted interpretation is that Sunnifa became an official part of the legend in the first part of the twelfth century, and this is the view adopted here. In this chapter, I suggest that the shaping of the magnificent terrace at the sanctuary, completed in the early twelfth century or around 1150, was carried out as part of the creation of an identity and memory of the Selja saints. First and foremost was St Sunnifa, whose relic was later moved to Bergen, but also the Seljumenn, whose relics were kept and worshiped at Selja after Sunnifa's *translatio* of AD 1170. Archaeological and written sources from AD 200/400 to *c*. AD 1170 will be considered. The year 1170 is chosen as a cut-off point for this paper because of the *translatio* to Bergen, which created a new dynamic both for the sanctuary at Selja and for the cult as a whole. The period after 1170 at Selja will be briefly referred to but not discussed in detail, except for sources from this period which throw light on activities prior to 1170. The development of the cult outside of Selja will also not be explicitly discussed. After 1170 Sunnifa became the patron saint of the town and diocese of Bergen and was venerated throughout Norway, and even across all Nordic countries as well as northern Germany (Hommedal 1997b).

In addition to Selja and Bergen, the cult of St Sunnifa and the Seljumenn is found on a third and smaller site, the island of Kinn (Fig. 4.1) where, according to legend, some of the Irish refugees who followed St Sunnifa by boat came ashore. The legend does not tell, however, of any martyrising there. The sanctuary at Kinn consists of an early twelfth-century stone church overlooking the ocean and a cave *c.* 30m further up the hillside behind the church. The location at Kinn is very similar to Selja, though with a smaller and less developed sanctuary. Fragments of masonry and cultural deposits have also been documented in the cave at Kinn (Christie 1983b) but it has never been properly investigated. Though Kinn is part of the cult of the Seljumenn, it will not be discussed extensively here.

In Norway, the Middle Ages is defined as the period when Norway was a Catholic country – AD 1000–1537 – while the earlier centuries are defined as the Early Iron Age, 500 BC–AD 550, and the Late Iron Age, AD 550–1000.

## Selja as an ecclesiastical centre: an overview

Selja lies in a wild and barren coastal landscape just south of the Stad peninsula. The island's western side, with the caves and ecclesiastical complex, faces the Atlantic Ocean and the most treacherous navigable waters along the entire Norwegian coastline (Figs. 4.1 and 4.2). The location of the sanctuary is thus very similar to certain other maritime monasteries and sanctuaries such as Skellig Michael in Ireland; Lindisfarne, Iona and St Michael's Mount in Great Britain; and Mont Saint Michel in France.

The present cultural heritage site at Selja consists of two groups of visible masonry remains. The first group are the remnants of the sanctuary associated with the rockshelter and caves. The second group is situated on flat ground beneath the sanctuary and is connected with the Benedictine monastery. The monastery was rebuilt in the thirteenth and fourteenth centuries, i.e. the period after the main focus of this article and *c.* 200 years after the Benedictine foundation. A new monastic stone conventual quadrangle with a cloister was then erected (Fig. 4.2), incorporating a late eleventh-century stone basilica which was probably erected originally as the bishop's cathedral at Selja but also functioned as the monastic church (Nybø 2000; Hommedal *in press*). The original late eleventh-century Benedictine monastery, probably connected to this church, must have consisted primarily of wooden buildings of which no trace now survives. The Benedictine complex will not be discussed further here, but the status of the Benedictines before 1170 will be incorporated into the discussion where relevant (i.e. the fact that the abbey was not dedicated to St Sunnifa but rather to the prominent English cleric, St Alban).

## 'A cave by the ocean': the sanctuary today and in the Middle Ages

Viewed from the Benedictine monastery, the sanctuary today stands out as a massive grey stone wall in a funnel-shaped crevice in the mountain to the east. The sanctuary is dominated by a huge masonry terrace now surviving as three artificial levels (Fig. 4.5). On the innermost and highest level, the ruins of a small stone church dedicated to St Sunnifa are located (Figs. 4.4 and 4.6). Located on a higher level, to the east of the church, are the two caves with a rockshelter outside, at *c.* 60m above sea level. All areas of the sanctuary are connected by flights of stone stairs. The sanctuary commands panoramic views over the Atlantic Ocean, entirely justifying what is possibly the oldest description of the site as 'a cave by the ocean'.

### *Archaeological surveys*

In what follows, some of the cultural heritage history of the sanctuary will be incorporated into the discussion. Early excavations conducted by the officer Carl O. Krefting and the theologian V. Koren were carried out between 1866 and 1868. The quality of their archaeological field methods can be illustrated by the fact that the 1866 work was carried out by 50 men over five days (Krefting 1868; Koren 1869; Nicolaysen 1892; Hommedal 1996, 25). In 1935–1940, the building engineer Cato Enger carried out further excavations and restorations. It was then that parts of the rockshelter masonry walls and the stone terrace were given their present and partially reconstructed form. The church ruins were restored in 1909 and 1967 (Enger 1949; Hommedal 1996).

In 1990–1992 archaeological excavations were carried out by the present author as part of an architectural and archaeological research project at Selja (Nybø 2000; Hommedal 1996; 1997a; *in press*). Excavations in the sanctuary concentrated on the area of St Sunnifa's church, with the main excavation to the north of the church (Figs. 4.4 and 4.7). Due to an absence of cultural deposits in the rockshelter and caves, no excavations were carried out there apart from test drilling in the sand floor of the main cave to document natural sediments. The outer terrace area was not examined as it had been rebuilt in the 1930s, though a visual examination of the lower and original parts of the masonry walls was conducted.

### *Written sources*

Some medieval texts, in Latin and Norse, will be considered. Critical editions of most of the manuscripts are edited in Rindal (1997), combined with critical Norwegian translations. The quotes provided here in English are translations for this article by the author, unless otherwise stated. The Latin *Acta Sanctorum in Selio* ('The legend of the holy people on Selja'), written *c.* AD 1170 as the Church's official account, has already been mentioned. The sanctuary was also described in two Norse versions of the story, incorporated into two different sagas of King Óláfr I Tryggvason (Rindal 1997a, 267–269; Ommundsen 2011, 32). The oldest of these two sagas was originally composed in Latin by the Icelandic monk Oddr Snorrason (*c.* 1190), but is now lost. However, a Norse translation from *c.* AD 1200 was transcribed in three later manuscripts, one of which (Stockholm perg. 18 4°), written *c.* 1300, preserves a

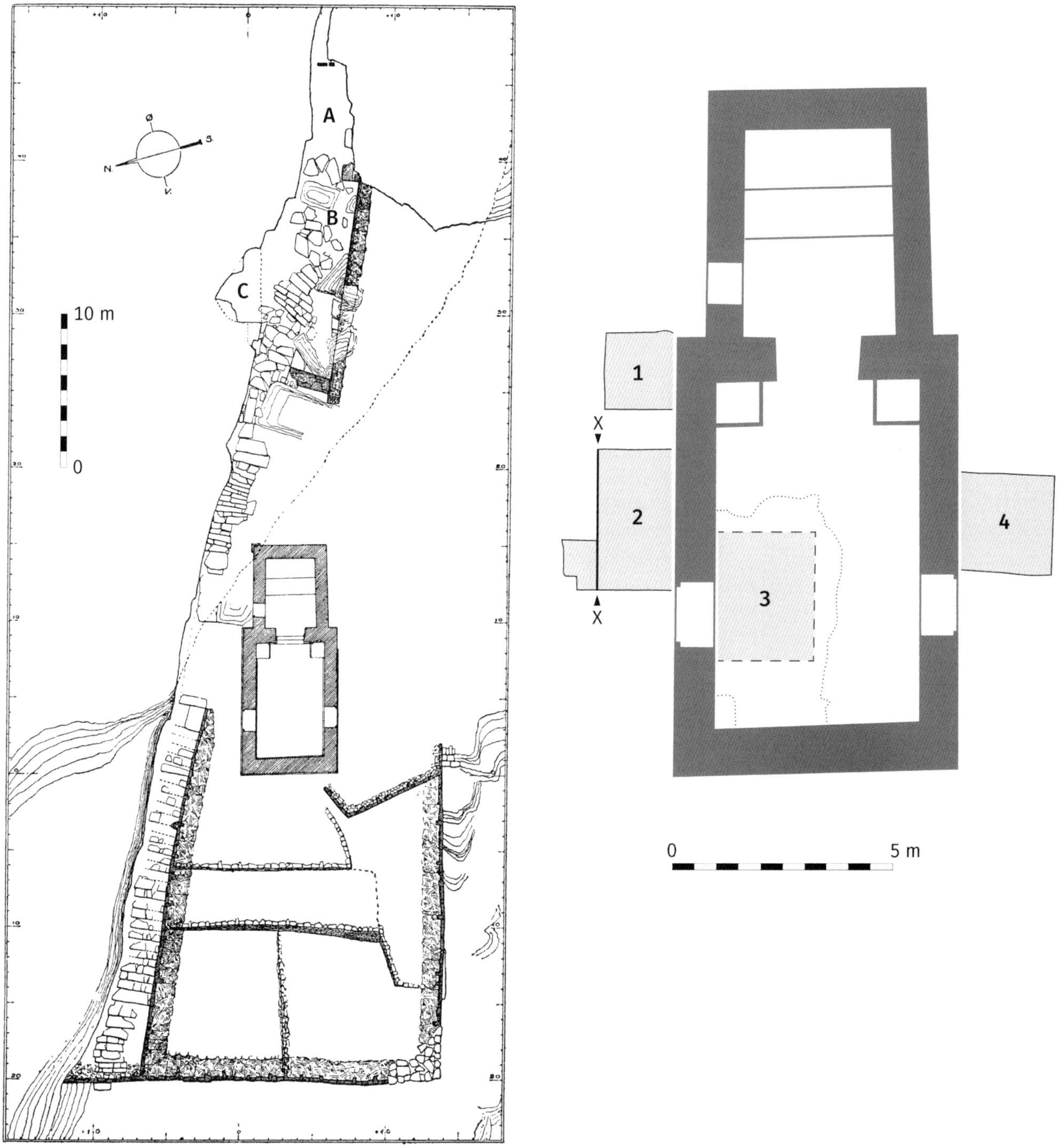


*Figure 4.4: The Sanctuary at Selja. To the left: the overall layout of the sanctuary with the rockshelter, St Sunnifa's church and the stone terrace with its different levels (compare to Fig. 4.5). In the rockshelter the main cave (A, see also Fig. 4.9), the outer rockshelter (B, see also Fig. 4.8) and the north cave (C) can be seen. To the right: Close-up of St Sunnifa's church with the layout of the archaeological excavation trenches 1990–1992. The main excavation took place in Areas 2 and 3. X-X marks the location of the section drawing shown in Fig. 4.7. The perforated line in Area 3 marks the irregular boundary of the site due to the embankment of stones. The dotted line marks the extension of slabs in the floor (in its form from 1909 and 1967) lifted in 1990–1992 in order to inspect the stone embankment and to adjust the excavations of Area 3. Illustrations: to the left, C. Enger, 1949, revised. To the right, A.T. Hommedal and P. Bækken.*

*Figure 4.5: The Sanctuary at Selja view to the north-east, with the restored stone terrace in three levels, the ruin of St Sunnifa church (on the upper, level) and the rockshelter. Compare to Fig. 4.4. Photo: A.T. Hommedal, 1991.*

*Figure 4.6: The chancel and eastern part of the nave in St Sunnifa's church, with the rockshelter behind it. Photo, A.T. Hommedal.*

section that mentions both the rockshelter's morphology and function and the church of St Sunnifa. The other saga, *Óláfs saga Tryggvasonar en mesta* ('The greatest saga of Óláfr Tryggvason'), was composed anonymously at the beginning of the fourteenth century and handed down in several fourteenth-century manuscripts. One of these manuscripts, *Flateyjarbók*, written in the 1380s, is of special interest here in that it mentions the terrace and also the location of St Sunnifa's church. The two sagas were written in Iceland and, at least for *Óláfs saga Tryggvasonar en mesta* (1958, 252) the writer had not been to Selja as it refers to people who had been there and were familiar with the site. We must assume that the writer relied on first-hand information as the descriptions are accurate based on what survives in the landscape today.

## The rockshelter and caves: morphology and function

The rockshelter area can be divided into three parts: the outer rockshelter, the main cave and the smaller northern cave (Figs. 4.4, 4.8 and 4.9). The outer rockshelter is on average 12.5m long (east-west) and 5m wide, created by an overhanging rock that slopes down to the north to form a roof (Figs. 4.4.B and 4.8). The space is several metres higher towards the south and west, creating a lofty chamber defined on these sides by constructed masonry walls. To the west is the entrance with stone steps leading down into the lower parts of the sanctuary. The masonry walls were partly restored in the 1930s, but the original medieval masonry is preserved in the lower courses and was documented in the nineteenth and twentieth centuries indicating that originally walls more or less enclosed the space (Krefting 1868, 5–6; Enger 1949, 10–11; Hommedal 1996, 25–27). Because of the different heights of the huge stone blocks that comprise the floor, the space is on two levels with the lower western section connected by seven stone steps to the upper section.

The main cave is approximately 6m long, 2.5m wide and *c.* 2m high (Figs. 4.4.A and 4.9). It is a narrower, eastern extension of the outer rockshelter, and the floor slopes downward *c.* 1 m compared to that in the rockshelter. The less clearly defined north cave (Fig. 4.4.C) extends from the western part of the outer rockshelter and is created by the northernmost and lowest overhanging part of the rock. This north cave had, at the time of excavation in the 1860s, a *c.* 1.8m-high and 6.2m-wide entrance opening onto the outer rockshelter. The cave itself was *c.* 3.7m wide and up to *c.* 2.5m high (Koren 1869, 9; Hommedal 1996, 25). Today, the north cave is partly filled with stones and thus appears smaller.

The rockshelter area is nowadays cleared of archaeological deposits, as was documented in 1990–1992. The excavations in 1866–1868 and 1935 removed deposits interpreted as sheep dung together with gravel and sand. Rocks believed to have collapsed in more recent centuries were broken up and removed (Enger 1949, 10; Hommedal 1996, 25). The

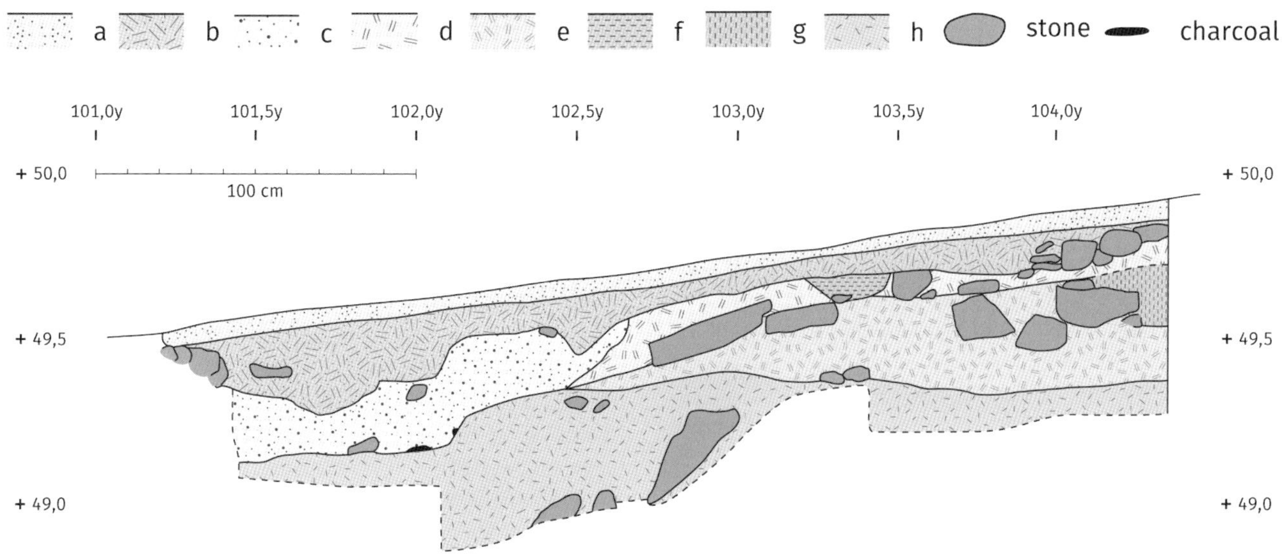


*Figure 4.7: The soil embankment on the north side of the nave of St Sunnifa church (see Fig. 4.4), seen from the south. Under the turf (a) come layers of humus and stones (b, f), interpreted as disturbed in the 1930s at the latest. The following layers (c, d, e, g) are interpreted as filled-in natural material. This human-made embankment was levelled in one round, possibly in two or three rounds. No artefacts were found in the layers. Only fragments of the new, levelled surface after the fill-in were preserved, due to truncation by the younger, modern stratigraphic layer (b). Charcoal from the observed surface-fragments (not within the drawn section) are radiocarbon dated (T-9320, T-9321, see Table 1) to the Viking Age. The original ledge, before the levelling, consists of composed soil (h). Charcoal from the documented surface before the levelling are radiocarbon dated (Tua-476, T-10047, see Table 4.1) to the Early Iron Age. Illustration: A.T. Hommedal and P. Bækken.*

interpretation of the deposits as dung from grazing sheep seeking shelter in post-medieval times must partly be correct. It seems clear, however, that cultural deposits from both the Middle Ages and earlier periods were also removed during these investigations. Alas, most of the documentation from the 1930s is now missing.

In the *Saga Ólafs Trygvasonar af Oddr Snorrason Munk* (1932 see also Rindal 1997b) the rockshelter area is described in the following manner:

> *I þeim dyrliga helli er þa fell er nv gíor kapella er þeir kalla salinn er hellirinn annaR veggrinn en annarR er af steini gávr ok inn ibergit er skvti oc fellr þar vr litill løkr oc fa þar margir heilso ok er þar gørt alltari iþeiri kappello ok er þat upp i fiallit fra hófvð kirkione. Slikt sama er þessi sveit dyrkvð iKinn.* (Rindal 1997b, 306)
>
> In the precious rockshelter which collapsed [when Sunnifa and the Seljumenn were martyred], there has now been built a chapel called 'Salinn'. The rock forms one wall, the other is built in stone. A cave leads into the rock face, and from it flows a small stream. Many people are cured there. In this chapel stands an altar, and it is located up in the mountain, away from the main church [i.e. the Benedictine abbey church]. In the same way these people are venerated in Kinn. (My translation after Rindal 1997c, 310)

The dating of this text is debatable. The saga was written *c.* 1190 and the text may provide an insight into the rockshelter area as it was in the late twelfth century. However, since this part of the saga is only preserved in the manuscript *Stockholm perg.18 4°*, the description might be a text addition of *c.* 1300. We must therefore assume that the text describes the sanctuary *c.* 1300 at its latest. The cave and well are also mentioned *c.* 1300 in *Óláfs saga Tryggvasonar en mesta* (Rindal 1997d).

In what follows, I will discuss different elements of the rockshelter area and how they can be related to the medieval written sources.

### *Salinn chapel*

Oddr Snorrason's description confirms that the rockshelter functioned as a chapel called *Salinn*, probably meaning 'place of dwelling' (Djupedal 1966, 20). It is, however, not clear whether Oddr's reference to a cave relates to the main cave or the north cave. One would automatically imagine that it is the main cave, as this is the most visible of the caves today and is an extension of the outer rockshelter. But this latter fact also leaves open the possibility that the main cave was incorporated into the definition of *Salinn*. Enger (1949, 8, 10) suggested that the main cave and outer rockshelter together formed the chapel, resembling the form of a church with the outer rockshelter being the nave and the main cave serving as the smaller and narrower chancel to the east (Fig. 4.4.A–B). Enger based his theory on some intentionally placed stones that he interpreted as a southern

*Figure 4.8: 'In the precious rockshelter as collapsed, there now is built a chapel called "Salinn". The rock is one wall, the other is built in stone'.* Salinn *is here seen towards the main cave in the east. Photo: A.T. Hommedal.*

narrowing of the crossing between the outer rockshelter and the main cave, with the rock formation on the northern side creating 'a chancel opening'.

Enger's argument also applies to a potential altar, a stone measuring 0.20m × 0.60m × 0.80m, now standing upright in the easternmost part of the main cave (Fig. 4.9). In the 1860s another stone slab, and in the 1930s two smaller stones embedded in mortar, were observed close by – all are now missing. The stones were interpreted by Enger (1949, 10) and others as parts of an altar. These slabs might be fragments of a block altar consisting of several stones, as the rather flat standing slab by itself would not have met the required shape of a main altar in the Middle Ages. On the other hand, in the 1860s Krefting (1868, 13) seems to have interpreted the now-missing slab as a horizontal altar stone (*mensa*). If this is correct, the T-shaped construction could have formed a simple table altar. This type is known from Romanesque Scandinavia, especially in Denmark. However, these are all of a more developed form (Jensen

*Figure 4.9:* Salinn. *The main cave view to east, from outer rockshelter. The 'altar basement' is located in the centre, in front of a narrow crack continuing eastwards into the rock. Photo: T. Bickhardt.*

*et al.* 1940, 273, 300, 507) than the potential rustic altar pillar at Selja, which even lacks a base. In general, an altar would have been supported by four columns or by one thick central pillar. The presumed altar at Selja, supported by a slab, has no European parallels (for medieval altar types, see Braun 1924, vol. I). Due to the proximity of the single surviving vertical stone to the rock wall, it also seems unlikely that there would have been room for a *mensa* of the size required (*c.* 1.5m × 1.2m) for a modest Romanesque freestanding main altar. There would not have been sufficient room to walk around the altar spreading incense at the start of the Mass as should happen (Kroesen and Steensma 2012, 46). The single standing stone is therefore most likely not an altar fragment. A more pragmatic explanation may be more probable, since the rectangular slab fits a *c.* 0.5m-wide crack that continues into the rock as an eastern extension of the main cave. The stone may therefore have been erected in post-medieval times to prevent sheep from entering the fissure.

If the altar mentioned by Oddr Snorrason was not located in the main cave, the most probable site would have been in the eastern part of the outer rockshelter. No trace of an altar has been documented there, even though the area was examined in the 1860s when wood, interpreted as the remains of a floor, was found (Koren 1869, 10). However, there is a possibility that the area examined did not include the easternmost part of the outer rockshelter. In fact, it is possible that the intentionally placed stones – interpreted by Enger as a narrowing of the opening of the cave giving a 'church-like layout' – are part of the floor in the outer rockshelter. This interpretation presupposes that stones in this easternmost section of the floor, with the supposed altar foundation, have been removed. This seems likely due to the present irregular nature of the floor towards the main cave. An altar located in this easternmost part of the rockshelter implies that the ceiling above the altar was low and emphasises the cave shape of *Salinn*. The main cave, probably perceived as the location where St Sunnifa's body was found and thus the holiest part of the chapel, would then have appeared as a *sanctuarium* and *oratorium* behind the altar. Since the written sources only mention one altar, we must assume that *Salinn* had only one.

### A 'side chapel' in Salinn? The north cave with its 'løkr'

What about the holy well? The main cave is dry at present and it appears unlikely that a well was located there in the Middle Ages. However, a well was documented in the north cave during excavations in the 1860s, occurring as a *c.* 15cm-deep basin in the rock (Koren 1869, 9). This basin was interpreted as the well filling the *løkr* (stream) mentioned by Oddr Snorrason. In the 1860s, water disappeared from the well and flowed into an adjacent crack in the rock face. It probably continues to flow underground into the stream that runs along the flight of steps for the sanctuary complex. It seems likely that Oddr Snorrason's *skvti* (cave) and *løkr* (Rindal 1997b, 306) can be identified as the north cave, its basin and the stream flowing from it. This theory is strengthened by a reference in *Flateyjarbók*: '*spretti vatn or berginv. ok rennr þadan litill lækr*' / 'there springs a well from the rock, and from there leaps a little stream' (Rindal 1997d, 321, my translation after Mundal 1997c, 328). Like Oddr Snorrason's saga, the *Flateyjarbók* manuscript also emphasises that sick people who drank from the water were cured.

The north cave, therefore, seems to have been an integral and important part of *Salinn*, probably as some form of 'side chapel'. This is also indicated by the stone steps connecting the elevated eastern part of the outer rockshelter to the lower western part, as the lower steps are partly oriented towards the north cave and then towards the well (Koren 1869, 10; Enger 1949, 11). It is, in fact, a possibility that the north cave with its well was perceived as the principal cave in *Salinn*.

Another point of interest is that the outer rockshelter and the north cave seem to have been whitewashed. Fragments of whitewash and plaster were observed during investigations both in the 1860s and the 1930s. According to Enger (1949, 10), the whitewash on the walls of the outer rockshelter was bright red. Red and white patches of whitewash were observed in the 1990s, together with white plaster on the original parts of the masonry walls. It seems most likely that the original colour was white. The red coloured fragments may be original, but the colour more probable reflects post-medieval graffiti, which seems to have been a ferruginous colour.

### Floors

Little can be said about the original floor in the north cave due to nineteenth-century backfilling, but we could at least expect the area around the holy well to consist of bare rock. In the main cave, a compact layer of gravel has been interpreted as the original floor (Koren 1868, 11; Enger 1949, 10). If the intention was to retain a cave-like environment, we might expect the gravel to constitute the floor level; if not, the gravel probably formed the foundation for a wooden or stone floor, now lost. In the outer rockshelter, as discussed, the huge stone blocks that comprise the present-day floor levels may also originally have functioned as a floor, partially covered with stone slabs as at present. The stone blocks may, however, have been the foundation for a wooden floor, at least in the upper and eastern area where fragments interpreted as raft beams and floor planks were found in several places in 1868 (Koren 1869, 10). Regardless, parts of the stone blocks must, in the

Middle Ages as now, have risen above the floor level as a reminder of the chapel's rockshelter character.

### *Archaeological artefacts*

We know very little about small finds from the excavations. In 1868 two pieces of carved wood interpreted as decorative elements of the chapel were found but are now lost (Koren 1869, 10). In the same year, thirteenth-century silk textile fragments, probably Italian or Spanish, were found in a hollow in the north cave. We can assume that these were parts of liturgical vestments from *Salinn* or other churches at Selja, probably a chasuble or cope. Helen Engelstad (1941, 40) has suggested that the textile fragments may be from a clerical grave in the cave, but this seems unlikely as they were found together with a broom (Koren 1869, 9; Hommedal 2009).

### *The sanctuary of the rockshelter*

We can then summarise our knowledge about the rockshelter sanctuary, *Salinn*, as follows: the main part of the chapel comprised the outer rockshelter. The altar most likely stood in the eastern part of this space. The main cave, presumably perceived as the original tomb of St Sunnifa, acted as an *oratorium* behind the altar. The north cave contained the well and stream with its healing waters, and as such was incorporated into the main chapel as a side chapel or *sanctorium*. *Salinn*, at least the outer rockshelter and probably also the north cave, seem to have been whitewashed. The main cave may also have been whitewashed, unless this holy 'tomb' of St Sunnifa was intentionally left more cave-like as a contrast to the proper chapel. The floors may have consisted of the natural stone or gravel surface. The upper and eastern part of the rockshelter, however, seem to have had a wooden floor at some point, perhaps to emphasise this elevated area if the altar was located here. According to documentary sources, water from the well supposedly had healing properties, something that indirectly tells us that *Salinn* was a place of pilgrimage.

According to the narratives, *Salinn* existed in this form *c*. 1300 at the latest, but the same morphology may have existed in the 1190s if the description came from Oddr Snorrason's original text. The character of the medieval masonry in the southern and western walls of the rockshelter indicate, however, that these were built in the first part of the twelfth century at the same time as the present terrace walls (see below) and therefore, the description of the morphology of *Salinn* probably dates to before the *translatio* of St Sunnifa to Bergen in 1170. Presumably the original rockshelter would have been demarcated by a wooden boundary, if not from the very beginning of the chapel's existence then at least in the period before the stone walls were erected. This chapel, with its overhanging rock roof, was once characterised by the author Sigrid Undset (2006 [1926], 290; 2006 [1929], 549, my translation) as: 'the oldest church vault we have left in this country' and 'today, there are no church vaults left in Norway that we know for sure that St Óláfr has bowed himself under, except for the rock here over the shelter', referring to King Óláfr II Haraldsson's fortunate arrival on his island of *Felicitas* in 1015.

### *The dedication of Salinn*

Oddr Snorrason mentions *Salinn* as a chapel but he does not mention its dedication. However, he lists the island's churches by their dedication (Rindal 1997b, 306). Having eliminated other possibilities, *Salinn* must have been dedicated to either St Mary the Mother of Christ, or St Michael the Archangel. In early scholarly discussions, it was even suggested that *Salinn* was dedicated to both saints and thus comprised two chapels – St Michael's chapel in the north cave and St Mary's chapel in the main cave (Krefting 1868, 15; Koren 1869, 11).

The prevailing theory has been that St Michael the Archangel, whose cult is often located in caves or on peaks, was the patron saint of *Salinn* (Nielsen 1905, 177; Enger 1949, 8; Djupedal 1966, 20–21, 39; Hommedal 1997a, 46). The author Vera Henriksen (1992, 22, 68–69) has argued for a St Mary affiliation at Selja based on a hypothesis that Irish monks may have been present on the island from an early period, but in the end she concludes that a dedication to St Michael is most probable. Henriksen also offers an interesting observation: according to the oldest version of the legend of the holy people at Selja, the saints-to-be called on God that He, '*sepulturam uero corporibus super eos cadentbus angelico preberet officio*' / 'with the help of angels would give their bodies a tomb underneath fallen rocks' (Borgehammar 1997a, 281, my translation after Tosterud 1997, 396). Henriksen (1992, 69) thus seems to suggest that the chapel was originally dedicated to St Mary with a secondary dedication to St Michael in reference to the angel of the legend.

I think it is more likely that *Salinn* was originally dedicated to St Michael the Archangel as the archangel's dedications, as mentioned, often relate to caves or peaks, as pointed out by Nielsen (1905, 177; Hommedal 1996, 48–49). St Michael was also considered the commander of the army of angels and as the struggling defender of the faith (Fredriksen 2004, 29–31). St Michael as the dragon slayer, struggling with the evil, is also known from late Viking Age and early medieval ornaments in Scandinavia (Pedersen 2014, 220), and church dedications to St Michael seem to have been relatively common in Norway (Fredriksen 2004, 89, 136–137; Ommundsen 2010, 71). The St Mary dedication, an even more widespread church dedication in Norway (Fredriksen 2004, 38, 136–137) and not so associated with caves, was probably attached to the other church at Selja which has no known dedication, that is, the parish church situated on the eastern side of the island. Henriksen (1992, 71) also considered this interpretation plausible. I find it likely that the St Michael dedication relates to the Benedictines at Selja (Hommedal, *in press*) as the religious historian Gro Steinsland (2012, 170), amongst others, has suggested. She also points to the frequent European combination of St Michael with a female saint, often St Mary, and puts forward the interesting theory that St Michael and St Sunnifa are to be viewed as a couple at Selja. A double dedication of *Salinn* to St Michael and St Sunnifa has been suggested (Nielsen 1905, 177), and this might be expected if Sunnifa had originally been part of the legend. However, there are no reliable indications of the original dedication of *Salinn* to Sunnifa. Rather, her church was located in front of the rockshelter.

## St Sunnifa's church

The stone church is set as far as possible into the mountainside beneath the rockshelter on the most level part of the terrace (Figs. 4.4 and 4.6). The ruins consist of a Romanesque church with a rectangular chancel (internal dimensions 4.6m × 3.4m) and a rectangular nave (7.5m × 4.6m), with walls preserved to a height of between 0.6m and 2.45m. The remains were somewhat damaged during restoration work in 1909 and further restored in 1967 but the general appearance seems accurate (Hommedal 1996, 38–43).

Three altars have been documented. In the nave, two foundations for side altars have been preserved in the traditional position on each side of the opening into the chancel where the foundation (*c.* 1.56m × 0.94m) for the main altar, now lost, was documented in the nineteenth century (Krefting 1868, 11). This altar was located in front of a 0.65 m high and 1.26 m deep stone catafalque occupying the easternmost part of the chancel (Figs. 4.4 and 4.6). The church has three doorways: a north portal in the chancel, and a north and a south portal facing one another in the western part of the nave. The floor consists of stone slabs with three steps leading up to the elevated chancel.

The dedication of the church to St Sunnifa seems probable. Oddr Snorrason mentions, '*Svnnifo k.*' / 'Sunnifa's church' (Rindal 1997b, 306, my translation after Rindal 1997c, 310), but does not pinpoint its location. *Flateyjarbók*, on the other hand, states that '*En SvNifo kirkia er vpp ifjallit hia klaustrinu*' / 'but Sunnifa's church is in the mountain above the monastery' (Rindal 1997d, 321, my translation after Mundal 1997c, 328). Even though it is debatable whether the church in this description was inside the mountain, i.e. *Salinn*, the identification of the stone church as that of St Sunnifa seems probable. Since the church appears to be older than the postulated official incorporation of St Sunnifa into the legend, it was most likely dedicated to the *Seljumenn* originally. This would be in accordance with Oddr Snorrason's information that the first church erected at Selja, in AD 996, was dedicated to '*þessum monnum*' / 'those [God's] men' found there and not to St Sunnifa (Rindal 1997b, 304, my translation after Rindal 1997c, 309).

The dating of St Sunnifa's church has been extensively debated. It varies from identifying the present church with King Óláfr I Tryggvason, i.e. AD 996, to suggestions it was built in the thirteenth century (Enger 1949, 14). Original masonry combined with the layout, craftsmanship and character of the building (e.g. that the church has both an external and internal plinth) indicate, however, that the church was constructed around AD 1100 or in the last decade of the eleventh century (Hommedal 1996, 45–52), and thus is contemporary with the basilica in the monastery (Nybø 2000, 206). A date at the end of the eleventh century is strengthened by a coin fragment (Fig. 4.10) minted for King Óláfr III kyrri ('the peaceful', ruling AD 1066–1093), which was found in the levelled stone plateau upon which the church was directly constructed (Hommedal 1997a, 48; 1998, 113, see also below).

The layout of St Sunnifa's church seems to reflect its function as a pilgrimage church with a rather large, rectangular chancel compared to other Norwegian Romanesque churches, caused by the catafalque filling the chancel's eastern part (Fig. 4.4). Opposing nave doorways and the lack of a west portal are not unknown in early twelfth-century Norwegian churches but the combination is uncommon. The lack of a west doorway could be explained by the harsh and windy weather at Selja, but then one might expect the same to apply to the basilica in the monastery and this has a west doorway (Nybø 2000). As has been discussed by this author (Hommedal 1997a, 52; and see below), the doorways or portals probably gave an 'ambulatory' character to St Sunnifa's church for pilgrims on special feast days. A small stone circle found in the floor of the nave in 1909 and interpreted as a 'basin' (Hommedal 1996, 39–42) would, if this interpretation is correct, probably have been a basin for holy water collected from *Salinn*'s well, and as such is another distinctive feature linking the church to pilgrims.

The catafalque has been interpreted by most scholars as the place where reliquaries were placed and, first and foremost, St Sunnifa's shrine. Art historian Marit Nybø (2000, 207), however, believes that St Sunnifa's shrine was usually located in the Benedictine St Alban's church and only brought to St Sunnifa's church and *Salinn* on liturgical feast days. I consider this interpretation unlikely as it presupposes processions where the shrine would be carried up and down some rather steep steep paths and steps to and from the sanctuary. In my opinion, the reliquary for Selja's main saint was permanently located in the church dedicated to her name and could be carried in processions onto the terrace. This location, close to the rockshelter as the martyr site, must also have been important. After the *translatio* in 1170, reliquaries of the Seljumenn must have occupied the catafalque. St Sunnifa's church, therefore, seems to

Figure 4.10: Both sides of the fragment of a coin minted for King Óláfr III kyrri (1066–1093), found in 1992 on the innermost part of the terrace, 1.5m to the south of St Sunnifa's church. The coin has been inscribed with runes, of which five still survive on the fragment, (GUNNA)R OWNS (THIS) STAMP. The Gunnar in question is, from other finds of coins, known as one of King Óláfr's mint masters (Hommedal 1998, 113). Photo: S. Skare, University Museum of Bergen.

have been built in the last decade of the eleventh century or around 1100 as a pilgrimage church accommodating reliquaries for the saints from Selja. In the decades prior to 1170, when the cardinal saint had been incorporated into the cult, the catafalque was probably the resting place of the relics of St Sunnifa herself.

## The stone terrace

The terrace is today divided into three levels (Figs. 4.4 and 4.5). The western section is *c.* 22m wide and 6m high, and the total surface area of the terrace is *c.* 380 square metres. When partly restored in the 1930s, the lower parts of the terrace's original masonry walls were still intact. During restoration works only original stones from the collapsed wall material were used. The main form of the restored terrace walls thus seems to correspond with the original structure, though the original height of the walls is not known. At the north side of the terrace the original stone steps lead up to the sanctuary. Beside these steps, to the north, flows the stream partly covered by the rocks with most of the water probably issuing from the well in the north cave.

The terrace is mentioned in *Flateyjarbók* as follows:

> *framan kirkíu þa er fram er af hellínum let ol. konungr (gera) æitt mikit griothlad ok sua hátt ok Ramgert sem hit sterkazsta virki segía sua sumir men at þat se æitt hit mesta mannuirke aþann hatt sem þat er gert undir þessu hlade edr uirkí er sett klaustrit er upp at ganga til hinnar efri kirkíunnar med bekkínum mille ok hladsíns.* (Rindal 1997d, 322)

> In front of the church, which is situated by the rockshelter, King Olaf [I Tryggvason] had made a great stone revetment as high and strong as the most solid of fortresses. Some people say that this is supposed to be one of the greatest constructions that people have created of its kind. Below this stone revetment or fortress the monastery is placed. Between the stream and the stone revetment a path leads up to the upper church. (My translation after Mundal 1997c, 328)

The magnificence of this construction is underlined in *Flateyjarbók* by the writer's uncertainty when describing the terrace. The edifice seems to be so unusual that he struggles for words to describe it, calling it a stone revetment and even a fortress. This naturally raises the question: what did this great stone revetment or fortress really look like, and what was its function?

According to Enger (1949, 19), who examined the terrace remains during its reconstruction in the 1930s, it seems to have been extended and completed in several phases. As the archaeological records of the investigations are now missing, we do not know the details of the original fabric encountered but some internal walls were documented (see Fig. 4.4) supposedly indicating the process of expansion in several stages. Enger's (1949, 16) idea that the terrace in its final phase consisted of a single horizontal level is debatable. The terrace wall towards the west would then have been *c.* 12m high, about twice its present height. As discussed in an earlier article (Hommedal 1997a, 42) it is most likely that the terrace, in the Middle Ages as today, was divided into different levels even though this would reduce its magnificence. It is difficult to say more about the shape of the upper level of the original terrace. We cannot tell whether the upper level was open as in its present form or if, for instance, some houses stood there as the foundations would have disappeared. This monumental construction is also too extensive to have been built as a basement or foundation for St Sunnifa's church. Rather, the terrace can be explained in a liturgical context as a gathering place in front of the holy rockshelter for pilgrims travelling to Selja. Furthermore, the terrace would have been suitable for liturgical processions, as without this area it would have been impossible to hold processions in the rocky terrain surrounding the sanctuary. St Sunnifa's church would have been too small to accommodate everyone seeking sanctuary, at least on the cult's main liturgical feast, *Seljumannamess*, July 8th. The church, with its opposed doorways in the nave, would have functioned as a simple 'ambulatory' where pilgrims could pass through to see or perhaps even touch the holy shrine of St Sunnifa or of the Seljumenn on the catafalque in the chancel. In this way the terrace would have served a similar function to a church nave with St Sunnifa's church located as a separate large 'relic shrine' at the innermost part of the terrace.

The terrace's final form, as described in *Flateyjarbók*, was probably completed in the first part of the twelfth century or in the 1150s at the latest. The *Flateyjarbók* scribe attributes the construction to King Óláfr I Tryggvason in the 990s. For this scribe it must have been of great importance to connect this magnificent building to the king of the saga. At the very least, the statement shows that the real builders and building period had been forgotten by the 1380s, indicating that the terrace was already old by that time.

The masonry in the original parts of the terrace walls seems to be a reliable source for dating the final phase of the terrace. The outer terrace walls are built of roughly hewn gneiss placed in slightly irregular yet distinctive courses. The same type of stone and masonry are found in the walls of the rockshelter and in the extant west tower of the Benedictine St Alban's church. Nybø (2000, 204) has dated this tower to between 1120 and 1160 according to changes in building styles in Bergen, which Selja has close ties with. This is also in accordance with the notion that the terrace was completed before, and not after, the *translatio* of St Sunnifa in 1170 (Hommedal *in press*). It is less likely that such a large building project would have been performed after the sanctuary had lost its cardinal saint to Bergen.

## The dawn of a sanctuary: the archaeological background

Excavations in 1990–1992 took place on the inner terrace and to the north, south and inside the present St Sunnifa's church (Fig. 4.4). To the north of the church a natural narrow earthen ledge was documented, sloping to the west and south, where packing material had been deliberately filled in between huge, naturally fallen boulders to form the inner terrace. In its youngest phase this inner platform of the terrace formed the foundation for the present church. This stone packing is dated to the last decades of the eleventh century or the very beginning of the twelfth century. On the natural ledge to the north of the church excavations shed light on prehistoric activities in the vicinity of the rockshelter. The stratigraphic record combined with radiocarbon dating and a few small finds indicate activities in front of the rockshelter during the period *c*. 100–1000 AD, and thus surely indicates settlement in the caves and rockshelter.

The archaeological data obtained can be divided into three phases:

### *Phase 1: An early local cave-dwelling*

On the original earthen ledge surface a possible hearth was discovered consisting of a concentration of heat-shattered stones and charcoal of a deciduous tree species, likely hazel (*Corylus avellana*), radiocarbon dated to 475–375 BC (T-10046), (see Table 4.1). This may indicate that activities had taken place in front of the rockshelter during the Pre-Roman Iron Age or earlier.

The principal activity documented is interpreted as a typical western Norwegian cave dwelling used during the fishing and hunting seasons during the period AD 100–550, i.e. the Early Iron Age. Two samples of charcoal from the original narrow earthen ledge surface have been radiocarbon dated to AD 120–330 (TUa-476) and AD 115–370 (T-10047), (see Table 4.1). No artefacts were found in this stratigraphic context. However, in the upper stratigraphic layers, scattered over the inner parts of the terrace restored in the 1930s, the 1990–1992 excavations uncovered seven sherds of bucked-shaped pots (B15273/1-7) dating from the fourth to the early sixth century, and a whetstone (B15273/8) dating to the Early Iron Age in general (Hommedal 1997a, fig. 8; Kristoffersen and Magnus 2010 and Siv Kristoffersen, Bente Magnus and Else J. Kleppe, pers. comm.). The artefacts may originally have come from inside the caves or rockshelter but were removed during the 1860s or 1930s excavations and secondarily deposited on the terrace.

These results fit well with the fact that caves and rockshelters were commonly used for short-term occupation along the coast during the Early Iron Age in western Norway

*Table 4.1: Radiocarbon dates from the Sanctuary at Selja. The ledge lies in front of the rockshelter, to the north of the St Sunnifa's church. Radiocarbon dates of the surface of the ledge before levelling (T-10046, T-10047) with a possible hearth (TUa-476) and after levelling (T-9320, T-9321). The other dates are from the stone filling underneath St Sunnifa's church (T-10052, T-10053)*

| *Lab no.* | *Context: the Sanctuary, Selja* | *The area according to Figure 4.4* | *Age BP* | *Calibrated age BC/AD* | *Sample material* | *Determination of wood* |
|---|---|---|---|---|---|---|
| Tua-476 | Ledge before levelling | Area 2 | 1800 ± 70 | AD 120–330 | Charcoal | Birch |
| T-10046 | Hearth? | Area 2 | 2335 ± 85 | 475–375 BC | Charcoal | Floriferous tree, hazel? |
| T-10047 | Ledge before levelling | Area 2 | 1785 ± 95 | AD 115–370 | Charcoal | Pine? |
| T-9320 | Ledge after levelling | Area 2 | 1210 ± 155 | AD 660–990 | Charcoal | Pine |
| T-9321 | Ledge after levelling | Area 2 | 1175 ± 75 | AD 770–965 | Charcoal | Pine |
| T-10052 | Stone filling | Area 3 | 1070 ± 85 | AD 885–1020 | Charcoal | Pine |
| T-10053 | Stone filling | Area 3 | 1160 ± 85 | AD 775–980 | Charcoal | Pine |

(e.g. Brøgger 1911; Odner 1969; Bakka 1973; Østebø 2008; Bommen 2009). Interestingly, in some of these coastal caves human skeletal remains have been found, such as in Sauehelleren, Skjonghelleren and Hamnsundhelleren to the north of Selja (Bergsvik 2017). A case in point is Skongeneshelleren, a remote cave situated immediately south-west of Selja and directly visible from it (Fig. 4.1). Here, remains of at least six individuals were recovered from cave deposits together with sherds of bucked-shaped pots dated to *c*. AD 500 (Brøgger 1911, 5–7). This suggests that people were buried in Skongeneshelleren at the same time that activities are taking place in the caves and rockshelter at Selja. As both sites are caves, share similar locations, and both produced bucket-shaped pottery, one might suggest that the cave at Selja was also used as a burial site during the Early Iron Age. In both instances bucked-shaped pottery may have accompanied the deceased as gravegoods. If correct, human skeletons of ordinary local Early Iron Age people may – when found five or six centuries later – have been reinterpreted and considered relics by the royal and clerical elite.

### *Phase 2: The need for an extension of the area*

During the Viking Age, i.e. in the ninth, tenth or early eleventh century at the latest, the ledge seems to have been extended and raised with a soil embankment towards the west (Fig. 4.7) and a stone and earth embankment to the south. This extension may have taken place in more than one phase. Tiny fragments of a possible fire were noted in this new and levelled surface, and two samples of charcoal (pine) were radiocarbon dated to AD 660–990 (T-9320) and AD 770–965 (T-9321), (see Table 4.1). An overall evaluation of the two dates suggests that both probably relate to the Viking Age (AD 800–1000/1030) or just before (Steinar Gulliksen pers. comm.). Two other samples of charcoal (pine) were radiocarbon dated to AD 885–1020 (T-10052) and AD 775–980 (T-10053), (Table 4.1). Both fragments came from the stone embankment to the south of the soil embankment, i.e. from the excavation in the north-western part of the present church's nave (Fig. 4.4, area 3). The embankment here consisted of huge naturally collapsed rocks in a matrix of stone and earth. The two charcoal samples were retrieved from soil fill between the rocks indicating that the extension was carried out during the Viking Age or the dawn of the Middle Ages.

In total, then, we have four radiocarbon determinations indicating that extension work was carried out some time from the mid-seventh to the beginning of eleventh century, and probably within a more limited period of *c*. 250 years from the end of the eighth to the beginning of the eleventh century. Unfortunately, no small finds were recovered from these stratigraphic contexts. However, a whetstone (B 15273/9) dated to the Late Iron Age or Middle Ages can be linked to the rockshelter area indicating Viking Age/medieval activity, similar to one found at Skrivarhelleren in Sogn (Prescott 1991). Even though we must be careful when drawing conclusions, it seems reasonable to suggest that the area in front of the rockshelter was not only used but was also intentionally extended to the west and the south within the Viking Age or the very earliest Middle Ages.

The question still remains: can this extension be related to pagan or Christian activities? And is it possible to connect the documented activity to the legend – either to the possible Irish refugees or the story of King Óláfr I Tryggvason and his kinsmen finding the relics? The martyrdom took place, according to the legend, in the middle of the tenth century and the saints were discovered in AD 996. The archaeological material is broadly contemporaneous with the period in which the legend supposedly originated. Regarding the questions posed above, the archaeological evidence does not support the theory of Norse pagan activities or foreign activities such as some kind of Irish settlement.

The first extension seems to have been carried out to address the need for a greater area in front of the rockshelter in the centuries before the Christianisation of Norway or in early Christian times. Activities at other western Norwegian rockshelters and caves are known from the Viking Age and early Middle Ages where they have been used, for example, as shielings or smithies (Bergsvik and Hansen 2015), but there are no indications of such usage at Selja. The character of the embankment and the extension at Selja is exceptional. The levelling must thus be seen as an expression of the very special status of the rockshelter, and the apparent systematic levelling may indicate the presence of an organising figure.

All scholarly discussions of the legend and sanctuary's early history have been concerned with the location of King Óláfr I Tryggvason's church at Selja, mentioned by Adam of Bremen *c*. 1080. Even though the legend does not tell us directly, it has generally been deduced that King Óláfr's church was built in front of the rockshelter, though possibly on another part of the island such as on the lower flat stretch of land were the Benedictine monastery was later built (Nicolaysen 1892, 6–7; Enger 1949, 14; Undset, 2006 [1929], 543–544; Djupedal 1966, 23; Hommedal 1997a, 66). From general knowledge of the earliest Viking Age and early Middle Age churches in Norway, we can assume that a church built *c*. AD 1000 at Selja would have been wooden – a stave church constructed with upright posts placed in postholes and with stones supporting the posts (e.g. Christie 1983a; Jensenius 2010; 2015). There was no archaeological evidence that such a building was erected in the excavated parts of the earthen embankment, and no postholes were encountered.

According to Enger (1949, 14) the excavations in the 1930s revealed a fire-layer, measuring up to 10cm thick, to the north of St Sunnifa's church, which he interpreted as from a burnt building, tentatively King Óláfr I Tryggvason's church. No traces of such a fire layer, neither *in situ* or in the disturbed layers were observed during the excavation 1990–1992. If at all existing, the fire-layer found during the 1930s must have been totally removed from within the excavation area. It is not likely the tiny fragments of charcoal (of these two are dated: T-9320; T-9321, see Table 4.1) stem from such a thick fire layer. The possible fire-layer thus cannot be verified.

In conclusion, we have no reliable archaeological indications that the extension work relates to the construction of a building on this artificial platform, although the fire-layer mentioned in the 1930s might indicate that a wooden building once existed there. The platform may, however, have functioned as a gathering place in front of the rockshelter. What is significant, however, is the fact that activities are archaeologically documented here for the Viking Age. In the first Christian phase, in accordance with the western Norwegian traditions of the Christianisation period (Gabrielsen 2002), a wooden or stone cross may have been erected on the platform requiring only one posthole.

### *Phase 3: Early medieval development in front of the rockshelter*

In the present St Sunnifa's church the north wall of the nave is located more or less at the edge of the Viking Age earthen embankment. As expected, it is documented that the church is stratigraphically later than the embankment since the foundation trench of the nave's north wall truncates the embankment. The nave's south wall, however, does not have a foundation and rests directly on the stone embankment constituting the inner part of the terrace. Within this stone embankment, and 1.5m south of the nave's south wall (Fig. 4.4, area 4), the fragment of a coin minted for King Óláfr III kyrri was found in an apparently undisturbed context (Fig. 4.10). According to the Norwegian numismatist Svein Harald Gullbekk (2011, 521), it is unlikely that the coins minted for Óláfr III kyrri were in circulation for more than a few decades after the king's death (1093), and thus not many decades into the twelfth century. It seems, therefore, that the earliest stone fill was altered and given its present level and form in the eleventh century or the beginning of the twelfth century at latest. Of course, a theoretical wooden church might originally have stood on this new level when the coin was deposited, later to be replaced by the stone church, but as discussed, this seems unlikely as no trace of a foundation for a wooden church was encountered in the excavated parts of the terraces. This may then indicate that the stone church was erected within or shortly after the circulation period of the coin minted for King Óláfr III kyrri.

It is generally accepted amongst historians that it was King Óláfr III kyrri who established the first West Norwegian episcopal seat at Selja *c.* 1070 (Helle 1997, 243–245; Ommundsen 2010, 79). The bishop's cathedral can, in all likelihood, be identified as the late eleventh-century basilica in the Benedictine monastery at Selja (Nybø 2000, 194). The King Óláfr III kyrri coin seems to indicate that the development of the sanctuary was also carried out as a part of the establishment of the episcopal see. The coin seems to support the hypothesis that the sanctuary at Selja was the main reason for the location of the West Norwegian bishop's first *cathedra* at Selja (Hommedal 1997a, 72–73). It seems then that area in front of the rockshelter was given its current form, with stone platform and stone church, in the late eleventh or early twelfth century, probably originally planned to promote the sanctuary as part of King Óláfr III kyrri's establishment of an episcopal see at Selja (Hommedal *in press*).

## The caves and rockshelter: from pagan to Christian sanctuary?

Let us then, using non-archaeological sources, look into the possibility that the first embankment and extension was connected to a pagan ritual site subsequently taken over by a Christian cult. As the fragmented archaeological material from the rockshelter provides no indication of a pre-Christian cult, the possibility has only been mentioned but not discussed to any extent in the archaeological literature (Hommedal 1996, 1997a, 66–67). This lack of archaeological evidence of a pre-Christian cult may, however, be a result of medieval renovation and the nineteenth-century removal of cultural deposits rather than a reflection of prehistoric activity at the site.

Discussion of a possible pagan cult relates to the deduction that the rockshelter chapel at *Salinn* was dedicated to St Michael, a saint often identified as a Christian struggling with evil. Historian Yngvar Nielsen suggested that the rockshelter had been a pagan sanctuary where St Michael replaced pre-Christian gods, even though he did not reject the possibility that King Óláfr I Tryggvason also discovered human bones there (Nielsen 1905, 168, 177–181; Hommedal 1996, 48–49). After Nielsen's discussion, the theme of a pagan cult at Selja was not much debated until Steinsland (1997; 2012) and the Old Norse philologist Else Mundal (1997a; 1997b) reintroduced the topic in the 1990s. Like Nielsen, both Steinsland and Mundal took St Michael as a starting point, and Steinsland also considered the combination of the cave, martyrdom, holy well and holy women. She compared these elements in the Christian legend to corresponding elements in Norse mythology. Steinsland saw the combination of St Michael and Sunnifa as a form of fertility, also found in other Christian sanctuaries where the combination seems to be St Michael and St Mary, and where even the Virgin Mary can be related to a cave, as discussed in the case of Selja. In Norse mythology, Njǫrðr and Skaði are a similar fertility couple but as Steinsland points out, there are no place names connecting these two gods to Selja. Steinsland therefore emphasises that she does not argue for any existence of their cult on the island. She also highlights the *jǫtun* (giant) women's association with caves in Norse mythology, and discusses the similarities between the Norse god Heimdallr and the Christian St Michael (*eschatology*, the role of the lure blower, the struggle with evil), suggesting the Christian saint replaced the Norse god. However, Steinsland did not find any substantial arguments for a cultic transition from Norse paganism to Christianity in connection with the cave at Selja. Based on the Norse sagas, Mundal (1997a) also suggested the possibility of a pagan cult in the cave at Selja related to food sacrifice for the *landvættir* (spirits) in caves and rockshelters. Mundal noted that several texts convey the idea that dead forefathers lived in holy mountains/rocks, and she indicates that abandoned but still familiar prehistoric settlements in caves and rockshelters could have been sites of ancestor worship (Mundal 1997a, 37–39). Of course, this is especially interesting in the case of Selja considering the archaeologically documented Iron Age settlement at the site.

As the archaeological material from the rockshelter does not clarify the possibility of a pre-Christian cult we must draw the same conclusion as Steinsland: 'Although we have followed these lines of enquiry and tried to make them clearer, we cannot point to Selja and say with certainty that here, in this cave, pagan rites were carried out. We lack clear evidence for that' (Steinsland 1997, 31–32, my translation). Nonetheless, the similarities mentioned above open up ways of thinking about *Siðaskipti*, i.e. the transition from Norse paganism to Christianity. When St Sunnifa became the patron saint of seafarers, by the late twelfth century at the latest, she may have taken over the role that Njǫrðr held in the Viking Age, as god of boats and the coastal landscape (Steinsland 2012, 165).

## The creation of identity and memory: the sanctuary up to 1170

I have put forward the theory that the purported relics found in front of the rockshelter represented a local prehistoric group living in the rockshelter at least 400 years before St Sunnifa and the Seljumenn are supposed to have been martyred on the island. As philologist Jan Erik Rekdal (1997, 120) has pointed out, such prehistoric material had to undergo a transformation – an *interpretatio Christiana* – to become relics. Therefore, an explanation – a core *narratio* – had to be present. How then does the archaeological understanding of the sanctuary correspond with the interpretation of other sources when it comes to the legend's origin, historical core and development? In other words: what was the first core *narratio* at Selja?

The oldest version of the Selja legend was, as mentioned, transcribed in the second half of the twelfth century almost 200 years after the relics were supposedly discovered (Ommundsen 2011, 32). The legend corresponds with other medieval legends of Irish saints elsewhere in Europe. It also bears similarities to virgin legends, not least that of St Ursula and the 11,000 virgins (Germany), as well as the legend of St Modwenna (Scotland) (Storm 1880, XXXXIV; DuBois 2008, 70; Simek 2013, 3–6). From the nineteenth century onwards, scholars, particularly historians, have repeatedly discussed the core of the Selja legend based on the written sources, and debated to what extent the legend is based on actual historic events. Interpretations have varied from the contention that the legend relates the actual historical event, to the claim that it is pure fantasy created to meet the needs of the new church in Norway. Between these extremes, it has been suggested that the legend has some foundation in the possible presence of Irish hermit monks on the island. Earlier scholars have also suggested, but without supporting archaeological evidence, that a local prehistoric settlement was located at the rockshelter (Hommedal 1996, 27–33, 45–52; Rekdal 1997, 115–119).

It seems probable that the legend of St Sunnifa and the Seljumenn developed over the course of the eleventh century and the first part of the twelfth century, until it was fully formed as the oldest version handed down at the time of the *translatio* in 1170. St Sunnifa herself seems to be a secondary twelfth-century addition to an earlier legend, which originally referred only to the Seljumenn (Johnsen 1968; Hommedal 1997a; O'Hara 2009; Ommundsen 2010; 2011; Steinsland 2012; Berle Nilsen 2013). According to Mundal (1997b, 92), a group of people in Norse accounts always has a leader, which suggests that the fictional main figure (Sunnifa) may have existed for a time as a popular tradition before being included in the Church's official legend. Other researchers think, like Mundal, that Sunnifa never existed as a person, but raise the possibility that the protagonist of the legend was incorporated as early as the middle of the eleventh century (e.g. Borgehammar 1997b, 143). The Old Norse philologist Rudolf Simek even claims the possibility that the legend's fictional protagonist goes back to the 990s, taking direct inspiration from the German legend of St Ursula and the 11,000 virgins (Simek 2013, 2, 15).

### *A story from Germany*

Simek's interpretation seems, however, to be inconsistent with the oldest documented reference to the saints in the *Gesta Hammaburgensis ecclesiae pontificum* (*Deeds of the Bishops of Hamburg*) by the German historian Adam of Bremen (died *c.* 1081) (Adam 1917; 1959; 1993). Mention of the holy men related to Selja can be found in the fourth book's 32nd chapter of the Gesta, and more precisely in a *scholion* (number 145), i.e. an added comment in the text from *c.* 1080 (Borgehammar 1997a, 141, note 44).

*Scholion* 145 reads as follows:

> *Paulus in Historia Longobardorum affirmat in ultimis partibus septentronis inter Scritefingos in quadam spelunca*

> *oceani iacere VII viros quasi dormientes, de quibus est opinion diversa, et quod predicaturi sunt illis gentibus circa finem mundi. Dicunt alii ex XI milibus virginibus illuc pervenisse aliquas, quarum cetus et naves monte obrutae sunt, ibique fieri miracula. Ubi et ecclesiam construxit Olaph.* (Adam 1917, 266)
>
> Paul affirms in his History of the Lombards that in a cavern off the ocean in the farthest northern parts among the Skritefingi [i.e. the Sámi] seven men lie as if asleep. About them there are divergent opinions, including the belief that they are going to preach to those heathens about the time the world will end. Others say that some of the Eleven Thousand Virgins came to this region and that their attendants and ships are buried in a mountain and that miracles are wrought there. In that place Olaf also built a church. (Adam 1959, p. 213)

Adam, or a different scribe who added the *scholion*, seems uncertain as to who these holy men are (see also Johnsen 1968, 47). If the legend already had a protagonist before the writing of the *scholion*, and the legend's figure was inspired by a German ecclesiastical milieu, the writer would most likely have known about the figure. Borgehammar's (1997b, 142) suggestion that the writer had heard about Sunnifa and Selja but had forgotten the names of the saint and the site seems unlikely to me. If information on the Norwegian saints had reached Germany *c.* 10 years before the writing of the *scholion*, as Borgehammar suggests, the story of the holy men would presumably also have been written into the main body of the text from the 1070s and not in an added *scholion*. This would especially hold true as the writer was living in the archbishopric of the metropolitan of which the church in Norway was then a part. The writer proposes a connection between the saints in Norway and the legend of St Ursula, but he only raises the possibility that some of the 11,000 virgins, i.e. some of the followers of St Ursula, had reached this location.

The writer of the *scholion* is so unsure in the interpretation that he also indirectly presents another possibility: that the holy people are connected to the Seven Sleepers of Ephesus (see discussion of *scholion* 129 below). The writer of *scholion* 145 seems convinced, however, when relating that Óláfr built a church at that place. If the writer knew about this church he would also have known about St Sunnifa if she was part of the Church's official narrative by that time. Mention of Óláfr's church also makes it probable that the site under consideration is Selja, even though the writer makes no direct mention of the island. According to historian Anders Winroth (2012, 123–124), Adam of Bremen seems to have had a negative view of King Óláfr I Tryggvason and all Anglo-Saxon missionary journeys to Norway. The writer of the *scholion*, a part of the same milieu, may thus have withheld some of his knowledge about a British-influenced sanctuary at Selja and through the legend of St Ursula tried to promote a German influence instead. However, if there was a main protagonist in the legend of Selja, he would not have missed the opportunity to make an even stronger parallel with the German St Ursula. We may then conclude that St Sunniva does not seem to have existed as a figure in the Selja legend at the time of Adam of Bremen's writings.

*Scholion* 145, concerning the site where Óláfr built his church, refers to an even older and less reliable narrative of seven holy men sleeping. This narrative is the Lombard monk Paul the Deacon's (*c.* 725–795) *Historia Langobardorum* from the 790s. Here he refers to the Mediterranean legend of the Seven Sleepers of Ephesus (Mundal 1997a, 40; DuBois 2008, 66). In another *scholion* (number 129) in *Gesta Hammaburgensis*, these seven individuals are said to sleep among the *Scritefingorum* – the Nordic peoples (Adam 1917, 250; 1959, 202; 1993, 201). As historian Alexander O'Hara (2009, 110) points out, the story is remarkably similar to that of the *Seljumenn*, and Ommundsen (2010, 76–77) even suggests that the text is a vague reference to the Selja saints. If so, the reference must be secondary to Paul the Deacon's original late eighth-century text. As Borgehammar (1997b, 141) has pointed out, however, it seems very unlikely that there is any connection between Paul the Deacon's story and Selja. The connection seems to be the result of associations by the writer of the *scholion* in *Gesta Hammaburgensis*. It seems, therefore, to be a coincidence that at the end of the eighth century Paul the Deacon mentions an occurrence that was later associated with Selja. A further coincidence is that Paul writes at a time when the archaeological material at Selja indicates the possibility that extension works were carried out in front of the rockshelter. Based on *Gesta Hammaburgensis*, we can conclude that in the second half of the eleventh century the sanctuary at Selja was so well established that it was known even in Germany, but not to the point where a completely accurate version of the tale was known.

How then to conclude on the extension of the area in front of the rockshelter in the centuries preceding the *Sidaskipti* in Norway *c.* 1000? This extended area is surely in some way connected to the veneration of saints suggested by the clergymen in Germany writing some generations later.

### *The idea of holy men from Ireland*

As discussed in an earlier article (Hommedal 1997a, 67–69), the tradition of Irish hermit monks choosing to live in isolated places was known to the Norse population in the early Middle Ages. In Iceland, these were referred to as *papar* in the sagas (e.g. Crawford 1997, 163–167). It is fair to assume that they could also have found their way to Norway, for example, in the ninth century. Considering sea currents and topography, it would have been natural for Irish hermits to settle on the wild coast at Selja. We cannot, therefore, completely discount the possibility that the legend is based on historic fact, namely that the island hosted an Irish hermitage of which no identifiable traces survive today. It is, however, just as likely that the Irish connection is based on knowledge the Norse had about Celtic saints and monasteries such as St Ninian at Withorn, Scotland (Hommedal 1997a, 69). Rekdal (2004) also suggests an influence on the Selja legend from Gaelic legends and traditions in the Norse-Gaelic colonies in Scotland and northern England towards the end of the tenth century, for instance, the Irish legend of St Donnán who was martyred on the island of Eigg in the Hebrides. We must likewise be aware of the possible influence of cave dwelling traditions connected to Christian cults and saints in Britain and Ireland, and within the areas of Norse-Gaelic colonies in eastern Scotland, as discussed by historian Barbara Crawford (1997). According to Crawford (1997, 178) these Celtic cave saints are all men, but according to Steinsland (2012, 162), women were also central to this tradition. It therefore seems just as likely that any Norsemen finding human remains in a prehistoric cave settlement (AD 100–550) at Selja may have interpreted them in light of their knowledge of Irish legends, cave settlements and ecclesiastical traditions. In turn this may have – through an *interpretatio Christiana* – given rise to the legend of the holy people of Selja.

An important feature of Selja was undoubtedly the strategic location of the island, just south of the treacherous stretch of sea at Stad (Figs. 4.1 and 4.2). All vessels following the shipping lane along the Norwegian coast had to pass here, and Selja formed a natural haven for northbound ships waiting for favourable weather. We also know that Stad was one of the leaving or arrival points used by ships travelling to and from Britain, as illustrated in the introductory story about King Óláfr II Haraldsson. On the mainland east of Selja there was a pagan ritual site at Hove during the Viking era, and the meeting place of an assembly at Dragseidet in Stad in AD 997. In pre-Christian times Selja appears to have functioned as a hub for a greater area, and to have been a centre of communication and transport. This made the island well suited as a bridgehead in the process of Christianisation.

Returning to Norway from Britain in 995 to unite Norway and convert the country to Christianity, King Óláfr I Tryggvason must, through Anglo-Saxon saint traditions, have been aware of the role played by relics in the religious life of Christian countries and in the political agendas of Christian kings (Crawford 1997, 170–176; Hommedal 1997a, 69–71). In such a context any relics found at Selja in 996 must have been perceived as 'manna from Heaven', whether one wished to establish a holy place on the basis of an actual find of prehistoric human bones or on the basis of a tradition of holy people. Rekdal (2004, 192) even suggests that King Óláfr I Tryggvason actively created the Selja legend from the Donnán legend on his way to Norway as a necessary tool for the introduction of Christianity to Norway. I would question, however, the notion that the king and his bishops consciously and deliberately created a legend for Norway. We must be aware of the fact that missionaries travelling westwards to Norway in the tenth and eleventh centuries, including the entourage of King Óláfr I, would surely be familiar with Celtic legends and ecclesiastical traditions. With this knowledge, they presumably would have been inspired to 'draw their own conclusions' from any human remains found at Selja and interpret them as deriving from the holy men of Celtic origin. From this point of view Selja would have been of utmost importance to King Óláfr I and his entourage in the early introduction of Christianity to Norway, not only as a future shrine but also as a means of aiding the unification of the country (Hommedal 1997a, 69–71). The importance of Selja is also clearly symbolised in the introductory story about King Óláfr II Haraldsson's return to Norway in 1015 and reaching the island of *Felicitas*.

Historian Arne Odd Johnsen (1968, 58–62) argues convincingly that the core of the legend of the holy people from Selja dates from around AD 1000 or shortly thereafter (see also Rekdal 1997, 118–120). It was not, however, until the early twelfth century that Sunnifa took over as the central figure of the Selja cult, probably between 1100 and 1140. Both of the other early Norwegian episcopal sees, Niðarós (Trondheim) and Oslo, already had historical figures as patron saints – St Óláfr and St Hallvarð respectively. It may therefore have been desirable for the diocese in western Norway to have its own individual saint with a legend that could appeal to people's emotion and imagination in a much more powerful way than the more anonymous Seljumenn. Ommundsen (2010, 88) even suggests that the bishop's see of Bergen 'invented' Sunnifa after 1100 in order to provide Bergen with the relics of a patron saint like the ones in the other Norwegian bishop sees. If Sunnifa was still not an official part of the late eleventh-century version, this may be one of the reasons why the Benedictine monastery, when founded in this period, was not dedicated to Sunnifa at Selja but to the English St Alban (Hommedal, *in press*). Incorporating this English saint into the legend seems to have been subsequently problematic. Oddr Snorrason claims that St Alban was the brother of Sunnifa and that his remains were found in the rockshelter with her (Rindal 1997c, 310). *Óláfs saga Tryggvasonar en mesta*, however, contests this and concludes that, '*En þvi er her ecki af honum s(agt) at þat syniz efanligt*' / 'nothing is told about him [St. Alban] here because this [that he is one of the legend's holy men] seems unlikely' (Rindal 1997d, 321, my translation after Mundal 1997c, 327).

By the time the shrine of St Sunnifa was moved to Bergen in 1170, this virgin queen had, according to Johnsen, already become the protagonist of the legend while the Seljumenn had been reduced to a lesser role as her followers. O'Hara (2009, 116) has argued that Sunnifa, when coming to the fore of the legend in the twelfth century, was seen as a figural representation of the coming of Christianity to Norway. As such, she was a personification of the Christian faith and therefore characterised as a woman by the hagiographer and given an Anglo-Saxon name (*sungefa*) meaning 'gift of the sun'. As discussed by both O'Hara (2009) and Ommundsen (2011, 37), this fits very well with the religious symbolism that flourished in Norway in the middle of the twelfth century. One example is the poem *Geisli* from 1152 where St Óláfr is compared to a ray of sunshine. The liturgy of St Óláfr's feast day on the 29th July, written shortly afterwards, is also built around the word and the idea of light, *lux*, as in the sequence *Lux illuxit* ('the light shone forth'). The later liturgical sequence of St Hallvarð's feast day has *Lux illuxit* as its theme (Ommundsen 2009, 169). The religious symbol of light is, with regards to Selja, not only connected to the name of Sunnifa but also to the liturgy of St Sunnifa and the Seljumenn. It is interesting to note that one of the miracles concerns a girl born blind who, after spending a night in St Sunnifa's church, had her eyes healed to enjoy the miraculous light (Storm 1880, 152; Hommedal 1997b, 197).

The great stone terrace at Selja providing the present-day layout of the sanctuary seems to have been built in the first half of the twelfth century when Sunnifa seems to have been given a more prominent role in the legend. This must be more than a coincidence. The creation of this great stone revetment as high and strong as the most solid fortress seems to have been carried out as part of the establishment of St Sunnifa as the main figure in the legend. There is a possibility that the terrace functioned in the introduction of the personified St Sunnifa. According to such an interpretation, the *translatio* to Bergen could only take place after the establishment of the sanctuary and the terrace. It was at Selja that the legitimisation of Sunnifa had to take place. The *translatio* could only happen after Sunnifa had been inexorably linked to the cult of the holy men at Selja. Likewise, it was only after the virgin queen had taken on such a central role in the cult that she could stand on her own two feet and bear to be separated from her followers. The relics of the Seljumenn remained on Selja, however, and formed the basis of the continuation of the cult at its original site, together with the relic of St Alban in the Benedictine monastery.

The fully developed sanctuary with its associated liturgical life must thus have played an important part in the legitimisation of this new aspect of the cult. The sanctuary would stand as a symbol and reminder of what everyone knew to be true: that Selja was the place of martyrdom of the holy virgin queen now resting in the cathedral of Bergen. If anyone had any doubts, they need only look to Selja and see! In this way, the magnificent terrace, together with the rockshelter and the rest of the sanctuary, was key to the creation of the identity and memory of St Sunnifa and the Seljumenn. Plaster fragments on the original terrace masonry indicate that the huge terrace wall was whitewashed making it stand out in the landscape most of the year. This place of martyrdom would also be more visible to passing ships travelling along the west coast of Norway. If St Sunnifa, who, according to legend, came by boat across the sea, was a patron saint of the ocean (Johnsen 1968, 40–62; Crawford 1997, 179), this visual connection with the sanctuary would have been even more vital for mariners just before or after passing the treacherous stretch of sea at Stad (Hommedal 1997b, 193–194). The liturgy for the saint's main feast day, Seljumannamess on July 8th, seems to have incorporated a reminder of Sunnifa as the patron saint of sailors. The liturgy for the divine office tells of a miracle where a damaged ship did not sink until both the crew and cargo were rescued because they pleaded to St Sunnifa for help (Ommundsen 2011, 41).

The liturgy of Seljumannamess even seems to have incorporated reminders of the sanctuary at Selja itself. The Benedictine monks, first on Selja and later in Bergen, were essential in the development of the liturgy and the understanding of the Selja saints. According to Ommundsen (2011, 41–43), the liturgy seems to have been written shortly after the *translatio* in 1170 as the *officium*, i.e. the liturgy for the divine office only tells of miracles that took place at Selja and not at Bergen (Storm, 1880, 152, 283–289; Ommundsen 2010, 87–88). This seems probable, but the focus on Selja may also have served as a reminder of Sunnifa's connection to the sanctuary on this holy island. For instance, the miracle of the blind girl directly mentions St Sunnifa's church (Storm 1880, 152; Ommundsen 2010, 87). The present church, dating back to *c.* 1100, was supposedly originally dedicated to the holy saints of Selja and later taken over by St Sunnifa. The church with this dedication and the catafalque in the chancel would also have been a sign of memory and identification. Another miracle tells of a small boy who fell off a stone wall and died, but with the help of the holy men was brought back to life and returned to his mother on Selja (Storm, 1880, 152; Ommundsen 2010, 87). It was not stated directly that the boy's death took place at Selja, just that the miracle occurred there, but reference to a stone wall high enough to endanger would surely act as a reminder of the mighty masonry of the terrace. In this way the *officium* is directly connected to the sanctuary. The liturgy performed throughout Norway and Scandinavia in the centuries after 1170 would, in this manner, emphasise Selja's role as the ideological origin for the cult of St Sunnifa and the Seljumenn. The Benedictines at Selja must have been the main protagonists in this almost 200-year-long 'creation and birth process' prior to 1170, at least after the establishment of the Benedictine monastery in the late eleventh century. We must, however, assume that Benedictines, in their role of missionaries, were present at Selja from the very first *interpretatio Christiana* of the relics related to this holy island. The Benedictines seem to have been principal to developing the legend of St Sunnifa and the Seljumenn, but also in the construction of the sanctuary and the development of the liturgy giving the saints from Selja their identity and memory (Hommedal *in press*).

## Summary and conclusions

Archaeological finds and cultural deposits in front of the rockshelter and caves at Selja show that human activities took place at the site during at least two periods in the first millennium AD. Between AD 100 and 550 the settlement seems to have followed a pattern common to western Norway functioning as a shelter during fishing and hunting activities. In the centuries preceding the Christianisation of Norway *c.* 1000, however, the site does not appear to have followed the general pattern of activities by local people in rockshelters and caves. The soil embankment and extension works carried out just before or during the Viking Age (800–1000/1030) are quite unique. Even though we cannot pinpoint the exact nature of activities, this was most likely connected, in one way or another, to the dawn of the rockshelter and cave as a sanctuary related to the legend we are familiar with today.

Even though the legend of St Sunnifa and the Seljumenn seems to be fictional, at its core it may relate to the discovery of human bones in the rockshelter or, more probably, inside the caves. The bones, subsequently interpreted as holy relics, are in this article presumed to be human remains from Iron Age burials. Iron Age people lived here at least 400 years before St Sunnifa and the Seljumenn are reputed to have come to the island. As a part of the *interpretatio Christiana*, when found the bones were perceived as relics of Christian refugees from the west who were martyred in the caves. This association seems to have been inspired by the site's location in a wild and barren landscape near the open seas, while also linking in with Irish and British hagiography and cave dwelling traditions.

According to subsequent narratives, the *interpretatio Christiana* at Selja happened in 996 and King Óláfr I Tryggvason is credited with finding the relics, which for him as a Christianising king would have been 'heaven-sent'. The new religion would consequently also be rooted in Norwegian soil at Selja. The king is credited with having built a church on the island, often interpreted as having been erected in front of the rockshelter. However, the archaeologically documented extension of the area in front of the rockshelter, which most likely took place during the Viking Age, has not revealed any proper indications of a building connecting the embankment to the narratives in the legend. The platform cannot be related to any Irish settlement, e.g. of hermit monks (*papar*) either. What can be concluded, however, is that the Christian sanctuary connected to the rockshelter was so well established in the last decades of the eleventh century that a stone platform was constructed as the innermost part of the present terrace, probably in connection with the construction of the present stone church. This may have been carried out as part of the establishment of the West Norwegian diocese and ecclesiastical centre at Selja at the time of King Óláfr III kyrri (1066–1093). During this period, the legend and sanctuary were also so well established that they were recounted by Adam of Bremen or another writer in the archbishopric of Hamburg-Bremen *c.* 1080, but not so well established that the information given about the Norwegian saints was accurate.

The sanctuary at Selja was built in the eleventh and twelfth century and was completed by 1170 at the latest. The holy rockshelter, with its two caves and a holy well, functioned as a chapel called *Salinn* and was probably dedicated to St Michael the Archangel. There was, and still is, a well where the water was said to have healing properties. The stone church in front of the rockshelter was originally probably dedicated to the Seljumenn and later taken over by St Sunnifa. The chancel has a catafalque where the shrine of St Sunnifa probably stood, behind the main altar, before her *translatio* to Bergen in 1170. The small church, with opposing doorways in the nave, seems to have served as a simple ambulatory, where pilgrims could pass through to see, or perhaps touch, the holy shrine of St Sunnifa in the chancel. This ambulatory was connected to the large stone terrace in front of the church, which functioned as a liturgical space for processions and gatherings in front of the holy rockshelter, e.g. for pilgrims coming to Selja on *Seljumannamess* on July 8th, the main feast day of the cult. St Sunnifa's church would have been too small to accommodate those seeking sanctuary, at least on liturgical feast days. In this manner, the terrace resembled the function of a church's nave with St Sunnifa's church standing as a separate large 'shrine' on the innermost part of the terrace.

The development of the sanctuary was carried out as part of the consolidation of the Selja saints and in establishing St Sunnifa as the main figure in the legend. The site developed from the rockshelter and caves and expanded to include a stone church and an enormous terrace forming a very special and distinctive site, which provided a permanent monument to the martyrdom of St Sunnifa and the Seljumenn. The sanctuary, and especially the terrace, thereafter stood as a symbol and reminder of what everyone knew to be true: that Selja was the place where the holy virgin and cave queen, now resting in Bergen, was martyred. In this way, the terrace played a conclusive role in the creation of the legacy, identity and memory of St Sunnifa and the Seljumenn.

## Acknowledgements

I would like to thank the editors, Knut Andreas Bergsvik and Marion Dowd, for inviting me to contribute to this book though I did not take part in the EAA conference, and likewise for their comments and discussions regarding the paper. I also wish to thank the Norse philologist Else Mundal, and the art historian Justin Kroesen, for discussions and comments on sections of the text.

## References

*Adam von Bremen. Hamburgische Kirchengeschicte*. 1917. Gesta Hammaburgensis ecclesiæ pontificum, ed. B. Schmeidler. Hannover und Leipzig: Hansche Buchhandlung.

*Adam of Bremen. History of the Archbishops of Hamburg-Bremen*. 1959. Transl. F.J. Tschan. New York: Colombia University Press.

*Adam av Bremen. Beretningen om Hamburg stift, erkebiskopenes bedrifter og øyrikene i Norden*. 1993. Transl. and publ. A.K. Frihagen and K. Tosterud. Thorleif Dahls Kulturbibliotek. Oslo: Aschehoug.

Bakka, E. 1973. Omkring problemet om kulturdualisme i Sør-Noreg. *In*: P. Simonsen and G.S. Munch, eds. *Bonde-veidemann, bofast-ikke bofast i nordens forshistorie*. Tromsø: Universitetsforlaget, 109–128.

Bergsvik, K.A., 2017. Caves and rockshelters in Iron Age coastal Norway – at the margins of the society? *In*: S. Semple and C. Orsini, eds. *Life on the Edge. Neue Studien zur Sachsenforschung*. Hannover: Hannover Museum Press, 317–334.

Bergsvik, K.A. and Hansen, G., 2015. Medieval Rockshelters in Western Norway – activities, functions and social identities. *In*: I. Baug, J. Larsen, and S.S. Mygland, eds. *Nordic Middle Ages – Artefacts, Landscapes and Society. Essays in Honour of Ingvild Øye on her 70th Birthday*. UBAS 8. Bergen: University of Bergen, 49–76.

Berle Nilsen, K., 2013. Sankta Sunniva – er hun en historisk person? Thesis (MA), NLA University College, Bergen.

Bommen, C. 2009. Bruken av hellarar i eldre jernalder i Sunnhordland. Thesis (MA), University of Bergen.

Borgehammar, S. 1997a. Den latinska Sunnivalegenden. En edition. *In*: M. Rindal, ed. *Selja – heilag stad i 1000 år*. Oslo: Universitetsforlaget, 270–292.

Borgehammar, S., 1997b. Sunnivalegenden och den benediktinska reformen i England. *In*: M. Rindal, ed. *Selja – heilag stad i 1000 år*. Oslo: Universitetsforlaget, 123–159.

Braun, J., 1924. *Der christliche Altar in seiner geschichtlichen Entwicklung*, 2. Binde. München: Karl Widmann.

Brøgger, A.W., 1911. Vestnorske hulefund fra ældre jernalder. *Bergen Museums Aarbog*, 1910, 3–22.

Christie, H., 1983a. Den förste generasjon av kirker i Norge. *Hikuin*, 9, 93–100.

Christie, H., 1983b. A 301 Borni-helleren på Kinn. Innberetning fra undersøkelser 8. August 1983. Unpublished report on file in the Topographical Archive, University Museum of Bergen.

Crawford, B., 1997. Hellige steder på De britiske øyene. Noen paralleller til Selja. *In*: M. Rindal, ed. *Selja – heilag stad i 1000 år*. Oslo: Universitetsforlaget, 160–182.

Djupedal, R., 1966. *Selja i tusen år. Eit minneskrift om kloster og kyrkjer*. Selje: Boktrykk – Bergen.

DuBois, T.A., 2008. Sts. Sunniva and Henrik: Scandinavian martyr saints in their hagiographic and national contexts. *In*: T.A. DuBois, ed. *Sanctity in the North. Saints, Lives, and Cults in Medieval Scandinavia*. Toronto–Buffalo–London: University of Toronto Press, 65–99.

Engelstad, H., 1941. *Messeklær og alterskrud. Middelalderske paramenter i Norge*. Oslo: Cammermeyers Boghandel.

Enger, C., 1949. Helligdommen på Selja. *Fortidsminneforeningens Årbok* 102(1946), 5–48.

Fredriksen, P. H., 2004. Helgener og kirkededikasjoner i Norge i middelalderen. Thesis (MA), University of Oslo.

Gabrielsen, K.H., 2002. Vestlandets steinkors. Monumentalisme i brytningen mellom hedendom og kristendom. Thesis (Cand. Philol), University of Bergen.

Gullbekk, S.H., 2011. Myntenes omløpshastighet i norsk middelalder: Middelalderens økonomiske system. *Historisk Tidsskrift* 90, 511–529.

Helle, K., 1997. Det første bispedømmet på Vestlandet. *In*: M. Rindal, ed. *Selja – heilag stad i 1000 år*. Oslo: Universitetsforlaget, 240–251.

Henriksen, V., 1992. *Selja og Stad – legender, saga og historie*. Naustdal: Sogn og Fjordane Forlag.

Hommedal, A.T., 1995. Selja i Nordfjord. Som Moster eit bruhovud i kristningsprosessen. *In*: H.-E. Lidén, ed. *Møtet mellom hedendom og kristendom i Norge*. Oslo: Universitetsforlaget, 143–169.

Hommedal, A.T., 1996. Selja. Helgenstad i tusen år. Eit forskingshistorisk bidrag om minnesmerket på øya Selja i Nordfjord. *Fortidsminneforeningens Årbok*, 150, 17–60.

Hommedal, A.T., 1997a. Bakgrunnen for helgenanlegget på Selja og staden si rolle i den tidlege kristninga av Vest-Noreg. *In*: M. Rindal, ed. *Selja – heilag stad i 1000 år*. Oslo: Universitetsforlaget, 43–76.

Hommedal, A.T., 1997b. 'Dei heilage frå Selja'. Vurdering av kulten rundt St Sunniva og Seljumennene og Selja si rolle som pilegrimsmål i mellomalderen. *In*: M. Rindal, ed. *Selja – heilag stad i 1000 år*. Oslo: Universitetsforlaget, 183–199.

Hommedal, A.T., 1998. The value of a coin. *In*: A. Ågotnes, ed. *The Story Behind. Archaeological Finds from the Middle Ages in Bergen*. Bergen: Bryggens Museum, 112–115.

Hommedal, A.T., 2009. 'Nogle stykker silkedamask' frå Selja. *In*: J.L. Zehetner, ed. *Bling. Pynt og klær i middelalderen*. Bergen: Bymuseet, 36–39.

Hommedal, A.T., 2015. Øya der kristendommen kom i land. Newspaper chronicle. *Bergens Tidende*, April 4th, 16–17.

Hommedal, A.T., *in press*. St Alban's Abbey. The Benedictines and the sanctuary at Selja, Norway. *In*: E. Bhreathnach, M.K. D'Aughton and K. Smith, eds. *Monastic Europe AD 1100–1700: Landscape and Settlement*. Turnhout: Brepols.

Jensen, C.A., Moltke, E., and Schultz, C.G., 1940. *Danmarks kirker, Thisted Amt 1*. Copenhagen: G.E.C. Gades Forlag.

Jensenius, J. 2010. Bygningstekniske og arkeologiske bemerkninger om trekirker i Norge i vikingtid og middelalder. *Collegium Medievale* 23, 147–178.

Jensenius, J., 2015. Wooden churches in Viking and Medieval Norway: two geometric and static strategies. *In*: E. Khodakovsky and S.S. Lexau, eds., *Historic wooden architecture in Europe and Russia*. Basel: Birkhauser, 20–27.

Johnsen, A.O., 1968. Når slo Sunniva-kulten igjennom? *In*: P. Juvkam, ed. *Bjørgvin bispestol. Frå Selja til Bjørgvin*. Bergen: Universitetsforlaget, 40–62.

Koren, V. 1869: 'Personel kapellan V. Korens indberetning'. *Fortidsminneforeningens Årbok (Aarsberetning)* 1868, 6–12.

Krefting, O. 1868: *Selje Klosterlevninger*. Indberetning om Antikvariske Undersøgelser 1866–1867 i Selje Kirke- og

Klosterruiner. Foreningen til Norske Fortidsmindesmerkers bevaring. Kristiania: Trykt hos Carl C. Werner & Ko.

Kristoffersen, S. and Magnus, B., 2010. *Spannformete kar. Utvikling og variasjon*. AmS-Varia 50. Stavanger: Museum of Archaeology, University of Stavanger.

Kroesen, J.E.A. and Steensma, R., 2012. *The interior of the Medieval village church*. 2nd edn. Leuven–Paris–Walpole, MA: Peeters.

Mundal, E., 1997a. Heiden kult som kan knytast til holer og hellerar. *In*: M. Rindal, ed. *Selja – heilag stad i 1000 år*. Oslo: Universitetsforlaget, 34–42.

Mundal, E., 1997b. Legender, helgenkult og misjonsstrategi i kristningstida. *In*: M. Rindal, ed. *Selja – heilag stad i 1000 år*. Oslo: Universitetsforlaget, 77–101.

Mundal, E., 1997c. Soga om Sankta Sunniva [Norwegian translation]. *In*: M. Rindal, ed. *Selja – heilag stad i 1000 år*. Oslo: Universitetsforlaget, 323–328.

Nicolaysen, N., 1892. *Om ruinerne paa Selje*. Udgivet af Foreningen til Norske Fortidsmindesmærkers bevaring. Medfølger Foreningens Aarsberetning for 1891. Kristiania: Carl C. Werner & Co.'s Bogtrykkeri.

Nielsen, Y., 1905. De gamle helligdomme paa Selja. *In*: *Historiske afhandlinger tilegnet Professor Dr. J. E. Sars paa hans syttiende fødselsdag den ellevte oktober 1905 af venner og Disciple*. Kristiania: Aschehoug, 164–181.

Nybø, M., 2000. Albanuskirken på Selja. Klosterkirke eller bispekirke? Thesis (Dr. Art.), University of Bergen.

Odner, K. 1969. *Ullshelleren i Valldalen, Røldal*. Bergen: Norwegian Universities Press.

O'Hara, A., 2009. Constructing a saint: The legend of St Sunniva in the twelfth-century Norway. *Viking and Medieval Scandinavia* 5, 105–121.

*Óláfs saga Tryggvasonar en mesta*, 1958. Publ. Ó. Halldórsson. Vol. I. Copenhagen: Ejnar Munksgaard.

Ommundsen, Å., 2009. A Saint and his sequence: Singing the legend of St Olaf. *Viking and Medieval Scandinavia* 5, 151–176.

Ommundsen, Å., 2010. The cult of Saints in Norway before 1200. *In*: H. Antonsson and I.H. Garipzanov, eds. *Saints and their Lives on the Periphery: Veneration of Saints in Scandinavia and Eastern Europe (c. 1000–1200)*. Turnhout: Brepols, 67–93.

Ommundsen, Å., 2011. Ei heilag jomfru til bispesetet – Sankta Sunniva og Bergen i mellomalderen. *In*: A. Ågotnes and I. Øye, eds. *Fra kongssete til kuturminne. Håkonshallen og Bergenshus-området gjennom 750 år*. Bergen: John Grieg Forlag, 30–45.

Østebø, K. 2008. *Hellerbruk i vestnorsk eldre jernalder belyst ved lokalisering*. Thesis (MA) University of Bergen.

Pedersen, A., 2014. Late Viking and Early Medieval ornaments: A question of faith. *In*: I. Garipzanov and R. Bonté, eds. *Conversion and Identity in the Viking Age*. Turnhout: Brepols, 195–223.

Prescott, C. 1991. *Kulturhistoriske undersøkelser i Skrivarhellaren*. Arkeologiske rapporter 14. Bergen: Historical Museum, University of Bergen.

Rekdal, J.E., 1997. Legenden om Sunniva og Seljemenneskene. *In*: M. Rindal, ed. *Selja – heilag stad i 1000 år*. Oslo: Universitetsforlaget, 102–122.

Rekdal, J.E., 2004. Sunnivalegenden – irsk rekved mellom norrøne fjæresteiner? *In*: J.V. Sigurðsson, M. Myking, and M. Rindal, eds. *Religionsskiftet i Norden. Brytninger mellom Nordisk og Europeisk kultur 800–1200 e.Kr.* Senter for studier i Vikingtid og Nordisk Middelalder. Skriftserie nr. 6. Oslo: University of Oslo, 159–196.

Rindal, M., ed., 1997. *Selja – heilag stad i 1000 år*. Oslo: Universitetsforlaget.

Rindal, M., 1997a. Sunniva–tekstar frå Mellomalderen. Innleiing. *In*: M. Rindal, ed. *Selja – heilag stad i 1000 år*. Oslo: Universitetsforlaget, 265–269.

Rindal, M., 1997b. Soga om seljumennene og Sunniva [Norse original text]. *In*: M. Rindal, ed. *Selja – heilag stad i 1000 år*. Oslo: Universitetsforlaget, 303–306.

Rindal, M., 1997c. Soga om seljumennene og Sunniva [Norwegian translation]. *In*: M. Rindal, ed. *Selja – heilag stad i 1000 år*. Oslo: Universitetsforlaget, 307–310.

Rindal, M., 1997d. Soga om Sunniva [Norse original text]. *In*: M. Rindal, ed. *Selja – heilag stad i 1000 år*. Oslo: Universitetsforlaget, 311–322.

Simek, R., 2013. An Irish princess in Norway – and her German origins. *In*: R. Simek and A. Ivanova, eds. *Between the islands - and the Continent: Anglo-Hiberno-Continental relations in the Early Middle Ages*. Vienna: Fassbaender, 252–270.

*Saga Ólafs Trygvasonar af Oddr Snorrason Munk*, 1932. Publ. F. Jónsson. Copenhagen: Gads Forlag.

Steinsland, G., 1997. Huleheligdommen på Selja. På leting etter førkristne spor – en vandring i myter, makter og tegn. *In*: M. Rindal, ed. *Selja – heilag stad i 1000 år*. Oslo: Universitetsforlaget, 11–33.

Steinsland, G., 2012. *Mytene som skapte Norge. Myter og makt frå vikingtid til middelalder*. Oslo: Pax Forlag A/S.

Storm, G., ed., 1880. *Monumenta historica Norvegiæ: latinske Kildeskrifter til Norges Historie i Middelalderen*. Kristiania: Brøgger.

Tosterud, B., 1997. Legenden om Sunniva [Norwegian translation]. *In*: M. Rindal, ed., *Selja – heilag stad i 1000 år*. Oslo: Universitetsforlaget, 293–298.

Undset, S. 2006 [1926]. Sommerdage paa Sankta Sunnivas ø. *In*: L. Bliksrud, ed., *Sigrid Undset. Essays og artikler 1920–1929*. Oslo: Aschehoug, 281–293.

Undset, S. 2006 [1929]. Sankta Sunniva og Seljemændene. *In*: L. Bliksrud, ed., *Sigrid Undset. Essays og artikler 1920–1929*. Oslo: Aschehoug, 531–551.

Winroth, A., 2012. *The Conversion of Scandinavia. Vikings, Merchants, and Missionaries in the Remaking of Northern Europe*. New Haven–London: Yale University Press.

# Chapter 5

# Signs from the Pictish underground: early medieval cave ritual at the Sculptor's Cave, north-east Scotland

*Lindsey Büster and Ian Armit*

*The Sculptor's Cave, Covesea, on the Moray coast in north-east Scotland, was used as a mortuary site from the Late Bronze Age to the Roman Iron Age, but it is the early medieval ('Pictish') symbols carved into its entrance walls that give the cave its name. Though no artefacts or other signs of activities of that date have been found within the cave, the carvings attest to its endurance as a ritual arena during the early medieval period. This chapter examines the Pictish symbols at the Sculptor's Cave, which are potentially among the earliest known in the corpus, in the context of the later prehistoric activities that preceded them.*

## Introduction

The Sculptor's Cave in Moray, north-east Scotland, derives its name from a series of Pictish symbols carved into its entrance walls (the Pictish period dates broadly to *c*. AD 400–900). The cave lies a few metres above sea level at the foot of 30m-high sandstone cliffs, and faces north across the Moray Firth to Wick and Thurso (Fig. 5.1). Access today involves scrambling down an artificially enhanced cleft ('the Lummie') in the sandstone cliffs in an adjacent bay, roughly 100m east of the Sculptor's Cave, or a much longer walk across the uneven shingle and slippery rocks of the shoreline. The bay in which the cave is situated is cut off for up to three hours either side of high tide; relative sea levels have changed little since later prehistory, and the same is likely to have been the case in the Pictish period. It is unlikely, therefore, that access was ever straightforward and this may be a primary factor in the cave's use as a place of funerary ritual during the Late Bronze Age and Roman Iron Age (see below). In turn, this funerary role may have subsequently attracted those who carved the Pictish symbols into the cave walls.

The cave measures approximately 20m deep by 13.5m wide, and the roof rises to a maximum height of about 5.5m. Unlike the other large, open sea caves along this stretch of coast, the Sculptor's Cave has an unusual twin entrance passage arrangement (Fig. 5.2). The passages are each between 2–3m wide and are large enough to walk through comfortably. During the early medieval period, however, these passages were choked with (now excavated) later prehistoric deposits, which would have raised the floor level and darkened the interior. Indeed, Allen and Anderson (1903, 130), who visited the cave prior to the removal of deposits by excavation, described the passages as being just 'eight feet' (*c*. 2.5m) high.

Following earlier recordings of the carvings (Stuart 1867; Allen and Anderson 1903, 129–131), the cave saw three campaigns of excavation (two formally recorded, one informal). The first, undertaken between 1928 and 1930 by Sylvia Benton, was prompted by a visit to see the renowned Pictish carvings, during which it was observed that the 'floor was strewn with human bone' (Benton 1931, 177). Benton excavated the majority of the cave interior, leaving much of the material in the entrance passages intact for future work. Threats to these surviving deposits from casual visitors prompted further excavations by Ian and Alexandra Shepherd in 1979 (Shepherd and Shepherd 1979), which effectively cleared the cave of all remaining anthropogenic deposits. At some point between these two 'official' excavation campaigns, a local amateur archaeologist, Mr George Leslie Darge, undertook excavation in caves adjacent to the Sculptor's Cave (Keillar 1969), and may have

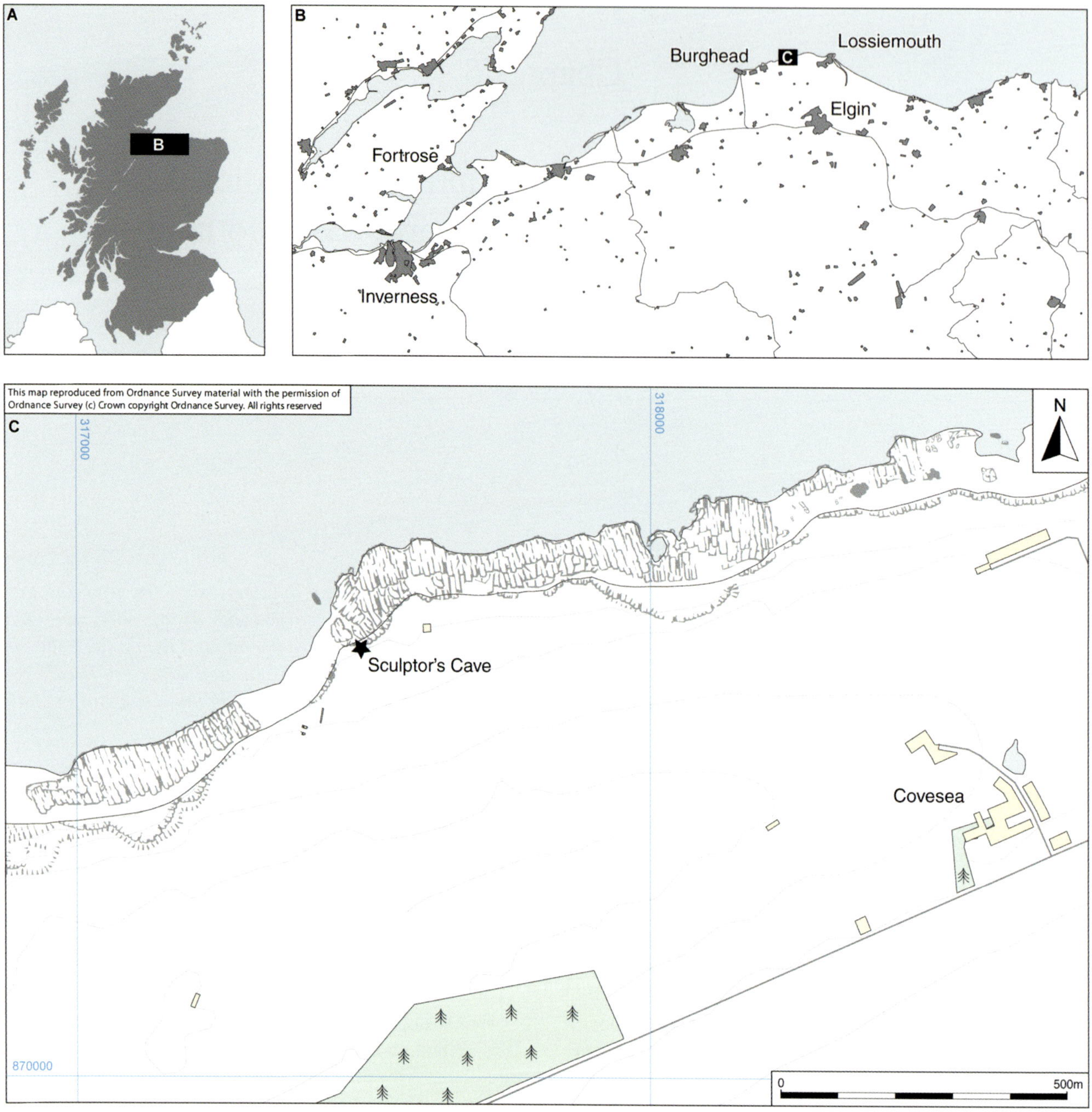


*Figure 5.1: Location map.*

dug in the Sculptor's Cave itself, as evidenced by modern disturbance to the sections drawn by the Shepherds in 1979. The Shepherds' excavation archive is currently being analysed by the present authors at the University of Bradford as the basis for a major reassessment of the archaeology of the Sculptor's Cave (Büster and Armit *in press*).

Although none of the artefacts or human remains found within the cave appear to date to the early medieval period, the Pictish carvings on the entrance walls attest to the enduring significance of the site at this time. These carvings are particularly important as they include some unusual motifs and have been argued to represent some of the earliest Pictish carvings in the corpus (Henderson and Henderson 2004, 171). Indeed, Alcock (1996) included the Sculptor's Cave carvings in his category of '*ur*-symbols': a small group that he saw as original, primal and ancestral to the more formalised symbols on Pictish stones (see below). This paper examines the nature of the Pictish carvings at the Sculptor's Cave and the potential motivations for their creation. In order to understand the possible reasons behind the carvings, however, it is first essential to explore the nature of later prehistoric activities in the cave.

*Figure 5.2: The Sculptor's Cave: a) general view from shoreline; b) twin entrance passages; c) view of entrance passages from cave interior. Photos: L. Büster and I. Armit.*

## Prehistoric use of the cave

The Sculptor's Cave appears to have witnessed over a millennium of ritual use prior to the carving of the Pictish symbols. Evidence from the major excavations, along with subsequent reanalysis of the human remains (Armit *et al.* 2011), has produced a reasonably clear outline of the sequence of human activities, represented principally by mortuary remains and the deposition of unusual and exotic metalwork and other artefacts. Although activities may have been broadly continuous, there were two discrete episodes of particular importance: the Late Bronze Age (1050–900 BC) and Roman Iron Age (AD 100–400).

### *Late Bronze Age activity*

Late Bronze Age deposits were dominated by a substantial human bone assemblage of more than 1600 fragments, most of which were recovered during Benton's excavations and subsequently discarded (Armit *et al.* 2011). A smaller assemblage of Late Bronze Age human remains was also recovered by the Shepherds from material left in the entrance passages by Benton (1931). Both the Benton and Shepherd assemblages were characterised by a preponderance of juvenile remains and some evidence for the selection/removal of skeletal elements. There was, for example, a significant under-representation of cranial fragments. Despite this, the close proximity of mandible and cranial fragments in the entrance passages, together with precious items of personal adornment such as gold-covered copper alloy 'hair-rings', led I.A.G. Shepherd (2007, 199) to conclude that juvenile skulls, probably fleshed and adorned with finery, had been displayed at the cave entrance. The fact that such precious items, presumably displayed in the open air rather than being buried, survived looting in the Late Bronze Age (and subsequent periods) attests to the significance of the site and the respect it was afforded.

### *Roman Iron Age activity*

AMS dates suggest continuity of activity during the Early and Middle Iron Age. The next period of intensive deposition, however, appears to have taken place during the Roman Iron Age, over a millennium after the initial Late Bronze Age funerary activity. Numerous small objects were deposited, presumably as votive offerings, including proto-handpins, 'tweezers', the bolt and key of a 'barrel lock', and glass beads (Benton 1931). A series of human cervical vertebrae bearing cutmarks indicative of decapitation from behind, found during Benton's excavations, have also recently been AMS-dated to this period (Armit *et al.* 2011). These represent a minimum of six individuals (four adults and two children or young adolescents). The nature and position of the cutmarks are consistent with beheading as a mode of execution. The vertebrae include elements that would have been removed with the head, and others that would have remained in the decapitated body. This strongly implies that the beheadings were conducted in the cave itself – rather than the cave being, for example, a place to display trophy heads from the battlefield. The AMS dates are sufficiently tightly grouped as to suggest that these decapitations might represent a single event which took place during the third century AD.

Whilst the curation and display of juvenile skulls at the cave entrance in the Late Bronze Age could be interpreted as a respectful way to honour and remember the dead, it is unlikely that the same explanation applies to the decapitations of the Roman Iron Age. Decapitations from Roman Britain are not uncommon, but generally the removal of the head was carried out post-mortem as part of non-normative funerary rites (e.g. Montgomery *et al.* 2011, 151). That was patently not the case in the Sculptor's Cave. Although one might suggest that the decapitated individuals here represent executed prisoners or criminals, the manifest ritual importance of the cave, with its deep funerary history, suggests otherwise. Human bone would probably have been very evident within the cave even at that time, while the presence of votive objects, and the inherent difficulty in transporting victims to the place of execution (rather than executing them in a more accessible, public place), suggests that these decapitations were (at least partially) ritualistic in nature.

The killings within the Sculptor's Cave occurred during a period of social and political upheaval following the final Roman withdrawal from southern Scotland. Given the undoubted ritual significance of the cave and its proximity to what was later to become the major northern Pictish stronghold at Burghead (some 6km to the west), it is possible that these individuals were executed as part of a political or dynastic struggle. Alternatively, their deaths may have been religiously inspired. These two hypotheses are not, of course, mutually exclusive.

Interestingly, the cave appears to have retained some ritual significance after the period of these decapitations, as attested by the deposition, a century later, of more than 200 coins; the northernmost deposit of coins of this date currently known (F. Hunter 2007, fig. 15). Only a handful of these are official Roman issues, the remainder representing indigenous copies. Some also feature perforations and chain-links, suggesting that they were used for personal adornment rather than as currency. The spatial distribution of the coins, as recorded in Benton's archive, does not suggest that they were necessarily deposited as a single hoard.

## The Pictish symbols

The term 'Picts' (*Picti*, probably meaning 'the painted ones') first occurs in a panegyric by the Roman writer Eumenius in AD 297. It appears to have been used by the Romans to refer to the barbarian inhabitants of Scotland north of the Forth-Clyde isthmus, though it is unlikely that these groups had much sense of their own collective identity before at least the late seventh century AD (Foster 2004, 9). Subsequently, however, the Pictish kingdom developed into a powerful and enduring political and cultural force (Fraser 2009).

'Pictish symbols' are a group of motifs which occur predominantly in north-east Scotland (Henderson and Henderson 2004). They include a mix of abstract symbols, naturalistic depictions of animals, and what appear to be highly conventionalised renderings of objects such as mirrors and combs. They are most commonly found on free-standing slabs, known as 'symbol stones', which are conventionally divided into two categories. Class I are the earliest, dating from around the sixth–eighth centuries AD and comprise symbols carved on undressed stones (i.e. stones which have not been shaped). Class II date from the eighth–ninth centuries AD and comprise dressed cross-slabs, featuring Pictish symbols and/or figurative scenes alongside Christian iconography. Pictish symbols are also found occasionally on portable artefacts, such as the two silver plaques and a silver pin from the Norrie's Law hoard in Fife (Graham-Campbell 1993).

Much debate surrounds the meaning of the symbols. They have been argued to be, *inter alia*, symbols of clan affiliation, profession, totem or rank (e.g. Thomas 1963; Foster 2004, 70; Carver 2008, 94). A particularly compelling interpretation by Samson (1992) suggests that the frequent pairing of motifs on symbol stones may reflect their use to denote two-part personal names. Samson believes that the symbol stones were essentially funerary monuments, but there is no particular reason (even accepting that the paired symbols denote personal names) why some might not have been territorial markers, religious dedications or memorials to various events. There is no consensus, and it is probable that the symbols and the stones that bore them were employed for a range of purposes, albeit mostly associated with power, status and religion (cf. Foster 2004, 76–77).

Like all rock art, the carved symbols are difficult to date directly, which makes rare instances of their presence on typologically dateable artefacts, such as those in the Norrie's Law hoard (most likely deposited in the seventh century AD; Graham-Campbell 1993), particularly significant. The earliest securely dated example currently known is a crude double-disc on a stone from the floor of Structure 23 at Pool in Orkney, probably built during the sixth century (J. Hunter 2007, 99–101). Some have argued, however, for a fifth-century origin, based on parallels between some of the symbols and artefacts of Roman Iron Age date. Laing and Laing (1984, 269), for example, suggest that some Pictish 'mirror' symbols depict Roman *paterae*. Conceivably, they may have their ultimate origins even earlier, pre-dating the carved stones on which they are most commonly found. Thomas (1961, 57) has suggested that the symbols may have originated as tattoo motifs, whilst Henderson and Henderson (2004, 84) have suggested that the stylised nature of many of the motifs, particularly the animals, could indicate their use as a decorative feature of textiles. Certainly the presence of incised Pictish symbols on animal bones from the Broch of Burrian and Pool, Sanday (Henderson and Henderson 2004, fig. 251) could suggest that such motifs were commonly used to decorate a range of perishable organic materials that have not survived in the archaeological record. Pictish symbols may thus ante-date Class I symbol stones by centuries rather than decades.

Pictish symbols at the Sculptor's Cave are located primarily on the walls of the twin entrance passages (Fig. 5.3). No definitive Pictish carvings have been found in the main body of the cave, despite careful inspection with floodlights during the 1979 excavations (Fraser 2008, 106). Given that the interior walls are significantly less eroded than those at the exposed entrance passages, it seems highly probable that the present distribution of carvings is a genuine reflection of their original distribution.

It is difficult to ascertain the definitive number of carvings in the cave, partly because different numbers have been recorded in various surveys (Stuart 1867; Allen and Anderson 1903; Fraser 2008; RCAHMS 2011, cat. no. SC1468820), and there is uncertainty as to which carvings are considered Pictish in date. For instance, Fraser's (2008, 106–107) descriptive list does not tally exactly with the numbers of symbols depicted in the accompanying illustrations – which are mainly from Stuart (1867). Based on those symbols illustrated in Fraser (2008) the cave contains: two fish

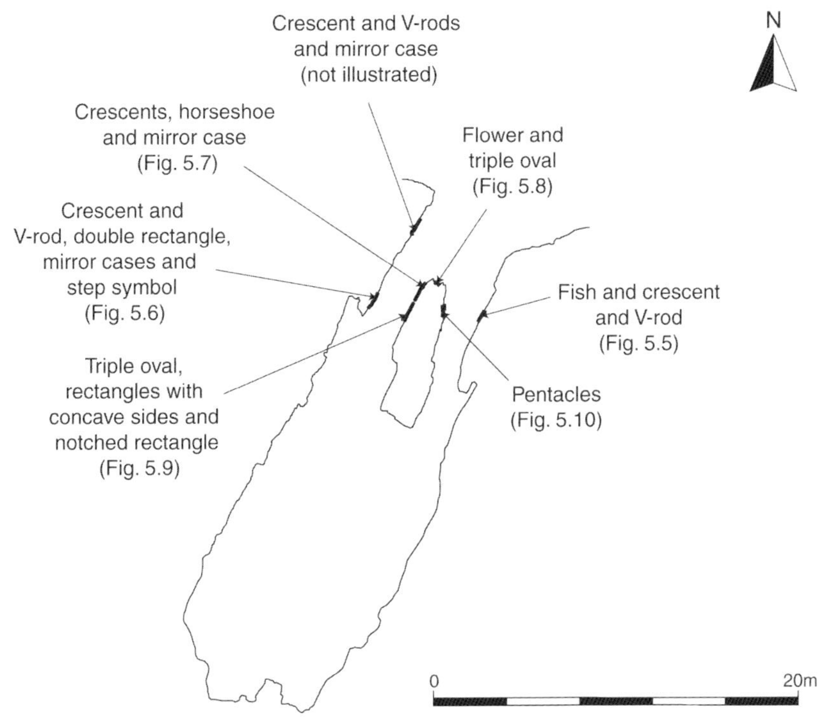


*Figure 5.3: Location of the Pictish symbols within the Sculptor's Cave. Plan based on terrestrial laser scan image courtesy Bradford Visualisation, University of Bradford.*

symbols; five crescents, four with associated V-rods; one 'horseshoe' symbol; two triple oval symbols; three mirror cases; one flower symbol; one double rectangle symbol; one 'step symbol'; two pentacles; and 'two small rectangles with concave long sides'. The RCAHMS (2011) survey additionally records a notched rectangle on the east wall of the West Passage, adjacent to one of the rectangles with concave sides. The cave also contains several simple (and thus chronologically undiagnostic) crosses; one large 'carpet cross' (considered to be later medieval on stylistic grounds); a seventeenth-century 'curse'; and a great deal of graffiti from the nineteenth century onwards. Discussion of these later carvings is outside the scope of the current chapter (see Armit and Büster in press, chap. 3).

Some of the Pictish symbols at the Sculptor's Cave appear rather crude in comparison with the better-preserved examples on many of the surviving symbol stones. While this may reflect their original appearance and quality, it needs to be borne in mind that wind erosion of the coarse-grained sandstone in the entrance passages has undoubtedly had a significant effect. Despite the general perception of the Sculptor's Cave carvings as rather poorly executed, Shepherd described certain examples, such as the flower and triple oval (see below), as 'stylish and orthodox' (1993, 81). Nonetheless, when compared to some of the finer examples of Pictish carving in the region, e.g. a bull symbol from the nearby stronghold of Burghead (Fig. 5.4), the Sculptor's Cave symbols appear relatively crude.

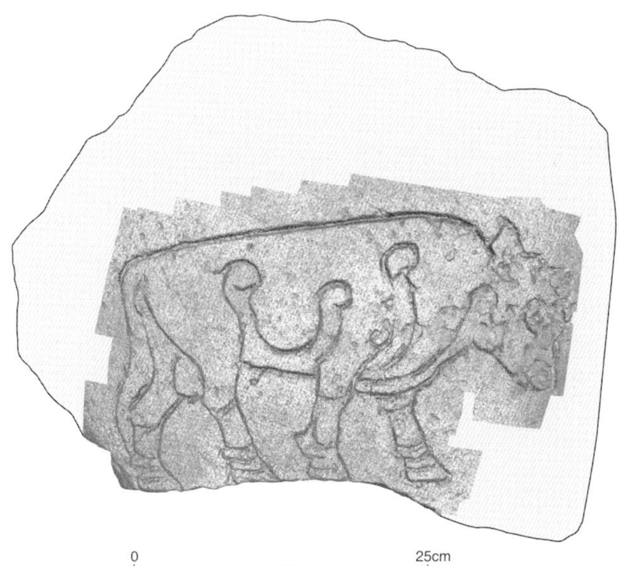


*Figure 5.4: A structured light scan of a bull motif from the Pictish stronghold at Burghead. Courtesy Fragmented Heritage and Bradford Visualisation, University of Bradford, and Elgin Museum.*

The following sections describe the principal symbols found in the Sculptor's Cave. The descriptions follow the groupings outlined by Fraser (2008) – groupings which are also, in the main, followed in the later RCAHMS survey.

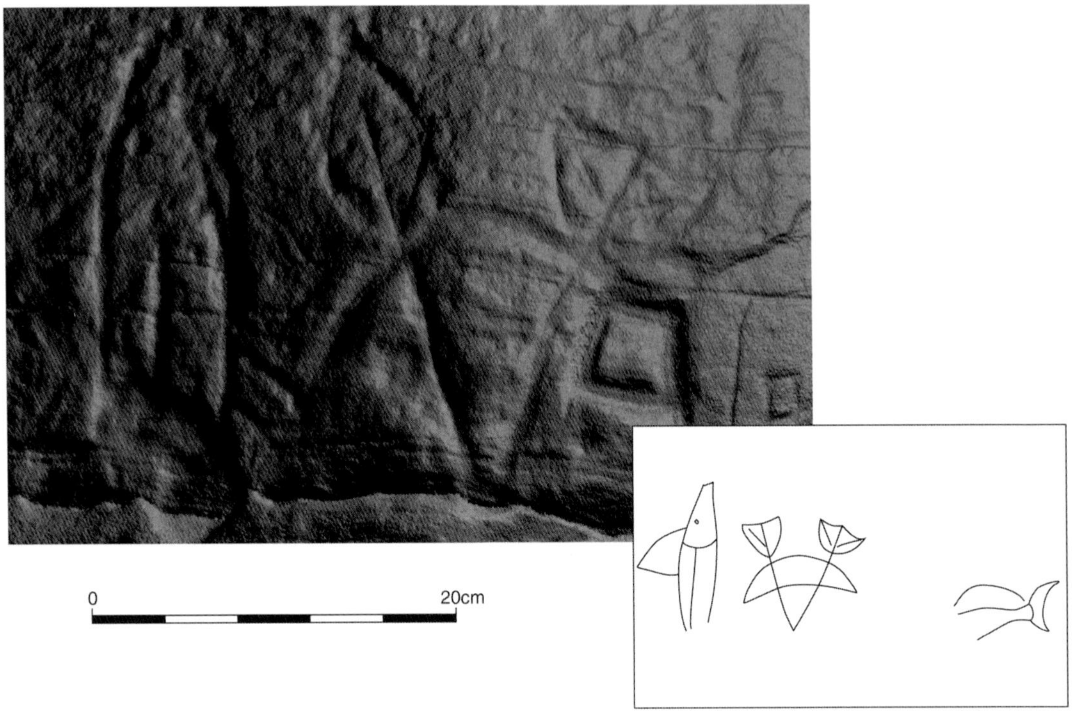


*Figure 5.5: A virtual RTI (Reflectance Transformation Imaging) rendering, from structured light scan data, of the paired fish and 'crescent and V-rod' symbols on the east wall of the East Passage of the Sculptor's Cave. Courtesy Fragmented Heritage and Bradford Visualisation, University of Bradford; inset: the same motifs (with additional fish symbol) redrawn from Stuart (1867, pl. 37).*

### *Fish and crescent and V-rod (Fig. 5.5)*

The first group of symbols encountered on entering the cave through the East Passage are two fish motifs bracketing a crescent and V-rod. The northernmost fish symbol is vertical, while the southernmost lies in the more common horizontal position.

The fish, the only animal motif amongst the Sculptor's Cave carvings, is one of the more common creatures represented in the corpus of Pictish symbols, featuring 14 times on Class I stones (Hicks 1993, 196) and occurring widely across eastern Scotland, from Caithness to Angus (Alcock 1988, 18). Only the top half of the vertical fish at the Sculptor's Cave is visible. Although the lower part may have been lost to erosion, it could be intended to depict a salmon in the act of leaping from the water. It is also worth noting that the unusual beak-shaped nose is suggestive of a bottlenose dolphin, still observed along the Moray coast today. The position of the fins, however, suggests that a salmon is the more likely interpretation.

The crescent and V-rod is relatively common in the repertoire of Pictish carvings, occurring on more than 20 symbol stones (Foster 2004, 71). The leaf-shaped terminals of the V-rod motif have led to its interpretation as a broken arrow, though others would prefer to see V-rods as representing sceptres, based on comparison with depictions in illuminated early medieval manuscripts such as the *Book of Kells* (Stevenson 1993, 17). In the Sculptor's Cave example, the lower right portion of the crescent has been damaged by later carving. The V-rod features large stylised leaf-shaped terminals, but the intricate decoration which normally fills the associated crescent is absent. While this may be due to erosion, Alcock has argued that the simple, unfilled crescents are, in fact, typical of the earliest group of *ur*-symbols and reflect the early date of this example; potentially, according to Alcock (1996, 1), the fifth century. Unfilled crescents are rare on symbol stones, with only a few identified (e.g. Henderson and Henderson 2004, figs. 50, 86) from the very large corpus of this motif.

### *Crescent and V-rod, double rectangle, mirror cases and step symbol (Fig. 5.6)*

Two further crescent and V-rod motifs occur on the west wall of the West Passage and are associated with a double rectangle and two mirror case symbols. Both are simpler than those associated with the fish motifs on the east wall of the East Passage, since they comprise unfilled crescents and V-rods that lack elaborate terminals.

The double rectangle symbol contains a central keyhole-shaped depression – suggestive of a miniature version of a mirror case symbol. Visual comparison (supported by the structured light scan in Fig. 5.6) of this symbol with others in the cave indicates it was rendered with more deeply incised

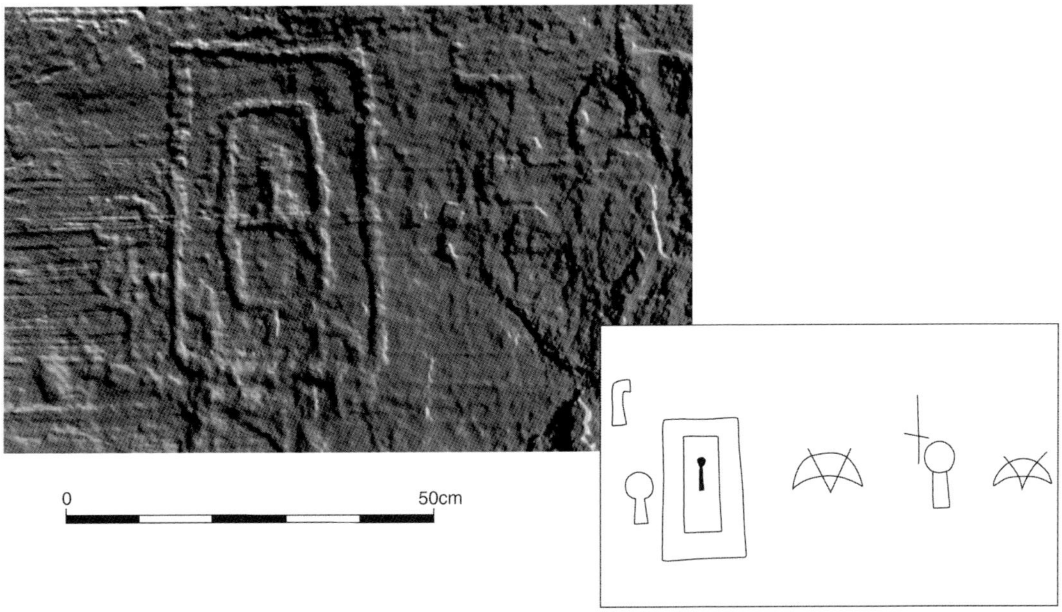


*Figure 5.6: A virtual RTI (Reflectance Transformation Imaging) rendering, from structured light scan data, of the paired double-rectangle and mirror/mirror case symbol (and partial crescent and V-rod) on the west wall of the West Passage of the Sculptor's Cave. Courtesy Fragmented Heritage and Bradford Visualisation; University of Bradford; inset: the same group of symbols (with additional mirror cases and crescents and V-rods) redrawn from Stuart (1867, pl. 37).*

lines, which could indicate some form of re-cutting after initial carving. The rectangle motif is uncommon but does occur at Wemyss Caves (see below), although the internal decoration is somewhat different from that of the Sculptor's Cave example. Rectangle symbols have sometimes been interpreted as shields (Ritchie 1969; Fraser 2008, 36), as worn, for example, by Pictish warriors on the stone from the Brough of Birsay, Orkney (Henderson and Henderson 2004, 65, fig. 78). Other interpretations are certainly possible, however; these motifs may represent books or perhaps specifically the Bible (Samson 1992, 40). Though Fraser (2008, 122) describes the figures on the cross slab from Fowlis Wester, Perth and Kinross, as holding shields, it appears in this example that at least one of the rectangular objects is a book satchel. Alternatively, the double rectangle at the Sculptor's Cave could represent a door, in which case it may have served as a metaphorical link between two worlds.

To the south of the double rectangle, above one of the mirror case symbols, is an enigmatic step motif. Like the double rectangle, this is not a common Pictish symbol.

### *Crescents (and V-rods), horseshoe and mirror case (Fig. 5.7)*

Another two examples of the crescent (one with V-rod and one without) occur with a horseshoe symbol and further mirror case motif on the east wall outside the West Entrance. A further crescent (without V-rod) also occurs below this central crescent. The horseshoe symbol is rare in the Pictish corpus, yet appears both in the Sculptor's Cave and in Court Cave, Caiplie, Fife (Fraser 2008, 66). To the south of the horseshoe lies a small symbol represented by three vertical lines joined by a single horizontal crossbar.

### *Flower and triple oval (Fig. 5.8)*

On the canopy of rock above and between the two entrance passages is an enigmatic 'flower' symbol, which lies immediately west of a triple oval symbol. In general terms, the flower is a highly stylised motif and essentially comprises a curvilinear frond, occasionally embellished with secondary fronds (as in the Sculptor's Cave example), and often includes internal decoration. Although not one of the most common Pictish symbols, the flower is distributed reasonably widely on Class I stones from Angus to the Western Isles, usually in association with a range of other symbols. It also appears in the corpus of carvings at Wemyss Caves, Fife (Fraser 2008, cat. no. 81.2). While Laing and Laing (1984, 268) have suggested that the Pictish flower symbol has its origins in stylised plant iconography on Roman artefacts, such as a fourth-century AD silver dish from Corbridge, others note that the form of the symbol is 'hardly botanical' (Thomas 1963, 57). A range of rather speculative interpretations have included its identification as some form of wooden churn or 'sprinkler' (Brodie 1996, 24), or even the hindquarters of a seal (Thomas 1963, 57). Perhaps the most convincing interpretation is by Thomas (1963), who suggests that the symbol probably belongs to the group of motifs portraying metal objects, in this

*Figure 5.7: Photograph of the crescents (and 'V-rods') and 'mirror case' in 1979. Illustration: Shepherd archive; inset: the same group of symbols (with additional crescent) redrawn from Stuart (1867, pl. 37).*

case perhaps an archaic form of a bronze harness mount (cf. Fox 1958, 130 and pl. 75), although the resemblances are hardly strong.

The triple oval symbol comprises, as the name suggests, three identical vertical ellipses in a horizontal line. Unlike many other examples, the ellipses here are void of internal decoration. The triple oval has been interpreted as representing an armlet of the 'massive metalwork' tradition (e.g. Thomas 1963, 57), though Hunter (2006, 150) suggests that this is unlikely based on the 'marginal resemblance' and very different geographical distributions of the two phenomena.

### *Triple oval, rectangles with concave sides and notched rectangle (Fig. 5.9)*

A second example of the triple oval symbol occurs high on the east wall of the West Passage. As with the triple oval symbol on the overhang outside the cave entrance (Fig. 5.8), this motif is formed of pointed ellipses without internal decoration. This triple oval symbol is however associated with two rare symbols, each comprising a pair of concave parallel lines. Although rare, this motif is depicted (horizontally rather than vertically, as in the Sculptor's Cave) on a symbol stone from Kintore (3), Aberdeenshire (Fraser 2008, 28) and, in more elaborate, form on a stone from Dairy Park, Dunrobin, Sutherland (Henderson and Henderson 2004, fig. 71).

A small rectangle with one concave or notched side lies immediately north of the smaller of the two rectangles with concave sides, and the possible remains of another symbol can be seen immediately below the larger of the two double crescents; superficially, the latter appears similar to the leaf-shaped terminal of a V-rod, though upside down.

### *Pentacles (Fig. 5.10)*

Two pentacles occur in close juxtaposition, high on the west wall of the East Passage. The northernmost is depicted by Allen and Anderson (1903, fig. 135a) as containing a central dot, though this feature is absent in recordings of the carvings by both Stuart (1867, pl. 37) and RCAHMS (2011). Pentacles are not included in what is usually regarded as the formal repertoire of Pictish motifs but are nonetheless accepted as Pictish by most authorities (e.g. Thomas 1961, 24). A pentacle occurs, for example, alongside other crudely rendered Pictish symbols on a small pebble from the Broch of Burrian, North Ronaldsay (Fraser 2008, 139). Alcock (1996) also considered pentacles as part of his original *ur*-symbol repertoire, albeit a motif that did not become established in the more formalised corpus featured on the Class I symbol stones.

## Other caves with Pictish symbols

The Sculptor's Cave is highly unusual in its association with Pictish carvings, since only a few other cave sites are currently known to contain them. One is the Clashach Cove, a natural sea arch (though probably formerly a cave) approximately 1.5km west of the Sculptor's Cave, which contains a single, heavily eroded crescent and V-rod

*Figure 5.8: A virtual RTI (Reflectance Transformation Imaging) rendering, from structured light scan data, of the paired 'flower' and triple oval symbols on the canopy of the rock between the two entrance passages at the Sculptor's Cave. Courtesy Fragmented Heritage and Bradford Visualisation; University of Bradford. These symbols were not recorded by Stuart (1867).*

(Fraser 2008, 106). Two of the Caiplie caves in Fife each contain a single symbol: a horseshoe in the East Cave, and a Z-rod overlying an unidentifiable symbol, obscured by later superimposed crosses, in the Chapel Cave (Fraser 2008, 66). On the west coast of Scotland, simple animal motifs are found among the Iron Age or early medieval carvings at the King's Cave, Arran (e.g. Thomas 1961, 23) but characteristic Pictish symbols are absent.

Most important, however, is the Wemyss Caves complex in Fife (Ritchie and Stevenson 1993; Gibson and Stevens 2007), which comprises 12 sea caves cut into a 2km stretch of sandstone cliffs on the north coast of the Firth of Forth. The name 'Wemyss' is a derivative of the Gaelic *uiams*, meaning 'caves'. Five of the caves (Jonathan's Cave, Michael's Cave (now collapsed), Court Cave, Western Doo Cave and Sliding Cave) contained Pictish carvings when documented by James Young Simpson in 1866 (cited in Gibson and Stevens 2007, 91). Jonathan's Cave contains

*Figure 5.9: Photograph of a) triple oval; b) double-crescent, notched rectangle and previously unrecorded 'leaf-shaped' symbol. Illustration: Shepherd archive. These symbols were not recorded by Stuart (1867).*

by far the most symbols and has, like the Sculptor's Cave, two entrances (Gibson and Stevens 2007, 96).

The symbols represented in the Wemyss Caves encompass a broader range than those at the Sculptor's Cave, and include a number of the more conventional Pictish motifs, e.g. the 'Pictish beast', fish, serpent, Z-rod, sun, comb case and double disc. The Wemyss Caves also, like the Sculptor's Cave, contain less common motifs that are not represented on Pictish symbol stones. Jonathan's Cave, for example, features the earliest depiction of an oared vessel in Britain, assuming, as seems likely, that it dates to the same period as the other carvings (Ritchie and Stevenson 1993).

*Figure 5.10: Photograph of two pentacles on the west wall of the East Passage at the Sculptor's Cave. Illustration: Shepherd archive; insets: the same symbols redrawn from Stuart (1867, pl. 37).*

One specific parallel between the Sculptor's Cave and Wemyss Caves is the occurrence at both sites of the unusual rectangle motif. At Wemyss the motif occurs in Sliding Cave, though unlike that in the Sculptor's Cave, it comprises a single rectangle with internal decoration (Ritchie and Stevenson 1993, 207, fig. 25.7). Ritchie and Stevenson (1993, 205) suggest that these rectangular symbols represent shields, as portrayed on several of the symbol stones (see above). Interestingly, at both sites the rectangle motif is more deeply incised than any of the other symbols (see Fig. 5.6).

As at the Sculptor's Cave, evidence for contemporary Pictish activities within the Wemyss Caves is scant. Limited excavations have revealed Iron Age activity in and around Well Cave and Sliding Cave, while two medieval inhumations have been found outside Jonathan's Cave (Gibson and Stevens 2007, 92), suggesting a long sequence of human activity. The specific role of the cave complex at any given time is, however, unclear.

## Discussion

The Sculptor's Cave and the Wemyss Caves represent unusual contexts for Pictish symbols, which are much more commonly found on free-standing stone monuments or portable objects. Other kinds of early medieval carvings do, however, occur in a number of Scottish caves outside Pictland, such as those previously described at the King's Cave, Arran. Although differing in the type and range of symbols represented, this phenomenon clearly reflects shared underlying beliefs and practices in relation to caves in early medieval Scotland.

Caves have always been special places in the landscape; liminal places representing the interface between the everyday world of the living and the Otherworld of gods, ancestors or supernatural beings (e.g. Moyes 2012). It is notable that caves containing Pictish symbols appear to lack any other evidence for early medieval activities, though, as at the Sculptor's Cave, they may have been a focus for earlier ritual. The creation of complex carvings around cave entrances may have been viewed as a means of sealing these conduits to the underworld, or as warnings to the unwary. Despite the similarities between the Sculptor's Cave and Wemyss Caves, the specific reasons for carving symbols can only be understood in the context of individual cave biographies. In the case of the Sculptor's Cave, the date of the symbols is potentially significant.

The problems involved in dating Pictish symbols have already been discussed. This is not easy when it comes to symbol stones, but it is even more difficult for the few incidences of symbols carved on cave walls. The relatively early origin for the symbols proposed by Thomas (1963) and others seems highly likely. Alcock (1996) placed the Sculptor's Cave carvings among his assemblage of *ur*-symbols, which he saw as ancestral to the formalised repertoire later found on the symbol stones. The Wemyss Caves carvings are also included in this group (see below), as is a curious collection of simple 'plaques' from an inaccessible sea-stack at Dunnicaer in Aberdeenshire (Alcock and Alcock 1992, 276–282), and certain symbols carved on portable objects, such as the small stone from Pool in Orkney (J. Hunter 2007, 99). Alcock's (1996) *ur*-symbols share a number of features including: a lack of decorative infilling; the presence of non-canonical symbols (such as the pentacle and triangle) and associations (such as an equilateral triangle in place of the expected V-rod on one of the symbols from Dunnicaer); and symbols with central dots (as present in an early recording of one of the pentacles from the Sculptor's Cave (Allen and Anderson 1903, fig. 135a) and several symbols from Dunnicaer and the Wemyss Caves). Although one cannot be certain about the date of *ur*-symbols, Alcock's (1996) assertion that they pre-date symbol stones, and the early stratigraphic date for the symbols at Pool, suggest that, if they do indeed belong to this group, the Sculptor's Cave examples probably date no later than the sixth century, and potentially even a few centuries earlier.

If we follow Samson (1992) in taking the pairs of symbols to denote personal names, then some of the symbols in the Sculptor's Cave might be taken to commemorate individuals. These would potentially include the fish/crescent and V-rod; the flower/triple oval; rectangles with concave sides/triple oval; mirror case/crescent and V-rod; and (based on closest juxtaposition) double rectangle/mirror case. Many of the symbols (including some of those cited above), however, occur singly or in scattered groups and thus break the semantic 'rules' elucidated by Samson (1992, 40–41). This is not necessarily surprising, as Samson's interpretation relates specifically to the meaning of the stones, rather than necessarily all contexts in which symbols appear. Furthermore, if Alcock's (1996) identification of the Sculptor's Cave carvings as *ur*-symbols is correct, then we should not expect them necessarily to be used in the same way as the later, formalised repertoire. Nonetheless, it is not impossible that at least some of the symbols carved around the entrance to the Sculptor's Cave represent specific, named individuals.

In this respect, the earlier use of the cave for highly distinctive and visible mortuary rites cannot be overlooked. The overtly ritualised nature of the death (Roman Iron Age) and display (Late Bronze Age) of individuals at the cave, together with the quantity and quality of material culture deposited (e.g. Late Bronze Age gold-covered hair-rings and several hundred Roman Iron Age coins) must presumably have been recognised. Whilst the specific nature of the Late Bronze Age mortuary practices may not have been evident to Pictish visitors, remains of Roman Iron Age activities may well have been visible. The human bones seen on the cave floor by Benton (1931, 176) were probably equally evident in the Pictish period. It may even have been that they were familiar with, and recognised, indicators of decapitation. Though little is known of the folkloric tradition of the Picts, scant contemporary evidence survives in Anglo-Saxon and Scandinavian sources that attests to the continued perception of caves as liminal places closely connected with the Otherworld (e.g. Gummere 2001; Semple 2013, 72); this must only have added to the ritually-charged nature of the cave. The names of those decapitated during the Roman Iron Age may even have been remembered through story, myth or genealogy and then represented in the Pictish carvings. If the Roman Iron Age decapitations represent a single event of political and/or religious significance, then the circumstances of this group's demise may have been well known.

The Pictish power base at Burghead, *c.* 6km west of the Sculptor's Cave, appears to have been built between the fourth and sixth centuries AD (Harding 2004, 248). It is not inconceivable, then, that the decapitations in the cave during the third century relate to the factional conflicts that ultimately resulted in the establishment of this key centre of Pictish power. The Pictish period was certainly no less politically turbulent than the preceding sub-Roman period, and it may be that those who now occupied positions of power wished to commemorate their fallen political or genealogical allies.

## Conclusion

The symbols at the Sculptor's Cave may have been carved simply to mark an important and long-venerated gateway to the underworld; a known place of religious and cosmological power, associated with the dead and the ancestors. The carvings may even have had a magical or religious role, in ritually sealing the cave and preventing incursions between the two worlds. If the double rectangle symbol is interpreted as a Bible, then perhaps the symbols pre-figure the later crosses, marking some early attempt to Christianise a dark and pagan place. Alternatively, the symbols may have had a rather more specific purpose as memorials to the dead; perhaps to specific lineage founders known or thought to have died there. In this sense, the Sculptor's Cave could have been transformed, through the deployment of symbols, from a liminal place inappropriate for the proper burial of a political elite, to a formal and properly demarcated funerary site. In this manner, a previously hidden and 'forgotten' group may (even in death) have been recognised, remembered and reintegrated into the Pictish political sphere.

## Acknowledgements

The *Sculptor's Cave Publication Project* (2014–2017) is funded by Historic Environment Scotland. All original illustrations were produced by Rachael Kershaw, University of Bradford. Scanning and processing of the carvings was undertaken by Adrian Evans, Tom Sparrow and Rachael Kershaw, courtesy of Fragmented Heritage and Bradford Visualisation, University of Bradford. Thanks to Hugh Brown and John Buchannan at Gordonstoun School for access permission; Kevin Rutherford for access assistance; The Moray Society, Elgin Museum and Janet Trythall for allowing and facilitating scanning of the Burghead symbol stone; and John Borland for providing information on the RCAHMS survey of the Sculptor's Cave carvings. The authors would also like to thank Andrew Wilson, Chris Gaffney and Randolph Donahue for their assistance with digitisation aspects of the work, and Bruce Mann at Aberdeenshire Council for his assistance with the fieldwork elements.

## References


Alcock, E., 1988. Pictish stones Class I: where and how? *Glasgow Archaeological Journal* 15, 1–21.

Alcock, L., 1996. *Ur*-symbols in the pictograph-system of the Picts. *Pictish Arts Society Journal* 9, 2–5.

Alcock, L. and Alcock, E.A., 1992. Reconnaissance excavations on Early Historic fortifications and other royal sites in Scotland, 1974–84; 5: A, Excavations & other fieldwork at Forteviot, Perthshire, 1981; B, Excavations at Urquhart Castle, Inverness-shire, 1983; C, Excavations at Dunnottar, Kincardineshire, 1984. *Proceedings of the Society of Antiquaries of Scotland* 122, 215–287.

Allen, J.R. and Anderson, J., 1903. *The Early Christian Monuments of Scotland: A Classified Illustrated Descriptive List of the Monuments with an Analysis of their Symbolism and Ornamentation (Pt 3)*. Edinburgh: Society of Antiquaries of Scotland/Neill & Co.

Armit, I., Schulting, R., Knüsel, C.J. and Shepherd, I.A.G., 2011. Death, decapitation and display? The Bronze and Iron Age human remains from the Sculptor's Cave, Covesea, North-east Scotland. *Proceedings of the Prehistoric Society* 77, 251–278.

Armit, I. and Büster, L., *in press*. *Darkness Visible: Later Prehistoric Ritual and Identity at the Sculptor's Cave, North-East Scotland*. Edinburgh: Society of Antiquaries of Scotland.

Benton, S., 1931. The excavation of the Sculptor's Cave, Covesea, Morayshire. *Proceedings of the Society of Antiquaries of Scotland* 65, 177–216.

Brodie, J., 1996. Ancient pictorial carvings on stones in Scotland – some observations on their meaning. *Pictish Arts Society Journal* 9, 21–28.

Carver, M., 2008. *Portmahomack: Monastery of the Picts*. Edinburgh: Edinburgh University Press.

Foster, S., 2004. *Picts, Gaels and Scots*. London: B. T. Batsford/Historic Scotland.

Fox, C., 1958. *Pattern and Purpose: A Survey of Early Celtic Art in Britain*. Cardiff: The National Museum of Wales.

Fraser, I., ed., 2008. *The Pictish Symbol Stones of Scotland*. Edinburgh: Royal Commission on the Ancient and Historical Monuments of Scotland.

Fraser, J.E., 2009. *From Caledonia to Pictland. Scotland to 795*. Edinburgh: Edinburgh University Press.

Gibson, C. and Stevens, S., 2007. Iron Age and Pictish activity at Wemyss Caves, Fife. *Tayside and Fife Archaeological Journal* 13, 91–99.

Graham-Campbell, J., 1993. The Norrie's Law hoard and the dating of Pictish art. *In*: R.M. Spearman and J. Higgitt, eds. *The Age of Migrating Ideas: Early Medieval Art in Northern Britain and Ireland*. Edinburgh–Stroud: National Museums of Scotland/Alan Sutton Publishing Ltd, 115–127.

Gummere, F. B., transl., 2001. *Beowulf*. Vol. XLIX, Part 1. The Harvard Classics. New York: P.F. Collier & Son.

Harding, D.W., 2004. *The Iron Age in Northern Britain: Celts and Romans, Natives and Invaders*. London: Routledge.

Henderson, G. and Henderson, I.M., 2004. *The Art of the Picts: Sculpture and Metalwork in Early Medieval Scotland*. London: Thames and Hudson.

Hicks, C., 1993. The Pictish class I animals. *In*: R.M. Spearman and J. Higgitt, eds. *The Age of Migrating Ideas: Early Medieval Art in Northern Britain and Ireland*. Edinburgh–Stroud: National Museums of Scotland/Alan Sutton Publishing Ltd, 196–202.

Hunter, F. 2006. New light on Iron Age massive armlet. *Proceedings of the Society of Antiquaries of Scotland* 136, 135–160.

Hunter, F., 2007. *Beyond the Edge of Empire – Caledonians, Picts and Romans*. Rosemarkie: Groam House Museum.

Hunter, J., 2007. *Investigations in Sanday, Orkney: Excavations at Pool, Sanday – A Multi-Period Settlement from Neolithic to Late Norse. Volume 1*. Orcadian: Kirkwall.

Keillar, I., 1969. Covesea, Parish of Duffus, Caves. *Discovery and Excavation in Scotland* 1969, 34.

Laing, L. and Laing, J., 1984. The date and origin of the Pictish symbols. *Proceedings of the Society of Antiquaries of Scotland* 114, 261–276.

Montgomery, J., Knüsel, C., and Tucker, K., 2011. Identifying the origins of decapitated male skeletons from 3 Driffield Terrace, York through Isotope Analysis: reflections of the cosmopolitan nature of Roman York. *In*: M. Bonogofsky, ed. *The Bioarchaeology of the Human Head: Decapitation, Decoration and Deformation*. Gainesville, FL: University of Florida Press, 141–178.

Moyes, H., ed., 2012. *Sacred Darkness: A Global Perspective on the Ritual Use of Caves*. Boulder, CO: University Press of Colorado.

Ritchie, J.N.G., 1969. Shields in North Britain in the Iron Age. *Scottish Archaeological Forum* 1, 31–40.

Ritchie, J.N.G. and Stevenson, J.N., 1993. Pictish cave art at East Wemyss, Fife. *In*: R.M. Spearman and J. Higgitt, eds. *The Age of Migrating Ideas: Early Medieval Art in Northern Britain and Ireland*. Stroud: Alan Sutton Publishing Ltd, 203–208.

RCAHMS (The Royal Commission on the Ancient and Historical Monuments of Scotland). 2011. *Sculptor's Cave, Covesea, Plan and Sections SC1256010*. Available from: http://canmore.rcahms.gov.uk/en/site/16278/digital_images/sculptor+s+cave+covesea/ [accessed 23 February 2013].

Samson, R., 1992. The reinterpretation of the Pictish symbols. *Journal of the British Archaeological Association* 145, 29–65.

Semple, S. 2013. *Perceptions of the Prehistoric in Anglo-Saxon England: Religion, Ritual and Rulership in the Landscape*. Oxford: Oxford University Press.

Shepherd, I.A.G., 1993. The Picts in Moray. *In*: W.D.H. Sellar, ed. *Moray: Province and People*. Edinburgh: Scottish Society for Northern Studies, 75–90.

Shepherd, I.A.G., 2007. 'An awesome place'. The Late Bronze Age use of the Sculptor's Cave, Covesea, Moray. *In*: C. Burgess, P. Topping, and F. Lynch, eds. *Beyond Stonehenge: Essays in the Bronze Age on Honour of Colin Burgess*. Oxford: Oxbow Books, 194–203.

Shepherd, I.A.G. and Shepherd, A.M., 1979. Sculptor's Cave, Covesea (Drainie), Occupational/Ritual Site. *Discovery and Excavation in Scotland* 1979, 14.

Stevenson, R.B.K., 1993. Further thoughts on some well known problems. *In*: R.M. Spearman and J. Higgitt, eds. *The Age of Migrating Ideas*: *Early Medieval Art in Northern Britain and Ireland*. Edinburgh–Stroud: National Museums of Scotland/Alan Sutton Publishing Ltd, 17–26.

Stuart, J., 1867. *The Sculptured Stones of Scotland*. Edinburgh: The Spalding Club.

Thomas, C., 1961. Animal art in the Scottish Iron Age and its origins. *Archaeological Journal* 118, 14–64.

Thomas, C., 1963. The interpretation of the Pictish symbols. *Archaeological Journal* 120, 31–97.

# Chapter 6

# Marking caves in Scotland and Iceland: characterising an early medieval phenomenon

*Kristján Ahronson*

*Early medieval religious impulse marked hundreds of special places with simple sculpture across the Irish and Scottish littoral zone. In Scotland, marking caves with rock-cut early Christian carvings was a discrete subset within a wider early medieval monastic tradition. Looking to Iceland, we discover a similar phenomenon. Recent research identifies what appears to be the earliest human presence on the island at, and in the immediate vicinity of, a cave site, around AD 800. Detailed analysis of the sculpture suggests that the Scottish and Icelandic phenomena are connected.*

## Introduction

Those of Scotland's caves marked with early Christian sculpture are, on the one hand, a subset of wider cave use in Britain and Ireland, and on the other hand, a subset of a broader early medieval monastic tradition of placing sculpted stones and carving simple rock-cut sculpture at hundreds of early Christian sites. This broader monastic tradition was productive from the sixth to ninth centuries, with the vast majority of such sculpture on the island of Iona, for instance, likely pre-dating the Viking age (Thomas 1971, 112; Campbell 1987, 112; Fisher 2001, 10–11). As Ian Fisher puts it: 'the simple crosses associated with this ascetic monasticism extend … from Loch Lomond to St Kilda … [and provide] the most widespread, indeed at most sites the only physical evidence of early Christianity in western Scotland' (Fisher 2001, 1). Inter-disciplinary survey suggests that the presence of early Christian motifs in Scottish caves indicates places for seclusion rather than isolation (see below). In contrast, southern Iceland's nearly 200 artificial caves have, remarkably, been little-studied. Set against this background, detailed research at the cross-marked Seljaland caves (Vestur-Eyjafjallahreppur, south Iceland) has identified a number of typological parallels with sculpture across the Irish and Scottish littoral zone, and indicates particular connections with early medieval monastic sites in western Scotland. Using tephrochronology, human activity has been identified in the late eighth to early ninth centuries at the Seljaland caves as well as in the local environment, with possible indications of woodland clearance and the introduction of domesticated non-indigenous herbivores. Particular care should be taken when interpreting these results, however, as they suggest what may be the earliest human activities yet discovered in Iceland at *c*. AD 800.

## Scotland's marked caves

Within a British context, cave sites with early Christian sculptural motifs have long been recognised to have a northern distribution, specifically in Scotland and its islands (Ahronson and Charles-Edwards 2010). We owe this realisation to the innovative work of some of archaeology's key nineteenth-century thinkers. Daniel Wilson, for instance, proposed that some of Scotland's caves were, 'the retreats which the primitive confessors of Scotland excavated or enlarged for their oratories or cells' (Wilson 1851, 89), and James Young Simpson observed that, 'we have various alleged instances of caves being thus employed as anchorite or devotional cells, and some of them still show rudely-cut altars, crosses &c' (Simpson 1859, 522). As a consequence of this and subsequent work in Scotland, it has been tempting to identify cave use as a phenomenon or practice associated with early medieval 'northern' Christianity; however, we should be wary of such an interpretation. As Thomas Charles-Edwards and I have argued elsewhere (Ahronson and Charles-Edwards 2010), a survey including medieval literature indicates a more extensive distribution for early medieval cave use in Britain. Thus, though references in medieval literature are limited, we can nonetheless recognise that descriptions of monastic cave use are sparse across insular Britain. Granted that the *Miracula Nynie Episcopi* describes St. Ninian's devoted studies in south-west Scotland 'in a cave of horrible blackness' (MacQueen and MacQueen 2005, 101), but we should also look at how the *Annals of the Four Masters* describe early medieval ascetics in Ireland betaking themselves, 'to caves, natural or artificial, and using them for their houses and oratories' (Simpson 1859, 522). Instead, and more precisely, it is the marking of these caves with distinctive early Christian sculptural motifs that appears to be an aspect of 'northern' Christianity. In other words, the early medieval use of British cave sites by early Christian communities is described in medieval literature, but it is a subset of this practice, namely the marking of these sites with sculpture, that appears to be distinct to early Christian northern Britain. Well-known examples of such marked caves in the west of Scotland include, for example, St Columba's Cave with its rock-cut crosses and altar on the shore of Loch Caolisport; St Ciaran's Cave with its elaborate marigold-carved boulder on the east coast of Kintyre; Nun's Cave and Scoor Cave with their many rock-cut crosses on the Ross of Mull; and St Molaise's Cave with its numerous rock-cut early medieval crosses and thirteenth-century Norse runic inscriptions and graffito crosses on Holy Island, off Arran (Fisher 2001, 4).

Late Antique and medieval literature provides valuable insights into understanding this northern distribution. For instance, analysis of surviving early medieval sculpture, such as the Nigg cross slab, suggests that Jerome's St Paul had some popularity in northern Britain (Mowbray 1936), and literature tells us that his eremitical life was spent in what was called a cave (Migne 1844-1864, ch. 5, cols. 20–21). Generally, seclusion appears to be the dominant theme. In the *Life of St Samson*, the saint withdraws to a cave on two distinct occasions (Taylor 1991 [1925], 42–43, 50–52; Flobert 1997, 204–206). In both stories his cave usage is part of a two-step disengagement from the world. On the first occasion, Samson and three companions leave his monastery of Ynys Bŷr to find a place of seclusion near the Severn; then he leaves his companions to wander through the woods to a large and 'very lonely cave'. On the second occasion, Samson triumphs over a serpent in its cave in Cornwall, then takes over the cave as an ascetic satellite settlement to the nearby monastery which he orders his men to build (Taylor 1991 [1925], 42–43, 50–52; Flobert 1997, 204–206).

Along similar lines, the anonymous *Life of St Cuthbert* describes the hermitage on Farne Island and how the saint put devils, 'to flight' and then dug down through 'very hard and stony rock, he made a space to dwell in … from which he could see nothing except the heavens above' (Colgrave 1940, 96–97). Felix's *Life of St Guthlac* carries an echo of this in that it provides an account of the saint improving a hole dug into a mound by treasure hunters, by 'building a hut over it' and then how he 'began to dwell' there (Colgrave 1956, 92–95). A common idea has been that remote and inaccessible cave sites were favoured for early Christian activity and that cave use may be understood in this context (see for instance Wilson 1851 and Simpson 1859). Certainly, a wider monastic impulse for isolation seems to be associated with extreme 'desert places in the ocean' (Fisher 1994, 35–36, 2001, 1; O'Loughlin 1997, 11–23), such as the very small Atlantic island of North Rona, 70km north-north-east of the island of Lewis and north-west of mainland Scotland. However, the aspect of monasticism associated with a desire for isolation is at odds with the cave-use literature touched upon here, which points to relative seclusion rather than isolation, and this is also suggested by analysis of the Royal Commission on the Ancient and Historical Monuments of Scotland's Historic Land Use Assessment data. For example, King's Cave on Arran, with its walls marked by early Christian sculpture, is located within an area of settlement and agriculture (0.5km from cultivation ridges by the shore) and is only 1.5km from a fortified site, the later prehistoric hillfort of Drumadoon (Fisher 2001, 65). The *Life of St Illtud* offers further nuance to this theme of seclusion (not isolation) from the violence of the world (Wade-Evans 1944, 220–227). With a local king fixed on killing him, Illtud flees from 'the excited people, who caused hindrance to his prayers' and took up life by the River Ewenni in a cave (Wade-Evans 1944, 221).

A further point is that rock-cut sculpture is not a feature of these stories, nor does rock-cut sculpture feature in caves with early Christian associations in Ireland and in parts of Britain outside Scotland. Thus we are reminded that the presence of sculpture is but one measure of early medieval monastic activity at a cave site, though one that conveniently provides both a chronological anchor and clearly identifies early Christian usage. Early medieval sculpture sites are generally associated with good arable land, which in Argyll tends to have a coastal distribution (Campbell 1987, 107); Early Medieval cave use appears to follow this pattern. Study of site distributions and locations, as well as National Museum of Scotland collections from caves, revealed that geology and the environs of a site clearly have a bearing on a cave's suitability for human use – and the coastal distribution mentioned above for Argyll is likely indicative of these factors (Ahronson *et al.* 2006). However, we have only a limited grasp of the range of criteria that determined the suitability of a cave site for Scotland's medieval populations generally, and for early

Christian communities specifically. We can nevertheless look to the National Monuments Record of Scotland for a broad indication of suitable caves for human use. Across Scotland 402 cave sites are listed in the National Monuments Record of Scotland. The greatest concentrations are in the west: more than half are located in Argyll and Bute. Most excavated sites with Iron Age or medieval phases were investigated in the late nineteenth and early twentieth centuries: 25 sites had potential Iron Age assemblages; 15 had potential early medieval assemblages; and 11 contained potential Norse/Hiberno-Norse assemblages. In line with general cross-period trends, there is also a west coast concentration of caves with early Christian associations, which correlates with descriptions in medieval literature as well as the area's rich contemporary sculptural tradition (e.g. Fisher 2001). Nonetheless, there are significant outliers beyond this region, such as the east coast Caiplie Caves in East Fife, discussed since the nineteenth century (e.g. Simpson 1865). In one study (Ahronson *et al.* 2006), we targeted eight west coast sites for detailed study, based on the presence or proximity of sculpture, including Bagh na h-Uamha on Rum, Uamh Righ on Jura, St Columba's Cave in Knapdale, St Ciaran's Cave and Keil Cave in Kintyre, St Molaise's Cave on Holy Island (off Arran), St Medan's Cave in the Rhins of Galloway and St Ninian's Cave near Whithorn (Fig. 6.1).

Analysis of the assemblages suggests certain trends for Scotland's early medieval cave use. Branigan and Dearne (1992) proposed models for cave use that included expected artefact characterisations, which they developed in order to investigate Romano–British sites. Their models are both temporal (permanent: high quantity, chronological continuity; episodic: low quantity, chronological discontinuity, possible pointers to seasonality) and functional (domestic occupation: cooking, storage and eating vessels, food debris, wide range of other artefacts; workshop: tools/moulds/waste/raw materials, unfinished or multiple products; shelter: few and random, food debris, but few cooking and storage vessels; shrine: absence of domestic assemblage, unusual groups/clusters or items, votives etc.; burial: human bones, personal jewellery, may be low amounts of pottery), and we sought to apply these classifications to our selected cave assemblages with early Christian associations.

There are, of course, difficulties in applying Romano-British models to our selected assemblages. For instance, large parts of western Scotland were largely aceramic within our chosen time-frame, therefore the presence of pottery would be a poor indicator of function, unlike for Roman Britain. Furthermore, older excavations employed a variety of techniques that did not favour good recovery of artefact assemblages and ecofacts. Chronology also presents its own problems. With older investigations, only a poor record of the stratification of archaeological deposits survives. Additionally, even supposedly secure analyses can be ripe for reinterpretation. For example, radiocarbon dating of 'early prehistoric' cave burials from Oban in Argyll has led to the discovery of a previously unidentified Iron Age phase of cave use (Saville and Hallén 1994). Artefact mobility within cave sediments is also a concern, exemplified at Keil Cave where fragments from a single bone comb were recovered from the top and bottom of the main cultural deposit (Ritchie 1968, 2002). We can, nonetheless, point to certain trends. In contrast with the Iron Age material, early Christian cave assemblages are small and restricted in scope. In general, the number and character of the excavated finds support Branigan and Dearne's model of religious and small-scale domestic usage, which chimes with the aforementioned literature-derived insights. One exception is the substantial multi-period collection from Keil Cave, which suggests the potential diversity of early medieval cave use in this region of Scotland.

Most of the cave sites we have been discussing have attracted scholarly attention from some of Britain's leading archaeologists since the nineteenth century, including the internationally important Wilson and Simpson, as well as nationally significant figures such as John Stuart (1856–1867, I and II, 41–44, 47, lxxxvii–xciv) and Joseph Anderson. In his 1880 Rhind Lecture on *Scotland in Early Christian Times*, Anderson paid special attention to the significance of early medieval cave sculpture (Anderson 1881, 183–187). And yet our understanding of the nature of the ritual expression suggested by the sculpture remains elusive. Within Britain, the marking of caves with rock-cut sculpture appears an impulse specific to northern Britain. How do we explain this local or regional impulse? On the one hand, early medieval Irish canon law sets out the critical importance of the cross symbol as well as the concept of hierarchies of sacred places (Wasserschleben 1885, 175, pl. xliv, 3 and 5). Furthermore, the use of simple cross-marked stones has been characterised as a new kind of monument use in order to mark out 'protected' spaces (Davies 1996), to identify holy ground and the Christian dead, or to indicate church landownership (Edwards 2001). We might also wonder about the extent to which this 'northern' tradition of marking caves is a survival of early pre-Christian practice. For instance, pre-Christian Pictish sculpture can be found decorating a number of Scotland's caves, including the Sculptor's Cave at Covesea (see Büster and Armit this volume) and the Caiplie Caves of East Fife. As mentioned earlier, the Caiplie Caves were studied by Simpson, where he noted:

> cave figures consist of animals, as the elephant, – exactly of the form seen on the Sculptured Stones [referring here to Stuart's *Sculptured Stones of Scotland*], – the deer, the dog, the swan, the peacock, fish, serpents, and monsters, a tripod, jar, &c., &c. … we see also representations of the mirror, comb, and arch or horse-shoe … [and] many specimens of

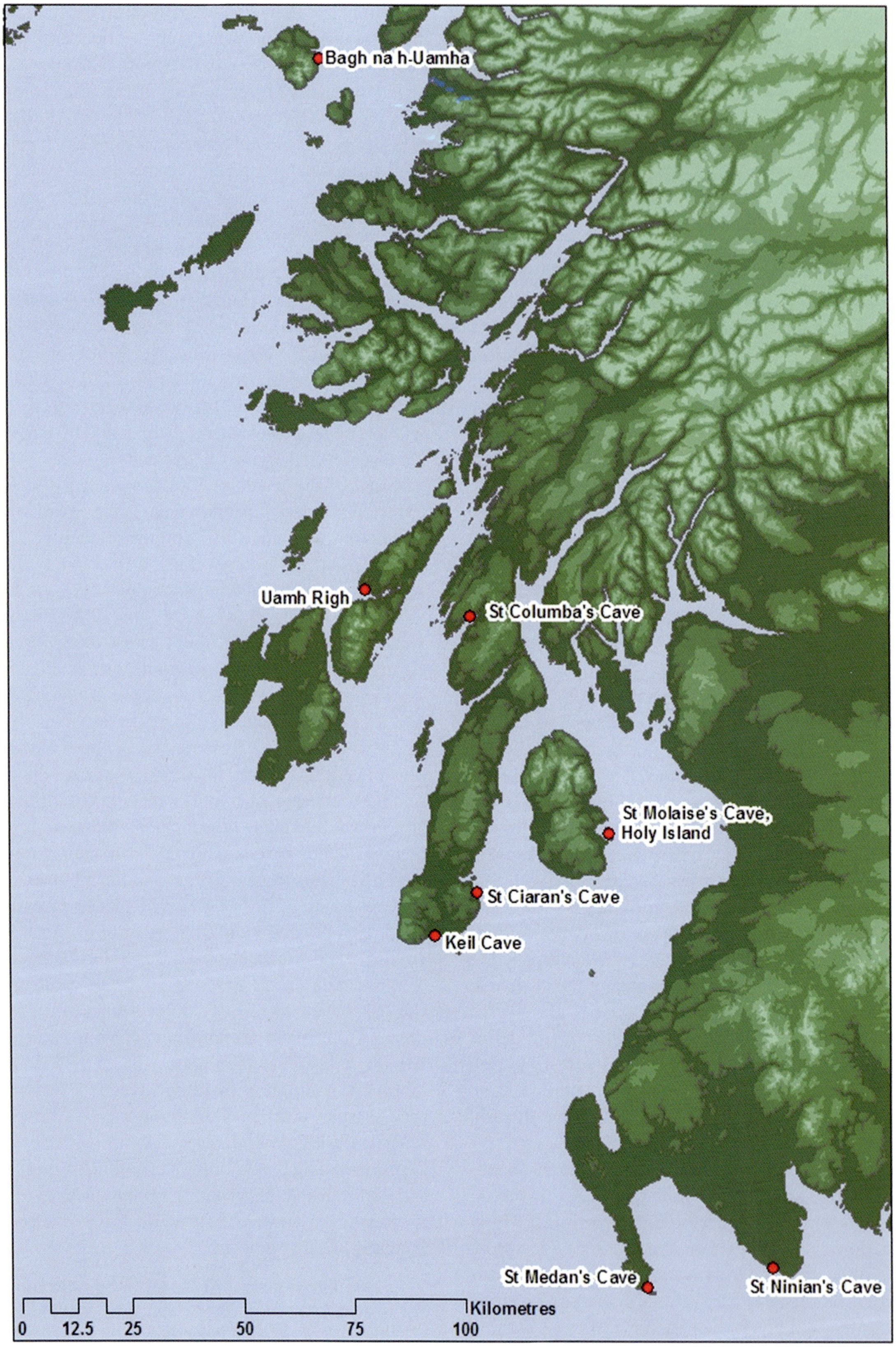


*Figure 6.1: Left: Selected cave sites on Scotland's west coast, based on the presence or proximity of early medieval sculpture. Locations derived from information held in the National Monuments Record of Scotland. Illustration prepared by S.M. Orr. Right: Sculpture carved into cave wall of the King's Cave, Arran. Not to scale, approximate dimensions of expanded terminal incised Latin cross: 1.05m × 0.57m (Stuart 1856–1867 vol ii pl. 36).*

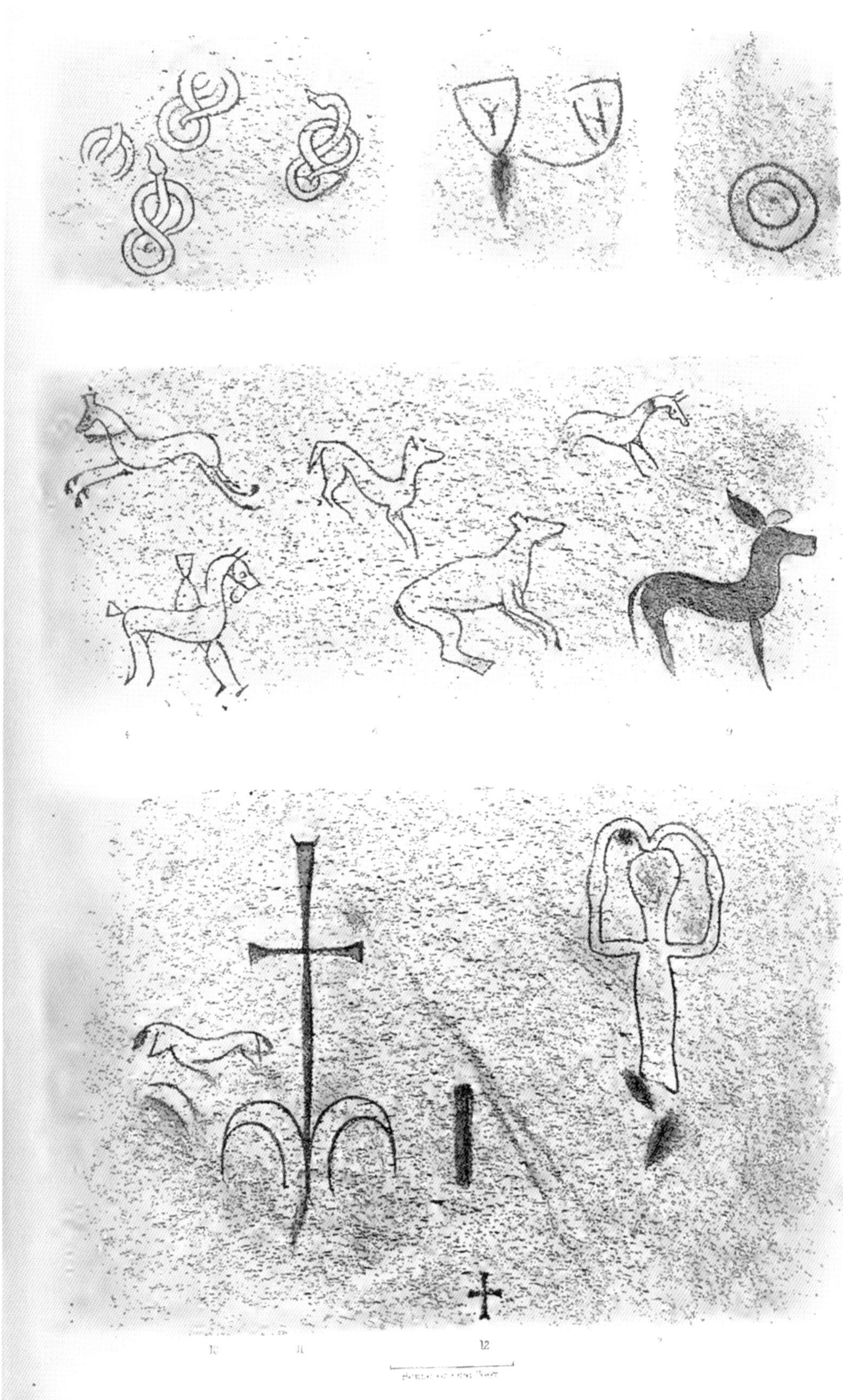

*Figure 6.1:* (Continued).

> the spectacle ornament are to be found on their walls with and without the intersecting Z sceptre (Simpson 1865, 137).

Simpson continued to record that there are also 'crosses of various forms' (1865, 137).

To what extent did this pre-Christian practice influence Scotland's early Christian tradition of marking caves? We might also consider the wider significance of the literature discussed earlier: Samson's triumph over the cave serpent in Cornwall, and how Cuthbert put devils 'to flight' and then dug down into the earth to make a space to dwell. Are we seeing here traces of an early Christian impulse to appropriate places of pagan ritual? Or are we dealing with an entirely early Christian phenomenon, drawing upon Mediterranean and Europe-wide impulses, to manifest within northern Britain's early medieval monastic communities – and only a coincidental occurrence with earlier pre-Christian usage of some cave sites? Whatever its origins, Scotland's early Christian cave sculpture seemingly marks sites for seclusion (and not for isolation), as suggested by the survey of late Antique and medieval literature above, and forms part of a discrete subset within a distinctive early medieval tradition that marked special or sacred places with simple sculpture. In this way, the cross-marked St Columba's Cave in Knapdale is part of a wider landscape of special places marked with simple early Christian sculpture, incorporating the neighbouring burial ground and possible chapel at Lochead, and the burial ground and enclosure at Cladh a'Bhile, Ellary (Fisher 2001, 141–143, 151).

## Iceland's marked caves

Looking north to southern Iceland's almost 200 artificial caves, we discover a similar phenomenon and enigma: some are marked by simple sculpture. These person-sized artificial caves have been cut into one of two lithologies: either palagonite tuff or soft sandstone, though we may note that the extreme concentration of caves in southern Iceland is not determined by the island's geology (Fig. 6.2). For instance, the Holocene lithology of south-eastern and north-eastern Iceland, where caves are rare or non-existent, is comparable in many ways to that of southern Iceland. In other words, the geology of those areas means that it would have been possible for people in south-eastern and north-eastern Iceland to have dug out artificial caves, but they did not. This distribution is noteworthy considering Branigan and Dearne's (1992, 38) suggestion that 'the distribution of utilised caves … broadly reflect the geology' and this certainly appears to have been the case in Scotland, with more than half of all sites located in Argyll and Bute where regional geology favours cave formation. However, there is no clear physical or cultural explanation for the discrete clustering of artificial caves in southern Iceland. One key difference is that in Iceland we are dealing with a constructed site type, rather than the Scottish use of natural caves (though often with some modification). These sites therefore present a tantalising problem: artificial caves are among Iceland's best preserved and most numerous surviving medieval structures, yet are some of the least understood, despite being sites of interest to pioneering figures in Icelandic archaeology. For example, over a century ago Brynjúlfur Jónsson posited that these caves may have been constructed by Irish-speaking peoples, previous to Iceland's Norse settlement:

> *Mér liggur við að efast um, að hellarnir séu frá Íslands bygðar tíma. Mundi ekki hugsanlegt, að þeir gæti verið eldri? Mér hefir dottið í hug, að þeir kunni, ef til vill, að vera eftir … hina Írsku men, sem hér voru fyrri en vorir norrænu feður* (Jónsson 1902, 29).

> I have begun to doubt whether these caves are from Iceland's [Norse] settlement period. Is it not conceivable that they could be older? It has occurred to me that they could have been made by … the Irish men who were here before our Norse fathers (Friðriksson 1994, 24).

Recent scholarship has focussed afresh on the process of Iceland's settlement by Viking-Age Scandinavians and their relationships across the Irish, British and north Atlantic islands with early medieval monastic communities of the 'Irish school' (called *papar* in later Norse literature). And, given that the shelter provided by human constructions, such as pithouses, longhouses or caves, is key to the survival of people in Iceland, cave buildings are long overdue in-depth study. A critical question is *when* artificial caves were constructed. Intriguingly, Icelandic cave use is described in early literature about medieval Scandinavia. Though fantastical in places, Adam of Bremen noted that Icelanders 'live in underground caves, glad to have roof and food and bed in common with their cattle' (Schmeidler 1917, 272; Tschan 1959, 217). Given Adam of Bremen's account, added to the evidence that caves played a role in early medieval British and Irish society, Jónsson's thoughts on the potential antiquity of Iceland's cave sites warrants careful consideration. The Seljalandshellar caves at Seljaland (Fig. 6.3) are of particular interest in this regard, with their three distinct chambers, chimney and 105 cross carvings on the surviving walls (Figs. 6.4 and 6.5) (Ahronson 2015). Though the Seljaland caves of Seljalandshellar and Kverkarhellir have been used in the recent past for farming activities (i.e. to shelter animals, store goods and for drying or smoking foods), they have also previously been used for other purposes (i.e. to house an outlaw in the sixteenth century and as a nineteenth-century *þingstaður*, or local parliament place) (Árnarson 1993 [1856], 200–202; Tómasson 1997, 151). Seljaland sculpture comprises a robust corpus of 24 larger crosses, comparable with rock-cut crosses from other sites in southern Iceland including, for example, the Westman Islands Heimaklettur site, Skollhólahellir cave, Berustaðahellir cave, Efri-Gegnihólar cave, and Árbæjarhellir cave. For instance, the expanded terminal style identified at the Hetta and Skollhólahellir sites is also seen at Seljaland, in both incised and sunken variants (Ahronson 2015, 174, 186–188). There

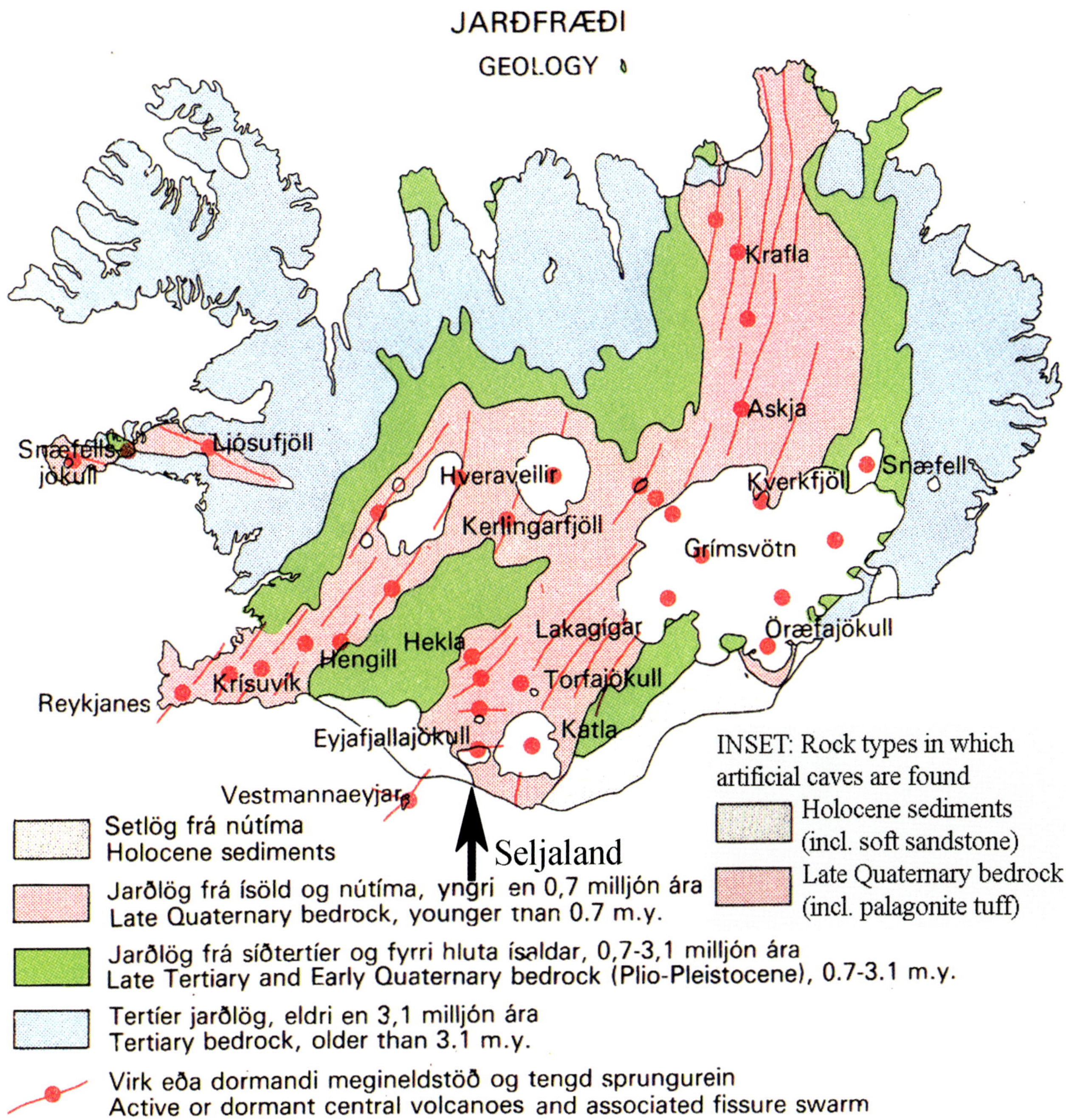


*Figure 6.2: Geology of Iceland, with inset detailing Holocene sediments in which artificial cave sites are found and arrow indicating location of Seljaland. Adapted from Landmælingar Íslands 1:500.000 topographic sheet, fifth edition 1991, based on data from National Land Survey of Iceland (www.lmi.is/wp-content/uploads/2013/10/License-for-use-of-free-NLSI-data-General-Terms.pdf).*

is, therefore, a coherent body of cross-marked artificial caves and exposed alcoves in southern Iceland illustrating early Christian religious activities.

## Sculptural parallels

The earliest of the surviving Scandinavian rune stones with simple cross inscriptions date to *c.* AD 975–1050 (Lager 2000; Sawyer 2000). In the Seljaland corpus, the cross forms appear different to the rune stone cross forms, and without their typical associated runic band. For instance, the Swedish Småland stone Sm69 seems to feature an equal-armed Greek sunken or outline form (Lager 2000, 121), whereas the Norwegian cross slabs fail to demonstrate convincing parallels (Birkeli 1973; Gellein 2007). More significant, however, is the host of additional features that the Seljaland crosses share with the western Scotland corpus. Ian Fisher has examined the Seljaland sculpture and pointed to a

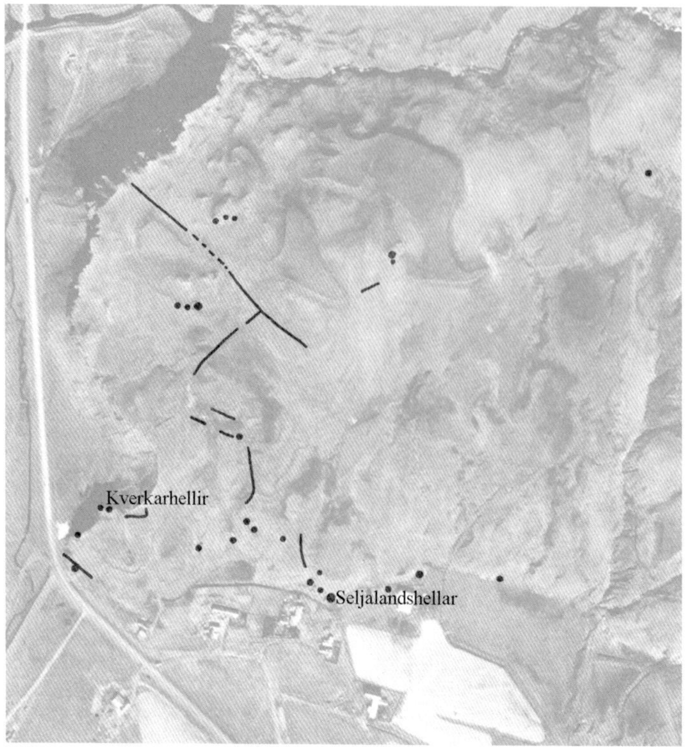


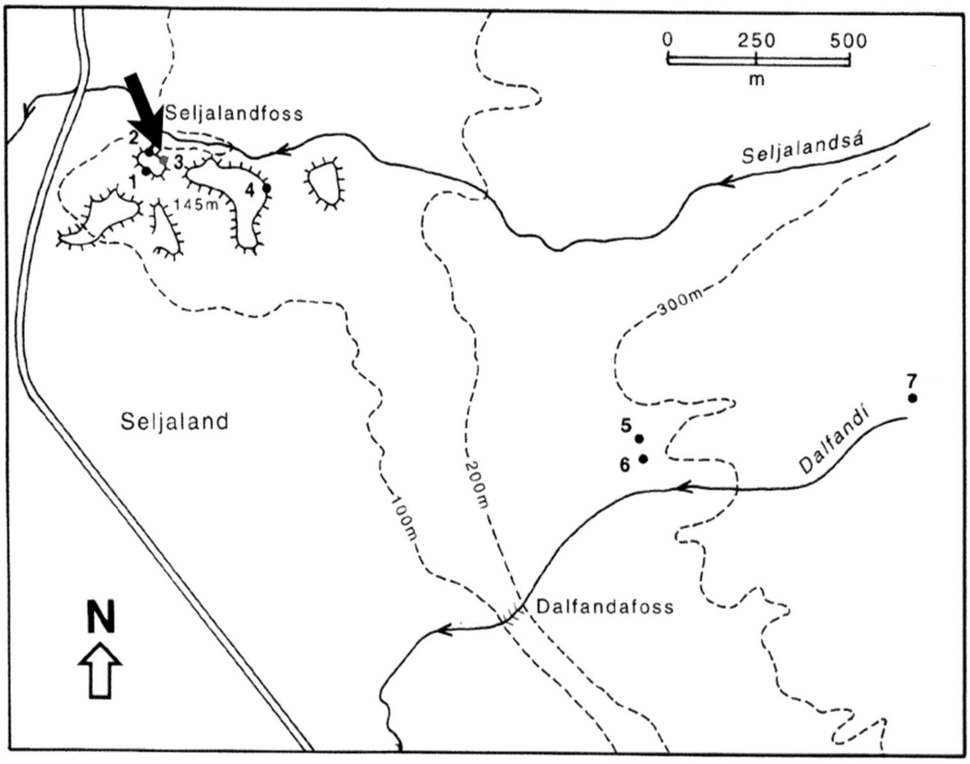


*Figure 6.3: Above: Adapted aerial photograph of Seljaland, locating surveyed features and including Kverkarhellir and Seljalandshellar caves. Based on data from National Land Survey of Iceland (1984 series) (www.lmi.is/wp-content/uploads/2013/10/License-for-use-of-free-NLSI-data-General-Terms.pdf). Scale 1:10000. Below: Map locating Ashburn* et al.*'s profiles at Seljaland. Adapted from Ashburn* et al. *(2003, 83). Profiles 1–4 (within the 100–200m contour lines) had a distinctive lightening of colour in early ninth-century sediments; this colour change is widespread in post-*landnám *sediments and associated with human impacts upon the environment. Indicated with an arrow, tephra contouring trenches were sited adjacent to Ashburn* et al*'s profile 3.*

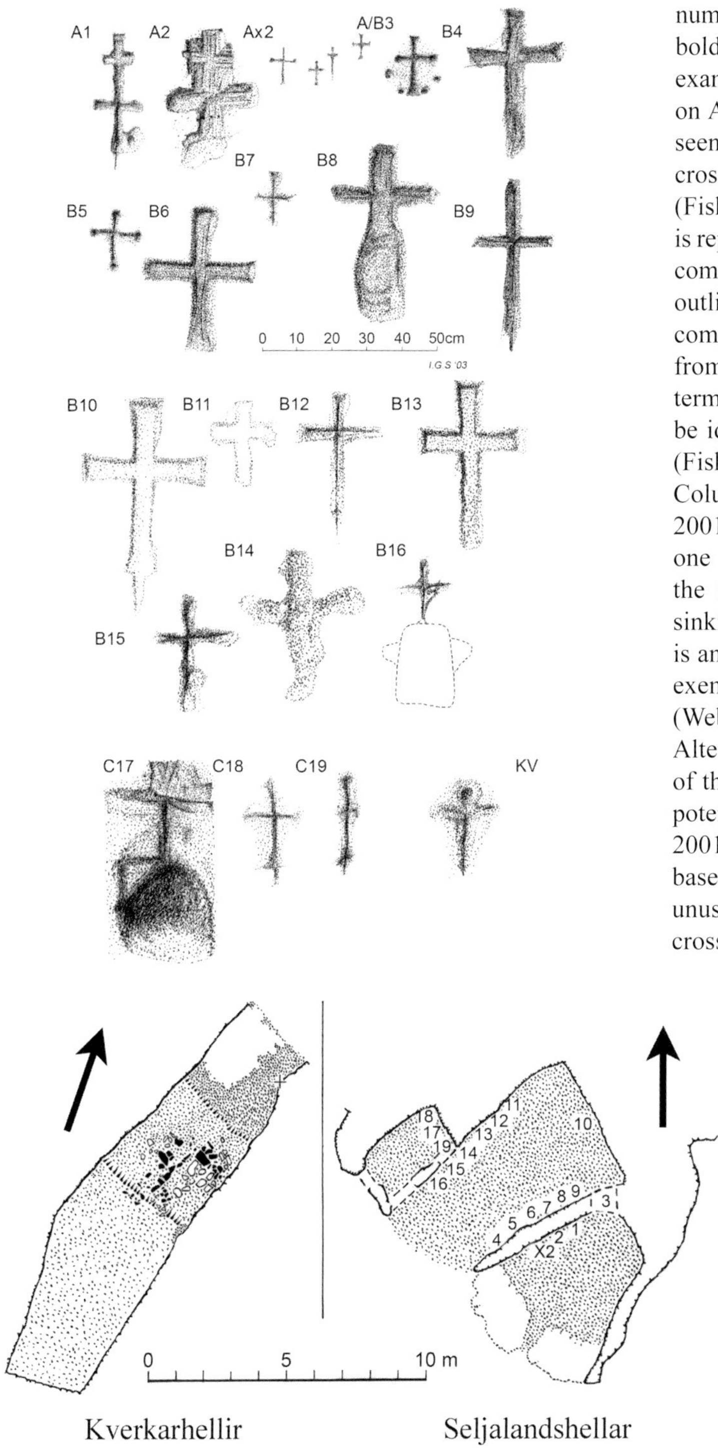


*Figure 6.4: Seljalandshellar cave and Kverkarhellir cave, at Seljaland, Vestur-Eyjafjallahreppur, southern Iceland. Plans (with arrows indicating north) and sculpture illustrations. The crosshair at the eastern wall of the Kverkarhellir cave mouth indicates the site of cross KV. The numbering of the Seljalandshellar plan indicates crosses A1 to C19 as well as the four mid-sized crosses represented by Ax2, with the initial lettering refers to the cave chamber within which each cross is located: the south-eastern cave chamber (the* gapi*) is indicated by A, the middle chamber by B, and the north-western chamber (the* stúka*) by C. Illustration: I.G. Scott).*

number of similarities (Fisher personal communication). The bold V-cut and the pointed base of a number of Seljaland examples are similar to a cross cut into a wall of King's Cave on Arran (Fisher 2001, fig. 31MM); the bold V-cut is also seen in other carvings, such as the rock-cut Aird a'Mhòrain cross from North Uist, marking a well and a landing place (Fisher 2001, fig. 31N). Furthermore, the pointed-base form is repeated on a stone from Cladh a'Bhile, Ellary, though this comparison is problematic as the Cladh a'Bhile carving is an outline cross (Fisher 2001, fig. 33U[17]). A more convincing comparison is the pointed base on one face of another stone from Cladh a'Bhile (Fisher 2001, fig. 31E[13]b). Pitted terminals, seen on a handful of Seljaland crosses, may also be identified on 'Eithne's Grave' from Eileach an Naoimh (Fisher 2001, fig. 30A) as well as on two crosses from St Columba's Cave (Fisher 2001, fig. 30B, 30C; Tolan-Smith 2001, 28). Furthermore, the armpit sinkings associated with one of the St Columba's Cave crosses can be compared to the Seljaland cross with pitted terminals and associated sinkings. The spiked socket base of three Seljaland crosses is an unusual feature, conceivably inspired by a metalwork exemplar or processional crosses such as the Rupertus Cross (Webster and Backhouse 1991, 170–173; Fisher 2001, 172). Alternatively, Fisher has noted a small cross bar at the foot of the cross shaft at Cladh a'Bhile and Achadh na Cille as potentially representing the foot rest of Christ's cross (Fisher 2001, figs. 31Ec and 31JJ, 12). The Seljaland spiked socket bases may be related to either of these suggestions. Another unusual feature is the oval-headed Kverkarhellir cross. The cross head bears some similarity to a small, outline, oval-headed cross from St Molaise's Table on Holy Island (Arran) (Fisher 2001, fig. 63B), though this should not be overly stressed.

Turning to the sunken cross form, a number of similar examples can be identified for this predominantly western Scotland type. For instance, a cross from the isolated monastic site on North Rona (Fisher 2001, fig. 32R[2]) is of sunken form and convincingly similar to Seljalandshellar B6. Furthermore, the Seljaland examples of this type see generalised comparison to the sunken crosses from St. Molaise's Cave on Holy Island (Arran) (Fisher 2001, fig. 32AA). In addition, the high central position of the sunken B10 cross in Seljalandshellar cave B is paralleled by the high central position of a sunken cross in St. Molaise's Cave (Fisher 2001, fig. 61B). Further afield, sunken forms with socket (or metalwork type) bases from the Breton collection of early Christian sculpture share some affinities with the Seljaland cross B10. Specifically, the seventh- to tenth-century Rimoette cross may be a good comparison, though fuller illustration of that cross is needed, and the similarly dated *croux Prostlon*'s sunken form also

*Figure 6.5: Three-chambered artificial cave of Seljalandshellar. Photograph looking north-west (© Kristján Ahronson).*

features a socket base (Davies *et al.* 2000, 244, 224). The two double-armed and footed-base crosses from Seljaland appear to be unique, though some comparison may be made with what appear to be similarly paired footed cross forms from Berustaðahellir cave. Limited comparison of double-armed examples may be made to two incised crosses from Cladh a'Bhile and Lochead (Fisher 2001, fig. 30GG[12]b, HH[1]), though this is far from convincing. Comparison may also be made to the Breton Langombrac'h cross, with its sunken form and double arms (Davies *et al.* 2000, 202). This Breton cross, however, is defined by arcs whereas the Seljaland examples are not, thus limiting the value of this comparison. Another Breton sunken cross, that which fronts the Crac'h stone, is a better comparison with its multiple arms and footed base (Davies *et al.* 2000, 174). In the western Scotland corpus, the sunken footed form – but not the double arms – is also present at St. Molaise's Cave (Fisher 2001, fig. 61C).

As demonstrated, a host of parallels for the Seljaland carvings are available across the insular world (if Brittany can be included as such), with particular similarities between the Seljaland and western Scotland material. Insular crosses of sunken form are concentrated in Scotland, with roughly twenty examples illustrated in Fisher's corpus of west Highland and island sculpture, and seven clear examples of the type survive at Seljaland. Prominence of the sunken form in both western Scotland and the Seljaland corpus suggests particular connections between the cross sculpture of southern Iceland and western Scotland, as do the numerous shared features discussed above (expanded terminals, bold V-cuts, and sinkings). The surviving cross sculpture as well as the orientation and layout of the smallest chamber in Seljalandshellar, suggests that this particular chamber may have functioned as a chapel. Certainly, such use has analogies in western Scotland, such as at St Columba's Cave and St Molaise's Cave – and it is worth noting that rock-cut sculpture at both of these sites includes notable typological parallels with the Seljaland caves, as described above.

## Dating cave construction in southern Iceland

Fortunately, chronological precision is possible for many events because of the excellent sequence of *tephrae* at Seljaland. Within the historic period, tephra deposits include twelve layers clearly separated by aeolian sediments, from the AD 1947 Hekla tephra layer to the *c.* AD 870 Vatnaöldur tephra layer, also known as the 'Settlement layer'. In other words, this stratified sequence of dated tephra layers can provide a chronological framework within which to place events identified from the sedimentary record.

Tephrochronology is a stratigraphy-based technique that sometimes deploys geochemical analysis to resolve ambiguities in field identifications. It must be stressed, however, that geochemical analysis alone is insufficient for application of this technique: the stratigraphic sequence of tephrae in a section is the basis for interpretation. Through stratigraphic and geochemical analyses, the first task for excavations at Seljaland's Kverkarhellir cave, therefore, was to relate the Seljaland profile to a stratified sequence of tephra deposits intercalated with aggrading sediments from outside the cave mouth (Fig. 6.6; Dugmore 1987). The Seljaland profile shows that, in this area, very few

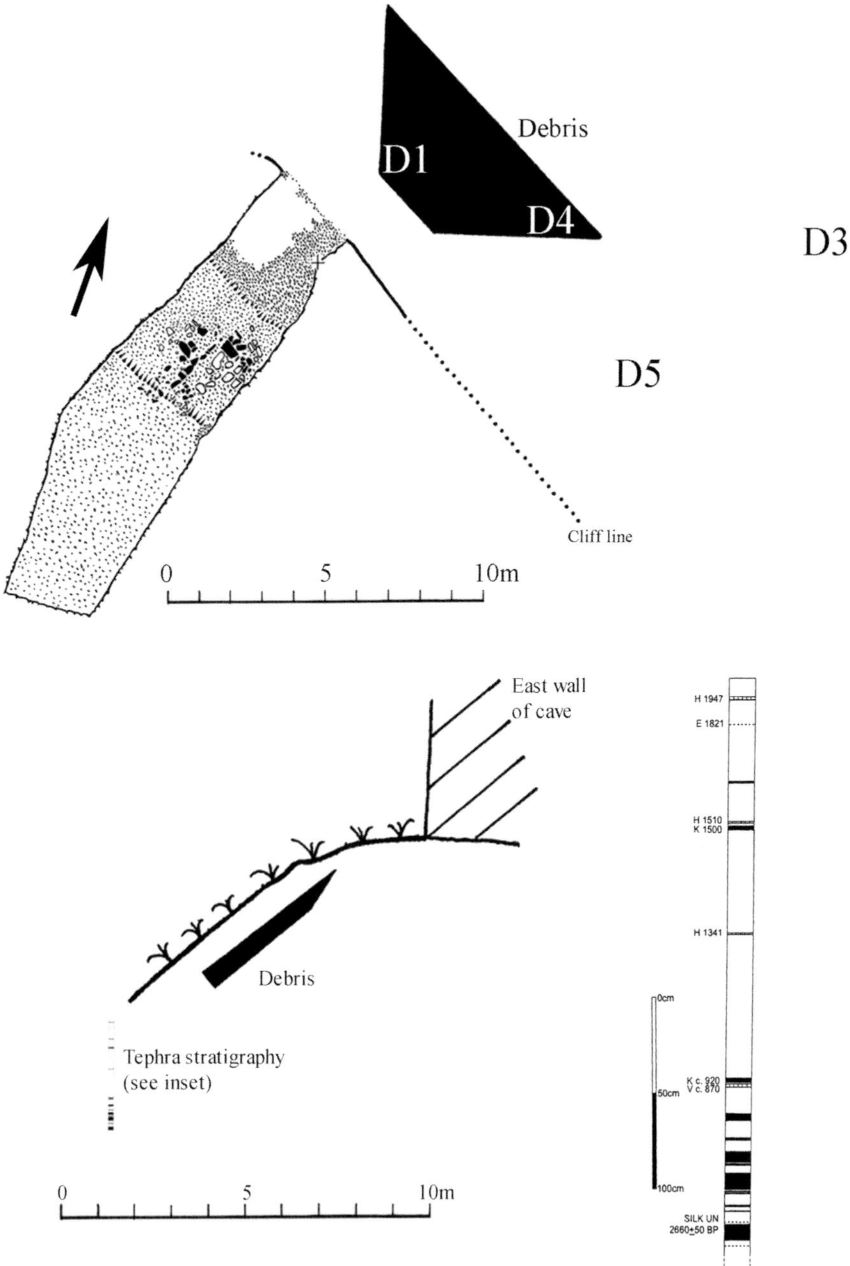


*Figure 6.6: Above: Location of trenches near Kverkarhellir cave. Below: Sketch profile of northwest-facing section showing the mouth of Kverkarhellir cave and the steep descent, as well as the predicted apron of waste and a generalised stratigraphic profile (note the different scale) for Seljaland-area tephra layers. Tephra stratigraphy inset illustration from Dugmore 1987.*

black Katla tephra layers have been recorded in the soils in historic time. The distinctive key historical layers are predominantly from Hekla: H1947 (coarse grey-brown pumice), H1510 (coarse grey-brown pumice) and H1341 (fine blue-grey tephra). K1500 is a relatively coarse black tephra layer from Katla. A pair of distinctive tephra layers (V870 and K920) is found at about the time of Norse settlement of the island (*landnám*). The V870 tephra layer (or 'Settlement' tephra layer) is from the Barðarbunga-Veiðivötn system and is generally understood to seal the prehistoric sequence from the Viking-age Scandinavian 'Settlement' period (Vésteinsson 1998, 3–4). This greenish brown tephra, with a small pale silica-rich component, has been dated to AD 871 ± 2 and AD 877 ± 4 (Grönvold *et al.* 1995; Zielinski *et al.* 1997). Katla erupted approximately 50 years later (*c.* AD 920), producing a black tephra. Thick (often greater than 10cm) coarse black tephra layers from the Katla central volcano dominate the prehistoric sequence, clearly distinguishable from the series of tephra deposits post-dating the period of human settlement.

As part of research at Seljaland, test trenches at the mouth of Kverkarhellir cave identified debris from the cave's construction within sediments including a dated sequence of tephrae. Applying tephrochronology to establish an episode of cave construction followed earlier efforts to date human activity at another southern Icelandic cave site, Kolsholtshellir in the Villingaholshreppur district of Árnessýsla. At Kolsholtshellir, Holt and Guðmundsson test trenched an '*allstór* öskuhaugur' (a fairly large ashheap) related to the cave (Holt and Guðmundsson 1980, 19–25). Their work recovered cultural material from a stratified deposit, including a tephra layer suggested to be AD 1500 Katla tephra. They also identified a small oval-shaped lens of the *c.* AD 870 Vatnaöldur tephra near the base of the deposit, and used this to imply that cave use began at that site sometime before *c.* AD 870 (Holt and Guðmundsson 1980, 19–25). However, if this isolated deposit is indeed *c.* AD 870 Vatnaöldur tephra, a further complication lies in the potentially complex provenance for a single lens: in addition to primary deposition as airfall, sources also include the reworking of older material, such as preservation within a later turf cutting.

Returning to Kverkarhellir cave, we may note that the cave fabric is a palagonite tuff and is assumed to have been dug out by iron-headed tools. The earliest phase may have extended a natural relict sea-cut alcove, and involved digging an area approximately 2m high × 2m long × 3m wide resulting in the production of at least 12 cubic metres of debris. A rock-cut cross on the eastern wall may be associated with this phase of construction. It could be suggested that the construction of Kverkarhellir with iron-headed hand tools would have produced palagonite debris consisting largely of angular medium pebbles to small cobbles (roughly 10–120 mm), accompanied by substantial amounts of finer pebbles (2–10 mm) and later infilled with aeolian material. Debris could include artefacts associated with construction such as damaged iron tools; however, considering the importance of recycling iron and the general rarity of artefacts from archaeological investigations in Iceland, the recovery of such material is unlikely. As a rule, the expected lithic debris (especially that produced by construction on this scale) should be dumped nearby, though avoiding access routes and activity areas (Schiffer 1987, 58–64). In the case of Kverkarhellir, topography presents limited possibilities, suggesting an apron of waste would have been deposited on the slope outside the cave mouth with a thickness, perhaps, of between 0.5m and 1m (Fig. 6.6).

In an attempt to relate Kverkarhellir cave to the well-dated tephrochronological sequence for the area, a hypothesis was formulated as follows: if a well-stratified sequence of sediments exists in the vicinity of Kverkarhellir, and includes prehistoric and historic tephrae (which may be identified through stratigraphic and geochemical analyses), then locating a dump of debris-type material within this sequence and in areas generally predicted by our depositional model would date an episode of construction at Kverkarhellir. This proposal was tested by excavating a number of trenches and by assessing particle size distribution for individual contexts. The tephra sequence in the immediate area of Kverkarhellir was found to include key historical tephrae, such as the *c.* AD 870 Vatnaöldur and *c.* AD 920 Katla couplet, and a number of thick prehistoric tephrae. Dated by this sequence of tephrae to *c.* AD 800 (or earlier), a deposit of debris-type thickness and character was identified within the predicted 'apron of waste' for the early digging out of Kverkarhellir. This thick debris-type context appears to be part of a dump of construction debris because comparable material was not found elsewhere. Sections revealed a thick context of angular palagonite pebbles and cobbles beneath tephrae produced by the eruptions of AD 1597 Hekla, *c.* AD 920 Katla and *c.* AD 870 Vatnaöldur (Fig. 6.5). The 50–75cm-thick deposit of angular pebbles and small cobbles was discovered to lie up to 25cm beneath the *c.* AD 920 Katla and *landnám* couplet, with the K920/V870 tephrae running intermittently across the trench and therefore understood to result from *in situ* airfall deposition of those tephra layers, and so significantly predating the *c.* AD 870 Vatnaöldur tephra layer. Uncertainties remain, however, on just how long before *c.* AD 870 this debris-type material was deposited. Based on Dugmore and Erskine's (1994) estimates for sediment accumulation rates at Seljaland, the 25cm of aeolian sediments sealed by the 'Settlement' tephra layer suggest a date several decades earlier than AD 870, if not a century or more. As an estimate then, the debris-type material would have been deposited by *c.* AD 800 and possibly before.

Given the scale of work outlined here, the case for this thick debris-type deposit being part of a construction dump is a good one. Though satisfying expectations of location, thickness and particle size distribution, a continuing concern was that this deposit could have been produced by a natural erosion episode from the escarpment face. Correspondingly, excavation revealed the local character of erosion deposits, and samples were processed to provide particle size distributions. Field examination of this pebble and cobble layer noted its similarity to the cave interior fabric at Kverkarhellir and both *in situ* examination and laboratory analyses demonstrated this layer to be of radically different character from the naturally-eroded deposits – thus we may conclude that the debris-type deposit was not produced by a natural erosion episode of the escarpment face: the postulated debris-type context was unlike erosion-origin material and was thus interpreted as construction debris from the digging out of Kverkarhellir. The outlined hypothesis has so far withstood testing and the resulting date for construction at Kverkarhellir raises important questions.

As noted earlier, the Viking-age Scandinavian 'Settlement' period of Iceland is generally understood to post-date the *landnám* or 'Settlement' tephra layer of *c.* AD 870. Though suggestions for early cave use in southern Iceland have been previously made, this chapter details the most comprehensive investigation yet undertaken (see also Ahronson 2015). The application of tephrochronological techniques to date Kverkarhellir has profited from the maturity of this area of research and from important earlier work at Seljaland (e.g. Dugmore 1987; Dugmore and Erskine 1994; Smith and Ahronson 2003). Care must be taken with these results, however, as they identify what may be the earliest human presence on the island *c.* AD 800, or earlier.

Though the Seljaland investigations are thus far the clearest indicator for people in Iceland at this early period, work in the Westman Islands and Reykjavík tentatively suggests complementary dates. Suggestions made for the Westman Islands have proved controversial (Hermanns-Auðardóttir 1989; 1991; 1992; Vilhjálmsson 1992, 167–181), while more recent fieldwork in Reykjavík has identified a field boundary sealed by a tephra layer suggested to be *in situ c.* AD 870 Vatnaöldur tephra – and thus interpreted to date this feature to, perhaps, *c.* AD 850 (Roberts *et al.* 2002, 35–39). Perhaps more relevant, however, is the local palaeoenvironmental change identified *c.* AD 800 at Seljaland (Dugmore and Erskine 1994, 69–73; Ashburn *et al.* 2003, 88), and potentially related to human activity in the landscape. If Kverkarhellir was indeed constructed in the eighth century, immediate questions arise as to by whom.

## The Seljaland caves and the wider landscape

The Seljaland caves of Seljalandshellar and Kverkarhellir are among the artificial caves of southern Iceland (see Figs. 6.2 and 6.3) that range from small shelters to large two-storied chambers (Hjartarson *et al.* 1991). Iceland experienced significant environmental and ecological changes in the first centuries of human colonisation (e.g. Ahronson 2015), and efforts to understand the human use of southern Iceland's artificial caves therefore encourage a consideration of environmental contexts. New discoveries indicate that Seljaland is the oldest recorded farm name in its regional unit of Vestur-Eyjafjallahreppur, and Seljaland is among the oldest placenames in Iceland, probably dating from at least the twelfth century (Ahronson 2015, 78–79; *contra* Sveinbjarnardóttir 1991, 76). An established approach has been to project patterns of land use and land division described in late medieval literature back into the Viking-age 'Settlement' period (*landnám*) of Iceland, based upon the idea that late medieval land use and land divisions derived from decisions made in preceding centuries (Vésteinsson 1998, 6). Certainly, important ecological niches converge at Seljaland – namely areas of highland, lowland plain, cliff, river, marshland and nearby coast – and Viking-Age colonists are thought to have consistently exploited the varied resources found in these habitats (Vésteinsson 1998, 6–12), thereby encouraging Seljaland's selection for early settlement. The island was transformed over these centuries: birch woodland was cleared, domesticated animals and crops introduced, native mammal, bird and fish populations over-exploited, natural vegetation cover stripped, and soils destabilised. Human impacts set in motion or accentuated processes that resulted in the unstable soils and eroded landscapes of present-day Iceland. Throughout this period, a dynamic natural environment bounded the Markarfljót and Eyjafjallasveit area of Iceland. Hekla lies to the north, while to the east the landscape is dominated by the glaciers Eyjafjallajökull and Mýrdalsjökull as well as the active central volcano of Katla. The escarpment that forms Seljaland is itself a landmark, looking west over the glacial river Markarfljót and the lowland coastal plain (*sandur*), as well as south-west to the nearby Westman Islands. Today constrained to one powerful channel, the Markarfljót exemplifies environmental change over historical time, having flowed through winding and migrating channels across a large delta at the time of early settlement.

As alluded to above, palaeoenvironmental changes have been detected in the early ninth century and have been claimed to relate to human activity in the landscape (i.e. the introduction of domesticates and woodland clearance). Clearly, consideration of potential evidence for human activity in the immediate environs of the Seljaland caves is an important aspect of our efforts to understand what was going on at the Seljaland caves *c.* AD 800. The new technique of *tephra contouring* provided unexpected results, suggesting structural changes in vegetation cover both before *c.* AD 870 and again in the decades leading up to *c.* AD 920.

Dugmore and Erskine (1994, 73–74) proposed that windblown sediments started moving around the landscape in the ninth and tenth centuries – eroding in one place and accumulating elsewhere. At Seljaland, this geomorphological change is revealed by a distinctive lightening of colour, which is well-represented in the post-*landnám* sediments with earlier occurrences identified in early ninth-century sediments at sites situated between 100 and 200 m above mean sea level (Fig. 6.3) (Dugmore and Erskine 1994, 72; Ashburn *et al.* 2003, 83). Furthermore, Ashburn *et al.* (2003, 92) studied the magnetic susceptibility of these lighter deposits and favour the idea that the consistently low values obtained result from human impacts upon these soils and from the introduction of animal waste and decaying vegetation from disturbance caused by introduced herbivores. They link these windblown sediments with domesticated animals because of the high organic content of the sediments. It is possible that we are seeing the effect of domesticates on a fragile woodland ecosystem and the consequent breaking up of soil cover. Regionally, two ecological zones are understood to have characterised the landscape around Seljaland prior to human settlement: a zone of raised woodland dominated by birch (*betula*) and willow (*salix*), and another zone of vegetation without raised woodland, subdivided into lowland coastal plain and upland components (Dugmore *et al.* 2000, 29). Situated on well-drained slopes between 10 and 300 m above sea level, the area of woodland may be quantified as covering roughly 300 hectares (Amanda Thomson, pers. comm.). This scenario of a 'pre-settlement' landscape dominated by woodland is supported by the island's earliest literature, which claims Norse settlers encountered '*viði vaxit á miðli fjalls ok fjøru*' (woods between mountains and shore) (Benediktsson 1969, 5). It is presumed that this woodland was quickly reduced by human populations, in some cases to create arable land, as attested to in the later *Grágás* legal code (Finsen 1974 [1852], 448). Figure 6.7 models vegetation cover for those landscapes sealed by the K920 and V870 tephra layers.

Careful examination of the character of local tephra horizons supports the idea of a wooded landscape: 'holes' in the *landnám* and older prehistoric tephra layers may be interpreted as tree casts, and thus evidence for forest cover. Additionally, undulating and discontinuous soil–tephra contact surfaces have also been noted for the *landnám* and prehistoric layers, and would be expected for tephra deposited in birch woodland with lush understorey. A problem for the idea of extensive late ninth-century woodland areas at Seljaland, however, is the early ninth-century lighter deposits (and corresponding change in geomorphological process) discussed earlier – and most visible in the postulated heart of this birch woodland (i.e. between 100 and 200m above sea level). The sedimentary record at Seljaland therefore suggests structural changes in vegetation cover and an influx of aeolian sediment that has not been sufficiently incorporated into models of past landscapes, perhaps because its precise nature and timing is poorly known.

The assumption that reduction of woodland in the ninth and early tenth centuries would have been determined by intensive human use is a potential problem. However, considering the relative stability of the north Atlantic climate throughout the ninth, tenth and eleventh centuries (Ogilvie *et al.* 2000), relating tree cover reduction to human activity has gained widespread support among palaeoecology researchers in southern Iceland. Haraldsson (1981, 41–42), for instance, concludes that birch woodland on raised areas of the Landeyjar coastal plain experienced steady growth in extent and trunk diameter between AD 800 and 900, with reduction and extinction of that woodland by AD 950, coinciding with Norse settlement there. Thus, the background trend of steady growth in woodland throughout the ninth century for the coastal plain (which Seljaland overlooks) points to the robustness of this assumption that people were instrumental in the destruction of forest environments. In other words, since a natural trajectory of woodland growth is widespread prior to human colonisation, then the reduction of woodland when people arrive in that landscape suggests humans to have been a major cause of woodland loss. Another possibility, more difficult to assess, however, is that woodland might also have been encouraged by human land management strategies: in other words, that a stand of woodland could be maintained or fostered as a result of human use rather than despite human use.

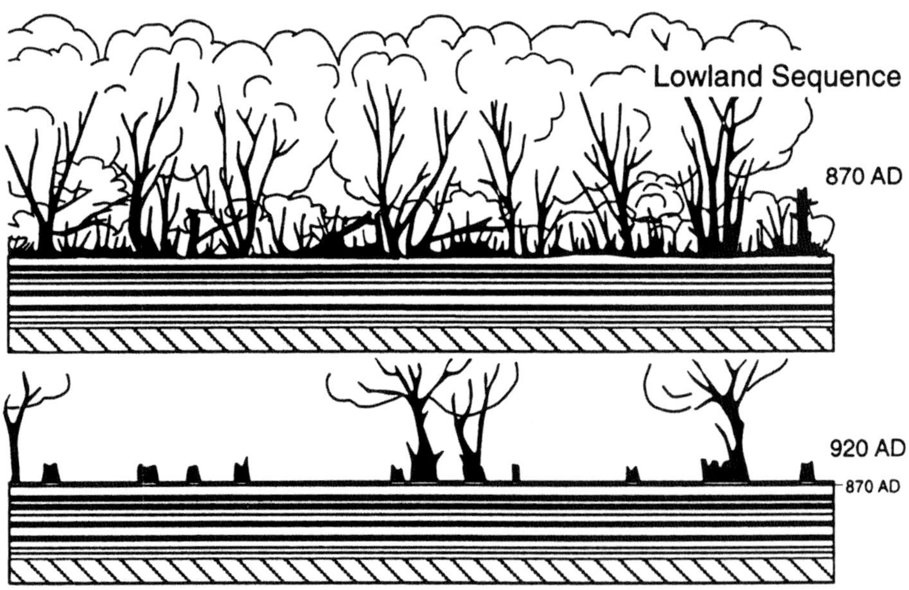


*Figure 6.7: Modelled vegetation structure for lowland area of Seljaland at the time of the deposition of the V870 and K920 tephrae. Detail from Dugmore and Simpson's composite presentation of historic vegetation models. Illustration: Dugmore and Simpson, forthcoming.*

At Seljaland, contours were obtained for centimetre-scale and continuous tephra layers identified as *in situ* airfall deposits from eruptions of Katla *c*. AD 920, as well as Vatnaöldur *c*. AD 870. The small scale of the tephra-contoured area excavated at Seljaland presents statistical limitations to wider interpretations; however, our results were clear and are presented visually in Figures 6.8, 6.9, and 6.10. In the K920 tephra layer, two 5–9cm circular 'holes' were interpreted to be trunk casts of thin trees while a number of medium-sized irregularly shaped gaps in the tephra layer were interpreted as the result of a lush understorey of vegetation which prevented deposition of tephra within these features. Additionally, a spike at this location in the magnetic susceptibility of sediments *c*. AD 920 may have resulted from the burning of woodland at that time (Ashburn *et al*. 2003, 92–93). Furthermore, since tephra contours for the K920 layer have 'photographed' what appears to be a small area of young woodland with lush understorey, consideration of Ashburn *et al*.'s results lead to the suggestion that it was this woodland that later burned. In contrast to K920, the contoured surface of the V870 tephra layer suggests a different vegetative structure for that landscape. Contouring this *landnám* layer, deposited *c*. AD 870, revealed a continuous and well-defined surface without 'holes' or irregular gaps. Interpretation of this data suggests an open grassland environment without tree cover. As these results run counter to the vegetation cover modelled in Figure 6.7 (and apparently well-established for this area of southern Iceland), two main possibilities present themselves: first, that we have contoured a natural clearing in woodland cover; and second, that this 3m × 2m area was cleared of birch trees by people before the *landnám* tephra was deposited. This second possibility could also help explain the change in sedimentation processes identified at this site in sediments dated to *c*. AD 800, and proposed to reflect the impact of people on the local environment and the introduction of non-indigenous herbivores into the landscape (Ashburn *et al*. 2003).

If this latter possibility were the case, such clearance would probably have occurred several decades before AD 870 in order to produce such an open and well-defined tephra layer. Additionally, unexpected linear depression features were found in this tephra layer – their size, shape and distribution hold out the possibility that these were created by medium-sized herbivores, such as sheep or small- to medium-sized cattle, treading upon freshly deposited tephra.

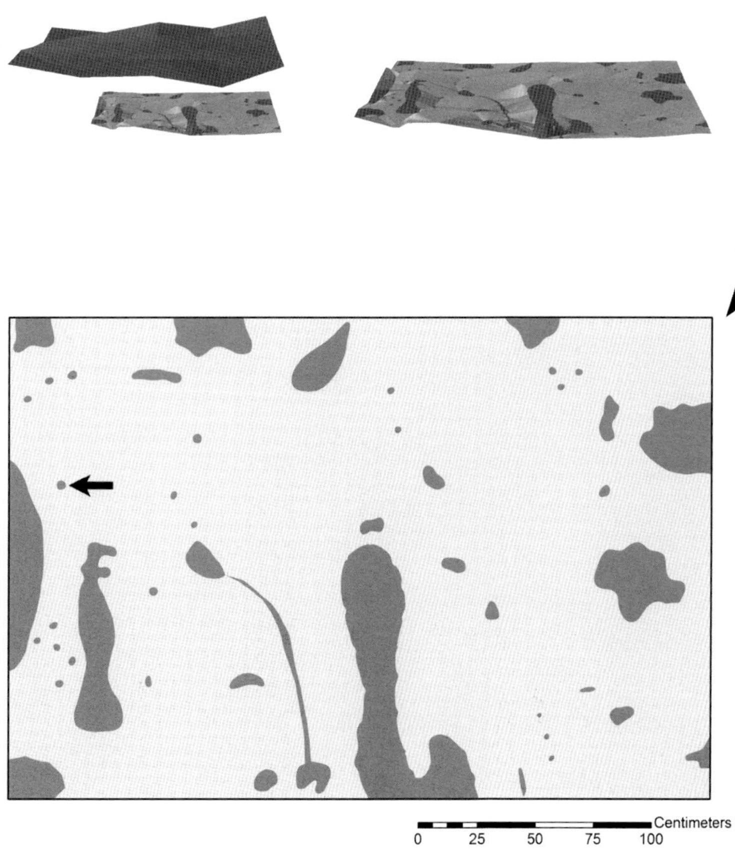


*Figure 6.8: Above left and right: Oblique images of modern grassed land surface and surface of the K920 tephra layer. 'Holes' in the tephra horizon are identified in shaded grey; a ground-level understorey of vegetation probably prevented the deposition of K920 tephra within these features. Below: Surface of K920 tephra layer. A single 5cm diameter tree cast is identified by an arrow. Illustration: J. Higdon.*

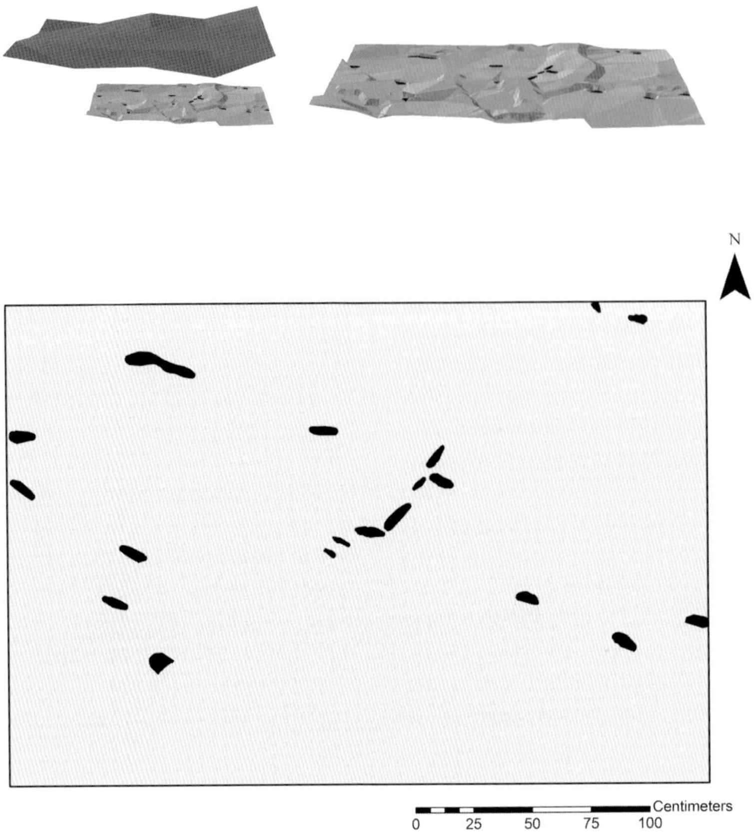


*Figure 6.9: Above left and right: Oblique images of modern grassed land surface and of the surface of the V870 tephra layer. 'Depressions' in the tephra horizon are shaded black. Regularly spaced and arranged in linear patterns running across the excavation area, these features may be preserved animal tracks. Below: Surface of V870 tephra layer. Illustration: J. Higdon.*

*Figure 6.10: Oblique views of surface contours of the following three tephrae: K1500 (uppermost surface contour), K920 (middle surface contour), and V870 (lowermost surface contour). Looking west-southwest.*

Though land mammals of this size are not native to Iceland, this idea of early 'herbivore tracks' in the *landnám* tephra layer is made plausible by the recent discovery mentioned above of a field boundary (indicative of farm animals) in Reykjavík dated to *c.* AD 850 (Roberts *et al.* 2002, 35–39).

Furthermore, this interpretation might in turn strengthen the second possibility, i.e. that we have excavated a landscape cleared of tree cover by people rather than a natural open area in woodland. These ideas would profit from further excavation of tephra contouring trenches at Seljaland, but the data provided by our trial seems to support the hypothesis that tree cover at Seljaland was reduced before AD 870–920 and that intensive use of the landscape was underway by that time. Intriguingly, the growth of young woodland with lush understorey by *c.* AD 920 may suggest abandonment of Seljaland and its caves in the AD 870–920 period, or alternatively, a change in land management at that time. In light of the alternate place-name of Papahellir (i.e. '*papar*' cave) to denote the three-chambered Seljalandshellar cave as well as its folkloric association with early Christian Irish-speaking peoples or *papar* (Hálfdan Ómar Hálfdanarson pers. comm.), one bold idea is that these Seljaland cave sites were built by early Christian communities as a 'desert place in the ocean' – potentially comparable to settlements on North Rona and elsewhere in Atlantic Scotland and Ireland. Recent work, for instance, considers similarly early dates for cereal pollen along these lines, suggesting early Christian monastic settlement and farming in the Faroe

Islands (Jóhansen 1985; Hannon and Bradshaw 2000; Edwards *et al.* 2005).

## Conclusion

The previous section of this chapter considered environmental changes in the centuries surrounding Viking-Age Scandinavian settlement in order to contextualise human activity at the Seljaland caves and in southern Iceland's artificial cave sites more generally. To assess ninth- and tenth-century palaeoenvironmental change, application of tephra contouring suggests early- to mid-ninth century clearing of woodland at Seljaland to create an open grassland environment suitable for grazing, and potentially identified the presence of non-indigenous herbivores by *c.* AD 870. Unexpectedly, land use at Seljaland appears to have changed by *c.* AD 920, with the growth of young woodland with lush understorey. If sustained by later work, this change might relate to the area's abandonment (and perhaps also abandonment of the Seljaland caves) during the Viking-Age Scandinavian 'Settlement' period, or to a change in land management strategies at that time. In other words, these results may be viewed alongside the early date for activity at Kverkarhellir cave – which may be the earliest human activity in Iceland.

There are connections that can be drawn between the marked caves of Scotland and Iceland, with both now appearing to have been used contemporaneously. In Scotland, early Christian cave sculpture appears to have marked places for seclusion, and yet:

> The Irish church was often dismissed by its opponents for occupying the remotest corner of the world, but its clerics carried the symbol of the cross to the furthest islands, perhaps consciously protecting Christendom against the dark forces of the ocean (Fisher 2001, 1).

A suite of typological similarities makes a persuasive case for connections between the Icelandic and Scottish cave sites: a number of shared features such as the distinctive sunken form, expanded terminals, bold V-cuts and sinkings indicate particular connections between the Seljaland caves and western Scotland, as well as wider connections to the Irish and Scottish littoral zone more generally. However, there are also regional differences: we have been discussing the *artificial* caves of southern Iceland, for instance, in relation to largely *natural* caves in Scotland – is this regional difference meaningful or simply practical, given the postulated rarity of appropriate natural caves in southern Iceland, alongside the suitability for cave construction of that region's palagonite tuff and soft sandstone? We might also wonder about how the theme of relative seclusion (rather than isolation), discussed in the British context, relates to the artificial caves of Iceland, which then of course highlights the unresolved question of how the early cave use identified at Seljaland might relate to any contemporary open-air settlements, or to the island's late ninth-century phase of Scandinavian settlement.

## References


*Adam von Bremen. Hamburgische Kirchengeschicte.* 1917. Gesta Hammaburgensis ecclesiæ pontificum, ed. B. Schmeidler. Hannover und Leipzig: Hansche Buchhandlung.

*Adam of Bremen. History of the Archbishops of Hamburg-Bremen.* 1959. Transl. F.J. Tschan. New York: Colombia University Press.

Ahronson, K., 2015. Into the Ocean. Vikings, Irish and Environmental Change in Iceland and the North. Toronto: University of Toronto Press.

Ahronson, K., and Charles-Edwards, T.M., 2010. Prehistoric annals and Early Medieval monasticism: Daniel Wilson, James Young Simpson and their cave sites. *Antiquaries Journal* 90, 455–466. Available from: http://dx.doi.org/10.1017/S0003581510000028 [accessed 1 December 2016].

Ahronson, K., Gillies, W. and Hunter, F., 2006. Early Christian activity at Scottish cave sites. *Church Archaeology* 7/8/9, 123–125.

Anderson, J., 1881. *Scotland in Early Christian Times. The Rhind Lectures in Archaeology for 1879.* Edinburgh: David Douglas.

Árnarson, J., 1993 [1856]. Íslenzkar þjóðsögur og ævintðri IV. *In*: Á. Böðvarsson and B. Vilhjálmsson, eds. *Íslenzkar þjóðsögur og ævintðri IV. New Edition.* Reykjavík: Bókaútgáfan þjóðsaga Prentsmiðjan Hólar H.F.

Ashburn, D., Kirkbride, M.P., and Dugmore, A.J., 2003. Post-settlement land disturbance indicated by magnetic susceptibility of aeolian soils at Seljaland. *In*: K. Ahronson, ed. *Atlantic Peoples between Fire, Ice, River and Sea. Past Environments in Southern Iceland. Northern Studies* 37, 81–94.

Benediktsson, J., 1969. Landnámabók: some remarks on its value as a historical source. *Saga-Book*, 17, 275–292.

Birkeli, F. 1973. *Norske steinkors i tidlig Middelalder. Et bidrag til belysning av overgangen fra norrøn religion til kristendom.* Oslo: Universitetsforlaget.

Branigan, K., and Dearne, M.J., eds., 1992. *Romano-British Cavemen. Cave Use in Roman Britain.* Oxbow Monograph 19. Oxford: Oxbow Books.

Campbell, E., 1987. A cross-marked quern from Dunadd and other evidence for relations between Dunadd and Iona. *Proceedings of the Society of Antiquaries of Scotland* 117, 105–117.

Colgrave, B., ed. and transl., 1940. *Two Lives of Saint Cuthbert: A Life by an Anonymous Monk of Lindisfarne and Bede's Prose Life.* Cambridge: Cambridge University Press.

Colgrave B., ed. and transl., 1956. *Felix's Life of St Guthlac.* Cambridge: Cambridge University Press.

Davies, W., 1996. 'Protected' space in Britain and Ireland in the Middle Ages. *In*: B. Crawford, ed. *Scotland in Dark Age Britain*, St John's House Pap 6. St Andrews: Scottish Cultural Press, 1–19.

Davies, W., Graham-Campbell, J., Handley, M., Kershaw, P., Koch, J. T., Le Duc, G. and Lockyear, K., 2000. *The Inscriptions of Early Medieval Brittany/Les inscriptions de la Bretagne du Haute Moyen Âge.* Celtic Studies Publications V. Aberystwyth, Wales: Celtic Studies Publications.

Dugmore, A.J., 1987. *Holocene Glacier Fluctuations around Eyjafjallajökull, South Iceland: A Tephrochronological Study.* Thesis (PhD), University of Aberdeen.

Dugmore, A.J. and Erskine, C.C., 1994. Local and regional patterns of soil erosion in southern Iceland. *In*: J. Stötter and J.F. Wilhelm, eds. *Environmental Change in Iceland*. Munich: Münchener Geographische Abhandlungen, 63–78.

Dugmore, A.J., Newton, A.J., Larsen, G. Larsen and Cook, G.T., 2000. Tephrochronology, environmental change and the Norse settlement of Iceland. *Environmental Archaeology* 5(1), 21–34.

Dugmore, A.J. and Simpson, I.A., 1200 years of Icelandic landscape change reconstructed using tephrochronology. *Earth Surface Processes and Landforms*.

Edwards, K.J., Borthwick, D., Cook, G., Dugmore, A.J., Mairs, K.A., Church, M.J., Simpson, I.A., and Adderly, W.P., 2005. Landscape change in eastern Suðuroy, Faroe Islands: a hypothesis-based approach to the determination of natural processes and human artifice. *Human Ecology* 33(5), 621–650.

Edwards, N., 2001. Early-Medieval inscribed stones and stone sculpture in Wales. *Medieval Archaeology* 45, 15–40.

Finsen, V., ed., 1974 [1852]. *Grágás: Konungsbók*. Odense: Odense Universitetsforlag.

Fisher, I., 1994. The monastery of Iona in the eighth century. *In*: F. O'Mahony, ed. *The Book of Kells: Proceedings of a Conference at Trinity College Dublin 6–9 September 1992*. Aldershot: Scolar Press for Trinity College Library Dublin, 33–47.

Fisher, I., 2001. *Early Medieval Sculpture in the West Highlands and Islands*. Monograph 1. Edinburgh: Royal Commission on the Ancient and Historical Monuments of Scotland/Society of Antiquaries of Scotland.

Flobert, P., ed. and transl., 1997. *La vie ancienne de Saint Samson de Dol*. Paris: CNRS.

Friðriksson, A., 1994. *Sagas and Popular Antiquarianism in Icelandic Archaeology*. Avebury: Ashgate.

Gellein, K., 2007. *Kristen innflytelse i hedensk tid? En analyse med utgangspunkt i graver fra yngre jernalder i Hordaland*. UBAS Hovedfag/Master 2. Bergen: University of Bergen. Available from: http://bora.uib.no/handle/1956/11216 [accessed 1 December 2016].

Grönvold, K., Óskarsson, N., Johnsen, S. J., Clausen, H. B., Hammer, C. U., Bond, G. and Bard, E., 1995. Tephra layers from Iceland in the Greenland GRIP ice core correlated with oceanic and land based sediments. *Earth and Planetary Science Letters* 135(1–4), 149–155. Available from: http://dx.doi.org/10.1016/0012-821X(95)00145-3 [accessed 1 December 2016].

Hannon, G.E. and Bradshaw, R.H.W., 2000. Impacts and timing of the first human settlement on vegetation of the Faroe Islands. *Quaternary Research* 54, 404–413.

Haraldsson, H., 1981. *The Markarfljót Sandur Area, Southern Iceland: Sedimentological, Petrological and Stratigraphical Studies*. Striae vol. 15. Uppsala: Striae.

Hermanns-Auðardóttir, M., 1989. *Islands tidiga bosättning. Studier med utgångspunkt i merovingertida-vikingatida gårdslämningar i Herjólfsdalur, Vestmannaeyjar, Island*. Umeå: Umeå Universitet Arkeologiska Institutionen.

Hermanns-Auðardóttir, M., 1991. The early settlement of Iceland: results based on excavations of a Merovingian and Viking farm site at Herjólfsdalur in the Westmen Islands, Iceland. *Norwegian Archaeological Review* 24(1), 1–33.

Hermanns-Auðardóttir, M., 1992. The beginning of settlement in Iceland from an archaeological point of view. *Acta Borealia* 9, 85–135.

Hjartarson, Á., Guðmundsson, G.J., and Gísladóttir, H., 1991. *Manngerðir hellar á Íslandi*. Reykjavík: Menningarsjóður.

Holt, A. and Guðmundsson, G.J., 1980. *Um manngerða hella á Suðurlandi* (Framlag til alþýðlegra fornfræða 1). Reykjavík: Sögufélag.

Jóhansen, J., 1985. *Studies in the Vegetational History of the Faroe and Shetland Islands*. Annales Societatis Scientarum Faeroensis Supplementum XI. Tórshavn: Føroya fróðskapparfelag.

Jónsson, B., 1902. Rannsókn í RangárÞingi sumarið 1901. *Árbók hins Íslenzka Fornleifafélags* 1902, 1–32.

Lager, L. 2000. Art as a reflection of religious change. *Archaeological Review from Cambridge* 17, 117–132.

Migne, J.P., ed., 1844–1864. *Vita S. Pauli Primi Eremitæ* in *Patrologia Latina* 23, cols 17–30.

Mowbray, C., 1936. Eastern influence on carvings at St Andrews and Nigg, Scotland. *Antiquity* 10(40), 428–440.

MacQueen, J. and MacQueen,W., 2005. *St Nynia, with a translation of the Miracula Nynie Episcopi and the Vita Niniani*. Edinburgh: Birlinn.

Ogilvie, A.E.J., Barlow, L.K., and Jennings, A.E., 2000. North Atlantic climate *c*. AD 1000: millennial reflections on the Viking discoveries of Iceland, Greenland, and North America. *Weather*, 55 (2), 34–45. Available from: http://dx.doi.org/10.1002/j.1477-8696.2000.tb04028.x [accessed 1 December 2016].

O'Loughlin, T., 1997. Living in the ocean. *In*: C. Bourke, ed. *Studies in the Cult of St Columba*. Dublin: Four Courts Press, 11–23.

Ritchie, J.N.G., 1968. Keil Cave, Southend, Argyll: A late Iron Age cave occupation in Kintyre. *Proceedings of the Society of Antiquaries of Scotland* 99, 104–110.

Ritchie, G. 2002. Excavation archives: preservation and chance. *In*: B. Ballin-Smith and I. Banks, eds. *In the Shadow of the Brochs: The Iron Age in Scotland, a Celebration of the Work of Dr Euan MacKie on the Iron Age of Scotland*. Stroud, Gloucestershire: Tempus 206–208.

Roberts, H.M., Snæsdóttir, M., and Vésteinnsson, O., eds., 2002. *Fornleifarannsóknir við Aðalstræti 2001. Áfanfaskýrsla./ archaeological investigations in Aðalstræti 2001. Interim report*. Reykjavík: Fornleifastofnun Íslands.

Saville, A. and Hallén, Y., 1994. The 'Obanian Iron Age'. *Antiquity* 68, 715–723.

Sawyer, B., 2000. *The Viking-Age Rune-Stones: Customs and Commemoration in Early Medieval Scandinavia*. Oxford: Oxford University Press.

Schiffer, M.B., 1987. *Formation Processes of the Archaeological Record*. Albuquerque, NM: University of New Mexico Press.

Simpson, J.Y. 1859. On an old stone-roofed cell or oratory in the island of Inchcolm. *Proceedings of the Society of Antiquaries of Scotland* 1859, 489–528.

Simpson, J.Y., 1865. Notices of some ancient sculptures on the walls of caves in Fife. *Proceedings of the Society of Antiquaries of Scotland* 6 (appendix), 135–140.

Smith, K.T. and Ahronson, K., 2003. Dating the cave? The preliminary tephra stratigraphy at Kverkin, Seljaland. *In*: K. Ahronson, ed. *Atlantic Peoples between Fire, Ice, River and Sea. Past Environments in Southern Iceland. Northern Studies* 37, 71–80.

Stuart, J., 1856–1867. *Sculptured Stones of Scotland.* 2 vols. Edinburgh: Spalding Club.

Sveinbjarnardóttir, G., 1991. Shielings in Iceland: an archaeological and historical survey. *Acta Archaeologica* 61, 73–93.

Taylor, T., 1991 [1925]. *The Life of St. Samson of Dol.* Felinfach: Llanerch.

Thomas, C., 1971. *The Early Christian Archaeology of North Britain: the Hunter Marshall Lectures Delivered at the University of Glasgow in January and February 1968.* London: Oxford University Press.

Tolan-Smith, C., 2001. *The Caves of Mid Argyll: An Archaeology of Human Use*. Monograph 20. Edinburgh: Society of Antiquaries of Scotland.

Tómasson, Þ., 1997. *Setið við sagnabrunn.* Reykjavík: Mál og Mynd.

Vésteinsson, O., 1998. Patterns of settlement in Iceland. A study in prehistory. *Saga-Book* 25, 1–29.

Vilhjálmsson, V.Ö., 1992. The early settlement of Iceland: wishful thinking or archaeological innovation. *Acta Archaeologica* 62, 167–181.

Wade-Evans, A.W., ed. and transl., 1944. *Vitae Sanctorum Britanniae et Genealogiae*. Cardiff: University of Wales Press.

Wasserschleben, H., ed., 1996 [1885]. *Die irische Kanonensammlung.* Leipzig: Nabu Press.

Webster, L. and Backhouse, J., eds., 1991. *The Making of England: Anglo-Saxon Art and Culture, AD 600–900.* London: British Museum Press.

Wilson, D., 1851. *Archæology and Prehistoric Annals of Scotland.* Edinburgh: Hugh Paton.

Zielinski, G.A., Mayewski, P.A., Meeker, L.D., Grönvald, K., Germani, S. Whitlow, S., Twickler, M.S. and Taylor, K., 1997. Volcanic aerosol records and tephrochronology of the Summit, Greenland, ice cores. *Journal of Geophysical Research* 102(C12), 26625–26626.

# Chapter 7

# Saintly associations with caves in Ireland from the early medieval period (AD 400–1169) through to recent times

*Marion Dowd*

*Ireland has a rich tradition of cave usage from the Mesolithic through to modern times. During the early medieval period (AD 400–1169) the long-standing prehistoric associations between caves and the ritual and funerary aspects of life witnessed a change. Caves now began to be used for a much more disparate range of secular functions. Notwithstanding, there is clear evidence that some caves – typically small sites in relatively isolated locations – were perceived as sacred places, typically through their association with a local Christian saint, and came to be venerated places in association with early monasteries. In later centuries, these same sites continued to be ritual foci in the landscape and were visited as part of popular Catholic pilgrimages.*

## Introduction

Caves played an active role in the lives and cultural landscapes of communities and individuals in early medieval Ireland. Some caves were used for short-term settlement and storage, others functioned as workshops and hideaways, while a small number fulfilled a religious or ritual role (Dowd 2015). This chapter focuses on the latter aspect, specifically exploring the manner in which certain caves became places where early Irish saints were commemorated and celebrated from the advent of Christianity in the early fifth century through to the arrival of the Anglo-Normans in 1169. Many of the sites in question continued to be ritual foci in the landscape through the medieval period and into post-medieval and modern times. The origin of religious associations of certain caves that were visited as part of popular post-medieval Catholic pilgrimages ('patterns') is unclear: some may have become sacred places only in relatively recent centuries, while others may trace their origin as places of Christian devotion back to the early medieval period. Conleth Manning (2005) was the first to document the corpus of Irish caves associated with saints, and the topic has also been explored by Dowd (2004, 2015). This present contribution expands on previous work, both in terms of the number of sites involved and the discussion around this specific site type. The early medieval period in Ireland is generally considered 400–1169, the medieval period is 1169–1550, and the post-medieval period spans 1550–1800.

Many early Christian eremitics across Europe and the deserts of North Africa used caves as places of solitary prayer, religious contemplation and a retreat from daily life. In Ireland, a significant number of caves are associated with Christian saints, monasteries and religious foundations, though when such associations originated is often unclear (Fig. 7.1). A small number of early medieval documentary sources attest to a relationship – real or perceived – between caves and saints, where caves were believed to have acted as places of spiritual retreat, contemplation and penitence for a saint, ultimately allowing him to come into closer contact with God. Other caves were incorporated into early medieval monastic complexes and it is reasonable to infer that these were also perceived as sacred places. It is possible that certain other caves, linked to saintly figures in medieval and post-medieval Ireland, may represent continuations of much earlier traditions.

### Early literary sources: saintly hermitages and Lenten retreats

A number of early medieval manuscripts, principally from the twelfth century, contain references to seven caves that

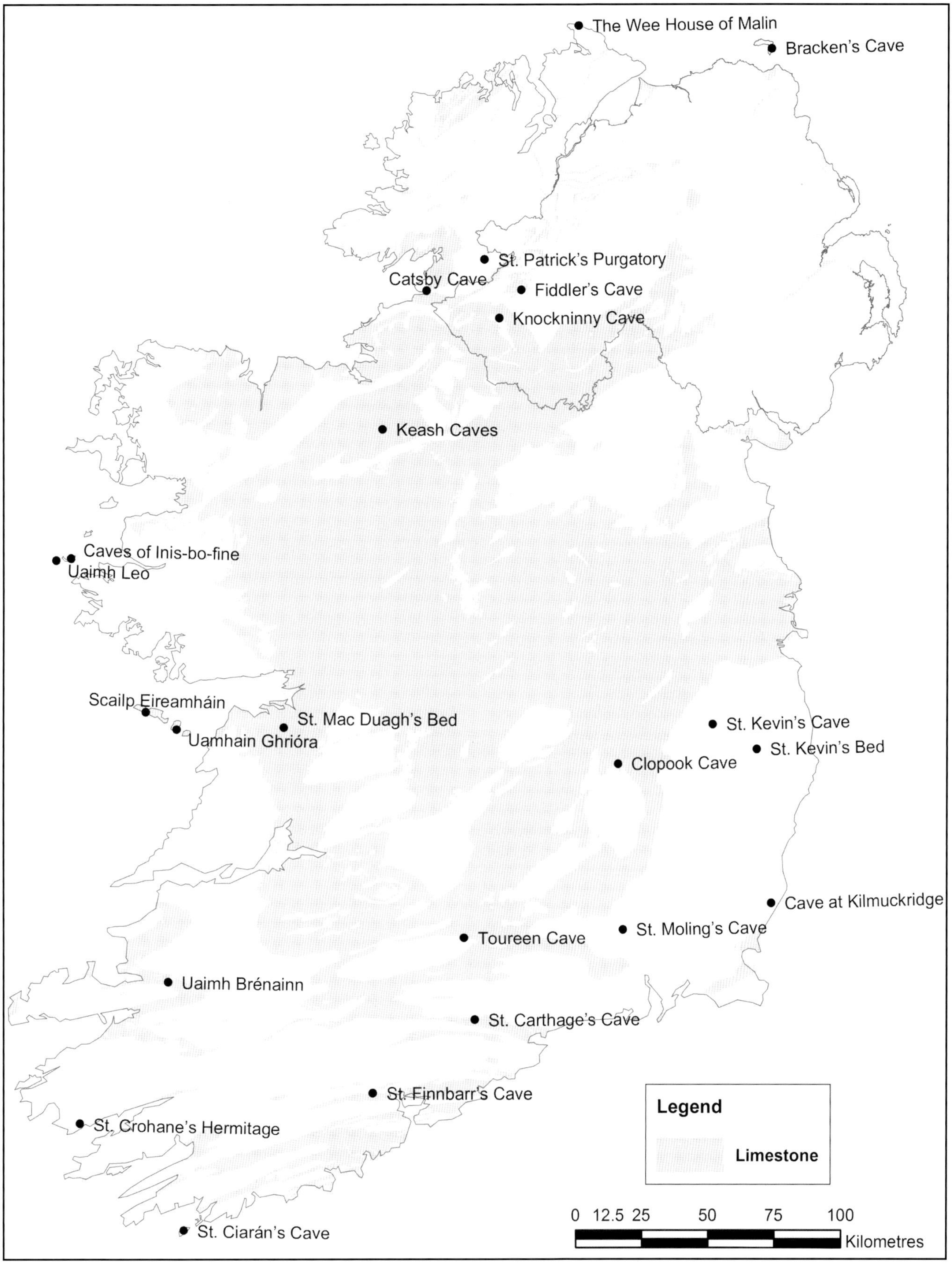


*Figure 7.1: Principal sites mentioned in the text.*

*Figure 7.2: Clopook Cave, Co. Laois. Photo: Marion Dowd.*

were associated with Christian saints. Only two of those caves can be identified in the landscape at present. One of these is Clopook Cave, Co. Laois, a small chamber that measures 2.5m high, 3.6m wide and 15m deep (Fig. 7.2). The site has never been archaeologically excavated and the only sign of human activity is the date '1881' carved into the cave wall (Sean Murray pers. comm.) and drystone walling towards the rear of the chamber reputedly constructed to prevent livestock from venturing deeper inside (Byrne 1852, 298). It is dry, spacious and well-lit and could conceivably have been used for occupation. In the ninth- or tenth-century *Vita Tripartita*, St Patrick, the patron saint of Ireland, is advised by Sechnall to give his chariot to St Fíacc of Sletty who had spent Lent or Shrove Saturday in a cave on the hill of Druim Coblai (*Uaimh Cnucc Dromma Coblai* – 'the cave of the hill of Druim Coblai'), identified as Clopook Cave, approximately 16km from St Fíacc's monastery in Sleaty, Co. Laois (O'Curry 1861, 607; Manning 2005, 110). Fíacc was traditionally associated with St Patrick and was portrayed as one of the first converts to Christianity, becoming abbot and bishop at Sleaty. He reputedly died *c*. AD 510–520 (Ó Riain 2011). St Patrick's *Vita* claims that St Fíacc would go to Clopook Cave on Shrove Tuesday, bringing with him five barley loaves mingled with ashes (Stokes 1887, 242–243). He was said to spend the 40 days and nights of Lent there before returning to Sleaty to celebrate Easter Mass with his brethren, taking with him from the cave a portion of one of the loaves (Comerford 1886, 129). The notion of St Fíacc emerging from this dim subterranean chamber into the world of the living on Easter Sunday morning carrying bread undoubtedly made explicit reference to the resurrection of Jesus Christ from his burial tomb or cave, bringing with him salvation and hope, ultimately symbolised by the 'bread of life'. Additionally, it draws attention to the self-imposed austerity of Fíacc's act of penance: over the course of 40 days he did not even use up all of the meagre five loaves allowed.

The same Lenten penitence theme is associated with a cave that 'faced' the River Boyne in the east of Ireland. The twelfth-century *Life of St Colmán mac Lúachán* mentioned that St Colmán was believed to have spent three Lenten periods in a cave here (McConkey 2012, 196). The location of this site is not known, but the close association between the Boyne and the Neolithic passage tombs at Newgrange, Knowth and Dowth, and the fact these three sites were referred to as 'caves' in medieval manuscripts (Lucas 1971/1973, 171), may indicate that the saint was linked to one of these prehistoric monuments rather than to a natural cave. Significant in this regard is that the Irish word for cave, *úam*, can also mean – amongst other things – a grave, tomb, cellar, crypt, vault or underground passage. When mentioned in medieval texts, therefore, it is sometimes ambiguous whether *úam* refers to a natural or humanly constructed feature (Dowd 2015, 6, 54). The broadly contemporaneous twelfth-century *Book of Leinster* contains a reference to a story titled *Uath ecalra imchummair* ('the cave of the church of Inchummar'). Though only the title survives, and the location of the 'cave' is unknown, here is another instance of a real or perceived early medieval association between a cave and a religious foundation (O'Curry 1861).

A cave–church connection is found in yet another twelfth-century text, the *Life of St Brendan*. Here we are told that Bishop Erc ordered the sixth-century St Brendan to spend a night in solitude in *Uaimh Brénainn* ('the cave of Brendan') at Ballymacelligott, Co. Kerry, as penance for striking a girl who had attempted to climb onto his chariot (Haren and de Pontfarcy 1988, 9). A church was subsequently constructed on or near the site of the cave and was referred to in the Ecclesiastical Taxation of 1302–1306 as *Ecclesia de Antro Sancti Brandani* ('the church of the cave of St Brendan') (Manning 2005, 115). Up to the nineteenth century it was known in the locality as *Uaimh Brénainn* (Hickson 1883/1884, 302). This now-destroyed limestone cave is also associated with the seventh-century St Moling. Transcribed in 1628–1629 from an older manuscript, *The Birth and Life of St Moling* recounts that Moling was the son of Fáelán and his wife's sister, Emnait. The baby was born by night in the extreme cold and deep snow. Feeling ashamed for betraying her sister, Emnait left her infant son Moling to perish and then tried to kill him, but he was protected by angels and a dove. According to the story, mother and child were subsequently rescued by a priest named Collanach who brought them to *Uaimh Brénainn* where the boy was raised for the first seven years of his life (Stokes 1907, 9–13).

St Moling is also associated with a second cave, St Moling's Cave at Mullennakill, Co. Kilkenny. Here the addition of drystone walling to a rockshelter has led to the creation of a part-natural, part-artificial cave (Carrigan 1905, 192; Manning 2005, 114). St Moling's Cave lies some 400m west of St Moling's holy well and 1.4km west of an ecclesiastical complex associated with the saint. A popular Catholic pilgrimage (known as a *pattern*) was held on Mullennakill Hill on the first Sunday after 24th August

(St Bartholomew's Day) until its suppression in 1867. Afterwards, and up to the 1940s, it was held on the second or third Sunday of July. The holy well and cave were visited on that day, and pilgrims knelt and prayed on a large flat stone located inside the cave (MacNeill 1982, 232, 575).

In 1137, an Augustinian monastery was constructed on or near the site of St Finbarr's Cave at Gill Abbey in Cork city; the monastery was known as *De Antro Sancti Barri* ('the abbey of St Finbarr's Cave') (O'Sullivan 1943, 15; Ó Riain 1994, 25–26). The cave was so called because it had supposedly been the retreat of the sixth-century St Finbarr. This tradition seemingly continued for several more centuries because in 1306 a Cork merchant bequeathed in his will 40 pence to 'the male anchorite of St Finbarr's Cave' (Ó Clabaigh 2010, 165). Writing in 1644, French aristocrat François de la Boullaye-Le Gouz stated that St Finbarr's Cave 'extends far underground' and noted that in former times St Patrick had retired there to pray (Crofton Croker 1837, 29).

The medieval *Life of St Kevin* described Glendalough, Co. Wicklow, as one of the four major places of pilgrimage (Harbison and Lynam 2002, 32). The founder of the monastery, the sixth-century St Kevin, reputedly spent a number of years as a recluse in at least two caves there – St Kevin's Cave and St Kevin's Bed. St Kevin's Cave penetrates a steep rocky cliff face on the eastern side of a narrow valley. It consists of a small natural cave that measures 3.7m × 2m and decreases in height from 2.2m to 1.7m. The saint is believed to have slept there (Grogan and Kilfeather 1997, 155). The twelfth- or thirteenth-century Irish and Latin *Lives of St Kevin* make reference to St Kevin's Bed as part of the hermitage of Temple-na-Skellig (Ó Carragáin 2010, 269). The site consists of a small chamber located on a sheer cliff face almost 10m above Lugduff Lake, the Upper Lake at Glendalough, and can only be accessed by boat (Fig. 7.3) (Hemp 1937, 290; Manning 2005, 110). It is a small rock-cut chamber that measures 2m deep, 0.9m high and 0.76m wide. It has been suggested that St Kevin's Bed may originally have been a prehistoric mine (Grogan and Kilfeather 1997, 140). Analysis by Manning (2005, 113, 117) confirms it is artificially rock hewn, probably with iron tools, but when the chamber was cut out of the cliff face has not been determined, though he suggests it may have been deliberately carved as a penitential bed in or before the twelfth century. Oral traditions from the nineteenth century claimed that having been tempted by a beautiful woman, St Kevin resolved to devote his time 'on his knees in the interior of his cave, condemning himself to undergo the severest penance' (Arlincourt 1844, 168). The woman in question either slipped and fell – or in most versions was thrown – into the lake below (Coyne and Bartlett 1842, 175–176; Harbison and Lynam 2002, 33). St Kevin's Bed was later used by St Laurence O'Toole (b. 1128), an abbot at Glendalough. The twelfth-century Latin *Vita* of his life claims that he regularly spent 40-day retreats in the cave, even after he became archbishop of Dublin in 1162. A wooden ladder allowed him to access the cave from the lake (Manning 2005, 110–113).

*Figure 7.3: St Kevin's Bed, Glendalough, Co. Wicklow: associated with St Kevin and the Lenten retreat of St Laurence O'Toole in the twelfth century. Reproduced with permission of the Photographic Unit, National Monuments Service.*

Several Irish and Latin versions of the *Life* of the 7th century St Mochuda (St Carthage) survive, apparently originally deriving from an 11th or 12th century version. This saint is said to have retired to a cave in 'a remote and lonely place' to escape the noise of building operations during construction of his monastery at Lismore, Co. Waterford. He used the cave as a hermitage for 18 months, occasionally visited by senior monks to whom he gave 'sound, sweetly-reasoned advice' (Power 1914, 145). Power suggested this now-destroyed cave was immediately north of the 12th century St Carthage's Cathedral in Lismore town, close to the bank of the River Blackwater (1914, 194).

Though not an early medieval text, the early seventeenth-century *Annals of the Four Masters*, in an entry for the year AD 898, refer to the deaths of four religious recluses in addition to 'Caenchombrac of the Caves of Inis-bo-fine' (Simpson 1859, 522). The location in question is the island of Inishbofin off the Connemara coast, less than 1km east of the island of Inishshark where the cave retreat of St Leo is situated. Inishbofin has numerous natural sea caves and two ecclesiastical complexes, both possibly originating in the early medieval period, one associated with St Scáithin and the other with St Colmán (Gosling 1993), but there appears to be no surviving reference to a St Caenchombrac.

An unusual example of where an elusive documentary reference to a cave may tentatively be connected to archaeological material and recent folk tradition is found at the Keash Caves, Co. Sligo (Fig. 7.4). Here, a series of 17 cave entrances breach a limestone cliff running across Keshcorran Mountain. An entry in the *Annals of the Fours Masters* probably refers to one of these caves: 'The Age of Christ, 1007. The sixth year of Brian. Muireadhach, a distinguished bishop, son of the brother of Ainmire Bocht, was suffocated in a cave, in Gaileanga of Corann' (O'Donovan 1851, 759). In terms of archaeological evidence, a human tibia from Cave O at Keshcorran returned an early medieval radiocarbon date of 963±33 BP (UBA-6680) while a tenth- to thirteenth-century iron socketed armour-piercing projectile head, possibly a crossbow bolt, was found in Cave J (Coffey Cave) some 65m to the north (Dowd 2013). From at least the early nineteenth century, Cave E – the largest of the cave entrances at Keshcorran – has been known as 'the Hermit's Bedroom' and is annotated as such on the 1830s Ordnance Survey map. Hardman (1892, 376) explained that a hermit resided there in solitude 'some years ago' but was trapped in the cave during a snow storm and died from hunger and exposure. One wonders whether the tibia might reflect the remains of the unfortunate bishop, and whether the nineteenth-century hermit might be an echo of this holy man who met his end in a cave in the area. In cases like this, any connection between documentary sources, archaeological evidence, and post-medieval folklore are highly tenuous, to say the least, and even further archaeological excavation is unlikely to clarify the issue. That said, a link between these disparate sets of data cannot be dismissed entirely.

Two aspects are worth noting about the caves discussed above that are documented in the early medieval texts. Firstly, four of these cave sites form part of early medieval and/or medieval ecclesiastical complexes. Secondly, the associated saints are generally 'early', typically holy men who lived during the sixth or seventh centuries. These points are relevant when assessing the caves discussed below that are associated with saints and form components of early medieval religious complexes. Though we cannot know for sure when these caves assumed a religious significance (i.e. during the early medieval, medieval or post-medieval period), the balance of evidence strongly argues that religious associations originated in the early medieval period when the foundations in question were constructed. For instance, nineteenth-century folk tradition claimed that in the 'distant past' a saint used to retire to Clopook Cave, Co. Laois, to pray and fast, after which he returned to his church via a subterraneous passage (Comerford 1886, 129). This folk memory is significant considering the ninth- or tenth-century manuscript references recounting that St Fíacc spent the 40 days of Lent in Clopook Cave.

## St Patrick's Purgatory, Co. Donegal: a cave of renown in early medieval and medieval Ireland

The most renowned cave from a Christian perspective in early medieval, medieval, post-medieval and modern Ireland is St Patrick's Purgatory, Co. Donegal. Medieval documentary sources record that noblemen from across Europe, Gaelic kings, higher ecclesiastics, monks and members of the lay population all went on religious pilgrimage to St Patrick's Purgatory. These medieval 'journeys of faith' were undertaken as acts of devotion or to serve penance, assuage guilt, seek miracles or appeal for healing (Turner and Turner 1978, 232–233; Hopper 2002, 3, 7). St Patrick's Purgatory is located on one of the numerous small islands scattered across Lough Derg lake, but there is confusion as to whether the purgatory was originally on Saint's Island or on Station Island. An early medieval monastery seems to have been located on Saint's Island and in the 1130s the Augustinians established a house here. The chief function of this house was apparently to minister to the needs of pilgrims attending the purgatory on the adjacent Station Island (Kenney 1979, 355; Lacy *et al.* 1983, 280–282). However, in 1735 a writer stated that the purgatory had originally been on Saint's Island but was later transferred to Station Island, a contention supported by nineteenth- and twentieth-century folk tradition (Pinkerton 1856, 104; O'Connor 1931, 113; Harbison 1991, 65).

The earliest reference to the pilgrimage is contained in *De Purgatorio Patritii* dating to *c.* 1120 and written by David Scottus of Würzburg (Kenney 1979). It was, however, an account penned by a Cistercian monk, Henry of Saltrey, in 1184 that brought European attention to St Patrick's Purgatory. In his book *Tractatus de Purgatorio Sancti Patricii*, Henry provides a portrayal of a fifth-century St Patrick who was led by Christ to a 'dark pit in a deserted place' – the island cave. Whoever spent a day and a night in the pit would supposedly experience, 'the torments of the wicked and the delights of the blessed' and would be absolved of sin (Haren and de Pontfarcy 1988, 8). A seventeenth-century account claimed that Patrick retired to the cave where he prayed that the pains of purgatory might be revealed to him. His wish was granted and after receiving a number of visions, the saint declared the island a terrestrial purgatory where sinners could repent (Seymour 1918, 11).

*Figure 7.4: The Keash Caves, Co. Sligo. Photo: Thorsten Kahlert.*

Henry of Saltrey also detailed a pilgrimage made to St Patrick's Purgatory by an English knight named Owein in 1146 or 1147. During his 24-hour solitary stay in the cave, the knight recorded witnessing devils torturing sinners. Tormented souls were nailed to the ground with red-hot irons. People were immersed in molten metal and freezing water. Sinners were beaten by devils and gnawed by serpents and toads. The knight was repeatedly dragged by devils to the entrance of hell but each time escaped by uttering the name of Christ. He also described visions of a paradise brimming with flowers and perfumes. He was given heavenly food to eat before returning to the mouth of the cave (Pinkerton 1856, 111). This account of the knight's experiences achieved widespread popularity across medieval Europe, leading to the compilation of numerous versions and translations. It appears to have influenced Dante's *Divine Comedy* (Turner and Turner 1978, 126). It may also have provided inspiration for a fourteenth-century fresco at Todi, Italy that depicts St Patrick looking over the entrance to purgatory – represented as a cave with seven chambers each containing one of the seven deadly sins (Harbison 1991, 57–58). Henry's narrative prompted a large number of overseas visitors to undertake the pilgrimage to Lough Derg. Written accounts dating to between the twelfth and fifteenth centuries survive detailing the experiences of 27 pilgrims from England, France, Hungary, Italy, the Netherlands, Switzerland and Belgium (Haren and de Pontfarcy 1988, 5–6; Easting 1991, xviii). Some pilgrims spent 24 hours in the cave where they described having visions of purgatory or experiencing physical torments. Others met and spoke with dead friends and family members while underground (Curtayne 1976, 37).

No trace now survives of the original cave that was the site of the early medieval and medieval pilgrimage but various writers provided descriptions. Henry of Saltrey wrote of 'a round pit, dark inside' (Haren and de Pontfarcy 1988, 8). In 1411 an Italian pilgrim recorded that the cave was low but could contain nine people (Pinkerton 1857, 71). In the 1540s it was likened to 'an old coal pit' and some 25 years later to 'a closet of stone' (Pinkerton 1857, 63–64). A description dating to *c.* 1600 referred to the 'door of the cave' and the need to spend 'twenty-four hours in either of the two caves' (Harbison 1991, 62). Even though the purgatory is represented as a natural cave in a fifteenth-century illustration (Fig. 7.5), most of the documented descriptions suggest an artificial subterranean stone structure. The underlying geology of the Lough Derg islands comprises schist and gneiss, rock types not

*Figure 7.5: A fifteenth-century depiction of St Patrick's Purgatory, Co. Donegal. After Pinkerton 1856, 110.*

conducive to the formation of caves. Notwithstanding, the medieval accounts of the purgatory consistently refer to it as a 'cave' and it is clear that it was *perceived* as such. For early medieval and medieval pilgrims it may have been considered more fitting that encounters with the Christian Otherworld were experienced in a natural cave rather than in an artificial structure created by human hands. What is clear is that the 'cave' of St Patrick's Purgatory was an established place of pilgrimage in the twelfth century. There is no indication that it necessarily developed from an earlier tradition. In fact, it may have been a product of the focus on penance and pilgrimage following the twelfth-century church reform (Harbison 1991).

## Caves as components of early medieval and medieval religious complexes

The construction of churches or monasteries on the location of a cave physically and spiritually capitalised on the sanctity of these hermitages and their associations with early saints, though whether natural caves actually existed at some of these locations, or whether they were ever actually utilised as religious retreats, is far from certain. Such associations may also reflect a deliberate attempt by the church to develop the cult of a saint centuries after his death by linking him to a particular topographical feature in the landscape and a specific place within an ecclesiastical complex. A prime example is St Colmán Mac Duagh's Cave, annotated *St Mac Duagh's Bed* on the 1830s Ordnance Survey maps, at Keelhilla, Co. Clare (Fig. 7.6). The cave forms part of an isolated hermitage complex including a twelfth-century church in addition to a graveyard, holy well, bullaun stone (a boulder with a circular depression that holds water, typically associated with early monasteries; the water is traditionally believed to have curative properties) and penitential stations. The cave is small (max. 2m × 1m) and it is difficult to imagine it could have been occupied, though it is large enough to permit an adult to sit or lie there. According to folk tradition, St Colmán spent seven years fasting in the cave, adopting a life of solitude and prayer. The saint obtained all the food, drink and clothing he required in the adjacent forests, in addition to the building materials required to construct an oratory. He was eventually discovered by a local king who persuaded him to accept the position of bishop of the wider territory after which he moved to Kilmacduagh, Co. Galway (Fahy 1911, 368–369).

A cave was also apparently part of the early medieval monastic complex at Toureen, Co. Tipperary, which also includes a church, cross, bullaun stone, holy well and ecclesiastical enclosure. The complex is associated with St Beccán who was said to have 'practised austerities' in the cave, but no trace of a cave survives at present (MacNeill 1982, 642–643). From at least 1684, a sea cave on the coast of Inishshark Island, Co. Galway, known as *Uaimh Leo* or *Fuaig Leo* ('the cave of Leo'), was believed to be a place where St Leo spent time in solitary prayer and meditation (Hardiman 1846, 115). It is immediately beside a holy well, *Tobar Leo* ('the well of Leo'), and lies approximately 100m east of an early medieval monastic enclosure dedicated to the saint (Gosling 1993, 124). In both these instances, the associations with early medieval monasteries strongly suggest that the caves dedicated to the saints Beccán and Leo were ritually significant places in early medieval times.

Not surprisingly, St Patrick, the patron saint of Ireland, is linked to several caves. He is said to have occupied Catsby Cave (Fig. 7.7), a small cave on the bank of the Abbey River immediately outside the enclosing wall of Assaroe Abbey, Co. Donegal – a Cistercian monastery founded in 1178. The saint is believed to have used the cave as a chapel and baptistery. St Columba is also said to have lived in Catsby Cave for a period (Wakeman 1896, 294–295; MacNeill 1982, 601). A holy well in the form of two artificial stone basins or bullauns is located on a rock ledge inside the cave. The hollows are filled with fresh water dripping from the cave roof (Fig. 7.7). The ledge is locally known as 'the altar' (Lacy *et al.* 1983, 307). In the nineteenth century Wakeman (1875, 470; 1896, 295) described a cross carved into the rock near the two bullauns but this is no longer visible. Up until relatively recent decades, popular Catholic pilgrimages (patterns) were annually made to the holy well in Catsby Cave between the 10th of June and the 20th of September, but particularly on 15th August, attracting crowds of pilgrims from within a 50km radius (Ó Muirgheasa 1936, 144). There is also a tradition that the dead were brought by boat across the River Erne estuary to Catsby. Funeral prayers were then recited at the cave before bringing the corpse to the graveyard located overhead in the grounds of Assaroe Abbey (Lockwood 1901, 182). Mass was reputedly celebrated in Catsby Cave during Penal times (1695–1829) when Catholicism was prohibited in Ireland. This little cave, therefore, has multiple religious

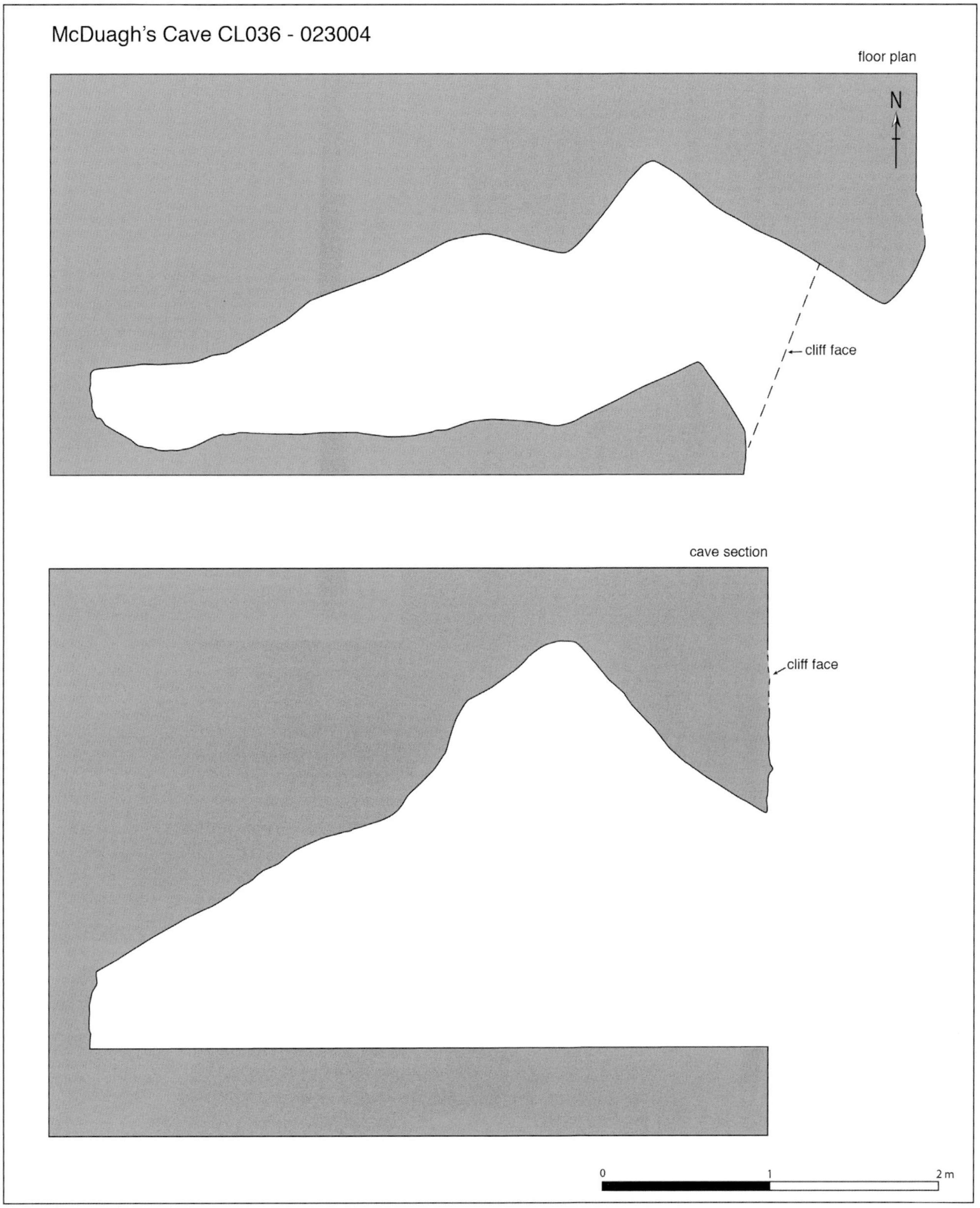


*Figure 7.6: Plan and longitudinal profile of Colmán Mac Duagh's Bed, Co. Clare. Illustration: Michael Lynch.*

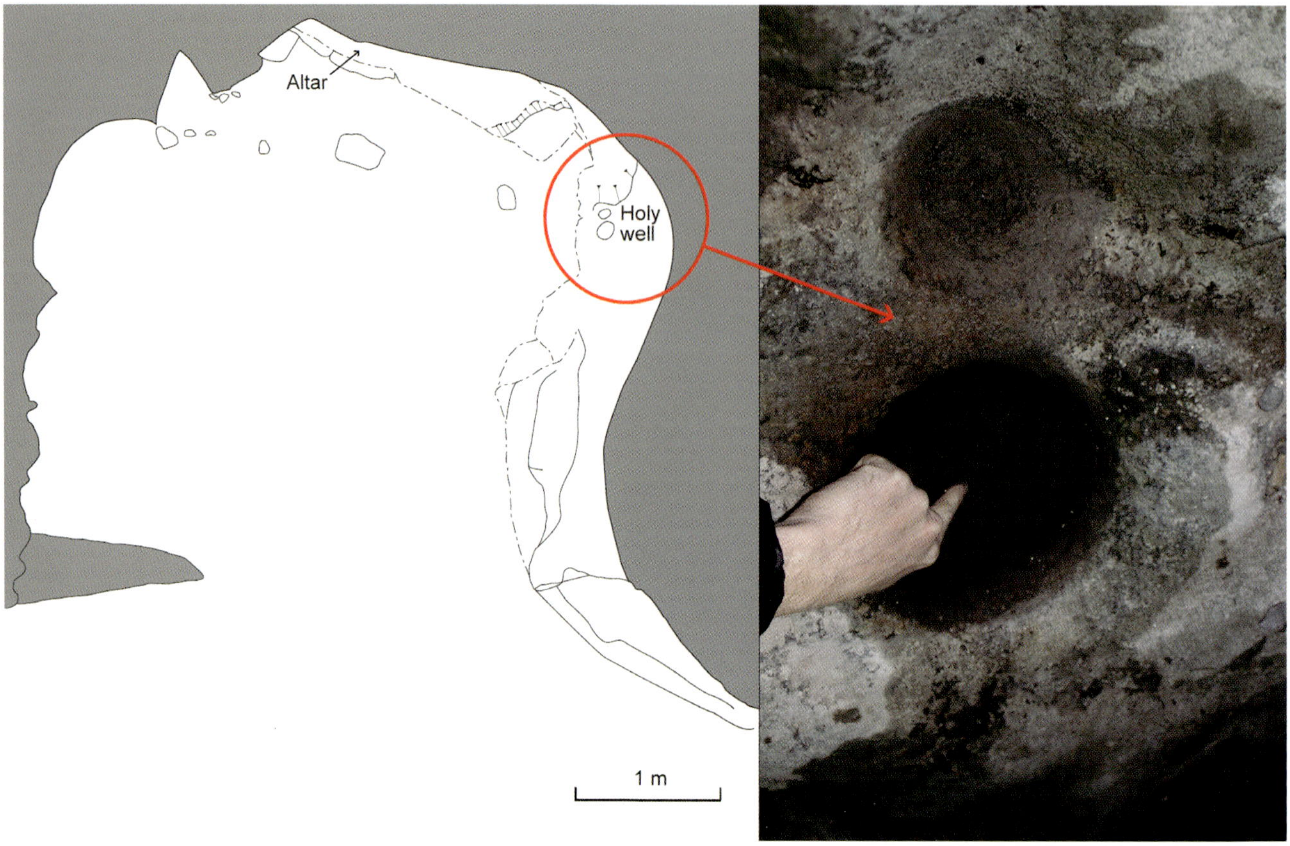


*Figure 7.7: Plan of Catsby Cave, and the two bullauns that comprise the holy well in the interior. Illustration: Richie Hinchy, photo: Marion Dowd.*

associations all indicating it was a sacred place in the landscape associated with saints, the dead, the celebration of Mass, and popular Catholic pilgrimage. Considering Assaroe Abbey was constructed in the late twelfth century, it is likely that the cave emerged as a ritually significant place at that time, if not earlier, and continued to be of religious significance throughout the medieval period and up to post-medieval and modern times.

A second pilgrimage cave is *The Wee House of Malin*, a semi-artificial cave on the Donegal coast at the most northerly tip of Ireland. Like Catsby Cave it is small, measuring just 2.75m deep, 1.3m wide and 2.25m high (Lacy *et al*. 1983, 242), yet in local folklore the cave, 'holds all that goes into it, and the more goes into it, it holds the more' (Beattie *et al*. 2000, 40). Crude drystone benches are located in the interior. The cavern is located immediately behind a medieval church associated with St Muirdhealach who died in 1088 (Ó Muirgheasa 1936, 160–161). This hermit saint reputedly lived in the cave (Fitzgerald 1975, 2), and it is also associated with St Morialagh of Clonca (Rowan 1979, 418). Further along the seashore is a holy well called *Malin Well* or *Tobar Muireadagh* ('the well of Muirdhealach'), which is covered by the sea at high tide and is therefore frequently rendered inaccessible (Lacy *et al*. 1983, 301). Water from the well was said to have been blessed by St Muirdhealach and stories circulated about its miraculous properties for those of ill health (Ó Muirgheasa 1936, 160). The traditional popular Catholic religious pattern at this complex took place on 15th August, though formerly it supposedly occurred on the festival of Bealtaine (eve of 1st May) and at midsummer (Ó Muirgheasa 1936, 160; Fitzgerald 1975, 2). On pilgrimage day penitents prayed and spent time in the cave and bathed in the holy well (Logan 1980, 61). In 1752, the English Bishop Pococke wrote that St Muirdhealach had lived in a cave in the cliff where poor people stayed when they came for a cure from the adjacent holy well (Logan 1980, 26).

Fiddler's Cave at Kiltierney, Co. Fermanagh, is a more substantial cave than those mentioned previously, measuring at least 40m in length, but is active and has a small river flowing through it (Fig. 7.8). Though it is no longer visible, a stone bearing two hollows believed to be the imprints of St Patrick's knees where he knelt in prayer was once reputedly located at the cave entrance (MacNeill 1989, 123). Significantly, the cave is located approximately 100m south-west of a Cistercian abbey and grange. There can be little doubt that it attracted the attention of the monastic community as it would have provided a valuable supply of

*Figure 7.8: Fiddler's Cave, Co. Fermanagh, where the patron saint of Ireland, Patrick, reputedly knelt in prayer. Photo: Marion Dowd.*

fresh water throughout the year. Its proximity to the abbey, two holy wells, and the folkloric link to St Patrick all suggest Fiddler's Cave was perceived to be of some religious importance either during or subsequent to the occupation of the abbey in medieval times.

On Cape Clear Island, Co. Cork, a cave dedicated to St Ciarán of Saighir was reputedly located beside a medieval church, which is also dedicated to this fifth- or early sixth-century saint (Seward 1795). The cave is no longer visible. Interestingly, the twelfth-century *Martyrology of Gorman* records February 24th as the feast day of *Ciarán of Uamha*, that is, 'Ciarán of the Cave' (Stokes 1895, 42). The same manuscript refers to another saint, *Mo Conóc Uamach* ('the cave-dweller of Kilmuckridge'), whose feast day was celebrated on December 19th (Stokes 1895, 221, 243, 347).

*Figure 7.9: Bracken's Cave on the coast of Rathlin Island, Co. Antrim. A holy well located inside the cave is dedicated to St Breacán. Photo: Andy McInroy.*

## Caves associated with the popular religious pattern in post-medieval times

The Irish *pattern* essentially celebrated the feast day of the local saint. This annual vernacular festival involving assemblies of many hundreds, and sometimes thousands, of people incorporated elements of official Christian ritual, popular Christian ritual, healing, carnivalesque celebrations, economic activities, the enactment of kinship, class contention, religious contention and cultural hybridity (Ó Cadhla 2002, 57). The origin of the pattern is unclear, though documentary references as early as the seventeenth century indicate its widespread popularity throughout Ireland, and in 1704 an act was passed (but failed) to suppress the tradition (Ó Cadhla 2002, 54). Many of the caves mentioned above in relation to early medieval and medieval ecclesiastical complexes formed part of popular devotions on the pattern day allowing the penitent to pay homage to their local saint and to kneel in prayer at a place he was believed to have visited. In these cases I would argue that while the pattern may be of post-medieval origin, the religious significance of these particular cave sites stems back to the date of the associated monastery or church. However, a small number of caves form part of patterns that, while associated with saints, have no associated early medieval or medieval religious complex. In these instances, the cave in question, like the pattern itself, may only have originated as a holy place in post-medieval centuries.

The aforementioned St Kevin's Bed, Co. Wicklow, is partially if not entirely an artificial chamber created at an unknown date, but by the end of the early medieval period and certainly by medieval times it was likely perceived as a natural cave and not a humanly manufactured feature. In a similar vein, St Crohane's Hermitage, Co. Kerry, has always been regarded as a cave though it is, in fact, a prehistoric copper mine measuring 2.2m × 4.8m and 2.1m in height. It was used as a forge in 1808 (O'Sullivan and Sheehan 1996, 76) and further mining may have taken place here during the nineteenth century (Cole 1922, 58). Despite this secular usage, it has been linked to religious activities since at least the mid-eighteenth century. In 1756, Charles Smith recorded that the 'stalactical exudations of the above mentioned cell are held in great estimation by the country people, who carefully preserve them, as imagining them to have many virtues in them, from the supposed sanctity of the place they grow in' (MacNeill 1982, 649). In 1758, Pococke stated that 'the people by their devotions have worn it so smooth as to give it a polish', and that St Ciarán of Saighir lived and composed his monastic rule in 'St Crohan's Cave' (Ó Maidín 1959, 36). Folk tradition relates that St Crohane spent his life in the 'cave' and left an impression of his back on the cave wall (Bland 1825, 117; MacNeill 1982, 649).

A popular Catholic pilgrimage known as *Pátrún Chróchháin* (St Crohane's pattern) traditionally took place from July 29th to August 1st, during which time pilgrims visited St Crohane's Hermitage and carved crosses on stones located outside the entrance (BBG 1915, 120; Ó Maidín 1959, 36). Two stone walls extend from the mine face creating a more chamber-like effect, and a stone step is located at the rear (O'Sullivan and Sheehan 1996, 76). Once more, the question arises as to *when* this artificial cave achieved religious and saintly associations. Adjacent to the hermitage is a holy well (*Tobar Chróchháin* – 'the well of Crohane') and bullaun stone (*Carraig Chróchháin* – 'the rock of Crohane') – features often associated with early medieval monastic and ecclesiastical sites. A medieval church and graveyard (recorded in the Papal Taxation List of 1302–1306), a cross slab, holy well and sacred ash tree dedicated to the saint are located 1km to the south-east (O'Sullivan and Sheehan 1996, 76). Was St Crohane's Hermitage a ritual focus in the early medieval or medieval landscape? Or did it only become associated with this local saint in recent centuries as part of the popular religious pilgrimage?

Other associations between caves, saints and holy wells are of similarly unknown origin. A holy well known as *Bracken's Well* is located at the rear of Bracken's Cave – a sea cave on Rathlin Island off the Co. Antrim coast (Fig. 7.9). According to folk tradition, St Brecán reputedly lived in this cave. When he found himself without water he lifted a stone whereupon the miraculous spring well (which subsequently became the holy well) appeared. Water from this holy well is believed to provide a cure for warts (Williams 1990, 50). St Ninnidh spent the 40 days of Lent praying and fasting in a cave on Knockninny Hill, Co. Fermanagh (Fogg and Fogg 2001, 111), while St Carthage retired to a cave near Lismore, Co. Waterford (Coleman 1965, 30). St Gregory sought seclusion in *Uamhain Ghrióra* ('the cave of Gregory') on the island of Inis Meáin, Co. Galway (Robinson 1990, 22). Another recluse, St Éireamhán, retreated to *Scailp Eireamháin* ('the cave or cleft of Éireamhán') on the adjacent island of Inis Mór. Both of these island caves are on the coast, locations that symbolically reinforce the isolation and wilderness of eremitic life in contrast to contemporaneous settlements that would be located away from the coastline.

## Discussion

Considering approximately 470 caves on the island of Ireland can be classified as relict caves, i.e. dry and habitable (Dowd 2015, 52–53), only approximately 25 of these (or 5%) are associated with saints in historical documentation or in popular Catholic religious practice. Though a relatively small group, the sites in question share a number of features. They principally consist of small, cramped chambers that are unsuitable for occupation if compared to the available floor space and height of the caves that typically produce evidence of early medieval settlement (see Dowd 2015, ch. 8). That said, their small size may have been perceived as important in emphasising and symbolising the discomfort experienced by saints on their spiritual quests. Several sites display some form of modification: drystone walls enclose the entrances of more open sites that might be better considered rockshelters rather than caves proper, and crude walling or 'benches' occasionally occur.

The Irish expansion from the kingdom of Dál Riada in Co. Antrim to a much larger area of the same name in Argyll, Scotland, in the fifth century coincided with the Irish conversion to Christianity. The monasticism brought from Ireland to Scotland consciously followed the ascetic and meditative ideals of the desert fathers (Fisher 2001, 2–3). The solitary life of meditation was highly valued in the early Irish church, and thus isolated caves provided the ideal environment for such practices. Fisher (2001) documents nine Scottish caves with early Christian carvings but rightly notes that this is uncommon elsewhere in Ireland and Britain. Some of the Scottish sites are associated with the same saints that are linked to Irish caves. Thus we have a St Ciarán's Cave on the Kintyre coast, a St Molaise' Cave on the coast of Holy Island (off Arran), and a St Columba's Cave on the Mid-Argyll coast (Fisher 2001, 62, 118, 151). What is notable, however, is that unlike some of the Scottish caves, no early medieval religious carvings have yet been recorded in an Irish cave. At Catsby Cave a cross was noted carved into the cave wall in the nineteenth century, but no trace of this now survives and there is nothing to suggest that it is early medieval or even medieval in date. It was more likely associated with post-medieval and modern religious pilgrimage. Another possible example is Lettered Cave on Knockmore Mountain, Co. Fermanagh, but the Christian carvings there probably relate to the celebration of Mass in Penal times (Dowd 2015, 241), though Shee Twohig (2004, 228) has considered the Lettered Cave carvings may potentially be early medieval or medieval in date.

The majority of the Irish and Scottish caves associated with saints are located in isolated and distinctly liminal places in the landscape: in hilly rocky terrain where no settlements occur, on the sea shore, and on islands. While this to some extent reflects the preferred choice of location for early medieval monasteries more broadly in both countries, it also emphasises the concept of the hermitage as a *dísert*, a 'place apart'. Figure 7.1 also clearly illustrates a western bias in the location of these saintly caves, one that does not correspond with the presence of limestone, but rather reflects the high number of early medieval monastic hermitages and retreats that run along the west coast of Ireland and its offshore islands. Almost all of the Irish cave sites are located in close proximity to an early medieval or medieval ecclesiastical complex, typically within 1km. Usually the cave is located some distance from the main ecclesiastical centre, with several penitential stations in between that serve to physically connect the cave with the main complex. Where early documentary references do not exist, we cannot definitively date when the caves in question took on a religious significance, but certainly by the eighteenth and nineteenth centuries all were linked to saints and/or popular Catholic pilgrimages. It is not unreasonable to suggest that these associations may have originated when the monastery or religious house in question was first established. The legends and names attributed to these caves all place the cave as the focal point of the ecclesiastical complex or popular religious pilgrimage: this was the special religious retreat of the saint. The cave could be read as a topographical representation ('proof') of the presence of the saint at a site and thus 'justification' for the subsequent establishment of a monastery, church or abbey at that location. It must be considered, however, that the post-medieval 'readings' of these caves as religious foci may not have existed in the early medieval period. Some of the caves discussed here may have played no part in the establishment and operation of early monasteries, and only became linked to these complexes many centuries later after the monastery had been abandoned and had become part of popular Catholic religious practices.

The early medieval literary references and the folk traditions of more recent centuries provide a single basic narrative about how saints used these sites: the cave was used as a spiritual retreat where the saint retired for prayer, penance or during the Lenten fast. The implication is that the cave provided shelter and distance from the human world, and granted the saint solitude and a space wherein he came into closer contact with God. While all the saints linked to caves in the Irish tradition are exclusively male (mirroring the correlation between holy wells and male saints – Carroll 1999, 25), some of the more recent folktales contain references to women or girls, typically in the context of temptation. This is the reverse of the numerous stories in early medieval and medieval texts, as well as in more recent folklore, where caves are presented as abodes of supernatural women who frequently challenge mortal males. In these contexts, the male is victorious if he can draw the omnipotent female out of her cave (Dowd 2015, chs. 9 and 10).

There is a strong correlation between the caves discussed here and holy wells. Some caves contain a holy well while others are located in proximity to holy wells and both were visited as part of popular Catholic practices related to the saint in question. In recent centuries these caves were visited at various times of the year but particularly as part of the annual popular Catholic pattern when pilgrims typically entered the cave, knelt there and prayed to the relevant saint. When patterns originated is once again shrouded in darkness: holy wells are notoriously difficult to date and are probably multi-period sites. The 'pagan survivals' theory rose to prominence in the nineteenth century (Carroll 1999, 6) and continues to be fashionable, particular with the neo-Pagan revival of rituals at some holy wells. However, a prehistoric date for the vast majority of Irish holy wells is unlikely, though Kelly (2002) has argued that such veneration was introduced into Ireland from Roman Britain in the Iron Age. Manuscript references from the seventh century onwards refer to saints blessing and creating wells, suggesting early medieval and medieval origins for some of the 3000 holy wells documented on the island (O'Sullivan and Ó Carragáin 2008, 328; Ray 2011). In contrast, Carroll (1999) contends that the holy well tradition only originated after the Council of Trent (1545–1563) and was developed by Anglo-Irish and Gaelic-Irish elites in the later sixteenth and seventeenth centuries. This potential span of dates for holy well traditions likely mirrors the date range of when the caves discussed in this chapter took on a religious significance: some may have been ritual foci in prehistoric times; others may have been developed as religious sites in early medieval times when they became part of a monastic establishment; others may have been interpreted as holy places in the medieval period, possibly because of their physical proximity to earlier ecclesiastical complexes; while some other caves may only have become associated with saints in post-medieval centuries through their incorporation into popular Catholic religious practices.

Unfortunately, none of the Irish caves associated with saints have ever been excavated, and none have produced datable archaeological material. Conversely, none of the Irish caves that have produced archaeological artefacts, human bones or structures are linked to a saint or to any early medieval religious activity (apart from the Keash Caves). This may be a product of the type of cave that has been the subject of antiquarian and archaeological excavation in the past. The very small chambers associated with saints would not have attracted the attention of antiquarians driven by palaeontological concerns or those searching for early prehistoric remains. Similarly, the small size of the majority of the caves in question mean they are of no interest to cavers and thus archaeological material, which can often be inadvertently discovered in the course of speleological activities, will not be exposed in these sites by cavers. Finally, archaeologists interested in early medieval monasticism and ecclesiastical sites tend to focus more attention on the built heritage rather than on natural features and are less likely to be interested in excavating a cave as opposed to a church site or similar.

Without excavation, the possibility that folk traditions claiming a saint occupied a cave thereby converting it into a holy place cannot be tested. Archaeological excavation is also necessary to assess whether some of these sites may have been ritual places prior to the advent of Christianity, sites that because of their earlier significance were subsumed and adopted into the new religious belief system. Taylor (1993, 163) has argued that in the Holy Land:

> Christians 'discovered' that they [caves] were in fact once used by saints, or in a significant biblical event, and that they therefore deserved redemption. As more and more pagans embraced Christianity, more and more caves were 'saved' and turned into Christian holy places.

In an Irish context, however, we need to be careful not to assume that all caves with saintly associations had originally been places of pre-Christian significance – a belief too commonly encountered in popular texts. Many places of popular Catholic devotion may have acquired religious status in relatively recent centuries – as argued by Carroll (1999) – and do not have long histories of sacred associations.

Ultimately, the only manner in which we can hope to gain further insight into those Irish caves that are closely associated with saints is through excavation – both of the interior and the external area outside the entrance. Occupation debris related to the saint purported to have stayed in the cave is not likely to be encountered. It may be possible, however, to recover material that might shed light on *when* the cave in question became a holy place, and what form that veneration took. We should also be open to the possibility that early Christian carvings remain to be discovered on cave walls with the aid of techniques such as laser scanning, high-resolution photography, infra-red imaging and photogrammetry if no longer visible to the naked eye. The references to cave dwelling saints in the early medieval and medieval manuscripts, combined with the fact that the majority of these sites are located within early medieval or medieval complexes, strongly suggest that we should not be surprised to find evidence indicating that the majority of these caves were the focus of Christian veneration in early medieval Ireland.

## Acknowledgements

My sincere thanks to Terry O'Hagan for so generously sharing his time and expertise with me, and for bringing relevant references in the *Martyrology of Gorman* to my attention. His feedback and comments on an earlier draft have greatly improved this contribution (though all errors in fact or interpretation are mine alone). My thanks to Karen Lysaght for making me aware of material related to St Mochuda. I am grateful to the following for permission to use their images: Séan Murray, the National Monuments Service, Thorsten Kahlert, and Andy McInroy. My thanks to Michael Lynch and Richie Hinchy for their surveys of two sites and for permission to reproduce same here. I am grateful to James Bonsall for his comments on the text, and for producing Figure 7.1.

## References

Arlincourt, C.V.P., 1844. *The Three Kingdoms: England, Scotland, Ireland*. London: Richard Bentley.

B. B. G., 1915. Kilcrohane. *Kerry Archaeological Magazine* 3(14), 119–122.

Beattie, S., Lynch, M., and Harvey, R., 2000. *Inishowen*. Donaghadee: Cottage Publications.

Bland, F.C., 1825. Description of a remarkable building on the north side of Kenmare river, commonly called Staigue Fort. *The Dublin Philosophical Journal and Scientific Review* 1, 108–119.

Byrne, D., 1852. On the duns of Cloch-an-Phuca and Log-an-Chorain. *Transactions of the Kilkenny Archaeological Society for the year 1851* 1, 298–300.

Carrigan, W., 1905. *The History and Antiquities of the Diocese of Ossory, Volume IV*. Dublin: Sealy, Bryers and Walker.

Carroll, M.P., 1999. *Irish Pilgrimage, Holy Wells and Popular Catholic Devotion*. Baltimore, MD: Johns Hopkins University Press.

Cole, G.A.J., 1922. *Memoirs of the Geological Survey of Ireland. Mineral Resources*. Dublin: The Stationery Office.

Coleman, J.C., 1965. *The Caves of Ireland*. Tralee: Anvil Press.

Comerford, M., 1886. *Collections Relating to the Dioceses of Kildare and Leighlin. Third Series – Diocese of Leighlin*. Dublin: James Duffy and Sons.

Coyne, J.S. and Bartlett, W.H., 1842. *The Scenery and Antiquities of Ireland, Volume I*. London: George Virtue.

Crofton Croker, T., 1837. *The Tour of the French Traveler M. de la Boullaye le Gouz in Ireland, A. D. 1644*. London: T. and W. Boone.

Curtayne, A., 1976. *Lough Derg, St Patrick's Purgatory*. Omagh: Graham and Sons Ltd.

Dowd, M., 2004. *Caves: Sacred Places on the Irish Landscape*. Thesis (PhD), University College Cork.

Dowd, M., 2013. The archaeology and mythology of the Keash Caves, Co. Sligo. *In*: M.A. Timoney, ed., *Dedicated to Sligo: Thirty-Four Essays on Sligo's Past*. Sligo: Publishing Sligo's Past, 75–80.

Dowd, M., 2015. *The Archaeology of Caves in Ireland*. Oxford: Oxbow Books.

Easting, R., 1991. *St Patrick's Purgatory*. Oxford: Early English Text Society 298.

Fahy, M., 1911. St Colman's oratory, in Burren, County Clare. *Journal of the Royal Society of Antiquaries of Ireland*, 41, 368–370.

Fisher, I., 2001. *Early Medieval Sculpture in the West Highlands and Islands*. Edinburgh: Society of Antiquaries of Scotland.

Fitzgerald, J., 1975. *Holy Wells of Inishowen*. Carndonagh: Foyle Press.

Fogg, P. and Fogg, T., 2001. *Beneath our Feet: The Caves and Limestone Scenery of the North of Ireland*. Belfast: Environment and Heritage Service.

Gosling, P., 1993. *Archaeological Inventory of County Galway (West Galway): Volume 1*. Dublin: Stationery Office.

Grogan, E. and Kilfeather, A., 1997. *Archaeological Inventory of County Wicklow*. Dublin: Stationery Office.

Harbison, P., 1991. *Pilgrimage in Ireland*. London: Syracuse University Press.

Harbison, P. and Lynam, J., 2002. *St Kevin's Way, Hollywood to Glendalough, Co. Wicklow*. Kilkenny: Heritage Council.

Hardiman, J., 1846. *A Chorographical Description of West or h-Iar Connaught, written A. D. 1684, by Roderic O'Flaherty esq*. Dublin: Royal Irish Society.

Hardman, E.T., 1892. The limestone caves of Sligo. *In*: W.G. Wood-Martin, ed., *History of Sligo, Volume 3*. Dublin: Hodges, Figgis & Co., 375–378.

Haren, M. and de Pontfarcy, Y., 1988. *The Medieval Pilgrimage to St Patrick's Purgatory Lough Derg and the European Tradition*. Enniskillen: Clogher Historical Society.

Hemp, W.J., 1937. St Kevin's Bed, Glendalough. *Journal of the Royal Society of Antiquaries of Ireland* 67, 290–294.

Hickson, M.A., 1883/1884. Notes on Kerry topography, ancient and modern. *Journal of the Royal Historical and Archaeological Association of Ireland* 6, 295–305.

Hopper, S., 2002. *To Be a Pilgrim*. Gloucestershire: Sutton Publishing Ltd.

Kelly, E.P., 2002. Antiquities from Irish holy wells and their wider context. *Archaeology Ireland* 16(2), 24–28.

Kenney, J.F., 1979. *The Sources for the Early History of Ireland*. New York: Columbia University Press.

Lacy, B., Cody, E., Cotter, C., Cuppage, J., Dunne, N., Hurley, V., O'Rahilly, C., Walsh, P. and Ó Nualláin, S., 1983. *Archaeological Survey of County Donegal*. Lifford: Donegal County Council.

Lockwood, F.W., 1901. The remains of the Abbey Assaroe, Ballyshannon, in the County of Donegal. *Ulster Journal of Archaeology* 7, 178–185.

Logan, P., 1980. *The Holy Wells of Ireland*. Buckinghamshire: Colin Smythe Ltd.

Lucas, A.T., 1971/1973. Souterrains: the literary evidence. *Béaloideas* 39/41, 165–191.

MacNeill, M., 1982. *The Festival of Lughnasa*. Dublin: UCD Department of Folklore.

MacNeill, M., 1989. The musician in the cave. *Béaloideas* 57, 109–132.

Manning, C., 2005. Rock shelters and caves associated with Irish saints. *In*: T. Condit and C. Corlett, eds., *Above and Beyond: Essays in Memory of Leo Swan*. Wicklow: Wordwell Ltd., 109–120.

McConkey, R., 2012. The caves of Rathlin. *In*: W. Forsythe and R. McConkey, eds., *Rathlin Island, an Archaeological Survey of a Maritime Landscape*. Belfast: Northern Ireland Environment Agency, 190–208.

Ó Cadhla, S., 2002. *The Holy Well Tradition: The Pattern of St Declan, Ardmore, County Waterford, 1800–2000*. Dublin: Four Courts Press.

Ó Carragáin, T., 2010. *Churches in Early Medieval Ireland: Architecture, Ritual and Memory*. New Haven, CT: Yale University Press.

Ó Clabaigh, C., 2010. Anchorites in late medieval Ireland. *In*: L.H. McAvoy, ed., *Anchoritic Traditions of Medieval Europe*. London: Boydell & Brewer Ltd., 153–177.

O'Connor, D., 1931. *St Patrick's Purgatory, Lough Derg: Its History, Traditions, Legends, Antiquities, Topography, and Scenic Surroundings; With Some Account of its More Notable Pilgrims, and a Detailed Description of the Authorised Devotions Performed at its Venerable Shrine*. Dublin: James Duffy and Co.

O'Curry, E., 1861. *Lectures on the Manuscript Materials of Ancient Irish History*. Dublin: James Duffy.

O'Donovan, J., 1851. *Annals of the Kingdom of Ireland, by the Four Masters (volume II), [AD 903–1171]*. Dublin: Hodges and Smith.

Ó Maidín, P., 1959. Pococke's tour of south and south-west Ireland in 1758. *Journal of the Cork Historical and Archaeological Society* 64, 35–56.

Ó Muirgheasa, É., 1936. The holy wells of Donegal. *Béaloideas* 6, 143–162.

Ó Riain, P., 1994. *Beatha Bharra, Saint Finbarr of Cork. The Complete Life*. London: Irish Texts Society.

Ó Riain, P., 2011. *A Dictionary of Irish Saints*. Dublin: Four Courts Press.

O'Sullivan, A. and Sheehan, J., 1996. *The Iveragh Peninsula: An Archaeological Survey of South Kerry*. Cork: Cork University Press.

O'Sullivan, D., 1943. The monastic establishments of mediaeval Cork. *Journal of the Cork Historical and Archaeological Society* 48, 9–18.

O'Sullivan, J. and Ó Carragáin, T., 2008. *Inishmurray: Monks and Pilgrims in an Atlantic Landscape*. Cork: Collins Press.

Pinkerton, W., 1856. Saint Patrick's Purgatory. *Ulster Journal of Archaeology* 4, 40–52, 101–117, 222–238.

Pinkerton, W., 1857. Saint Patrick's Purgatory. *Ulster Journal of Archaeology* 5, 61–81.

Power, P. 1914. *Life of St Declan of Ardmore and Life of St Mochuda of Lismore*. Irish Texts Society 16. London: David Nutt.

Ray, C., 2011. The sacred and the body politic at Ireland's holy wells. *International Social Science Journal* 62(205–206), 271–285.

Robinson, T., 1990. *Stones of Aran, Pilgrimage*. London: Penguin.

Rowan, A., 1979. *North West Ulster: The Counties of Londonderry, Donegal, Fermanagh and Tyrone*. London: Penguin.

Seward, W.W., 1795. *Topographia Hibernica, or the Topography of Ireland, Ancient and Modern.* Dublin: Alex Stewart.

Seymour, J.D., 1918. *St Patrick's Purgatory, a Medieval Pilgrimage in Ireland.* Dundalk: Dundalgan Press.

Shee Twohig, E., 2004. An enduring tradition: incised rock art in Ireland. *In*: H. Roche *et al.*, eds., *From Megaliths to Metals: Essays in Honour of George Eogan*. Oxford: Oxbow Books, 222–229.

Simpson, J.Y., 1859. On an old stone-roofed cell or oratory in the island of Inchcolm. *Proceedings of the Society of Antiquaries of Scotland* 2, 489–528.

Stokes, W., 1887. *The Tripartite Life of Patrick: With Other Documents Relating to that Saint, 2 Volumes*. Rerum Britannicarum Medii Aevi Scriptores 89. London: Eyre and Spottiswoode.

Stokes, W., 1895. *Félire húi Gormáin: The Martyrology of Gorman, from a Manuscript in the Royal Library, Brussels*. Henry Bradshaw Society 9. London: Harrison.

Stokes, W., 1907. *The Birth and Life of St Moling*. London: Harrison and Sons.

Taylor, J.E., 1993. *Christians and the Holy Places*. Oxford: Clarendon Press.

Turner, T. and Turner, E., 1978. *Image and Pilgrimage in Christian Culture*. New York: Columbia University Press.

Wakeman, W.F., 1875. On certain markings on rocks, pillar-stones, and other monuments, observed chiefly in the County Fermanagh. *Journal of the Royal Society of Antiquaries of Ireland* 13, 445–474.

Wakeman, W.F., 1896. Lough Erne and Ballyshannon excursion. *Journal of the Royal Society of Antiquaries of Ireland* 26, 279–300.

Williams, B., 1990. The archaeology of Rathlin Island. *Archaeology Ireland* 4(2), 47–51.

# Part II
# Iberia and the Mediterranean

# Chapter 8

# Hidden in the depths, far from people: Funerary activities in the Lower Gallery of La Garma and the use of natural caves as burial places in early medieval Cantabria, northern Spain

*Pablo Arias, Roberto Ontañón, Enrique Gutiérrez Cuenca, José Ángel Hierro Gárate, Francisco Etxeberria, Lourdes Herrasti and Paloma Uzquiano*

*The discovery in 1995 of the skeletons of five young individuals dating to the seventh–eighth centuries AD in the Lower Gallery at La Garma, a place that is only accessible by descending two shafts 7m and 13m deep, provided solid archaeological evidence for the use of natural caves in Cantabria (northern Spain) for burial during the early medieval period. Recent excavation of similar contexts, such as the caves of Las Penas or Riocueva, together with the re-analysis of formerly known sites, is disclosing new, apparently heterodox, funerary behaviour during that period. This includes intriguing features such as the systematic crushing of human skulls, and the association of burned grain with bodies. Further analysis reveals that this form of funerary activity is not restricted to Cantabria. Evidence for such atypical burials can be found in other parts of the Iberian Peninsula and elsewhere in south-west Europe. This paper attempts to address the reasons behind such unusual funerary behaviour. Why were the bodies of some individuals hidden in remote areas of natural caves rather than being buried in ordinary cemeteries? Some hypotheses are discussed here and further lines of research are proposed.*

## Introduction

La Garma is a hill 186m high, 5km from the modern coast of Cantabria, and 12km to the east-south-east of the city of Santander in northern Spain (Fig. 8.1). It is the location of thirteen archaeological sites (most of them caves) that have yielded evidence of human activities from the Lower Palaeolithic to the Middle Ages, including most of the intermediary periods – one of the richest and most detailed archaeological sequences in Europe (Arias 1999; Arias *et al.* 1999; Arias and Ontañón 2012). It is particularly important because of one exceptional site, the Lower Gallery, a cave whose original entrance was blocked at the end of the Pleistocene, which has allowed the conservation of Upper Palaeolithic floors and structures in a state that can be considered unique (Ontañón 2003; Arias 2009; Arias *et al.* 2011), as well as one of the greatest ensembles of Palaeolithic rock art and portable art (Arias 1999; González Sainz 2003; Arias and Ontañón 2004, 2013). On the basis of its importance, La Garma has been listed as a UNESCO World Heritage site (Ontañón *et al.* 2008). The Lower Gallery at La Garma does not only contain prehistoric remains; two funerary areas dating to the seventh or eighth century AD have also been found, together with abundant evidence throughout the cave of human activities during that period. This paper describes the available evidence for an early medieval presence at La Garma, focusing on ritual activities. Its significance in light of comparable contexts found elsewhere in Cantabria and Spain will also be discussed.

## The Lower Gallery at La Garma

The Lower Gallery is one of the caves in the La Garma karst system. It is a large passage about 300m long (Fig. 8.1)

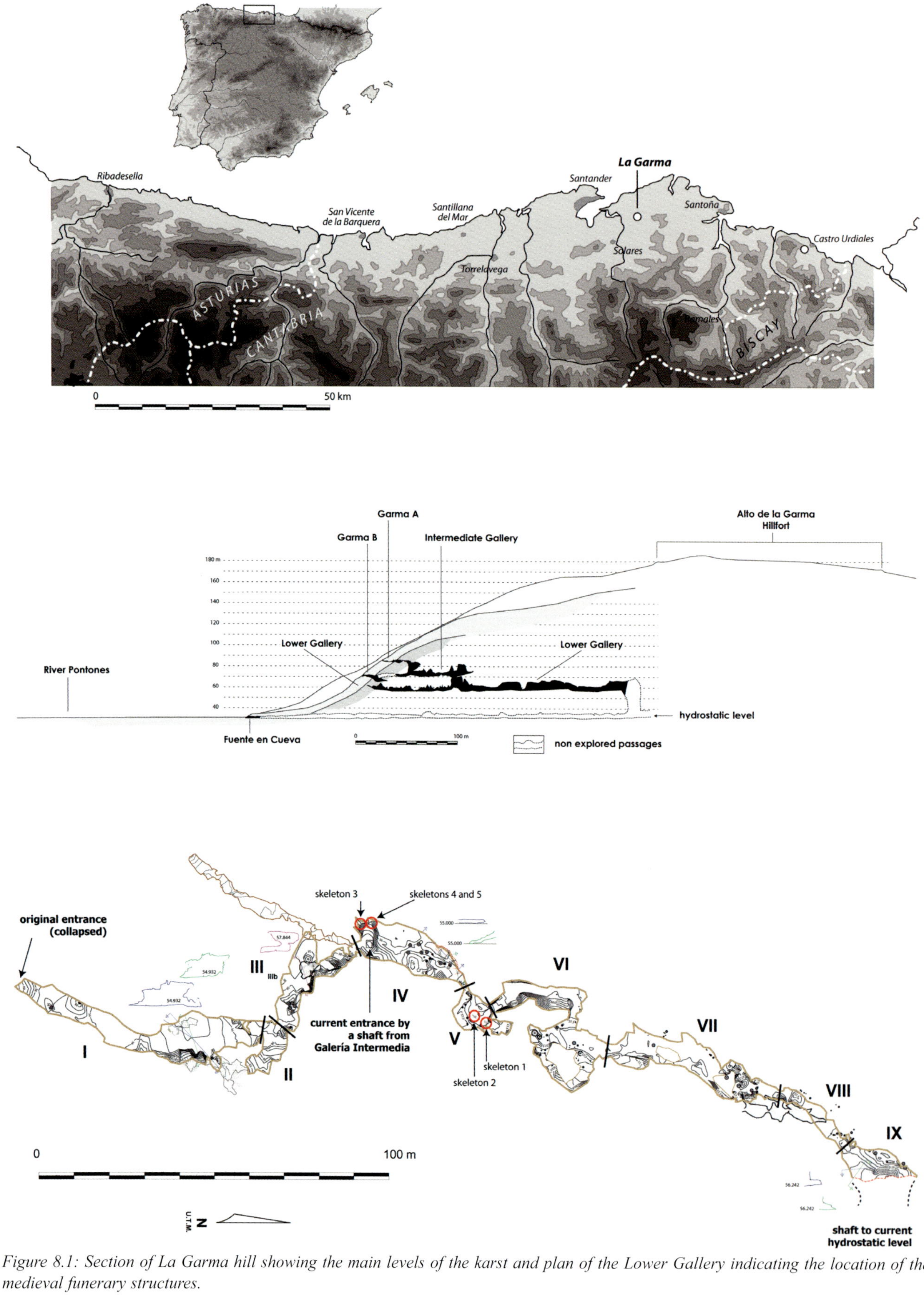


*Figure 8.1: Section of La Garma hill showing the main levels of the karst and plan of the Lower Gallery indicating the location of the medieval funerary structures.*

whose natural entrance, at 55m above sea level, became blocked in the late Pleistocene. The only access today (and in the Middle Ages) is through an entrance 25m higher, known as La Garma A. Before the archaeological excavations that began in 1995, this entrance was a narrow hole about 50cm in diameter, as the prehistoric deposits practically filled the outermost part of the cave. The first chamber is the Entrance Hall, 4.4 × 2.0m in size, where some medieval artefacts were found in the upper level, although these are somewhat more modern (tenth to twelfth century) than the period the present study refers to, according to the typology of the pottery retrieved (Bohigas 2002) and the thermoluminiscence (TL) dates obtained (Table 8.1). The back of the Entrance Hall leads to a narrow passage through which it was necessary to crawl prior to archaeological excavations. In some places the passage was so low (about 40cm) that visitors' backs rubbed against the roof when crawling along the floor. This second constriction leads to a slightly larger second chamber (6.0 × 2.8m) where an object was found that might be contemporaneous with the early medieval remains described below. This was a ribbed metal bead, supposedly of gold although it may actually have been of brass (this object, now lost, was found in an earlier survey and we have never had the opportunity to examine it).

The cave continues through a third narrow and awkward passage, two metres in height, constricted by speleothems that are probably Pleistocene in age. Apparently, it was widened by breaking some stalagmites, probably in the early Middle Ages, as the length of the new spelaeothems that grew after that episode is similar to many others in the Lower Gallery that started some 1300 years ago (see below).

After dropping to the floor of the passage, the top of the first shaft is reached, which is 7.35m deep and connects via a steep ramp to the Intermediate Gallery. This comprises another level in the system, whose original entrance was La Garma B, a small cave with Bronze Age burials, which still connected with the Intermediate Gallery about 30,500 cal BC, as shown by the radiocarbon determinations on *Ursus arctos* skeletons in the passage. The connection was blocked by the growth of speleothems, probably at some time in the Late Glacial period or early Holocene. The Intermediate Gallery continues in a straight line, with a level floor, easily negotiated by visitors. However, the route to the Lower Gallery (about 40m long) is interrupted about half way along its length by a group of stalagmites; although they are not a particular obstacle for visitors, they would undoubtedly have made movement more difficult when carrying a heavy load, such as a corpse.

The Intermediate Gallery ends in a second shaft, 12.84m deep, which opens into the middle of the Lower Gallery. Once there, movement is easy as it is a large passage with high roofs and floors that are generally horizontal, apart from some piles of blocks such as those at the foot of the shaft from the Intermediate Gallery. As Figure 8.1 illustrates, the Lower Gallery was formed by the union of two approximately straight parallel passages running in a south west–north east line. For descriptive purposes, it has been divided into nine sections along its length (Zones I to IX), corresponding to chambers or sections of passage separated by lower sections or other divisions (e.g. block piles, groups of stalagmites etc.). In any case, these are not an obstacle for movement through the cave, nor were they in the Middle Ages.

*Table 8.1: La Garma. Radiometric dates for medieval contexts at La Garma*

| *Context* | *Material* | *Species* | *Individual* | *Method* | *Reference* | *Determination (BP)* | *Intervals (cal. AD/AD)* 1σ | 2σ |
|---|---|---|---|---|---|---|---|---|
| Lower Gallery Zone V | bone | *Homo sapiens* | 1 | $^{14}$C AMS | AA-45589 | 1426 ± 59 | 577–658 | 432–761 |
| Lower Gallery Zone V | bone | *Homo sapiens* | 2 | $^{14}$C AMS | AA-45590 | 1348 ± 36 | 645–758 | 625–768 |
| Lower Gallery Zone IV | bone | *Homo sapiens* | 3 | $^{14}$C AMS | AA-45592 | 1269 ± 56 | 665–800 | 658–881 |
| Lower Gallery Zone IV | bone | *Homo sapiens* | 5 | $^{14}$C AMS | AA-45591 | 1288 ± 42 | 672–767 | 653–863 |
| Lower Gallery Zone IV | bone | *Homo sapiens* | 4 | $^{14}$C AMS | OxA-7249 | 1115 ± 40 | 891–981 | 778–1016 |
| Lower Gallery Zone IX | charcoal | *Corylus avellana* | | $^{14}$C AMS | AA-78255 | 1263 ± 35 | 688–770 | 666–867 |
| Lower Gallery Zone IX | charcoal | Indeterminate | | $^{14}$C AMS | AA-45563 | 1275 ± 31 | 685–767 | 661–855 |
| Lower Gallery Zone VIII | charcoal | *Corylus avellana* | | $^{14}$C AMS | AA-78254 | 1267 ± 35 | 686–769 | 664–865 |
| Lower Gallery Zone VII | charcoal | *Corylus avellana* | | $^{14}$C AMS | AA-78253 | 1562 ± 46 | 429–542 | 404–593 |
| Lower Gallery Zone VI | charcoal | *Corylus avellana* | | $^{14}$C AMS | AA-78252 | 1235 ± 35 | 694–863 | 686–881 |
| Lower Gallery Zone V | charcoal | *Corylus avellana* | | $^{14}$C AMS | AA-78251 | 1202 ± 38 | 773–880 | 690–945 |
| Lower Gallery Zone IV | charcoal | *Corylus avellana* | | $^{14}$C AMS | AA-78250 | 1293 ± 42 | 669–767 | 651–862 |
| Lower Gallery Zone IV | charcoal | Indeterminate | | $^{14}$C AMS | AA-45593 | 1282 ± 33 | 679–767 | 657–800 |
| Lower Gallery Zone IV | charcoal | Indeterminate | | $^{14}$C AMS | AA-20042 | 1281 ± 57 | 664–773 | 653–880 |
| Lower Gallery Zone IV | charcoal | Indeterminate | | $^{14}$C AMS | AA-45574 | 1279 ± 33 | 681–767 | 659–854 |
| Lower Gallery Zone IV | charcoal | Indeterminate | | $^{14}$C AMS | AA-45582 | 1266 ± 46 | 672–774 | 662–876 |
| Lower Gallery Zone IV | charcoal | Indeterminate | | $^{14}$C AMS | AA-20041 | 1220 ± 44 | 720–879 | 679–938 |
| Lower Gallery Zone I | charcoal | *Corylus avellana* | | $^{14}$C AMS | AA-78256 | 1321 ± 35 | 657–764 | 650–769 |
| Intermediate Gallery | charcoal | Indeterminate | | $^{14}$C AMS | OxA-6890 | 1210 ± 40 | 770–880 | 687–940 |
| La Garma A | painted pottery | | | TL | MAD-558 | 1043 ± 92 | 862–1046 | 770–1138 |
| La Garma A | painted pottery | | | TL | MAD-559 | 1023 ± 92 | 882–1066 | 790–1158 |
| La Garma A | pottery | | | TL | MAD-649 | 855 ± 64 | 1080–1208 | 1016–1272 |
| El Valladar | pottery | | | TL | MAD-557 | 1026 ± 101 | 870–1072 | 769–1173 |

It should be noted that this difficult route was the only possible way through which people could have reached the Lower Gallery during the early medieval period, as none of the other original entrances were still open at that time. In addition to the difficulties described above, four constrictions in La Garma A and the Intermediate Gallery, and the shafts, would have existed at this time. The constrictions in La Garma A are caused in two cases by speleothems present since the Pleistocene, and in the Intermediate Gallery and the shafts they are caused by prehistoric accumulations of sediment, as Bronze Age deposits dated to the mid-second millennium cal BC were found on the surface. This is confirmed by the presence of archaeological material on the cave floor contemporaneous with the early medieval deposits in the Lower Gallery: in La Garma A is the aforementioned bead, and in the Intermediate Gallery are fireplaces (Fig. 8.2), charcoal marks on walls, and abundant charcoal on the floor. Owing to their specific composition (identical to the early medieval charcoal from the Lower Gallery – see below) and the radiocarbon determinations (Table 8.1), these may be considered evidence of the same groups who descended into the Lower Gallery.

It should also be pointed out that the Lower Gallery has remained practically unaltered since the period referred to here (seventh–eighth centuries), apart from a slight regrowth of the stalagmites, varying between 3cm and 10cm in height, according to observation of the numerous stalagmites broken at that time and the more precise observations made of stalagmite GAR-01, of which twenty dates have been obtained by uranium-series dating for a palaeoclimate study (Baldini *et al.* 2010; Baldini *et al.* 2015). However, this is insignificant from the point of view of human movement or the appearance of the cave, and it can be taken that its present state is practically identical to that which existed 1300 years ago. Furthermore, the Lower Gallery has been closely monitored by archaeologists and heritage authorities ever since it was discovered on 2 November 1995. Therefore, the post-Palaeolithic archaeological alterations described below (broken stalagmites and disturbed pieces of flowstone) can be confidently attributed to early medieval visitors, as we are reasonably sure that the cave has not been visited in recent times by unauthorised individuals.

## Early medieval remains in the Lower Gallery

Four types of archaeological evidence dated to the early medieval period have been observed in the Lower Gallery: charcoal, evidence of the breakage and removal of speleothems, disturbance to pieces of flowstone and stone on the floor, and funerary deposits. Footprints of bare feet are also visible in areas of a soft floor in Zones I and VI but, as yet, it has not been possible to attribute these to either the Palaeolithic or the medieval visitors.

### *Torches and stalagmites: non-sepulchral medieval evidence in the Lower Gallery*

The most ubiquitous and abundant medieval remains at La Garma are pieces of charcoal found throughout the passage, from the talus cone that sealed the original Palaeolithic entrance to the shaft at the end of the passage. Both of these points are marked by fireplaces and particularly dense concentrations of charcoal. The end of the passage is interrupted by an impressive deep chasm (20m deep); charcoal is located on the sides and ledges of the shaft suggesting medieval visitors looked in over this dangerous pit, perhaps searching for a way to continue their explorations. In any case, in all areas of the cave, without exception, numerous pieces of charcoal are found in isolation or in small concentrations (Fig. 8.3, 6–9).

A large proportion of the charcoal preserved in the Lower Gallery has been analysed by one of the present authors

*Figure 8.2: Remains of a fire against the wall of the Intermediate Gallery, just above the chasm to the Lower Gallery. Observe some other concentrations of charcoal on the floor and on the large fallen stalagmite on the left side of the image.*

*Figure 8.3: Pieces of hazel charcoal on the floor of the Lower Gallery.*

(P.U.) and 14 pieces have been radiocarbon dated (Table 8.1). With the exception of some from the Magdalenian floors in Zone IV (dated to about 14,500 cal BC and belonging to the *Juniperus* genus), the anthracological study has shown that all identifiable specimens correspond to hazel (*Corylus avellana*), and all derived from very young branches as the fragments display extremely rapid growth in their general ligneous plane. It appears likely that hazel branches were gathered to make torches for lighting the cave during visits, as well as to make small fires. The charcoal resulted from torches fragmenting and breaking off as wood burnt. These fragments did not completely combust when they fell onto the damp floor and were thus conserved.

Hazel has been an abundant species in the area since the early Holocene, so its wood would have been easily obtained. It also burns easily, especially in the case of thin branches such as those documented from La Garma, and would therefore have been suitable for illumination. There is some ethnographic documentation for its use in this way in Cantabria during the twentieth century, as reported by M. Pardo de Santayana (2008, 87). However, combustion is relatively rapid, which might explain the abundance of charcoal in the cave. Moreover, this suggests that visitors brought with them a large quantity of wood to light torches and fires, seemingly suggesting a planned exploration of the cave rather than mere occasional visits.

At the end of last glaciation, the Lower Gallery at La Garma experienced a major process of karst reconstruction. Increased humidity caused the growth of large groups of stalactites and stalagmites. In many cases, the latter grew over Magdalenian floors and reached considerable heights (often up to 80cm) or joined with stalactites to form columns. These formations attracted the attention of medieval visitors, as often occurred in historic times (there are even examples of industrial extraction, as at the Grande Grotte de Arcy-sur-Cure in the eighteenth century; see Baffier and Girard 1998, 59–60), and many were deliberately broken. In some chambers, especially in Zone V, this damage takes on the appearance of systematic destruction, as patently seen in the broken stalagmites and stalagmite pieces piled up in several areas of the cave (see, for instance, Fig. 8.4). The activities of medieval visitors are easily recognisable because of the growth of the stalagmites: many continued to develop, but a hiatus can be seen by the difference in colour and opacity between the early Holocene formations and those from the last 1300 years. Occasionally, this is particularly conspicuous because a new stalagmite grew on blocks or speleothem fragments that had been moved in the medieval period (Fig. 8.5). At La Garma, as well as 'cave vandalism', the breakage of stalagmites served a practical purpose – many pieces were moved and reused in various ways. Some were piled in certain parts of the cave, which may have served to mark the route through the passage (Fig. 8.6). Others were used to mark out or manipulate human remains, as in the case of Skeletons 1 and 3. The former (Fig. 8.7) is surrounded by a series of stalagmite fragments and the feet rest on a piece of stalagmite. These may have marked the funerary space or perhaps acted as weights to hold down a shroud. With Skeleton 3, a speleothem fragment rested on smashed pieces of the skull (Fig. 8.8). As discussed below, this may have been the object used to destroy the cranium.

*Figure 8.4: Zone IV. Reconstructed broken stalagmite near a Palaeolithic 'mask' representing a bison head.*

It was not only broken stalagmites that were removed by medieval visitors. In some places, pieces of flowstone on the cave floor were disturbed. Much of the floor in the Lower Gallery is covered by a thin film of manganese oxide, a dark grey patina that is particularly conspicuous on pieces of flowstone and speleothems. In the case of the Magdalenian bones, it is occasionally found on concretions that cover them. This film, covering the Palaeolithic floors, must have formed at a very humid time, probably in the early and middle Holocene, and certainly before the medieval phase. In some places this coating is on the underside of Palaeolithic objects, showing that they had been turned over, either deliberately or

*Figure 8.5: Artificial accumulation of stalagmites in Zone VI.*

*Figure 8.6: Funerary context of the Zone V. In the foreground, Skeleton 2; in the background, Skeleton 1. Photo: Pedro Saura.*

*Figure 8.7: Funerary structure 1.*

*Figure 8.8: Funerary structure 3. Note the fragment of stalagmite on the remains of the skull.*

accidentally. As with the broken speleothems, it seems that no one else could have been responsible for this other than the medieval visitors, bearing in mind that all visits to the Lower Gallery have been monitored since its discovery in 1995.

### *The funerary deposits*

The funerary deposits are located in the central part of the Lower Gallery in Zones IV and V (Fig. 8.1). The best preserved are in Zone V (Fig. 8.6), an approximately circular chamber about 9.5m in diameter. The bodies of two individuals were placed on the calcite floor here, aligned with the orientation of the cave, with the heads to the north-east. Skeleton 2, a sub-adult male about 1.60m tall, with an estimated age at death of 18–20 years, lies on a small prominence approximately in the centre of the chamber. The skeleton is in correct anatomical position, lying on the left side with arms and legs flexed, and with the pelvis resting on a small stalagmite that existed at the time of the burial. Abundant remains of putrilage can be seen in the area of the torso. Despite the excellent state of preservation of most of the bones, the skull and jaw are crushed to powder, apart from a small piece of the mandible. Yet the remains of the skull are still in correct anatomical position, in the form of a stain which approximately reproduces the shape of the head. The left femur shaft is also crushed, possibly by trampling.

Skeleton 1 is at the north-eastern end of the chamber, opposite its entry, at the start of a short blind passage (Fig. 8.6–7). The body was deposited on a gentle slope, which probably contributed to some post-depositional alterations. The skeleton is also of a sub-adult male about 18–20 years of age, in this case very gracile and about 1.52cm tall. The remains are in correct anatomical order, in a supine position, with the right arm separated from the trunk (Fig. 8.7). However, some *post-mortem* alterations are evident. Much of the right hand is missing and some of these bones were found at the end of the blind side-passage. The left patella was displaced by 87cm. The coccyx had moved 50cm and lay between the two tibiae. The leg bones had separated, particularly the fibulae. Finally, the jaw is in the area of the right humerus. More striking is the apparently deliberate destruction of most of the skull and upper part of the torso. As with Skeleton 2, remains of putrilage can be seen in the area of the pelvis and amongst the ribs. Differences in the colour of the bones are particularly conspicuous between the femora and the tibiae, suggesting this individual was covered by some kind of garment that reached the knees, causing differences in the decomposition processes. Several fragments of stalagmites and a limestone block around the body may have served to mark out the funerary space or to hold down a shroud or covering. It is interesting that the individual's feet must have been resting against fragments of stalagmite, as the metatarsals are in an almost vertical position against the stalagmite whereas the phalanges have fallen to the other side of it. Some 12cm to the west of the right knee, a small iron bar of unknown function is the only piece of material culture found in this chamber. It may be a small awl or punch. A blackish substance is preserved at one end – probably related to the presence of a handle or adhesive.

It is worth considering that the position of the two bodies in Zone V had a deliberate scenographic intention. From the chamber entrance these skeletons are highly visible, especially as this area is approached from a higher level and therefore the funerary deposits are viewed from a height on arriving to Zone V (Fig. 8.6). The human bodies immediately attract attention, especially Skeleton 1, which lies directly opposite and is more visible because of its inclined position. Obviously, in a cave visibility depends on lighting, but the chamber is small and the torches that appear to have been used may have been sufficient to illuminate the human remains.

As stated above, stalagmites in this part of the cave were systematically broken. This can be observed, for instance, in the stalagmite beside the right arm of Skeleton 1 (Fig. 8.7) where the remains of the original late Pleistocene/early Holocene stalagmite broken by the medieval visitors, with its characteristic blackish manganese-oxide coating, contrasts with the translucent white new growth of the last 1300 years. The broken fragments were probably used for the feature that surrounds Skeleton 1 or were piled up in other parts of the chamber (see Figs. 8.6 and 8.7).

The funerary area in Zone IV is located 40m to the south-west, at the foot of the shaft from the Intermediate Gallery. This part of the cave contains a large pile of blocks reaching a height of about 4 m above the normal level of the passage, on which a huge slab of limestone fell from the wall during the Pleistocene (Palaeolithic representations were painted on it, and bear bones have been found dated to about 15,000 cal BC). Medieval bodies were deposited around this huge slab: one (Skeleton 3) on the south-west side, on the normal floor level at the start of a short side-passage, and the other two (Skeletons 4 and 5) in a small space between the block pile and the west wall of the cave.

Skeleton 3 is a young individual who died at about 12 years of age. The remains are in correct anatomical position, lying on the right side with flexed arms and legs, and resting on the stony floor of an approximately triangular area bounded by the large slab mentioned above and the cave wall. The body was placed with its back very close to the wall and with its feet almost touching it. The head faced south (Fig. 8.8). The state of the skeleton is very poor and the bones have generally suffered post-depositional fragmentation in the form of splintering. The skull was affected to a much greater degree; it was crushed to powder leaving a white shadow that suggests its shape. A speleothem fragment was placed, on its narrow side, over the remains of the skull. This fragment must have been deposited by a human hand after the body had decomposed and the skull had been destroyed; it could not be the result of accidental collapse from the large slab, and it could not possibly have been placed on a convex surface, such as a human head.

There are also numerous pieces of hazel charcoal in this area (Fig. 8.8). Many are later than the decomposition of the body, as fragments occur on top of the crushed skull. The only other object associated, at least spatially, with this skeleton is a shell of the marine gastropod lined top shell (*Phorcus lineatus*). This species was very rare on the Cantabrian coast in the Pleistocene (Álvarez Fernández 2011) so it is very unlikely that its presence in the Lower Gallery can be attributed to Palaeolithic activities. It may come from the Mesolithic shell midden at the entrance of La Garma A, where this species is abundant, but even then it must have been medieval visitors who transported it to the Lower Gallery, as no sign of human activities dating to between the Upper Palaeolithic and the Middle Ages has been detected in the inner part of La Garma A or in the Intermediate Gallery. This has been confirmed by

*Figure 8.9: Natural niche with skeletons 4 and 5. Observe the belt buckle in the foreground.*

*Figure 8.10: Visigothic style damascened lyriform buckle from Zone IV. Photo after restoration.*

the radiocarbon date on the shell dated to 8369 ± 37 BP; 6815–6565 cal BC at 95.44% probability (OxA-32289), which is strictly coeval with the Mesolithic layers at the entrance of La Garma A.

Skeletons 4 and 5 are on a rocky ledge at the foot of the shaft connecting the Intermediate and Lower galleries. Here, the cave wall and one of the large slabs in the collapse form an approximately circular space about a metre in diameter (Fig. 8.9). Some bones, probably belonging to Skeleton 4, fell from its northern edge towards a lower step of the passage. Skeleton 5 is apparently an individual under 14 years of age. Skeleton 4 can only be classified as a sub-adult. The poor state of preservation of both skeletons does not allow a precise interpretation of how they were deposited. However, they seem to have been placed in opposite positions: Skeleton 5 nearer the large slab with its head towards the south, and Skeleton 4 beside the wall with its head towards the north. Some remains from Skeleton 4 overlie those of Skeleton 5, but it is quite likely that the two bodies were deposited at the same time. As seen in Figure 8.9, the funerary space contains limestone blocks and pieces of speleothem about 15–20cm long. These are located around the skeletons and on top of them, especially in relation to Skeleton 4. This is apparently the result of deliberate action, although there is not enough evidence to determine whether these are the remains of a structure covering the corpses or of some activity that followed decomposition of the bodies. However, those blocks in the centre and on the west side seem to support the second hypothesis. It is also difficult to determine whether the skeletal remains were manipulated in any way. The skulls are again very fragmented but, owing to the poor state of preservation, it cannot be ascertained whether they were deliberately destroyed.

A lyre-shaped belt buckle was found on the eastern side of this space and, to the north of it, small pieces of iron oxide that might have come from the same item (metal rivets?). Judging by its position, this buckle is likely to have formed part of the attire of Skeleton 5, which would at least confirm that this individual was dressed when deposited. As described in detail elsewhere (Arias *et al.* 2012), the buckle is made of iron with damascened decoration in silver and brass, the latter being composed of about two or three parts Cu for each one of Zn, according to the semi-quantitative analyses with an energy dispersive x-ray detector, EDAX, fitted to a scanning electron microscope. It consists of a lyre-shaped plate, with which a hinge articulates an oval clasp and a prong with a rectangular base (Fig. 8.10). The decoration consists of a Greek cross inside a square, flanked by two spoked wheels. The iconography is obviously Christian and is often found on similar objects from Visigothic Spain and Merovingian Burgundy. However, it should be noted that the technique of damascened decoration on iron is relatively rare in Hispano-Visigothic buckles, which are usually made from bronze. These objects have been documented from sites all over the Iberian Peninsula and in southeast France, the old Visigothic Septimania, and can therefore be considered a type of personal adornment found throughout the kingdom of Toledo.

### Chronology

The interpretation of the early medieval activity at La Garma depends largely on the chronology of the different archaeological elements. Are we looking at a single episode, in which five bodies were all deposited at the same time, or the repeated use of a funerary space? It is equally important to establish whether the other evidence of early medieval human activities (charcoal, broken stalagmites, alterations of the Palaeolithic floors) is coeval with the funerary usage.

Certain elements of relative chronology enable an initial archaeological estimation. Most of these suggest the cave was used on several occasions during the Middle Ages. This includes the presence of charcoal, presumably from torches, on top of the bones and putrilage of the five individuals; and the rock on the decomposed skull of Skeleton 3. To these can be added the destruction of some skeletal parts (especially the skulls, but also the femur of Skeleton 2) which, if assumed to be caused by anthropic activity, would confirm that at least one visit was made to the cave after the bodies had become skeletonised. In contrast, the positions of Skeletons 4 and 5 appear to be compatible with simultaneous deposition of two bodies rather than two separate events.

A series of 19 radiometric determinations has been obtained from bones of the five individuals and 14 pieces of charcoal collected along the Lower Gallery, between the original entrance to the shaft at its end, as well as from the fireplace in the Intermediate Gallery (Fig. 8.11). Their interpretation is not simple because, despite being very precise (the standard deviations are all less than five per cent of the age of the sample), the large oscillation in the relevant section of the calibration curve, caused by a sudden drop in atmospheric $^{14}C$ concentrations in the mid-eighth century, produces very wide calibrated ranges, which at 95.4% probability (2σ) often exceed two centuries. It is thus not possible to reach precise conclusions about the chronology of activities. Statistical analysis confirms that, with the sole exception of the charcoal from Zone VII mentioned below, all the dates of historical age obtained in the Lower and Intermediate galleries are compatible. The maximum probability lies in the late seventh and early eighth centuries. If the hypothesis that they all correspond to a short period of funerary activity were true, there would be a 44.4% probability that this took place between AD 693 and 726, and lower probabilities for two intervals in the mid-eighth century (14.3% for 737–749 and 8.9% for 764–771). However, the probability of the latter two ranges is supported by the date of Skeleton 4, which is not compatible with the older range. In any case, the probability that this activity took place between AD 688 and 754 is very high (78.8%).

This chronology is compatible with independent sources of information. The belt buckle associated with Skeleton 5 corresponds to a relatively late type datable, according to Ripoll's (1998) systematic study of these objects, to the second half of the seventh century and the first decades of the eighth century, although other studies suggest that they may have continued in use until the late eighth century (Gutiérrez Lloret *et al.* 2003, 162–163). A second source of evidence is the radiometric date for the breakage of stalagmite GAR-01 in Zone IV. According to the uranium-series dates obtained for this speleothem (Baldini *et al.* 2015), the break occurred sometime between the determinations: 1874 ± 15 BP; AD 105–165 (BIG-UTh-A650) and 958 ± 22 BP; AD 1007–1095 (BIG-UTh-A649). The interpolation of the growth rate of the stalagmite over this span of time (about 27.3μm per year) allows the time of the fracture of the speleothem to be estimated more precisely to about AD 758.

In sum, the chronological evidence indicates that the funerary activity in the Lower Gallery at La Garma may be dated to the late seventh century or, more probably, to the early eighth century – the last years of the Visigothic kingdom of Toledo or the beginning of the kingdom of Asturias.

It is more difficult to determine the frequency of usage during the medieval phase of activity. This is a problem that the current resolution of $^{14}C$ is not capable of resolving, as the uncertainty derived from the method itself is, in this case, aggravated by the problem of the oscillations in the calibration curve during the period in question. An example is given by considering determinations AA-45593 and AA-45592. The former comes from a charcoal fragment found on the crushed remains of Skeleton 3, and therefore it should be more recent than the latter date on bone. As AA-45593 is a sample from a branch of a species with a relatively short lifespan (hazel), it is highly unlikely that this could be considered a case of the 'old wood effect' (Schiffer 1986; Cook and Comstock 2014). However, as seen in Table 8.1, this is not the case, although in reality the two dates are statistically indistinguishable. It is clear that the span of time between the two 'radiocarbon events' (*sensu* Van Strydonck *et al.* 1999) is below the method's capacity of resolution.

A similar problem is the disparity between the dates obtained for Skeletons 4 and 5, which appear to contradict the hypothesis of their contemporaneity. However, this may be another effect of the oscillation mentioned above. The decline in atmospheric $^{14}C$ concentration responsible for the inflection in the curve (at about AD 740–760) was followed by a sudden and very sharp increase (around 14‰) in AD 774–775 (probably in the Northern Hemisphere spring of 775) (Miyake *et al.* 2012; Güttler *et al.* 2015). This would result in an apparent reduction in the age of a sample from that period of around 165 years, which would perfectly account for the apparent anomaly of the date of Skeleton 4. Indeed, this might suggest a real age of around AD 775 for Skeleton 4.

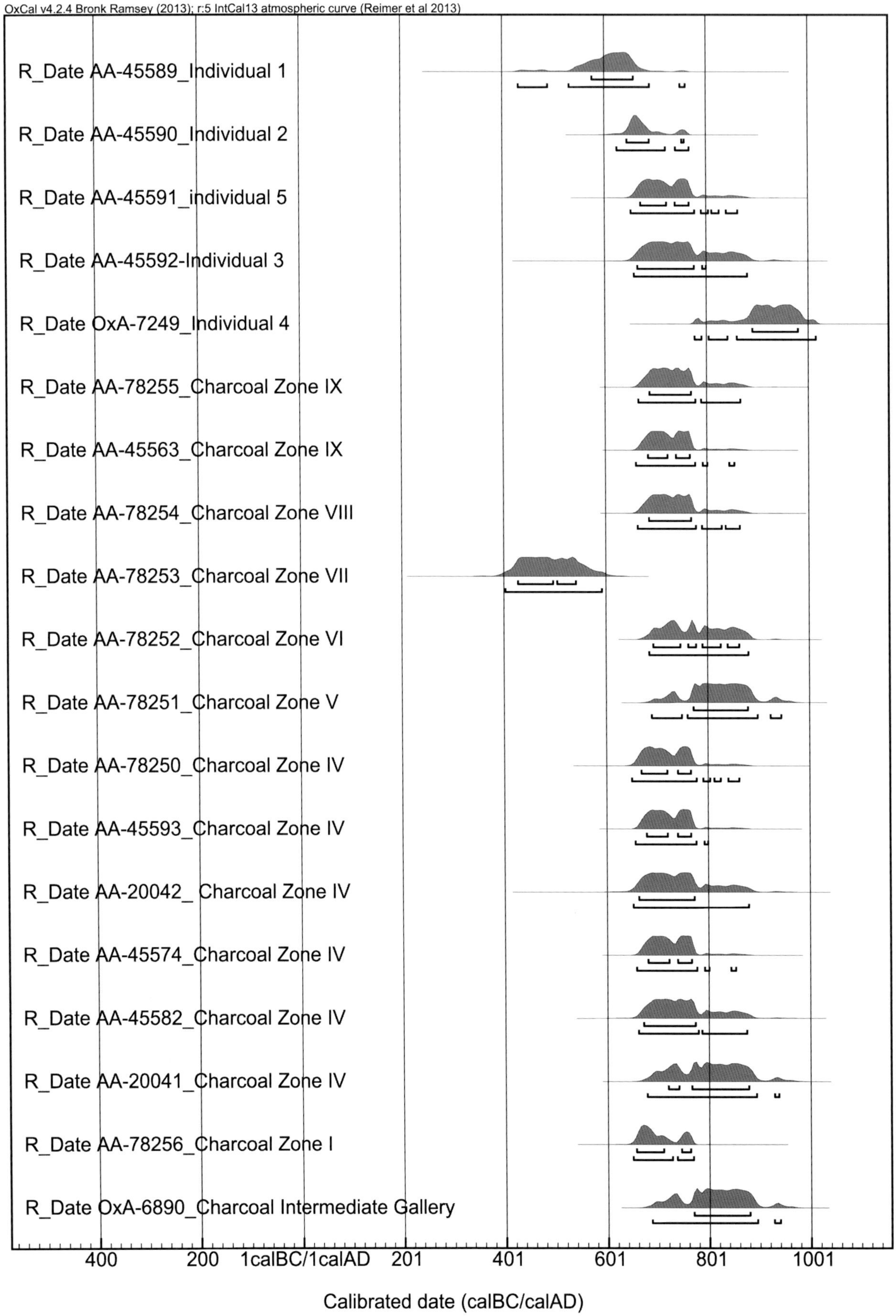


*Figure 8.11: Medieval radiocarbon dates for the Lower Gallery and the Intermediate Gallery at La Garma.*

Statistical analysis using the Bayesian method proposed by Bronk Ramsey (2009a) confirms that, with the sole exception of determination AA-78253 for hazel charcoal from Zone VII, all the medieval dates in the Lower and Intermediate galleries are compatible. The exception may indicate that there was previous exploration of the cave, in the fifth or sixth century, but this may simply be an anomaly or outlier (*sensu* Bronk Ramsey 2009b). In any case, as explained above, $^{14}C$ does not allow a definite conclusion to be reached as to whether there was a single visit or several successive visits – both scenarios are compatible with the statistical distribution of the existing dates. However, the available information suggests at least two separate events: one involving the deposition of bodies and, later, visits to the cave when the remains may have been damaged, corresponding to some of the dates on charcoal and stalagmite breakage.

### *Overview*

To summarise the information about the medieval funerary deposits at La Garma, several points should be stressed. All the individuals were young, children or sub-adults, and where sex could be determined, they were males. In two cases (Skeletons 5 and 1) there is evidence that the bodies may have been clothed. The corpses were carefully deposited, but their postures vary (supine decubitus and both right and left lateral decubitus have been documented), possibly influenced by the morphology of the cave. In at least one case (Skeleton 1), the body seems to have been delimited or covered. However, the most striking aspect is evidence for the subsequent manipulation of bodies after skeletonisation, which appears to have involved the deliberate destruction of the skulls. Some pieces of charcoal dispersed over the floor of the Lower Gallery may be attributed to these later visits.

## Regional context: burial caves in the Visigothic period

The burials in the Lower Gallery at La Garma are not unique in the region: four other Cantabrian caves are known with evidence of funerary use in the seventh and eighth centuries AD: Cudón, El Juyo, Las Penas and Riocueva (Gutiérrez Cuenca and Hierro 2012) (Fig. 8.12).

Several bronze and iron objects of Visigothic typology were found in association with human remains in Cudón (Miengo) in the 1920s, including a belt buckle, a small bronze jug, a spindle hook and a set of tools (Alcalde del Río 1934). They were found in the area of the current entrance, which almost certainly was blocked at the time of deposition. Recent explorations have uncovered pottery sherds dispersed throughout the cave, some of which correspond to types compatible with the early medieval period. These include a small jar (Peña 2006), a fragment of an 'S-profile' pot with undulating incised decoration (Morlote *et al.* 1996, 228) and, in particular, a sherd dated radiometrically that corresponds to the fourth-seventh centuries: 1501 ± 97 BP (UAM-10023T) (Table 8.2).

In El Juyo (Camargo), in a small chamber deep inside the cave, the remains of a woman and three children were found in the 1950s. Associated with the human remains were several glass beads belonging to a necklace dated in the Visigothic period (Maza 1957, 103; Janssens and González Echegaray 1958, 9–10), now missing.

The most important parallel for La Garma is probably Las Penas (Piélagos) (Serna *et al.* 2005; Hierro 2011). This cave is about 200m long with a small entrance (little more than half a metre high and a metre wide) and a first low passage through which it is necessary to crawl. At the end of the main passage a deposit dated in the Visigothic period, consisting of human remains and a large variety of objects, was discovered in 2004. The site was excavated by Valle and Serna in subsequent years. The human remains derived from 13 individuals: five infants, including a foetus or neonate, and eight sub-adults and young adults, all under 30 years of age, whose bodies had been laid on the cave floor. With a few exceptions, the bones had been moved from their original positions by flooding. None of the individuals displayed pathologies or wounds that might reveal the cause of death (Carnicero 2006). No complete skull was found, only small fragments concentrated in a particular part of the cave (a narrow passage connecting with the funerary space in two places), and they displayed signs of having been subjected to fire. Objects associated with the bodies included five complete belt buckles, four of bronze and one with an iron plate bearing inlaid decoration in a Christian theme, and a bronze clasp. The assemblage included objects of personal adornment, such as rings, ear-rings and beads; tools and implements, such as a fire striker, spindles and a barbed axe; and various receptacles such as ceramic pots, wooden cauldrons and a small iron pail plated with copper alloy. In addition, the remains of two hens (*Gallus gallus*), bear (*Ursus arctos*) claws and a large accumulation of carbonised cereal grains – barley (*Hordeum vulgare*), spelt (*Triticum spelta*), einkorn (*Triticum monococcum*), undetermined wheat (*Triticum* sp.) and millet (*Panicum miliaceum*), as well as flax seeds (*Linum usitatissimum*) (identified by Inés L. López-Dóriga), were found in the same place as the burnt skull fragments. The five radiometric dates, obtained on the human bones, remains of leather attached to one of the belt buckles, hen bones and a cereal grain (Table 8.2), are consistent and place the funerary use of the cave in the period AD 666–778 (87.9% probability).

Riocueva (Entrambasaguas) – frequently misspelt as Recueva – is a karst system nearly 3.5km long. Its small entrance leads into a tiny chamber with a low passage through which it is necessary to crawl to reach *Galería del Campamento*, a passage whose first 60m contained early

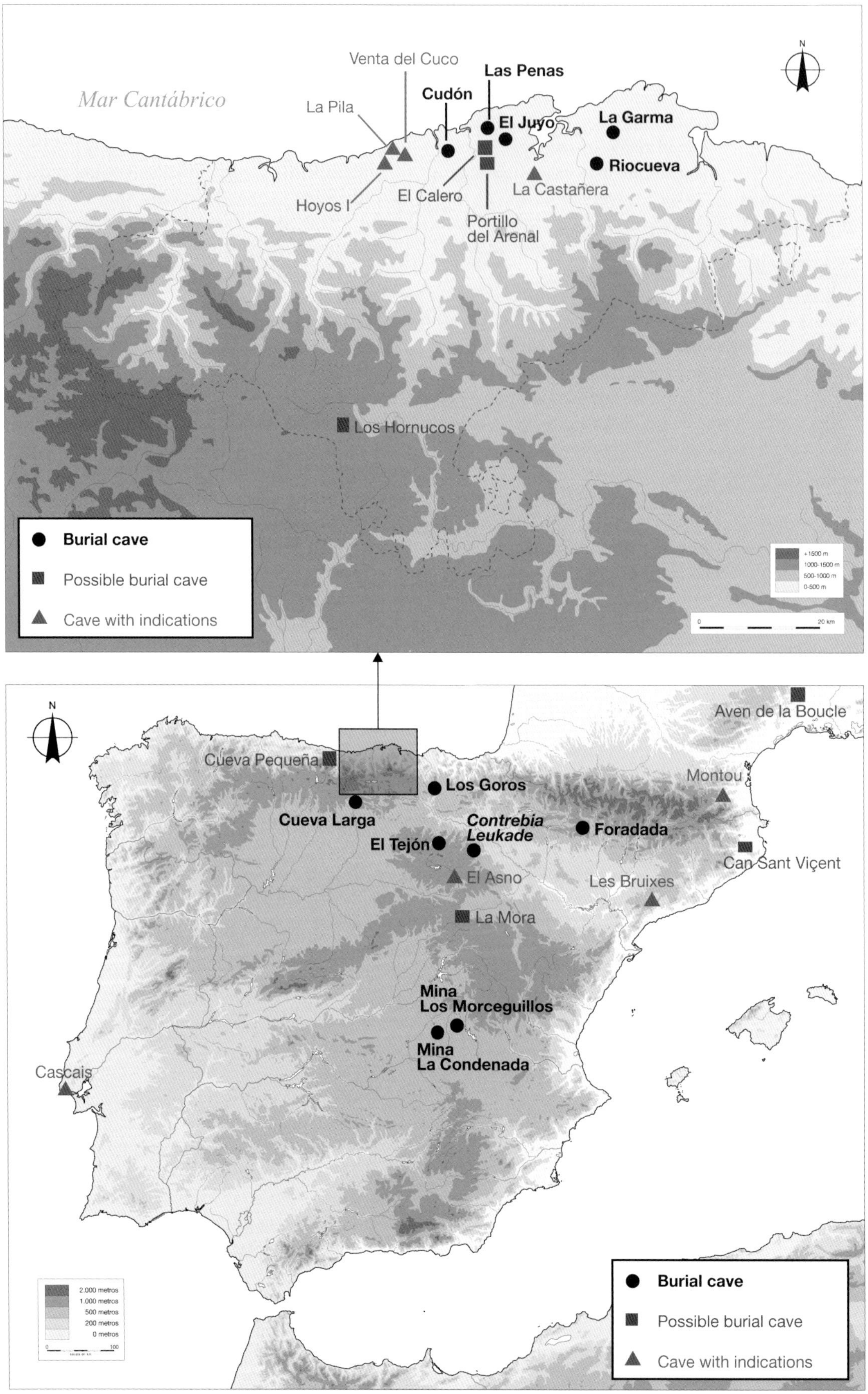


*Figure 8.12: Burial caves dating to the seventh and eighth centuries AD in the territory of the Visigothic kingdom of Toledo.*

*Table 8.2: Radiometric dates for medieval funerary contexts in Cantabria*

| *Site* | *Material* | *Species* | *Method* | *Reference* | *Determination (BP)* | *Intervals (cal AD/AD)* 1σ | 2σ |
|---|---|---|---|---|---|---|---|
| Cudón | pottery | | TL | UAM-10023T | 1501 ± 97 | 408–602 | 311–699 |
| Las Penas | bone | *Homo sapiens* | $^{14}$C AMS | Poz-10412 | 1270 ± 30 | 687–768 | 663–859 |
| Las Penas | bone | *Homo sapiens* | $^{14}$C AMS | Poz-10414 | 1275 ± 30 | 685–767 | 661–800 |
| Las Penas | leather | | $^{14}$C AMS | Poz-7526 | 1265 ± 35 | 687–769 | 665–866 |
| Las Penas | bone | *Gallus gallus* | $^{14}$C AMS | OxA-29210 | 1273 ± 25 | 688–767 | 672–772 |
| Las Penas | seed | Cerealia | $^{14}$C AMS | Poz-10413 | 1250 ± 30 | 687–775 | 676–870 |
| Riocueva | bone | *Homo sapiens* | $^{14}$C AMS | Poz-39142 | 1380 ± 30 | 638–668 | 606–680 |
| Riocueva | bone | *Homo sapiens* | $^{14}$C AMS | Poz-46496 | 1265 ± 30 | 689–769 | 666–863 |
| Riocueva | bone | *Homo sapiens* | $^{14}$C AMS | Poz-46497 | 1305 ± 30 | 665–764 | 658–769 |
| Riocueva | seed | *Setaria italica* | $^{14}$C AMS | Poz-49634 | 1300 ± 30 | 669–764 | 660–770 |
| Riocueva | pottery | | TL | MADN-6061.BIN | 1345 ± 77 | 589–743 | 512–820 |

medieval deposits. It was discovered in the 1950s by a group of explorers employed by the Deputation of Santander. Later, members of the *Seminario Sautuola*, at the Prehistory and Archaeology Museum of Cantabria, opened several trial pits at the entrance and first part of the passage, where they found prehistoric layers and remains from the Visigothic period (Peñil and Ruiz 1971). In the early 1980s, archaeologists from CAEAP (*Colectivo para la Ampliación de Estudios en Arqueología Prehistórica*) re-explored the cave and found a deposit of pottery sherds on the surface associated with human bones, which they attributed to the Iron Age (Morlote *et al.* 1996), although a later reappraisal by one of the authors of this paper suggested a Visigothic date (Hierro 2002). Since 2010, the archaeology of this cave has been studied by two of the present authors (J.A.H.G. and E.G.C.) within the framework of the *Mauranus* research project (Gutiérrez Cuenca and Hierro 2010/2012). This study has succeeded in identifying a funerary deposit dated to the seventh–eighth centuries. However, the actions of burrowing animals and the frequent entry of visitors in recent decades has resulted in human remains becoming fragmented and dispersed, with very few first order anatomical connections identified. According to a study carried out by S. Carnicero, the remains correspond to at least four individuals, all under 20 years of age: a perinatal individual, a child between 2 and 3 years of age, a child between 6 and 11 years of age, and an individual between 12 and 18 years of age. Similar to Las Penas, no complete skulls have been found, only small fragments that are often burnt. Parts of the post-cranial skeletons also exhibit signs of fire, at a temperature oscillating between 300 and 600 °C, when the bones had already lost their flesh. This may have been because they were beside the skulls when they were burnt. Together with the human remains, artefacts such as ceramic sherds, the foot of a glass cup, fragments of an iron cauldron plated with a copper alloy, iron knives, spindle hooks, and a fishhook have been found. The most outstanding artefacts, however, are undoubtedly the personal adornments: iron shoe studs, a copper buckle prong with a shield-shaped base, a bronze chain, several glass beads from a necklace, and an exceptional gold ring with an inscription that may be read as PAVL(*a*) (a personal name). A small textile fragment was also found, perhaps part of a handkerchief or a piece of linen cloth (Gutiérrez Cuenca *et al.* 2014), in which were wrapped numerous carbonised grains of millet (*Panicum miliaceum*) and foxtail millet (*Setaria italica*) (identification by Lydia Zapata and Inés L. López-Dóriga). Charred grains of barley (*Hordeum vulgare*) were also recovered from the funerary area. The radiometric dates for human bones and a carbonised foxtail millet grain are all internally consistent to the period cal AD 666–778, with which the TL determination of a potsherd is in agreement (Table 8.2).

In addition to sites in the vicinity of La Garma, other examples of the funerary use of caves in the Iberian Peninsula during the Visigothic period can be mentioned, most of which are located in the eastern part of the Meseta (the Spanish central plateau) and in the Ebro Valley (Fig. 8.12). The nearest site to La Garma is Cueva Larga in the La Horadada karst (Villaescusa de las Torres, Palencia). A rectangular chamber, 27m inside the cave entrance, contained the remains of dozens of individuals, sherds from several vessels, two bronze rings, an iron buckle, tools, and the remains of wood, one of which was dated to a quite imprecise interval in Late Antiquity or in the early Middle Ages: 1440 ± 110 BP; 356–863 cal AD (I-11113) (Santonja *et al.*1982). Further east, human remains representing three individuals, and several metal objects, were found in one of the lower passages in Los Goros (Hueto Arriba, Álava), which is accessed from a shaft several metres deep. The artefacts included an iron belt buckle with inlaid decoration in silver and brass, and a battle axe (Palol 1957a, 1957b).

Another interesting funerary deposit dated to the early medieval period was found in the Ebro Valley, at the old Celtiberian-Roman town of Contrebia Leucade (Aguilar del Río Alhama, La Rioja). The deposit was located inside an artificial cave associated with an Iron Age house. Here, a multiple burial dated in the Visigothic period contained numerous individuals accompanied by a belt buckle with a fixed plate and a coin minted in the reign of the Visigothic king Wittiza (AD 698–710) (Hernández Vera *et al.* 2007). Also in La Rioja, in Cueva del Tejón (Ortigosa de Cameros), a bronze belt buckle with a fretted fixed plate, with the inscription *XRSSIT/TECUMX*, was found. Dated to the seventh century AD (Garín 1913, Ripoll 1998, 98), it was associated with human remains.

At Cueva Foradada (Sarsa de Surta, Huesca) in the Pyrenees, Visigothic remains were found in an internal chamber at the end of a long narrow passage where in some places it is necessary to crawl. The assemblage included bones of numerous, mostly juvenile and infantile, individuals (only one was over 30 years of age). Artefact finds included a lyre-shaped buckle, a *tremissis* of Wittiza (minted at Gerunda in the first decade of the eighth century), a bone spindle whorl, remains of several bronze rings, glass paste beads from a necklace, iron utensils and numerous fragments of ceramic and glass vessels (Barandiarán 1973). Remains of burials corresponding to the Visigothic period were also found in several parts of La Condenada Mine (Osa de la Vega, Cuenca). In another mine in the same region, Los Morceguillos (Alconchel de la Estrella, Cuenca), several artefacts of Visigothic age associated with human remains were collected in a non-scientific investigation (Bernárdez and Guisado 2014).

Other cave sites are known where Visigothic artefacts have been found, often relating to clothing and personal adornments, or where seventh-/eighth-century dates have been obtained (see Hierro 2011 for further details). Although there is no clear evidence of funerary usage in these instances, the nature of the artefacts and their similarities to the better-known sites described above, suggest that 'dressed burials' might provide a valid interpretation. However, the existence of late prehistoric burials in some of these caves cautions prudence. This group include the caves of Portillo del Arenal, El Calero II, and Los Hornucos in Cantabria; Cueva Pequeña in Asturias; La Mora in Soria; Can Sant Vicenç in Catalonia; and Aven de la Boucle in the French Department of Gard. More doubtful are the sites of Hoyos I, Venta del Cuco, La Pila, and Abrigo de la Castañera in Cantabria; El Asno in Soria; Les Bruixes in Tarragona; Montou in Pyrénées-Orientales (France); and Cascais in Estremadura (Portugal) (Fig. 8.12).

In general, caves used for funerary purposes, both in Cantabria and in the rest of the Iberian Peninsula during the seventh and eighth centuries AD, share a number of common characteristics that depart from what is usual in cemeteries of that time, especially regarding certain features of the funerary record (Hierro 2011; Gutiérrez Cuenca and Hierro 2012). In most cases the caves are barely habitable or totally unsuited for secular human activities. In many cases, funerary spaces are located in remote locations that are difficult to access, often far from entrances. In some instances, of which the most characteristic is the Lower Gallery at La Garma, the funerary passages or chambers can only be reached after descending one or more shafts several metres deep, while at other sites the places where bodies were deposited seem to have been blocked off by stone walls, such as at Las Penas, Cueva Foradada and Contrebia Leucade.

The funerary deposits in caves generally appear to have consisted of multiple burials, with the number of individuals varying from three or four at Los Goros, to dozens at Cueva Larga. In some cases, such as Las Penas, evidence suggests a single brief period of usage. In others, bodies may have been deposited in several phases, as at La Garma and Riocueva. However, in the latter, funerary activity does not appear to be the result of extended continuous use as a sepulchral place, but rather several short episodes. Regarding the ages of those interred in caves, at the best-known sites – Riocueva, La Garma, Las Penas, Cueva Foradada and Cueva Larga – only individuals under 30 or 35 years of age are represented, in many cases children and adolescents, whereas mature and elderly adults are absent. The presence of the latter has only been documented at Cueva Larga, although in very small percentages, as only 15 per cent of the individuals were more than 30 years of age. The demographic profile is one of the main differences that can be observed between these caves and open-air cemeteries in the seventh and eighth centuries. In the latter, all age groups are usually represented from infants to elderly individuals; in caves, only young individuals are found.

Elements related to clothing and personal adornment stand out amongst the objects accompanying the deceased in caves, particularly belt buckles, rings, ear-rings and beads. In some cases, it could even be said that such objects are over-represented. In Las Penas, for example, the buckle to body ratio is very high, with six items for thirteen individuals. If we exclude the children and the neonate, we obtain a ratio of 75% of dressed burials for the sub-adult and young adult individuals in the cave, a much higher ratio than is usual for the first decades of the eighth century. In fact, it is at this time that dressed burials tend to become scarcer in open-air cemeteries, which makes the excessively adorned nature of some of the cave burials quite striking. Another feature, probably related to this, is that in many cases funerary deposits in caves include everyday objects such as items for making cloth, carpenter's tools, knives, axes, farm tools, cooking pots, metal and wooden containers, glasses etc. In contrast, such objects are practically non-existent in the graves of seventh- and eighth-century cemeteries in the Iberian Peninsula, except perhaps for pots and knives, and even then, only in a few cases.

## An attempt to interpret the data

The presence of Hispano-Visigothic items in caves and mines in northern Spain has attracted the attention of researchers since the first part of the twentieth century, as it was not easy to explain the existence of human activities in such unusual locations. One line of explanation, proposed by Alcalde del Río (1934), associated these sites with possible Christian hermitages. In turn, Carballo (1935) considered that they reflected the use of caves as temporary dwellings in times of political and social instability, and associated them with the Islamic invasion of AD 711. A third, later, interpretation saw these caves as settings for pagan ritual practices, both religious and funerary (González Echegaray 1966), which were supposedly maintained at a relatively late date in scarcely Romanised regions of northern Spain where the penetration of Christianity was limited (González Echegaray 1988). More recently, explanations have been proposed within the framework of the profound social and economic changes that Western Europe underwent after the fifth century. From this point of view, caves were considered in terms of the occupation and exploitation of areas that until then had been regarded as marginal (Quirós and Alonso 2007). Finally, the information gathered over the last 20 years at such sites as the Lower Gallery at La Garma, Las Penas and Riocueva, has clearly demonstrated that caves were also used for funerary purposes (Hierro 2011).

For a better understanding, it is necessary to explore the nature of the broader funerary record of this period. Some examples of cemeteries dated to the Visigothic period (late sixth to early eighth century AD) in Cantabria include Santa María de Hito, El Conventón in Rebolledo, and Santa María de Retortillo (Gutiérrez Cuenca and Hierro 2007). In general, they are related to the ruins of older Roman buildings, showing some continuity in the occupation of territories, though the function of sites had then changed. Roman buildings occasionally determined the internal organisation of cemeteries. Graves usually consist of simple pits, pits associated with low walls or with a wooden coffin, and possibly stone sarcophagi. Orientations vary, but burials orientated east predominate. They occur in complex stratigraphic contexts, often beneath long cist graves corresponding to later medieval cemeteries. Objects of personal adornment are scarce, with rings more common than belt buckles, but with no pottery or glass vessels, weapons or utensils. However, deer antlers and animal teeth (e.g. carnivore canines and herbivores molars) are found, perhaps used as amulets. Although it is difficult to isolate demographic profiles in the early phases of sites that witnessed prolonged usage, they seem to match demographic tendencies of the time, with infant mortality at about 20–25 per cent, and the presence of all age groups. About the early eighth century, certain elements indicate a change was taking place. Long cist burials appear and objects related to clothing and personal adornment become scarcer until they disappear completely, with everyday garments probably replaced by simple shrouds. In addition, cemeteries were located around churches. From this time onwards, long cist graves and sarcophagi, practically the only types of tomb known, were aligned with these new places of worship. Despite the changes, cemeteries founded in the Visigothic period continued in use, uninterruptedly at least until the middle medieval period.

In short, in Cantabria, the open-air funerary record of the sixth to eighth century is characterised by cemeteries that were similar to those in other parts of the Iberian Peninsula. This appears to have been the usual form of burial for the rural Christian communities that comprised the majority of the population in the region. There is reasonable evidence to propose that some significant changes took place in funerary behaviour at the end of this period, particularly the change from dressed burials to the use of shrouds. Certain differences with funerary caves are apparent. How can we explain such variability in funerary behaviour within the same chronological, geographic and cultural setting? We believe that the ordinary, usual and regulated behaviour was inhumation in individual graves in cemeteries close to a church. Funerary deposits in caves might thus be considered different from the general rule, a kind of deviant burial or *Sonderbestattung* (Müller-Scheeßel 2013). Instead of a necropolis near a village in open land accessible to the community, these burials were inside caves, in places difficult to access, sometimes even walled off. Instead of long cist graves and sarcophagi, with bodies placed in an extended position with the head to the west, corpses were left on cave floors, grouped in small spaces, without any particular orientation and in a variety of positions. Instead of burial with a shroud, bodies were apparently dressed and adorned. Instead of an almost total absence of artefacts in graves, a large number of objects of various kinds – significantly including utensils connected to daily chores – were left with the corpses. Therefore, instead of a panorama of normality, we find a very different or ‘atypical’ scenario.

How can this be explained? So far, three kinds of hypotheses have been put forward. The most traditional one derives from the classic studies of González Echegaray (1966, 1988), who proposed continuity between the Iron Age populations in this part of northern Spain, the *Cantabri*, and early medieval groups. This line of explanation was echoed in regional literature, largely influenced by the tendency of historiography in those years to attribute a great weight to indigenous tradition in shaping the political and social characteristics of the early medieval period in northern Spain (Barbero and Vigil 1979). From this standpoint, practices such as those documented at La Garma, Riocueva and Las Penas were considered evidence of the survival of pagan funerary practices amongst at least a part of the regional population.

From a quite different perspective, Gutiérrez González (2010, 70–73) proposed a hypothesis that the outstanding artefacts of Visigothic chronology found in underground sites (including mines) could be interpreted as privileged burials of local élites who aimed to differentiate themselves from the rest of the population through funerary practices that differed from the norm, in the style of exceptional practices such as ship burials, for example, at Sutton Hoo in England. In the same line, García and Muñiz (2010, 342) proposed that the possible prestigious nature of cave burials was restricted to privileged groups.

Recently, one of the present authors (J.Á.H.) has put forward another hypothesis to explain funerary deposits in caves. These could be burial places of victims of an epidemic, with caves chosen because of their distance from dwellings, revealing the fear of contagion amongst the groups from which the deceased originated (Hierro 2008). The death in exceptional circumstances of some individuals led to their exclusion from ordinary cemeteries, which in the seventh and eighth centuries was the usual burial place for the Christian faithful.

Nowadays, the debate appears to focus on the latter two hypotheses, as the notion of possible paganism in Visigothic Cantabria seems unlikely in the light of recent research. In the first place, studies have shown that Romanisation was not so superficial in the north of Spain (Aja *et al.* 2008; Fernández Ochoa *et al.* 2008), and the region even maintained a certain level of urbanisation, which continued through the Visigothic period until the establishment of the kingdom of Asturias (Menéndez Bueyes 2001). It is therefore unlikely that paganism played a significant role in society at that time, apart from the survival of aspects that by then had lost a formal religious character and had become popular 'magic' or 'superstitious' religious practices. This is confirmed by the presence of Christian iconography on some of the objects found with the cave burials (see above). It should be added that there is no clear evidence of a late prehistoric funerary tradition of cave burial; it is necessary to go back to the Bronze Age to find systematic use of caves for this purpose (Ontañón and Armendariz 2005/2006).

Gutiérrez's hypothesis is more difficult to assess, as the quality of the available archaeological information is poor. However, the evidence is not entirely convincing. Many of the sites he mentions are older than the period in discussion here (they correspond to the fourth and fifth centuries) and their funerary character is unproven (Chapipi, Peña Forua and Los Husos), or at least the association between burials and Late Antique or medieval archaeological materials and radiocarbon dates is uncertain (L'Alborá, Cueva Pequeña). In fact, in some caves where human bones have been dated, they have been found to be prehistoric, as occurred at El Cantal, Ñobre and el Portillo del Arenal (Gutiérrez Cuenca and Hierro 2010/2012). It is also worth adding that weapons, one of the indicators of social status mentioned by Gutiérrez, are rarely found in caves. Among the materials dated to the seventh–eighth centuries, only one case can be mentioned: the battle axe from Los Goros. It is true that in some caves used for funerary purposes objects that can be considered 'prestige items' were found (buckles with inlaid decoration, gold rings, bronze jugs). However, this might simply indicate the inclusive character of cave burials, with all types of individuals sharing the same underground space. An example might be La Garma itself, where only one of the five bodies was fitted with a belt with a decorated buckle. Furthermore, it is not clear to what extent some objects, like buckles or glass vessels, were exclusive to élites or might have been available to wider sectors of society. From another perspective, it seems paradoxical that a burial intending to display power and wealth would be placed in inconspicuous sites such as remote cave passages that are difficult to access. Another aspect that is difficult to reconcile with this hypothesis is the age distribution of the human remains from the well-documented sites: these are significantly biased in comparison to the general demographic profile.

In our opinion, the available evidence more closely matches the hypothesis advanced by Hierro (2008). Features such as the difficulty of accessing the burial places, the atypical demographic profile, and the nature of the associated artefacts (clothing, personal adornments, domestic utensils) fit the notion of funerary practices associated with exceptional situations that produced fear and rejection among the wider population. These situations may well have been some of the numerous epidemics known to have occurred at that time, as Hierro (2008) proposes, but may also include other types of 'bad death' (Gutiérrez Cuenca and Hierro 2012), perhaps related to certain forms of behaviour condemned by the ideology of the time (e.g. witchcraft, delinquency). This seems to be consistent with the post-burial behaviour documented at some sites (and which is absent in open-air cemeteries), such as destruction or burning of human bones after skeletonisation, and the presence of carbonised cereal grains. With regard to the former, La Garma must obviously be mentioned, but also Las Penas, where all the skulls were grouped in a particular part of the funerary passage, then smashed and burnt. Very similar behaviour has been documented in Riocueva. This intentional destruction of bones, which must have been carried out some time after bodies were deposited, may be evidence of necrophobic behaviour possibly aimed at eliminating the potential threat these bodies represented to the communities they belonged to in life (Hierro 2011; Arias and Ontañón 2012). The presence of carbonised cereals (einkorn, spelt, barley and millet at Las Penas; millet, foxtail millet and barley at Riocueva) associated with bodies, and very probably with the action of burning bones, also supports the interpretation. This was an action repeatedly condemned in early medieval penitentials from the seventh century onwards. Therefore, it seems to have been a recognised custom, apparently intended to guarantee the well-being of the living against threats from the dead, in exceptional circumstances (Hierro 2011; Gutiérrez Cuenca and Hierro 2012).

## Conclusion

The use of caves for funerary purposes in Cantabria and the wider territory of the Visigothic kingdom of Toledo and its Asturian successor, in the seventh and eighth centuries AD, generally appears to have been a response to exceptional circumstances in rural communities, and may be interpreted as an example of 'deviant burial' with profound symbolic significance. From the choice of place – an underground site separated from the village – to the violent actions meted out to corpses and the unusual disposal of personal and everyday objects, all the aspects of the phenomenon attest to a series of beliefs about the dead that would not be unusual to the early medieval mentality. Sites like the Lower Gallery at La Garma, Las Penas and Riocueva, which are among the best documented for the period, provide details about this modality of deviant burial that, judging by its wide geographic distribution, may not have been as unusual as previously believed. All the sites that have been identified display patterns that are best explained as practices intended to prevent the dead 'returning' to disturb the living.

Unfortunately, the absence of information about this behaviour in written documents from the period greatly hinders interpretation. Many questions remain unanswered and, at the present time, our research continues to seek answers. One important line of inquiry is the determination of the causes of death as this could be a key factor in understanding the phenomenon. Attempts are currently being made to identify DNA from pathogen species in the anthropological material, which might contribute new insights on early medieval beliefs and attitudes towards death.

## Acknowledgements

The archaeological work at La Garma has been funded by the Government of Cantabria in the framework of several agreements with the University of Cantabria. Archaeological research at Riocueva has also been funded by the Government of Cantabria. The graphics in this paper were produced, unless otherwise specified, by Luis C. Teira at the Cantabrian International Institute of Prehistoric Research (IIIPC). All the calibrations are referred to the IntCal13 curve (Reimer *et al.* 2013), except for the *Phorcus lineatus* shell of Zone IV, which has been calibrated with the Marine13 curve (Reimer *et al.* 2013), using the value of ΔR calculated by Mestres and Arias (2006) for the southern coast of the Bay of Biscay. They have been processed with the OxCal (version 4.2) programme (Bronk Ramsey 2009a).

## References

Aja, J.R., Cisneros, M., and Ramírez, J.L., eds., 2008. *Los cántabros en la Antigüedad: la historia frente al mito*. Santander: Servicio de Publicaciones de la Universidad de Cantabria.

Alcalde del Río, H. 1934. Varios objetos de los primeros tiempos del cristianismo en la Península. *In*: *Homenaje a Mélida*. Madrid: Anuario del Cuerpo de Archiveros, Bibliotecarios y Arqueólogos, 149–160.

Álvarez Fernández, E., 2011. Humans and marine resource interaction reappraised: archaeofauna remains during the late Pleistocene and Holocene in Cantabrian Spain. *Journal of Anthropological Archaeology* 30(3), 327–343.

Arias, P., 1999. La Garma (Kantabrien/Spanien): Eiszeitliche Wandkunst und Wohnplätze in einer verschlossenen Höhle. *Jahrbuch des Römisch-Germanischen Zentralmuseums Mainz* 46, 3–20.

Arias, P., 2009. Rites in the dark? An evaluation of the current evidence for ritual areas at Magdalenian cave sites. *World Archaeology* 41(2), 262–294.

Arias, P., González Sainz, C., Moure, A. and Ontañón, R., 1999. *La Garma. Un descenso al pasado*. Santander: Consejería de Cultura y Deporte del Gobierno de Cantabria.

Arias, P. and Ontañón, R., eds., 2004. *La materia del lenguaje prehistórico. El arte mueble paleolítico de Cantabria en su contexto*. Santander: Consejería de Cultura, Turismo y Deporte del Gobierno de Cantabria.

Arias, P. and Ontañón, R., 2012. La Garma (Spain): Long-term human activity in a karst system. *In*: K.A. Bergsvik and R. Skeates, eds. *Caves in Context: The Cultural Significance of Caves and Rockshelters in Europe*. Oxford: Oxbow Books, 101–117.

Arias, P. and Ontañón, R., 2013. Cantabrian portable art in its context: an approach to the study of Palaeolithic graphic expression in northern Spain. *In*: A. Pastoors and B. Auffermann, eds. *Pleistocene Foragers on the Iberian Peninsula: Their Culture and Environment. Festschrift in Honour of Gerd-Christian Weniger for his Sixtieth Birthday*. Mettmann: Neanderthal Museum, 261–281.

Arias, P., Ontañón, R., Álvarez Fernández, E., Cueto, M., Elorza, M., García-Moncó, C., Güth, A., Iriarte, M.J., Teira, L.C. and Zurro, D., 2011. Magdalenian floors in the Lower Gallery of La Garma. A preliminary report. *In*: S. Gaudzinski-Windheuser, O. Jöris, M. Sensburg, M. Street and E. Turner, eds. *Site-Internal Spatial Organization of Hunter-Gatherer Societies: Case Studies from the European Palaeolithic and Mesolithic*. Mainz: Verlag des Römisch-Germanischen Zentralmuseums, 31–51.

Arias, P., Ontañón, R., Gutiérrez Cuenca, E., Hierro, J.Á. and Pereda, E.M., 2012. El broche de cinturón de tipo visigodo de la Galería Inferior de La Garma. *In*: B. Arízaga *et al.*, eds. *Mundos Medievales: Espacios, sociedades y poder: Homenaje al Profesor José Ángel García de Cortázar y Ruiz de Aguirre*. Santander: PUbliCan, 335–353.

Baffier, D. and Girard, M., 1998. *Les cavernes d'Arcy-sur-Cure*. Paris: La maison des roches.

Baldini, L.M., McDermott, F., Arias, P., García-Moncó, C., Baldini, J.U.L., Mattey, D., Hoffmann, D., Richards, D. and Müller, W., 2010. Climate in northern Spain through the Younger Dryas and Holocene preserved in a precisely dated speleothem from La Garma cave, Cantabria. *Geophysical Research Abstracts* 12, EGU2010-14937.

Baldini, L.M., McDermott, F., Baldini, J.U.L., Arias, P., Cueto, M., Fairchild, I.J., Hoffmann, D., Mattey, D., Müller, W., Nita, D.C., Ontañón, R., García-Moncó, C. and Richards, D.A., 2015.

Regional temperature, atmospheric circulation, and sea-ice variability within the Younger Dryas Event constrained using a speleothem from northern Iberia. *Earth and Planetary Science Letters* 419, 101–110.

Barandiarán, I., 1973. Restos visigodos en la cueva Foradada (Sarsa de Surta, Huesca). *In*: *Estudios de Edad Media de la Corona de Aragón, IX*. Zaragoza: Consejo Superior de Investigaciones Científicas-Escuela de Estudios Medievales, 9–48.

Barbero, A. and Vigil, M., 1979. *Sobre los orígenes sociales de la Reconquista*. Barcelona: Ariel.

Bernárdez, M.J. and Guisado, J., 2014. La Moneda Visigoda en Cuenca y su contexto arqueológico. El hallazgo del tesorillo de tremises visigodos de la mina romana de *lapis specularis* de La Condenada en Osa de la Vega (Cuenca). *In*: E. Gozálbez, J.A. Hernández Rubio, and J.A. Almonacid, eds. *Cuenca: La historia en sus monedas*. Cuenca: Ediciones de la Universidad de Castilla-La Mancha, 159–190.

Bohigas, R., 2002. La cerámica Medieval de la cueva de La Garma (Omoño, Ribamontán al Monte, Cantabria). *In*: R. Bohigas, ed. *Trabajos de arqueología en Cantabria V*. Santander: R. Bohigas, 109–113.

Bronk Ramsey, C., 2009a. Bayesian analysis of radiocarbon dates. *Radiocarbon* 51(1), 337–360.

Bronk Ramsey, C., 2009b. Dealing with outliers and offsets in radiocarbon dating. *Radiocarbon* 51(3), 1023–1045.

Carballo, J., 1935. La caverna de Suano (Reinosa). *Altamira* II(3), 233–252.

Carnicero, S., 2006. Estudio antropológico del yacimiento arqueológico Cueva de Las Penas (Mortera, Piélagos, Cantabria). *Sautuola* XII, 295–300.

Cook, R.A. and Comstock, A.R., 2014. Evaluating the old wood problem in a temperate climate: a Fort Ancient case study. *American Antiquity* 79(4) 763–775.

Fernández Ochoa, C., Gil, F., and Orejas, A., 2008. Veranes (Gijón, Asturias, Spain). A rural landscape through time. *In*: C. Bartels, Ruiz del Árbol, H. van Londen and A. Orejas, eds. *Landmarks. Profiling Europe's Historic Landscapes*. Bochum: Deutsches Bergabau-Museum, 63–73.

García Álvarez-Busto, A. and Muñiz López, I., 2010. *Arqueología Medieval en Asturias*. Oviedo: Trea.

Garín, J., 1913. Hebilla epigráfica cristiana del s. V hallada en Ortigosa de Cameros (Logroño). *Boletín de la Real Academia de la Historia* LXIII, 105–106.

González Echegaray, J., 1966. *Los Cántabros*. Madrid: Guadarrama.

González Echegaray, J., 1988. Los cultos religiosos y el proceso de romanización en Cantabria. *Altamira* 47, 27–45.

González Sainz, C., 2003. El conjunto parietal paleolítico de la Galería Inferior de La Garma (Cantabria). Avance de su organización interna. *In*: R. de Balbín and P. Bueno, eds. *Arte prehistórico desde los inicios del s. XXI. Primer Symposium Internacional de Arte Prehistórico de Ribadesella*. Ribadesella: Asociación Cultural Amigos de Ribadesella, 201–222.

Gutiérrez Cuenca, E. and Hierro, J.Á., 2007. Nuevas perspectivas para la reconstrucción histórica del tránsito entre la Antigüedad y la Alta Edad Media en Cantabria: la necrópolis de Santa María de Hito. *Nivel Cero* 11, 97–116.

Gutiérrez Cuenca, E. and Hierro, J.Á., 2010–2012. Nuevas evidencias sobre el uso de las cuevas de Cantabria durante la Tardoantigüedad y la Alta Edad Media. Primeros resultados del Proyecto Mauranus. *Sautuola* XVI–XVII, 263–280.

Gutiérrez Cuenca, E. and Hierro, J.Á., 2012. El uso de las cuevas naturales en Cantabria durante la Antigüedad Tardía y los inicios de la Edad Media (siglos V–X). *Kobie. Serie Paleoantropología* 31, 175–206.

Gutiérrez Cuenca, E., Hierro, J.Á., and Alfaro, C., 2014. Restos textiles de la cueva de Riocueva (Entrambasaguas, Cantabria). *In*: C. Alfaro, M. Tellenbach, and J. Ortiz, eds. *Production and Trade of Textiles and Dyes in the Roman Empire and Neighbouring Regions. Purpureae Vestes IV*. Valencia: Universitat de València, 73–81.

Gutiérrez González, J.A., 2010. Arqueología tardoantigua en Asturias. Una perspectiva de la organización territorial y del poder en los orígenes del reino de Asturias. *In*: J.I. Ruiz de la Peña and J. Camino, eds. *La Carisa y La Mesa. Causas políticas y militares del origen del reino de Asturias*. Oviedo: Asociación Amigos de La Carisa, 52–83.

Gutiérrez Lloret, S., Gamo, B., and Amorós, V., 2003. Los contextos cerámicos altomedievales del Tolmo de Minateda y la cerámica altomedieval en el sudeste de la Península Ibérica. *In*: L. Caballero, P. Mateos, and M. Retuerces, eds. *Cerámicas tardorromanas y altomedievales en la Península Ibérica. Ruptura y continuidad*. Madrid: Consejo Superior de Investigaciones Científicas, 119–168.

Güttler, D., *et al.*, 2015. Rapid increase in cosmogenic $^{14}C$ in AD 775 measured in New Zealand kauri trees indicates short-lived increase in $^{14}C$ production spanning both hemispheres. *Earth and Planetary Science Letters* 411, 290–297.

Hernández Vera, J.A., Núñez, J., and Martínez Torrecilla, J.M., 2007. *Contrebia-Leucade, guía arqueológica*. Logroño: Gobierno de La Rioja.

Hierro, J.Á., 2002. Arqueología de la Tardoantigüedad en Cantabria: yacimientos y hallazgos en cueva. *Nivel Cero* 10, 113–128.

Hierro, J.Á., 2008. *La utilización de las cuevas en Cantabria en época visigoda. Los casos de Las Penas, La Garma y El Portillo del Arenal*. Thesis (MSc), Universidad de Cantabria.

Hierro, J.Á., 2011. La utilización de las cuevas en Cantabria en época visigoda. Los casos de Las Penas, La Garma y El Portillo del Arenal. *Munibe (Antropologia-Arkeologia)* 62, 351–402.

Janssens, P. and González Echegaray, J., 1958. *Memoria de las excavaciones de la Cueva del Juyo (1955–56)*. Santander: Patronato de las Cuevas Prehistóricas de la Provincia de Santander.

Maza, T., 1957. Manifestaciones de la economía montañesa desde el siglo IV al XVIII. *In*: *Aportación al estudio de la historia económica de La Montaña*. Santander: Banco de Santander, 81–143.

Menéndez Bueyes, L.R., 2001. *Reflexiones críticas sobre el origen del Reino de Asturias*. Salamanca: Ediciones Universidad de Salamanca.

Mestres, J.S. and Arias, P., 2006. Datación por Radiocarbono y calibración de las fechas radiocarbónicas aplicadas a materiales de origen terrestre y marino procedentes de la región Cantábrica. *In*: I. Clemente, ed. *Explotación de recursos litorales y acuáticos en la Prehistoria. Workshop, Barcelona 15–16 abril 2005*. Barcelona: Departament d'Arqueologia i Antropologia-Institució Milà i Fontanals CSIC, 7–10.

Miyake, F., Nagaya, K., Maduda, K. and Nakamura, T., 2012. A signature of cosmic ray increase in AD 774–775 from tree rings in Japan. *Nature* 486, 240–242.

Morlote, J.M., Muñoz, E., Serna, M.L. and Valle, Á., 1996. Las cuevas sepulcrales de la Edad del Hierro en Cantabria. *In*: *La arqueología de los Cántabros. Actas de la Primera Reunión sobre la Edad del Hierro en Cantabria: Santander, mayo de 1995*. Santander: Fundación Marcelino Botín, 195–279.

Müller-Scheeßel, N., ed., 2013. *'Irreguläre' Bestattungen in der Urgeschichte: Norm, Ritual, Strafe ...? Akten der Internationalen Tagung in Frankfurt a. M. vom 3. bis 5. Februar 2012*. Römisch-Germanische Kommission, Kolloquien zu Vor- und Frühgeschichte 19, Bonn: Dr. Rudolf Habelt.

Ontañón, R., 2003. Sols et structures d'habitat du Paléolithique supérieur, nouvelles données depuis le Cantabres: la Galerie Inférieure de La Garma (Cantabrie, Espagne). *L'Anthropologie* 107, 333–363.

Ontañón, R. and Armendariz, Á., 2005/2006. Cuevas y megalitos: los contextos sepulcrales colectivos en la Prehistoria reciente cantábrica. *In*: *Homenaje a Jesús Altuna, vol. II: Arqueología*. San Sebastián: Sociedad de Ciencias Aranzadi, 275–286.

Ontañón, R., García de Castro, C. and Llamosas, A., 2008. *Palaeolithic Cave Art of Northern Spain (Extension to Altamira). Proposal of Inscription of Properties in the UNESCO List of World Heritage*. Santander: Comisión de Coordinación del Bien 'Arte Rupestre Paleolítico de la Cornisa Cantábrica'.

Palol, P. de, 1957a. Bronces con decoración damasquinada en época visigoda. *In*: *Actas del V Congreso Nacional de Arqueología*. Zaragoza: Secretaría General de los Congresos Arqueológicos Nacionales, 292–305.

Palol, P. de, 1957b. Los objetos visigodos de la Cueva de Los Goros (Hueto Arriba-Álava). *Boletín de la Institución Sancho el Sabio* 1–2, 73–84.

Pardo de Santayana, M., 2008. *Estudios etnobotánicos en Campoo (Cantabria): conocimiento y uso tradicional de las plantas*. Madrid: Consejo Superior de Investigaciones Científicas.

Peña, R., 2006. Perfil de olla y orza. Cueva de Cudón, en Cudón (Miengo, Cantabria). *In*: P.Á Fernández Vega, ed., *Apocalipsis. El ciclo histórico de Beato de Liébana*. Santander: Gobierno de Cantabria, 181.

Peñil, J. and Ruiz, F., 1971. Reseña arqueológica de Recueva. *Cuadernos de Espeleología* 5–6, 129–133.

Quirós, J.A. and Alonso Martín, A., 2007. Las ocupaciones rupestres en el fin de la Antigüedad. Los materiales cerámicos de Los Husos (Laguardia, Álava). *Veleia* 24–25, 1123–1142.

Reimer, P.J., Bard, E., Bayliss, A., Beck, J., Blackwell, P., Bronk Ramsey, C., Grootes, P.M., Guilderson, T., Haflidason, H., Hajdas, I., Hatté, C., Heaton, T., Hoffmann, D., Hogg, A., Hughen, K., Kaiser, K., Kromer, B., Manning, S., Niu, M., Reimer, R., Richards, D., Scott, E., Southon, J., Staff, R., Turney, C. and van der Plicht, J., 2013. IntCal13 and Marine13 Radiocarbon Age Calibration Curves 0–50,000 Years cal BP. *Radiocarbon* 55(4), 1869–1887.

Ripoll, G., 1998. *Toréutica de la Bética (siglos VI y VII D.C.)*. Barcelona: Reial Acadèmia de Bones Lletres.

Santonja Gómez, M., Santonja Alonso, M., and Alcalde, G., 1982. Aspectos de la ocupación humana antigua del cañón de la Horadada (Palencia). *Publicaciones de la Institución Tello Téllez de Meneses* 47, 337–392.

Schiffer, M.B., 1986. Radiocarbon dates and the 'Old Wood' problem: the case of the Hohokam chronology. *Journal of Archaeological Science* 13(1), 13–30.

Serna, M.L., Valle, Á and Hierro, J.Á., 2005. Broches de cinturón hispanovisigodos y otros materiales tardoantiguos de la cueva de *Las Penas* (Mortera, Piélagos). *Sautuola* XI, 247–277.

Van Strydonck, M., Nelson, D.E., Crombé, P., Bronk Ramsey, C., Scott, E.M., van der Plicht, J. and Hedges, R.E.M., 1999. What's in a $^{14}$C date? *In*: J. Evin, C. Oberlin, J. Daugas and J. Salles, eds. *3ème Congrès International $^{14}$C et Archéologie. Lyon 6–10 avril 1998*. Rennes: Société Préhistorique Française (Mémoire XXVI) – Groupe des Méthodes Pluridisciplinaires Contribuant à l'Archéologie (G.M.P.C.A.), 433–448.

# Chapter 9

# Christian and Muslim patterns of secular and religious cave use in the Iberian Peninsula in Late Antiquity and the Early Middle Ages (fifth/sixth to eleventh/twelfth centuries AD)

*Manel Feijoó*

*The Iberian Peninsula displays a wide and varied range of human uses of natural and artificial caves in Late Antiquity and the early Middle Ages to fulfil a variety of functions. Two different cultures, Christian and Muslim, co-existed in the peninsula, each with its own particular expression of domestic activities and devotional or ascetic rites. The aim of this contribution is to examine the human use of caves from the fifth/sixth to the eleventh/twelfth century, and their range of functions. The sites are mainly located along the north, south and the eastern coast of the Iberian Peninsula.*

## Introduction

This chapter is concerned with the religious use of caves in Late Antiquity and the early Middle Ages by the cultures and religions that inhabited the Iberian Peninsula, beginning with the spread of Christianity and, subsequently, with the consolidation of Islam in large parts of the peninsula, the so-called *al-Andalus*. As we shall see, both religions held an attraction for caves, to a large extent linked to ascetic practices. The ways in which these underground spaces were adapted to traditional religious architecture and belief will be analysed. Religious practices were, however, not the only reason for occupying and using caves. Some caves were used for permanent occupation or short-term shelter for both people and animals; other caves functioned as storage spaces for food and materials. The location of certain sites suggests a defensive aspect, especially as this period was largely characterised by episodes of instability and military conflict.

## Caves in Christian Iberia

The Late Antique period (fourth to eighth century AD) is characterised by a major transformation in rural settlement patterns. In tandem with the emergence of new farming settlements and the abandonment of earlier habitation patterns that had been based on the centrality of Roman villas, came a growth in the number of fortified settlements and an increase in cave occupation. The use of caves in Late Antiquity and the early Middle Ages in the Iberian Peninsula has not received much scholarly attention. Up to the 1970s, archaeological research on caves was concerned primarily with prehistoric material. In recent years that focus has shifted, and there is now a growing interest in cave use in historic times (e.g. López Quiroga and Martínez Tejera 2014).

### *Christianity and caves*

With the emergence of Christianity, a rich and complex symbolism developed associating caves with concepts of regeneration, death and resurrection (Molina 2006a, 650). Such associations were already present in the Judeo-Christian tradition: according to the Old Testament in the Bible it was in a cave that Lot and his daughters found shelter after the destruction of Sodom and Gomorrah (*The Holy Bible* [King James version] Genesis 19:30), and the prophet Isaiah contemplated the birth of the Messiah who would get refuge in the fortresses of rock, 'his place of defence shall be the munitions of rock' (Isaiah 33:16–17) or, at least, in this way is how the Apostolic Father Barnabas interpreted this prophecy of Isaiah. Barnabas wrote (Epistle

XI:5): 'And again the Prophet says: ... You will dwell in a high cave, built of solid rock' (Ehrman 2005, 53). That Jesus was born in a cave was particularly significant. Although in the New Testament in the Bible the Gospel of St Luke placed this event in a manger (Luke 2:7), and the Gospel of St Matthew (Matthew 2:11) simply mentions a *oikia* (house), the Apocryphal gospels describe the birth in a cave: (Pseudo-Gospel of James 18; Pseudo-Matthew 13; Santos Otero 1963, 68–69 and 90–92). In the mid-third century and according to Origen of Alexandria in his *Contra Celsum* I, 51 (Against Celsus), the cave where the birth of Jesus took place was identified (Chadwick 1953, 47–48) and in the fourth century, Helen, mother of Emperor Constantine, built a basilica on the spot. The emperor ordered the construction of another basilica on the supposed burial place of Christ, as recounted by his biographer Eusebius of Caesarea (Molina 2006b, 866–867).

St John the Baptist can be considered the forerunner of the eremitic tradition. He lived and preached in the desert, far from mundane life, creating the prototype of the austere way of life that was later imitated by anchorites: 'John's clothes were made of camel's hair, and he had a leather belt around his waist. His food was locusts and wild honey' (Matthew 3:4). In monastic literature, caves exercised the same fascination as abandoned pagan temples or the desert inhabited by demons. Monasteries or hermitages in caves represented the objectification in stone of an ascetic, genuinely religious, feeling (Molina 2006a, 671). The retreat of a Christian hermit to a cave was akin to withdrawing to the wilderness, where the anchorite overcame the temptations of the earthly world and attained spiritual perfection.

A key feature of the hermit's life was to escape from the world and society and live a life of solitude, as described by Isidore of Seville (*Etymologies* 7, 13): '*Anachoritae sunt qui post coenobialem vitam deserta petunt et soli habitant per deserta; et ab eo, quod procul ab hominibus recesserunt, tali nomine nuncupantur*' (Oroz and Marcos 2004, 672): 'anchorites are those who, after a community life, seek out deserted places and live alone in the wilderness. Because they withdraw far from people they are named with this name' (Barney *et al.* 2006, 172).

### Christian cave hermitages in northern Spain

A fundamental problem in the study of caves is to refine the chronology of usage. In the case of Iberian eremitism, several pieces of evidence allow us to date their use from at least as far back as the fifth century, through the Visigothic period (sixth–eighth century), and into high and late medieval times. It is relatively common to find reuse and reworking of a cave, a process that can destroy evidence of previous activities. Many of these sites, however, lack scientific archaeological investigation but some written sources allow a closer estimation of the chronology of particular hermitages, and also aid in the identification of the hermit who occupied the cave (Fig. 9.1).

Numerous caves with evidence of use in Late Antiquity are found in the Ebro Valley and incorporate architectural elements related to Christian worship. One of the sites that has received the most attention is San Millán de la Cogolla, in the province of La Rioja (Fig. 9.2, 12). Documentation attests to the existence of a monastic community there from at least the first half of the tenth century. It is difficult to establish whether there was any earlier monastic activity there as the introduction of Islamic power in northern Spain in the early decades of the eighth century may have led to the abandonment of any such monastery. Regardless of a community organised around a monastic rule, archaeology has proved the existence of eremitic practices there from the fifth/sixth century. This cave was the retreat of the hermit Aemilianus (hence the current name of the monastery, *San Millán*), as described by Braulio, Bishop of Zaragoza (episcopate AD 631–651), who endeavoured to build the hagiography of this hermit saint (Castellanos 1999). Braulio completed it 50 years after the death of the hermit, collecting oral information from those who knew him, and so his account is relatively reliable.

Aemilianus began his spiritual preparation for ascetic practise with another hermit named Felices, who would later retreat to the so-called *Castellum Billibium*, about 40km north of San Millán de la Cogolla (Fig. 9.2, 7), and around which archaeological investigations have documented the existence of a Late Antique population and church (Martínez and Cepeda 1996; Pascual *et al.* 2006). In the countryside around this *castellum*, a small cave (Cueva de Páceta) was identified as a hermitage but given its orientation, altitude and shallowness, it is difficult to imagine that this cave was occupied.

After completing his education with Felices, Aemilianus went into solitary retreat and at the end of his life he may have been buried in a tomb in one of the rock cavities of San Millán de la Cogolla (Sáenz Rodríguez 1997, 54–55). The surviving building is an eleventh-century construction. Also located here is a series of artificial or semi-artificial caves on two levels; there may also have been a third, lower level that was destroyed by remodelling in later centuries (Monreal 1989, 168–169). These caves served as a place for monks who, on the death of the saint, occupied this area thereby preserving his burial place and memory. Three chambers, of different shapes and sizes were connected by a corridor. Other individual cells may have been located on the mountainside nearby (Monreal 1988, 81–87). Two cavities were probably used as chapels or churches. Successive reforms carried out in this area demonstrate its importance to subsequent communities. One roughly quadrangular church has a small altar; the second church is oblong, also with an altar niche, and provides access into a small atrium. Archaeological investigations in the 1970s revealed the

*Figure 9.1: Iberian Peninsula with the main sites mentioned in the text.*

presence of a necropolis. The earliest graves date to the sixth and seventh centuries, confirming the proposed first phase of religious use of this area, which subsequently led to the construction of a Mozarabic monastery in the eleventh century (Andrío *et al.* 1996).

In the province of La Rioja, various groups of caves are scattered from San Millán de la Cogolla in the north-west (Fig. 9.2, 12) to Arnedo in the south-east (Fig. 9.2, 32). Up to recent decades, cave dwelling was a typical settlement pattern in these areas. Some of these caves also appear to have been used for medieval religious and ascetic purposes (Abad 1999). In the case of the fifteenth-century monastery at Vico (Fig. 9.2, 35), near Arnedo, evidence points to an earlier eremitic retreat. Two caves are located to the south-east of the monastery, one with evidence of agricultural activity (a tank presumably linked with a wine press, discussed below), although the period of use is not known as it was used by farmers until recently. Another cavern seems to have functioned as a church in Late Antiquity. Putlog holes at the entrance point to a possible porch or *narthex*, although it is difficult to pinpoint the period of construction. The church consists of a nave and apse, occupying an area about 20m long and 5m wide. Barrel vaulting in the ceiling was increased in height by over one metre in the apse creating a more prominent space. Latin crosses are inscribed on the wall of this apse.

A series of openings dug into the walls of this cave are difficult to interpret, though they probably represent small niches to hold objects. González Blanco suggested the openings in the southernmost wall were used to install wooden elements that formed part of a wine press (González Blanco *et al.* 1999, 274). One interpretation is that a press was installed there after the church had been abandoned. Alternatively, it may have been in operation

*Figure 9.2: Distribution of caves to the south of the river Ebro in the province of La Rioja during Late Antiquity and the early Middle Ages (Sáenz 2005 after González Blanco* et al., *1979; printed with permission of the authors). The following sites are referred to in the text: 7. Páceta Cave and Castellum Billibium; 8. Nájera; 12. San Millán de la Cogolla; 19. Albelda; 32. Arnedo; 35. Vico Monastery.*

while the church was active. Other examples can be cited of the use of religious spaces to carry out production activities, though always related to the manufacture of items essential for the celebration of the Eucharist, namely bread and wine. Examples include the presence of a small grape treading press and/or an oven for the production of liturgical bread in church buildings in the East (Palmer 1990, 214). Furthermore, very close to this cave-church is another much smaller cave (approx. 3.5 × 3m), which may have been used as a store related to the aforementioned possible produce. Today this small cave is used by local farmers to store straw.

Between the two levels of the cave is a vent that serves to oxygenate the cave (González Blanco *et al.* 1999). Ventilation valves are also found in Santa Lucía de Ocón, about 20km northwest of Arnedo (Pascual and González Blanco 1999); in the monastery of San Martín de Albelda (Fig. 9.2, 19), between Arnedo and San Millán de la Cogolla (Ramírez and González Blanco 2014); and in the so-called cave hermitage of Albojarico (Jordán and González Blanco 1985), in the province of Albacete and near Camareta Cave and the Coín complex (Málaga), discussed below. To the west of the monastery, there is a group of smaller caves with evidence of human adaptation in the form of niches, walls and an access stairway. The sizes and location also suggest ascetic occupation (Monreal 1989, 215–216).

### *Multi-purpose caves*

In La Rioja several clusters of caves can be found along the Najerilla, Iregua and Cidacos rivers – all tributaries of the Ebro River, and to a lesser extent in the Jubera and Leza basins (Fig. 9.2). Along the middle stretch of the Cidacos River, passing through the meadows of Arnedo, are outcrops of sedimentary sandstone that provided ideal conditions for the manufacture of hundreds of artificial caves. The marks of the metal tools used for rock cutting are evident at all sites. Even if some were originally natural cavities, they were all totally remodelled (Puertas 1974, 11). Not all were necessarily used for religious or ascetic purposes. The diversity of shapes, sizes and locations have made them suitable for multiple purposes: permanent residences, barns, cellars, warehouses, yards and dovecotes (Eguizábal 2014). In the town of Nájera (Fig. 9.2, 8), about 15km north-east of San Millan, Puertas examined a series of caves that are situated on a hillslope and are difficult to access. At one site, known as *El Castillo*, the cave dwellings were divided into four galleries that gradually increase in height. All are rectangular in shape and show evidence of having been modified by metal tools. In these caves at Nájera the outer openings indicate modifications to maximise shelter from inclement weather (Puertas 1974). The galleries of El Castillo are divided into small independent living spaces that have partition walls, which create small rooms and compartments for daily use.

Sometimes it is extremely difficult to determine if a cave served a religious function or was a dwelling. For example, Cueva de San Miguel and Cueva de La Cienta, both in Arnedo, may have been used to store utilitarian objects, but it has also been suggested they were used to house relics (González Blanco 2014, 22). Crosses or Christian inscriptions carved into the walls of some of these caves have been documented, supporting a monastic function, but the presence of Christian symbols alone is not sufficient to rule out their use as simple dwellings of a secular Christian family or individual (Figs. 9.3 and 9.4).

With reference to the settlement of Las Gobas (Burgos), in the upper Ebro valley, I would like to draw attention to an important but often overlooked factor in the evaluation

*Figure 9.3: Cueva de la Cienta (Arnedo). The carved holes in the walls (and on the pillar, in the next figure) may have been used as simple shelves to leave objects of daily use, but it has also been suggested that they were used to store relics. Photo: C. Sieiro, with permission.*

*Figure 9.4: Cueva de San Miguel (Arnedo). Photo: C. Sieiro, with permission.*

of cave occupation. Since the first investigations at this site in the late 1960s, archaeological research has revealed cave churches and thus the settlement was considered an eremitic centre (Azkárate and Solaun 2008, 143). Recent archaeological excavations, however, have shown the existence of other domestic spaces, not in caves but on flat terrain in the vicinity, namely a hut built on thick wooden posts with storage spaces and a hearth. A funerary area has also been documented. The ceramic assemblage reveals use from the seventh/eighth to the tenth century. The religious use of some of these cavities is without question, but the relationship between religious buildings and rural peasant settlements has been raised (Azkárate and Solaun 2008). This perspective highlights the need for extensive excavation at such sites, because not only could it change our view of how caves functioned, it might also provide insight into the strategies of rural populations – an understudied aspect of Late Antique Hispania.

### *Cave hermitages and monasteries in southern Spain*

Leaving the northern region, other examples in the Iberian Peninsula include a cave-hermitage in the cliff of Ares del Bosc in the province of Alicante. It is a small hermitage consisting of a rectangular space with two annexed rooms or chapels. Latin crosses are engraved into the walls, and the main chamber has a bench running along the perimeter – a functional element present in other caves of religious character (Ferrer 1991). This small simple oratory was presumably focussed on seclusion and solitude. Other hermitages have greater architectural and ornamental wealth, such as in the town of Coín in the province of Málaga, Andalusia. This site consists of five rectangular rooms with adjoining cavities. Three of the chambers are interconnecting and are particularly large. The five entrances were cut through a large rock outcrop that measures approximately 30m long and 14m high, giving the complex an imposing, even monumental, character. The building also features arches, niches, buttresses, a gabled roof, a bench and an arch framing the apse. A vent opened into one of the chambers, similar to that at Vico. The Coín complex is likely to date to the tenth century, which is the Mozarabic period when Christian communities lived under Muslim rule, although the existence of an earlier place of worship cannot be discounted (Puertas 1986, 2003; Marmolejo 2008).

In the province of Jaén, also in Andalusia, several examples of natural caves are known that were modified to create a hermitage or monastic space, or to be used as dwelling places. The hermitage of Valdecanales (Rus, Jaén) is well known (Fig. 9.5). This complex comprises three artificial caves carved into a rocky outcrop of sandstone, with a structure that has now disappeared but was probably a wooden porch represented by putlog holes. The space used for liturgical rites boasts a decorated arch, while the other

*Figure 9.5: Hermitage of Valdecanales (Rus, Jaén). Photo: M. Feijoó.*

chambers have been interpreted as dwellings for a small community of hermits. The main cave consists of three units: a large rectangular chamber divided into three sections, and two small secondary chambers. A series of twelve arches are carved into the façade of the main chamber and the decorative motifs place the hermitage in the seventh century (Hauschild and Schlunk 1970; Vañó 1970).

Close to Valdecanales is the Giribaile plateau (Vilches, Jaén) where an interesting set of caves has been documented, apparently occupied in Late Antiquity. Detailed descriptions of this settlement are available (Gutiérrez Soler *et al.* 2005), but here I will only mention the sites that show evidence of use for liturgical purposes. The so-called 'Cueva de las Mujeres' has five chambers artificially excavated from a natural cavity. The complex is perfectly symmetrical, even in the aesthetic and functional features, such as niches. In contrast, other caves are characterised by an absence of decorative elements and the presence of storage pits or wall cupboards. The presence of a necropolis used in Late Antiquity seems to corroborate the Visigothic date of these caves. It has been suggested, however, that based on the morphological arrangement of some parts of the settlement and its association with certain types of *al-Andalus* caves (primarily the so-called *habitats de falaise* explored below), that it was used in the Islamic period (Ribera 2010, 360 and footnote 66). In fact, a *hisn* (castle or fortress) was built on top of the plateau during the Islamic period (Castillo *et al.* 2010). In this instance, we cannot discount continuous occupation from the Visigothic to the Islamic periods, as the use of caves in Andalusian culture was a common phenomenon among the rural population.

## Caves in Islamic Iberia: the case of *al-Andalus*

The dynamics of Islamic settlement in the Iberian Peninsula (*al-Andalus*) reveal the use of caves for a variety of functions as a common phenomenon in early medieval and later medieval times. There have been some attempts to synthesise the evidence for cave use in Christian Hispania (e.g. López Quiroga and Martínez Tejera 2014), but that has not been the case with the Muslim evidence though the number of sites is gradually increasing. Here I will present some examples that reveal the functional diversity of caves in *al-Andalus*. Before that, however, I will outline the significance of caves in Islamic religion.

### *Islam and caves*

As we have seen, caves held spiritual connotations for Christians and similarly, in Muslim culture, caves also served an important role in religious life. The origin of the Islamic religion can be traced to a cave located on Mount Hira, about 3km north-east of the city of Mecca (now Saudi Arabia). It was there, in AD 616, that the archangel Gabriel conveyed the divine revelation to the Prophet Muhammad who then became a messenger of Allah. Soon after, another cave called *Jabal Tawr* provided shelter for Muhammad and his companion Abu Bakr al-Siddiq (who later became the first Muslim caliph) when they were persecuted and fled from Mecca to Medina, as stated in the Quran:

> If you help him not, then know that Allah helped him even when the disbelievers drove him forth while he was one of the two when they were both in the cave, when he said to his companion, 'Grieve not, for Allah is with us'. Then Allah sent down His peace on him, and strengthened him with hosts which did not see, and humbled the word of those who disbelieved (*The Holy Qur'an*, *al-Tawba*, IX, 40).

Another significant example of caves in sacred Islamic texts is a *surah* (chapter) which speaks of the 'Men of the Cave' (*The Holy Qur'an*, *Surat al-Kahf*, XVIII). This text takes a pre-Christian legend that features the so-called Seven Sleepers of Ephesus. There are several versions of this legend in different languages, which probably originated in Syrian fifth- and sixth-century hagiographic texts (Fudge 2007, 68–70). The context is the persecution of Christians ordered by Emperor Decius in the middle of the third century. A group of young people fled to take refuge in a cave to avoid being forced to worship pagan idols. Once in the cave, they fell into a deep sleep from which they only awoke three centuries later when disputes were taking place between Christians about the resurrection of the dead on the Day of Judgment. The Seven Sleepers revealed that God had woken them to prove the truth of the Resurrection. While retaining the broad outline of the Christian legend, the Quran version differs (Massignon 1954). The message of the resurrection on the Day of Judgement remains, although only the Seven Sleepers provide evidence of the final resurrection, while the resurrection of Jesus Christ is not acknowledged. This is what Van Staëvel (2010, 319) has termed '*imitatio Muhammadi*', and was an early influence on Muslim eremitism, carried out in pursuit of *Tawakkul* – the abandonment of the material world and spiritual commitment to God (Pénicaud 2008, 6–7). This legend flourished following Islamic conquests and spread through different territories. Many sites claimed to be the true location of the Cave of the Seven Sleepers, including the town of Loja in the province of Granada (Bejarano 1993, 325).

### *The religious aspect of Andalusian caves*

In *al-Andalus* there are some examples of caves with evidence of religious activities. Cueva de la Camareta in the province of Albacete (Fig. 9.6) is an artificial cave carved into a perpendicular scarp about 30m high (González Blanco 1983; González Blanco *et al.* 1993). It consists of a central chamber which provides access into a series of smaller rooms. One chamber is significantly smaller and smoke on its walls indicates it housed a hearth. The most interesting characteristic of this space are the large number of inscriptions and graffiti spanning pre-Roman times through to a set of Latin inscriptions and up to the Muslim period (Bejarano 1993). The Latin inscriptions belong mostly to the seventh century (Velázquez 1993) and include Greco-Latin names (*Aurelius*, *Asturius*, *Sidonia*, etc.) as well as some of Germanic origin (*Lubigildo*). Christian expressions have been documented and an inscription that mentions an individual named *Cila*, who is rated '*sanctus vir Dei*' (The Holy man of God), suggests the possibility that this space was occupied by a Christian hermit (Velázquez 1993, 316–318). The same possibility applies in the case of the Arabic inscriptions (Fig. 9.7), the earliest of which might belong to the ninth century. The orientation of the cave to the east follows the Islamic canonical rule but it has not been possible to establish the presence of a *mihrab*, the architectural space towards which faithful Muslims should face when praying. However, in circumstances where it was not possible to have a *mihrab*, it was sufficient to mark the direction in which the prayer was performed by something else. In fact, Islamic tradition states that the prayer space of the Prophet Muhammad in Medina was marked by a simple stone on the ground; the same phenomenon can still be found among some nomadic Muslims in the Sahara Desert (Carmona 2012, 257). Furthermore, although no *ribat* (a space for religious practices or oratory) has been found in Cueva de la Camareta, it should be noted that one of the inscriptions refers to *rabit* (hermit) and there are references to Allah and the prophet Muhammad (Bejarano 1993, 326).

One final site, the Cueva de Extremadura in the Andalusian town of Priego de Córdoba, suggests even more strongly that it was an Islamic hermitage. Recent studies have documented more than 30 caves in this region that were occupied between the tenth and eleventh centuries (Cano 2010). Cueva de Extremadura was discovered and investigated in 2011 (Carmona 2012). It consists of three main chambers. Most of the pottery fragments recovered

*Figure 9.6: Plan and section of Cueva de la Camareta (Albacete) (after González Blanco* et al.*, 1993, with permission). Most of the inscriptions are located in room A, facing east and with a carved column (no. 6) at the entrance.*

during excavations belonged to domestic jars and pots, but some fine wares and storage containers were also represented. The abundance and dispersal of material rules out use of the cave as a place of sporadic refuge, and the constricted morphology excludes its use as a common dwelling place. Researchers have argued for a religious function associated with ascetic practices. It is worth noting that in one of the rooms a space that may represent a *mihrab* has been documented (Fig. 9.8) – a modified natural niche of the approximate dimensions of a traditional *mirhab* (2m high, 0.80m wide, 1m deep). Carmona, after consulting Islamic religious texts, concluded the niche was probably used for an oil lamp, as stated in a *sura* (chapter) of the Quran: 'Allah is the Light of the heavens and the earth. The similitude of His light is as a lustrous niche, wherein is a Lamp. The lamp is in a glass. The glass is as it were a glittering star' (Carmona 2012, 249).

While the canonical *mirhab* must face Mecca, this is not the case with the hypothetical *mirhab* of Cueva de Extremadura. However, this precept is not a strict obligation and al-Andalus mosques often diverge from this rule. In addition to the difficulties of precise orientation inside a cave, this is also a natural structure not built by the faithful, although certainly manipulated and adapted by them as much as possible in accordance with the Quran. The exact orientation at the moment of prayer, and therefore in the architectonic model, is a less important element as justified in the Islamic text: 'To Allah belong the East and the West;

*Figure 9.7: Arab inscription in Cueva de la Camareta (Albacete) (after González Blanco* et al.*, 1993, with permission) and interpretation of the same inscription (Bejarano, 1993, 358–359, with permission). Text: 'Ahmad ibn ... went into this room/Ibn Ahmad went into the rooms/God bless, in the name of God, to / Mu[hammad]'. This is one of the most extensive inscriptions in the cave. The name 'Ahmad' recurs in many other inscriptions.*

so withersoever you turn, there will be the face of Allah' (*The Holy Qur'an*, *Sura* 2 'of the Cow' *–al-Baqarah-*, *ayah* 115).

With respect to the ceramic material, we must consider the significant presence of fine ceramic tableware, which does not belong to the assemblage of coarse domestic pottery (Fig. 9.9). This reveals a certain 'purchasing power' of users of this cave, which does not necessarily contradict their ascetic role as we know many affluent individuals, or those close to palatine circles, decided to practice spiritual retreat. This is mirrored in Ibn Hayyan's reference in *Muqtabis V* to followers of Ibn Masarra (Carmona 2012, 252). It is in this territory that Sufi doctrine was preached and spread during the tenth century, Ibn Masarra being the main proponent. Ibn Masarra became leader of a religious community with ascetic tendencies and, after his death, his followers remained loyal to his doctrine in the territories of Córdoba, then spreading to other regions of *al-Andalus*. Anchorites and hermits devoted to contemplation and the practice of virtue attracted popular attention, and were a counterpoint to the moral laxness of the ruling oligarchy. Biographical repertoires of Ibn Faradi, Ibn al-Abbar and al-Humaydi, among others, sometimes used Sufi technical terminology to refer to Hispanic characters, pioneers of this kind of spiritual behaviour (De Santiago 1981, 270).

*Figure 9.8: Supposed mihrab in Cueva de Extremadura (Córdoba) (after Carmona 2012, with permission). In the lower image, note some evidence of human manipulation, showing the importance given to this natural niche. Above it is a small opening that was probably used for an oil lamp.*

## *Defence, domestic and storage functions*

The Andalusian world was not exempt from territorial disputes and armed conflicts and it is therefore not surprising that some Islamic settlements in rock cavities are of a defensive and/or military nature. One such example is Cueva del Harzal (Olmedillas, Guadalajara), situated in a narrow gorge near the Alboreca River, a tributary of the Henares, at the boundary between the provinces of Soria and Guadalajara. This cave has four openings but only two are accessible: one is located at ground level while the second can only be accessed via an artificial ramp. The large quantity of ceramic fragments in the adjacent field probably reflects debris and waste from the cave (Valiente and García-Gelabert 1983, 8–9). This cave, as well as others in the vicinity, was used until recently to shelter livestock, which had a negative impact on archaeological strata. Pottery from the cave and adjacent field corresponds to Islamic styles, namely from the Caliphate period (tenth/eleventh centuries), with similar finds from other cave settlements in the province such as Cueva de los Casares, but also prominent centres such as Medina Azahara (Córdoba) and Medinaceli (Soria), and military buildings such as Gormaz Castle (Cabré 1934). The role of Cueva del Harzal as a shelter must be related to its orientation towards Christian territories, as it is located along the natural route through the Henares River valley to Soria and the so-called Upper March (the northern border of Muslim territories). It was this very route that the Christian King Alfonso III took in 876 to carry out his military offensive against the territories of the peninsular central region, as would his successor, King Ordoño II (Valiente and García-Gelabert 1983, 22–23). This historical rivalry and territorial threat between Christians and Muslims likely encouraged the creation of refuges in caves in territories that faced military threat.

Bertrand (2000) has conducted detailed analysis of cave settlements in the territories of the Guadix-Baza plateau, Andalusia. Islamic occupation of these caves began in the late tenth and early eleventh centuries, coinciding with the end of the Umayyad caliphate in the peninsula and its division into small kingdoms (the *Taifa* period). At this time, two significant and interrelated events occurred: the arrival of a large contingent of North African Berber people and the appearance of a type of rock construction known as *graniers* or *magasins de falaise* (cliff granary) (Gattefosse 1934) or, as preferred by Bertrand (2000), *covarrones-refugio* (refuge caves). These are situated in difficult to access locations and have a clear defensive purpose. Described as 'authentic troglodytic strongholds' (Bertrand 2000, 29), they are technically very sophisticated and located at different heights. These artificial caves had stables in the lower levels and internal rock-cut stairs gave access to second-level chambers where food stocks were kept, as evidenced by excavated silos some four or five metres in depth. Vertical tunnels provided access to the uppermost levels, which provided refuge if needed (Bertrand 2000, 28–29). These *covarrones-refugio* served no permanent residential function, as the population would

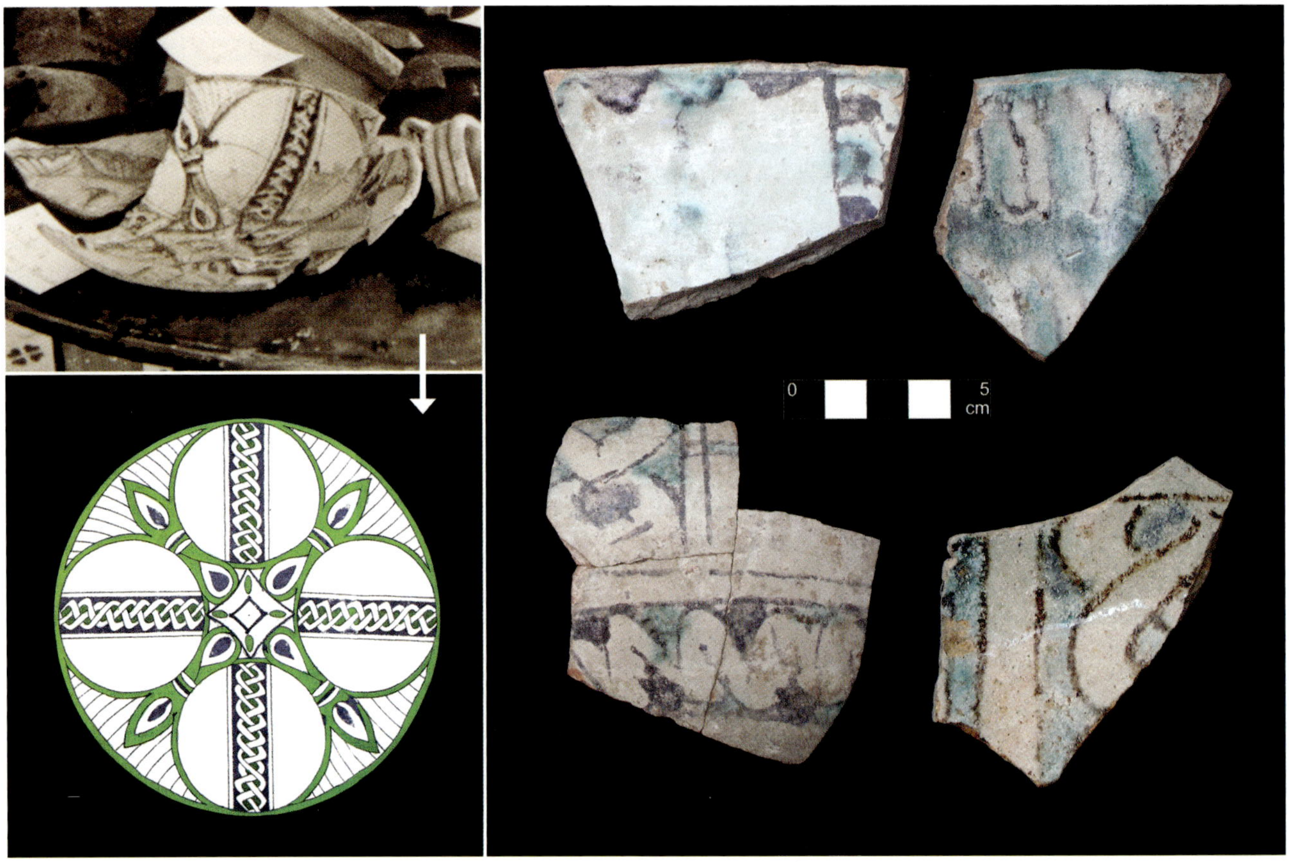


*Figure 9.9: Fine tableware pottery from Cueva de Extremadura (Córdoba) (after Carmona 2012, with permission) illustrating the purchasing power of users of this cave.*

have occupied *alquerías* (farmsteads) or isolated dwellings in the adjacent landscape.

In the twelfth century, coinciding with the arrival of the Almohads from North Africa, a new type of cave occupation site was introduced that bore some similarities with the *covarrones-refugio*, but now displayed a clear permanent residential function. These were clusters of housing units on three, four or even five levels. Each unit had a homogeneous morphology and internal distribution. The ground floor usually accommodated a stable and often a kitchen that opened onto a small terrace. The first level provided storage and work space, while the principal occupation chambers were on the second level. The uppermost chambers again functioned as a last resort in terms of refuge for inhabitants. Small rock-cut stairs and overhanging wooden cornices permitted communication between housing units, and these shelters can be compared with examples that exist today in some parts of Algeria, Libya and Morocco (Bertrand 1990, 2000, 31). Significantly, residential occupancy of these caves coincides with a reduced occurrence of farmhouses and other settlements in the surrounding landscape, indicating a movement towards the greater shelter and protection provided by caves.

Other Iberian regions also have examples of caves used for storage but with no evidence of occupation. One example, located in an area of rugged terrain on the Mediterranean seaboard about 70km north-west of Valencia, is Cuevas de Benaxuay. Approximately 1km away is the fortification of *Torrecilla* where excavations revealed Andalusian dwellings and abundant material from the Almohad period (twelfth–thirteenth centuries) (Ribera 2010, 345). The caves are located along a cliff comprising a series of small interconnecting chambers. Archaeological material is scarce, but this is partly related to a lack of concerted excavation. Ceramic finds mostly correspond to domestic and storage vessels. Rock-cut or stone-built silos are also a feature, as are remains of wooden structures and brick compartments associated with storage. Archaeological finds suggest the final usage of the caves was around the mid-twelfth century. The population who used Cuevas de Benaxuay probably dwelt in the nearby town of Chelva (Ribera 2010).

## Conclusions

I have attempted here to document human occupation in natural and artificial caves in Late Antiquity and the early Middle Ages in the Iberian Peninsula. Cave occupation was a well-known phenomenon throughout the Mediterranean basin. The symbolic associations with caves from prehistoric times were likely inherited by subsequent cultures though incorporating new meanings and symbolism from their own religious traditions. The use of caves as shelters for hermits or coenobitic groups is an established aspect of Christianity, usually linked to ascetic activities by seeking seclusion and solitude to achieve spiritual perfection and closeness to the divine. This aspect has been extensively studied in terms of Hispanic Christianity, but only recently has it been researched from an archaeological perspective in terms of cave hermitages or monasteries. These same ascetic or religious practices in caves are also present in Muslim religious practice in the Islamic lands of the Iberian Peninsula, *al-Andalus*. This has received little archaeological attention but some examples are presented here that will hopefully encourage further study and analysis.

Apart from religious activities, caves were used for a variety of other purposes. They functioned as places of refuge in times of social and political instability and military threat, both in Christian territories as well as in *al-Andalus*. Different forms of occupation are apparently dependant on the social, political and military context. Across both cultures and territories, caves were sometimes adapted as places of permanent or temporary residence, and in other instances used for storage or activities related to farming and husbandry. This chapter is not an attempt to create an exhaustive catalogue of cave settlements in the Iberian Peninsula, but rather to present an overview of the heterogeneous characteristics and variables of Christian and Muslim use of caves in Late Antiquity and the Early Middle Ages.

## References

Abad León, F., 1999. Expansión de la vida eremítica y monástica en La Rioja. *In*: A. González Blanco, ed. *Los columbarios de La Rioja*. Murcia: Universidad de Murcia, 285–312.

Andrío, J., Martín, E., and Souich, Ph. 1996. La necrópolis Medieval de San Millán de la Cogolla de Suso (La Rioja). *Berceo* 130, 49–106.

Azkárate, A. and Solaun, J. L., 2008. Excavaciones arqueológicas en el exterior de los conjuntos rupestres de Las Gobas (Laño, Burgos). *Archivo Español de Arqueología* 81, 133–149.

Barney, S.A., Lewis, W.J., Beach, J.A. and Berghof. O., eds., 2006. *The Etymologies of Isidore of Seville*. Cambridge: Cambridge University Press.

Bejarano, I., 1993. Las inscripciones árabes de la Cueva de la Camareta. *In*: A. González Blanco, R. González Fernández and M. Amante Sánchez, eds. *La Cueva de la Camareta (Agramón, Hellín-Albacete)*. Murcia: Universidad de Murcia, 323–377.

Bertrand, M., 1990. Les habitats de falaise d'occupation almohade et proto-nasride dans la depression de Guadix-Baza (Province de Grenade). *In*: J. Bermúdez and A. Bazzana, coords. *La maison hispano-musulmane. Apports de l'archeologie*. Granada: Publicaciones del Patronato de la Alhambra y Generalife, 47–71.

Bertrand, M., 2000. Cuevas d'Al-Andalus et cuevas chrétiennes: origines et évolution de l'habitat troglodytique des hautes plateaux de Grenade. *Castrum* 6, 27–52.

Cabré, J., 1934. Las cuevas de los Casares y de La Hoz. *Archivo Español de Arte y Arqueología* 10, 225–234.

Cano, E., 2010. *La ocupación de cuevas naturales durante la Edad Media andalusí en el entorno de Madinat Baguh (Priego de Córdoba)*. Granada: Alhulia.

Carmona, R., 2012. Ascetas, devotos y misticismo islámico: nuevas perspectivas sobre la ocupación de cuevas naturales en madinat Baguh (Priego de Córdoba). *Antiquitas* 24, 223–264.

Castellanos, S., 1999. *Hagiografía y sociedad en la Hispania visigoda. La* Vita Aemiliani *y el actual territorio riojano (siglo VI)*. Logroño: Instituto de Estudios Riojanos.

Castillo, J.C., Gutiérrez Soler, L.M., and Gutiérrez Calderón, M.V., 2010. El asentamiento islámico de Giribaile (Jaén). De asentamiento de altura a castillo almohade. *Cuadernos de Madinat al-Zahra'* 7, 239–262.

Chadwick, H., ed., 1953. *Origen: Contra Celsum*. Cambridge: Cambridge University Press.

De Santiago, E., 1981. Sufismo en Al-Andalus: evocación histórica. *Cuadernos de Estudios Medievales y Ciencias y Técnicas Historiográficas* 6–7, 269–275.

Eguizábal, D., 2014. Panorama rupestre del Valle Medio del Cidacos. *In*: J. López Quiroga and A.M. Martínez Tejera, eds., In concavis petrarum habitaverunt. *El fenómeno rupestre en el Mediterráneo Medieval: de la investigación a la puesta en valor*. Oxford: Archaeopress, 218–223.

Ehrman, B.D., ed., 2005. *The Apostolic Fathers, volume II*. Cambridge, MA–London: Harvard University Press.

Ferrer, P., 1991. L'eremitori rupestre d'Ares del Bosc. *Alberri. Quaderns d'investigació del Centre d'Estudis Contestants*, 111–123.

Fudge, B., 2007. The men of the cave: Tafsir, tragedy and Tawfiq al-Hakim. *Arabica* LIV(1), 67–93.

Gattefosse, J., 1934. Les graniers de falaise, forme ancienne d'agadir collectif. *Bulletin de la Societé de Préhistoire du Maroc* 3–4, 91–102.

González Blanco, A., 1983. La Cueva de la Camareta, refugio ibérico, eremitorio cristiano y rincón misterioso para árabes y foráneos hasta el día de hoy. Sus graffiti. *In*: *XVI Congreso Nacional de Arqueología* (Cartagena-Murcia 1982). Zaragoza: Universidad de Zaragoza, 1023–1033.

González Blanco, A. 2014. La cronología de las cuevas artificiales. *In*: J. López Quiroga and A.M. Martínez, eds. In concavis petrarum habitaverunt. *El fenómeno rupestre en el Mediterráneo Medieval: de la investigación a la puesta en valor*. Oxford: Archaeopress, 18–28.

González Blanco, A., Espinosa, U., and Sáenz, J. M., 1979. La población de La Rioja durante los siglos obscuros, *Berceo* 96, 81–111.

González Blanco, A., González Fernández, R., and Amante Sánchez, M., eds., 1993. *La Cueva de La Camareta (Agramón, Hellín-Albacete)*. Murcia: Universidad de Murcia.

González Blanco, A., Faulín García, C., Cinca Martínez, J.L. and González Fernández, R., 1999. Una nueva iglesia en el monasterio de Vico (Arnedo-La Rioja). *In*: A. González Blanco, ed. *Los columbarios de La Rioja*. Murcia: Universidad de Murcia, 259–277.

Gutiérrez Soler, L.M., Rueda Galán, C., Beatriz Luna, M. and Díaz García, M.J., 2005. Las cuevas de Giribaile: nuevas aportaciones para el estudio del poblamiento eremítico en Andalucía Oriental. *Arqueología y Territorio Medieval* 12, 13–37.

Hauschild, Th. and Schlunk, H., 1970. *Die Höhlenkirche beim Cortijo de Valdecanales*. Heidelberg: F. H. Kerle.

Jordán, J.F. and González Blanco, A., 1985. Probable aportación al monacato del SE peninsular: El conjunto rupestre de la Muela de Alborajico. *In*: R. C. Alonso de Cruz, ed. *Del* conventus carthaginiensis *a la* chora *de Tudmir*. Murcia: Universidad de Murcia, 334–363.

López Quiroga, J. and Martínez Tejera, A.M., eds., 2014. In concavis petrarum habitaverunt. *El fenómeno rupestre en el Mediterráneo Medieval: de la investigación a la puesta en valor*. Oxford: Archaeopress.

Marmolejo, F., 2008. *Informe sobre las cuevas rupestres de Coín*. Málaga: Fundación García Agüera. Available from: http://www.fundaciongarciaaguera.org/cuevas-rupestres.php [accessed 3 July 2016].

Martínez, A. and Cepeda, J.J., 1996. Conjunto arqueológico de Buradón (Salinillas de Buradón, Labastida). *Arkeoikuiska* 96, 183–189.

Massignon, L., 1954. Les Sept Dormants d'Ephèse (Ahl al-Kahf) en Islam et en Chrétienté: Première Partie. *Revue des Études Islamiques* 22, 61–110.

Molina, J.A. 2006a. Recorrido por la geografía del monacato rupestre cristiano. Una interpretación histórica. *In*: E. Conde, R. González, and A. Egea, eds., *Espacio y tiempo en la percepción de la Antigüedad Tardía*. Murcia: Universidad de Murcia, 649–675.

Molina, J.A. 2006b. La cueva y su interpretación en el cristianismo primitivo. *In*: E. Conde, R. González and A. Egea, eds., *Espacio y tiempo en la percepción de la Antigüedad Tardía*. Murcia: Universidad de Murcia, 861–880.

Monreal, A., 1988. San Millán de Suso. Aportaciones sobre las primeras etapas del cenobio emilianense. *Príncipe de Viana* 43, 70–96.

Monreal, A., 1989. *Eremitorios rupestres altomedievales (El Alto Valle del Ebro)*. Bilbao: Universidad de Deusto.

Oroz, J. and Marcos, M.A., eds., 2004. *Isidoro de Sevilla. Etimologías*. Madrid: Biblioteca de Autores Cristianos.

Palmer, A., 1990. *Monk and Mason on the Tigris Frontier: The Early History of Tur âAbdin*. Cambridge: Cambridge University Press.

Pascual, M.P. and González Blanco, A., 1999. El monasterio dúplice de Santa Lucía de Ocón (La Rioja). *In*: A. González Blanco, ed., *Los columbarios de la Rioja*. Murcia: Universidad de Murcia, 249–258.

Pascual, M.P., García Ruiz, P., Cinca Martínez and Pascual González, H., 2006. La Cueva de Páceta: Castro Bilibio, La Rioja. ¿Un eremitorio rupestre? *In*: E. Conde, R. González, and A. Egea, eds., *Espacio y tiempo en la percepción de la Antigüedad Tardía*. Murcia: Universidad de Murcia, 719–737.

Pénicaud, M., 2008. Réflexions sur la diffusion géographique des Sept Dormants. *Aurora* 4, 2–13.

Puertas, R., 1974. Cuevas artificiales de época altomedieval en Nájera. *Berceo* 86, 7–20.

Puertas, R., 1986. Los conjuntos rupestres mozárabes de Coín y Archidona. *Cuadernos de La Alhambra* 22, 11–54.

Puertas, R., 2003. El conjunto rupestre mozárabe de Coín. *In*: J.A. Martín Ruiz, ed., *Arqueología y patrimonio en la Algarbía malagueña*. Málaga: Diputación de Málaga, 41–56.

Ramírez, T. and González Blanco, A., 2014. San Martín de Albelda. *In*: J. López Quiroga and A.M. Martínez Tejera, eds., In concavis petrarum habitaverunt. *El fenómeno rupestre en el Mediterráneo Medieval: de la investigación a la puesta en valor*. Oxford: Archaeopress, 197–217.

Ribera, A., 2010. Las cuevas de Benauxay. Un grupo de cuevas-ventana andalusíes en el río Chelva (Valencia). *Cuadernos de Madinat al-Zahra'* 7, 343–367.

Sáenz Rodríguez, M., 1997. El cenotafio de San Millán de la Cogolla en el Monasterio de Suso, *Berceo* 133, 51–84.

Sáenz, C., 2005. La Antigüedad Tardía. *In*: J. G. Moya and B. Arrué, eds. *Historia del arte en La Rioja. Tomo I: De la prehistoria a la antigüedad Tardía*. Logroño: Fundación CajaRioja, 175–203.

Santos Otero, A., ed., 1963. *Evangelios apócrifos*. Madrid: Biblioteca de Autores Cristianos.

*The Holy Bible* (King James version), 1978. Nashville, TN: The Gideons International.

*The Holy Qur'an*, 2004. Tilford, Surrey: Islam International Publications Ltd.

Valiente, J. and García-Gelabert, M.P., 1983. La cuva Harzal de Olmedillas. Resultados de una prospección (Sigüenza, Guadalajara). *Wad-al-Hayara* 10, 7–24.

Van Staëvel, J.-P., 2010. La caverne, refuge de 'l'ami de Dieu': une forme particulière de l'érémitisme au temps des almoravides et des almohades (Maghreb Extrême, XIe–XIII e siècles). *Cuadernos de Madinat al-Zahra'* 7, 311–325.

Vañó, R., 1970. Oratorio rupestre visigodo del Cortijo de Valdecanales, Rus (Jaén). *Madrider Mitteilungen* 11, 213–222.

Velázquez, I., 1993. Las inscripciones latinas de la Cueva de la Camareta. *In*: A. González Blanco, R. González Fernández and M. Amante Sánchez, eds. *La Cueva de la Camareta (Agramón, Hellín-Albacete)*. Murcia: Universidad de Murcia, 267–321.

# Chapter 10

# The occupation and use of natural caves in the Ligurian-Piedmontese region between Late Antiquity and the Early Middle Ages (fifth to late seventh century AD)

*Paolo de Vingo*

*The reoccupation of caves, a widespread phenomenon that developed after prehistoric times in southern Europe, is quite interesting in terms of the distribution of settlements and how the Ligurian-Piedmontese region was utilised. The reuse of caves is documented in many parts of Liguria, the north-western Italian–French Alpine area, the region of southern Jura, and in Provence. The use of caves for defence or for occasional shelter only partially explains such reoccupation in historic times, especially considering the large quantity of archaeological deposits corresponding to this period. Rather, the reuse of some caves should be considered within an economic framework that, between Late Antiquity and the early Middle Ages (fifth to late seventh century), expanded into hills and mountains and was linked to a widespread resurgence of the exploitation of woods and forests and the breeding of goats, sheep and semi-feral pigs.*

## Introduction

The problem of the reuse of caves in historic periods is well-known and has generally been linked to political instability that drove local populations to seek refuge in remote settings that were easy to defend. These settlement choices are confirmed by the archaeological deposits in Provence (Demians d'Archimbaud 1972, 635–657; Boyer *et al.* 1978) and in the region of southern Jura and Savoie (Gagnière and Granier 1963; Paunier 1978, 306) in France, and in Friuli in Italy. These deposits date to between the late third and early fifth centuries, a period in which the sources record the first incursions of the Alamanni and the Visigoths (Maselli Scotti 1992, 370; Ruggini 1995, 540–545).

A similar situation occurs at Angera in Lombardy. Here, materials reflecting a settlement phase and small-scale metalworking activities date to the fourth–fifth centuries (Sena Chiesa 1995, 59). An interesting site in north-central Piedmont in terms of its Late Antique and early medieval phases is a cave known as Ciota Ciara in Monfenera in Valsesia (Fedele 1975, 231–244; Micheletto 1998, 63), while in Liguria the phenomenon is documented in both the eastern part of the region (Val Maremola and Val Frascarese) and the western part (Finale Ligure), where Arene Candide Cave parallels the Piedmont site (Gardini 1987, 149; Gardini and Murialdo 1994, 177–178; Murialdo *et al.* 2001, 64; Christie 2006, 473–484; de Vingo 2011, 197) (Fig. 10.1).

To examine this particular form of settlement, it is worth remembering that, in many cases, repeated reuse of caves over centuries altered archaeological deposits. Many of the caves can be studied based only on nineteenth-century reports that are often imprecise; hence, artefacts can only be generically dated to sometime between Late Antiquity and the modern era. In the past, it was theorised that reoccupation of the Ligurian caves had to be considered within a post-classical economic context: these caves served as temporary and occasional shelters during the exploitation of wooded areas and the open breeding of goats, sheep and pigs (Castiglioni *et al.* 1992, 296–297; Murialdo 1996, 72; Murialdo *et al.* 2001, 64), and caves in Piedmont may have been inhabited by hermitic monks (Micheletto 1998, 63).

In the case of the sites examined, the dominant materials found in Ligurian-Piedmontese caves are containers for preserving and/or producing food, or vessels for the table. Rather than reflecting a Roman type of diet, they provide

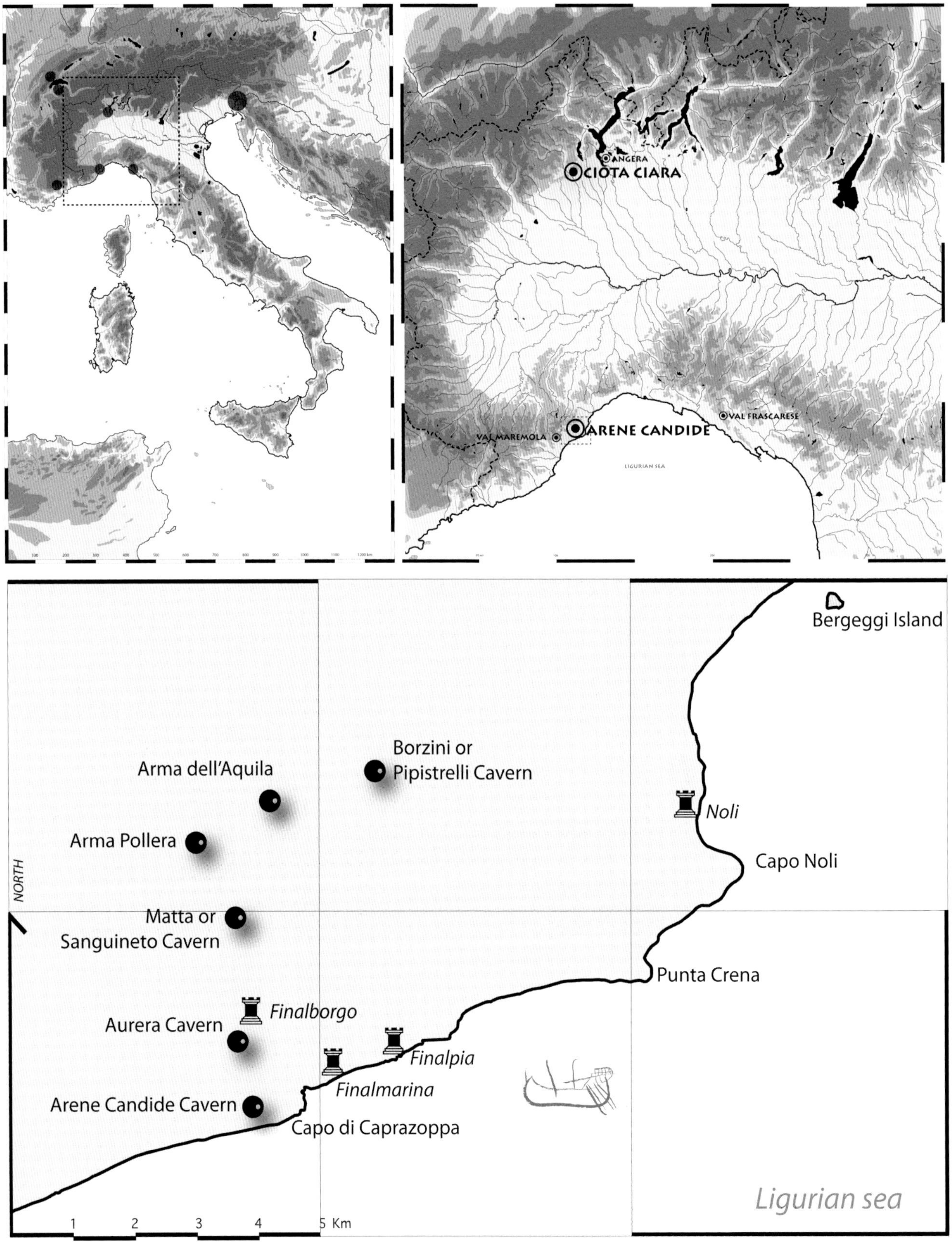


*Figure 10.1: Italy (1), North-central Italy (2) with the location of sites mentioned in the text. © Rossana Managlia.*

evidence of the transition to an early medieval nutritional system in which meat, with its high protein content, was the daily staple. This would explain the presence of soapstone as privileged cooking ware and amphorae to contain wine and oil, complementary elements of the daily diet.

## Late Antique and early medieval pottery from caves and sites in coastal Liguria

In the Finale Ligure area, several caves with significant prehistoric and early historic archaeological deposits have yielded artefacts pointing to continuous occupation from the Roman and post-classical period through to the Middle Ages and into the modern era (Issel 1908, 375–376; Bernabò Brea 1947; Murialdo *et al.* 1986, 237). Based on the large quantity of material that has been found, we can suggest phases of intense occupation in Late Antiquity for Arene Candide Cave, which will be explored in detail below. In the area of Perti and the nearby Aquila Valley, another series of gorges with archaeological evidence point to cave use in Late Antiquity and the early Middle Ages, such as Pollera Cave and the Matta, Aquila and Pipistrelli caverns, although the quantity of artefacts from each site varies (Bernabò Brea 1947, 43–49, 52–54, 61–63).

Pollera Cave yielded a basal fragment of a soapstone vessel (type IVa) with incised lines on the internal surface, and compact fluting with a rounded and uniform profile on the outside. The exterior of the base is characterised by signs of detachment via chiselling with a thin tip that produced incisions with rounded edges, arranged in an oblique pattern (Murialdo 1988, 241). Fragments of Late Antique/early medieval soapstone also came from the Matta or Sanguineto cavern, together with various specimens of coarseware with an everted rim made on a slow wheel, as well as a moderate number of amphorae and glazed ceramics from the late Middle Ages and the modern era. The site, situated on the slope of Bric di Sant'Antonino facing the Aquila torrent, has yielded at least five soapstone vessels of different origin: a Val d'Aosta lithotype (type IVa), as well as various kinds of grey soapstone (types II and IIIa–IIIb) (Murialdo 1988, 241; Biagini 2002, 157–158). Finally, African amphora (Beltran 59/Keay LXII), datable to between the fifth and the mid-seventh centuries, were found in both Aquila Cave and Pipistrelli Cave (Murialdo *et al.* 1986, 236–241; Long and Volpe 1998, 332–336; Murialdo 2001a, 264–267).

The archaeological data allow us to link the reoccupation of these caves with the parallel phenomenon of the reoccupation of certain sites on high ground that had been previously used in the proto-historic period. This seems to be the case with Aurera Cave on the Caprazoppa ridge, which is the source of a fragment of African red slip A (Lamboglia 54/Hayes 61A form), datable to between AD 325 and 400–420, as well as a stamped coarseware bowl that has been dated to AD 625 using thermoluminescence

*Figure 10.2: Entrance to Arene Candide Cave. Photo: © Paolo Biagi.*

(Castiglioni *et al.* 1992, 296–297; Olcese 1993, 145–148; Olcese *et al.* 1998, 246; Murialdo *et al.* 2001, 63–64; Wickham 2009, 518–519). Finds from Arene Candide Cave, explored in the nineteenth century and archaeologically excavated in the mid-twentieth century (Fig. 10.2), included soapstone, pottery, amphorae and fragments of African red slip D ware from 'Layer I', attributed to the Roman era, for which three different strata have been identified: a whitish layer (with traces of ash and carbon in the northern part of the deposit) situated between two layers of reddish clayey soil with an abundance of loose stones (Bernabò Brea 1947, 25–26). The nature of this deposit, and probably also a lack of knowledge at that time regarding post-Roman artefacts, does not permit a more precise chronological distinction of the possible occupation phases of the cave (Murialdo *et al.* 1986, 238) (Fig. 10.3).

In Arene Candide Cave, African amphorae accounted for 78.4% of the pottery present based on a minimum number of vessels (MNV), and thus they constitute the largest number of transportation containers identified here. The data that has been obtained permits assessment of the final production phases of these containers, supplementing the chronological and typological sequences sketched out in the past. In this period, the production areas of these vessels seem to be concentrated in northern Tunisia (around Carthage, Nabeul and Sidi Zahruni) and the central area of Roman activities (*Leptis Minor*, *Sullechtum* and *Thaenae*) (Bonifay 2004, 9–15; Gandolfi *et al.* 2010, 34–35). Some of the amphorae are thought to have been produced in the area of Tripolitania, based not only on the fact that they are made of greyish brown clay with a surface characterised by fine quartz crystals smaller than 0.05mm associated with ferrous rock, lime and rare mica, but also based on typological elements (Peacock 1984, 18; Peacock and Williams 1996, 167–168; Bonifay 2004, 479; Gandolfi and Murialdo 2004, 98). The geological area of the clay with Aeolian quartz and carbonate-marly limestone must still be defined; when fired, it turned into a light brown or yellow paste and was

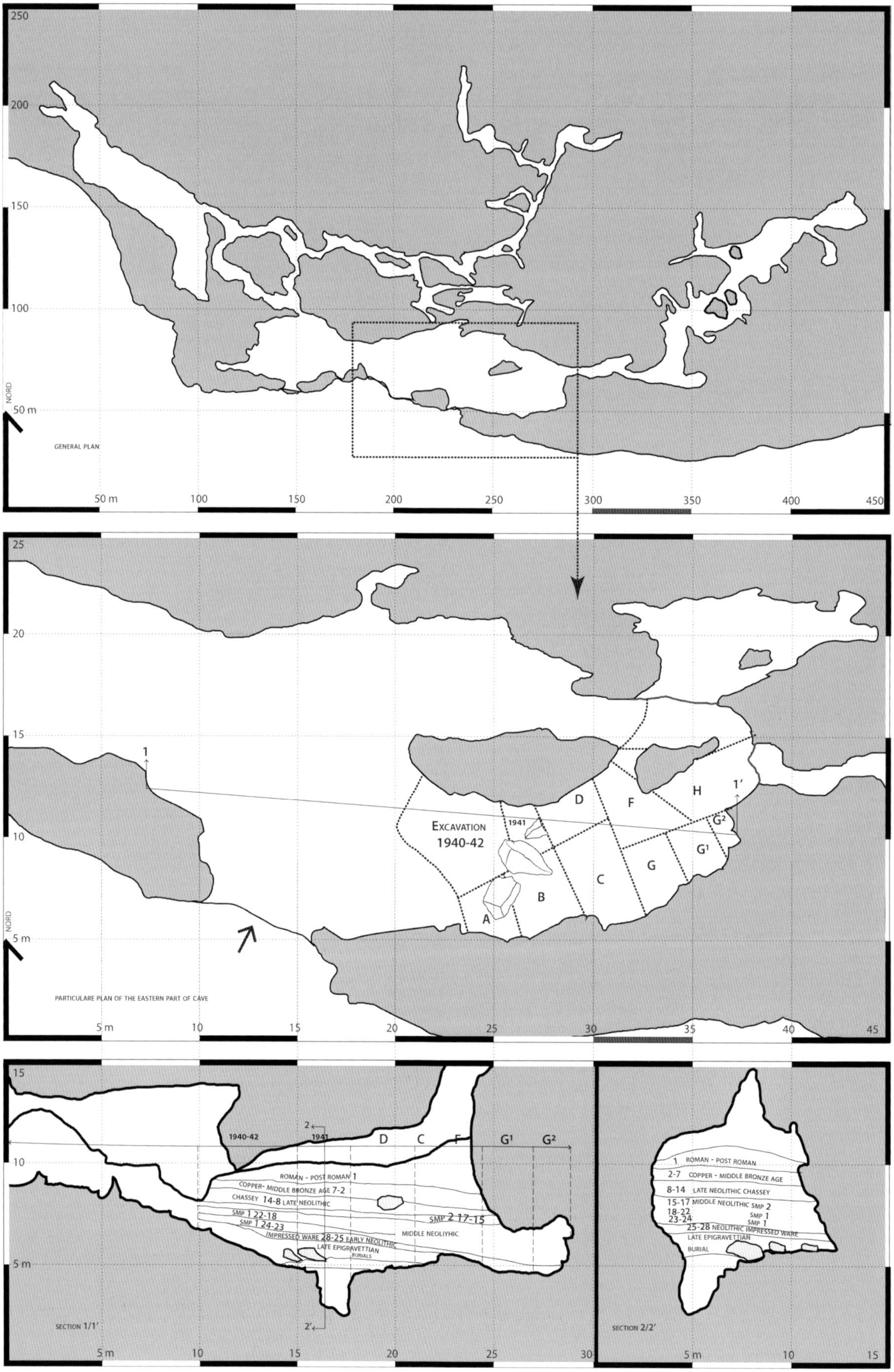


*Figure 10.3: Plan of Arene Candide Cave. © Rossana Managlia.*

utilised to produce small tapered containers (Peacock 1984, fabric 2.5, 17). The sporadic presence of augite in some of the samples led to speculation that this came from north-east Tunisia and Tripolitania, although it is impossible to exclude a possible provenance from other parts of North Africa (Murialdo 1995a, 216; Murialdo *et al.* 2011, 69).

Pottery vessels from Arene Candide come in two rim types: Keay LV A and LVI B (Keay 1984, 289–298), attributable to large cylindrical receptacles produced in Africa and then exported to Catalonia in the late fifth century (Keay 1984, 293; Long and Volpe 1998, 317–318; Vallverdú Remolà 2000, 154–155) and to southern France at the end of the fifth century and, particularly, during the sixth century in association with the earliest variants of Keay LXII (Long and Volpe 1994; Bonifay and Piéri 1995, 103; Long and Volpe 1998, 339–342; Vallverdú Remolà 2000, 159–160; Gandolfi *et al.* 2010, 35). In Liguria, they characterise 'Layer IA' at the Terme excavation in Ventimiglia (Gandolfi 1986, 297–298, fig. 26.3), while a specimen was reused in a sixth-century burial in the northern aisle of the basilica of Riva Ligure (Martino 1988, 263–264, fig. 11; Frondoni *et al.* 2013, 1290).

The Keay LVI B rim from Arene Candide Cave (Murialdo 1995a, 217–218, fig. 1.1; Pastorino 1997, 626, fig. 2.5) (Fig. 10.4) shows specific morphological analogies with the rim found at the fortified farmstead of Nador in *Mauretania Caesariensis*, an area in which this type of amphora is extensively documented, which would point to an Algerian rather than a Tunisian provenance (Manacorda 1989, 179–181, fig. 42, no. 227). Keay LVI specimens appeared in Carthage between AD 450 and 500 (Keay 1984, 293–298; Peacock 1984, 130; Vallverdú Remolà 2000, 155). Two amphorae of this type were also found in the vault of the baptistery in Albenga (Pallarés 1987, 282–283, figs. 9–11, nos. 1–2) associated with Keay XXXV A, LVII, LVI B, LXII Q, XXVI/*spatheion* 2A, VIII B, XXXII/Nador 225 produced in Africa, so the roof of the early Christian complex should probably be dated to the second half of the fifth century and possibly even the late fifth/early sixth century (Murialdo 1995a, 217; Murialdo 1995b, 435; Long and Volpe 1998, 321–322; Bonifay 2004, 137; Gandolfi *et al.* 2010, 34).

Type LXII rimmed cylindrical North African amphorae represent 59.5% of those identified in Catalonia (Keay 1984, 423–424), in southern France (Bonifay 1986, 287), and in Arene Candide (Fig. 10.5). Based on the presence of Keay LV–LVI types associated with a cup (Hayes form 94–108/ Fulford 50, 70), a plate (Hayes form 105/Atlante Plate XLIII, nos. 3–5/Fulford 66) and a vase – a *listello* (Hayes

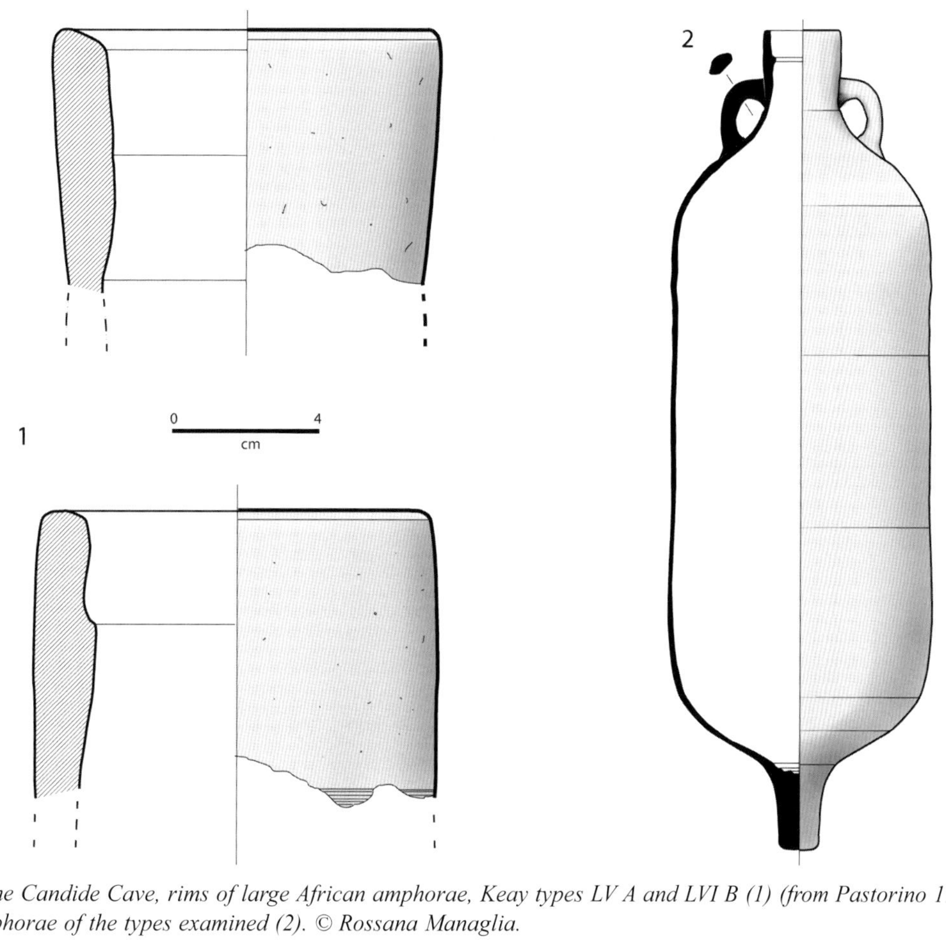


*Figure 10.4: Arene Candide Cave, rims of large African amphorae, Keay types LV A and LVI B (1) (from Pastorino 1997, figs. 2.5, 2.6, 626), sample amphorae of the types examined (2). © Rossana Managlia.*

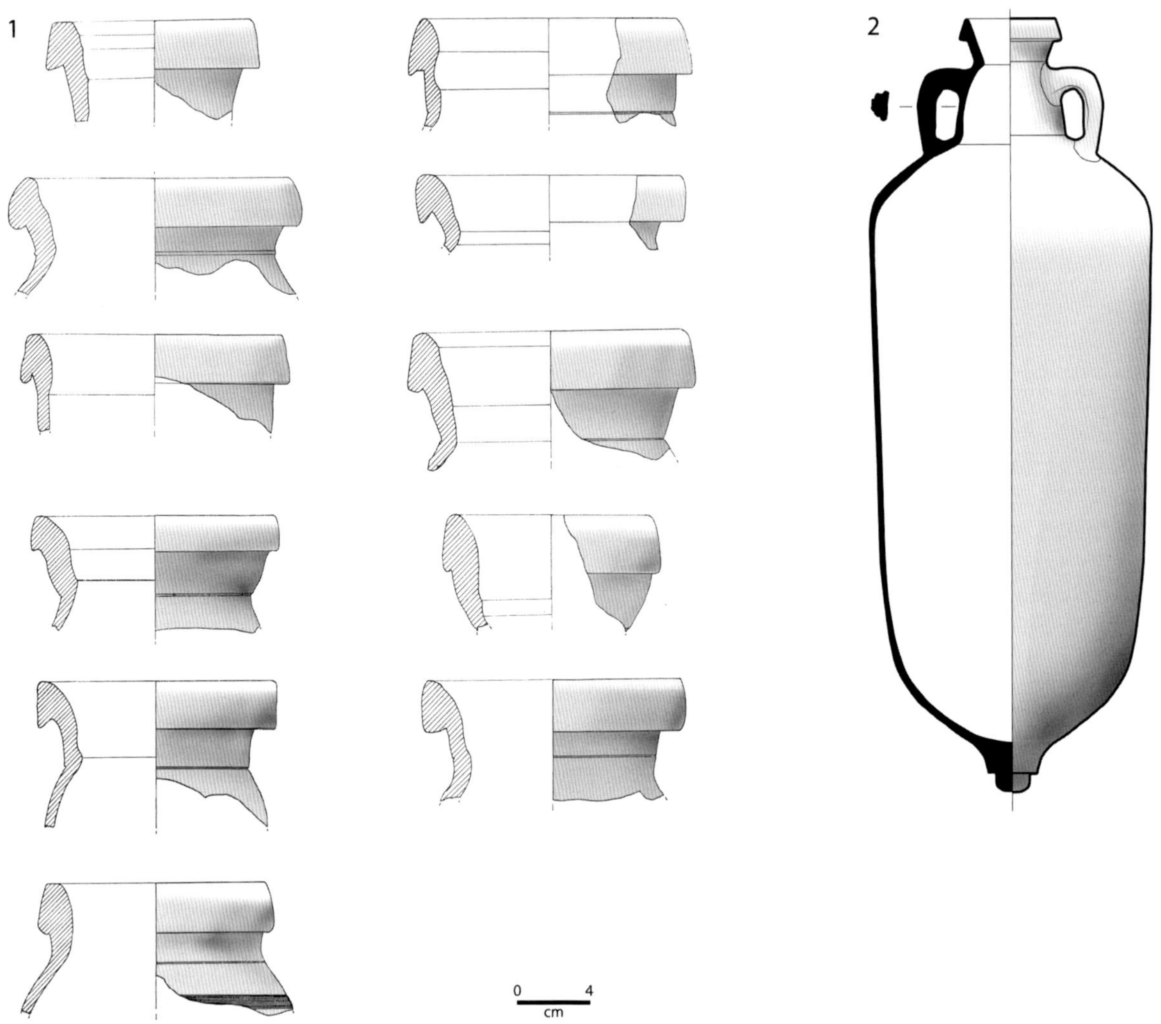


*Figure 10.5: Arene Candide Cave, rims of large African amphorae, Keay type LXII A-D-Q (1) (from Pastorino 1997, figs. 1.5–15, 624), sample amphora of the type examined (2). © Rossana Managlia.*

form 91C/Lamboglia 24/25–38) in African red slip D, the Arene Candide context can be dated to around the second half of the sixth century (Murialdo 1988, 238–239, 1995a, 220; Bonifay 2004, 135–137) (Fig. 10.6).

The two main forms of Keay LXII appear for the first time in Carthage around 450–475 (Peacock 1984, 125) and represent the most widely documented African amphorae during the sixth century in Catalonia (Keay 1984, 418) and coastal Liguria (Lusuardi Siena *et al.* 1991, 124–139; Murialdo 1995b, 435–436, 2001a, 264–267; de Vingo 2005, 345–348; Gandolfi *et al.* 2010, 37). They do not seem to have appeared in southern France before the early sixth century and, in association with Keay LXI, they represent the most numerous containers between the late sixth and early seventh centuries (Bonifay 1986, 287–304; Long and Volpe 1998, 321–322; Bonifay 2004, 137–140).

The Hayes 105 pottery form from Arene Candide Cave corresponds to that of a large plate with a thick quadrangular rim that is flattened on the inner edge and sometimes along the lower one, is convex on the outside and distinguished by a side that is slightly hollowed or has a step with a base of medium height that is thickened and rounded. It was produced in red slip D[2] with thin paint of rather low quality, applied to the interior surface and the rim and sometimes with drips on the outside (Bertolotto and Murialdo 2001, 333). The proposed dating of AD 580/600–660 is confirmed by other data obtained from Carthage, but the initial phase should probably be moved to the mid-sixth century or even AD 520–540 (Hayes 1972, 166; Fulford 1984, 74; Lund 1995, 537–538; Bonifay 2004, 185). Furthermore, considering its distinctive functional features, this form displays widespread circulation not only in Tunisia and North Africa (Lund 1995, 537) but also in parts of the western Mediterranean (Cartagena in Spain, southern France, and Italy) (Bonifay and Pelletier 1983, 317–321; Cavaillés Lopis and Vallauri 1994, 102; Reynolds 1995, 10,

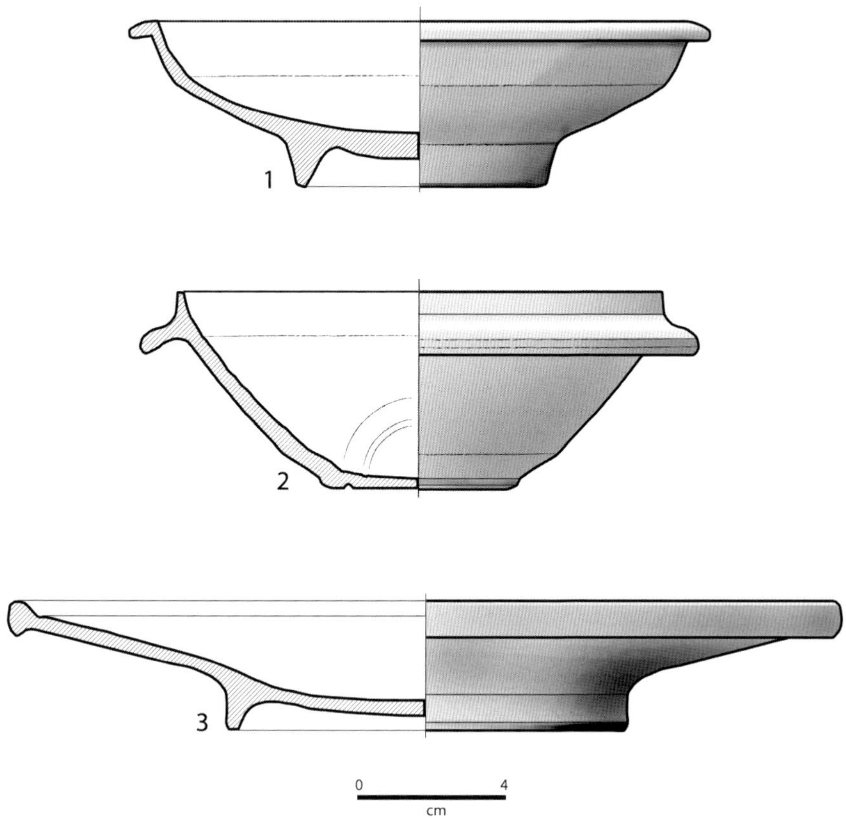


*Figure 10.6: Arene Candide Cave, cup (1), vase a* listello *(2), plate in African red slip D (3). © Rossana Managlia.*

fig. 39; Tortorella 1998, 55; Járrega Domínguez 2000). Small quantities also reached the Po Valley (Brescia, Castelseprio) (Massa 1999, 111), the Alpine foothills (Invillino), the upper Adriatic (Pirano-Trieste) and the Istrian area (Capodistria, Brioni) (Mackensen 1987, 233; Cunja 1996, 98–99; Pröttel 1996, pl. 30). This plate also circulated widely in the east, where it appeared in various contexts dating to the late sixth and early seventh centuries (Greece, Turkey, Jordan). Its ongoing production and exportation during the second half of the seventh century is confirmed by its presence in Saraçhane, the *Crypta Balbi* in Rome (Saguì 1995, 124, fig. 3.1; 1998, 307–310) and the shipwreck at Yassi Ada dated to AD 625 (Bass 1982, 157).

Alongside large cylindrical amphorae, a significant part of Finale's trade with North Africa involved small and medium-sized cylindrical or tapered containers, the so-called *spatheia*/Keay XXVI forms, which characterise the fifth-century levels in various contexts in the western Mediterranean and, to a lesser extent, the eastern Mediterranean (Manacorda 1977, 211–221; Panella 1983, 178–180; Keay 1984, 212–219; Carignani 1989, 76–78; Murialdo 1995b, 443; Long and Volpe 1998, 346; Vallverdú Remolà 2000, type B, 237; Romei 2004, 279–282; Murialdo 2007, 18; Gandolfi *et al.* 2010, 40), and for the Byzantine phase by amphorae that, starting in the final decades of the sixth century, seem to have maintained the same functions. In the case of material from Arene Candide, the small and medium-sized *spatheia* typical of the fifth century are not well represented, with only a rim fragment attributable to Keay XXVI G (Pastorino 1997, 625–626 variant fig. 2.7, 626) (Fig. 10.7).

The seventh-century archaeological cultural layer in the Arene Candide cave is characterised by two different types of containers. The first is a type of globular amphora with an umbonate and umbilicate bottom, the presence of which seems to reflect a profound transformation in production activities and in the modes of transport of North African goods in the seventh century, with the progressive abandonment of large cylindrical containers and the use of a globular model, probably eastern in origin (Murialdo 1995a, 230; Keay 1998, 148; Saguì 1998, 315–317; Murialdo 2001a, 291–293, types 47–48, figs. 18–19; Bonifay 2004, 151–153; Saguì 2004, 285; Murialdo 2007, 18; Ricci 2007, 166, fig. 2.15.23; Gandolfi *et al.* 2010, 39–40). The second type is also globular but is known as 'Carthage Late Roman 2'. Featuring a shoulder decorated with one or more bands of comb-like grooves, these represent the main containers of the Aegean area; production centres have been identified in Chio and in Argolide, on Kounoupi (Peacock and Williams 1986, 182–184; Arthur 1989, 82–83; Murialdo

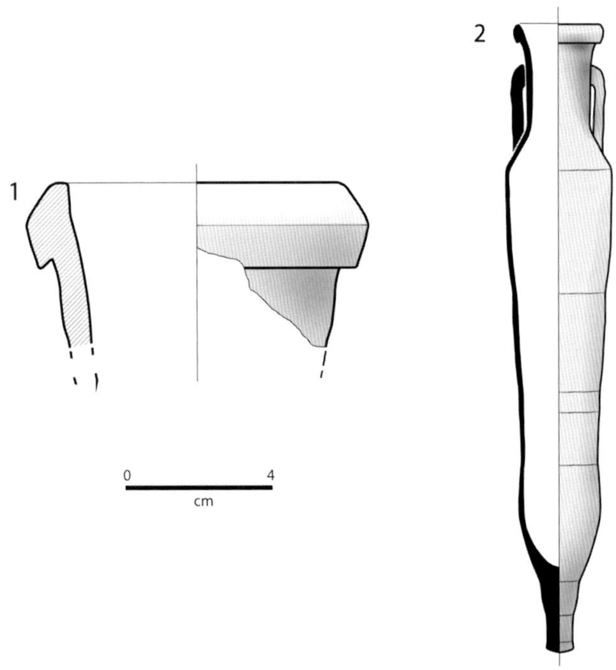


*Figure 10.7: Arene Candide Cave, rim of a* spatheion, *Keay type XXVI G (1) (from Pastorino 1997, fig. 2.7, 626), sample amphora of the type examined (2). © Rossana Managlia.*

1995a, 233; Pieri 2005, 85–91) (Fig. 10.8). Their dubious appearance in the fourth century has been suggested in the areas closest to assembly workshops, whereas in Carthage a sharp increase in imports is documented only around the middle of the sixth century, continuing to the beginning of the following century (Riley 1981, 115; Peacock 1984, 119). A similar trend has been observed for Catalonia where this amphora is not widely documented (Keay 1984, 352–357), and for southern France (Bonifay and Villedieu 1989, 25–27; Vallverdú Remolà 2000, 206–208). The classic type appeared in Marseille in the early sixth century whereas a later variant, with a vertical neck and a small everted rim, is documented in the seventh century (Bonifay 1986, 273, 302–304; Bonifay and Piéri 1995, 109–111; Long and Volpe 1998, 337; Pieri 2005, 88–89).

In the eighth century and subsequent centuries, the trade with the Aegean area that is extensively documented in central-southern Italy does not seem to have reached Liguria and the Finale area, where the significant resumption of commercial relations with the Aegean is represented by Byzantine coins (tenth century and the first three decades of the eleventh) from Perti, as well as fragments of fluted amphorae found in nineteenth-century deposits in the sea cave of Punta Crena in Varigotti (Gardini 1993, 52–54).

An amphora rim (resembling type Zemer 57) from Arene Candide, dated to between the third and sixth centuries, can be traced to the Aegean area and has parallels with unpublished material from the Agora of Athens (Zemer 1977, 70). As opposed to what has been found in other Late Antique centres, so far the Finale caverns have yielded very few Late Roman 1 amphorae, confirmed as being produced in the region of Antioch and outlying areas (Seleucia), in Ismeler, in Caria, and on Cyprus and Rhodes (Empereur and Picon 1989, 236–243; Panella 1993, 665–666; Pieri 2005, 69–70, 2007, 613–614). They have been dated to between the late fourth/early fifth centuries and the middle of the seventh century, with possible differentiations among the main variants (Riley 1976, 213–216, 1981, 120–121; Peacock 1984, 119; Long and Volpe 1998, 336–337; Pieri 2005, 70–77). This pottery type appeared in Rome between the late fourth century and the first few decades of the fifth century, increasing between AD 440 and 480 (Carignani and Pacetti 1989, 11). Compared with what has been found in other locations around the central Mediterranean but to a lesser extent in Catalonia (Keay 1984, 428; Vallverdú Remolà 2000, 215–225), this constitutes the main amphora imported into Marseilles in the fifth century, with a dramatic reduction in its presence in the sixth and particularly the seventh centuries (Bonifay 1986, 302–304; Bonifay and Pieri 1995, 108). A similar trend has been confirmed for Naples (Arthur 1985, 250–252). In the ancient Roman *municipia* of the *IX Regio*, this is the eastern container most extensively documented in the sixth-century layers in Luni (Lusuardi Siena *et al.* 1991, 131, pl. 5.1–5.4, 129) and Genoa (Gardini and Melli 1988, 161–162, fig. 3.3), and in the infill of the dome of the Albenga baptistery, with only one example of type A (Pallarés 1987, 285, no. 24, fig. 8; Murialdo 1995a, 236; Pieri 2005, 70–74).

The analysis method implemented has led to a rather precise definition of the sub-regional areas and in some cases the production centres of a few types of North African amphorae, datable to between the end of fifth and the seventh centuries, found in Arene Candide Cave, even though the limited quantity of vessels from the eastern Mediterranean provides evidence of the heterogeneity of the context examined as regards single trade flows. The characterisation of the wares confirmed the driving economic force of the African provinces, making it possible to distinguish the products of two central Tunisian centres, located a few kilometres apart (*Leptis Minor*, *Sullechtum*), from those of northern Tunisia (Sidi Zahruni, Port Prince). The area of Nabeul would seem to be the origin not only of some types of medium and large-sized cylindrical amphorae, but also of smaller vessels that correspond to the *spatheia*. Such information is very important because it offers new perspectives for studying the economic situation in the western Mediterranean for the period in question. First and foremost, the data indicates that Carthage did not play an exclusive role in the marketing of agricultural surplus during the Late Antique centuries (as had always been hypothesised), but also that the eastern amphorae were used by Byzantine authorities as a strategic economic choice to

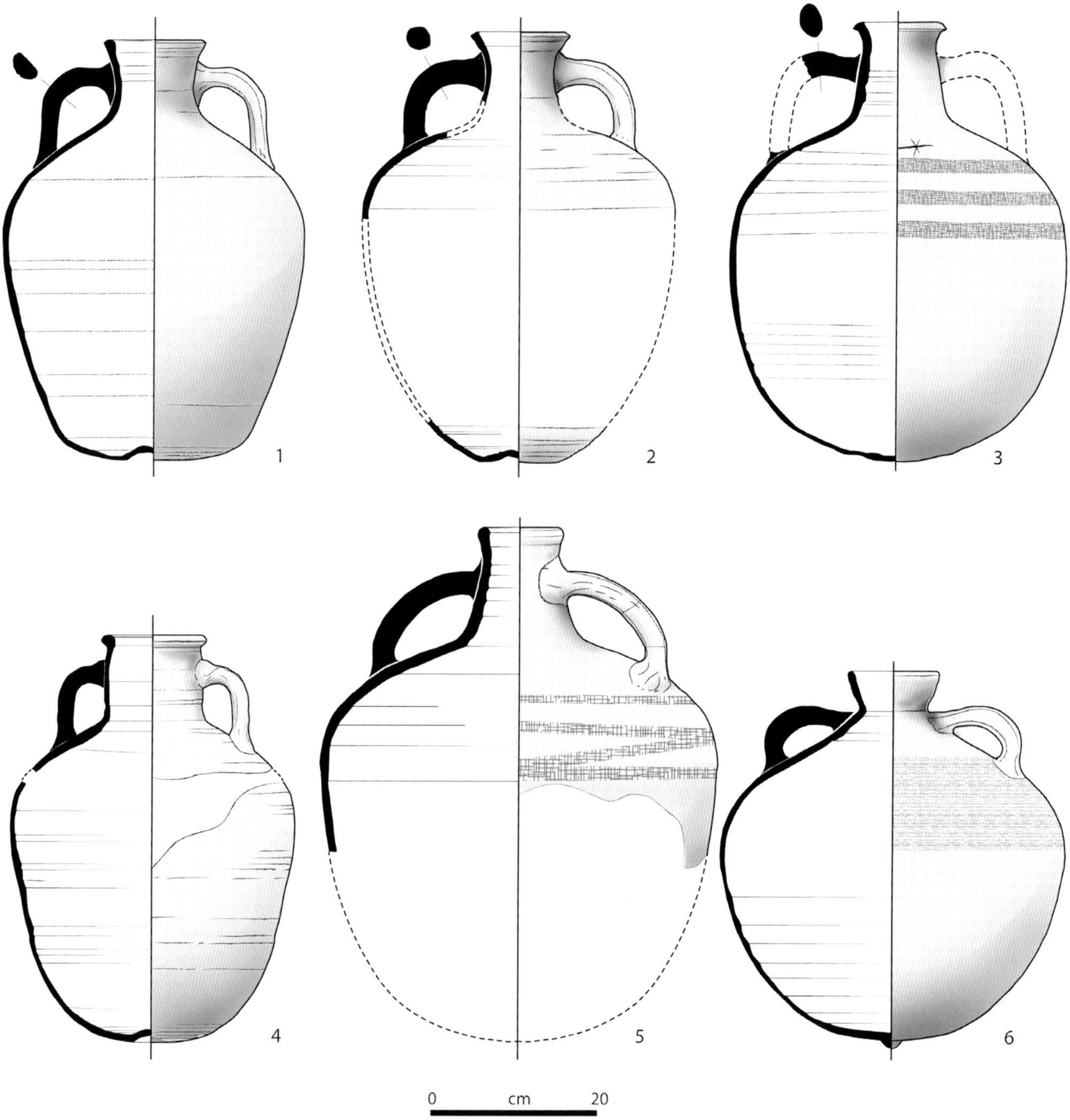


*Figure 10.8: Arene Candide Cave, North African globular amphorae (1–5) and Middle Eastern Late Roman 2 A amphora (6). © Rossana Managlia.*

rebalance the loss in control over the African provinces even if such a decision remained merely an 'attempt'.

## Late Antique–early medieval pottery from Ciota Ciara and related sites at Monfenera

On the west face of Monfenera (Vercelli), an isolated mountain that dominates the narrow plain of Borgosesia (Vercelli) in the Sesia river valley, there is a series of caves at an altitude of 650–700m above sea level. Substantial historic deposits have been found in the caves of Ciutarun, Ciota Ciara and Belvedere, where systematic archaeological investigations were conducted between the mid-1960s and the early 1970s, completing and integrating previous work, including excavations in Ciutarun that commenced in 1860 (Fedele 1975, 271–278). Analysis of the strata excavated in the Belvedere rock overhang is especially interesting, revealing the presence of *in situ* structures and hearths attributed to two different phases: the first is from the Gothic period, with glazed ceramics and a coin from the fifth century, while the second – more problematic – is datable to either between the sixth and seventh centuries or between the tenth and twelfth centuries (Fedele 1975, 276). For the second phase, it has been theorised that there was an actual dwelling beneath the rock overhang, to which the iron nails and Roman *tegulae* may relate (Micheletto 1998, 63) (Fig. 10.9).

In Ciota Ciara, which was excavated in two phases between the 1970s and 1990s (Gambari 1994, 345), the team's interest in the prehistoric phases meant that the historic ceramics and metals were not examined closely. However, the latter findings make it possible to reconstruct – in excellent detail – the way of life of a small group of people who occupied the cave from the late fifth century to the middle of the sixth (Brecciaroli Taborelli 1995, 79–105). Unglazed common ware comprised over 90 per cent of local or regional ceramics, whereas the remainder is represented by glazed receptacles. In both cases the morphological repertoire is quite limited, in keeping with a trend documented at other Late Antique sites in the northern part of the Italian peninsula (Negro Ponzi 2004, 28–30). Moreover, it can also be observed that the two vessel styles are quite similar from a technological standpoint, making it possible to suggest that a large proportion of the receptacles came from the same workshop. All the material was produced with a type of temper containing a significant quantity of inert material (granules of porphyry, polycrystalline quartz, feldspar, fine and medium laminas of muscovite and biotite), made on a wheel and smoothed with wet hands or a damp cloth, and then fired in an oxidised atmosphere (Brecciaroli Taborelli 1998b, 570) (Fig. 10.10).

The glazed ware from Ciota Ciara – with a glaze ranging in colour from dark yellowish brown to yellow, applied evenly on the internal surfaces of the vessels and along the outside rim – includes three main forms: a double-handled globular olla (1), a vase *a listello* (2), and small jugs with a globular pouring spout (2). The first two forms display parallels with similar material from the Ticino, Lombard and Piedmont area dating to between the fourth and the fifth/sixth centuries, whereas the area has not yielded any glazed vessels resembling the two jugs (Brecciaroli Taborelli 1998b, 572). Common cooking ware, storage vessels and tableware represent the most significant occupation debris from Ciota Ciara and it is not possible to distinguish different

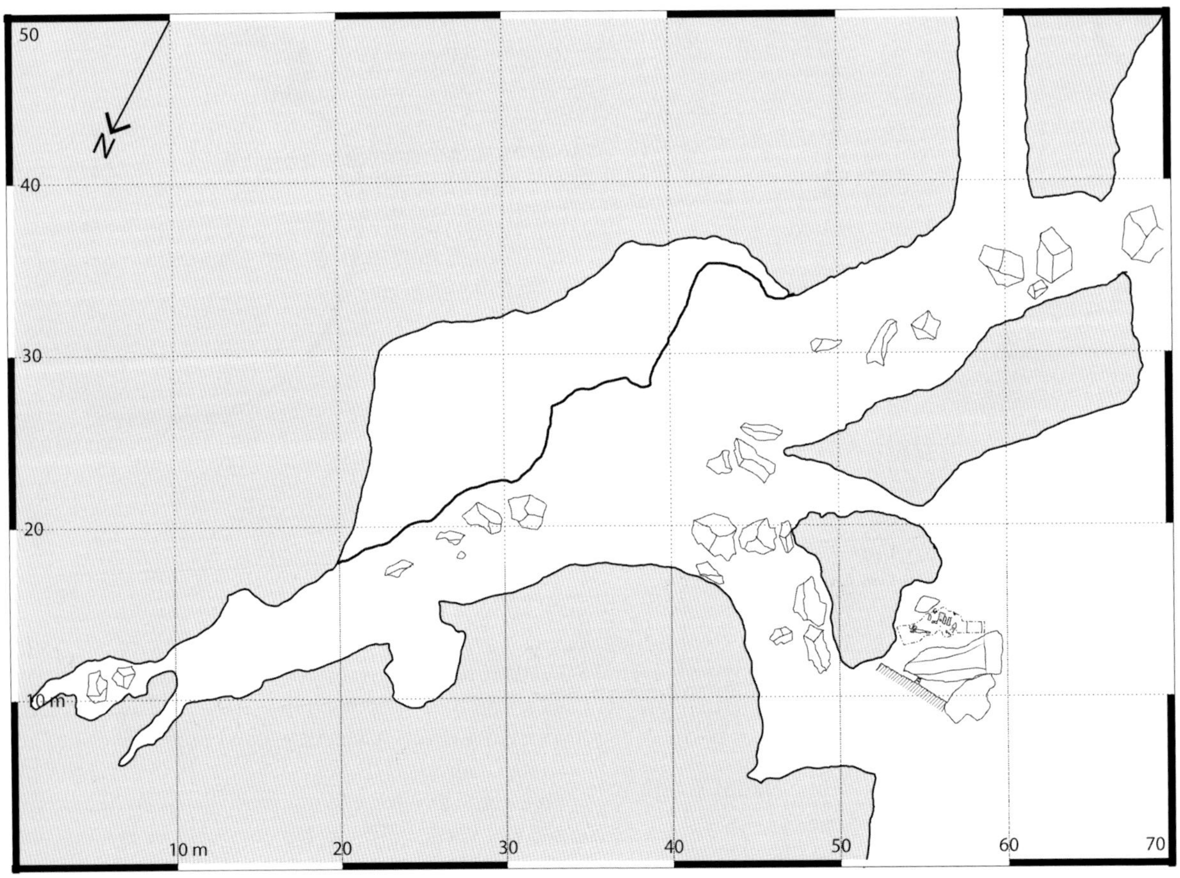


*Figure 10.9: Plan of Ciota Ciara. © Rossana Managlia.*

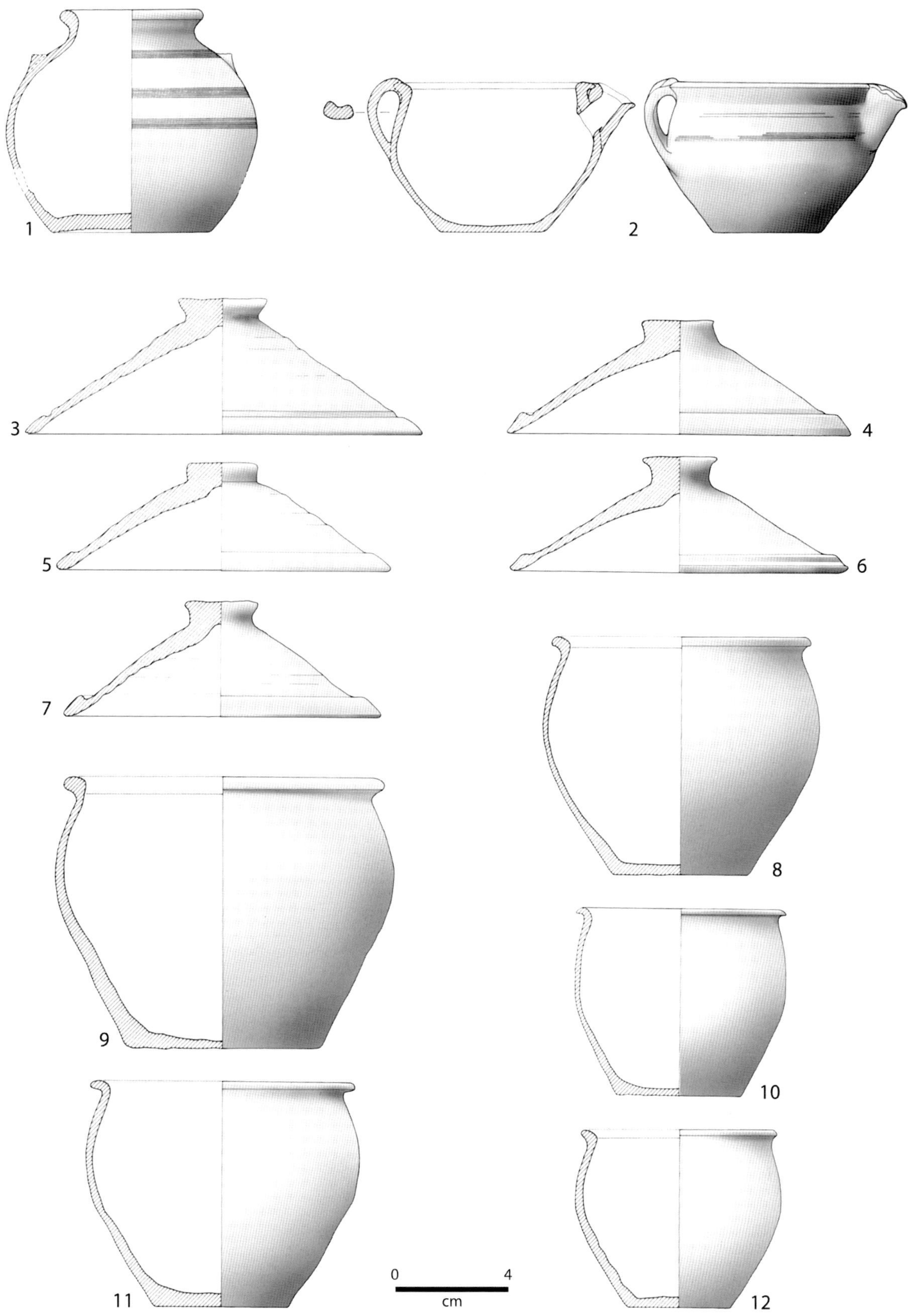


*Figure 10.10: Ciota Ciara Cave, kitchen ware for food storage, glazed ceramic vessels (1–2), lids (3–7), ollae (8–12). © Rossana Managlia.*

types of use, also due to the fact that it would be reasonable to assume that nearly all the vessels were employed for multiple purposes. The repertoire includes a few simple forms with typological variants that can be noted in the most representative groups, such as ollae, lids and lid-bowls. The 60 olla vessels can be ascribed to three formal types, based on rim and body shape, where these survive. Nearly all the 30 complete lids are represented by a truncated-cone model with a sub-cylindrical grip and a rim with a shaped band. Their diameters almost perfectly match those of the ollae and they are similar to unpublished specimens from Piedmont. In addition to intact lids, there are also small isolated fragments that represent other lid forms and lid-bowls, but they are certainly characteristic of the Late Roman production phase (Brecciaroli Taborelli 1998b, 575).

In Ciota Ciara, the vases *a listello* constitute a morphologically differentiated group represented by three forms (bowl, basin, small olla) typical of the Late Antique contexts of the northern Italian peninsula; among these, the basins are the most problematic due to functional considerations. How they were utilised is a highly-debated issue: in this case, the lack of traces of smoke, which would occur if they were used to cook food, allows us to theorise that they were used as storage containers or to prepare raw food, but also – and possibly primarily – as tableware (Brecciaroli Taborelli 1998b, 575). The array of ceramics is completed by a large handled bowl, most of which is missing, for which no significant comparisons have been found in terms of form, and by a pitcher with a trefoil outline, the typological models of which have been recognised in the Late Roman glazed production of the Transpadane area (Micheletto 1998, 63).

The pottery also includes a small bowl in African red slip D (Hayes 94–108/Fulford 50, 70) with a rim that is horizontal or sloped downward and varying in thickness, with a wall that is generally rounded and a tall tapered foot; the inner surface of the bottom is decorated with a 'haloed cross-bearing angel' (Brecciaroli Taborelli 1995, 80–83; 1998a, 281; 1998b, 569–570). Based on the shape of the rim, the examined specimen has been attributed to subtype B (Hayes 94 B), which in Carthage is characteristic of the sixth century, rising to an incidence of around 25% of African red slip between AD 525 and 533 (Fulford 1984, 67–69, fig. 18). In Italy, this form appeared around AD 475 (Hayes 1972, 148) – as confirmed by 'assay P' at the Palatine in Rome (Carignani *et al.* 1986), Carminiello ai Mannesi in Naples (Soricelli 1994, 129), the fortified village of Sant'Antonino (Bertolotti and Murialdo 2001, 330) and the Roman *municipium* of *Albintimilium* in western Liguria (Gandolfi 1981, 112–113) – and it continued to be used until AD 600 (Lund 1995, 524–525). The stamped decoration is from phase II (450–550), when Christian symbols appear on the bottoms of cups, bowls and pateras in African red slip D, generally imprinted on the central internal medallion (Gandolfi 1994, 146; Bonifay 2004, 192–193; Gandolfi 2005, 217). The sole storage receptacle that has been found, a Late Roman 2, was imported from the east. For the period of the fifth and sixth centuries in Piedmont, it constitutes a unique presence given that, throughout the central-western Transpadane area, artefacts from the Aegean and eastern areas appear only in urban contexts (Milan, Brescia, Castelseprio, Monte Barro), and even there they are only present in very small numbers (Brecciaroli Taborelli 1998b, 570; Pieri 2005, 88–89).

One of the artefacts that best expresses the transition from Late Antiquity to the Early Middle Ages – but also the profound transformations in terms of diet – is the soapstone represented by three vessels from Ciota Ciara. The first is a sub-cylindrical pot made from talc carbonate rock from the northern Piedmont valleys of the Ticino and Toce rivers. The exterior is covered with extensive fluting done on a wheel and irregularly spaced, while the interior is almost smooth; the exterior of the base is coarse and was retouched with a pointed chisel. The other is a truncated-cone vessel made by working Group F chlorate-schist rock, with an exterior wall decorated with fluting grouped in bands on a smooth ground, while the interior is marked by light and unevenly spaced fluting. The surfaces of the first two containers are completely blackened, confirming continued use and prolonged direct contact with fire to cook food. The third is a small sub-cylindrical pot with the same lithotype as the previous one, likewise decorated with bands of fluting, a bottom distinguished by light undercutting and a base that is smooth, like the internal surface. In this case, we can exclude the possibility that the receptacle was utilised for cooking, making it likely that it was used to store food; in effect, the properties of soapstone made it ideal for this purpose (Brecciaroli Taborelli 1995, 101) (Fig. 10.11).

The ironwork documented at Ciota Ciara consists of bars at workmanship stage and the structural remains of a smithy, with a large quadrangular hearth that housed the forge, which resembles what has been documented in other villages in the Piedmont hills such as Peveragno and Belmonte (Micheletto 1998, 59–61). The tools that have been identified (axes, awls, chisels, shears) point to their use for crafts such as carpentry, spinning and weaving, the workmanship of leather and activities essentially tied to domestic settings, given that knives could be used to cut, slice or bone meat (Brecciaroli Taborelli 1995, 103) (Figs. 10.12–10.14).

## Discussion

The reuse of caves for the period examined here – as a form of stable settlement and not only occupied occasionally – cannot be explained in a single way. In Italy in the mid-1700s when antiquarian research began, much attention was focused on studying prehistoric cultures, and caves, as the

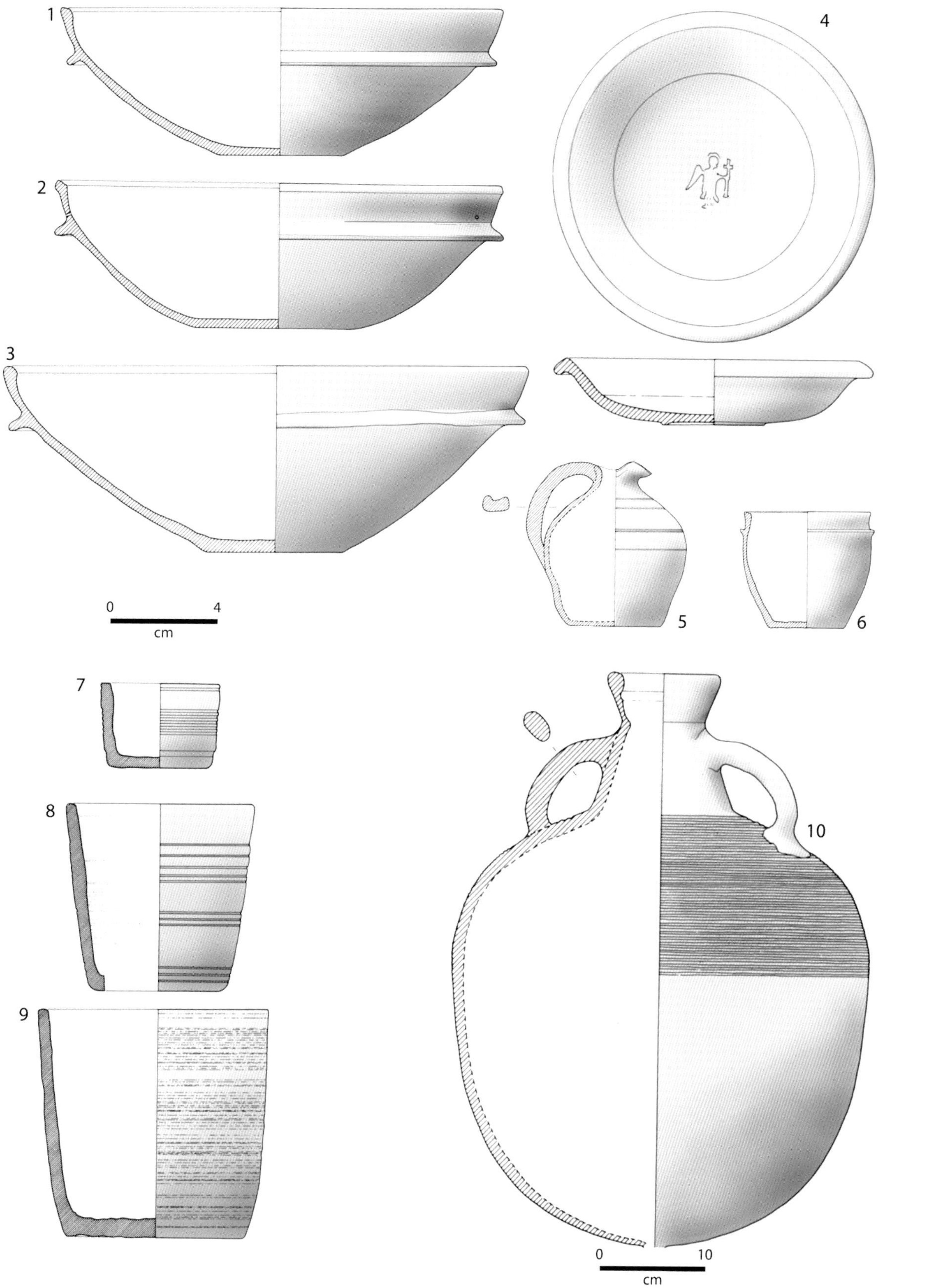


*Figure 10.11: Ciota Ciara Cave, kitchen ware for food preparation and transportation, vases* a listello *(1–3), African red slip D (4), pitcher (5), olla (6), soapstone containers (7), Late Roman 2 amphora (8). © Rossana Managlia.*

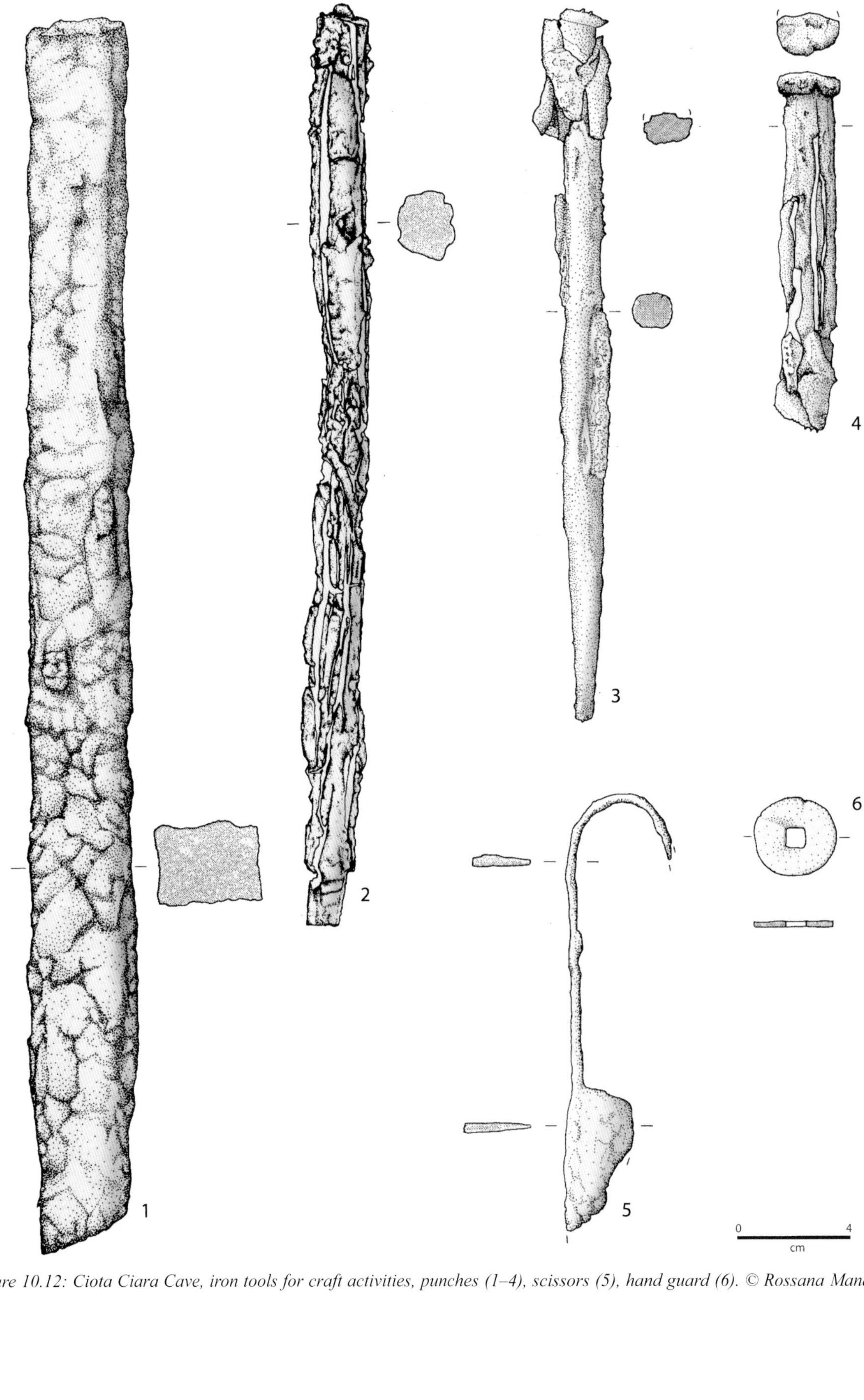


*Figure 10.12: Ciota Ciara Cave, iron tools for craft activities, punches (1–4), scissors (5), hand guard (6). © Rossana Managlia.*

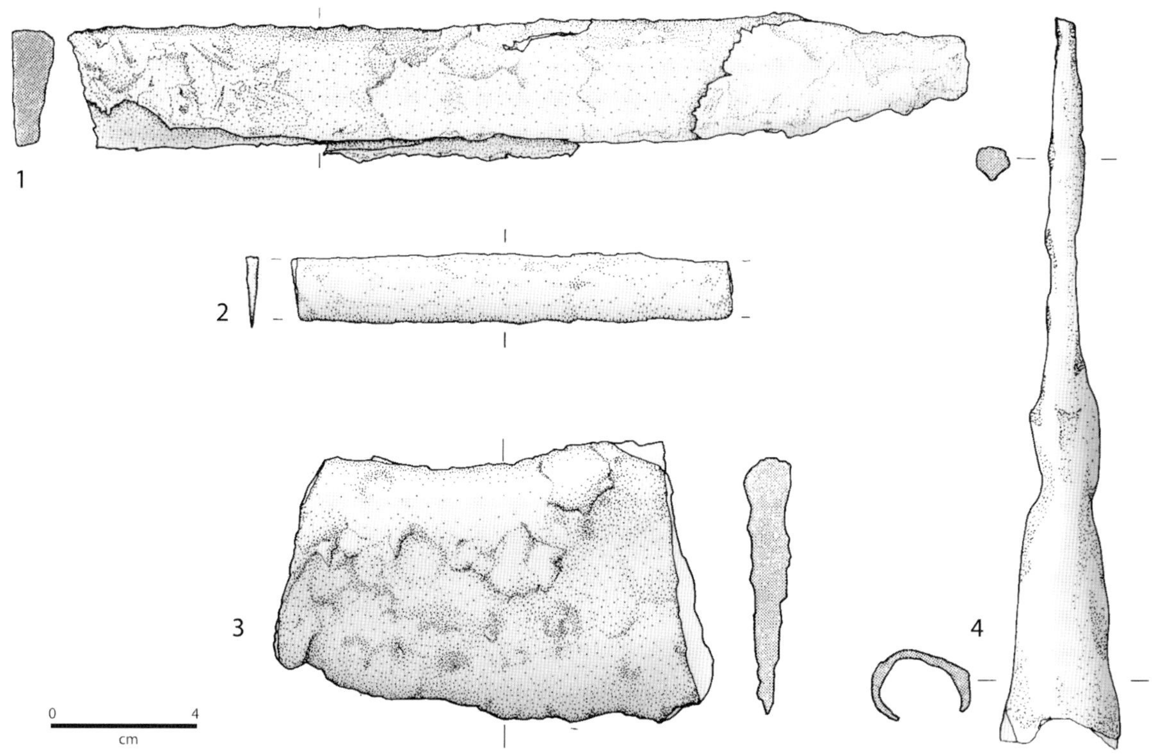


*Figure 10.13: Ciota Ciara Cave, iron weapons, blades (1–2), axe head (3), Roman* pilum *point (4). © Rossana Managlia.*

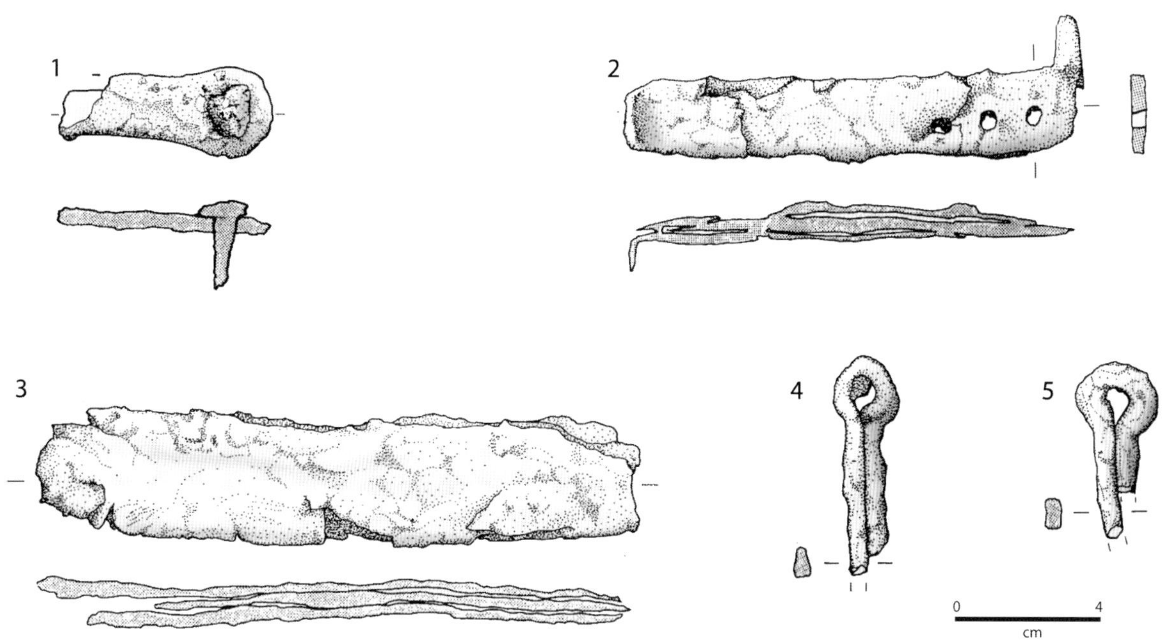


*Figure 10.14: Ciota Ciara Cave, iron connecting elements, hinges (1), hinge plates (2–3), cotter pins (4–5). © Rossana Managlia.*

perceived places where human civilisation had developed, were the subject of regular surveys but without rigorous excavation techniques. At that time, it was unimaginable that caves had also been used in the Roman era or the Middle Ages and, therefore, when efforts were made to locate prehistoric material, more recent layers containing amphorae, kitchen ware, storage vessels, soapstone and utensils were destroyed because they did not correspond to what antiquarians were seeking.

Artefacts dating to between the late fifth and the early seventh centuries from caves in Finale may reflect an archaeological situation that is far more complex than was previously believed. It offers us the opportunity to consider two different levels, one socio-economic and the other historical and political. Regarding the socio-economic levels, there is no question that this constitutes a tangible expression of unexpected abilities of African and Middle Eastern production centres to renew themselves and adapt, exploiting established and far-reaching commercial networks. We do not know with any certainty what might have been the relationship between the material, the caves and the communities that used it. These were probably agricultural communities, which were also able to develop trade and production activities. However, it is not easy to understand the socio-economic background of these communities as the archaeological data has been destroyed or disturbed in so many cases.

In particular, after the Vandalic War (June 533 to March 534 AD) and the Justinian reoccupation of part of the Iberian and Italian peninsulas, *Zeugitania* and *Byzacena* seem to have been the linchpins of a strategic system to control the Tyrrhenian sector and part of the western Mediterranean, based largely on the export of staples associated with subsidiary goods such as slip ware and common pottery (Mackensen 1998, 26–33; Bonifay 2004, 449–462; de Vingo 2005, 347–348). This role seems to have grown in the first half of the seventh century, particularly during the reign of Heraclius (AD 610–641), who began his conquest of power from Carthage (Murialdo 2001b, 301–302; Wickham 2009, 756–764). New forms of transportation containers – following cylindrical amphorae – appeared between the late sixth and early seventh centuries (and derived from Keay LXI and LXII, such as Keay VIII A but also forms totally independent of them), and the dating proposed for amphorae with an umbonate bottom at several Italian and Provençal sites post-dates the cessation of large scale Mediterranean trade in the Ligurian and Provençal areas until at least the second half of the seventh century. Indeed, it is possible that trade continued until the early eighth century (Murialdo 1995b, 447; Jézégou 1998, 345–346; Murialdo 2001b, 301; Wickham 2009, 816; de Vingo 2014, 298).

In general, commerce directed towards the western European coasts around the end of Late Antiquity – the products in these amphorae have yet to be fully defined – essentially reflect African workshops with large-scale production of pottery for the transportation of oil used chiefly for domestic lighting rather than as food (Bonifay 2004, 87–153, 2005, 453–456). The artefacts imported from the east can be associated with the supply of different wines, although we cannot reject the possibility that some types of amphorae contained prized oils (Arthur 1986; Arthur 1989; Bonifay and Villedieu 1989; Carignani and Pacetti 1989; Bonifay and Piéri 1995). The significant presence of eastern amphorae in North African urban centres close to local sources of intensive oil production seems to confirm this theory (Riley 1981; Panella 1983; Peacock 1984; Wickham 2009, 740–741).

As to the historical and political context, it is clear that materials found in the Finale caves can largely be ascribed to an urban material culture, although only for the amphorae from Arene Candide can we suggest a very intensive presence in Late Antiquity, perhaps in the form of a temporary deposit of easily perishable foodstuffs such as wine, which could be preserved in caves better and for a longer time due to the stable microclimate. Likewise, in the case of Arene Candide it was soapstone – and smaller quantities have also been found in nearly all the individual caves examined – that was employed not only to store solid foods and liquids, but especially for cooking, which points to the presence of a stable and sedentary community and not sporadic occupation. We must also consider that it is certainly not coincidence that this site is situated close to the main Roman coastal road, as if this settlement choice was made based on the ease and speed with which one could access the main roadway in order to ship goods. Thus, the reoccupation of the Finale caves should not be considered a result of traumatic or violent events, but perhaps a deliberate decision on the part of a local population that, evidently not solely for safety reasons but perhaps for economic convenience, opted for this solution based on the same logic that, during this same period, dictated the decision either to move to fortified villages on higher ground or to remain in towns on the coast. Despite the fact that all the guarantees provided by Rome had vanished, it is inconceivable that the settlement dynamics would have been similar and entirely oriented in the same direction. As is the case today, it is likely that different solutions were adopted to address various socio-economic needs that were unquestionably influenced – but not caused – by events linked with raids by the Visigoths and Alamanni.

With regard to the Late Antique and early medieval period in western Piedmont, no archaeological evidence confirms the involvement of the local population in the historical-political vicissitudes that affected the entire area of north-western Italy between the end of the fifth century and the first half of the sixth (de Vingo 2010, 21–28). As a consequence, the decision to establish cave settlements based on the exploitation of woodlands, flora and fauna, and in the Valsesia valley in particular, is hard to sustain given the proximity of towns that continued to thrive during the same period (Brecciaroli Taborelli 1995, 107).

In Late Antiquity and the early Middle Ages, monastic life, with its complex and profound religious and moral beliefs, developed in societies going through a profound crisis as a reaction to relations perceived as oppressive. In the Christian tradition, the eremitic lifestyle is a form of monasticism and a forerunner to the cenobitic monastic life in which hermits spent their entire lives dedicated to praising God through penitence and prayer. The main figures of these initial religious experiences, that developed in Egypt between the third and fourth centuries, came from various social origins and, for their sojourns, chose sepulchral environments or caves where they could meditate in the darkness and overcome temptations, sites often located in proximity to water resources where they cultivated what they needed to sustain themselves (Tabacco 2010, 62–70). The presence of vascular forms of type D African slip ware decorated with Christian symbols – and for this reason considered in relation to the celebration of religious ceremonies – had led in the past to the hypothesis of the presence of an eremitic monastic community, but other data of the material culture coeval with the previous African artefacts (weapons, utensils, eastern transport vessels and complex production structures) do not seem to confirm this theory and instead shift the focus to a settlement that was socio-economically self-sufficient.

In the case of Ciota Ciara, the diverse range of ceramic wares (vases *a listello*, small jugs, ollae, lids, lid/bowls) largely reflecting local tradition and with a minimal contribution of African artefacts (a bowl), limited to shipping containers (one eastern and one African-Tunisian), three intact soapstone vessels, weapons used for hunting rather than self-defence (a Roman javelin tip) and a smelting furnace with an array of instruments – to be examined in relation to crafts activities for the production of essential consumer goods – allow us to put forward a different social context. The data from this site seems to indicate the presence of a medium-sized farming community (similar to the coeval fortified villages of Peveragno and Belmonte in Piedmont), organised in spaces aimed at conducting production activities with domestic furnishings to meet community needs, with the self-production of dietary requirements – through the technological capacity to make iron implements – and with a commitment towards economic relations, although modest in scope and of little commercial value. Observations on Arene Candide and Ciota Ciara allow us to suggest that the transition from Late Antiquity to the early Middle Ages, at least in the western part of the Italian peninsula, was essentially an adaptation to the overall political and socio-economic changes faced by the European continent. This adaptation was determined by the need to establish a new way of life in which Rome was no longer the hub around which everything revolved, but the foundation on which a 'new world' was starting to be built (Wickham 2009, 861–867; Wickham 2014, 105–106).

## Conclusion

The main problem with the contexts examined here is the impossibility of defining with precision the relationship between materials found, regardless of type, and the original archaeological contexts due to the destruction that occurred when the first 'excavation' attempts were carried out. However, it is clear that the Piedmontese and Ligurian areas played a leading role from both socio-economic and production perspectives. We cannot say much about those who lived in these caves, but it is important to recognise that the various aspects represented (military, craftsmanship or commercial) reveal communities where individuals played several roles at the same time. These thoughts should be considered in relation to a difficult period, i.e., the transition between Late Antiquity and the early Middle Ages, during which the lack of a central power forced communities to assume several roles within the same political context, but within new living conditions.

## References

Arthur, P., 1985. Naples: notes on the economy of a dark age city. *In*: C. Malone and S. Stoddart, eds. *Papers in Italian Archaeology IV. The Cambridge Conference*. BAR International Series 246. Oxford: Archaeopress, 247–259.

Arthur, P., 1986. Amphorae and the Byzantine world. *Bullettin de Correspondence Hellenique* XIII, 655–660.

Arthur, P., 1989, Aspects of Byzantine economy: an evaluation of amphorae evidence from Italy. *Bullettin de Correspondence Hellenique*, XVIII, 79–93.

Bass, G.F., 1982. The Pottery. Cargo Amphoras. *In*: G.F. Bass and F.H. Vandoorninck Jr., eds. *Yassi Ada. A Seventh-Century Byzantine Shipwreck*. College Station, TX: University of Texas Press, 155–165.

Bernabò Brea, L., 1947. *Le caverne del Finale*. Bordighera: Istituto di Studi Liguri.

Bertolotti, F. and Murialdo, G., 2001. La ceramica fine da mensa: sigillata africana e sue imitazioni. *In*: T. Mannoni and G. Murialdo, eds. *S. Antonino. Un insediamento fortificato nella Liguria bizantina*. Bordighera: Istituto Internazionale di Studi Liguri, 317–337.

Biagini, M., 2002. Frequentazioni di età storica della grotta del Sanguineto o della Matta (Finale Ligure). *Quaderni del Museo Archeologico del Finale* 4, 157–161.

Bonifay, M. 1986. Observations sur les amphores tardives de Marseille d'après les fouilles de la Bourse (1980–1984). *Revue Archéologique de Narbonnaise* XIX, 269–305.

Bonifay, M. 2004. *Etudes sur la céramique romaine tardive d'Afrique*. BAR International Series 1301. Oxford: Archaeopress.

Bonifay, M. 2005. Observations sur la typologie des amphores africains de l'Antiquité Tardive. *In*: M.J. Esparraguera Gurt, J. Garrigòs Buxeda and M.A. Ontiveros Cau, eds. *LRCW 1. Late Roman Coarse Ware, Cooking Wares and Amphorae in the Mediterranean. Archaeology and archaeometry*. BAR International Series 1340. Oxford: Archaeopress, 451–472.

Bonifay, M. and Pelletier M., 1983. Eléments d'évolution des céramiques de l'Antiquité tardive de Marseille d'après les fouilles de la Bourse (1980–1981). *Revue Archéologique de Narbonnaise* XVI, 285–346.

Bonifay, M. and Piéri, D., 1995. Les amphores tardives à Marseille, état des recherches. *Journal of Roman Archaeology* 8, 94–120.

Bonifay, M. and Villedieu, F., 1989. Importations d'amphores orientales en Gaule (V[e]–VIIe siècle), *Bullettin de Correspondence Hellenique* XVIII, 17–46.

Boyer, R., Lagrand, Ch., and Michel, J.-M., 1978. Dérivées-des-Sigillées Paléochretiennes du Var. *Documents d'Archéologie Méridionale* 1. Paris: Editions de la Maison des Sciences de l'Homme, 189–223.

Brecciaroli Taborelli, L., 1995. Un insediamento temporaneo della tarda antichità nella grotta 'Ciota Ciara' (Monfenera, Valsesia). *Quaderni di Archeologia del Piemonte* 13, 73–135.

Brecciaroli Taborelli, L. 1998a. Il vasellame da mensa in età tardoantica. *In*: L. Mercando, ed. *Archeologia in Piemonte. L'età romana*. Torino: Umberto Allemandi, 271–289.

Brecciaroli Taborelli, L. 1998b. Un contesto ceramico di fine V-prima metà del VI secolo dalla grotta 'Ciota Ciara' del Monfenera (Valsesia-Piemonte). *In*: L. Saguì, ed. *Ceramica in Italia: VI–VII Secolo*. Proceedings of the Conference in honour of John W. Hayes. Comunicazioni, Rome, 11–13 May 1995. Biblioteca di Archeologia Medievale. Firenze: All'Insegna Del Giglio, 569–576.

Buisson, A., 1991. Les grottes refuges de l'époque romaine dans le Jura méridional et les Alpes du Nord françaises (Aine, Isère, Savoie, Haute-Savoie). *Caesarodunum*, 25, 51–66.

Carignani, A., 1989. Amphores. *In*: Ph. Pergola and C. Vismara, eds. *Castellu (Haute-Corse). Un établissement rural de l'Antiquité tardive. Fouilles récentes (1981–1985)*. Documents d'Archéologie Française 18. Paris: Editions de la Maison des Sciences de l'Homme, 75–89.

Carignani, A., Ciotola, A., Pacetti, F. and Panella, C., 1986. Il contesto del tempio della Magna Mater sul Palatino. *In*: A. Giardina, ed. *Società romana e impero tardoantico. III. Le merci. Gli insediamenti*. Roma-Bari: Laterza, 27–43.

Carignani, A., and Pacetti, F., 1989. Le importazioni di anfore bizantine a Roma fra IV e V secolo: le evidenze di alcuni contesti urbani. *Bullettin de Correspondence Hellenique* XVIII, 5–16.

Castiglioni, E., Cupelli, G., Falcetti, C., Ferretti, F., Fossati, A., Giovinazzo, R., Mannoni, T., Murialdo, G., Palazzi, P., Panizza, M., Parodi, L., Ricci, R. and Vicino, G., 1992. Il castrum tardoantico di S. Antonino di Perti, Finale Ligure (SV). Terze notizie preliminari sulle campagne di scavo 1982–1991. *Archeologia Medievale* XIX, 279–368.

Cavaillés Lopis, M. and Vallauri 1994. L. Les céramiques fines importées. *In*: G. Demians d'Archimbaud, ed. *L'oppidum de Saint-Blaise du V$^{e}$ au VII$^{e}$ siècle (Bouches-du-Rhône)*, Documents d'Archéologie Française 45, Paris: Editions de la Maison des Sciences de l'Homme, 86–115.

Christie, N., 2006. *From Constantine to Charlemagne. An Archaeology of Italy AD 300–800*, Cornwall: Ashgate.

Cunja, R., 1996. *Poznorimski in Zgodnjesrednjeveski Koper. Capodistria tardoromana e altomedievale*. Koper-Capodistria: Società storica del Litorale.

Dèmians d'Archimbaud, G., 1972. Le matériel paléocretien de la Grotte de l'Hortus. *Etudes Quaternaires* 1, 635–657.

de Vingo, P., 2005. Liguria in Late Antiquity and in the early Middle Ages: its trade relations with the western and eastern Mediterranean Sea through transport amphorae. *In*: J.M. Gurt, J. Garrigòs Buxeda and M.A. Ontiveros Cau, eds. *LRCW 1. Late Roman Coarse Ware, Cooking Wares and Amphorae in the Mediterranean. Archaeology and Archaeometry*. BAR International Series 1340. Oxford: Archaeopress, 341–353.

de Vingo, P. 2010. *From Tribe to Province to State*. BAR International Series 2117. Oxford: Archaeopress.

de Vingo, P., 2011. Late antique mountain settlements in the Savona area and central-western Liguria. *In*: I. Catteddu, P. de Vingo and A. Nissen Jaubert, eds. *On the Road Again. L'Europe en mouvement. Archaeology and Rural Landscape: Rural Settlements in their Natural, Economic and Social Environment*. 4th International Congress of Medieval and Modern Archaeology. Paris, 3–8 September 2007. Genova: De Ferrari, 193–212.

de Vingo, P., 2014. Production and importation of Late Antique and early medieval pottery in Liguria. *In*: J. Drauschke and R. Prien, eds. *Küche und Keller in Antike und Frühmittelalter. Produktion Vorratshaltung und Konsum in Antike und Frühmittelalter*. Gemeinsame Tagung mit der Arbeitsgemeinschaft Römische Archäologie. Friedrichshafen, 30 Mai–1 Juni 2012. Hamburg: Verlag Dr. Kovac, 257–303.

Empereur, J.-Y., and Picon, M., 1989. Les régions de production d'amphores impériales en Méditerranée orientale. *In*: Amphores romaines et histoire économique. Dix ans de recherche. *Collection de l'Ecole Française de Rome* 114, 223–248.

Fedele, F., 1975. Scoperte e ricerche di archeologia medievale sul Monfenera (Valsesia). *Bollettino storico bibliografico subalpino* LXXIII, 269–280.

Frondoni, A., de Vingo, P., and Gambaro, L. 2013. La basilica paleocristiana e l'area archeologica di Riva Ligure (Imperia): gli ultimi risultati di scavo. *In*: O. Brandt, S. Cresci, J.L. Quiroga and C. Pappalardo, eds. *Acta XV Congressus internationalis archaeologie Christiane. Episcopus, civitas, rerritorium*. Toleti 8–12.09.2008. Città del Vaticano: Pontificio Istituto di Archeologia Cristiana, 1290–1302.

Fulford, M.G. 1984. The coarse (kitchen and domestic) and painted wares. *In*: S.P.D. Peacock and M.G. Fulford, eds. *Excavations at Carthage: the British Mission. The Avenue du President Bourghiba, Salambo. The Pottery and Other Ceramic Objects from the Site*. Sheffield: The British Academy, 155–231.

Gagnière, S. and Granier, J. 1963. L'occupation des grottes du III$^{e}$ au V$^{e}$ siècle et les invasions germaniques dans la basse vallée du Rhône. *Provence Historique* XIII, 225–239.

Gambari, F.M., 1994. Borgosesia. Scavi nella grotta Ciota Ciara (campagne 1992–1993). *Quaderni della Soprintendenza Archeologica del Piemonte* 12. Notiziario, 345.

Gandolfi, D., 1981. La Terra Sigillata Chiara D proveniente dagli scavi di Albintimilium. *Rivista di Studi Liguri* XLVII, 53–149.

Gandolfi, D., 1986. La pietra ollare a Ventimiglia. *Rivista di Studi Liguri* LII, 269–302.

Gandolfi, D., 1994. La produzione ceramica africana di età medio e tardo imperiale: terra sigillata chiara e ceramica da cucina. *In*: S. Lusuardi Siena, ed. *Ad Mensam. Manufatti d'uso da contesti archeologici fra tarda antichtà e medioevo*. Udine: Del Bianco Editore, 127–156.

Gandolfi, D., 2005. Sigillate e ceramiche da cucina africane. *In*: D. Gandolfi, ed. *La ceramica e i materiali di età romana*. Bordighera: Istituto Internazionale di Studi Liguri, 195–232.

Gandolfi, D. and Murialdo, G., 2004. Produzione e circolazione della ceramica in Liguria tra tardoantico e altomedioevo. *In*: G. Pantò, ed. *Produzione e circolazione dei materiali ceramici in Italia settentrionale tra VI e X secolo*. Atti del II Incontro di Studio sulle ceramiche tardoantiche e altomedioevali. Torino 13–14 dicembre 2002. Documenti di Archeologia 35. Mantova: Società Archeologica Padana, 97–120.

Gandolfi, D., Murialdo, G., Capelli, C. and Bonifay, M., 2010. Anfore africane di tardo V–VII secolo in Liguria (Italia): un aggiornamento dei dati archeologici e archeometrici. *In*: S. Menchelli, S. Santoro, M. Pasquinucci and G. Guiducci, eds. *LRCW3. Late Roman Coarse Wares, Cooking Wares and Amphorae in the Mediterranean*. BAR International Series 2185 II. Oxford: Archaeopress, 33–56.

Gardini, A., 1987. Reperti medievali della Grotta Nera. *Archeologia in Liguria. Scavi e scoperte 1982–1986* III(2), 149.

Gardini, A., 1993. La ceramica bizantina in Liguria. *In*: S. Gelichi, ed. *La ceramica nel mondo bizantino tra XI e XV secolo e i suoi rapporti con l'Italia*. Florence: All'Insegna Del Giglio, 47–77.

Gardini, A. and Melli, P., 1988. Necropoli e sepolture urbane ed extraurbane a Genova tra tardo-antico ed alto-medioevo. *Rivista di Studi Liguri* LIV, 159–178.

Gardini, A. and Murialdo, G., 1994. La Liguria. *In*: R. Francovich and G. Noyé, G. eds. *La Storia dell'alto medioevo italiano (VI–X secolo) alla luce dell'archeologia*. Atti del convegno internazionale, Siena, 2–6 dicembre 1992. Florence: All'Insegna del Giglio, 159–182.

Hayes, J. W., 1972. *Late Roman Pottery*. London: British Museum Press.

Issel, A., 1908. Liguria Preistorica. *Atti della Società Ligure di Storia Patria* XL, 5–765.

Járrega Dominguez, R. 2000. Las cerámicas de importación en el nordeste de la Taraconense durante los siglos VI y VII d.C. Aproximación general. *In*: *V reunió d'arqueologia Cristiana Hispànica*, Cartagena, 16–19 d'abril de 1998. Barcelona: Universitat de Barcelona, 467–483.

Jézégou, M.P., 1998. Le mobilier de l'épave Saint-Gervais 2 (VIIe siècle) à Fos-sur-Mer (Bouches-du- Rhône). *Etudes Massaliètes* 5, 343–351.

Keay, J. S., 1984. *Late Roman Amphorae in the Western Mediterranean. A Typology and Economic Study: the Catalan Evidence*. BAR International Series 196. Oxford: Archaeopress.

Keay, J. S., 1998. African amphorae. *In*: L. Saguì ed. *Ceramica in Italia: VI–VII secolo*. Proceedings of the conference in honour of John W. Hayes. Comunicazioni, Roma, 11–13 May 1995. Biblioteca di Archeologia Medievale. Florence: All'Insegna Del Giglio, 141–155.

Long, L. and Volpe, G., 1994. Lo scavo del relitto tardoantico della Palud Isola di Port-Cros, Francia). Prime note sulla campagna 1993. *Vetera Christianorum* 31, 211–233.

Long, L. and Volpe, G., 1998. Le chargement de l'épave 1 de la Palud (VIe siècle) à Port-Cros (Var). Note preliminaire. *Etudes Massaliètes* 5, 317–342.

Lund, J. 1995. Hellenistic Roman and Late Roman fine ware from the Segermes Valley. Forms and chronology. *In*: S. Dietz, L. Sebaï Ladjimi, and H. Ben Hessen, eds. *Africa Proconsularis. Regional Studies in the Segermes Valley of Northern Tunisia*. Copenhagen: Aarhus University Press, 447–629.

Lusuardi Siena, S., Murialdo, G., and Sfrecola, S., 1991. Le ceramiche mediterranee in Liguria durante il periodo bizantino (VI–VII secolo). *In*: AIECM2, ed. *A cerâmica medieval no Mediterrâneo ocidental*. Lisboa, 16–22 novembro 1987. Mértola: Campo Arquelógico De Mértola, 123–146.

Mackensen, M., 1987. Mediterranee Sigillata, lampen und amphoren. *In*: V. Bierbrauer, ed. *Invillino-Ibligo in Friaul I. Die Römische Riedlung und das spätantik-frühmittelalterliche Castrum*. Münchner Beiträge zur vor- und Frühgeschichte (33). Munich: C.H. Beck, 229–265.

Mackensen, M., 1998. Centres of African red slip ware production in Tunisia from the late 5th to 7th century. *In*: L. Saguì, ed. *Ceramica in Italia: VI–VII secolo*. Proceedings of the conference in honour of John W. Hayes. Comunicazioni, Rome, 11–13 May 1995. Biblioteca di Archeologia Medievale. Firenze: All'Insegna Del Giglio, 23–39.

Manacorda, D., 1977. Anfore. *In*: *Ostia IV*. Studi Miscellanei 23, Rome: De Luca Editore, 117–254.

Manacorda, D., 1989. I materiali. *In*: D. Manacorda, ed. *Il castellum del Nador. Storia di una fattoria tra Tipasa e Cesarea (I–VI secolo)*. Monumenta Archaeologica Lybica XXIII, Rome: L'Erma di Bretschneider, 127–216.

Martino, P.G., 1988. Proposta per una cronologia-tipologia sepolcrale in alcuni complessi archeologici del Ponente Ligure. *Rivista di Studi Liguri* LIV, 249–268.

Maselli Scotti, F., 1992. Due fortificazioni tardoantiche ad oriente di Aquileia. *In*: G. Sena Chiesa and A.E. Arslan, eds. *Felix Temporis Reparatio*. Atti del Convegno, *Milano capitale dell'impero romano*. Milano 8–11 marzo 1990. Milan: Edizioni ET, 369–373.

Massa, S. 1999. La ceramica d'importazione africana. *In*: G.P. Brogiolo, ed. *S. Giulia di Brescia: gli scavi dal 1980 al 1992. Reperti preromani, romani e altomedievali*. Florence: All'Insegna Del Giglio, 101–117.

Micheletto, E., 1998. Forme di insediamento tra V e XIII secolo: il contributo dell'archeologia. *In*: L. Mercando and E. Micheletto, eds. *Archeologia in Piemonte. Il Medioevo*. Torino: Umberto Allemandi, 51–80.

Murialdo, G., 1988. Necropoli e sepolture tardoantiche del Finale. *Rivista di Studi Liguri* LIV, 221–242.

Murialdo, G., 1995a. Anfore tardoantiche nel Finale (VI–VII secolo). *Rivista di Studi Liguri*, LIX–LX, 213–246.

Murialdo, G., 1995b. Alcune considerazioni sulle anfore africane di VII secolo dal castrum di S. Antonino nel Finale. *Archeologia Medievale* XXII, 433–453.

Murialdo, G. 1996. Il vicus romano e gli insediamenti altomedievali. *In*: G. Murialdo, ed. *Perti. Un territorio rurale nel finale tra la preistoria e l'età moderna*. Bordighera: Istituto Internazionale di Studi Liguri, 53–72.

Murialdo, G., 2001a. Le anfore da trasporto. *In*: T. Mannoni and G. Murialdo, eds. *S. Antonino. Un insediamento fortificato nella Liguria bizantina*. Bordighera: Istituto Internazionale di Studi Liguri, 255–296.

Murialdo, G., 2001b. I rapporti economici con l'area mediterranea e padana. *In*: T. Mannoni and G. Murialdo, eds. *S. Antonino. Un insediamento fortificato nella Liguria bizantina*. Bordighera: Istituto Internazionale di Studi Liguri, 301–310.

Murialdo, G., 2007. Alto-Adriatico e Alto-Tirreno nel mondo mediterraneo: due mari a confronto tra VI e X secolo. *In*: S. Gelichi and C. Negrelli, eds., *La circolazione delle ceramiche nell'Adriatico tra tarda antichità e Altomedioevo*. Documenti di Archeologia 43, Mantova: Società Archeologica, 9–29.

Murialdo, G., Fossati, A., Falcetti, C. and Bonora, E., 1986. La pietra ollare nel Finale. *Rivista di Studi Liguri* LII, 217–242.

Murialdo, G., Palazzi, P., and Arobba, D. 2001. Archeologia del paesaggio finalese nell'antichità. *In*: T. Mannoni and G. Murialdo, eds. *S. Antonino. Un insediamento fortificato nella*

*Liguria bizantina*. Bordighera: Istituto Internazionale di Studi Liguri, 39–64.

Murialdo, G., Gandolfi, D., Mannoni, T. and Varaldo, C., 2011. La Liguria bizantina dopo un sessantennio di ricerche: dati acquisiti e prospettive future. *In*: C. Varaldo, ed. *Ai confini dell'Impero. Insediamenti e fortificazioni bizantine nel Mediterraneo occidentale (VI-VIII secolo)*. Atti del Convegno di studi. Genova-Bordighera, 14–17 marzo 2002. Atti dei Convegni IX. Bordighera: Istituto Internazionale di Studi Liguri, 25–88.

Negro Ponzi, M.M. 2004. Ceramica altomedievale nel Piemonte. *In*: S. Patitucci Uggeri, ed. *La ceramica altomedievale in Italia*. Quaderni di Archeologia Medievale VI, Florence: All'Insegna Del Giglio, 11–36.

Olcese, G., 1993. *Le ceramiche comuni di Albintimilium. Indagine archeologica e archeometria sui materiali dell'area del Cardine*. Florence: All'Insegna Del Giglio.

Olcese, G., Murialdo, G., Palazzi, P. and Parodi, L., 1998. La ceramica comune in Liguria nel VI e VII secolo. *In*: L. Saguì, ed. *Ceramica in Italia: VI–VII secolo*. Proceedings of the Conference in honour of John W. Hayes. Comunicazioni, Rome, 11–13 May 1995. Biblioteca di Archeologia Medievale. Florence: All'Insegna Del Giglio, 227–251.

Pallarés, F., 1987. Alcune osservazioni sulle anfore del battistero di Albenga. *Rivista di Studi Liguri* LIII, 269–306.

Panella, C., 1983. Le anfore africane della prima, media e tarda età imperiale: tipologia e problemi. *In*: *Actes du colloque sur la céramique antique*. Carthage 23–24 juin 1980. Carthage: Centre d'Étude de la Civilisation Classique et des Antiquités Romaines et Byzantines, 171–196.

Panella, C., 1993. Merci e scambi nel Mediterraneo tardoantico. *In*: A. Carandini, L. Cracco Ruggini, and A. Giardina, eds. *Storia di Roma. L'età tardoantica. I luoghi e le culture*. Torino: Giulio Einaudi Editore, 613–697.

Pastorino, A.M., 1997. Roman and Late Roman Layers in the cave of Arene Candide. *In*: R. Maggi, ed. *Arene Candide: A Funerary and Environmental Assessment of the Holocene Sequence*. Memorie dell'Istituto Italiano di Paleontologia Umana V, Rome: Il Calamo, 623–634.

Paunier, D., 1978. Un refuge du Bas-Empire au Mont-Musiège (Haute Savoie). *Museum Helveticum* 35, 295–306.

Peacock, S.P.D., 1984. The red-slipped wares. The amphorae. *In*: S.P.D. Peacock and M.G. Fulford, eds. *Excavations at Carthage: The British Mission. The Avenue du President Bourghiba, Salambo. The Pottery and Other Ceramic Objects from the Site*. Sheffield: The British Academy, 48–140.

Peacock, S.P.D. and Williams, D.F., 1986. *Amphorae and the Roman Economy*. London–New York: Longman.

Pieri, D., 2005. Le commerce du vin oriental à l'époque byzantine (V[e]–VIIe siècle). Le témoignage des amphores en Gaule. *Bibliothèque archéologique et historique* 174. Beirut: Institut Français di Proche-Orient.

Pieri, D. 2007. Les centres de production d'amphores en Mediterranée orientale durant l'Antiquité tardive: quelques remarques. *In*: M. Bonifay and J.-C. Tréglia, eds. *LRCW2. Late Roman Coarse Wares, Cooking Wares and Amphorae in the Mediterranean. Archaeology and Archaeometry*. BAR International Series 1662 II. Oxford: Archaeopress, 611–625.

Pröttel, P.M. 1996. *Mediterranee Feinkeramik des 2.-7. Jahrhunderts n. Chr. ins oberen Adriaraum und in Slowenien*. Kölner Studien zur Archäologie der Römischen Provinzen 2, Espelkamp: Verlag Marie Leidorf GmbH.

Reynolds, P. 1995, *Trade in the Western Mediterranean AD 400–700: the Ceramic Evidence*. BAR International Series 604. Oxford: Archaeopress.

Ricci, M., 2007. Il contesto del Mitreo. *In*: G.P. Brogiolo and A. Chavarría Arnau, eds. *I Longobardi. Dalla caduta dell'Impero all'alba dell'Italia*. Catalogo della mostra. Torino-Palazzo Bricherasio 28 settembre 2007–6 gennaio 2008. Novalesa-Abbazia dei Santi Pietro e Andrea 30 settembre–9 dicembre 2007. Mantova: Società Archeologica Padana, 161–169.

Riley, A.J. 1976. Late amphoras. *In*: J.M. Humphrey, ed. *Excavations at Carthage 1975 Conducted by the University of Michigan, Vol. I*. Ann Arbor, MI: The University of Michigan Press, 114–120.

Riley, A.J. 1981. The pottery from cisterns 1977.1, 1977.2 and 1977.3. *In*: J.M. Humphrey, ed. *Excavations at Carthage 1975 conducted by the University of Michigan, Vol. VI*. Ann Arbor, MI: The University of Michigan Press, 23–96.

Romei, D., 2004. Produzione e circolazione dei manufatti ceramici a Roma nell'altomedioevo. *In*: M.S. Arena, P. Delogu, L. Paroli, M. Ricci, L. Saguì and L. Venditelli, eds. *Roma dall'antichità al Medioevo. Archeologia e Storia*. Milan: Electa, 278–311.

Ruggini, L., 1995. *Economia e società nell'Italia Annonaria. Rapporti fra agricoltura e commercio dal IV al VI secolo*. 2nd ed. Bari: Edipuglia.

Saguì, L., 1995. L'esedra della Crypta Balbi e il monastero di S. Lorenzo in Pallacinis. *Quaderni di Archeologia Etrusco-Italica* 23, 121–129.

Saguì, L. 1998. Il deposito della Crypta Balbi: una testimonianza imprevedibile sulla Roma del VII secolo. *In*: L. Saguì, ed. *Ceramica in Italia: VI–VII secolo*. Proceedings of the conference in honour of John W. Hayes. Comunicazioni, Rome, 11–13 May 1995. Biblioteca di Archeologia Medievale. Florence: All'Insegna Del Giglio, 305–330.

Saguì, L. 2004. Ceramica fine da mensa. *In*: M.S. Arena, P. Delogu, L. Paroli, M. Ricci, L. Saguì and L. Venditelli, eds., *Roma dall'antichità al Medioevo. Archeologia e Storia*. Milan: Electa, 268–274.

Sena Chiesa, G., 1995. Angera romana: il vicus e l'indagine di scavo. *In*: G. Sena Chiesa and M.P. Lavizzari Pedrazzini, eds. *Angera romana. Scavi nell'abitato 1980–1986*. Rome: Quasar, 31–63.

Soricelli, G. 1994. Terra Sigillata della prima, media e tarda età imperiale. *In*: P. Arthur, ed. *Il complesso archeologico di Carminiello ai Mannesi, Napoli (Scavi 1983–1984)*. Lecce: Congedo Editore, 109–168.

Tabacco, G., 2010. L'egemonia greco-orientale e la formazione di un Occidente latino-germanico. *In*: G. Sergi, ed. *Alto Medioevo*. Torino: Utet Università, 49–102.

Tortorella, S. 1998. La sigillata africana in Italia nel VI e nel VII secolo: problemi di cronologia e distribuzione. *In*: L. Saguì, ed. *Ceramica in Italia: VI–VII secolo*. Proceedings of the conference in honour of John W. Hayes. Comunicazioni, Rome, 11–13 May 1995. Biblioteca di Archeologia Medievale. Florence: All'Insegna Del Giglio, 41–69.

Vallverdú Remolà, J.A., 2000. *Las ánforas tardo-antiguas en Tarraco (Hispanía Tarraconensis). Siglos IV–VII d.C.* Colleció Instrumenta 7. Barcelona: Universitat de Barcelona.

Wickham, C., 2014. *L'eredità di Roma. Storia d'Europa dal 400 al 1000 d.C.* Rome–Bari: Laterza.

Wickham, C., 2009. *Le società dell'alto medioevo. Europa e Mediterraneo (secoli V–VIII)*. Rome: Viella.

Zemer, A. 1977. *Storage Jars in Ancient Trade*. Haifa: National Maritime Museum.

# Chapter 11

# The culture of rock-cut cemeteries and artificial ritual caves in Roman and Byzantine Malta

*Mario Buhagiar*

*The Maltese islands have a rich tradition of rock-cut funerary architecture, which, in Late Antiquity, conditioned burial practice and associated rituals between approximately the first century BC and the seventh century AD. Caves were central to this development because cemeteries frequently evolved from the re-cutting and elaboration of natural caves or, in their absence, the creation of artificial ones to meet burial requirements. In both instances the architecture was a synthesis of Leventine Phoenico-Punic prototypes and Hellenistic influences that arrived by way of Sicily and North Africa. This chapter discusses the shift from the Carthaginian shaft-and-chamber tomb to the Late Roman and Early Christian miniature catacomb, and shows how the assimilation of different influences resulted in a diversified sepulchral richness. Architectural and decorative features are discussed while taking into account apotropaic and eschatological symbolism. Rock engravings and paintings are explored from an iconographic and art historical perspective. Special consideration is given to the ritual of funerary meals, which gave cemeteries the very special and almost unique feature of rock-cut cylindrical tables cut from a single piece with a U-shaped dining couch of the* stibadium *typology. This chapter provides a meaningful background to the cave-related practices that were a major phenomenon of late medieval and early modern Malta.*

The Maltese archipelago occupies an area of *c.* 316 sq. km and owes its importance in history to its strategic location in the centre of the western Mediterranean, 93km south of Sicily and 288km east of Tunisia (Fig. 11.1). The culture of rock-cut tombs has a long history and is rooted in the rich prehistoric period starting from around the sixth millennium BC (Trump 2002). The practice of underground burial places was facilitated by the availability of a malleable limestone that is easy to quarry and work. Many were re-cut from natural caves. The most noteworthy is the Hal Saflieni hypogeum, which dates to the Temple Period (4100–2500 BC) (Pace 2000). Also significant, albeit less spectacular, is the roughly contemporaneous Brochtorff Circle, a multiple-burial cave complex in Xaghra on the island of Gozo, which is still under investigation (Malone *et al.* 2009). The Phoenicians, who established contact with the islands in the first millennium BC, brought with them a typology of shaft-and-chamber tombs, which reflected the Levantine influence that characterised the west Mediterranean from around 900 BC to the second century AD (Sagona 2002, 4, 5). The Late Roman and Early Christian cemeteries are a development of the Phoenician layout and stylistic idiosyncrasies and, to a marked extent, an elaboration on their tomb typologies (Buhagiar 1986, 13–16).

## The Phoenician and Punic legacy

In spite of the Roman conquest of 218 BC, at the outbreak of the Second Punic War (*Livy. History of Rome* XXX, 51) Malta remained a centre of Punic culture (Gouder 1978), and it is significant that neo-Punic inscriptions have been noted in Romano-Hellenistic tombs until about the start of the first century AD (Sagona 2002, 4). Tombs are scattered all over the islands, but the largest and most important concentration is in the Tac-Caghqi district (now Old College Street and its environs) in the market town of Rabat, outside

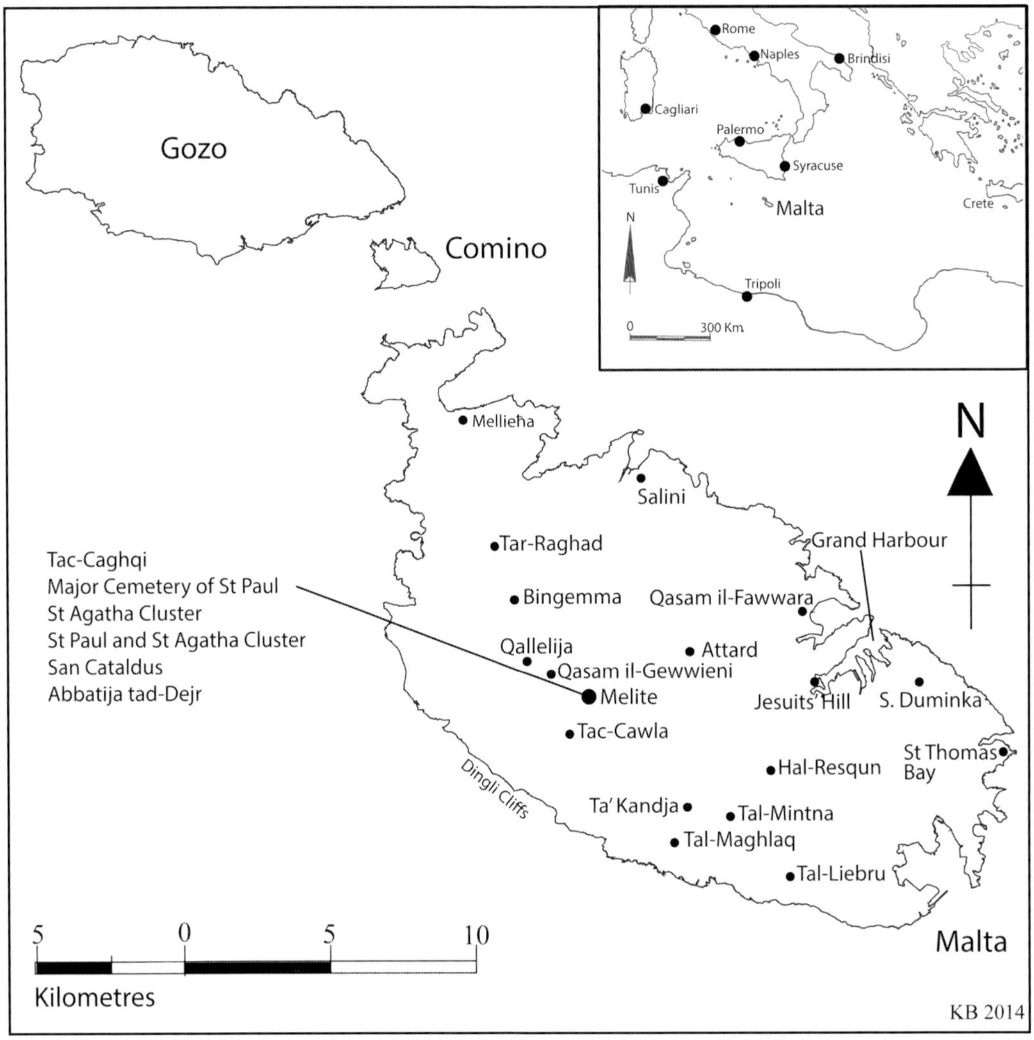


*Figure 11.1: The culturally strategic Central Mediterranean location of the Maltese Islands and map of Malta showing the distribution of the Punico-Hellenistic tombs and Late Roman and Byzantine hypogea discussed in the study.*

the ditch of the city of Melite. The standard typology of a shaft negotiated by foot-holes or precipitously narrow steps, and of one or sometimes more cubical chambers with mortuary couches, was hardly, if at all, affected by the influx of Alexandrian Hellenism, which started to impact on the islands from around the late fourth century BC (Fig. 11.2). The pioneering investigations of Themistocles Zammit suggested that for better protection the shafts had been filled with earth and stones and, in some instances, sealed by stone slabs marked by a low pyramidal mound made of mortar mixed with ground pottery. T. Zammit (1931a, 102) also talks, without further elaboration, of 'stone altars of the classical type found in the filled-up shafts'. He also recorded that a complete altar and fragments of several others (now unaccounted for) were on display at the Valletta Museum. Political affiliation to Sicily made the archipelago vulnerable to Hellenistic civilization, which remained a dominant cultural reality in Late Roman and Byzantine times. It was only in the course of the fifth century AD, when the islands were (seemingly) conquered by the Vandals of North Africa, that cemeteries started experiencing new architectural and iconographic influences, which were grafted onto the Phoenician-Punic prototype (Buhagiar 2014, 237–239).

## The Apotropiac Romano-Punic tomb

Several rock-cut tombs, dating approximately from the first century BC to the first century AD, show an apotropaic concern with appeasing the spirits of the dead or (more probably) frightening away the demonic powers of the underworld. The most significant known instance is a single-chambered cremation burial investigated by Zammit within a tight cluster of tombs at Tac-Caghqi at Malta (MAV Field notes of Themistocles Zammit 3 [1909–1912]; MAR 1909, 5–6). The chamber (Fig. 11.3) was decorated with a painted ceiling rosette composed of a crown of red fleshy

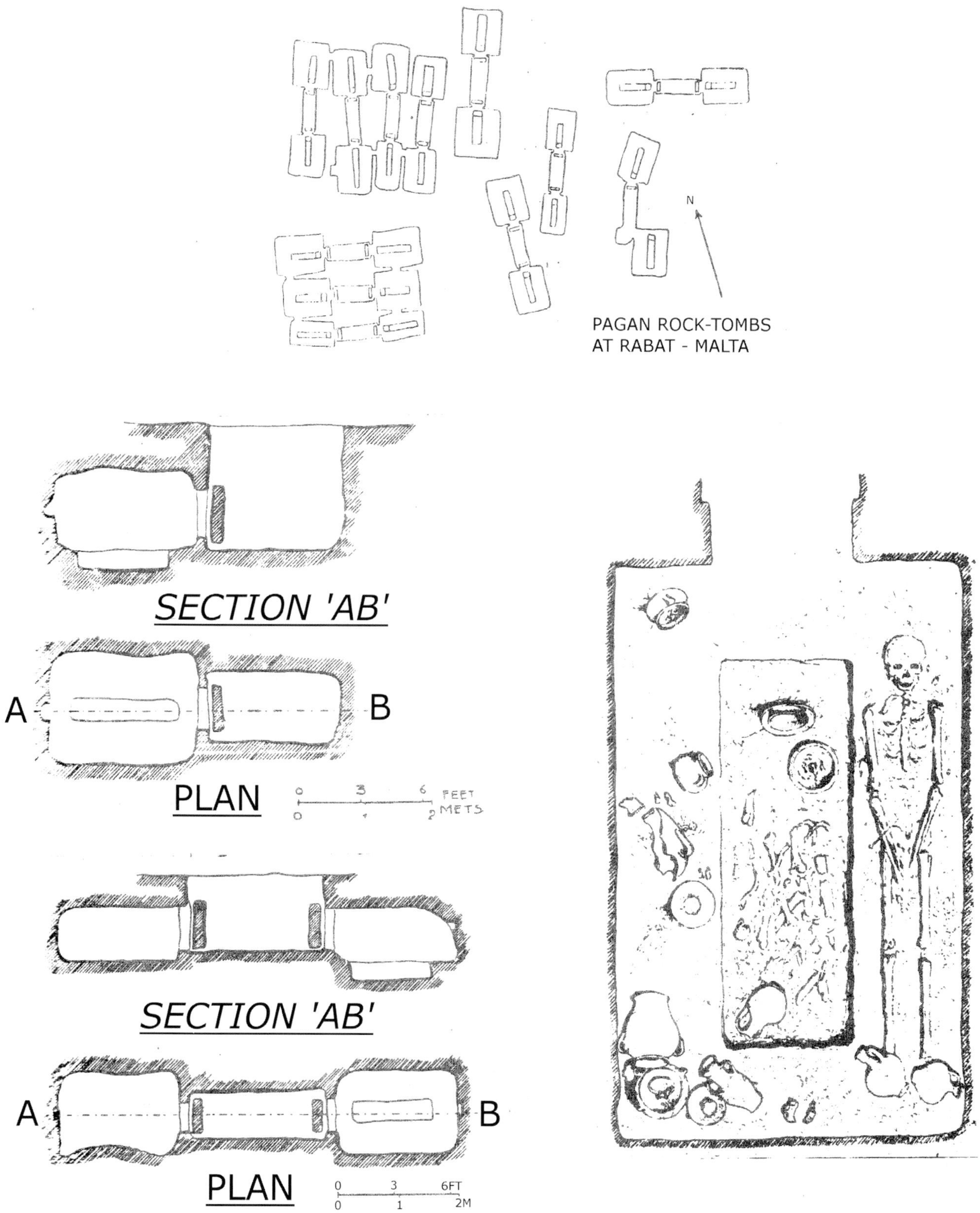


*Figure 11.2: The Tac-Caghqi Punico-Hellenistic Necropolis investigated by Themistocles Zammit in 1906. Based on* Bulletin of the Museum *1/3, 1931 (after Buhagiar 2014).*

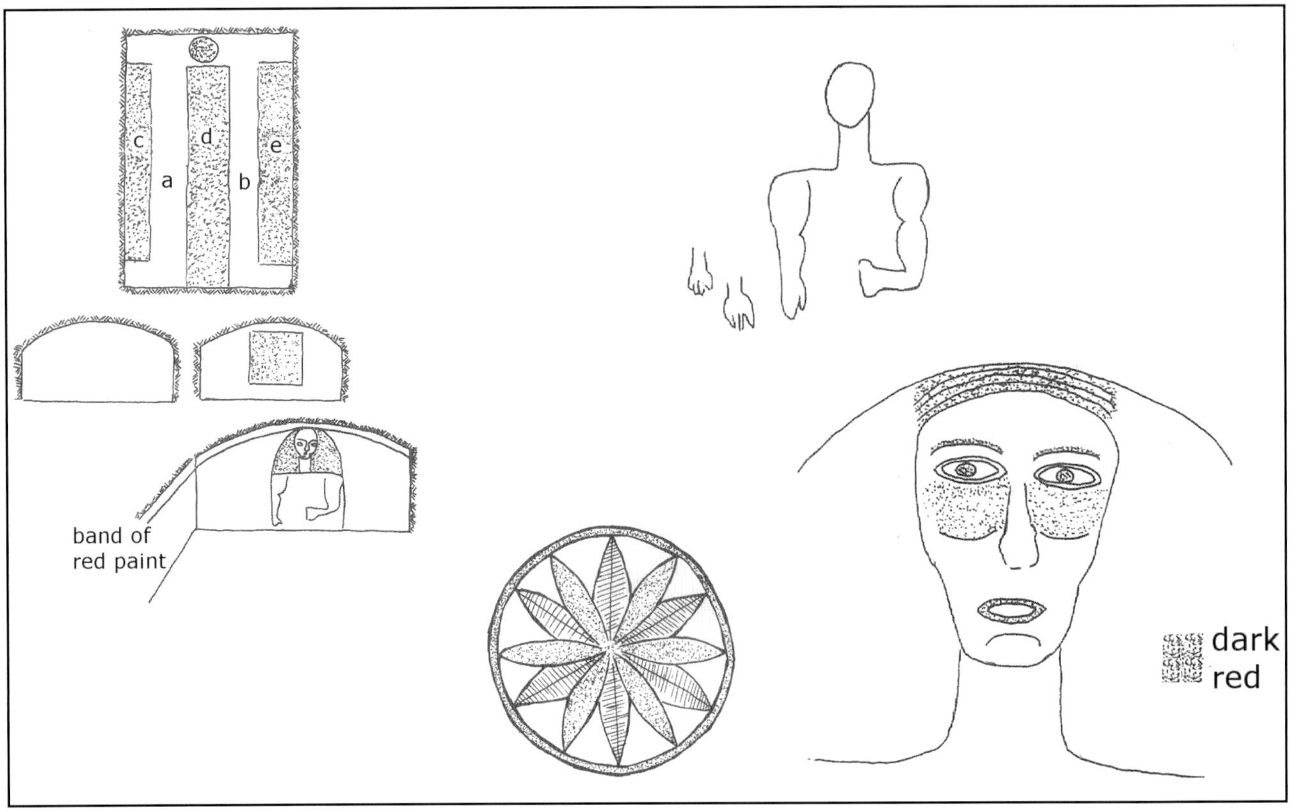


*Figure 11.3: Tac-Caghqi Punico-Hellenistic tomb with apotropaic figural relief and painted rosette. Based on Themistocles Zammit 1906 (after Buhagiar 2014).*

petals, but its most important feature was a low relief wall sculpture of a humanoid with a large pear-shaped head, an elongated neck, large almond-shaped eyes, a prominent nose, a heavy lipped mouth, and accentuated chin. The torso was vague and (apparently) in lower relief. One arm was folded over the breast while the other hung limply at the side. An apsed lunette at the back of the head gave it added prominence. The necromantic nature of the relief was heightened by red paint. The face was light red but a darker red was used for the cheeks, lips, eyebrows, pupils and hair. It stood guard over a cinerary urn placed into a purposely cut niche. Stylistically, the relief is related to the widely diffused typology of Punic figural stelae often associated, as in Carthage, with the *Tophet* (Moscati 1988, 304–327). One from Monte Sirai, Sardenia (Museo Archeologico Nazionale, Cagliari), representing a similarly schematised female form holding an apparent lotus flower, is closely comparable (Moscati 1988, 319). Approximate parallels can also be found on other Sardinian stelae and on some from Motya, Sicily (Moscati 1988, 319). No stelae have been reported from Malta and it is possible that they were replaced by figural reliefs or engravings in rock-cut tombs. No photographic documentation of the relief was found in the records of the Valletta Museum and T. Zammit's drawings are the only source of visual information. The tomb was rediscovered in the course of building works in 1951 but was sealed up again apparently without further investigation (MAR 1951–1952, viii).

A grotesque head (36 × 31cm), now in the National Museum of Archaeology, was carved in high relief on one corner of a mortuary couch in a two-chambered inhumation tomb at a burial site at Il- Qallilija, outside Rabat, investigated by Zammit in 1916. It presumably served a similar apotropaic function but there is no mention of colour (Field notes of Themistocles Zammit 5 [1916–1921], 32). The stylistic idiosyncrasies are again those of a figural stele. The necromantic figure of a nude male in Egyptian stylisation is boldly engraved in a single-chambered cave tomb discovered in 1989 in the town of Attard (Frendo 1997, 6). The man is performing a ritualistic dance. He has an erect penis and exaggeratedly large arms, one of which is raised in a threatening gesture. The torso is represented frontally but the head, which has a large eye, and the legs, one of which is menacingly thrust forward, are in profile.

A direct reference to the evil spirit that haunts the abode of the dead is contained in a four-line neo-Punic incantation, painted in bright red in the hall-like ante-chamber of a first-century BC to first-century AD hypogeum, discovered at Tac-Caghqi in 1951 and investigated by Charles George Zammit. The spirit is ordered to desist and be placated by a potent offering, presumably a libation, for which there is evidence on the sealing plugs of the burial cubicles (Borg and Rocco 1976, 61–64).

A rock-cut chamber, or perhaps a natural cave, was discovered in 1847 in a now unknown locality in the district of Qasam il-Gewwieni, outside Rabat. It excited antiquarian interest but the resultant reports are inadequate and confusing. They mention rock engravings in an Egyptian Phoenico-Punic style, but complain that the place was too dark to make out what they represented. The most trustworthy eye witness was Cesare Vassallo, Librarian and Keeper of Antiquities at the Royal Malta Library, who was of the opinion that the only (apparently) certain engraving was of an ibis, the bird sacred in Egypt because of its association with the god Thoth. The engraving stood out because it was highlighted in colour (Vassallo 1876, 49–51), presumably red ochre. The probability is that what he saw was an allegorical bird of a typology discussed below that was common in Early Christian hypogea. If this was indeed the case, it had no relation to Punic necromancy.

## The evolution of the catacomb, and tomb typologies

Themistocles Zammit believed, probably correctly, that the crowding of burials at Tac-Caghqi resulted in the accidental fusing of the burial chambers of adjacent tombs. This, in time, led to the practical and less space-consuming development of having tombs served by a common shaft (T. Zammit 1931a, 1/3, 100–130). His conjecture was confirmed by the presence on the site of a hypogeum with burial chambers arranged along the sides of a narrow gallery (Field notes of Themistocles Zammit 2 [1907–1908], 1–102; MAR 1907–1908, 6–7). Similar single gallery hypogea are common in the Maltese countryside and may have served as a prototype for subsequent developments (Fig. 11.4). In most cases this happened in an *ad hoc* manner with new spaces being added to cater for increased burial demand. The initial gallery was sometimes extended along its long axis but, in most instances, enlargements consisted of opening new galleries that branched off from it at right or obtuse angles.

### *Canopied (*baldacchino*) tombs*

In the larger and more important cemeteries of Melite, the galleries led to hall-like chambers which, with the exception of similar arrangements in the minor catacombs of eastern Sicily (Agnello 1970), are idiosyncratically Maltese. One of their most important characteristics is the presence of canopied (or *baldacchino*) tombs, usually arranged in rows, creating an axial grid-iron layout. The canopied tomb (Fig. 11.5) is a rock-cut sarcophagus with an arched superstructure that connects with the ceiling. Popular with both Christian and Jewish communities, it is space consuming, imposing and carries a sign of distinction. It does not seem to owe its origins to any known prototype and may have resulted from a synthesis of Punic and Hellenistic influences. Outside Malta the type is frequent in the small catacombs of the Sicilian countryside, but with the canopied top replaced by stocky corner pilasters (Agnello 1970). An isolated example has also been reported in the Roman catacomb of Peter and Marcellinus (Ferrua 1949, 509). This distinctive tomb typology was possibly of Maltese origin and reached Sicily and Rome through political and cultural channels. There is, however, no real supporting evidence.

### *Window tombs*

More insular and seemingly unknown outside Malta is the window tomb (Figs. 11.5–11.6). This is the most widely occurring tomb typology in Maltese cemeteries and is essentially a Late Roman development of the burial chamber in the Romano-Punic tomb. It gets its name from the window-like entrance to a usually oval funerary cell tunnelled into the walls of halls and galleries at an average height of 60–80cm above floor level. The chamber often has apsed head and foot recesses and there is usually a rock-cut pillow with two or more headrests (Buhagiar 2007, 24). In rural hypogea, window tombs are often the exclusive burial arrangement. In Melite cemeteries they compete for popularity with the less vernacular *arcosolium* (Fig. 11.5), which was in several instances the preferred option. There is, for example, only one window tomb in the major Cemetery of St Paul.

### *Arcosolia*

*Arcosolia* were often paired with canopied tombs and, in many instances, tunnelled in the walls of the same hall. Contrary to what one might expect, they are closer to the Roman and mainland Italian typology than to the Sicilian deeply tunnelled variety; multiple rows of rock-cut sarcophagi are a principal feature of the catacombs of San Giovanni and Vigna Cassia in Syracuse. The Maltese *arcosolium* normally does not have more than two or, at most, three sarcophagi. The only exception, in the major Cemetery of St Paul, is the presence of six examples but this is still too small to compare with Sicily. The standard *arcosolium* seems to be an imported tomb typology, which would explain its presence in Melite and the Grand Harbour region (Buhagiar 2014, 135–143) – areas more open to incoming cultural trends than the countryside. There is, in addition, a seemingly native variant where a mortuary couch, *c.* 80–100cm high and normally wide enough for two corpses, replaces the sarcophagi and is contained in a niche with a flattened arch. As with the window tomb, this native typology is rooted in the Punic tradition and it is possible to see in it an elaboration of the burial platform of the Romano-Punic tomb.

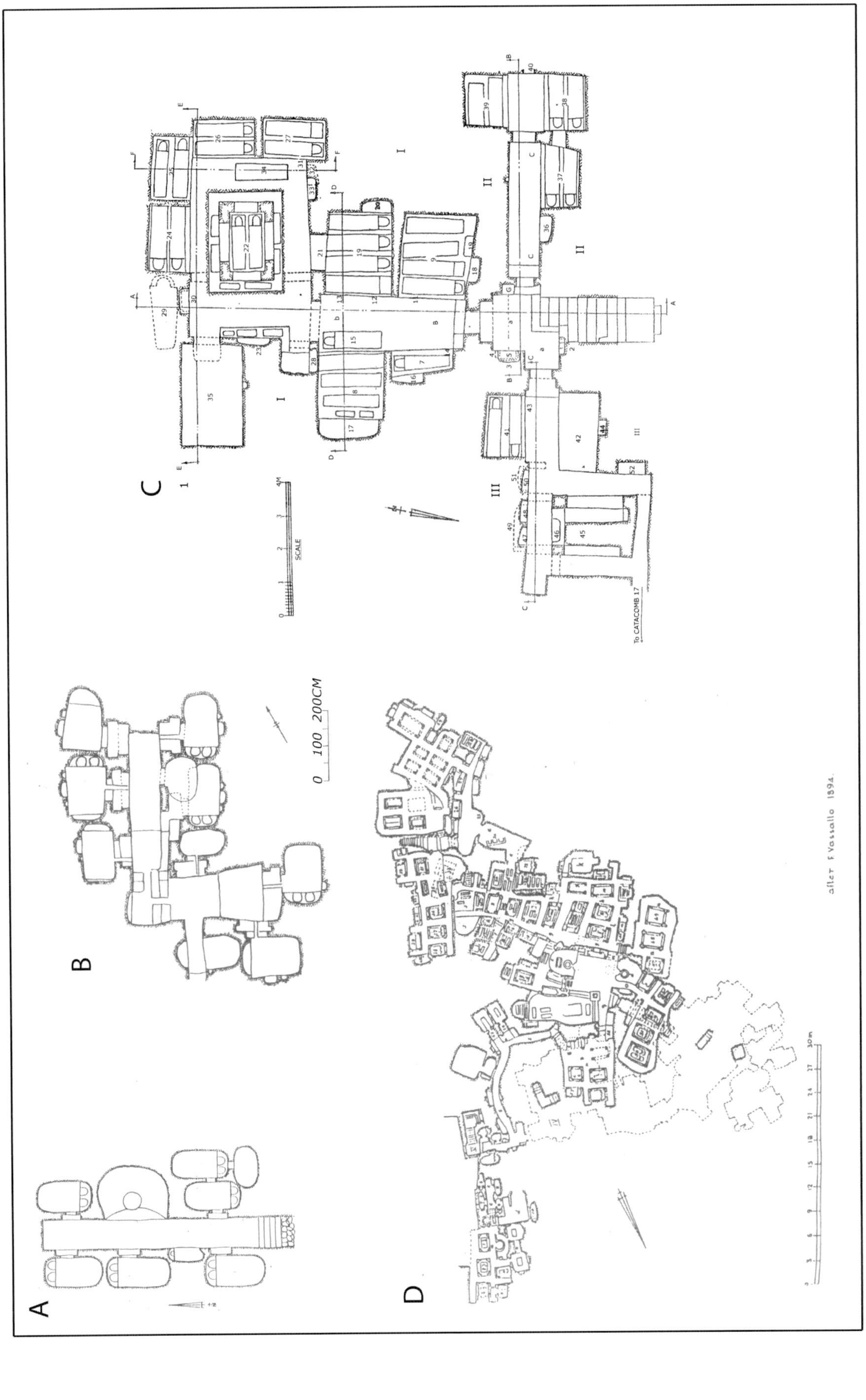


*Figure 11.4: Evolution of the Late Roman and Byzantine Hypogeum: a) One galleried hypogeum at Tac-Caghqi; b) Two-galleried hypogeum at Tal-Mintna, Mqabba; c) Complex Hypogeum 13 in the St Paul and St Agatha Cluster; d) Major Cemetery of St Paul (after Buhagiar 1986).*

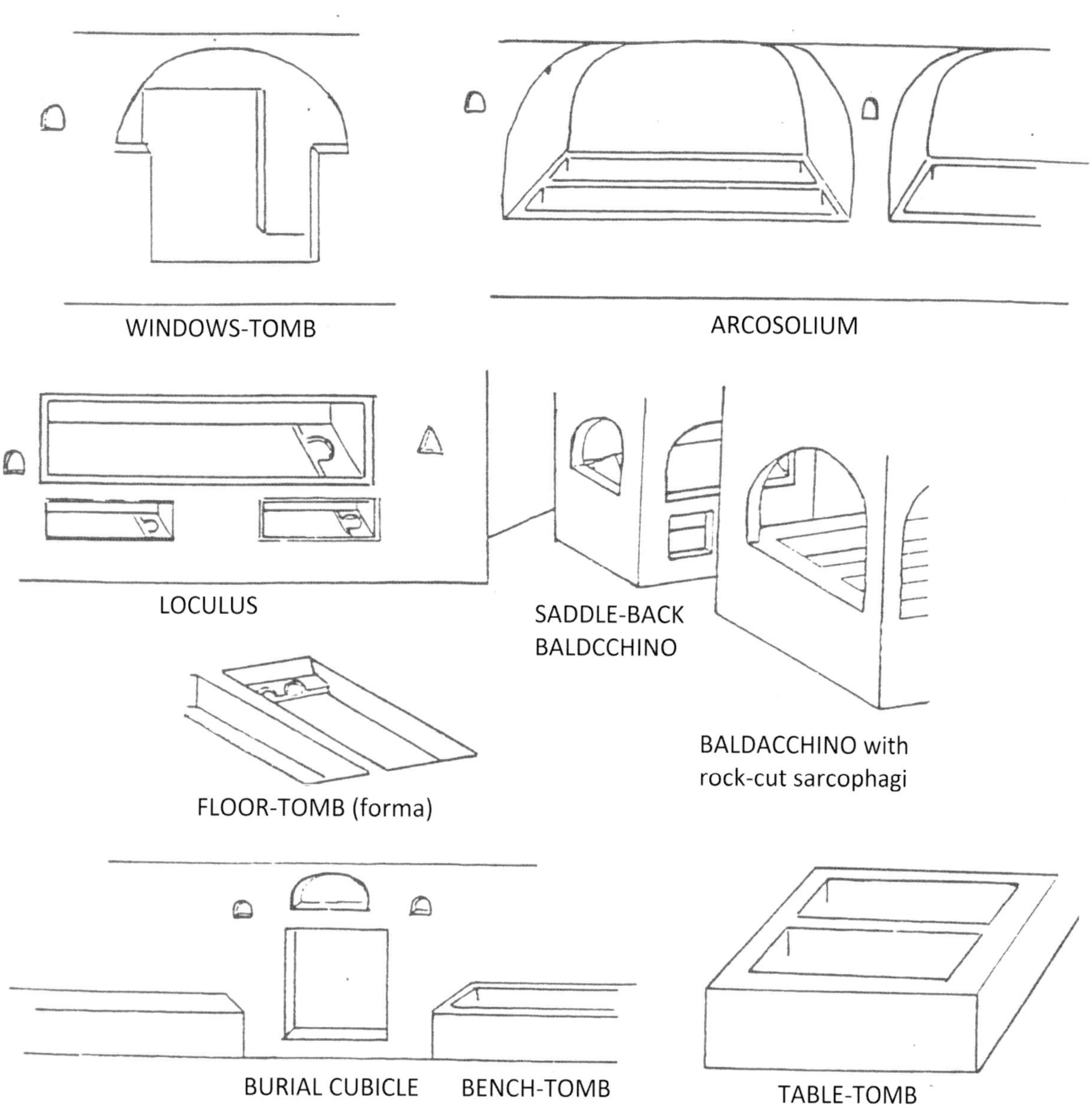


*Figure 11.5: Different tomb-typologies of the Late Roman and Byzantine hypogea (after Buhagiar 1986).*

### *Burial cubicles*

The burial cubicle (Fig. 11.5) that is the closest equivalent to, but still distinct from, the *cubiculum* of the Roman catacombs takes the language of selective borrowings a significant step further and merges the Romano-Punic burial chamber with the complex Late Roman and Byzantine catacomb. There are differences and elaborations, but the basic characteristics remain the same. Usually located at the end of a principal gallery, or in a hall with canopied tombs, it retains the same box-like proportions and is entered down three, or sometimes four, steep steps from a low square-headed window-door. Inside were three mortuary couches, under very flattened arches, grouped around a restricted central space that sometimes contained a pit serving as a water drain, or perhaps to hold funerary pottery. The window-door was sealed with a tight-fitting stone plug and was occasionally flanked by rock-cut benches. Sometimes (e.g. Hypogeum 6 in the St Paul and St Agatha cluster) it was recessed at the back of a flat-arched niche (Buhagiar 1986, 105). The burial cubicle continued to feature in seeming late contexts but with a number of variations to the standard typology. The mortuary couch at the back wall was, on occasion, replaced by a window tomb, and in one instance, at Tac-Cawla on the outskirts of Rabat, was replaced by a *loculus*-tomb (Buhagiar 1986, 198–200). In other cases, the mortuary couch was replaced by a floor burial complete with a rock pillow and normally two, or sometimes three, headrests. In one exceptional instance, in

*Figure 11.6: Window-tombs in Hypogeum 13 in the St Paul and St Agatha Cluster. Photo: K. Buhagiar.*

*Figure 11.7: Funerary-*triclinium *in the Major Cemetery of St Paul. Photo: K. Buhagiar.*

Jewish Hypogeum 12 in the St Paul and St Agatha cluster, two burial chambers under flattened arches have pillows with six and seven headrests respectively, and the tomb in the back wall is eliminated (Buhagiar 1986, 117).

## Loculus, forma *and bench tombs*

The *loculus*, which in mainland Italian, Sicilian and North African cemeteries was the most widely diffused tomb type (Fig. 11.5), was used in Malta almost exclusively for child burials. The number of known adult *loculi* is limited to approximately two dozen. The *forma* (or floor tomb) (Fig. 11.5) is equally rare and one gets the impression that it was adopted as a last resource after all other available burial space had been utilised. Excluding a few isolated instances where it occurs above ground (Buhagiar 1986, 24), *forma* tombs were usually dug into the floors of galleries or in passageways between canopied tombs. They were often provided with the customary pillow and headrests and had an average depth of around 70cm. This was insufficient for the accommodation of an adult body and to close the tomb it was necessary to lay the stone or terracotta sealing slabs in a pyramid-like arrangement. The *loculus* and the *forma* were both alien to the Romano-Punic tradition and, as in the case of the *arcosolium*, they resulted from the infiltration of new artistic currents. More vernacular is the bench tomb (Fig. 11.5) which, like the *forma*, stressed the need for maximising sepulchral space. It gets its name from a hollowed-out bench that sometimes skirted the walls of a burial hall. Only a handful, all in the Melite cemeteries, has been recorded and they are invariably of small size and intended for the body of a young child.

## Ritualistic rock-cut tables

The uniqueness of the Maltese cemeteries lies neither in their organic growth from a Romano-Punic nucleus nor in the richness of tomb types, but in the presence of a rock-cut table cut from one block associated with a low bench with sloping sides recalling the Roman *stibadium* or U-shaped dining couch. Table and bench are on several occasions contained within a cylindrical apsed niche prominently located either at the entrance of the catacomb or the beginning of a principal gallery. Sometimes they are found in spacious halls which, in Christian contexts, could have been intended for ritual meetings. On occasion they are furnished with rock-cut benches (Fig. 11.7). The larger cemeteries may have two or, in rare instances, three tables. Significantly they are absent in Jewish catacombs (Buhagiar 2011, 90). The tables were normally carefully finished and illuminated by oil lamps in strategically placed pyramid-shaped or cylindrical sockets. They usually have a flat top edged with a low ridge notched at one end. Most are cylindrical, but oval or horseshoe-shaped tables are not uncommon.

Clearly these tables had a ritualistic function. The most important burials were clustered in their immediate vicinity and were sometimes physically linked to them by drilling small openings through the walls of the cylindrical niche which itself often contained burials. Child *loculi* and window tombs were the most frequent, but *arcosolia* and canopied tombs were not uncommon. The table, bench and niche were normally rendered with a dark red or light brown cement, which could have served as a preparation for painted decoration. In one instance in Hypogeum 3 in the St Agatha cluster, a *trompe l'oeil* effect is achieved by giving the rock-cut niche the semblance of a flattened corbelled dome resting on a projecting rock ledge supported by two Doric pilasters engraved in relief (Buhagiar 1986, 75–76). One gets the feeling of a calculated effort to reproduce in a rock-cut setting the *triclinium* area of the average Roman *domus*. Fronting this table is a carefully finished aedicule (small shrine) with a painted allegory of the succour (*refrigerium)* of the soul. Similar but less elaborate aediculae are found in other hypogea and presumably related to the ritualistic significance of the tables.

The ritual function of these tables was first perceptively argued by Erich Becker who saw a connection with the custom, widespread in the ancient world, of holding *refrigeria*, or commemorative meals, on or near tombs on death anniversaries (Becker 2000, 97–103). Charles G. Zammit recognised them as funerary *triclinia* that reproduced, in a sepulchral environment, the dining arrangement (*triclinia*) of the average *domus* of the Imperial period (C.G. Zammit 1940, 293–296). The houses of Pompeii and Herculanium offer good examples of dining rooms in which the furniture consisted of three reclining couches arranged in a U-shaped formation around a small table. They were normally portable and made of wood or metal, but fixed couches in stone or brick, such as in the *triclinium* of the Cryptoporticus (Pompeii), are also known. Each couch normally accommodated three people reclined on the left elbow. In or around the second century AD the three-couch arrangement was replaced by a single couch, or *stibadium*, that remained in fashionable use throughout Late Antiquity. This limited the number of diners to six or seven individuals. In the late third or early fourth century Villa Heruclea at Piazza Armerina, Sicily, the *stibadia* were placed in apsed recesses (Gentili 1954). This reflects a development in dining room architecture that found its most significant expression in the Great Palace of Constantinople, where the complex built in the early fourth century by the mighty courtier Antiochus had two *triclinia* in apsed recesses (Bek 1983, 81–107).

Funerary meals were often represented in art. The earliest, and in a way the most eloquent, are the paintings in the fifth-century BC Tomb of the Diver, discovered in Paestum in 1968 (Napoli 1970). Belonging to a later period, but better related to incipient Christian practice, are the reliefs on a mausoleum at Amiternum (Février 1976, 30), and on the tomb of the young *aedile* G. Vestorius Priscus, near the Porta Vesuvius at Pompeii (Spano 1943, 237–316). The practice was widespread in the Romano-Hellenistic world. Funerary *triclina* have been reported from places as far removed as Porto on Isola Sacra near Rome (Février 1978, 211–224), Alexandria (Adriani 1966, 134) and Tripolitania (Di Vita 1978, 198–256). The ritual was an important event of the *Paternalia*, the annual festival of the dead, which reached a climax on 21 February when burial rites were renewed. The proclaimed intention was to strengthen the family bond, or *collegium*, with deceased members symbolically partaking of the meal through libations (Wolski and Berciu 1973, 370–379). In Malta there is evidence for libations in the Tac-Caghqi hypogeum with the Neo-Punic incantation (discussed above) where libation holes are drilled through the sealing plugs of the burial cubicles (Buhagiar 1986, 186). Less certain is the evidence from Hypogeum 3 in the St Paul and St Agatha cluster where another plug door has a neat circular hole drilled through its thickness. It fitted tightly into the window-door of the cubicle of a possible *collegium* of medical doctors (Buhagiar 1986, 99).

The ritual of funerary meals and libations may first have been adopted by early Christians as a commemoration of martyrs. Evidence of it in Rome is preserved in catacomb paintings in Callistus, Priscilla and Peter and Marcellinus, among others. There is, in addition, a clear reference to it in the Ad Catacumbas cemetery complex on the Via Appia, where graffiti scratched on an apparently third-century pilgrim's loggia commemorate *refrigira* in honour of the major apostles Peter and Paul who were, for some time, buried there (Kjaergaard 1984).

The ritual was tolerated as an expression of fraternal piety and love and seems to have been closely associated with the *Agape* or 'Love-Feast' celebration, which was an important feature of the Christian way of life and was at times inseparable from the Eucharistic mystery. The early fourth-century *Canons of Hippolytus*, which may have originated in Egypt, allowed the two rituals to be held together as an *amnesis*, or commemoration, of the dead (Borg 1986, 55). *Agape* celebrations sometimes led to excess and became a cause of serious embarrassment to the early church, but in spite of official censure and sometimes strict prohibitions, they were difficult to eradicate and in certain instances survived well into the seventh and eighth centuries (Buhagiar 2014, 169–172). There is no evidence for *Agape* celebrations in Malta and it is wrong (as has long been the case) to call the ritual tables 'Agape tables'. The nature and history of the Maltese funerary meal still needs to be properly investigated. Equally incorrect is the belief that the tables are proof of Christian identity (Buhagiar 1986, 29–34). It is now clear that they also featured in pagan contexts, such as in the case of the Ta' Marcell hypogeum in the Tac-Caghqi Romano-Punic necropolis discussed above (Buhagiar 2014, 170).

There is nothing similar to the Maltese ritual tables in mainland Italian and Sicilian catacombs. The closest parallel is in the necropolis of Porto on Isola Sacra where a late second-century AD burial chamber contains reclining stone benches (Février 1978). A large stone table outside the catacomb of Porta Ossuna near Palermo is more distinct (Agnello 1970, 230). Better related, but in an above ground context, are tables noted in Sardinia at Cornus (Giuntella *et al.* 1985), and in Spain in necropoli at Terragona (S. Fructuosus) (Baraal I Altet 1978, 49–60) and Cartagenia (Sammartin and de Palol 1972, 447–458). Spain and Sardinia had, like Malta, a close association with North Africa where the closest similarities have been reported (Buhagiar 2014, 243–244). The connection was again first made by Erich Becker who drew attention to a table and its apsidal context in the basilica of the virgin saint Salsa in Tipaza, Algeria, which he recognised from an excavation report (Gselle 1901, 336, pl. xcv). He perceptively commented that the description and annexed plate looked exactly like the Maltese ritual tables (Becker 1913, 98). He also drew attention to the study by Abbé Saint Gérand of the adjacent sepulchral basilica of Bishop Alexander with its tombs of nine *justi priores* who the historian Louis Duchesne (1843–1922) thought were bishops (Février 1978).

Of greater interest, but unknown to Becker, are *triclinia* of the *stibadium* typology in a pagan necropolis in the Sidret el-Balik region of Sabratha, Libya. Despite their similarity, these tables occur in above-ground cemeteries. The only known instance outside Malta of a table in an underground cemetery is in a small catacomb at Gargaresc, near Tripoli, Libya, where one is located in a burial chamber with a mural of the temptation of Adam and Eve (Di Vita 1978). There are, however, differences: the cylindrical niches are missing and, more importantly, the table and *stibadium* are not rock-cut from a single piece but comprise separate drystone units.

It is possible that the practice of funerary meals in Malta was consolidated by the Vandal invasion of AD 455, which brought the island in close contact with the African church (Buhagiar 2014, 243–244). It is also plausible that because of the remoteness of the island the ritual survived longer than in most other places. It is not known when the ritual fell out of use, but an official attempt to abolish it is suggested by the wilful mutilation of many tables. On some occasions, such as in Hypogeum 5 in the St Agatha cluster (Buhagiar 1986, 79), tables were completely destroyed to provide new burial space. In the major Cemetery of St Paul, the suppression of the table rituals created the need for a new ritual space with the placement of an altar beneath a *ciborium* or canopy (Buhagiar 2014, 230–233).

In spite of their evolution it is improbable, as sometimes suggested, that the tables were a late addition necessitating the destruction of pre-existing tombs (Borg 1986, 61–64). Many were the focal point of the catacomb, and to an extent conditioned its development. A departure from the standard shape are three square tables (Buhagiar 2014, 167), which are possibly earlier than the standard cylindrical form. None of the square tables has a *stibadium*. In one instance, in Hypogeum 21 of the St Paul and St Agatha cluster, it is replaced by two rock-cut seats. The square table in the pre-Christian Tac-Caghqi catacomb with the Neo-Punic incantation (discussed above), is of greater interest. It is cut from one piece of soft limestone and fits tightly into a cavity in the middle of a concave space that seems to anticipate the cylindrical apsed niche of the later catacombs (Buhagiar 1986, 185).

One final consideration is the nature of the funerary meal. A V-shaped perforation in the raised ridge of the table top was, presumably, a practical cleaning device for brushing away food particles. In one instance, in the one of the three rural hypogea at Tal-Mintna on the outskirts of Mqabba (Buhagiar 1986, 214–219), a hole is drilled through the thickness of the ridge to serve as a drain for liquids when the table was cleaned. Wine was probably drunk and a concave cutting at the front of the table might have served the purpose of an amphora stand. Seats at the extremities of the *stibadia* seem to suggest a presiding minister and assistant. Perhaps rather than a formal meal, one has to consider a ritualistic one, at least as far as the Christian tables are concerned.

## Physical characteristics of the Maltese catacombs

A striking characteristic of the Maltese catacombs is their compactness and intimate proportions. They lack the labyrinthine complexities of the catacombs of Rome, Naples, Syracuse and Hadrumentum. The major Cemetery of St Paul covers an approximate footprint of 2166 sq. m, while the neighbouring St Paul's Grotto catacomb is only 28m along its long axis. The larger cemeteries are the result of an *ad hoc* fusion of originally separate catacombs. The St Agatha cluster, which extends over an area of *c*. 3800 sq. m, is made up of over 20 separate catacombs each with its own shaft entrance (Buhagiar 1986, 69–93). In most cases the catacombs were intended for the restricted use of a family or guild (*collegium*), or to service small communities in outlying areas. Sometimes, as in the significant case of Tar Raghad at Mgarr (Buhagiar 2014, 161–163), it is still possible to see the demolished remains of the Romano-Punic tombs from which the catacomb evolved. The demand for burial spaces may in some instances have generated commercial activity. A deeply engraved Greek inscription [CIG IV, 9450/IG XIV, 603] on an apparent fifth-century catacomb in the Jesuits' Hill necropolis, on the Grand Harbour, records its purchase from the possible entrepreneurs Zosimetis and Anicetos (Buhagiar 2014, 137–138).

Not all cemeteries were of the shaft typology. Sometimes they were tunnelled into the face of a cliff, as happened on the Bingemma Ridge *c*. 4km west of Melite (Buhagiar 2014, 109–134) where most of the tombs were tunnelled into natural caves. At other times, as at the anchorage of Is-Salini on the north of the island, they were dug into the sides of a quarry (Buhagiar 1986, 338–350). A more significant quarry cemetery complex is Abbatija tad-Dejr (Buhagiar 2014, 197–211), where the main catacomb is unique for the regularity of its layout, the quality of its finish, and the marble rendering of the canopied tombs. The superior importance of this necropolis was emphasised by a monumental approach consisting of a colonnaded building with a mosaic floor.

## Painted decoration

The catacombs are not remarkable for their wealth of decoration but if we judge them only from the state in which they survive, we run the danger of forming an exaggerated idea of austerity. Fragments of paintings survive only in the cemeteries of Melite, but daubs of paint in several other burial sites suggest that painting tombs was not an uncommon practice. What little survives is of iconographic and art historical interest. The artists were, as was normal in sepulchral contexts, of varying skill. Some were presumably interior decorators in above-ground houses. The technique employed can loosely be called fresco, but in actual fact most paintings were produced *a secco* on a smoothened rock surface that had been rendered with a cement compound of ground pottery and lime. The subject matter is normally restricted to symbolic or purely decorative motifs. Old and New Testament scenes are absent. Figure painting is limited to two individuals. The better known, on the platform of a canopied tomb in the major Cemetery of St Paul, shows a person of undetermined sex sitting on a stool and resting his/her hands on a pillar-like object. Above it is a common Greek farewell salutation and an apparent anchor, perhaps a symbol of hope. The second painting (now lost) belonged to a canopied tomb and represented a diminutive standing figure (63.5 × 27cm) with the one surviving hand uplifted in prayer. This suggests an Orant; the Orant featured prominently in Early Christian iconography and is thought to represent the deceased in heavenly paradise. The painting is known from a rough sketch and a few scribbled notes by Themistocles Zammit who excavated the catacomb in 1905 (Field notes of Themistocles Zammit: 1 1905–1907, 12–13).

The painted scenes in this and other tombs reflects a knowledge of the linear style of interior decoration fashionable in the Late Imperial period (second–third century AD), which depended for effect on the intelligent application of a linear programme that divided the painted surface into a field of geometric shapes. In the Roman catacombs it was extensively used for the decoration of burial chambers (*cubicula*) and their *arcosolium* tombs (Liversidge 1963, 109). In Malta, the most notable surviving example is a canopied tomb in Hypogeum 2 in the St Agatha cluster where two birds, one a probable dove and the other an unknown species, feature in ornate frames on either side of the canopy. Two festive roses are painted inside the tomb. A neighbouring semi-detached canopied tomb had a now largely vanished painting of two genii carrying a plaque with a four-line Greek inscription commemorating a certain Leonias who was buried at an unknown date before the calends of September. Only a few daubs of paint survive. The genii were already in a bad state in 1910 when Becker saw them; he published a photograph but had to retrace the outlines of the figures to make them legible (Becker 1913, 223, pl. 2).

The most important surviving painting is in the seemingly ritualistic aedicule fronting the funerary table in Hypogeum 3 (discussed above) of the St Agatha cluster. It represents a large scallop shell (the symbol of life beyond the grave), beneath which two doves holding a flowering branch saunter solemnly in the direction of drinking cups (*proculae*), between which is the Chi-Rho monogram with an alpha and omega. The painting (Fig. 11.8) seems to be an allegory of the nourishment (*refrigerium*) of the soul in heavenly paradise. The outlines of a dove with an olive branch survive from a largely vanished painting on one side of the arch of a canopied tomb in the apsed niche of one of the ritualistic tables in the *triclinium* hall of the major Cemetery of St Paul. Two other doves, in a poor state of preservation, are painted on the front of the central canopied tomb of the nearby St Cataldus' catacomb. In 1830, another probable dove was noted in the arched surround of a window tomb in Hypogeum IV at Abbatija tad-Dejr where it accompanied a Latin inscription recording the names of several of the deceased (CIL X 7498) (Buhagiar 2014, 201–202).

*Figure 11.8: Painted aedicule with scallop shell and two doves in Hypogeum 3 in the St Agatha Cluster. Photo: K. Buhagiar.*

The potent allegorical significance of the dove provided Early Christian art with its most widely diffused iconographic symbol. Less common were the three horses painted in black outline, noted in 1973 by Director of Museums Tancred Gouder in an unpublished catacomb in the basement of a house at Tac-Caghqi (personal communication). The horse had an allegorical meaning common to different religious cultures. It was both a symbol of death and of freedom without restraint. In a Christian context it could mean life beyond the grave. On the other hand, the horses could, more prosaically, mean that the hypogeum belonged to a breeder of horses or, perhaps, that he was named Hippias or Ippolitus.

## Rock engraving

Paint was also used to highlight architectural detail. The best example is in a now inaccessible hypogeum dug into a quarry at Tal-Maghlaq on the outskirts of Qrendi and Siggiewi (Buhagiar 1986, 328–331), where the ridges of a scallop shell in the entrance apsed niche of a window tomb are painted bright red. This crisply carved shell is a notable example of rock engraving. It is surprising that the soft malleable Maltese limestone was not better exploited for rock engraving. It is only in the countryside that one encounters profuse use of carved decoration, and it is possible that the phenomenon reflects a folk tradition of ornamentation and an insular perpetuation of the Phoenician-Punic legacy. The catacombs of Melite and the harbour town on the Grand Harbour (Buhagiar 2014, 30–31) have, on the other hand, an ascetic sobriety that may reflect a more cosmopolitan Romano-Hellenistic influence. Rock carving there is often limited to a simple cross or iconographic motif in the Christian cemeteries, and to a seven-branch Menorah in the Jewish ones. Architectural ornament is also used with restraint usually on window tombs, which may have crisply carved miniature pilasters and columns. On rare occasions, the arch of a canopied tomb has a hood mould with end volutes. Scallop shells, of the Tal-Maghlaq typology, have ridges radiating from a spherical knob. In an apparent family catacomb outside Melite, investigated by Themistocles Zammit, two small roundels composed of a six-petalled floral motif seem to recall the painted roundel in the nearby Tac-Caghqi Romano-Punic tomb (discussed above) and one can conjecture a lingering Punic influence. More notable, and probably sharing a similar artistic legacy, is a more intricate roundel decoration of engraved and drilled circular motifs on the jambs of a window tomb in a wayside catacomb at Ta' Kandja on the outskirts of Mqabba (Buhagiar 1986, 321–323).

The Christian identity of the Ta' Kandja catacomb is emphasised by a prominently engraved Greek cross inscribed in a circle on the ceiling of the gallery. A similar cross is engraved in relief on the apsed head recess of a window tomb in the Tar-Raghad catacomb at Mgarr (Buhagiar 2014, 161). Less prominent rock-engraved crosses and cross monograms have been reported from several other cemeteries. Occasionally, as in the artistically refined decorative programme on the ceiling of a canopied tomb at Abbatija tad-Dejr (Buhagiar 2014, 205–206), they may be accompanied by an alpha and omega and a Chi-Rho monogram. More vernacular, but interesting for their different typologies, are the cross monograms in the Tal-Liebru hypogeum near Safi (Buhagiar 1986, 250–256), but there are doubts as to their date and it is possible they belong to a later medieval period when the site might have been used by an ascetic coenobitic community of Greek monks (Buhagiar 2007, 94).

Palm fronds, allegorising Victory over Death, are another potential indication of Christianity but this may not always be the case because the symbol was borrowed from the Greco-Roman world. They are encountered in several catacombs, notably Abbatija tad-Dejr, Hal Resqun and Tal-Liebru (Buhagiar 2014, 186). A palm tree with six fronds is, in addition, painted in an extension to the Tac-Caqghi catacomb with the Neo-Punic incantation, in what can arguably be an early Christian context (Buhagiar 1986, 190). In the Jewish catacombs, the seven-branched Menorah is usually prominently engraved above the entrance (Buhagiar 2011). There are a number of variants. Sometimes they are represented on a three-legged stand or, less commonly, as stylised seven-branched twigs. In Catacomb 13 in the St Paul and St Agatha cluster, they are rudely scratched on a canopied tomb, but the catacomb also contains a boldly engraved Menorah between the headrests of an *arcosolium* tomb.

A bestiary of symbolic birds and quadrupeds has greater iconographic appeal. The rock engraving is sometimes given an ochre fill to make it stand out. This is the case with two birds in catacomb 3 in the St Paul and St Agatha cluster where one of the fowl, a quail or perhaps a peacock, is skilfully rendered and its plumage highlighted with daubs of red ochre and black charcoal. Two large birds feeding a fledgling, in the wayside catacomb of Hal Resqun, Gudja (Fig. 11.9) (Buhagiar 1986, 246–249), seem to represent the well-known allegory of the pelican, an early symbol of the Eucharistic mystery, but the birds have peculiarities. One wears a branched horn like a stag's antler while the other has an apparent tail and four legs. It is possible that the creatures fuse into one iconographic motif the Early Christian symbols of the pelican and the stag. A similar synthesis of different allegories is repeated in two instances in the Salini Bay necropolis. The first, in catacomb 5, shows a quadruped in the act of grazing or drinking. A stag has been suggested (Musgrave 1979, 97), but the antlers are missing and a lamb appears more probable. The second, in tomb 15, is more enigmatic. This is a small engraving (*c.* 21cm high) which seems to represent a biped above which is a Chi-Rho monogram with an alpha and omega. Often thought to be a lamb (Lewis 1977, 148; Musgrave 1979, 92), it is hybrid creature with a humped back and an elongated snout that looks like a bird's beak. Its closest parallels are the Hal Resqun birds and it possibly has a close allegorical affinity (Serracino-Inglott 1964).

Two rock engravings stand out because of the presence of human forms that have the appearance of Orant figures. The first, deeply engraved on the entrance niche of a burial chamber at Xaghra ta' Santa Duminka, on the outskirts of Zabbar and Kalkara, has a stylised head with two outstretched arms emerging from a scallop shell (Fig. 11.9) (Buhagiar 2014, 191–195). The second, above the entrance to a burial chamber in the aforementioned Hal Resqun catacomb, is more complex. It shows three humanoids with globular heads and outstretched arms, who share the crammed space with a menagerie of quadrupeds, fowl and fish (Fig. 11.9). For economy of space some of the figures are engraved back to back and upside down. Themistocles Zammit interpreted this engraving as the biblical account of God's creation of the world (T. Zammit 1934, 189–195). Stevenson (1978, 63) suggested it was the 'naming of the

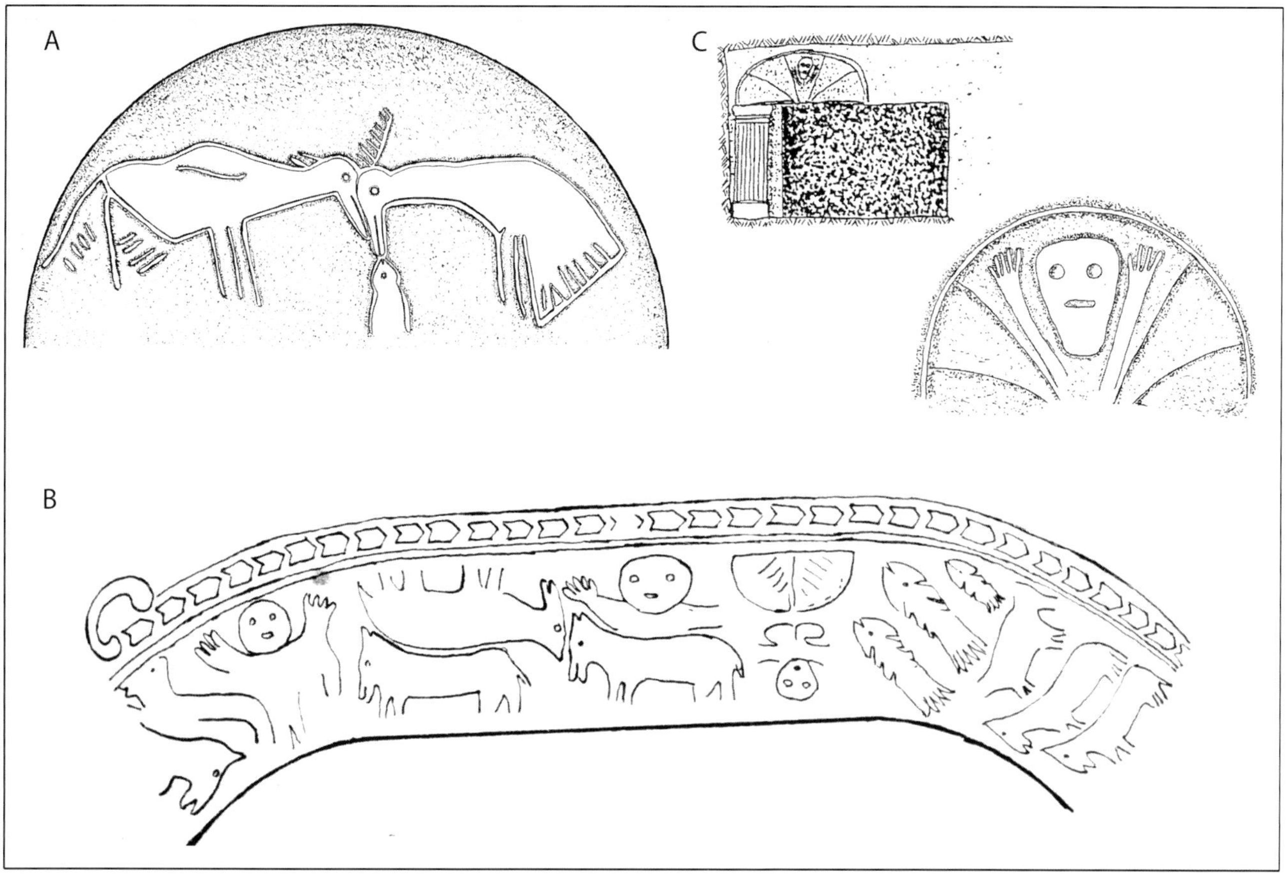


*Figure 11.9: Rock-engravings in the Late Roman and Byzantine hypogea a) Two birds feeding a fledgling, Hal Resqun hypogeum, b) Heavenly Paradise with Orants, Hal Resqun hypogeum. Orant emerging from a scallop-shell, Xaghra ta' Santa Duminka (after Buhagiar 2014).*

animals'. The upraised hands suggest, on the other hand, Orants while the menagerie is a probable allegory of the heavenly paradise as often represented in North African tomb mosaics, such as those from Tabarka and Kelibia in the Bardo Museum, Tunis. The Santa Duminika and Hal Resqun Orants are stylistically related. They share the same minimalist iconography and stylisation. Only the head and arms are represented. The heads have large mouths and saucer-like eyes but no nose, and the number of fingers varies from one hand to the next. They seem to point to a native style rooted in the Punic tradition that produced the Tac-Caghqi apotropaic humanoid. It may be no coincidence that the Santa Duminika Orant finds its closest affinity with the Monte Sirai figure stele in the Cagliari Museo Archeologico Nazionale discussed above.

Less visually stimulating but of greater socio-anthropological interest are engravings of tools that throw light on the trades and professions of the deceased. Farming tools predominate. The most interesting, in catacomb 16 in the St Agatha cluster, can only be studied from plaster casts in the St Agatha Museum, Rabat, because the catacomb is now inaccessible (Buhagiar 1986, 91). They include two varieties of sickle (*falx*) one of which, shaped like a curved knife with a short handle, is presumably the *falx strumentaria* or *messoria*. The second is longer and has a less pronounced curve but an equally short handle. Other tools include a two-pronged rake (*rastrum*), which could be used as a winnowing fork or to break large clods left by the plough when land was tilled. Two tools are difficult to identify. One may be a heavy type of hoe, perhaps a *ligo* or *bidens*, such as those used to tear up roots before land was worked. The other may be a ploughshare (*buris*), an essential part of the plough (*aratrum*) that could also in itself be used as a rudimentary plough. The Tac-Caghaqi catacomb with the Neo-Punic incantation has farming tools on the sealing plugs of two burial cubicles. They are engraved in relief and include a hoe and two sickles (Buhagiar 1986, 186–189).

Fourteen apparent surgical instruments engraved on the aforementioned plug door to a burial chamber in catacomb 3 of the St Paul and St Agatha cluster (Cassar 1974, 89–93) seem to mark the resting place of a *collegium* of physicians. They closely resemble a relief in the Roman catacomb of Praetextatus. Six large quarrying tools in the apsed niche of a ritual table in catacomb 23 of the St Paul and St Agatha cluster (Buhagiar 1986, 143) suggest that the neighbouring tomb was owned by a fraternity of quarrymen or stonemasons; Harrison Lewis proposed grave-diggers (*fossori*) (Lewis 1977, 148). Twenty-seven tools on a window tomb in a catacomb at Ghar Barca, investigated at the turn of the twentieth century, were associated by Themistocles Zammit with the trade of a tinsmith (Zammit 1931a; Buhagiar 1986, 200–201). This catacomb is now destroyed. A boat on a canopied tomb in Jewish catacomb 14 in the St Paul and St Agatha cluster may suggest a sailor or perhaps a merchant who plied his trade between Malta, Sicily and beyond (Buhagiar 2011, 88–89). The same may also be true of another boat with lateen sails at Abbatija tad-Dejr (Buhagiar 2014, 207).

### The epigraphic legacy

The corpus of known inscriptions from cemeteries amounts to a total of 39 texts, often very fragmentary (Buhagiar 1986, 392–401). Eighteen are Greek, fifteen Latin, and six Neo-Punic. The preponderance of Greek is indicative of a Hellenistic cultural bias. They are normally either scratched on the cement rendering of tombs or scribbled in red ochre paint on walls and sealing slabs. Only rarely are they engraved. The corpus includes four inscriptions on marble slabs and one on a lead plaque. The Christian and Jewish texts cover a time range from approximately the late fourth to the late sixth/early seventh centuries. They are, in the majority, simple farewell messages sometimes including the name and age of the deceased. Only a handful provide further information. One commemorates a kind Christian doctor named Domesticos (CIG, IV. 941). Another, deeply engraved in the aforementioned Jesuits Hill catacomb, records the sale of the burial plot from Zosimetis and Anicetos (CIG, IV. 9450). Of greater interest is a painted text on an *arcosolium* tomb in Jewish catacomb 13 in the St Paul and St Agatha cluster that records the resting place of the head of a synagogue (*gerousiarch*) and his wife Eulogia 'the elder' (*presbytera*) (Buhagiar 2011, 82–84). The most explicitly Christian text is deeply engraved in a catacomb in St Thomas Bay, Marsascala (Buhagiar 1986, 268). It reproduces the well-known verse from *Acts* III:6–7 (The Holy Bible): In NOMINE DNI HIS XI SURGES ET AMBLAS ('In the name of Jesus Christ, get up and walk') followed by an invocation that proposes a prayer formula popular in Early Christian Numidia: DNE SALBU ME FAC ('Lord save me') (Cabrol and Leclerq 1931, 1339).

### Architectural decoration

The use of marble for architectural enhancement has been reported from a number of catacombs. The most important is the main catacomb at Abbatija tad-Dejr where fragments of marble slabs, some still glued to the tombs, were noted in 1926 (Buhagiar 2014, 199). The stone was presumably reutilised. The Maltese islands are composed of sedimentary rocks and marble was a costly imported material several times recycled. In one of the catacombs near the church of St Cataldus outside Melite, a marble slab reutilised as a step contained a fragment of an inscription composed of letters, which Themistocles Zammit described as 'deeply engraved and beautifully shaped' (MAR 1910–1911, 9–10). Less common were terracotta floor tiles such as were used in the ritual table hall of catacomb 24 in the St Paul and St Agatha cluster (Becker 1913, 30–31). Ornate screens (*transennae*) may have been used in the larger catacombs to segregate areas of the cemetery. Their presence is suggested by rock engravings in imitation of latticed screens at Abbatija tad-Dejr (Buhagiar 2014, 205–206), Qasam il-Fawwara (Buhagiar 1986, 250), and other sites. The latticed motif is also recorded on a fragment of a now lost limestone slab that Becker (1913, 12, 110, 213) thought to be part of an altar, but which was more probably a surviving element of the lid of a sarcophagus. Becker perceptively called such motifs 'pseudo-transennae'. It is likely that he was thinking of Sicily where the remains of latticed screens have been noted in several catacombs (Agnello 1970, 233).

### Locking devices

One final consideration is the locking devices that secured the entrance to a catacomb and its burial chambers. Reference has been made to the bulky monolithic plugs that tightly fitted in the window-doors of burial cubicles. In Jewish catacomb 10 in the St Paul and St Agatha cluster, the entrance to the principal burial chamber was closed by a stone pivot door (137 × 66 × 18cm) cut from a single piece of hard coralline limestone and fitted with locking arrangements (Fig. 11.10). Such doors were common in Maltese Late Roman and Early Christian catacombs, but this is the only surviving *in situ* example. Further evidence of stone pivot doors is found in several other catacombs of suitable size. When the entrance opening was too large, stone doors were presumably replaced by strong wooden substitutes. This probably happened in the major Cemetery of St Paul where the entrance (107 × 288cm) could not be securely fitted with a stone door. In catacomb 3 in the Salini Bay necropolis small socket holes (3cm in diameter) suggest a wooden door that turned on iron pins. Approximately 20 catacombs are known with evidence for pivot doors of either stone or wood (Buhagiar 1986, 28). In some instances, such as catacomb 3 in the St Paul and St Agatha cluster, the ceiling at the back of the entrance was purposely heightened to allow the massive door to swing with ease.

*Figure 11.10: Stone pivot door to burial chamber in Hypogeum 10 in the St Paul and St Agatha Cluster. Photo: K. Buhagiar.*

## Conclusion

Archaeological and epigraphic data suggest that the rock-cut tombs and catacombs discussed in this study remained in use during most of the early Middle Ages. At a late stage in their development, around the sixth/seventh centuries, burial chambers in the major Melite cemeteries and possibly also in the Salina Bay necropolis were re-cut as Byzantine oratories (Buhagiar 2014, 230–235). Some cemeteries may have remained in use until the Muslim conquest of AD 870, but secure evidence is lacking. Following the Christian reconquest of 1127, communities of anchoritic Greek-rite monks migrating from the kingdom of Sicily squatted in some of the sites, which they used for coenobitic activities re-cutting burial chambers into ritualistic prayer halls that they decorated with icons of saints (Buhagiar 2005, 58–80). The most eloquent evidence for their activities comes from the cave-church in the St Agatha complex of catacombs and the two oratories at Abbatija tad-Dejr (Buhagiar 2005, 63–67; 2014, 202–208), both in the Melite area. The same coenobitic activity in the cave tombs and rock-cut cemeteries of Sicily has been studied and published by Aldo Messina (1979, 1994, 2001), who has also discussed the cultural affinity between Maltese and Sicilian cave-churches (Messina 1990, 109–120). The Greek monks, influenced by Near Eastern monasticism, especially Egyptian and Syrian, also introduced the practise of rock-cut churches that were sometimes, as in the case of Santa Maria tal-Virtú outside Melite, re-cut from tombs or expanded from natural caves. Cave-churches were scattered in several rural districts but were especially frequent in the rocky terrain of north Malta. Some, such as the cave-church of the Virgin at Mellieha, acquired a powerful cultic reputation (Buhagiar 2005, 63–67).

The adaptation of tombs and other burial places into cave settlements became common practice. Cave dwelling was a major phenomenon of late medieval and early modern Malta and was remarked upon by travellers to the island. The Bingemma ridge in the north of Malta is a good case study for the reutilisation of Late Roman and Early Christian tombs as places of habitation and stables for farm animals (Buhagiar 2005, 40–54). Another important but understudied site is Ta' Giampula on the outskirts of Rabat and Siggiewi, where a catacomb or perhaps a tomb cluster was drastically re-cut, first possibly for coenobitic activity and subsequently as a dwelling for farmers and their livestock. Such coenobitic and agricultural activities provided a new lease of life to these Late Roman and Early Christian burial places. Although this involved drastic re-cutting and structural modifications, it helps perpetuate an essentially Levantine tradition of rock-cut architecture and natural cave use introduced by the Phoenicians, into a characteristically Maltese late medieval phenomenon.

## References

### *Abbreviations*

CIG: Corpus Inscripionum Graecarum (1828–1877) 13 vols.
IG: Inscriptiones Graecae founded by Theodore Mommsen in 1847–1994. 49 vols.
MAR: Museum Annual Report, Valletta
MAV: Museum of Archaeology, Valletta
STM: Sunday Times of Malta

Adriani, A., 1966. *Repertorio d'arte dell'Egitto-greco-romano*, Scrie C. I II: Palermo: Universita di Palermo.

Agnello, G., 1970. Le catacombe di Sicilia e di Malta e le loro caratteristiche strutturali. *In*: *L'architettura a Malta dalla preistoria all'ottocento: Atti del XV congress di storia dell'architettura – Malta, 11–16 settembre 1967*. Rome: Centro di studi per la storia dell'architettura, 213–235.

Baraal I Altet, X., 1978, Mensae et repas funéraire dans les necropolis d'époque Chrétienne de la peninsula ibérique: Vestiges archéologiques. *In*: *Atti del IX Congresso di archeologia christiana, Rome 1975* II. Vatican City: Istituto pontificio di Studi di Archeologia Christiana, 198–256.

Becker, E., 1913. *Malta Sotteranea: Studien zur Altchristlichen und* Jüdischen *Sepulkralkunst.* Strasbourg: Heitz.

Becker, E. 2000. *Malta Sotterranea. Studies of its Early Christian and Jewish sepulchral art.* Transl. and ed. K. Fenech. Malta: Midsea Books.

Bek, L., 1983. Questiones Conviviales – The idea of the *triclinium and* the staging of the convivial ceremony from Rome to Byzantium. *Analecta Romana, Instituti Danici*, XII, 81–107.

Borg, V., 1986. Malta and its Paleochristian heritage. *In*: *Malta Studies of its Heritage and History.* Malta: Mid-Med Bank Ltd., 47–95.

Borg, V. and Rocco, B., 1976. L'Ipogeo di Tac-Caghki a Malta. *Sicilia archeologica - Rassegna. Periodica di studi, notizie e documentazzione a cura dell' E P T di Trapani*, Year V (18–19–20), 61–74.

Buhagiar, M., 1986. *Late Roman and Byzantine Catacombs and Related Burial Places in the Maltese Islands.* BAR International Series 302. Oxford: British Archaeological Reports.

Buhagiar, M., 2005. *The Late Medieval Art and Architecture of the Maltese Islands.* Malta: Fondazzjoni Patrimonju Malti.

Buhagiar, M. 2007, *The Christianisation of Malta. Catacombs, Cult Centres and Churches. Malta to 1530.* BAR International Series 1674. Oxford: British Archaeological Reports.

Buhagiar, M., 2011. The Jewish catacombs of Roman Melite, *The Antiquaries Journal* 91, 73–100.

Buhagiar, M. 2014. *Essays on the Archaeology and Ancient History of the Maltese Islands: Bronze Age to Byzantine.* Malta: Midsea Books.

Cabrol. F. and Leclercq, H., 1931. *Dictionnaire d'archéologie chrétienne et de liturgie,* vol. IV part II (15 volumes 1907–1953). Paris: Letouzey et Ane.

Cassar, P. 1974. Surgical instruments on a tomb-slab in Roman Malta. *Medical History* 18, 89–93.

Di Vita A., 1978. L'Ipogeo di Adamo e Eva a Gargaresc. *In*: *Atti del IX congress internazzionale di archeologia Christiana, Rome 1975.* Vatican City: Civilta Cattolica, 196–256.

Ferrua, A. 1949. Antichità Christiana: Le catacombe di Malta. *Civiltà Cattolica* 3(2381), 505–515.

Février, P.A., 1976. Naissance d'un art chrétienne, iconographie et histoire. *In*: A. Falon, ed. *Le dossiers de l'Archéologie* 18 (sept–oct 1976). Paris: Edicis, 18–33.

Février, P.A. 1978. Le culte des morts dans le communites chrétiennes durant le IIIe siècle. *In*: *Atti del IX congress internazzionale di archeologia christiano Roma 1975* I. Vatican City. Civilta Cattolica, 211–274.

Field Notes of Themistocles Zammit. Unpublished, MAV.

Frendo, H., 1997. *Attard. The Life of a Maltese Casale.* Malta: Arrard Local Council.

Gentili, G.V., 1954. *La villa imperiale di Piazza Armerina.* Rome: Universita di Studi.

Gselle, S., 1901. *Les monuments antiques de l'Algerie* II. Paris. Imprierie Franchise.

Giuntella, A.M., Borghetti, G. and Stiaffini, D., 1985. *Mensae e riti funerari in Sardegna.* Taranto: Istituto Pontificio di Archeologia Cristiana.

Gouder, T.C. 1978. Phoenician Malta. *In*: *Heritage: An Encyclopaedia of Maltese Culture and Civilisation* I. Malta: Midsea Books, 173–186.

Kjaergaard, J., 1984. From *Memoria apostolorum* to *basilica apostolorum.* On the Early Christian cult-centre on the Via Appia. *Analecta Romana Instituti Danici* XIII, 25–27.

Lewis, H., 1977. *Ancient Malta. A Study of its Antiquities.* Bucks: Colin Smythe.

Liversidge, J.L., 1963. Wall painting and stucco. *In*: M. Hening, ed. *A Handbook of the Visual Arts of the Roman World.* Oxford: Phaidon, 97–115.

Livy. *History of Rome*, Volume VIII. Books 28–30. Transl. F.G. Moore. The Loeb Classical Library 381. Cambridge, MA: Harvard University Press.

Malone, C., Stoddart, S., Bonnano, A. and Trump, D., eds., 2009. *Mortuary Customs in Prehistoric Malta. Excavations at the Broctorff Circle at Xaghra (1987–94).* Cambridge: McDonald Institute Monographs.

Messina, A., 1979. *Le chiese rupestri del Siracusano.* Palermo: Istituto Siciliano di Studi Bizantini e Neoellenici.

Messina, A., 1990, Trogloditismo medieval a Malta. *Melita Historica* X(2), 109–119.

Messina, A., 1994. *Le chiese rupestri del Val di Noto.* Palermo: Istituto Siciliano di Studi Bizantini e Neoellenici, Monumenti 4.

Messina, A., 2001. *Le chiese rupestri del Val Demone e del Val di Mazara.* Palermo: Istituto di Studi Bizantini e Neoellenici, Monumenti 7.

Moscati, S., 1988. Stelae. *In*: S. Moscati, ed. *The Phoenicians.* Milan: Bompiani.

Musgrave, G.H., 1979. *Friendly Refuge. A Study of St Paul's Shipwreck and his Stay in Malta.* Sussex: Heathfield Publications.

Napoli, M. 1970. *La Tomba del Tuffatore.* Bari: Ente per il turismo di Bari.

Pace, A., ed., 2000. *The Hal Saflieni hypogeum 4000 BC–2000 AD.* Valletta: National Museum of Archaeology.

Sagona, C., 2002. *The Archaeology of Punic Malta.* Leuven: Peeters.

Sammartin, P. and de Palol, P. 1972. Necropole paleochristiana de Cartagenia. *In*: *Atti del VIII. Congresso di archeologia Cristiana Barcellona 1969.* Vatican City–Barcelona: Istituto Ponificio di Archeologia Cristiana, 447–458.

Serracino-Inglott, G., 1964. The Salina necropolis. *Sunday Times of Malta.* 26 January 1964.

Spano, G., 1943. *La tomba dell'aedile C. Vittorio Prisco di Pompeii.* Atti della Real Accademia. Memorie Serie VIII, Vol. III(6). Rome: Istituto Ponificio di Archeologia Cristiana.

Stevenson, J., 1978. *The Catacombs. Rediscovered Monuments of Early Christianity.* London: Thames and Hudson.

Trump. D., 2002. *Malta Prehistory and Temples.* Malta: Midsea Books.

Vassallo, C., 1876. *De monumenti antichi nel gruppo di Malta. Cenni storici periodo fenicio ed egizio.* 2nd edn. Malta: Government Printing Office.

Wolski, W. and Berciu, I., 1973. Contribution au problem des tombes romaines a dispositive pour les libations funeraires. *Latomus. Revue et collection d'études latines*, XXXII, 356–402.

Zammit, C.G., 1940. I triclini funebri nelle catacomb di Malta. *In*: *Rivista di archeologia Cristiana* XVII. Rome: Istituto Pontificio di Archeologia Cristiana, 204–210.

Zammit, T., 1931a. The Maltese rock-cut tombs of a Late Pre-Christian type. *Bulletin of the Museum* (Valetta Museum), 1/3.

Zammit, T., 1934. An early Christian rock-tomb on the Hal Resqun Birdle Road at Gudja. *Bulletin of the Museum* (Valetta Museum) 1/4.

# Chapter 12

# Investigating cave dwelling in medieval Malta (AD 800–1530)

*Keith Buhagiar*

*The roots of Maltese high medieval cave dwelling probably lie in the twelfth and thirteenth centuries, and was the result of new attitudes adopted following the Norman conquest of 1127. A strong cave dwelling tradition during this period appears to reflect a coordinated effort at increasing the hydrological and agricultural output of specifically designated countryside areas of the Maltese archipelago. Considering the geographic proximity of Malta to southeast Sicily, it is probable that most influences filtered into Malta through direct contact with the neighbouring Sicilian island. This chapter seeks to investigate the Maltese medieval agricultural estate, or giardino, development as well as the closely-knit clusters of rock-cut dwellings and their adjoining cave churches. The water supplies of many giardini were obtained from a series of humanly excavated aquifer galleries, a number of which subscribe to qanat-type water extraction systems.*

## Introduction

This chapter examines the emergence of Maltese medieval cave dwelling by considering artificial caves utilised for both human habitation and religious worship, as well as cave typology, and the hydrological and agricultural infrastructure that enabled these rock-cut settlements to exist. The cave-dwelling phenomenon was widespread in the Mediterranean throughout the medieval period wherever environmental conditions proved favourable. Arid and semi-arid areas that suffered from a lack of timber, but offered plentiful natural rockshelters and an abundance of easily quarried stone, were instrumental in conditioning a type of architecture that was entirely stone-based in addition to encouraging cave-dwelling. For centuries during the high and late medieval period (the late tenth century to the first half of the sixteenth century), the Maltese archipelago was intimately drawn into the Sicilian sphere of influence. The archipelago's compact size and geographical proximity to its much larger neighbour directly contributed in placing Malta within the Sicilian orbit (Dalli 2008, 245). In fact, it is probable that most influences discussed below filtered into Malta through direct maritime contact with the south-eastern Sicilian region. Not all cave units included in this chapter can be directly linked to the high medieval period, but most can be considered representative of the nature of Maltese cave-dwelling during the period under investigation.

As the timeframe covered by the 'early', 'high' and 'late' medieval terminology employed in this chapter lacks standardisation, an explanation within the context of the Maltese medieval historical framework is necessary. 'Early medieval' encompasses the mid-sixth to the tenth century and includes the Byzantine and Early Muslim periods. 'High medieval' comprises the late tenth to the early thirteenth century and, in a local chronological framework, involved the Late Muslim and Norman periods. 'Late medieval' encompasses the late thirteenth century until the arrival of the Hospitaller Knights of the Order of St John in Malta in 1530. For data on Maltese caves and the utilisation of other subterranean spaces for the period preceding AD 800, see M. Buhagiar in this volume.

## Geological, hydrological and climatic context

The Maltese archipelago lies in the central Mediterranean Sea south of Sicily (Fig. 12.1). Its largest islands listed in descending order according to size are Malta, Gozo and Comino. The island of Malta, which is central to this paper's discussion, has a surface area of 153 sq. km and has a maximum length and width of 27.4km and 14.5km

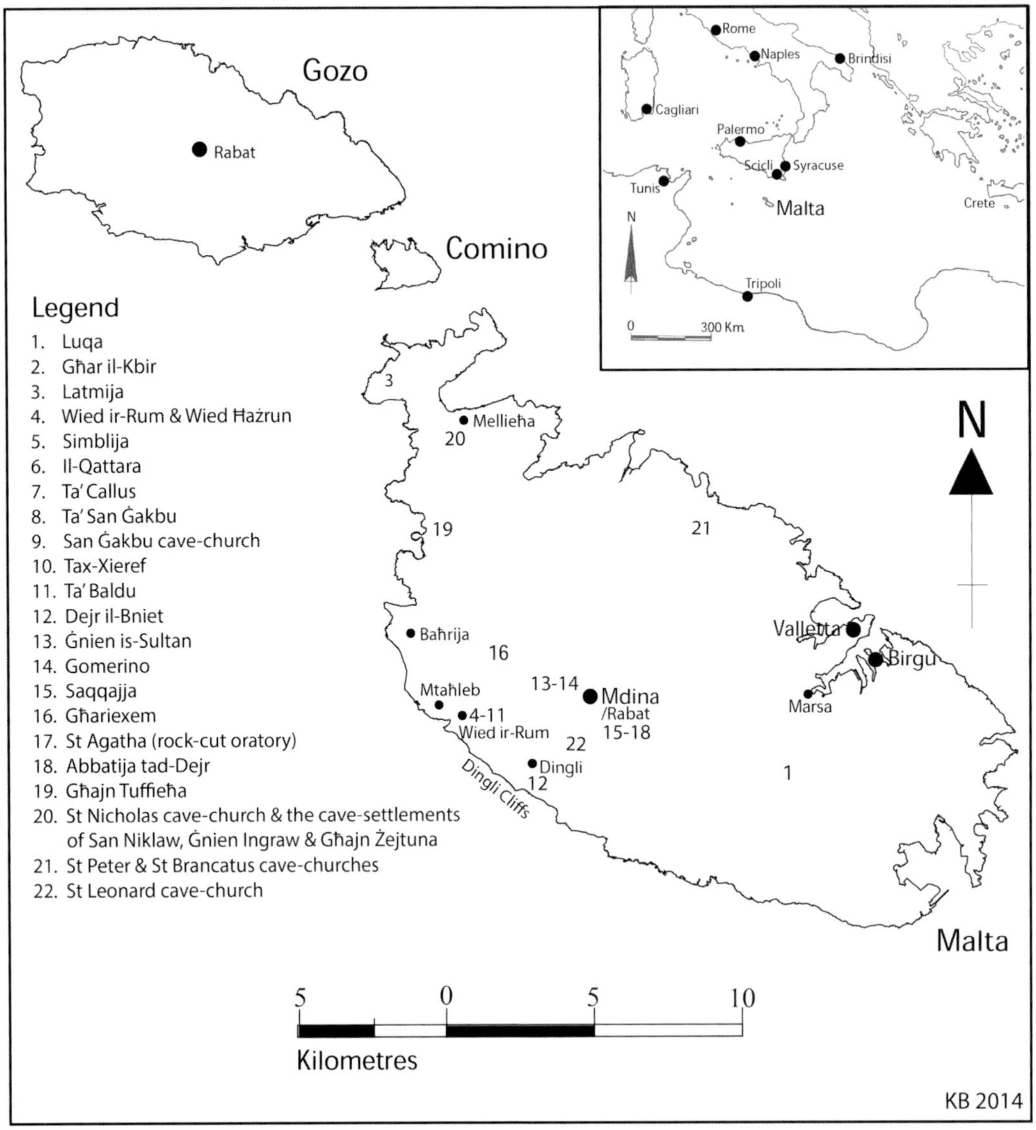


*Figure 12.1: Map of the Maltese archipelago showing the spatial distribution of place-names mentioned in the text.*

respectively. Geological deposits are almost exclusively sedimentary in formation and four distinct rock layers constitute the basic geology. When not disturbed by land faulting, the horizontal stratification from bottom to top consists of: (1) Lower Coralline Limestone; (2) Globigerina Limestone; (3) Blue Clay; and (4) Upper Coralline Limestone (Bowen-Jones *et al.* 1961, 25; Zammit-Maempel 1977, 18; Pedley *et al.* 2002, 35). Exposed Lower Coralline and Globigerina Limestone deposits mainly cover areas of central and southern Malta. However, it was Upper Coralline Limestone and Blue Clay availability that principally determined high and late medieval cave settlement location and distribution. Upper Coralline Limestone is the youngest rock formation and is carboniferous in nature. Four subdivisions of this rock stratum have been identified. Of particular importance to the understanding of the local cave dwelling phenomenon is the Mtarfa Member, in which the majority of the caves are located. The thickness of this stratum varies from 12–16m and is composed of thickly bedded carbonate mudstones and wackstones (Debono and Xerri 1993).

From a hydrological perspective, Blue Clay is one of the most important rock horizons available locally. Blue Clay is not evenly distributed, with the greatest concentrations present in the north and north-western areas of Malta. It is due to its presence and impervious qualities that an easily accessible water table, locally referred to as the 'perched aquifer', forms at the base of Upper Coralline Limestone formations (Morris 1952, 55). Water stored above Blue Clay has been recognised as a vital and easily accessible resource since antiquity. The perched aquifer was, until the latter half of the nineteenth century, the only reliable water source available in the archipelago, even during episodes of extended drought (Sapiano *et al.* 2006, 37; Sapiano 2008, 82; Buhagiar 2012a, 157–159). Whilst Upper Coralline Limestone formations occupy *c.* 36.32 sq. km of Malta's surface area, perched aquifers occurring within this zone, cover an area of *c.* sq. 31.69 km (Morris 1952, 55). Prior to the turn of the twentieth century, a successful mode of perched aquifer water extraction was through the utilisation of a wide-ranging network of subterranean water galleries, many of which tunnel into Mtarfa Member rock outcrops in order to extract a perennial water source; these are discussed below. An alternative aquiferous source available in Malta is the mean-sea-level aquifer. This consists of rainwater that percolates down to sea level and which, due to its lesser density, settles above the heavier salt water (Bowen-Jones *et al.* 1961, 43; Sapiano *et al.* 2006, 27). Even though occasionally tapped since at least the first decades of the seventeenth century, prior to the 1870s the dynamics behind the workings of the mean-sea-level aquifer remained practically unknown. The mean-sea-level aquifer is of little or no relevance to the Maltese high and late medieval cave dwelling phenomenon (Buhagiar 2014, 89–109).

Malta's climate is typically Mediterranean and is characterised by hot dry summers and warm wet winters (Bowen-Jones *et al.* 1961, 48–49). Air temperature conditions are stable and predictable, the warmest months being July and August when temperatures occasionally soar to around 40ºC. The annual temperature range is approximately 15ºC and an average precipitation of 550mm means rainfall is insufficient and erratic creating regular drought conditions (Skinner *et al.* 1997, 188; Sapiano *et al.* 2006, 21). Data gathered between 1947 and 2004 by the Luqa meteorological station revealed that annual precipitation can vary by as much as 300 mm more, or 250mm less, than the mean rainfall (Sapiano *et al.* 2006, 21; Sapiano 2008, 80–81). Rainfall readings for the Valletta weather station date back to 1841 and enable the computation of a reliable local climatic scenario for the past two centuries. Rainfall between September and November is fairly reliable in nature and is often characterised by heavy downpours, but progressively decreases during the spring months (Park 1977, 508–509). On average, the wettest month is December. July is the driest month during which drought has been registered for most years (Bowen-Jones *et al.* 1961, 48–49). In Malta, downpours are often localised and as much as 16 per cent of the rainwater is lost as surface run-off and 40% through evaporation (Azzopardi 1995, 75; Sapiano *et al.* 2006, 22–23).

The occurrence of climate shifts in the Mediterranean region since antiquity is subject to controversy and debate (Vita-Finzi 1969; Grove and Rackham 2001; Bolle 2003; Carroll *et al.* 2012; Lionello *et al.* 2012; McCormick *et al.* 2012). Nevertheless, based on sedimentation analysis and archaeological and historical evidence, it appears that Mediterranean climatic conditions in Late Antiquity were not appreciably different from those of the present-day, and were subjected to temporary and minor wetter interludes (Vita-Finzi 1969, 112–114; Grove and Rackham 2001, 145; Bolle 2003, 22–23; Carroll *et al.* 2012, 37; Lionello *et al.* 2012, xlv–xlvi; McCormick *et al.* 2012, 169–220). Recent local sedimentary analysis and radiocarbon dating from Marsa suggest an increase in sediment erosion, possibly because of more rainfall, at around 1000 years BP. This was followed by a warmer period, which in north Tunisia resulted in rising temperatures and an increase in humidity levels, at about 900 to 700 years BP (Fenech 2007, 112). In another study, the winter mean climate reconstruction between 1500 and 1995 was attempted for the wider Mediterranean region. No drastic temperature or rainfall changes were detected even though fluctuations were registered. The coldest winter was in 1891, the warmest in 1772, the wettest in 1684 and the driest in 1609 (Luterbacher and Xoplaki 2003, 133–153; Luterbacher and Xoplaki 2006, 27–97; Camuffo *et al.* 2010, 169–199).

## Cave settlement typologies and other characteristic features

It has been observed by Wettinger that the north-western part of Malta is 'strangely bare' of known *raħal* (village) settlement sites, either due to a defect in the surviving documentation, or because the Maltese countryside had been depopulated for so long that the surviving place-names dropped their *raħal* prefix (Wettinger 1975, 190; Fiorini 1993, 118–119). Fieldwork carried out by the present author in northern and north-western Malta was, in this respect, an 'eye opener' and revealed how it was the *għar* or cave-type settlements that prevailed in these areas.

For centuries, rural inhabitants of the island lived at an almost subsistence level. Humanly excavated cave settlements, like other surviving rural structures, display a marked absence of ornamentation. Cave dwellings were conceived to be practical rather than fashionable (K. Buhagiar 2007, 114). Each cave settlement is unique, and size, asymmetry and usage create endless combinations - often the result of successful human interactions with the landscape. The inhabitants of these cave settlements did not try to conquer or destroy nature, but attuned to the challenges posed by topography. In most instances, Maltese rock-cut settlements can be regarded as a continuum rather than an addition to the landscape. Almost none are visible from above the overhanging rock under which they are located, and most are not easily identified from a distance. Unfortunately, the study of Malta's cave settlements does not come without its setbacks. Cave re-occupation and enlargement often involved the destruction of earlier occupation phases and, in the absence of stratified deposits, scientific dating is difficult.

*Figure 12.2: The karst feature settlement of Għar il-Kbir. General view of the natural rock hollow into the sides of which are excavated a number of cave units. Photo: K. Buhagiar.*

*Figure 12.3: General view of a cliff-face settlement hewn into a Mtarfa Member deposit at Baħrija. The access to most caves is screened-off by means of dry-stone wall structures. Photo: K. Buhagiar.*

There are two distinct cave settlement typologies in Malta: (a) the adaptation of a natural karst depression for settlement purposes; and (b) cliff-face settlements. Cave usage varies from cultic worship, human habitation, animal pens, storage spaces related to agricultural activities, animal-driven mills (*centimoli*) and apiaries (*mġiebaħ*). The majority of Malta's medieval cave settlements are either entirely rock-cut or at least partially extended by human intervention. Examples of karst feature settlements are Għar il-Kbir and Latmija (Fig. 12.2). Both instances involved the occupation of one or more caves hewn into the sides of an open-air, natural rock-depression (Buhagiar 1997, 64–70). Karst subsidence structures initially form by the erosion of calcium carbonate deposits, which readily dissolve through the action of rainwater and gradually lead to the formation of subterranean caves (Dolgoff 1996, 426–428; Skinner *et al.* 1997, 164; Waugh 2003, 180–181). When structural collapse takes place, this leaves a large crater-like doline feature, which in the case of Għar il-Kbir and Latmija was utilised for the purpose of cave-dwelling. The majority of Maltese karst feature cave-settlements are located in areas featuring hard Upper Coralline deposits. These geological formations frequently restricted and minimised cave enlargement.

Cliff-face settlements are located along the sides of ridges and valleys and involved the occupation of natural or artificially enlarged caves (Fig. 12.3). Most of the Maltese cave dwelling sites fall into this category, and were most commonly hewn into a surprisingly brittle Upper Coralline deposit, locally identified as the Mtarfa Member (K. Buhagiar 2007, 111–112). This formation is too friable to quarry but can be easily dug out, making the process of cave excavation and enlargement not as labour intensive and time consuming as commonly perceived. The location of most cliff-face settlements implies that their occupants possessed a sound knowledge of the local geology. Mtarfa Member deposits are characteristically located only a few metres above the perched aquifer and through the excavation of underground galleries, these cave settlements and associated arable land had access to a constant water supply (Buhagiar 2012a, 157–159). Cliff-face settlements are frequently fronted by terraces. Apart from connecting two or more adjoining caves, terraces functioned as a communal gathering place and in periods of clement weather were utilised as an outdoor extension to the limited space offered by the cave interiors (K. Buhagiar 2007, 112).

Caves frequently cluster together into units, but isolated caves containing evidence of human or animal habitation are also quite common. Dry-stone and mortared stone walls were often built across cave entrances, with an arched or square-headed doorway as the only means of access (Fig. 12.4). Dry-stone constructions frequently divided cave interiors into a series of individual spaces. Entrance walls and parts of the cave interiors were occasionally plastered and whitewashed, but the extent of this practice is not known. Narrow slits sometimes acted as windows in the external walls, but generally speaking this appears to have been an uncommon feature (K. Buhagiar 2007, 112–113).

Maltese cave settlements were commonly accessed by means of one or more well-defined footpaths, some of which had a cobbled-type surface. In areas of difficult terrain access to cave settlements was facilitated through the construction of dry-stone ramps. These were built parallel to the cliff-face and are similar in the method of construction to dry-stone walls. The gap between the cliff-face and rubble wall was commonly bridged by a soil and rubble infill and capped by a cobbled surface (Buhagiar 2012a, 160).

Two distinct types of roofing strategies have been identified. When external dry-stone walls were built at a distance of not more than *c.* 0.6m from the overhanging rock ledge, the resultant gap was bridged and sealed by means of roughly sawn, thin ashlar slabs. These rested against the rock-face at an angle that generally varies between 20° and 40°. The roofing slabs were secured in place by mortar and made watertight through the employment of a mixture of ground pottery and lime known locally as *deffun* (K. Buhagiar 2012a, 160). This type of roofing technique was an extremely practical measure that allowed for the creation of greater internal cave space. In Sicily, an identical type of roofing technique was observed by this author at Scicli and in a cave at the Monastery of San Corrado Fuori le Mura in the territory of Noto (Buhagiar 2012b, 99–100), but the extent of this roofing method in Sicily has yet to be established (Fig. 12.5).

*Figure 12.4: Exterior view of a cave dwelling unit at Baħrija. A series of rock-hewn steps facilitate access to the cave interior. Photo: K. Buhagiar.*

External walls built at a distance of over 0.7m from the overhanging cave roof were covered by means of a light roof structure (Fig. 12.5). It is unlikely that any of the light roof structures recorded by this author pre-date the first decades of the twentieth century, but the materials utilised and the construction methods employed are probably similar to those used in the high and late medieval periods. Dead vegetal material, easily obtained from the surrounding countryside, was utilised. Due to the local unavailability of timber, unrefined carob and fig tree branches were often used as load-bearing elements, normally spaced 0.6 to 0.8m apart, and bridged by large quantities of dried reeds. A thick, compact layer of hay capped the roof, presumably tied to the beams to prevent dispersal during rough weather. In sites located close to easily accessible clay deposits, it is possible that a thin clay layer lined the roofs to improve waterproofing, but there is no surviving evidence for this. Wherever a cave roof extended above and beyond the light roof structures, the resultant space was frequently utilised for the storage of agricultural produce. In a handful of instances, steps on the external wall provided access to this storage space. Only a handful of light roof structures survive relatively intact, and unless preserved and adequately safeguarded, these will soon be lost (K. Buhagiar 2007, 114).

Rectangular recesses hewn into the walls of caves were frequently utilised for storage. Notarial deeds dating to the fourteenth and fifteenth centuries that describe the furniture content of Maltese late medieval above-ground houses lead us to believe that habitable caves also contained few items of furniture: perhaps a table, door and a couple of other wooden furnishings. Maltese cave settlements were

*Figure 12.5: Cave roofing strategies: A) ashlar slabs abutting the overhanging cave roof at a cave at San Corrado Fuori le Mura in the territory of Noto, Sicily; and B) a light roof structure constructed out of reeds and other perishable materials covering a portion of a cave interior at Mtaħleb. Photo: K. Buhagiar.*

sometimes spread out on two different levels, making the best possible use of the limited space available without encroaching upon any adjoining arable land.

The rural settlement of Simblija on the outskirts of Rabat (Malta), incorporates many of the above-mentioned features (Saliba *et al.* 2002). Simblija is an example of a late medieval agricultural territory, which still survives in its embryonic form, and consists of a combination of rock-excavated and dry rubble constructions. The focal node of the settlement was an open square containing a structure probably used as a church, a subterranean animal driven mill (*centimolo*), and a cistern for the storage of rain water (NLM, Treas. A. 74, f. 136; Fiorini 2003, 15–21; Buhagiar 2005, 51–54).

Many of the elements of cave architecture described above closely parallel south-eastern and central Sicilian cave dwellings and rock-cut oratories which, over the past decade, have been investigated by this author. Many of the Sicilian caves were similarly excavated into a brittle geological deposit, visually similar to the Maltese Mtarfa Member stratum. This was noted, amongst other areas, in various cave clusters at Enna, Pantalica, Cava d'Ispica, Scicli and its surrounding countryside (Buhagiar 2012b, 98–99). Terraces in front of caves likewise feature prominently in Scicli, Cava d'Ispica and other areas of south-eastern Sicily. The same applies to rock-cut apiaries (beehives) associated with a stone-built enclosure, which so far have only been observed at Scicli. Light roof structures have similarly been noted in the Scicli-Modica area of Sicily. The principal difference between these and the surviving Maltese examples is that in the former instance, the reed framework appears to have been frequently covered by a layer of lime and capped by clay roofing tiles or *tegole* (Buhagiar 2012b, 99–101).

Recent research on Maltese high- and late-medieval landscape development has revealed how cliff-face settlements where intimately connected to fertile agricultural estates or *giardini*, purposely positioned directly beneath cave dwelling sites (Buhagiar 2014). Apart from providing shelter to farmers engaged in the cultivation of these estates, most Maltese cliff-face settlements were conveniently placed directly above artificially excavated water galleries that supplied both the settlement and agricultural estate with a constant water supply. Upper Coralline Limestone areas commonly contain garigue-type ecosystems characterised by dense, low-growing shrubs, often aromatic in nature, such as the Mediterranean Thyme (Sultana and Falzon 2002, 23–24). Garigue areas overlying cliff-face settlements commonly served the purpose of rough grazing grounds for any herds of sheep and goats reared by the cave dwellers. It should be emphasised here that the scientific dating of these subterranean units is still a *desideratum*. With most caves being occupied continuously until the first decades of the twentieth century, it is unlikely that any stratified deposits survive within these sites. Nonetheless, an analysis of the landscape context in which the caves are situated, as well as an investigation of *giardino* development, provide a reliable dating indication.

### *A retrogressive analysis of the Maltese countryside and its agricultural estates*

As there is a lack of an equivalent English term for *giardino*, in this text the original word is used throughout. Similar but inexact modern equivalents include orchards, plantations, gardens, market gardens and even small land holdings. Whilst bearing in mind that a *giardino* place name does not necessarily signify the availability of a water source, detailed investigation of the *giardini* estates of north and north-western Malta found these to frequently contain spring water sources originating from within perched aquifer galleries (Buhagiar 2014, 119–121). Furthermore, the *giardini* of north and north-western Malta commonly contained orchard plantations focussed on fruit production. The cultivation of fruit trees requires a continuous water supply and was probably concentrated in these areas due to the availability of perennial water sources. Most *giardini* were located in valleys, which apart from providing shelter from the prevailing winds, allowed gravity-fed irrigation of the water captured by perched aquifer galleries to take place.

Perched aquifer galleries are generally easily identified by their rectangular shaped rock-cut entrance, which is on average 0.8m wide and little more than 1.5m high. The average gallery length is unknown, but several recorded water tunnels may well be a few hundred metres deep. Galleries are generally found level with the highest terraced fields in a valley, with water being gravity-fed to any adjoining and/or underlying fields by means of open stone canals (K. Buhagiar 2007, 118–122).

It is not uncommon for a gallery to diverge into one or more channels. Some only carry a small trickle of water, while in others the water level is too deep to wade through, making their investigation hazardous. The accurate mapping of flooded galleries has only been possible since 2008, through the employment of an experimental, remotely operated submersible device (ROV). Equipped with video and sonar sensors, digital compass, robotic arm and a Global Positioning System (GPS) locator, video footage and sonar scans of investigated galleries have been obtained (Olstad *et al.* 2010).

Subsurface investigation is central to most archaeology-related activities, and if key *giardini* sites in Malta are scientifically excavated, these could present the medievalist with much-needed data on Malta's rural medieval landscape development. However, when little is known about the existence of archaeologically relevant features in a landscape, as is the case with Maltese *giardini*, it is best for subsurface investigations to be preceded by a proper assessment of the above-ground evidence through systematic field research. This methodological approach views the landscape as a palimpsest, in which are preserved traces of earlier patterns of occupation and usage, making it possible to identify formerly unknown archaeological remains (Roberts 1987, 91; Aston 1997, 39–40). Taking the above into consideration, and in an attempt to better contextualise the antiquity of perched aquifer galleries and the *giardino* framework within which they are located, including cliff-face settlements, this section reflects upon the principal results obtained by the implementation of a retrogressive analytical approach aimed at investigating Maltese rural landscape development (Buhagiar 2014). Retrogressive analysis involves the removal of known dated features in a landscape to gain better knowledge of its components at an earlier period (Cousins 2010, 27; Vermeulen 2004, 125–127; Oosthuizen 2006, 77–79; Rippon 2012, 3–5).

*Figure 12.6: Terraced field cultivation at Wied ir-Rum. General view of the Tax-Xieref and the Ta' San Ġakbu giardini. Photo: K. Buhagiar.*

There is no fixed starting point or agenda for this method of investigation and only on completion of a landscape study will it be known how far back one is able to go. For this approach to succeed, and to view a particular landscape from the perspective of its occupants at the time, all available/known historical data have to be utilised (Oosthuizen 2006, 77–79; Cousins 2010, 25–27).

## The rock-cut galleries of Wied ir-Rum and Wied Ħażrun

In an attempt to contextualise *giardino* development and the water management strategies practiced in rural medieval Malta, Wied ir-Rum, an extensive valley system located in the territory of Rabat (Malta), is presented as a case study. Wied ir-Rum is a river valley carved out of an Upper Coralline Limestone outcrop by rainwater action. Together with the nearby Wied Ħażrun, it is one of the most fertile districts of Malta boasting a rich biodiversity and unspoilt landscape, and is renowned for its water sources and the quality of its cultivated crops (Fig. 12.6). The life source of both Wied ir-Rum and Wied Ħażrun are a series of rock-cut galleries, hewn into the brittle Mtarfa Member deposit, which capture perched aquifer water (Fig. 12.7). The volume of retrieved water varies from gallery to gallery, but most still yield a constant water supply sufficient to allow crop cultivation during the arid summer months. Water transportation from the gallery systems is often facilitated by a shallow canal cut into the gallery floor.

*Figure 12.7: A near-horizontal gallery extracting a perennial water source in the Ta' San Ġakbu giardino at Wied ir-Rum. It is located immediately below the recently identified Ta' San Ġakbu cave-church. Photo: K. Buhagiar.*

Wied ir-Rum comprises a number of adjoining *giardini*, which in 1647 were listed as *La Kattara*, *Tal Callus*, *Ta' Scieref*, *Di Baldu* and *Di S. Giacomo* (Abela 1647, 65). The modern equivalents of these placenames are: Il-Qattara, Ta' Callus, Tax-Xieref, Ta' Baldu and Ta' San Ġakbu. According to a seventeenth-century description of Wied ir-Rum and its environs: '*Valle de' Christiani Greci, amena e piena di giardini d'ambe le parti, che rappresentano all'occhio una bellissima veduta, e somministrano al gusto buonissime frutta*' (Abela 1647, 65); 'the valley of the Greek Christians, both sides of which are crowded with *giardini*-type agricultural estates, which produce tasteful fruit and present the eye with pleasant views' (my translation). The quote gives the impression of a series of long established *giardini* dependent upon reliable water sources. Another insight into the Wied ir-Rum *giardini* and settlements can be gleaned from a detailed plan of the Mtaħleb area drawn up in 1665 (AIM, Acta Civilia, vol. 171, Case 12). The plan's main focus is on the *giardini* of the Mtaħleb district, but it also indicates the location of many of the aforementioned *giardini* at Wied ir-Rum.

The agricultural importance of Wied ir-Rum and the fact that it contained *giardini* prior to 1530 are strongly hinted at in a number of cartographic representations of Malta and other documentary sources. In two different maps of Malta produced by Antonio Lafreri and Nicolò Nelli in 1551 and 1565 respectively (Agius-Vadalà and Ganado 1994, 29; Ganado 2008), it is significant that the spatial location of the only annotated valley, captioned as *Vallone giardini*, corresponds with that of Wied ir-Rum. The maps illustrate what appears to be a watercourse passing through the valley floor and trees are depicted flanking the southern side of the valley. Wied ir-Rum is not mentioned by name, but the valley morphology and its location on the west coast of Malta, between the settlements of Tartarni and Mġarr, leave little doubt as to its identity. The same applies to another map possibly produced by Tommaso Barlacchi and also dating to 1565. From the western region of Malta, only what appears to be the Wied ir-Rum valley system is illustrated in a clear and well-defined manner (Agius-Vadalà and Ganado 1994, 29), thus indicative of a major agricultural production site.

*Cabrei* (sing. *cabreo*) documents are a collection of maps, plans of buildings and landscape views representing public or privately owned property. In a Maltese context, these were commonly used by the Knights of the Order of St John throughout the seventeenth and eighteenth centuries as an inventory of the property administered by the Order. One particular *cabreo* volume (NLM, Treas. B. 289) dating to the early seventeenth century describes the Tal-Callus *giardino* at Wied ir-Rum in the following way: '*In detto Giardino ui sono due fontane la' grande sotto il balzo dalla parte di mezzo giorno, doue la sua' gebia per dentro la' rocca, l'altra dalla parte di ponente doue ui é ancora la gebietta*' / 'In the aforementioned *giardino* there are two water springs, the larger one of which originates from a cave below the southern ravine, inside which its water collecting reservoir is placed. The other spring/fountain is located to the west and for which there is still a water reservoir' (my translation). The *per dentro la' rocca* is a clear reference to the presence of at least one rock-cut perched aquifer gallery, at the entrance of which was a subterranean water reservoir. As this description of the Tal-Callus *giardino* was not accompanied by a plan of the property, the agricultural plot in question cannot be identified with certainty. This shortcoming was fortunately offset by the availability of three different plans of the Tal-Callus estate in two other *cabrei* manuscripts produced in the first decades of the eighteenth century. One of these plans (NLM, Treas. B. 290, f. 77) has made it possible to carry out a comparative study of the field boundaries of the Tal-Callus area of Wied ir-Rum and has pinpointed the exact spatial location of the estate illustrated in *cabreo* 290. Two other plans (NLM, Treas. B. 291, ff. 86–87), which are contemporaneous with the one formerly described, might in essence be draft versions on which the more artistically elaborate *cabreo* 290 plan was based. It was through these latter manuscripts that the two *fontane* (springs) mentioned in the *cabreo* 289 manuscript were identified and located (Buhagiar 2014, 176–183). One of the springs is indicated as a square-shaped box, annotated *fontana*, on the northern side of a country path close to the north-western boundary of the Tal-Callus property. The second *fontana* flanks the southernmost extent of the property, and is clearly indicated as originating from a perched aquifer gallery. Personal field research has confirmed that both *fontane* originate from perched aquifer galleries.

Other important evidence on the Tal-Callus estate comes in the form of a deed drawn up by notary Paulo Bonello in September 1467 (Fiorini 2005, 26–27). This documents the transfer of property between Antonius Busalib and Antonius Callus, both residents of the *Civitas* (Mdina). Busalib renounced all rights over a field and a meadow at Wied ir-Rum to Callus. Callus, on the other hand, renounced his rights over half the water-yield of a *fonte aquarum* called Il-Fawwara ta' Wied ir-Rum. A brief topographical description of the property in question makes it possible to identify this landholding with the *giardino* Tal-Callus and, probably, Il-Fawwara ta' Wied ir-Rum is a reference to one of the two water sources described above.

Another water source in the neighbouring Wied Ħażrun was described in an early seventeenth-century source as:

> *dalla parte di mezzo di nella strada publica ui e una fontana la quale sebene e nel publico nulla di mezzo appartiene a detto giardino dentro li quale giardino ui e anco una gebietta che racoghe l'acqua di detta fontana per seruitio di detto giardino.* (NLM, Treas. A. 74, f. 136)

> in the middle of the public road, outside the aforementioned *giardino* there is a spring which provides this *giardino* with a water supply which is harvested in a reservoir. (My translation)

Field research associated this *fontana* with a perched aquifer gallery located in the upper valley section of Wied Ħażrun. Its name remains unknown, but investigation of the gallery interior revealed significant quantities of calcite deposits on its floor and sides that are an indication of its antiquity (Fig. 12.8).

Water gallery distribution is not only limited to the Wied ir-Rum and Wied Ħażrun localities, but also to other areas of Malta and Gozo that have the same geological stratification.

*Figure 12.8: Interior view of a perched aquifer gallery located in the upper valley section of Wied Ħażrun. Thick calcite deposits cover the gallery floor and are an indication of its antiquity. Photo: K. Buhagiar.*

It is worth noting, however, that the largest known perched aquifer gallery concentration in the Maltese archipelago is found at Wied ir-Rum (K. Buhagiar 2007, 119–121).

## The Maltese medieval *giardino*-type agricultural estates

The picture that is emerging points decisively towards the existence of a series of well-established medieval *giardini* in Malta that were essentially determined by the presence of a constant water supply, and a number of which included rock-cut dwellings. The *giardini* of Dejr il-Bniet, Gomerino, Għajn Tuffieħa and Ġnien is-Sultan are cases in point. These were first mentioned in fourteenth-century documentation, but may have existed as early as the twelfth century. *Giardini* estates were frequently acknowledged to contain one or more *fontane* (K. Buhagiar 2014, 153–154). In medieval Latin, *fons* or *fontana* terminology can indicate the artificial tapping of an aquiferous source by means of wells or other humanly made constructions (Baxter and Johnson 1947, 177; Lockwood 1952, 279; Latham 1965, 196; Niermeyer 1976, 439). The same applies to late sixteenth- and early seventeenth-century Italian *fonte*, *fontana* and *fontanella* terminology (Florio 1598, 135, 1611, 192). Furthermore, the seventeenth-century Maltese historian, Gian Francesco Abela, mentions a number of *fontane* that flowed out of caves – an indirect reference to perched aquifer galleries (Abela 1647, 65–66). Extensive fieldwork by this writer has succeeded in the identification of many perched aquifer galleries that still supply land estates with a constant water supply. That a number of *giardini* were used in the cultivation of various crops, including fruit, during the late medieval period is revealed by a *Cancelleria Regia* entry dating to 7 June 1393 wherein the rights of the landholder over the acquired *giardini*, including the fruit produced from the land, are indicated (Fiorini 2004, 713, 715). Seventeenth-century documentation on the Saqqajja and Għariexem perched aquifer galleries at Rabat (Malta), also clearly indicates that these pre-date the Knights and can therefore be considered as being medieval water-related interventions in an agrarian landscape (Univ. 187 manuscript ff. 1–14).

## Rock-cut churches, oratories and the Siculo-Greek monastic connection

Maltese rock-cut churches can be divided into two main categories: urban and rural. Whilst the settings in which they are located are different, both share a number of common characteristics and are the product of the same religious pressures and socio-cultural circumstances. The urban churches lie within the precincts of palaeochristian hypogea and tend to show a greater preoccupation with architectural enhancement and elaboration than their rural counterparts (Buhagiar 2005, 58). Rural rock-cut churches are, in contrast, more simplistic and form an integral part of the cave-dwelling landscape in which they are located. Cave churches either form part of, or adjoin, cliff-face settlement sites and are almost exclusively excavated into Mtarfa Member rock. As is the case with the cave church dedicated to St Nicholas at Mellieħa, which gave its name to the valley below, cave churches must have been a landmark within the late medieval Maltese landscape (Fig. 12.9). The same applies to the cave churches of St Peter in the Naxxar territory and St Brancatus at Għargħur, the dedication of which was assimilated in the toponomy of the surrounding area (Buhagiar 1997, 84–86).

The dating of both urban and rural churches is a challenging issue and continuous reuse makes it improbable that any archaeologically relevant deposits survive. Rural cave churches are commonly fronted by a terrace, but in many instances these too have been disturbed, thus making the archaeological assessment of such areas a largely unproductive exercise. The assessment of cave typologies, as well as art historical analysis of preserved murals, where available, are the most reliable methods of dating. Abbatija tad-Dejr and the rock-cut oratory at St Agatha's catacombs, both at Rabat, are amongst the two most important urban cave church sites that survive. Analysis of the *sinopia* (a preliminary sketch on a wall that is about to be frescoed) of a possible Deësis (a representation of Christ making the sign of the cross, the Virgin Mary and St John the Baptist) located in the apsed niche of the east wall in Oratory I at Abbatija tad-Dejr, coupled with data provided by a nineteenth-century report on this fresco, hint at a work of art that stylistically comes from the milieu of Siculo-Norman Sicily. There, similar representations of Christ the Pantokrator are frequently encountered in the surviving rock-cut and built churches dating to between the eleventh and thirteenth centuries (Messina 1979, 49; Buhagiar 2005, 59–61).

Within the same oratory at Abbatija tad-Dejr are two other murals, probably depicting the Archangel Michael and St John the Evangelist. The icons are contained within a red frame that probably once bore the saints' names in Latin characters. The combination of Byzantine style with Latin text is another reliable dating element, even though this artistic style remained a standard practice locally until at least the fifteenth century (Buhagiar 2005, 61). Another fresco surviving in the adjoining Oratory II at Abbatija tad-Dejr is now on display at the National Museum of Fine Arts in Valletta. This shows the fusion of the Crucifixion and the Annunciation scenes. The amalgamation of these themes suggests a fourteenth-century date and parallels closely a painting at the *Grotta dei Santi at Monterosso Almo* at Ragusa, Sicily, which also seems to be contemporaneous (Messina 1979, 117). Similarly, another two Siculo-Byzantinesque icons survive in an oratory at St Agatha in Rabat (Malta). It is probable that these belonged to a more extensive fresco-cycle destroyed in the late-fifteenth or early sixteenth century to make way for a series of Late Gothic devotional images (Buhagiar 2005, 65–66).

*Figure 12.9: Dry-stone walls define the extent of the San Niklaw cave-church at Mellieħa. Traces of plastering and painted decoration survive within and a rock-cut terrace connects this enclosed area to other nearby caves. Photo: K. Buhagiar.*

Rural cave churches were of a rather intimate size, had a dimly lit interior, and were commonly accessed from a rock terrace that connected a series of two or more caves. As in the case of cave dwellings, the entrances to rock-cut churches were commonly screened off by a dry-stone wall, the only means of access being a narrow square-headed doorway. The deeply ingrained nature of cave dwellings and cave churches in northern and north-western Malta during the high and late medieval periods is best illustrated by the fact that the principal cave church of Mellieħa occupied the status of a parish church in the fourteenth century, and tended to the spiritual needs of the adjoining rock-cut settlements of San Niklaw, Ġnien Ingraw and Għajn Żejtuna (Buhagiar 2005, 72–74).

Both urban and rural cave churches were probably fitted with either masonry or wooden altars and in the case of the cave church of St Leonard in Rabat, and that dedicated to St Peter at Naxxar, there is evidence of an internal flagstone floor. In some churches a cobbled passageway facilitated access to the entrance, which was often difficult to reach. Cave church interior furnishing was probably sparse, with *dukkien* or bench accommodation sometimes cut into the rock-face along the walls. Several of the surviving churches were decorated with murals that survive in a precarious state of preservation. Like the urban cave churches, the surviving murals are Siculo-Byzantinesque in tradition and inspiration (M. Buhagiar 2007, 98).

The existence and location of a number of rural medieval cave churches faded from popular memory thus necessitating their rediscovery. A rural cave church recently identified by the author as that of San Ġakbu (St James) at Wied ir-Rum incorporates several of the aforementioned features. Access to this cave church is via a badly weathered footpath, which leads from the Ta' San Ġakbu plateau down to a terrace which connects the cave, which this study identifies as the cave church of St James, to two other caves. The most important cave is located on the westernmost part of the rock terrace and directly overlies a perched aquifer gallery. This cave is extremely well-cut, has a surprisingly high ceiling, and a floor level that is lower than that of its front terrace. The cave's entrance was originally screened off by means of a dry-stone wall and access to the interior was through a square-headed doorway. The interior refinement of this cave is remarkable, especially when considering that a sizeable portion of it, including the ceiling, was cut out of the hard Tal-Pitkal Member, Upper Coralline Limestone deposit (Fig. 12.10). The cave measures 8.05 × 6.11m and has an approximate height of 3.86m. Four animal feeding troughs flank the west and east walls of the cave and are probably the result of subsequent reutilisation of this cave. Well-defined tool marks preserved in the walls and roof hint that the layout is the result of a piecemeal development and, together with its typology, location and general setting, helped correlate it with the long-lost church of San Ġakbu.

This church was immortalised in history following the 1575 visitation report by Pietro Dusina who described it as follows:

> *Sancti Jacobi Apostoli Guedrum. Vistavit etiam Ecclesiam sub vocabulo Sancti Jacobi Apostoli, quæcaret introitibus, et rectore, pavimento, ostio, et ornamentis verum causa devotionis patroni viridariorum convicinorum in dicta Ecclesia in die festivitatis Sancti Jacobi celebrari faciunt missam, et à parte superiori intus defluit pluvia. Dominus mandavit nullo pacto in dicta Ecclesia amplius celebrari, nisi prius refectis portis ligneis, ac tecto, et pavimento restauratis.* (Dusina 1575 [1996], 168)

> Also visited the church dedicated to St James the Apostle, which is rural, and built in the place named Guedrum, which is without revenue, rector [priest], [*paved*] floor, door, ornaments, but where, because of devotion, the owners of the neighbouring orchards celebrated Mass within, on the feast day of St James; from the upper part, flows down rain. The lord [Bishop] said he would not authorise further celebrations in the church, until wooden doors, the floor and the roof were not restored. (My translation)

The San Ġakbu cave church was in a state of disrepair in the sixteenth century and it must have been deconsecrated and subsequently abandoned shortly after Dusina's visit. Particularly intriguing is a series of cross monograms carved into the west wall and ceiling including two Latin crosses and another tentatively identified as a cross potent. The assertion that the church ceiling had to undergo restoration works implies the possible presence of a light roof structure covering the outermost portion of this cave church. If this was the case, it is likely that this wooden roof was similar in typology to other light roof structures at cave dwelling units as described above. The interior of this presumed cave church closely parallels another rock-cut church dedicated to Maria di Piedigrotta at Scicli, Sicily. The importance of the cultic space at Ta' San Ġakbu is also hinted at by the presence of an underlying perched aquifer gallery. This water gallery set-up is identical to that of another late medieval cave church dedicated to St Leonard at Lunzjata. The Lunzjata gallery was partly investigated using a remotely operated submersible in 2009 and was found to be over 90m long, and possibly contains a series

*Figure 12.10: Interior view of the recently identified Ta' San Ġakbu cave-church. A dry-stone wall still partly screens the entrance and various cross monograms are carved on the cave's interior. Photo: K. Buhagiar.*

of circular shafts that connect this subterranean channel to the surface.

Even though there is no direct historical documentary evidence, it has been proposed that following the Norman reconquest of Malta in 1127, several of the Maltese cave churches were administered by Greek-rite Basilian monks (M. Buhagiar 2007, 317–338). This hypothesis is based on Sicilian and Pantellerian models where Greek-rite monks operating from rural monasteries and anchoritic stations saw to the spiritual needs of rural, often isolated, communities (Luttrell 1975, 37–38). Much of the argument centres round the meaning of the word *dejr*, which can mean either a cowshed/animal pen, or a monastic building/establishment (Wettinger 2000, 107–108). *Dejr* terminology was used all over the Islamic East, Spain and Muslim-period Sicily and is often associated with a Christian monastic establishment. Whilst making no distinction between Greek and Latin-rite clergy, Sicilian historical information favours the presence of Greek monks who carried out their evangelisation programme amongst Muslim communities of the island. The available local archaeological record does hint indirectly at the presence of Greek monasticism, but the issue is still the subject of scholarly debate and necessitates further academic investigation. So far, none of the known cave churches and adjoining rock-cut settlements can be securely associated with monastic establishments. On the other hand, of particular interest is the site of Abbatija tad-Dejr where a palaeochristian period burial complex was reutilised as a cult centre during the post-Muslim period, making it the foremost contender for a Greek-rite site at this time (M. Buhagiar 2005, 58–61, 2007, 95).

## Interpreting the evidence: making a case for the high and late medieval periods

A reconstruction of the Maltese landscape in Late Antiquity and the medieval periods remains a work in progress and the lack of concrete historic and archaeological evidence for Malta's high medieval period certainly does not help. An objective discussion of the known sources of evidence is necessary at this point, analysis of which allows some preliminary conclusions to be drawn. There is sparse documentation for ninth-century Malta, but the available archaeological and historical record hints at a clear-cut break between the Byzantine period, which ended in 870, and the Norman conquest of Malta, which commenced in 1091 but was mainly consolidated after 1127. The 870 expedition for the conquest of Malta was launched from Sicily and should probably be viewed in the context of Muslim territorial expansion following the fall of the settlement of Castrogiovanni (Enna) in 859. The Muslim conquest of Malta was marked by bloodshed and destruction, probable retaliation against the Christian inhabitants, and an orchestrated demographic resettlement programme, which included the death or exile of the local bishop, with the island or its main settlements reduced to a *hirba* or uninhabited ruin (Brown 1975, 81–84; Luttrell 1975, 21–28, 92, 100; Wettinger 1986, 90–91, 2012, 368–369; Metcalfe 2009, 25–26). Possibly the principal reason behind the Muslim conquest of Malta was not colonisation but the neutralisation of formerly Byzantine-held territory, including its military-related infrastructure.

The post-870 phase is sparsely documented and most of the tenth-century Muslim sources are silent on the period between 870 and 1048. In the latter part of the ninth century, Malta was probably located outside the main Sicilian-Ifrīqiyan shipping route. Additionally, political instability in Palermo, caused by the death of six governors within a three-year period, might have detracted attention from the newly acquired Maltese archipelago soon after its annexation within the Muslim sphere of influence (Metcalfe 2009, 26–28). One of a handful of known sources dating to this period, Ibn Hawqal, implies that Malta was an uninhabited island containing flocks of sheep, wild donkeys and an abundance of honey (Gabrieli 1961, 245–253; Dalli 2006, 27; Wettinger 2012, 369–371). According to a later source, Al Himyari, Malta was visited by ship builders because its wood was of the strongest kind, and by fishermen for the tastiness of its fish. He also mentions pine, juniper and olive trees (Brincat 1995, 11–12). It is unlikely that Malta was totally depopulated during this period (Molinari and Cutajar 1999, 9–16; Luttrell 2002, 100; Cutajar 2004, 58; Carroll *et al.* 2012, 27–38), but a drastic population decline is not improbable.

One hypothesis is that Muslim retaliation against the local population was primarily directed towards the urban centres of the archipelago, namely Mdina and Birgu in Malta, and the Citadel in Gozo. Even if an ethnic-cleansing policy was employed, it is doubtful that this would efficiently target more remote rural locations that could still provide for small communities accustomed to living at subsistence or near-subsistence level. Cliff-face settlements in remote areas of the Maltese countryside provide an excellent case in point, but the more accurate dating of most of these sites is still a *desideratum*. Anyone unfamiliar with Maltese topography and terrain would almost certainly overlook the presence of these inconspicuous cave-settlements, which blend in extremely well with the natural surroundings. Nonetheless, even if some remote rural rock-cut settlements remained in operation, the surviving inhabitants appear to have been too few in number to influence the subsequent course of events – not even leaving any trace of their existence in the spoken language (Wettinger 1986, 95). Linguistic analysis of the Maltese language excludes any signs of language stratification, with the linguistic base appearing to be of solely Arabic origin. There are also close parallels between Sicilian and Maltese toponyms, which suggest intimate Sicilian-Maltese linguistic connections (Brincat 1995, 1–7, 27; 2011, 33–62).

Historic documentary sources claim that Malta was once again repopulated by Muslims in 1048–1049, in time to ward off a Byzantine invasion – a fact that has been cautiously interpreted not necessarily as a sign of the island's depopulation in earlier centuries, but of a large-scale Muslim colonisation, which possibly took place as late as the early eleventh century (Dalli 2006, 58–62). The fact that women and daughters formed part of this wave of migration makes it improbable that the sole purpose behind the colonisation of Malta during this period was the establishment of a garrison. A number of variables may have contributed to this demographic expansion: (a) a period of economic prosperity in Sicily during the first half of the eleventh century; (b) the Sicilian civil war between the different Muslim caliphates, which commenced in 1038; and (c) fear of the Normans, whose territorial ambitions in the southern Italian peninsula made them a force to be reckoned with. The uncertainty caused by the impending Norman conquest of Sicily in the eleventh century forced a section of the wealthier Muslim families to emigrate from Sicily (Brincat 1995, 20–21; Von Falkenhausen 2002, 262; Metcalfe 2003, 28), and there is the possibility that several opted to settle in Malta.

Malta was far from a deserted place a century later when the Muslim geographer Al Idrisi speaks in terms of the archipelago as being:

> away from the island of Pantelleria at a distance of 100 miles towards the east one finds the island of Gozzo (Gozo) with a secure port. From Gozzo one goes to a small island named Kamuna (Comino). From there going eastwards one finds the island of Malta. It is large and has a sheltered place on the east side. Malta has a town and abounds in pastures, sheep, fruit and honey. (Wettinger 1986, 97)

Investment in agricultural intensification, which seemingly took place in the post-1127 period, appears to have been generally successful and succeeded in placing cotton cultivation to the forefront, an item of luxury trade, mention of which is made in a property inventory drawn up in Genoa in June 1164 (Dalli 2006, 158; M. Buhagiar 2007, 18, 40). It was during this period that a Latin garrison was presumably stationed on the island together with clergy responsible for attending to the spiritual needs of the soldiers. This probably marked the initial stages of the long drawn out Christianisation process of the island – a strategy that was finally successful during the thirteenth century, and which was possibly unduly delayed due to a strengthening in maritime ties with North Africa in the first half of the twelfth century (Luttrell 1975, 31; M. Buhagiar 2007, 82). Furthermore, it is significant that twelfth-century pollen samples retrieved from the Marsa plain adjoining the east coast of the island indicate an increase in wood, cereal and flax vegetation (Fenech 2007, 112), and appear to confirm the agricultural intensification process the island experienced during this period.

Any interpretation of Maltese landscape development must take into consideration contemporaneous developments in southern Italy and Sicily. Landscape evolution in southern Italy during the Norman period appears to have first centred on the development of *giardini*-type cultivations, then dry-farming, where agriculture is entirely dependent on the seasonal rainfall, and only at a later stage, the utilisation of waste land for rough grazing and wood gathering (Martin 2002, 19, 37). *Castra* (plural) or *castrum* (singular), small fortified settlements that were often perched on ridges and hilltops, appeared in the southern Italian landscape before the turn of the eleventh century, probably as a direct response to an increasing number of Muslim incursions. In the region of Benevento and Capua these not only provided protection, but also served as a centre of lordship and as a point of agricultural consolidation (Martin 2002, 27; Ramseyer 2006, 31). Sicily, having been exposed to Muslim influence since the mid-eighth century, offered different agricultural potential, where Muslim agricultural technology made it possible to grow citrus fruit, date palm and sugar cane (Martin 2002, 20). Reverting back to the Maltese situation, it appears that the Maltese rural economy and the administration of Crown estates were under the direct control of the urban inhabitants of the medieval Maltese capital of Mdina – the *Civitas* – which also received much of the profits (Wettinger 1982, 4).

It is possible that the fertile valleys of Wied ir-Rum and Wied Ħażrun, as well as other *giardino* areas that contained extensive field terraces, water galleries and rock-cut settlements, all formed part of this post-1127 agricultural intensification process. The majority of Maltese cliff-face cave settlements probably developed organically, closely associated with the development of *giardini* and perched aquifer galleries. In central and southern Malta, *raħal*-type masonry-built settlements dominated the late medieval landscape. Nonetheless, the near complete absence of *raħal*-type place names in the north and north-western parts of Malta can probably be explained by the fact that the exposed Mtarfa Member deposits and the easily accessible perched aquifer sources tapped by means of galleries, encouraged the inhabitants to resort to rock-cut, rather than above-ground, masonry-built, settlements.

Field terracing coupled with the hydrological intensification of an area entails a labour-intensive output, and it may take decades to completely transform a previously uncultivated landscape into an agriculturally productive one that caters for arable agriculture. Due to the availability of perennial water springs commonly originating from perched aquifer galleries, *giardini* are capable of producing a summer crop in an otherwise arid season, thus increasing the economic value of land. The Maltese *giardino* framework was possibly already in place by the thirteenth century. In 1241, the Maltese *secrezia*, administrators of royal rights and properties, received a total of 11,457 *tari* (the prevailing late medieval currency unit) from the leasing of gardens, but as the *masserie*, agricultural estates of the *curia* (the Crown), were administered directly, the exact revenue extracted is not known. Other documentary evidence reveals that in 1270 the castellan and the captain of Malta were instructed to look into the reinstatement of lands, including a *tenimentum* (estate) and 'garden' at Pwales at a place called *liburgnatum*, which had been confiscated during the reign of King Frederick II (Dalli 2006, 125–126). This hints at the presence of a *giardino* set-up at Pwales in the first half of the thirteenth century.

Malta's close ties with Sicily during the high and late medieval periods (Dalli 2008, 243–258) make it tempting to propose that perched aquifer gallery technology filtered into Malta through the archipelago's intimate ties with Sicily from the twelfth century. From the Norman period, Sicily, and presumably its smaller satellite island territories, was administered directly from the royal court, thus providing a context for organised agricultural investment (Houben 2002, 147–148). A matter worthy of consideration is that a substantial portion of appointees to Malta and landholders had a direct link with Sicily. In the 1230s, Frederick II's proctor (procurator) at Malta, Paolino de Malta, had close ties with both Malta and Sicily. Paolino de Malta was either Sicilian or Italian and in 1235 he was granted as fief the Sicilian *casale* of Stafenda – a *contrada* in south-east Sicily located between the settlements of Noto and Ispica (Luttrell 1976, 405–408). The same applies to Giliberto Abbate, Frederick II's governor in Malta, who was a member of the wealthy and influential Sicilian Abbate family from Trapani (Sciascia 1989, 1174–1181; Luttrell 1997, 3).

The timeframe for the local appearance of perched aquifer galleries is a complex matter that requires the consideration of a number of variables. In Sicily the dating of galleries is similarly problematic. The belief that this water capture infrastructure dates back to at least the Norman occupation of Sicily was confirmed by the identification of twelfth-century ceramics in a *qanat* system in Palermo (Biancone and Tusa 1997). However, Goblot advocates a ninth-century date for the introduction of these water systems in Sicily (Goblot 1979, 134; Todaro 1989, 115–117).

Fieldwork by this writer has determined the existence in Malta of two distinct types of perched aquifer galleries: (a) those containing shaft wells, which at intervals pierce the ceiling of the principal *qanat*-type gallery system; and (b) more crudely excavated perched aquifer gallery systems in which shaft wells are conspicuously absent. Field research has shown that the majority of the perched aquifer galleries containing shaft wells are either located below a principal high and late medieval settlement – as is the case with the *Civitas* and its suburb of Rabat – or are closely associated with Crown property estates. I suggest here that the perched aquifer galleries located in Crown property landholdings are the work of a specialised workforce, specifically commissioned to improve the hydrology of these designated areas during the high medieval period. In such a scenario, it is unlikely that the technical know-how necessary for the successful detection of a reliable water source and the excavation of *qanat*-type galleries containing shafts would have been available locally. In the absence of a competent local workforce, it is possible that technical expertise came from abroad, probably Sicily. Shaft-less perched aquifer galleries are in general shorter in length and are probably the work of a non-specialised workforce. Such subterranean galleries may have been purposely located in areas that already yielded small volumes of perched aquifer water, and were intended as a measure to increase water yield. Cases in point appear to be Wied ir-Rum and Wied Ħażrun where the majority of perched aquifer galleries appear to be shaft-less. It is likely that the workforce behind these systems comprised farmers, who even with a limited understanding of the local geology, could still boost the water yield of specifically designated areas.

## Conclusions

This study proposes that *giardino* development, the harnessing of perched aquifer resources via rock-cut galleries, cave settlements and cave churches are all the product of Norman or post-Norman period cultural influences and agricultural investment in Malta. All these features formed part of the same landscape transformation process, and cave settlements were strategically placed in unutilised ground within the *giardino* framework, directly above springs originating from humanly excavated perched aquifer galleries. It is hoped that the present research will lead to an increasing awareness of the archaeological potential that the Maltese countryside has to offer. None of the elements of these medieval landscapes have been scientifically dated, but comparative work as well as a retrogressive analytical approach has made it possible to link *giardino*, perched aquifer galleries and cave churches to the late medieval period. Furthermore, the investigation of Maltese cave settlements and their landscape context has brought to the fore a close relationship with neighbouring Sicily. In Sicily, a comprehensive investigation of medieval hydrological systems, and a more detailed study of cave typologies and landscape development of particular regions in the south-east of the island, are still necessary. This will undoubtedly lead to the exposure of more relevant data, allowing for better analogies between medieval Malta and medieval Sicily.

## References

### *Abbreviations*

AIM Archivum Inquisitionis Melitae
NLM National Library (Malta)
Univ. Università (Malta)

### *Unpublished sources*

AIM, Acta Civilia, vol. 171
NLM, Treas. A. 74

NLM, Treas. B. 289
NLM, Treas. B. 290
NLM, Treas. B. 291
Univ. 187 manuscript

Abela, G.F., 1647. *Della descrittione di Malta Isola nel Mare Siciliano con le sue Antichità ed altre notitie*. Malta: Midsea Books.

Agius-Vadalà, M. and Ganado. A., 1994. *A Study in Depth of 143 Maps Representing the Great Siege of Malta of 1565*, vol. 1. Malta: Publishers Enterprises Group.

Aston, M., 1997. *Interpreting the Landscape: Landscape Archaeology and Local History*. London: Routledge.

Azzopardi, A., 1995. *A New Geography of the Maltese Islands*. Malta: St Aloysius College.

Baxter, J.H. and Johnson, C., 1947. *Medieval Latin World-List from British and Irish Sources*. London: Humphrey Milford.

Biancone, V. and Tusa, S., 1997. *I Qanat dell'area centrosettentrionale della piana di Palermo', archeologia e territorio*. Palermo: G.B. Palumbo Editore, 375–389.

Bolle, H.J., 2003. Climate, climate variability, and impacts in the Mediterranean area: an overview. *In*: H.J. Bolle, ed. *Mediterranean Climate: Variability and Trends*. Heidelberg: Springer, 5–86.

Bowen-Jones, H., Dewdney, J.C., and Fisher, W.B., 1961. *Malta. Background for Development*. Durham: Dept. of Geography, University of Durham.

Brincat, J., 1995. *Malta 870–1054: Al-Himyarī's Account and its Linguistic Implications*. Malta: Said International.

Brincat, J., 2011. *Maltese and Other Languages: A Linguistic History of Malta*. Malta: Midsea Books.

Brown, T.S., 1975. Byzantine Malta: a discussion of the sources. *In*: A.T. Luttrell, ed. *Medieval Malta. Studies on Malta before the Knights*. London: British School at Rome, 71–87.

Buhagiar, K., 1997. *The Għar il-Kbir Settlement and the Cave-Dwelling Phenomenon in Malta*. Unpublished dissertation. University of Malta.

Buhagiar, K., 2007. Water management strategies and the cave-dwelling phenomenon in Late-Medieval Malta. *Medieval Archaeology* 51, 103–131.

Buhagiar, K., 2012a. Caves in context: The late medieval Maltese scenario. *In*: K.A. Bergsvik and R. Skeates, eds. *Caves in Context. The Cultural Significance of Caves and Rockshelters in Europe*. Oxford: Oxbow Books, 153–165.

Buhagiar, K., 2012b. Malta, an island satellite in the lee of Sicily: investigating the troglodytic context for the late medieval and early modern periods. *In*: I. Contino and F. Buschemi, eds. *L'insediamento rupestre di Monte S. Antonio a Regalbuto: Alle origini del Raḥal di 'Abbûd*. Enna: Università degli Studi di Catania, 95–118.

Buhagiar, K., 2014. Water Management Technology as a Contributing Factor in the Development of the Rural Landscape of the Maltese Archipelago. Making a Case for the Late Medieval Period. Thesis (PhD), University of Malta.

Buhagiar, M., 2005. *The Late Medieval Art and Architecture of the Maltese Islands*. Malta: Fondazzjoni Patrimonju Malti.

Buhagiar, M., 2007. *The Christianisation of Malta. Catacombs, Cult Centres and Churches in Malta to 1530*. BAR International Series 1647. Oxford: Archaeopress.

Camuffo, D., Bertolin, C., Barriendos, M., Dominguez-Castro, F., Cocheo, C., Enzi, S., Sghedoni, M., della Valle, A., Garnier, E., Alcoforado M.-J., Xoplaki, E., Luterbacher, J., Diodato, N., Maugeri, M., Nunes, M.F. and Rodriguez, R., 2010. 500-year temperature reconstruction in the Mediterranean Basin by means of documentary data and instrumental observations. *Climatic Change* 101(1–2), 169–199.

Carroll, F.A., Hunt, C.O., Schembri, P.J. and Bonnano, A., 2012. Holocene climate change, vegetation history and human impact in the Central Mediterranean: evidence from the Maltese Islands. *Quaternary Science Reviews* 52, 24–40.

Cousins, S.M., 2010. The Prudhoe landscape history project: a retrogressive study of the landscape history of part of Southern Northumberland. *In*: T. Faulkner, H. Berry, and J. Gregory, eds. *Northern Landscapes: Representations and Realities of North-East England*. Woodbridge: Oxford University Press, 25–39.

Cutajar, N., 2004. The archaeology of Malta's Middle Ages: documenting cultural change between the tenth and the thirteenth century. *In*: K. Gambin, ed. *Malta. Roots of a Nation: The Development of Malta from an Island People to an Island Nation*. Malta: Midsea Books.

Dalli, C., 2006. *Malta: The Medieval Millennium*. Malta: Midsea Books.

Dalli, C., 2008. Satellite, sentinel, stepping stone. Medieval Malta in Sicily's orbit. *In*: A. Bonanno and P. Militello, eds. *Malta in the Hybleans, the Hybleans in Malta*. Palermo: Officina Studi Medievali, 245–258.

Debono, G., and Xerri, S., 1993. *Geological Map of the Maltese Islands, 1:25.000*. Malta: Oil Exploration Directorate.

Dolgoff, A., 1996. *Physical Geography*. New York: Houghton Mifflin.

Dusina, P., 1996 [1575]. Apostolic visitation of Mgr. Pietro Dusina. *In*: S. Fiorini, and G. Aquilina, eds. *Documentary Sources of Maltese History: Part IV. Documents at the Vatican. No. 1 Archivio Segreto Vaticano Congregazione Vescovi e Regolari. Malta: Visita Apostolica no. 51 Mgr Petrus Dusina, 1575*. Malta: University of Malta.

Fenech, K., 2007. *Human-Induced Changes in the Environment and Landscape of the Maltese Islands from the Neolithic to the 15th Century AD*. BAR International Series 1682, Oxford: Archaeopress.

Fiorini, S., 1993. Malta in 1530. *In*: V. Mallia-Milanes, ed. *Hospitaller Malta 1530–1798: Studies on Early Modern Malta and the Order of St John of Jerusalem*. Malta: Mireva, 111–198.

Fiorini, S., 2003. X'nafu dwar Callus? *In*: C. Cassar and Y. Vella, eds. *Min kien Callus?* Malta: Klabb Kotba Maltin, 15–53.

Fiorini, S., 2004. *Documentary Sources of Maltese History: Part II. Documents in the State Archives, Palermo, No. 2, Cancelleria Regia: 1400–1459*. Malta: University of Malta.

Fiorini, S., 2005. *Documentary Sources of Maltese History: Part I. Notarial Documents – No. 3, Notary Paulo Bonello MS.588:1467–1517; Notary Giacomo Zabbara MS.1132: 1471–1500*. Malta: University of Malta.

Florio, I., 1598. *A Worlde of Wordes, or Most Copius, and Exact Dictionarie in Italian and English*. London: Arnold Hatfield.

Florio, I., 1611. *Queen Anna's New World of Words, or Dictionarie of the Italian and English tongues*. London: Melch Bradwood.

Gabrieli, F., 1961. Ibn Hawqal e gli Arabi di Sicilia. *Rivista Studi Orientali* 35, 245–253.

Ganado, A., 2008. *Għażla ta' mapep ta' Malta mill-kollezzjoni Albert Ganado*. Malta: Office of the Prime Minister.

Goblot, H., 1979. *Les Qanats: Une technique d'acquisition de l'eau*. Paris: Ecole Hautes Etudes Sciences Sociales.

Grove, A.T., and Rackham, O., 2001. *The Nature of Mediterranean Europe: An Ecological History*. London: Yale University Press.

Houben, H., 2002. *Roger II of Sicily: A Ruler between East and West*. Cambridge: Cambridge University Press.

Latham, R.E., 1965. *Revised Medieval Latin World-List from British and Irish Sources*. Oxford: Oxford University Press.

Lionello, P., *et al.*, 2012. The climate of the Mediterranean region in hisorical times. *In*: P. Lionello, ed. *The Climate of the Mediterranean Region: From the Past to the Future*. Amsterdam: Elsevier, xlv–xlvi.

Lockwood, J.F., 1952. *A Smaller Latin–English Dictionary*. London: John Murray.

Luterbacher, J. and Xoplaki, E., 2003. 500-year winter temperature and precipitation variability over the Mediterranean area and its connection to the large-scale atmospheric circulation. *In*: H.J. Bolle, ed. *Mediterranean Climate. Variability and Trends*. London: Springer, 133–153.

Luterbacher, J. and Xoplaki, E., 2006. Mediterranean climate variability over the last centuries: a review. *In*: P. Lionello, P. Malanotte-Rizzoli, and R. Boscolo, eds. *Mediterranean Climate Variability*. Heidelberg: Elsevier, 27–126.

Luttrell, A.T., 1975. Approaches to Medieval Malta. *In*: A.T. Luttrell, ed. *Medieval Malta. Studies on Malta before the Knights*. London: British School at Rome, 1–70.

Luttrell, A.T., 1976. Frederick II and Paolino di Malta. *In*: A.T. Luttrell, ed. *The Making of Christian Malta: from the Early Middle Ages to 1530*. Hampshire: Aldershot, 405–409.

Luttrell, A.T., 1997. Giliberto Abbate's report on Malta: circa 1241. *In*: K. Sciberras, ed. *Proceedings of History Week*. Malta: Malta Historical Society, 1–29.

Luttrell, A.T., 2002. *The Making of Christian Malta: From the Early Middle Ages to 1530*. Hampshire: Aldershot.

Martin, J.M., 2002. Settlement and the agrarian economy. *In*: G.A. Loud, and A. Metcalfe, eds. *The Society of Norman Italy*. London: Brill, 17–45.

McCormick, M., Büntgen, U., Cane, M.A. and Cook, E.R., 2012. Climate change during and after the Roman Empire: reconstructing the past from Scientific and Historical evidence. *Journal of Interdisciplinary History* 43(2), 169–220.

Messina, A., 1979. *Le chiese rupestri del Siracusano*. Palermo: Istituto Siciliano di Studi Bizantini e Neoellenici, Monumenti 2.

Metcalfe, A., 2003. *Muslims and Christians in Norman Sicily. Arabic Speakers and the End of Islam*. London: Routledge.

Metcalfe, A., 2009. *The Muslims of Medieval Italy*. Edinburgh: Edinburgh University Press.

Molinari, A. and Cutajar, N., 1999. Of Greeks and Arabs and of Feudal Knights. *Malta Archaeological Review*, 3, 9–16.

Morris, T.O., 1952. *The Water Supply Resources of Malta*. Malta: Government of Malta.

Niermeyer, J.F., 1976. *Mediae latinitatis lexicon minus*. Leiden: Brill.

Olstad, C.S., White, C., Hiranadani, D., Buhagiar, K, Gambin and Clark, C.M., 2010. The Malta cistern project. Underwater robot mapping and localisation within ancient tunnel systems. *Journal of Field Robotics* 27(4), 399–411.

Oosthuizen, S., 2006. *Landscapes Decoded. The Origins and Development of Cambridgeshire's Medieval Fields*. Hatfield: University of Hertfordshire.

Park, C., 1977. Island with few options. *Geographical Magazine* 49(8), 508–509.

Pedley, M., Clarke, M.H., and Gale, P., 2002. *Limestone Isles in a Crystal Sea*. Malta: Publishers Enterprises Group.

Ramseyer, V., 2006. *The Transformation of a Religious Landscape: Medieval South Italy 850–1130*. New York: Cornell University Press.

Rippon, S., 2012. *Historic Landscape Analysis: Deciphering the Countryside*. Oxford: Council for British Archaeology.

Roberts, B.K., 1987. Landscape archaeology. *In*: J.M. Wagstaff, ed. *Landscape and Culture. Geographical and Archaeological Perspectives*. Oxford: Basil Blackwell, 77–95.

Saliba, P.C., Magro Conti, J., and Borg, C., 2002. *A Study of Landscape and Irrigation Systems at Is-Simblija Limits of Dingli*. Malta: the authors.

Sapiano, M., 2008. Measures for facing water scarcity and drought in Malta. *European Water Resources Association* 23/24, 77–84.

Sapiano, M., Mangion, J., and Batchelor, C., 2006. *Malta Water Resources Review*. Rome: FAO.

Sciascia, L., 1989. I cammelli e le rose: gli Abbate di Trapani da Federico II a Martino il Vecchio. *In*: S. Manelli, ed. *Mediterraneo Medievale. Scritti im onore di Francesco Giunta* 3, Catanzaro: Centro di studi tardoantichi e Medievali di Altomonte, 1174–1181.

Skinner, M., Redfern, D. and Farmer, G., 1997. *The Complete A-Z Geography Handbook*. London: Hodder and Stoughton.

Sultana, J. and Falzon, V., 2002. *Wildlife of the Maltese Islands*. Malta: Birdlife Malta.

Todaro, P., 1989. Utilizzazioni del sottosuolo di Palermo in età medievale. *In*: C. Roccaro, ed. *Palermo Medievale: Testi dell'VIII colloquio Medievale, Palermo 26–27 aprile 1989*. Palermo: Officina di studi Medievali, 109–128.

Vermeulen, F., 2004. Roads for soldiers and civilians in the Civitas Menapiorum. *In*: F. Vermeulen, K. Sas, and W. Dhaeze, eds. *Archaeology in Confrontation: Aspects of Roman Military Presence in the Northwest*. Ghent: Academia Press, 125–142.

Vita-Finzi, C., 1969. *The Mediterranean Valleys – Geological Changes in Historical Times*. Cambridge: Cambridge University Press.

Von Falkenhausen, V., 2002. The Greek presence in Norman Sicily: the contribution of the archival material in Greek. *In*: G.A. Loud and A. Metcalfe, eds. *The Society of Norman Italy*. Leiden: Brill, 235–287.

Waugh, D., 2003. *The New Wider World*. Cheltenham: Nelson Thornes.

Wettinger, G., 1975. The lost villages and hamlets of Malta. *In*: A.T. Luttrell, ed. *Medieval Malta. Studies on Malta before the Knights*. London: British School at Rome, 181–216.

Wettinger, G., 1982. Agriculture in Malta in the late Middle Ages. *In*: M. Buhagiar, ed. *Proceedings of History Week 1981*. Malta: The Historical Society, 1–48.

Wettinger, G., 1986. The Arabs in Malta. *Malta. Studies of its Heritage and History*. Malta: Mid-Med Bank Ltd., 87–104.

Wettinger, G., 2000. *Place-Names of the Maltese Islands ca. 1300–1800*. Malta: P.E.G.

Wettinger, G., 2012. Malta in the High Middle Ages. *Melita Historica* 15(4), 367–390.

Zammit-Maempel, G., 1977. *An Outline of Maltese Geology and Guide to the Geology Hall of the National Museum of Natural History, Mdina, Malta*. Malta: Progress Press.

# Part III
# Central and Eastern Europe

# Chapter 13

# The use of caves for religious purposes in early medieval Germany (AD 500–1200)

*Mechthild Schulze-Dörrlamm*

*Between AD 500 and 1200, Christians in Germany used caves in three different ways: as hermitages, churches and as replicas of the Holy Sepulchre. Descriptions in the Lives of some missionaries from the seventh and eighth centuries provide us with the earliest indications of the use of caves as hermitages, which were inhabited for short periods only. As eremeticism was not of great significance within the Catholic Church of the Carolingian and Ottonian empire, reference to a hermitage in King Otto I's deed of donation from AD 956 attracts attention. According to this document, the cave beneath St Michael's mountain church near Blankenburg, known as the Volkmarskeller, was the cell of the cleric Liutbirg († c. AD 870). Eremeticism became more common between the eleventh and fifteenth centuries in Germany. The rock-cut hermitage near Bretzenheim is apparently the largest cave hermitage. From the tenth century some caves were developed into churches, of which the Steinkirche in the Harz Mountains is the most famous. The 'Holy Sepulchres', built in the twelfth century, provide the most spectacular testimony to the religious use of caves in the Middle Ages. They may well have played a role in the celebration of the Easter liturgy. Furthermore, two preserved complexes in Kastel-Staadt and in the Externsteine were decorated with stone reliefs alluding to Christ's death. As yet, there is no unequivocal proof for pagan cult practices in German caves during the early Middle Ages, nor after the fall of the Western Roman Empire (AD 476).*

## Introduction

The role of caves as places of religious, and especially Christian, activities in early medieval Germany (*c.* AD 500–1200) has never been systematically investigated. Written references on the topic are few, and though some oral traditions survive, these are less reliable. Some regional case studies, however, have revealed archaeological finds from the period in caves (Walter 1985, 1989, 119ff.; Bockisch-Bräuer and Zeitler, 91ff.; Wieland 1996, 54ff.; Stoll-Tucker 1997, 129ff.; Quast 2006, 82–83 with distribution map fig. 33, including a find list 165 no.14.5.7). The nature of the activities that resulted in the deposition of such finds is uncertain; for instance, could the material reflect religious activities or even cult practices (Stoll-Tucker 1997, 159–160; Kaulich 2001, 143)? Only cave chambers with clear evidence of cultic activities, such as those adorned with religious symbols or depictions, allow any discussion of a religious function, although rarely is there information on the origin and/or length of such usage.

This is the first attempt at an overview of caves in Germany that were used, or possibly used, for religious purposes in the Early Middle Ages. It begins in the former *Germania Libera*, the territory east of the Rhine and north of the Danube, where caves occur that may contain traces of pagan cultic activities; the population of this region converted to Christianity between the late sixth and eighth centuries. Following this is an overview of caves used by Christians between the seventh and the twelfth/thirteenth centuries as hermitages, churches and, in two instances, as replicas of the Holy Sepulchre.

## Caves with possible traces of pagan cult practices

According to contemporaneous reports, some communities in the former Roman frontier provinces west of the Rhine and south of the Danube practiced pagan cultic activities long after Christianity had been made the state religion (AD 392), in some instances even up until the ninth century (Ristow 2007, 3–4). Certain archaeological finds, in particular coins, reveal that people visited old temple districts for such purposes (Ristow 2007, 4).

Archaeological finds from some caves in *Germania Libera*, where the population did not convert to Christianity until at least the late sixth century, include sherds of hand-made pots and bowls of fourth-/fifth-century date (Schach-Dörges 2010, 644ff. figs. 12–17), occasional small military metal objects from the Roman frontier provinces (Schach-Dörges 2010, 633ff. fig. 8), and a number of graves that are usually interpreted as exceptional burials with no clear religious contexts (Quast 2006, 83). Worth mentioning are, for example, 12 graves from the first half of the fifth century in Sontheim Cave, Alb-Donau (Schach-Dörges 2010, 615ff. figs. 2–3), and the grave of a woman who was buried with a pearl necklace during the seventh century in Fischerhöhle (Fisher's Cave) near Heuchling, Hersbruck (Dannheimer 1962, 188 pl. 72B; Wieland 1996, 58, no. 738; Stoll-Tucker 1997, 129 pl. 41; Quast 2006, 83). There are neither written sources nor oral traditions as to why these individuals had been buried in caves. Perhaps they belonged to fugitive foreigners who wanted to protect or hide the graves of their relatives? Perhaps these were individuals who died from contagious diseases, such as leprosy? Or perhaps these people were excluded from their communities for altogether different (religious?) reasons. The motives behind these atypical burials are far from clear.

It is difficult to identify objects that could represent religious ceremonies in caves. One possibility, however, are finds of metal keys. For instance, an ornate brass key of sixth-century date with a bead-and-reel handle and T-shaped bit was found in an undisturbed ash layer hidden between larges stones in a small cave known as Clythenhöhle II, near Oelsen in Saale-Orla (Eastern Thuringia) (Eisel 1886, 61; Schmidt 1970, 95, no. 106 pl. 106.3; Arends 1978, no. 557, fig. 12.6; Steuer 1982, 232, no. 82, fig. 25.2; Walter 1985, 37, 40, 41, 82, fig. 30) (Fig. 13.1.1–2, 3a). In the sixth century, women wore keys as amulets (Ament 1992, 20–21), and

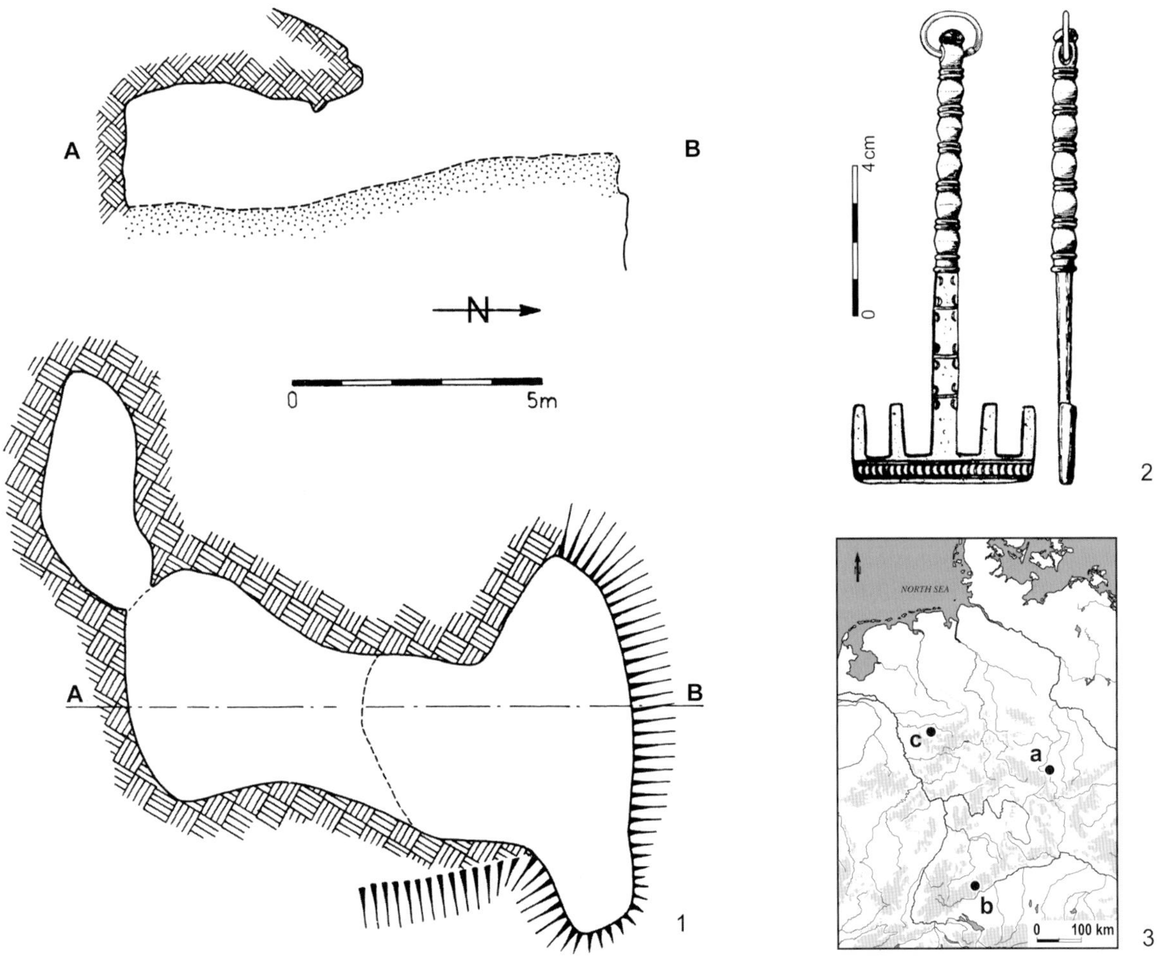


*Figure 13.1: 1. Clythenhöhle II near Oelsen, district Saale-Orla (Thuringia). Layout and longitudinal section A to B. 2. Sixth-century ornamental brass key with T-shaped bit and bead-and-reel handle from the undisturbed ash layer in Clythenhöhle II. Height 12cm (after Eisel 1886 and Walter 1985). 3. Caves in Germany with early medieval traces of pagan rituals (?): a) Clythenhöhle II near Oelsen; b) Lonsinger Höhle, district Reutlingen; c) Klusensteiner Höhle near Hemer. Illustration: M. Weber, RGZM.*

thus this decorative example may have been hidden during a magical summoning. It could have been utilised to help a woman conceive, or to provide relief during birth (Steuer 1982, 205). A similar motivation may have resulted in the deposition of a possible Merovingian period iron key with a T-shaped bit in Lonsinger Höhle, Reutlingen (Fig. 13.1.3b) (Arends 1978, 957 no. 454; Quast 2006, 83 and 246–247 pl. 47E; Schach-Dörges 2010, 642–643 fig. 10.1). These two keys potentially constitute traces of pagan, magical customs that did not survive the Christianisation of Germany.

The meaning of a bronze pseudo-coin fibula, dating to the second half of the ninth century, from Klusensteiner Höhle near Hemer, Märkischer, remains unclear (Fig. 13.1.3c) (Frick 1992/1993, 393 pl. 12, 23; Schulze-Dörrlamm 1999, 273ff. distribution map fig. 9 with find list no. 3, 12; Schulze-Dörrlamm 2008, 542ff. fig. 11.2). This cave was repeatedly visited from at least the pre-Roman Iron Age as evidenced by the discovery of animal bones and pottery sherds of Late Hallstatt and La Tène date (Hömberg and Laumann 1986, 271). The cave may, therefore, be an older ritual site, but, as the fibula is an isolated find, we cannot conclude that it represents a local survival of pagan activities into the Carolingian period.

## Caves with traces of Christian usage

To date, there is no archaeological evidence for the religious use of caves in the frontier provinces of the Western Roman Empire by early Christians. Without exception, all the evidence relates to later centuries. Not a single cave has yielded finds of liturgical implements comparable to, for instance, the fragment of a bell shrine from Kilgreany Cave, Ireland, the silver communion chalice from a cave near Trient, Switzerland, or the gilded bronze icon of St Michael from his cave on Monte Gargano, Italy (Schulze-Dörrlamm 2008, 547ff. fig. 15–16.18). Caves used by Christians are thus only identifiable when developed into hermitages, churches, or imitations of the Holy Sepulchre in Jerusalem (Fig. 13.2). Four such caves have been identified in Germany, all dating to the Middle Ages.

### *Cave hermitages*

Some Christians retired to caves with the intention of uniting with God, as well as attaining spiritual perfection and breaking ties with human society (Rahner 1959, 767). Hermitages are amongst the earliest evidence that caves were utilised by Christians for religious purposes and are especially widespread in the Near East, but not in German regions between the Alps and the North Sea.

Legend claims that about AD 600, the Frankish bishop St Arnulf († AD 640) from Metz installed a hermitage in the late Roman *mithraeum* in Halberg Mountain at Saarbrücken, which had been destroyed at the end of the fourth century (Schindler 1963, 135 figs. 5–6, 1966, 109). He is said to have used the hermitage as a base for his missionary activities in the region (Fig. 13.2.1) (Schröter 1852, 148; Schindler 1963, 135, figs. 5–6). This so-called Heidenkapelle ('pagan chapel') was consequently considered the oldest Christian cult site in the Saar river region (Klein 1923, 13ff.), but archaeological excavations do not support the tradition (Schindler 1963, 135). There are no traces of a seventh-century Christian hermitage; the earliest pottery sherds date to the eleventh/twelfth centuries. Late medieval pottery fragments and small votive finds confirm the written references that claim eremites settled here in the fifteenth century, and converted the site into a chapel for Christian pilgrims (Klein 1923, 20; Schindler 1963, 135–136 pl. 17–18).

Some Christian missionaries who came to Germany in the eighth century from Anglo-Saxon territories apparently lived in caves for short periods. Tradition records that the Anglo-Saxon St Sola († AD 794), a contemporary and companion of the Anglo-Saxon missionary and archbishop St Bonifatius († AD 754), lived in a cave until the construction of his monastery at Solnhofen, Weissenburg-Gunzenhausen, around AD 750 (Later 2011, 19, 24). Archaeological investigations revealed that a narrow corridor connected the cave named after the saint, Sola-Höhle, with the adjacent stone chapel, but the cave would have been too small and inadequate for occupation (Later 2011, 20). Furthermore, there is no archaeological evidence confirming the purported age of this complex (Fig. 13.2.2).

In contrast to Sola, the Anglo-Saxon monk Burkhardus, anointed first bishop of Würzburg by Bonifatius in AD 742, is said to have retired in old age to a cave known as Hohenburg, by the Main River, as a hermit to await his death (AD 755). The grotto of St Burkhardus (Fig. 13.2.4) has been identified as the dripstone cave beneath Homburg castle in Main-Spessart (Bockisch-Bräuer and Zeitler 1996, 92–93), but cannot be dated to that period by archaeological finds.

Eremiticism was not a significant aspect of monasticism within the Catholic Church of the Carolingian and Ottonian empire (Rahner 1959, 768), which would explain the scarcity of written records relating to cave hermitages. However, one of the oldest is a document dating to 5th December AD 956, which records that King Otto I endowed Quedlinburg monastery with St Michael's church and a nearby cell, in which St Liutbirg († *c.* AD 870) was said to have lived (Fig. 13.2.6): '*speluncam, ubi quedam Liutburg quondam fuit inclusa et ecclesiam ibidem in honorem Sancti Michaelis Archangeli constructam*' / 'the cave where a certain Liutburg once was enclosed along with the church constructed there in honour of St Michael the Archangel'. (Regesta Imperii II, 1 no. 253; Steinacker 1922, 195–196 fig. 144; Diestelkamp 1934, 106–107). Because of the precise description of the location, it must be Volkmarskeller, a limestone cave near Blankenburg in the Harz Mountains, above which are the ruins of St Michael's Church and the associated Michaelstein

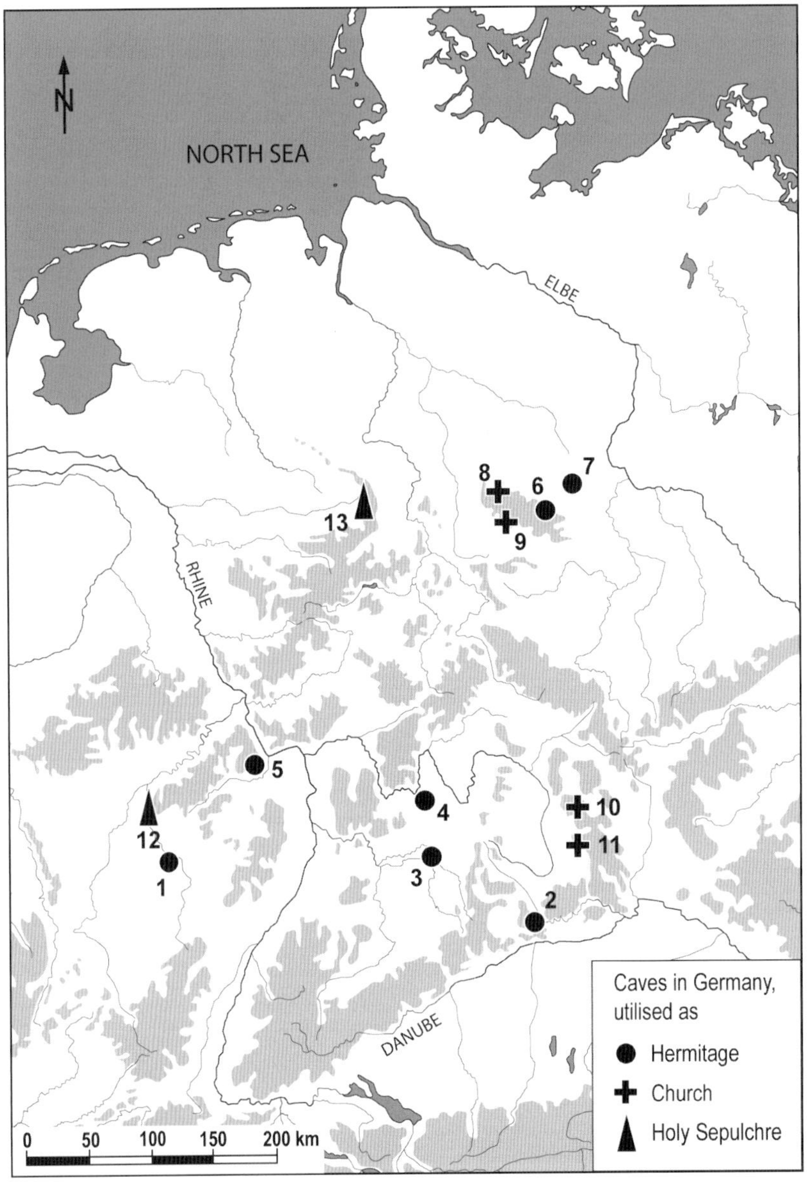


*Figure 13.2: Caves in Germany that have or are said to have been used by Christians for religious purposes in the early Middle Ages:* Hermitages*: 1.* Mithraeum *at Saarbrücken; 2. Sola-Höhle near Solnhofen; 3. Sankt Wendel zum Stein at Dörzbach; 4. Burkhardus grotto at Homburg/Main; 5. Felseneremitage near Bretzenheim; 6. Volkmarskeller near Blankenburg; 7. Klusberge near Halberstadt.* Churches: *8. Kluskapelle at Goslar; 9. Steinkirche near Scharzfeld; 10. Klauskirche near Betzenstein; 11. St Andrew's church near Rupprechtstegen.* Holy Sepulchres*: 12. Klause at Kastel-Staadt; 13. Externsteine at Horn-Bad Meinberg. Illustration: M. Weber, RGZM.*

monastery (Fig. 13.3.1). Although recent research rules out the possibility that this cave was St Liutbirg's hermitage (a close confidante of Bishop Haimo from Halberstadt and Bishop Ansgar from Bremen), there is evidence for its use as a hermitage during the Middle Ages (Schwineköper 1975, 328–329; Dehio 2002, 111). The hermit Bernhardus – *presbyter solitaries de Lapide s. Michaelis* († AD 1118), for example, lived here (Steinacker 1922, 196). It consists of a long cave with two exits and a vertical shaft in the ceiling. The connection between the cave and the monastery located overhead was investigated by Brinckmann between 1884 and 1887 (Steinacker 1922, 198–199). He found remnants of plastered masonry, several crosses hewn into the cave walls, skeletons representing at least six interments, and artefacts including pottery sherds, Saxon battle axes and a spur, which he dated to the Carolingian–Ottonian period. As the finds and records no longer survive, it is not possible to establish more precise dates, which is particularly unfortunate in terms of the carvings and burials. From the mid-tenth century, Volkmarskeller hermitage and the associated St Michael's Church served a religious function, and in 1147 they merged with the Cistercian monastery of Michaelstein

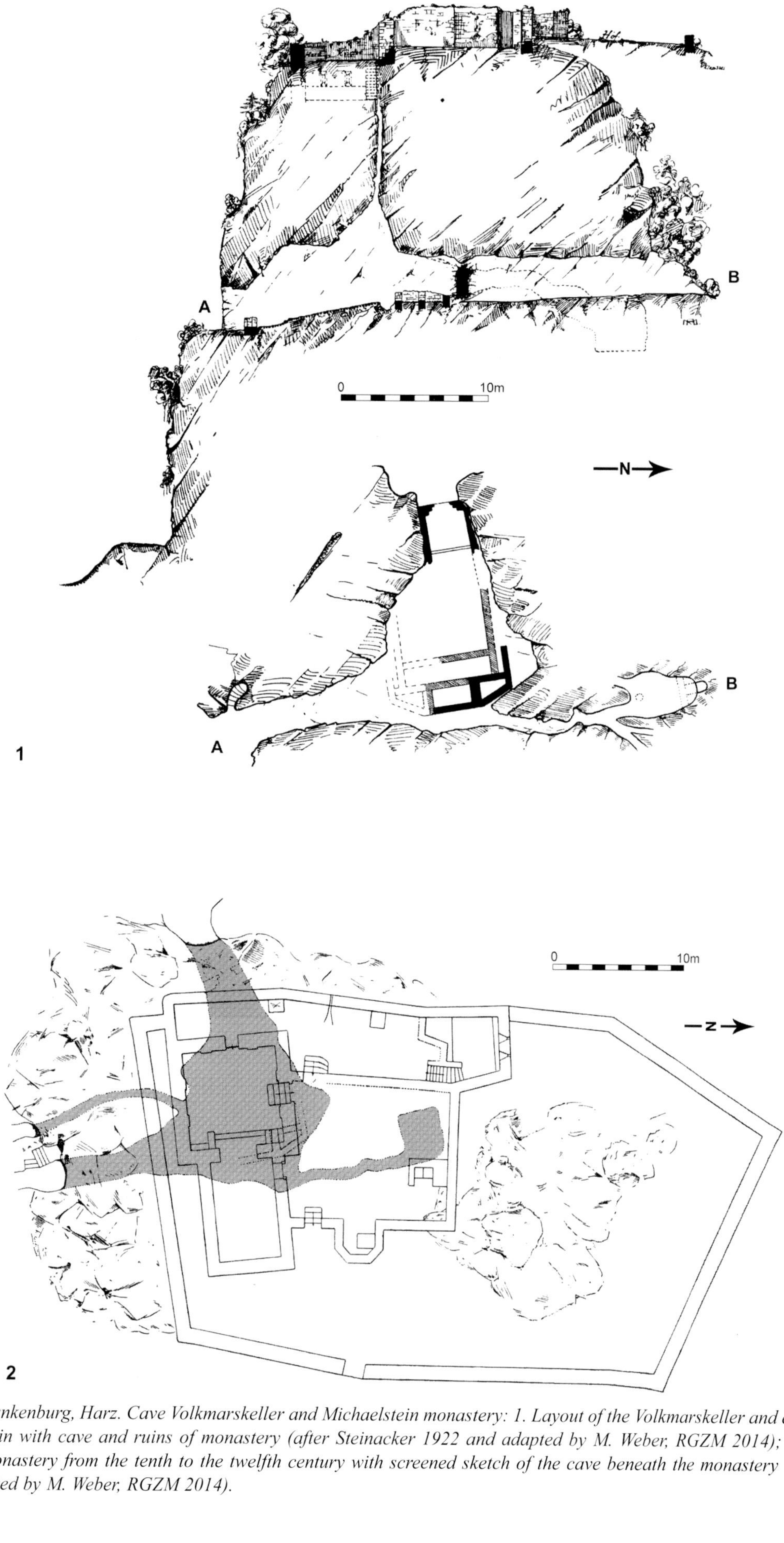


*Figure 13.3: Blankenburg, Harz. Cave Volkmarskeller and Michaelstein monastery: 1. Layout of the Volkmarskeller and east–west section through mountain with cave and ruins of monastery (after Steinacker 1922 and adapted by M. Weber, RGZM 2014); 2. Layout of the Michaelstein monastery from the tenth to the twelfth century with screened sketch of the cave beneath the monastery (after Steinacker 1922, and adapted by M. Weber, RGZM 2014).*

(Fig. 13.3.2) (Steinacker 1922, 202). The cave was then named after the cleric Volkmann, the younger patron of St Michael's Church (Steinacker 1922, 160–161). Both seem to have been abandoned over time rather than being violently destroyed (Steinacker 1922, 204).

Felseneremitage, near Bretzenheim on the Nahe River, Bad Kreuznach, is reputably the largest cave monastery north of the Alps (Fig. 13.2.5). After the last hermit, a monk of the order of Wilhelmites, died in 1827, it was dissolved and gradually deteriorated (Zimmermann 1935, 138–139 fig. 22). The monastery comprised a cave complex with stone and wooden buildings that are depicted in an 1875 sketch by A. M. Schwan but are now demolished (Zimmermann 1935, 138–139 fig. 89–90). The artificial rock-cut cave complex had two storeys and consisted of several interconnected chambers. Together, they provided a residential surface area of 90 square metres (Fig. 13.4) (Schulze-Dörrlamm 2008, 563–564 fig. 29). While it is not known when the hermitage was first established, the date of the altar can be estimated. A lead reliquary, discovered in the sepulchrum of the altar of St Antonius' Church, destroyed in 1567, is inscribed with the year '1043' (Zimmermann 1935, 139; Gaul 1954, 147; Schneider 2003, 28–29). Believing that the rock hermitage developed from an earlier refuge of a seventh-/eighth-century insular missionary, who might in turn have occupied a late Roman *mithraeum*, local historian Hans Schneider investigated the entire complex (Schneider 1994; Schneider 2003). He wrongly believed he found traces of a *mithraeum* and the basin of a Christian baptismal font, but no evidence to support his supposition was revealed. The original layout and actual date of the hermitage, which reached its current size in the sixteenth century and grew to become a place of pilgrimage by 1717, remain unknown.

Smaller complexes that we either do not know of, or have entirely forgotten, are also likely to have existed during the Middle Ages. Caves in the Klusbergen Hills to the south of Halberstadt town, for example, have not been investigated though one is said to have been a hermitage associated with Münzenberg monastery by the late eleventh century (Fig. 13.2.7) (Doering 1902, 503–504; Gaul 1954, 147). Its current appearance bears little resemblance to the original edifice as indicated by antiquarian illustrations (Mundhenk 1983, 24 n.17).

It remains unclear as to when the two caves beside the late Gothic pilgrimage church of Sankt Wendel zum Stein, near Dörzbach, Hohenlohe (Fig. 13.2.3), were inhabited (Fischer 1973, 181ff.; Illich 1975, 7ff.). The church, built on a rocky terrace at the river Jagst (Fig. 13.5.1–3) and beside a saltwater source, is dedicated to the patron saint of shepherds and, as legend goes, was established by a shepherd (Beschreibung 1883, 505–507). A preserved Romanesque arched window in its southern wall indicates that it was constructed in the eleventh/twelfth century (Fig. 13.5.1). Its western wall leans against a steep cliff between two caves, which are accessed by stone stairways. The smaller cave functioned as a hermitage, whereas the Gothic wall paintings and ceiling vault of the larger cave suggest it served as a chapel (Illich 1975, 7ff. sheet 1–2). No dateable finds or other indications survive to determine when this complex was established.

### *Cave churches*

In the early Middle Ages, few churches in Germany appear to have been constructed within caves. Of the small number on

*Figure 13.4: The Felseneremitage near Bretzenheim on the river Nahe, Bad Kreuznach. Comprehensive view of the two-storey complex, with front buildings removed. Photo: H. Schneider, Bretzenheim.*

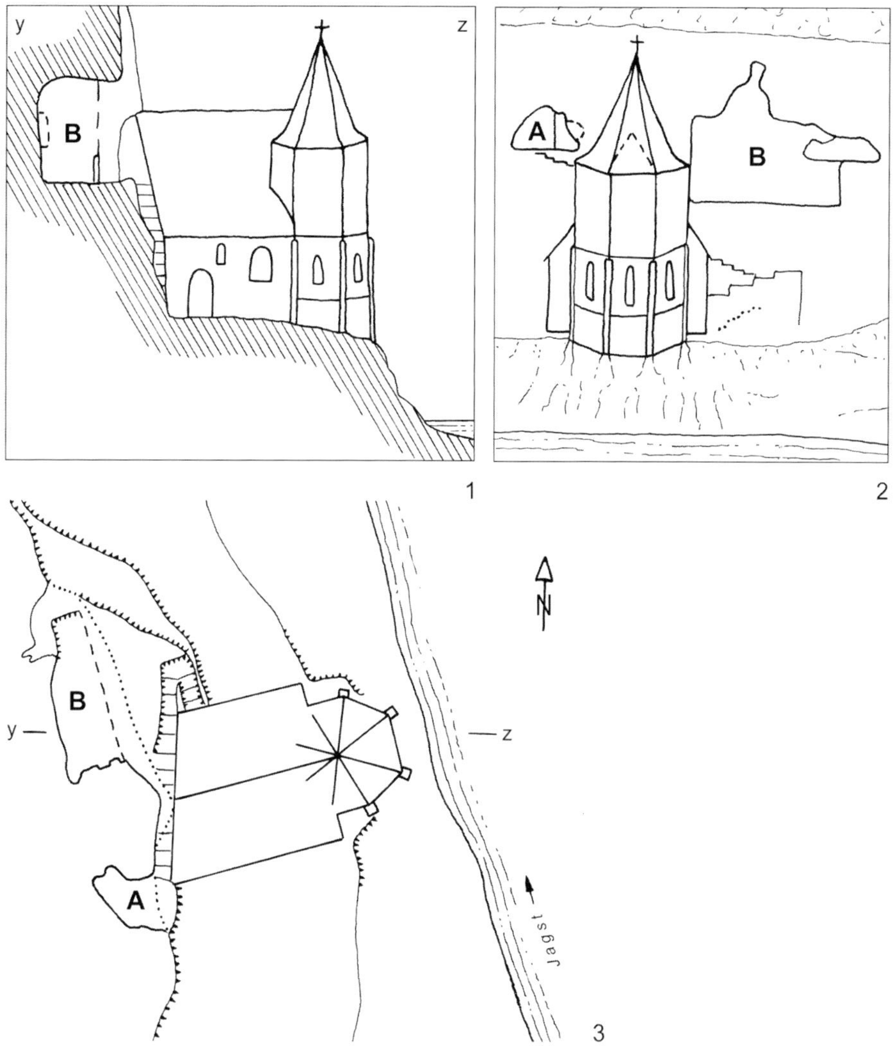


*Figure 13.5: Sankt Wedel zum Stein on the river Jagst near Dörzbach, Hohenlohe. Sketches of the church and its rear rock face: 1. Side view of the church from the south with a Y–Z section through the area; 2. Front view of the church choir, hermit's cave (A) and chapel (B) in the rock face; 3. Top view of the church and both caves. Illustration: M. Weber, RGZM, after H. Illich, 1975.*

record, the most famous is the Steinkirche near Scharzfeld, Osterode, in the Harz Mountains (Fig. 13.2.9). This church consists of a tunnel-shaped and barrel-vaulted cave with an altar and holy water font. A triangular platform in front of the entrance provides a space for the congregation and a pulpit was carved into rock here. According to local tradition, this church is the oldest in the Harz Mountains, having been founded by the Anglo-Saxon missionary Winfryth/Bonifatius in AD 732 after he had quarried it out with his own hands using only a hammer while on one of his missionary trips (Fig. 13.6) (Nowothnig 1978, 203ff. figs. 2–3; Schulze-Dörrlamm 2008, 553–554 fig. 21). This legend has been contradicted by excavations inside the cave and on the platform – the oldest pottery sherds recovered are from the ninth/tenth century (Schirwitz 1961, 5–6; Schulze-Dörrlamm 2008, 554). On the other hand, it is possible that prior to its religious role, the cave served as a refuge for people from surrounding areas during Hungarian raids on the Ottonian kingdom during the first half of the tenth century (Schulze 1984, 479ff. with historical maps figs. 6–8; Schulze-Dörrlamm 2006, 43ff. figs. 2–3, 2008, 554). Regardless, the cave must have been converted into a church, i.e. fitted with a nave, altar, holy water font and pulpit, before the twelfth century. Several graves outside and inside the cave, accompanied by coins, provide a *terminus ante quem*.

In all probability, the Steinkirche near Scharzfeld is a little older than the Kluskapelle on the northern outskirts of the Harz Mountains (Fig. 13.2.8). The latter was built into a grotto in Klus Rock near Goslar as Mary's Chapel, but was demolished in the nineteenth century (Griep 1960, 46ff.). The church owes its name to the cave, which probably served as a hermit's cell before the construction of the chapel (Griep 1960, 46ff.).

There are no concrete indications as to the age of Andreaskirche (Andreas' Church) in a cave near

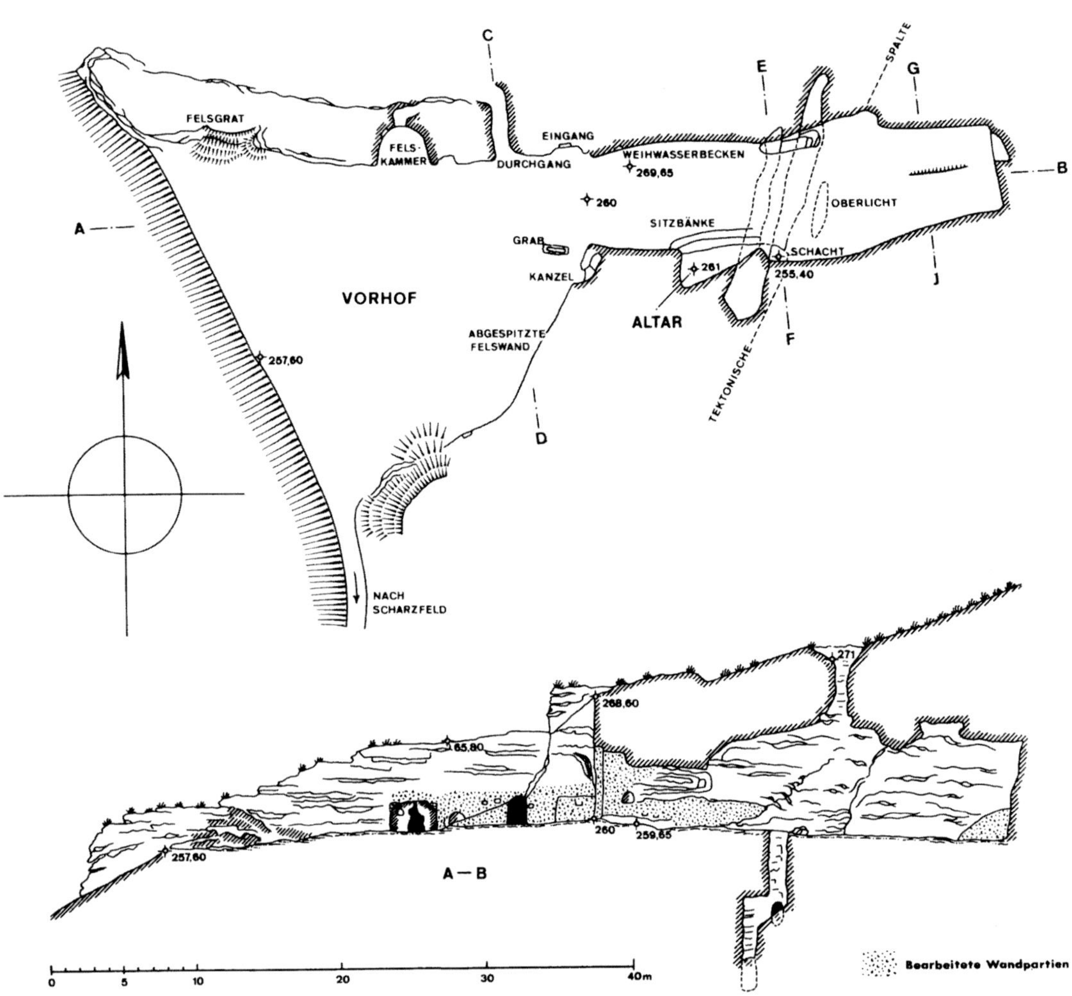


*Figure 13.6: The Steinkirche near Scharzfeld, Osterode am Harz. Layout of the cave church and section through the rock cave and its foreground (after Nowothnig 1978).*

Rupprechtstegen, Stadt Hersbruck, Nurnberg Land, or the Klauskirche (Klaus' Church) in the cave near Betzenstein, Bayreuth (Bockisch-Bräuer and Zeitler 1996, 92). Oral traditions that these cave-churches existed in the early Middle Ages have not been confirmed by excavation (Fig. 13.2.10–11).

## Replicas of the Holy Sepulchre

Pilgrimages to Jerusalem are generally thought to be the inspiration behind the emergence of holy sepulchres, which were located in the lateral nave or crypt of large churches or were constructed as detached stone buildings, from the tenth century onwards (Heimann-Schwarzweber 1970, 182ff.; Krause 2007, 274ff.; Kotzur and Ecker 2011, 245). In Germany they played an important role in the Easter liturgy, albeit with regionally differing manifestations. On Good Friday, the adoration of the cross was followed by the symbolic deposition of a dedicated host or cross into the artificial tomb of Jesus, which was then subsequently raised at Easter vigil (Jungmann 1960, 122). Easter Sunday morning then saw the dramatic re-enactment of the three Marys' visit to the empty grave (Kotzur and Ecker 2011, 244).

Between the twelfth and early thirteenth centuries in Germany, artificial caves were occasionally carved in picturesque elevated rocky landscapes as imitations of the Holy Sepulchre in Jerusalem. These were decorated with figural reliefs, seemingly to represent to pilgrims the holy sites at Jerusalem (Treude and Zelle 2011, 16). One such artificial cave was inserted into a steep cliff at Klausen-Staadt on the Saar River, Trier-Saarburg (Figs. 13.2.12 and 13.7.1) (Wackenroder 1939, 113ff. fig. 84–88; Böhner 1966, 179ff.; Mundhenk 1983, 52 fig. 12; Wegner 1994, 330–332; Bornheim gen. Schilling 2008, 5–6 figs. 13–14). It consisted of a square Kapelle der Kreuzauffindung ('Chapel of the Discovery of the Holy Cross') with a staircase leading to the higher Kreuzkapelle ('Holy Cross Chapel') (Fig. 13.7.3). From the latter, one could access the arcosolium, quarried into the southern exterior rock wall, which was intended to receive the cross or a wooden figure of the crucified (Fig. 13.7.2). A very weathered

*Figure 13.7: The Klause at Kastel-Staadt on the river Saar, Trier-Saarburg: 1. View of the caves of the Holy Sepulchre from around AD 1200 (right) and of the more recent Chapel of the Cross from AD 1600 (after Wackenroder 1939); 2. Layout of the rock chapel of the Discovery of the Holy Cross (right), from which the older Holy Cross Chapel is accessed by stairs (after Wackenroder 1939); 3. View onto the arch-shaped niche in the southern rock face, with the arcosolium and relief (after Bornheim gen. Schilling 2008); 4. Front view of the arch-shaped niche of the arcosolium and the relief (after Wackenroder 1939).*

1.95m wide and 1m high relief, dating from the late twelfth or early thirteenth century, in the arched niche above the arcosolium, provides an indication of the date of the complex. It represents the enthroned Mother of God with her child as well as the enthroned Christ, carried by angels in a mandorla (Wackenroder 1939, 117 figs. 86–87; Wegner 1994, 330; Bornheim gen. Schilling 2008, 6 figs. 16–17). It is closely related to the Holy Sepulchre referring, as it does, to Christ's birth and his glorification after the crucifixion and resurrection. Although there are no records as to who built the complex, the fact that the land then belonged to the Benedictine monastery of St Maximin at Trier (Bornheim gen. Schilling 2008, 6 figs. 16–17), and their capacity as an imperial abbey to finance the artistic decoration of the arcosolium, provide robust indications.

In 1600, the Franciscan Fr. Romery erected a two-storey chapel with a single nave and, above it, a refuge for a hermit on a rock outcrop beside the Holy Sepulchre (Fig. 13.7.1–2) (Wegner 1994, 330; Bornheim gen. Schilling 2008, 5 fig. 9). Romery dedicated both edifices to the Holy Cross and the holy empress Helena, who is supposed to have searched for, and found, the True Cross in Jerusalem. The chapel deteriorated during the French Revolution but was restored in 1835/1836 by the crown prince and, later, King of Prussia, Friedrich Wilhelm, based on the plans of his architect C.F. Schinkel (Bornheim gen. Schilling 2008, 6–8 figs. 7–10). Wilhelm had the remains of his ancestor, blind King Johann of Bohemia (1296–1346), buried in the basement; these were subsequently transferred to Luxembourg Cathedral in 1946 (Wegner 1994, 330; Bornheim gen. Schilling 2008, 10 figs. 18–22).

As the rock plateau upon which the Celtic Treveri had built a large *oppidum* was populated from the Roman Principate well into the Middle Ages (Böhner 1966, 180–181; Heyen 1988, 164; Koch and Schindler 1994, 128–130; Nortman 2005, 381–383) some historians suppose a continuity of cult. They assume that the rock outcrop over the Saar could have been an old pagan ritual site that was transformed into a Christian sanctuary (Wackenroder 1939, 113; Heyen 1988, 184), but there is no supporting evidence for this hypothesis.

The site of Externsteine, near Horn-Bad Meinberg, Lippe (Fig. 13.2.13), is better known but even more contested than the Klause hermitage in Kastel-Staadt (Hohenschwert 1994, 42ff.; Schulze-Dörrlamm 2008, 562ff.). From the seventeenth century, it was believed that this 38m-high sandstone rock face and its caves (Fig. 13.8) was an old Germanic ritual site later transformed by Charles the Great

*Figure 13.8: View of the Externsteine at Horn-Bad Meinberg, Lippe. Photo: A. Thünker after Archäologie in Deutschland 2006.*

(AD 768–814) into a Christian sanctuary following his victory over the Saxons. It may be here that the Saxon *Irminsul* stood, a venerated pagan tree or pillar destroyed on King Charles' orders in AD 772 (Springer 2000, 504–505). The fact that there are no oral traditions, written records or archaeological evidence for the ritual use of caves by Saxons on the Continent undermines the hypothesis of a Saxon ritual site (Mundhenk 1983, 88ff.; Schulze-Dörrlamm 2008, 564). Revealingly, excavations in the Externsteine caves (Fig. 13.9), which were particularly intensive during the Third Reich (Halle 2002; Pesch 2003, 575; Treude and Zelle 2011, 24; Linde 2013, 767–768, no. 696), did not yield finds from the period prior to the Saxon wars of Charles the Great, nor finds that might relate to an old Saxon sanctuary (Mundhenk 1983, 92–93). The runic inscription on an inaccessible area of rock, discovered in 1992, is a modern fake (Pesch 2003, 569ff. fig. 3). In fact, the earliest archaeological finds (pottery and metalwork) recovered from excavations outside the caves date to the late tenth century (Hohenschwerdt 1994, 92; Treude and Zelle 2011, 14 fig. 20). All recent scientific studies, including radiocarbon dating and thermoluminescence, confirm the results of the excavation. The first traces of fire found in the vaulted grotto (Fig. 13.9a) possibly originate from the Carolingian period (735 ± 180 BP), although with certainty only from Ottonian times (934 ± 94 BP) (Treude and Zelle 2011, 16). The vast majority of material can be attributed to the eleventh/twelfth century and the fourteenth/fifteenth century. There is, therefore, no unambiguous proof of religious activities at Externsteine in pre-Christian times.

Throughout the Middle Ages, Christians frequented the Externsteine for religious purposes and undertook several structural modifications of the cave system. At first it may simply have been a hermitage, which was then extended to an imitation of the Holy Sepulchre during the twelfth century (Gaul 1954, 148 figs. 65–67). Subsequently, the cave system in the main outcrop (Fig. 13.9.1) included an isolated vaulted grotto with a lateral arcosolium (Fig. 13.9a, 3) and a chapel with a vestry – interpreted as the grotto of the Discovery of the True Cross and Golgatha Chapel (Fig. 13.9b–c) – and a secluded recluse chamber (Fig. 13.9d). In front of the cave are the remains of a stone table and a wooden coffin (Fig. 13.9.4–5), and to the east is a cave chapel cut into rock (Fig. 13.9.6). The Christian use of these caves can be deduced from a Latin inscription in the chapel, according to which Bishop Heinrich (presumably Heinrich II from Paderborn) dedicated an altar in 1115 (Gaul 1954, 148–149; Mundhenk 1983, 15; Hohenschwert 1994, 41; Treude and Zelle 2011, 7; Linde 2013, 178). A 4.8m high and 3.7m wide impressive relief of the Deposition of Christ from the Cross, dated to the twelfth century, beside the entrance of the vaulted grotto (Fig. 13.9.2) testifies to the character of this complex as a Holy Sepulchre (Hohenschwert 1994, 44–45; Matthes and Speckner 1997; Linde 2013, 767–768 fig. 696).

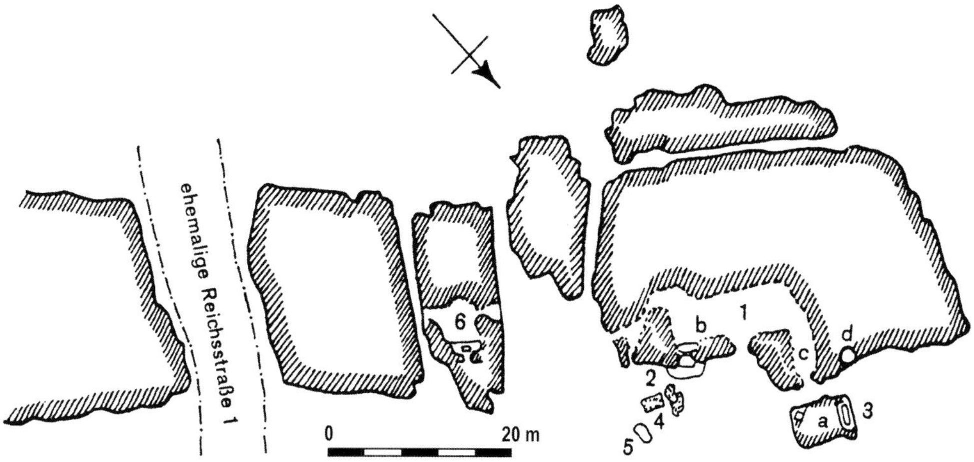


*Figure 13.9: The Externsteine. Section through the rocks and their caves: 1. Large lower system of grottos: a) vaulted grotto; b) chapel room; c) vestry; d) cell of retreat. 2. Relief of the deposition of Christ; 3. Arcosolium; 4. Remains of a stone table; 5. Trace of a tree trunk coffin; 6. Upper chapel. After Hohenschwert 1994, revised by M. Weber, RGZM, 2014.*

*Figure 13.10: View of the relief of Christ's deposition of the cross from around AD 1160/1170 between the entrances into the Holy Sepulchre of the Externsteine at Horn-Bad Meinberg. Height c. 5.5m. Photography: District Council Detmold, after Linde 2013.*

The hypothesis that this relief could date to as early as AD 820, i.e. during the Christianisation of Saxony (Matthes and Speckner 1997, 184ff.), can be refuted on stylistic terms. Art historians believe it was executed *c.* 1160/1170 (Fig. 13.10) (Treude and Zelle 2011, 4; Linde 2013, 768) making it the oldest monumental sculpture hewn into rock north of the Alps.

## Conclusion

In Germany, there are no written accounts or archaeological traces of pagan cult practices in caves between the fall of the late Roman empire and Christianisation. The deposition of isolated keys is but a weak suggestion and is in no way conclusive. While it is conceivable that magico-religious ceremonies (e.g. prayers, summonings, dances etc.) were practiced in some caves without leaving any physical trace, such rituals remain obscure. On the other hand, there are no concrete indications of the Christian adoration of Christ, Mary and other saints in caves in Late Antiquity and the early Middle Ages (approximately AD 400–900).

Information in the Lives of the saints that some Anglo-Saxon missionaries of the eighth century lived in caves may be correct, although the archaeological record does not confirm this. Permanent use of some caves as hermitages is only supported by evidence from the ninth/tenth century. In general, the frequency of hermits occupying caves probably remained comparatively low in the early Middle Ages (Fig. 13.2.1–7) (see also the compilation of cave hermitages by Mundhenk 1983, 24 n.15), increasing only during the Renaissance and Baroque eras. Churches appear to have been established in caves from the tenth century (Fig. 13.2.8–9). The early twelfth to early thirteenth century saw the conversion of caves in picturesque locations into imitations of the Holy Sepulchre in Jerusalem (Fig. 13.2.12–13) and their use as hermitages. In the case of Externsteine, the architects of the complex are said to have been the monks of Abdinghof monastery at Paderborn, and in the case of the Holy Sepulchre at Klausen-Staadt, the monks from St Maximin at Trier. They may have been inspired by corresponding expressions of veneration of the cross in the Near East.

This brief overview provides a highly incomplete picture as the interpretation of the archaeological finds is limited and research is lacking. It does, however, highlight the necessity of further detailed research in this area.

## Acknowledgements

This chapter was translated by Gwendolen Pare, Nackenheim.

## References


Ament, H., 1992. *Das alamannische Gräberfeld von Eschborn (Main-Taunus-Kreis)*. Materialien zur Vor- und Frühgeschichte von Hessen 14. Wiesbaden: Landesamt für Denkmalpflege.

Arends, U., 1978. Ausgewählte Gegenstände des Frühmittelalters mit Amulettcharakter. Thesis (PhD), Heidelberg University.

Beschreibung, 1883. *Beschreibung des Oberamts Künzelsau*. Stuttgart: Kohlhammer.

Bockisch-Bräuer, C. and Zeitler, J. P., eds., 1996. *Kulthöhlen. Funde – Deutungen – Fakten*. Exhibition Catalogue. Nürnberg: Graf.

Böhner, K., 1966. Kastel, Kr. Saarburg: Befestigung und Klause. *In*: Römisch-Germanisches Zentralmuseum Mainz, ed. *Führer zur vor- und frühgeschichtlichen Denkmälern 5. Saarland*. Mainz: Zabern, 179–183.

Bornheim, gen. Schilling, W., 2008. *Klause bei Kastel*. Burgen, Schlösser, Altertümer 12. Koblenz: Burgen, Schlösser, Altertümer Rheinland–Pfalz.

Dannheimer, H., 1962. *Die germanischen Funde der späten Kaiserzeit und des frühen Mittelalters in Mittelfranken*. Germanische Denkmäler der Völkerwanderungszeit Serie A, 7. Berlin: De Gruyter.

Dehio, G., 2002. *Handbuch der deutschen Kunstdenkmäler. Sachsen-Anhalt I, Regierungsbezirk Magdeburg*. Munich: Deutscher Kunstverlag.

Diestelkamp, A., 1934. Die Anfänge des Klosters Michaelstein. *Sachsen und Anhalt* 10, 106–118.

Doering, O., 1902. *Beschreibende Darstellung der älteren Bau- und Kunstdenkmäler der Kreise Halberstadt Land und Stadt*. Halle: Hendel.

Eisel, R., 1886. Höhlencultstelle bei Oelsen (Kr. Ziegenrück, Reg.-Bez. Magdeburg). *Zeitschrift für Ethnologie* 18 (Verhandlungen), 56–62.

Fischer, F., 1973. Höhle bei St. Wendel zum Stein nahe Dörzbach. *In*: Römisch-Germanisches Zentralmuseum Mainz, ed. *Führer zu vor- und frühgeschichtlichen Denkmälern 24. Hohenloher Land*. Mainz: Zabern, 181–184.

Frick, H.-J., 1992/1993. Karolingisch-ottonische Scheibenfibeln des nördlichen Formenkreises. *Offa* 49/50, 243–463.

Gaul, O., 1954. Neue Forschungen zum Problem der Externsteine. *Westfalen* 32, 141–164.

Griep, H.-G., 1960. Die Klus vor Goslar. *Goslarer Bergkalender* 310, 46–57.

Halle, U., 2002. *'Die Externsteine sind bis auf weiteres germanisch!'. Prähistorische Archäologie im Dritten Reich*. Bielefeld: Verlag für Regionalgeschichte.

Heimann-Schwarzweber, A. 1970. Grab, Heiliges. *In*: E. Kirschbaum and W. Braunfels, eds. *Lexikon der christlichen Ikonographie, 2. Rom, Freiburg, Basel*. Vienna: Herder, 182–192.

Heyen, F.-J., 1988. Kastel (Kreis Saarburg). *In*: L. Petry, ed. *Rheinland-Pfalz und Saarland. Handbuch der historischen Stätten Deutschlands* 5. Stuttgart: Krömer, 163–165.

Hömberg, Ph.-R. and Laumann, H., 1986. *Hemer (Klusensteiner Höhle). Ausgrabungen und Funde in Westfalen-Lippe* 4. Mainz: Ph. von Zabern, 271.

Hohenschwert, F., 1994. Externsteine. *In*: J. Hoops, ed. *Reallexikon der germanischen Altertumskunde* 8. Berlin, New York: De Gruyter, 37–46.

Illich, H., 1975. Sankt Wendelin-Höhlen bei Dörzbach/Jagst. *Beiträge zur Höhlen- und Karstkunde in Südwestdeutschland* 7, 7–11.

Jungmann, J. A., 1960. Heiliges Grab II. Liturgie. *In*: J. Höfer and K. Rahner, eds. *Lexikon für Theologie und Kirche* 5. Freiburg: Herder, 122.

Kaulich, B., 2001. Die archäologischen Funde aus dem Schnakenloch bei Peilstein, Gde. Neukirchen bei Sulzbach-Rosenberg, Lkr. Amberg-Sulzbach. der Naturhistorischen Gesellschaft Nürnberg. Fürth: VKA-Verlag, 127–144.

Klein, C., 1923. Die Ausgrabungen und Funde in der Heidenkapelle auf dem Halberg bei Saarbrücken. *Bericht I des Konservators der geschichtlichen Denkmäler im Saargebiet*, 13–20.

Koch K.-H. and Schindler R., 1994. *Vor- und frühgeschichtliche Burgwälle des Regierungsbezirks Trier und des Kreises Birkenfeld*. Trierer Grabungen und Forschungen XIII, Teil 2. Vor- und frühgeschichtliche Wehranlage im ehemaligen Stammesgebiet der Treverer. Mainz: Zabern.

Kotzur, H.-J. and Ecker, D., 2011. Das verschwundene Martinschörlein. Auf den Spuren eines architektonischen Kleinods. *In*: H.-J. Kotzur, ed. *Der verschwundene Dom. Wahrnehmung und Wandel der Mainzer Kathedrale im Lauf der Jahrhunderte*. Exhibition Catalogue Mainz. Mainz: Bischöfliches Dom- und Diözesanmuseum Mainz, 239–262.

Krause, H.-J., 2007. *Zur entwicklungsgeschichtlichen Einordnung und Datierung der Arkosolnische und der Phasen des Grabbaues*. *In*: H.-J. Krause and G. Voss, eds. *Das Heilige Grab in Gernrode. Bestandsdokumentation und Bestandsforschung*. Beiträge zur Denkmalkunde in Sachsen-Anhalt 3. Berlin: Deutscher Verlag für Kunstwissenschaft, 264–308.

Later, Ch., 2011. *Die Propstei Solnhofen im Altmühltal. Untersuchungen zur Baugeschichte der Kirche, zur Inszenierung eines früh- und hochmittelalterlichen Heiligenkultes und zur Sachkultur*. Kallmünz: Lassleben.

Linde, R. 2013. Die Kontroverse um die Externsteine. *In*: Ch. Stiegemann, M. Kroker and W. Walther, eds. *Credo. Christianisierung Europas im Mittelalter 2*. Exhibition Catalogue Paderborn. Nr. 696. Petersberg: Imhof, 767–768.

Matthes, W. and Speckner, R., 1997. *Das Relief an den Externsteinen*. Ostfildern: Edition Tertium.

Mundhenk, J., 1983. *Forschungen zur Geschichte der Externsteine IV. Die Geschichte der Externsteine in Schwerpunkten – eingeordnet in einen historischen Gesamtabriss*. Lemgo: F. L. Wagner.

Nortmann, H., 2005. Kastel-Staadt, Teilgemeinde Kastel, Kreis Trier-Saarburg. Eisenzeitliche Großbefestigung (Oppidum) mit römischer Nachfolgenutzung. *In*: J. Kunow and H.-H. Wegner, eds. *Urgeschichte im Rheinland. Jahrbuch 2005 des Rheinischen Vereins für Denkmalpflege und Landschaftsschutz*. Cologne: Rheinischen Vereins für Denkmalpflege und Landschaftsschutz, 381–383.

Nowothnig, W., 1978. Scharzfeld. 'Steinkirche', Ritterstein und Einhornhöhle. *In*: Römisch-Germanisches Zentralmuseum Mainz, ed. *Führer zu vor- und Frühgeschichtlichen Denkmälern 36, Westlicher Harz*. Mainz: Zabern, 203–212.

Pesch, A., 2003. *Noch ein Tropfen auf die heißen Steine ... Zur 1992 entdeckten Runeninschrift an den Externsteinen*. *In*: W. Heizmann and A. van Nahl, eds. *Runica – Germanica – Medievalia*. RGA Ergänzungsband 37. Berlin–New York: Walter de Gruyter, 567–580.

Quast, D., 2006. *Die frühalamannische und merowingerzeitliche Besiedlung im Umland des Runden Berges bei Urach*.

Forschungen und Berichte zur Vor- und Frühgeschichte in Baden-Württemberg 84. Stuttgart: Theiss.

Rahner , H., 1959. Einsiedler. *In*: J. Höfer and K. Rahner, eds. *Lexikon für Theologie und Kirche* 3. Freiburg: Herder, 767–769.

Ristow, S., 2007. *Frühes Christentum im Rheinland. Die Zeugnisse der archäologischen und historischen Quellen an Rhein, Maas und Mosel.* Münster: Aschendorff.

Schach-Dörges, H., 2010. Zu den Bestattungen frühalamannischer Zeit in der Sontheimer Höhle im Alb-Donau-Kreis. *Fundberichte aus Baden-Württemberg* 31, 615–664.

Schindler, R., 1963. Neue Untersuchungen am Mithrasheiligtum in Saarbrücken. Beiträge zur saarländischen Archäologie und Kunstgeschichte 10. *Bericht der Staatlichen Denkmalpflege im Saarland*, Saarbrücken: Staatliches Konservatoramt, 119–136.

Schindler, R., 1966. Die Mithrashöhle bei Saarbrücken. *In*: Römisch-Germanisches Zentralmuseum Mainz, ed. *Führer zu vor- und frühgeschichtlichen Denkmälern 5. Saarland.* Mainz: Zabern, 108–111.

Schirwitz, K., 1961. Zu den Ausgrabungen von 1937 vor der Steinkirche bei Scharzfeld am Harz. *Harz-Zeitschrift* 13, 1–8.

Schmidt, B., 1970. *Die späte Völkerwanderungszeit in Mitteldeutschland.* Katalog (Südteil). Veröffentlichungen des Landesmuseums für Vorgeschichte in Halle 25. Berlin: Landesmuseum für Vorgeschichte in Halle.

Schneider, H., 1994. *Vom heidnischen Heiligtum zur christlichen Wallfahrtsstätte. Zur Geschichte des kultisch-sakralen Teiles der Eremitage bei Bretzenheim.* Kl. Schriftenreihe Gesch. Eremitage in Bretzenheim 4. Bad Kreuznach: Privatdruck.

Schneider, H., 2003. *Die Felseneremitage in Bretzenheim a. d. Nahe: Einsiedelei, Felsenkloster und Wallfahrtsort vom frühen Mittelalter bis ins 19. Jahrhundert.* Bretzenheim a. d. Nahe: Privatdruck.

Schröter, F., 1852. *Über die römischen Niederlassungen und die Römerstraßen in den Saargegenden*, II. Saarbrücken: Hofer.

Schulze, M., 1984. Das ungarische Kriegergrab von Aspres-lès-Corps. Untersuchungen zu den Ungarneinfällen nach Mittel-, West- und Südeuropa (899–955 n. Chr.) mit einem Exkurs zur Münzchronologie altungarischer Gräber. *Jahrbuch des Römisch-Germanischen Zentralmuseums Mainz* 31, 473–514.

Schulze-Dörrlamm, M., 1999. Münzfibeln der Karolingerzeit. *Archäologisches Korrespondenzblatt* 29, 271–288.

Schulze-Dörrlamm, M., 2006. Spuren der Ungarneinfälle des 10. Jahrhunderts. *In*: F. Daim, ed. *Heldengrab im Niemandsland. Ein frühungarischer Reiter aus Niederösterreich. Mosaiksteine 2.* Mainz: Römisch-Germanisches Zentralmuseum 43–62.

Schulze-Dörrlamm, M., 2008. Zur Nutzung von Höhlen in der christlichen Welt des frühen Mittelalters (7.–10. Jahrhundert). *Jahrbuch des Römisch-Germanischen Zentralmuseums Mainz* 55, 529–675.

Schwineköper, B., 1975. Michaelstein. *In*: B. Schwineköper, ed. *Handbuch der historischen Stätten Deutschlands 11. Provinz Sachsen Anhalt.* Stuttgart: Kröner, 328–329.

Springer, M., 2000. Irminsul § 1 Historisches. *In*: J. Hoops, ed. *Reallexikon der Germanischen Altertumskunde* 15. Berlin, New York: De Gruyter, 504–505.

Steinacker, K., 1922. *Die Bau- und Kunstdenkmäler des Kreises Blankenburg.* Die Bau- und Kunstdenkmäler des Landes Braunschweig 6. Wolfenbüttel: Zwissler.

Steuer, H., 1982. *Schlüsselpaare in frühgeschichtlichen Gräbern - Zur Deutung einer Amulett-Beigabe.* Studien zur Sachsenforschung 3 . Hildesheim: Lax, 185–247.

Stoll-Tucker, B., 1997. *Nacheiszeitliche Höhlennutzung am Beispiel des oberen Pegnitztales (Nördliche Frankenalb).* Arbeiten zur Archäologie Süddeutschlands 4. Büchenbach: Faustus.

Treude, E. and Zelle, M., 2011. *Die Externsteine bei Horn.* Lippische Kulturlandschaften 18, Detmold: Lippischer Heimatbund.

Wackenroder, E., 1939. *Die Kunstdenkmäler des Kreises Saarburg.* Die Kunstdenkmäler der Rheinprovinz 15, 3. Abteilung. Düsseldorf: Schwann.

Walter, D., 1985. *Thüringer Höhlen und ihre holozänen Bodenaltertümer.* Weimar: Museum für Vor- und Frühgeschichte.

Walter, D., 1989, *Nacheisenzeitliche Höhlenfundplätze im Mittelgebirgsraum. In*: J. Herrmann ed. *Archäologie in der Deutschen Demokratischen Republik. Denkmale und Funde* 1. Archäologische Kulturen, geschichtliche Perioden und Volksstämme. Leipzig: Urania, 119–122.

Wegner, E., 1994. *Kreis Trier-Saarburg. Verbandsgemeinden Hermeskeil, Kell, Konz, Saarburg.* Kulturdenkmäler in Rheinland-Pfalz 12, 1. Worms: Wernersche Verlagsgesellschaft.

Wieland, G., 1996. *Die Spätlatènezeit in Württemberg.* Forschungen und Berichte zur Vor- und Frühgeschichte in Baden-Württemberg 63. Stuttgart: Theiss.

Zimmermann, W., 1935. *Die Kunstdenkmäler des Kreises Kreuznach.* Die Kunstdenkmäler der Rheinprovinz 18, 1. Düsseldorf: Schwann.

# Chapter 14

# Knights in the dark: on the function of Polish caves in the Middle Ages

*Michał Wojenka*

*This chapter discusses cave use in Poland during the Middle Ages, focusing on the Kraków-Częstochowa Upland in particular. The majority of material studied relates to later phases of the Middle Ages. Excluding a silver hoard deposited in Okopy Wielka Dolna Cave about 1095, most of the securely dated artefacts are linked to the so-called chivalric culture of the late thirteenth and first half of the fourteenth centuries AD, characterised primarily by finds of rowel spurs and two chivalric belt fittings. The remaining weaponry fragments mostly comprise boltheads, which cannot be dated more precisely than to the Middle Ages. Activities of armed groups in caves in the Kraków-Częstochowa Upland are not recorded in medieval texts. However, one legend records that the Polish duke Władysław, the 'Elbow-high', found refuge in a cave near Ojców village, possibly in the spring of 1306, as he struggled to wrest power from King Wenceslaus III in Krakow. Some military material from caves probably relates to this 'legendary' event.*

## Introduction

On a summer's day in 1871, Count Jan Zawisza, owner of the picturesque village of Ojców, began amateur investigations in caves that were located in the area. He probably had little awareness of the future archaeological significance of these caves and the locality he governed. That summer marked the beginning of Polish cave archaeology and Ojców, a small locality situated in the Jurassic region of the Kraków-Częstochowa Uplands, became one of the cradles of Polish prehistory. Over this 140-year history of cave archaeology in Poland, more than 180 caves have been explored. Almost from the beginning archaeological investigations in caves focused primarily on the search for Palaeolithic assemblages. This was undoubtedly a result of the remarkable Stone Age finds discovered in the caves of Mamutowa and Maszycka (Zawisza 1874; 1876; 1882; Ossowski 1884). Because of this focus, however, material relating to later periods of use received little or no attention, leading to a perception that caves were exclusively places of Palaeolithic activity (Wojenka 2011, 105; 2012a, 16).

This paper is an attempt to explore the medieval use of caves and rockshelters in Poland, focusing almost exclusively on sites situated within the Kraków-Częstochowa Uplands – a region in the central part of southern Poland (Fig. 14.1). This region is karst-rich with more than 1800 caves currently documented (e.g. Gradziński and Szelerewicz 2004, 75, tab. 2, cf. Kowalski 1951, 6). These caves became the subject of systematic archaeological excavations, with little investigation of caves elsewhere in Poland, though with some notable exceptions: Obłazowa and W Wąwozie Sobczańskim Dolna Cave in Nowa Biała; Magurska Cave in Zakopane; Raj Cave in Chęciny; Nad Stawem w Gackach Cave in Leszcze; and, to a certain extent, Zbójecka Cave in Łagów. The first three sites are located within the Pieniny (Nowa Biała) and Tatra Mountains (Zakopane) respectively, the cave in Leszcze lies in the River Nida region, and the latter two are situated in the Świętokrzyskie Mountains (Fig. 14.1). Smaller archaeological investigations carried out in four caves in the Sudety Mountains were of no archaeological significance (see below). Only three of the aforementioned sites produced medieval assemblages: Obłazowa, Nad Stawem w Gackach and Zbójecka.

Overall, evidence of medieval activities is currently recorded from 59 caves, of which only three are located

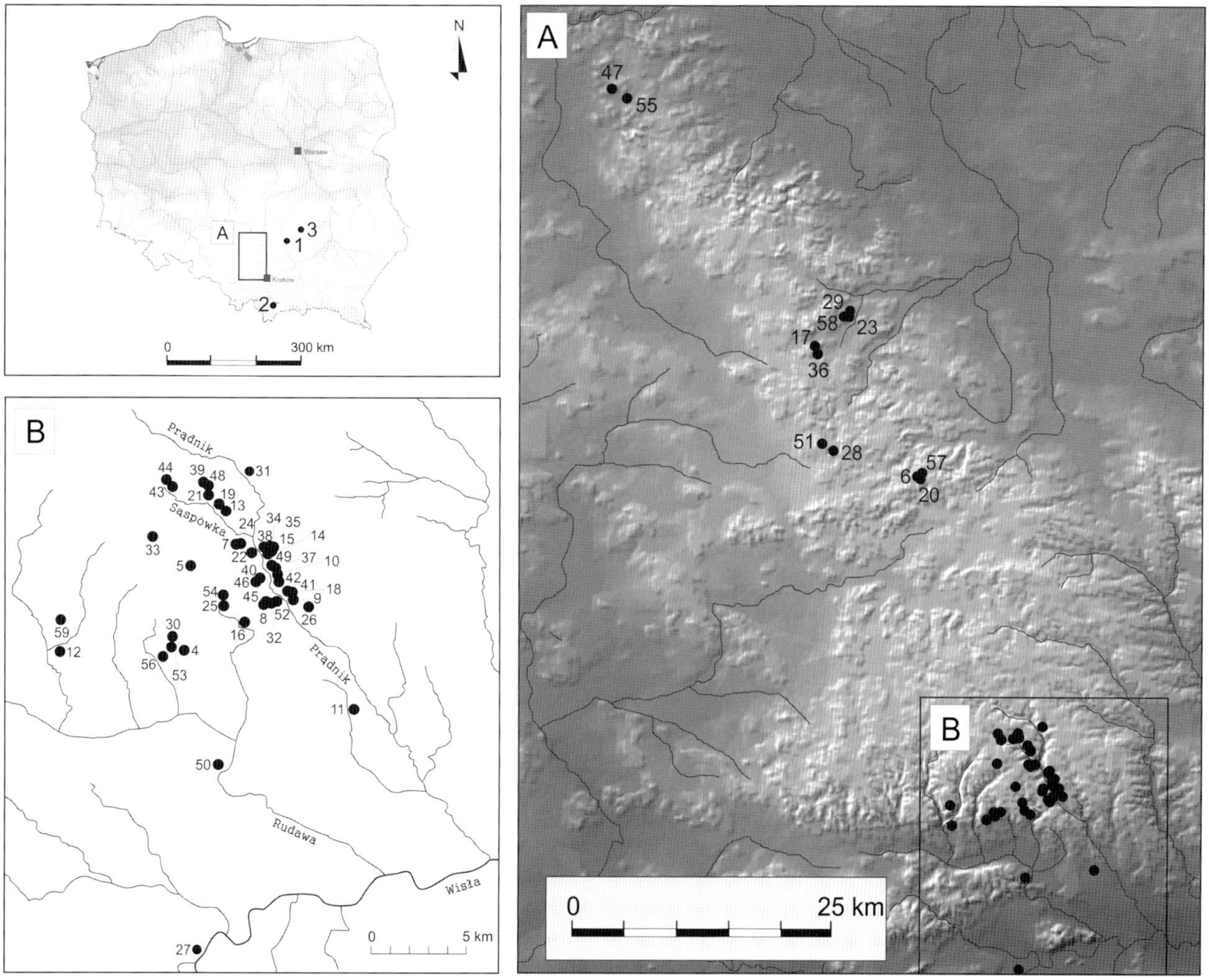


*Figure 14.1: The distribution of caves and rockshelters with medieval assemblages in Poland. 1. Nad Stawem w Gackach Cave, Leszcze; 2. Obłazowa Cave, Nowa Biała; 3. Zbójecka Cave, Łagów; 4. Bezimienna Cave, Bolechowice; 5. Bębłowska Dolna Cave, Bębło; 6. Biśnik Cave, Strzegowa; 7. Boczne przy Jaskini Łokietka rockshelter, Ojców; 8. Boczne przy Jaskini Sypialni rockshelter, Biały Kościół; 9. Boczne w Ogrójcu rockshelter, Prądnik Czajowski; 10. Borsucza w Górze Okopy Cave, Ojców; 11. Borsucza Cave, Podskalany; 12. Borsuka Cave, Radwanowice; 13. Bramka rockshelter, Sąspów; 14. Ciemna Cave, Ojców; 15. Dolne Zachodnie w Górze Koronnej rockshelter, Ojców; 16. Duża w Mącznych Skałach Cave, Biały Kościół; 17. Dziadowa Skała Cave, Skarżyce; 18. Górne w Kopcowej Skale rockshelter, Prądnik Czajowski; 19. Iłowe rockshelter, Sąspów; 20. Jasna Smoleńska Cave, Strzegowa; 21. Koziarnia Cave, Sąspów; 22. Krowia Cave, Ojców; 23. Krucza Skała rockshelter, Kroczyce; 24. Łokietka Cave, Ojców; 25. Mamutowa Cave, Wierzchowie; 26. Maszycka Cave, Maszyce; 27. Na Gołąbcu Cave, Piekary; 28. Na Górze Birów IV rockshelter, Podzamcze; 29. Na Górze Słupsko rockshelter, Kostkowice; 30. Na Kawcu Cave, Karniowice; 31. Nad Mosurem Starym Duża Cave, Grodzisko; 32. Nad Tunelem w Stodoliskach Cave, Biały Kościół; 33. Nietoperzowa Cave, Jerzmanowice; 34. Oborzysko Małe rockshelter, Ojców; 35. Oborzysko Duże rockshelter, Ojców; 36. Okiennik Wielki Cave, Żerkowice; 37. Okopy Wielka Dolna Cave, Ojców; 38. Pod Rękawicą rockshelter, Ojców; 39. Pod Tunelem Wielkim Cave, Sąspów; 40. Potrójne rockshelter, Ojców; 41. Północne w Kopcowej Górze rockshelter, Prądnik Czajowski; 42. Puchacza Cave, Ojców; 43. Sąspowska Wschodnia Cave, Sąspów, 44. Sąspowska Zachodnia Cave, Sąspów; 45. Sypialnia Cave, Biały Kościół; 46. Średnie w Korytanii rockshelter, Ojców; 47. Towarna Cave, Kusięta; 48. Tunel Wielki Cave, Sąspów, 49. W Okopach Górna Cave, Ojców; 50. W Skale Kmity rockshelter, Zabierzów; 51. W Skale Rzędowej rockshelter, Bzów; 52. W Stokowej Skale rockshelter, Prądnik Czajowski; 53. Wielka Strąka Cave, Kobylany; 54. Wierzchowska Górna Cave, Wierzchowie; 55. Zamkowa Dolna Cave, Olsztyn; 56. Zdaminowa Cave, Kobylany; 57. Zegarowa Cave, Strzegowa; 58. Złodziejska Cave, Kroczyce; 59. Żarska Cave, Żary. (**Częstochowa district**: Kusięta, Olsztyn; **Kielce district**: Łagów; **Nowy Targ district**: Nowa Biała; **Kraków district**: Bębło, Biały Kościół, Bolechowice, Grodzisko, Jerzmanowice, Karniowice, Kobylany, Maszyce, Ojców, Piekary, Podskalany, Prądnik Czajowski, Radowanowice, Sąspów, Wierzchowie, Zabierzów, Żary; **Olkusz district**: Strzegowa; **Zawiercie district**: Bzów, Kostkowice, Kroczyce, Podzamcze, Skarżyce, Zawiercie, Żerkowice.) Drawing: M. Wojenka.*

outside the Kraków-Częstochowa Uplands (Fig. 14.1). In this paper, the term 'medieval' relates to period from the sixth to the early sixteenth century, corresponding to the early Middle Ages (sixth to mid-thirteenth century) and late Middle Ages (mid-thirteenth to sixteenth century) in Poland. However, as will be outlined below, the earliest evidence for the medieval use of Polish caves is not until the ninth century, and the end of the Middle Ages (fifteenth to early sixteenth century) is not clearly represented at cave sites. Here I examine both natural caves and rockshelters, without discussing the differences between these categories (Grodzicki 1991; McNatt 1996; Matoušek *et al.* 2005, 13–17). Even though, according to some researchers, rockshelters can be considered a type of cave (e.g. Gradziński 2012), I will not depart from the term 'rockshelter' in cases where it is firmly rooted in the archaeological literature.

From the outset, it must be stated that it is presently difficult to identify instances of the ritual use of caves in Poland during the Middle Ages, though to some extent this may be a consequence of the history of cave research. The upper sediments in caves, which hypothetically might have contained remnants of medieval activities, were often the subject of investigations in the late nineteenth and early twentieth centuries when archaeological methods were not to modern scientific standards. Bearing in mind the imperfect methods of that time, it is plausible that archaeological material related to ritual may have been overlooked. At present the only approach to identifying potential medieval rituals in caves is to examine assemblages of undated human bones recovered from the upper strata of more than a dozen Polish cave sites, all but one of which are situated in the Kraków-Częstochowa Uplands. In each instance the archaeological context must be regarded as insecure and thus it is not possible to date these bones by association. Generally, the human remains in question were typically found in a disarticulated state and it is difficult to say what this represents – whether intact skeletons had been disturbed during subsequent human activities in a cave and/ or dispersed by natural post-depositional processes. Until now these skeletal remains have been largely neglected by researchers, with the exception of Stanisław Jan Czarnowski who considered skulls found in the Ojców area (Czarnowski 1903, 1904a, 1909).

## A brief history of cave research in Poland (with special regard to medieval archaeology)

The history of cave archaeology in Poland is, to some extent, coeval with the development of cave archaeology in the Kraków-Częstochowa Uplands (Fig. 14.1). This section begins with an attempt to summarise the work conducted in caves in the Uplands and is supplemented by a brief description of the archaeological excavations carried out in caves outside this region (see also: Rook 1980, 7–8; Partyka 1992; Lech 2001; Cyrek 2002, 9–15, 2007a, 2009; Lech and Partyka 2006; Stefaniak *et al.* 2009; Wojenka 2012a, 8–13).

The earliest published references to the archaeological significance of caves can be credited to M. Olszyński (1871) and J. Zawisza (1871) who describe fieldwork carried out by Zawisza in the vicinity of Ojców in 1871 (including Łokietka, Zbójecka and Nietoperzowa caves) (Fig. 14.2). From that point onwards, caves in Poland – and especially in the Kraków-Częstochowa Uplands – became the subject of scientific investigations (Partyka 1992, 73; Lech and Partyka 2006, 56). Zawisza's research campaign lasted for more than ten years and involved excavations at some important caves situated around Ojców: Mamutowa, Łokietka, Ciemna, Okopy Wielka, Dolna and Nietoperzowa caves (Wojenka 2012a, 8). At the same time, several small excavations were directed by other antiquarians in the southern part of the Uplands, such as at Smocza Jama Cave in Kraków and Na Łopiankach Cave in Mników. It is worth noting that, in contrast to Zawisza's work, these excavations consisted of formal institutional projects undertaken by the Anthropological Commission of the Academy of Arts and Sciences in Kraków.

Paradoxically, the initial period of scientific interest in caves coincided with the serious destruction of many sites, a consequence of the growth of the guano mining industry between 1872 and 1879 (Kowalski 1951, 36; Rook 1980, 7). The upper sediments of many sites were irretrievably lost – as was the case at Nietoperzowa Cave in Jerzmanowice, an important site now recognised for its Palaeolithic assemblages (Chmielewski 1961), and Koziarnia Cave in Ojców. These industrial activities attracted the interest of F. Roemer, a geologist and paleontologist from Wrocław, who published some of artefacts that were discovered,

*Figure 14.2: Fielwork of 1871 in Zbójecka Cave in Ojców. Source: Olszyński 1871, 373.*

including a medieval bolthead from Koziarnia Cave (Roemer 1884, pl. VI.8).

An important event occurred in 1879 when a well-known prehistorian, Gotfryd Ossowski, began his examination of caves in the Kraków area, which represented a turning point in the development of Polish cave archaeology. He excavated about 50 cave sites on behalf of the Academy of Arts and Sciences (Rook 1980, 7), including the famous Maszycka Cave in Maszyce, which yielded spectacular Upper Palaeolithic finds (Ossowski 1884, 70–85). Ossowski's work led to the first significant insight into the medieval usage of caves as a result of excavations at sites such as Na Gołąbcu Cave in Piekary, rockshelter W Skale Kmity in Zabierzów, and Wierzchowska Górna Cave in Wierzchowie (Ossowski 1880, 51–52, 1887, 19–25).

Medieval finds unearthed by Ossowski undoubtedly heralded the potential of caves as sources for the study of the archaeology of the Middle Ages. At the end of the nineteenth century an intensive programme of cave investigation led by Stanisław Jan Czarnowski was instigated in the Ojców area. Though not an archaeologist, Czarnowski had a deep interest in caves, especially in terms of their usage in late prehistoric and historic times. During his long-term fieldwork campaign, more than 50 caves and rockshelters were investigated for the first time (Lech 2001, 135). In some respects, Czarnowski continued the earlier efforts of Ossowski by examining sites situated in the southern part of the Kraków-Częstochowa Uplands. It should be mentioned that until 1918 the southern part of Uplands acted as the border between the Russian and Austro-Hungarian empires, thus the activities of both researchers were limited: Ossowski was active on the Austrian side, while Czarnowski worked on the opposite side of the border. In relation to medieval cave usage, Czarnowski's excavations were immensely important. He was one of few cave researchers interested in examining the upper layers in caves. The results of his fieldwork led to the publication of medieval artefacts found in the Ojców area at sites such as Okopy Wielka, Dolna Cave, Główna w Kopcowej Górze Cave, Łokietka Cave and Pod Rękawicą rockshelter (Czarnowski 1898, 1911a, 1914a, 1924). While allowing for problems with his excavation methodology, it must be emphasised that Czarnowski's work made a lasting contribution to the entire Holocene archaeology from Polish caves, including the Middle Ages.

One would be wrong to assume that the outcomes of Czarnowski's excavations laid the groundwork for subsequent archaeological studies in medieval cave use. His death in 1929 marked the end of an era: over the following decades, almost without exception, scholars were primarily interested in caves only in terms of Palaeolithic occupation (Cyrek 2007a). However, prior to World War II the principal caves in the Kraków-Częstochowa Uplands attracted the attention of Stefan Krukowski and Leon Kozłowski, including Ciemna and Nietoperzowa caves, which yielded interesting prehistoric finds (Kozłowski 1921; Krukowski 1948).

Cave research after 1945 continued to focus on the Palaeolithic. Jasna and Mroczna Cave in Strzegowa, explored by Sawicki (1949, 1953) and Stefaniak *et al.* (2009, 312–314), as well as Dziadowa Skała in Skarżyce and Nietoperzowa in Jerzmanowice, excavated by Chmielewski (1958, 1961), are known only for their Palaeolithic assemblages. The 1960s and 1970s witnessed an increase in archaeological research in caves. Intensive and multidisciplinary projects in the Sąspowska valley (the Ojców area), led by Chmielewski, involved the investigation of 13 caves and rockshelters including Sąspowska Zachodnia, Sąspowska Wschodnia, Koziarnia and Tunel Wielki. Unfortunately, the results of these excavations were never published in detail, though a short article refers to some medieval finds (Chmielewski 1988).

Only a few of the numerous cave excavations carried out from the 1960s to the 1980s are of interest in terms of medieval archaeology (Wojenka 2012a, 11–12). The Palaeolithic continued to be the focus of most fieldwork, with finds from later periods a by-product of this work (see Dagnan-Ginter *et al.* 1992, pl. 2). In several instances, however, the research goals were to recover evidence of later activities, as at Cave no. 1 in Tyniec (Fraś and Olszowski 1971), Wierzchowska Górna Cave in Wierzchowie (Mączyńska and Rook 1972), and Nad Mosurem Starym Duża Cave in Grodzisko, where attention was concentrated on Neolithic activities (Rook 1970a, 1970b). It is regrettable that the excavations carried out from 1969–1971 in Zamkowa Dolna Cave in Olsztyn did not result in the publication of material relevant to medieval research; the cave is said to have been used as a smithy by medieval inhabitants of Olstin/Holstain castle and was enclosed within its fortifications (Kopacz and Skalski 1971; Kopacz 1975, 71).

The state of research in medieval cave use improved during the 1990s largely as a result of excavations led by Muzolf in the central part of the Kraków-Częstochowa Uplands, within the area of Ogrodzieniec, where traces of thirteenth-/fourteenth-century occupation were found in Zegar Cave, W Pośrednicy rockshelter and Jasna Smoleńska Cave (Muzolf 1999; Stefaniak *et al.* 2009). At about the same time, medieval activities were identified in Biśnik Cave in Strzegowa, producing a thirteenth-/fourteenth-century assemblage most likely contemporaneous with the fortification located above the cave (Cyrek 2002, 23). Excavations in Łokietka Cave also shed new light on medieval cave use in the Ojców area (Sobczyk and Sitlivy 2001a, 2001b).

Cave research projects and excavations have continued to the present day including, for instance, excavations in Ciemna Cave in Ojców (Valde-Nowak *et al.* 2014; Wojenka 2013), Żarska Cave in Żary (Wojenka *et al.* 2011) and Na Górze Słupsko rockshelter in Kostkowice (Krajcarz *et al.* 2014).

Relevant to the above review are archaeological excavations carried out in caves situated outside the Kraków-Częstochowa Uplands. These sites, however, were rarely the subject of proper archaeological excavation. In the Polish Carpathians only three sites merit comment. Magurska Cave in Zakopane was excavated in 1937 but to poor archaeological standards (Jura 1949; Kowalski 1953, 17–18; Cyrek 2002, 10–11, fig. 1). W Wąwozie Sobczańskim Dolna Cave, excavated in 1985, yielded only paleontological material (Alexandrowicz *et al.* 1985). More can be said about Obłazowa Cave in Nowa Biała. This key cave site in the Pieniny Mountains has been excavated since 1985, yielding Palaeolithic and later assemblages including medieval artefacts (Valde-Nowak 2003, 72–73). Much less is known of four caves in the Sudety Mountains that were excavated before World War II: Radochowska Cave in Radochów, and W Połomie Południowa, Północna and Wschodnia caves in Wojcieszów (Zotz 1939; Kowalski 1954, 77–78; Cyrek 2002, 10–11, fig. 1; Bieroński *et al.* 2009). Contrary to the opinion of some scholars (see map in Cyrek 2002, 10–11, fig. 1), because of a lack of finds Niedźwiedzia Cave in Kletno is excluded from the register of archaeological sites (Stefaniak and Bieroński 2009, 517).

A similar state of research exists with regard caves in the Świętokrzyskie Mountains. The most famous cave in the region (and the only one that was archaeologically excavated) is Raj Cave in Chęciny, which was inaccessible during the late Holocene (Kozłowski 1972). More interesting for us is the discovery of medieval ceramics in Zbójecka Cave in Łagów (Hadamik 2013, 56-59). Medieval ceramic assemblages were also recovered from Nad Stawem w Gackach Cave in Leszcze during excavations in 1994 (Informator Archeologiczny 1998, 31–32).

## Polish caves in the Middle Ages: the archaeological evidence

The above outline of cave research in Poland clearly illustrates that cave use in medieval Poland can be studied almost exclusively based on sites in the Kraków-Częstochowa Uplands. The specific natural features of the Uplands, the relatively harsh climate and poor quality soils, probably made the region less attractive for the first Slavic settlers who came to southeastern Poland from the Dnieper basin in the early sixth century AD. This resulted in a hiatus of activity on most of the Uplands, which lasted at least until the second half of the eighth century and possibly into the ninth century when the first strongholds were established in the area. The earliest known medieval finds from caves date to this early stage of colonisation of the Uplands, represented only by about a dozen pottery sherds discovered in 2011–2012 in Na Górze Słupsko rockshelter in Kostkowice (Krajcarz *et al.* 2014, 25, fig. 5b). What is remarkable is that these appear to represent the same phase of settlement as the early medieval stronghold on the hill. The fortified site at Kostkowice has a somewhat broader date, spanning the ninth and tenth centuries, based on two iron deposits of so-called 'axe-like' *grivnas* (Zagórska-Telega and Bochnak 2001; Rozmus *et al.* 2006). The cultural material from the rockshelter can be interpreted as being associated with the occupants of the fortification.

The isolated finds from Na Górze Słupsko rockshelter testify to the use of caves in the pre-Christian or 'tribal' era (i.e. before the late tenth century), some two hundred years before the next evidence of cave usage. That next site, Okopy Wielka Dolna Cave in Okopy Hill in the Ojców area, produced material of an entirely different character (Fig. 14.3). A silver hoard was recovered there during excavations by Czarnowski in 1897 (Czarnowski 1898; Mycielska and Rook 1965, 156, 167–168; Reyman 1966, 23; Suchodolski 1987, 18–41; Reyman-Walczak *et al.* 2013, 127–130). The hoard, comprising 116 coins and two amorphous cast silver 'ingots' contained in a small clay vessel, was deposited in a shallow niche (Fig. 14.4.1) (Wojenka 2012b). The majority of the coins are relatively common issues of so-called cross pennies, but the presence of 26 rare specimens from the first private Polish coinage, minted by the powerful nobleman Sieciech, is remarkable. The latest coin in the hoard was minted in Hungary during the reign of Ladislaus I (1077–1095), which leads to the conclusion that the hoard was deposited at the very end of the eleventh century. A second coin hoard was found in 1912 when Czarnowski was exploring the nearby Pod Rękawicą rockshelter, about 600m from Okopy Hill. Four coins appear to have been discovered around a fireplace from which an iron arrowhead was retrieved (Czarnowski 1924, 21). The issuer of two of the coins was also the aforementioned Sieciech (Suchodolski 1987, 18; Reyman-Walczak *et al.* 2013, 130). In my opinion, the Pod Rękawicą

*Figure 14.3: The main entrance to Okopy Wielka Dolna Cave in Ojców (marked with an arrow). View from the west. Photo: M. Wojenka*

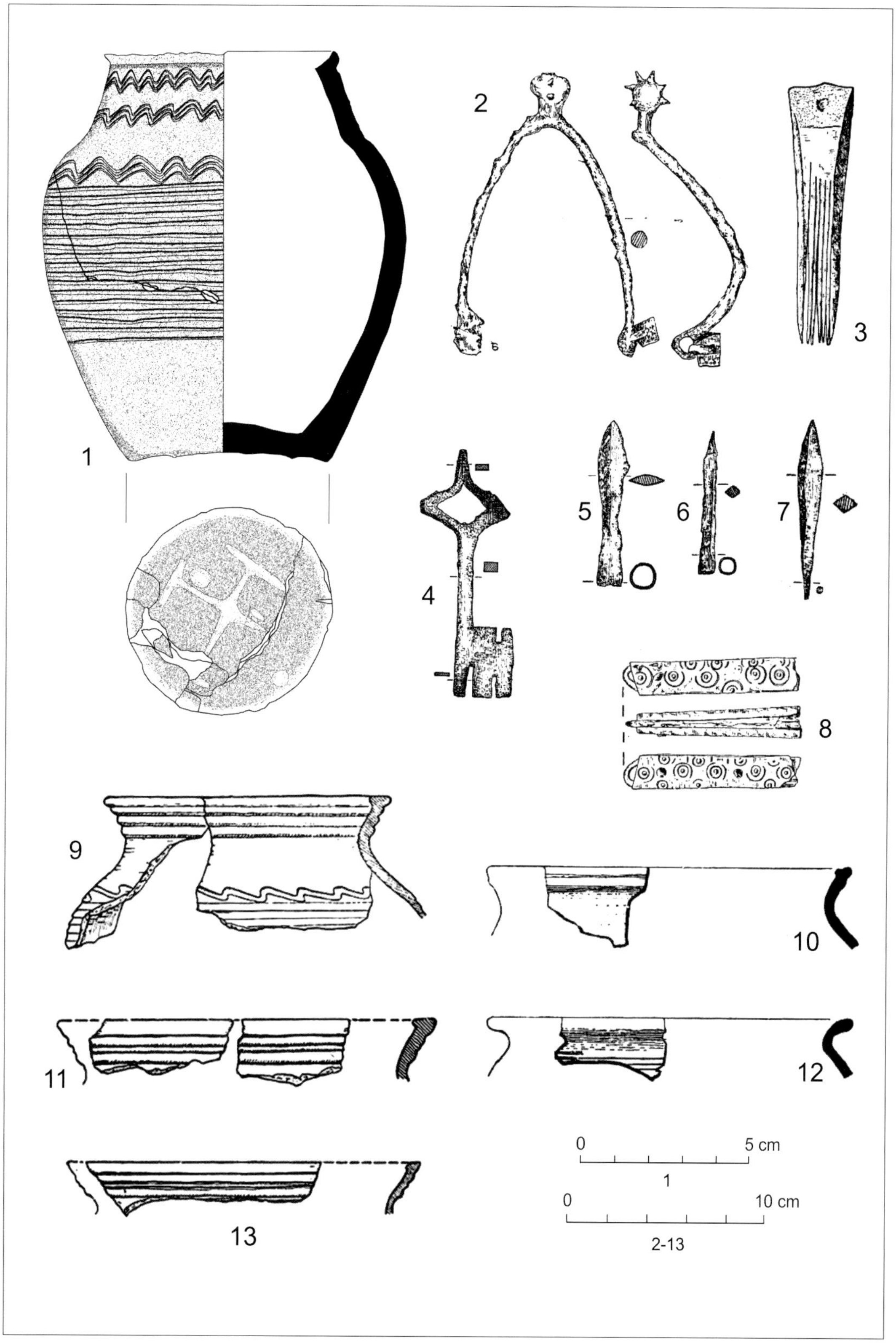


*Figure 14.4: Pottery and metalwork from Polish caves. 1, 9, 11, 13. Okopy Wielka Dolna Cave (after Mycielska and Rook 1965, pl. IX.8, 10, 14; Wojenka 2012b, 239, pl. 3); 10, 12. Oborzysko Małe rockshelter (after Rook 1964, pl. II.20, 22); 2, 4–7. Bębłowska Dolna Cave (after Rook 1963, pl. I. 6–12); 3, 8. Wierzchowska Górna Cave (after Mączyńska and Rook 1972, pl. XV.7–8). 1, 9–13. clay; 2, 4–7. iron; 3, 8. bone. Printed with permission from the Archaeological Museum in Kraków.*

coins should be considered the remnants of another hoard that was probably destroyed and scattered, possibly even during Czarnowski's explorations.

What is interesting about these two coin hoards is that an eleventh-century settlement is not confirmed in the Ojców area. The earliest historical records date only to 1231 when the adjacent village of Smardzowice is mentioned. Theoretically it might suggest that the deposition of coin hoards had nothing to do with settlement of the area. This might be true, but it should be kept in mind that the earliest historical records could have been written much later, after settlements had been established. In fact, an early medieval assemblage from a cave might indicate that surrounding villages were settled at a similar early date. For example, the earliest medieval pottery from Łokietka Cave dates to the eleventh-twelfth centuries (Rodzińska-Nowak *et al.* 2002, 321), while rural settlement in the vicinity is only confirmed at least 200–300 years later, including the nearest village, Czajowice, first mentioned as late as 1382. A similar situation occurs at Wierzchowska Górna Cave in Wierzchowie and Maszycka Cave in Maszyce where a few sherds of so-called 'white' early medieval pottery were found (Rook 1970c, 146; Mączyńska and Rook 1972, 133); these vessels date from the eleventh to the thirteenth century (Mączyńska and Rook 1972, 133) and it is likely that a similar timeframe applies to a decorated bone knife handle from Wierzchowska Górna Cave (Fig. 14.4.8). The date of material from these two sites is earlier than the first written records concerning the adjacent rural settlements. Some unspecified 'early medieval' pottery fragments are also mentioned from Dziadowa Skała Cave in Skarżyce, but it is difficult to date these more precisely (Chmielewski 1958, 26). A similar problem arises regarding the date of a bone comb from Wierzchowska Górna Cave (Fig. 14.4.3) (Mączyńska and Rook 1972, pl. XV.8; Wojenka 2012a, 25).

An intensification of cave use in the Kraków-Częstochowa Uplands took place during the late Middle Ages, particularly in the thirteenth and fourteenth centuries when a number of sites were in use. Later activities, from the fifteenth to the beginnings of the sixteenth century, are rare. Pottery fragments are the most frequent finds from the thirteenth and fourteenth centuries (Fig. 14.4.9–13). One ceramic assemblage that dates to this period was recovered from Łokietka Cave in Ojców. A pit dug into the floor of Krucza Skała rockshelter in Kostkowice produced pottery of thirteenth- to fourteenth-century date (Cyrek 1994, 41). Similarly, a pit in Biśnik Cave in Strzegowa contained pottery from the fourteenth/fifteenth centuries and an iron knife (Cyrek 2002, 23). In recent years, large quantities of medieval pottery have been retrieved during the archaeological investigations of Ciemna Cave in Ojców. Though this assemblage is currently under analysis, it principally appears to date to the thirteenth or early fourteenth centuries (Wojenka 2013, 258, fig. 8.6–8.10), and probably relates closely to metal artefacts from the site (see below). Some medieval pottery sherds of unspecified date have also been found in Okopy Wielka Dolna Cave (Fig. 14.4.9, 14.4.11, 14.4.13), Potrójne rockshelter, and a few other caves in the Ojców area (Wojenka 2012a, 25–26).

A little more can be said about an interesting ceramic assemblage from the Main Chamber of Żarska Cave, excavated by the present author and J. Wilczyński in 2012 and 2014 (Fig. 14.5). The pottery represents a typical wheel-made household assemblage (Fig. 14.6). The vessels are richly ornamented and well-fired. What is interesting is the large size of the pots (cf. Fig. 14.6.1, 14.6.4, 14.6.11), leading to a tempting conclusion that they functioned for storage. The vessels were mostly found in association with an extraordinarily large fireplace (at least five square metres) that contained large quantities of faunal remains, especially pig and poultry (the bones are currently under analysis). The form, fabric, rim profiles and olive-green glaze of the vessels from Żarska Cave date medieval activities at the site to the second half of the thirteenth century and first half of the fourteenth century. Regrettably, it is not possible to definitively attribute the few metal artefacts from this cave to the Middle Ages. Interestingly, the context of the medieval finds from Żarska Cave has parallels with other cave sites: hearths containing medieval pottery sherds of unspecified date have been discovered in Jasna Smoleńska Cave in Smoleń (Stefaniak *et al.* 2009), Złodziejska Cave in Kroczyce (Cyrek 2007b, 20), and Cave no. 4 in Birów (Mirosław-Grabowska *et al.* 2007, 25).

Though medieval assemblages from caves in the Kraków-Częstochowa Uplands frequently contain pottery, these are not easily dated owing to a generally poor chronological division of ceramic types. Fortunately, however, a group of metal finds (mostly iron) are also known. These include items such as a 'Gothic' key with rhomboidal handle from Bębłowska Dolna Cave in Bębło (Fig. 14.4.4) (Rook 1963, 339, tab. I.7), and a somewhat problematic anchor-shaped

*Figure 14.5: The main entrance to Żarska Cave in Żary (marked with an arrow). View from the north. Photo: M. Wojenka*

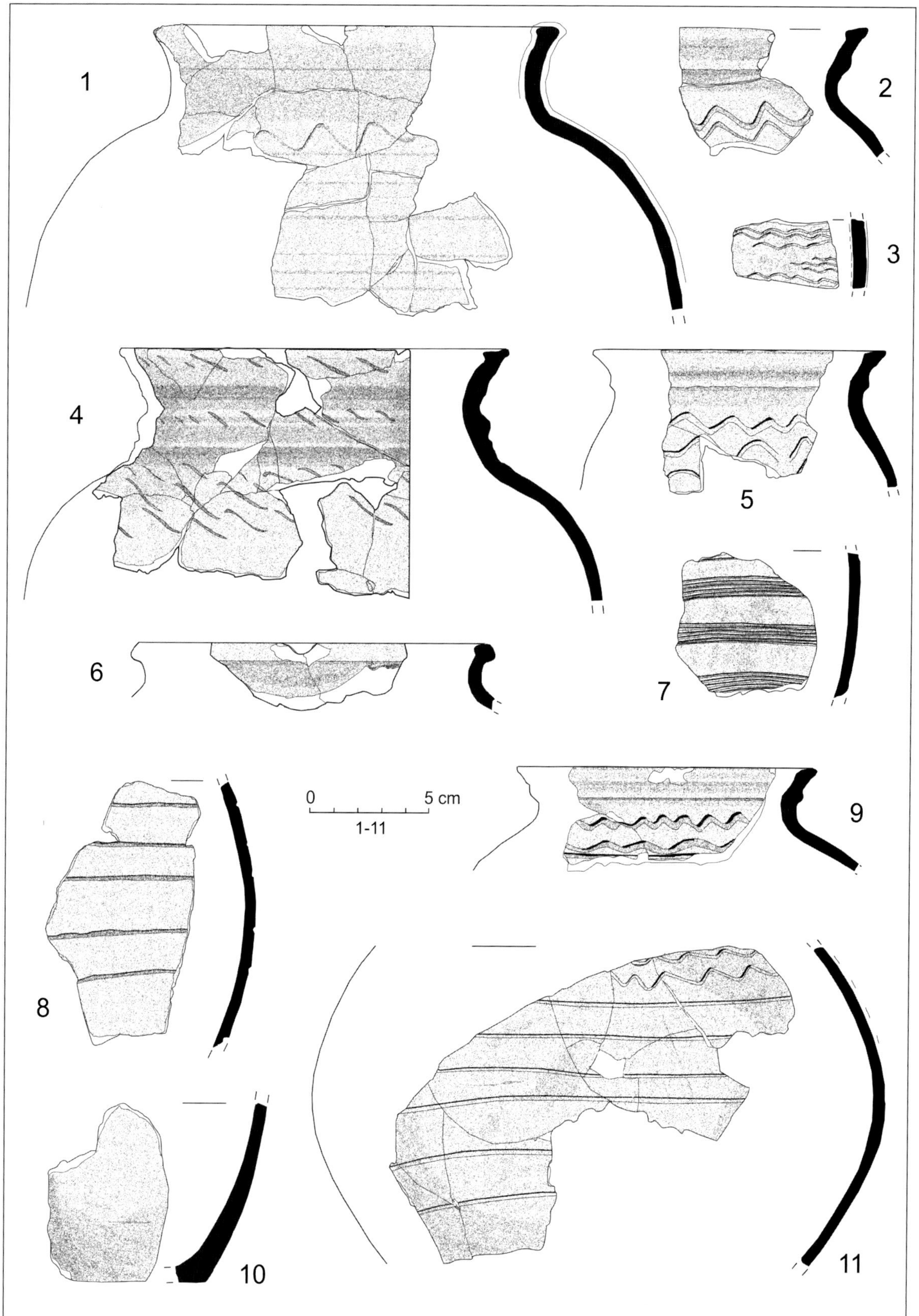


*Figure 14.6: Pottery assemblage from Żarska Cave. Drawing: M. Wojenka.*

key from Główna w Kopcowej Górze Cave (Czarnowski 1911a, 16) that may actually be of Iron Age date (Wojenka 2012a, 27). An iron pincher has been discovered in Boczne w Ogrójcu rockshelter in Maszyce (Czarnowski 1914b, 46, tab. VII.O.5), and three belt buckles that are difficult to date have been recovered from Okopy Wielka Górna Cave and W Stokowej Skale rockshelter in the Ojców area. They survive in the form of unclear photographs in antiquarian publications (Czarnowski 1902, 10, tab. 8.5; 1926, fig. 9.12). Luckily, the belt buckles from Jasna Smoleńska Cave derive from a sealed and stratigraphically secure medieval fireplace (Stefaniak *et al.* 2009). All of these metal finds were accompanied by sherds of pottery.

Another group of finds from caves could be described as belonging to a 'military horizon' and relating to activities of unspecified armed groups in caves. This is characterised mainly by finds of rowel spurs, currently known from at least ten sites (Wojenka 2012a, 28). Many of these derive from older excavations by Ossowski and Czarnowski, though one specimen was recently retrieved from Ciemna Cave (Fig. 14.7.6) (Wojenka 2013, 258, fig. 8.5) – a significant point that will be returned to later. Four spurs are recorded from Bębłowska Dolna Cave at Bębło (Fig. 14.4.2) (Rook 1963, 338–339, 341–342, pl. I.6), and a single example is known from Na Gołąbcu Cave in Piekary (Ossowski 1880, 51–52; Dąbrowska 1962, 56). Rowel spurs also surfaced in the adjacent rockshelter of Boczne w Ogrójcu (Czarnowski 1914b, 46, pl. VII.O.8). An unspecified spur, said to be 'historic' and as such presumably a rowel form, came from Oborzysko Wielkie near Ciemna Cave (Czarnowski 1924, 18). This specimen is now lost, as are finds from Wierzchowska Górna Cave at Wierzchowie (Ossowski 1887, 23; Mączyńska and Rook 1972, 122), and two unspecified spurs from Nad Bystrą Wodą Cave in Ojców (Czarnowski 1911b, 50; Czarnowski 1911c, 634). From brief literary references, we also know of incomplete spurs of thirteenth- to fourteenth-century date discovered quite a distance from the Ojców area in Jasna Smoleńska Cave, Strzegowa (Stefaniak *et al.* 2009, 263). Without exception, the published and surviving artefacts represent the older variant of the rowel spur, most likely attributable to type A–C, which dates from the mid-thirteenth to the mid-fourteenth century (Kołodziejski 1985, 166).

Other military finds from caves cannot be closely dated and include quite a few boltheads and arrowheads (Fig. 14.4.5–14.4.7) (Ossowski 1887, 23; Rook 1963, 339, pl. I.9–10, 12; Mączyńska and Rook 1972, 122; Dagnan-Ginter *et al.* 1992, 9, pl. II.5). As a rule, these are isolated finds. One exception is W Skale Kmity Cave, Zabierzów, which yielded more than 30 boltheads and two arrowheads with distinctive lozenge-shaped blades (Ossowski 1880, 52; Dąbrowska 1962, 75–78). The arrowheads may be of non-local provenance, very likely associated with the steppe/nomadic environment (Liwoch 2016; Świętosławski 1997, 65, 82). Two spearheads are also known from the rockshelters of Boczne w Ogrójcu and Boczne przy Jaskini Łokietka (Czarnowski 1914a, pl. XVI.1; 1914b, 46, pl. VII.O.7). Ossowski reported on a sword fragment from Na Gołąbcu Cave at Piekary (Ossowski 1880, 51–52), but this was not confirmed during a museum review by Dąbrowska (1962, 56). A fragment of chain mail is also known from Jasna Smoleńska Cave (Muzolf 1999, 14).

Returning to the rowel spur from Ciemna Cave, no other cave site has such a strong 'military horizon'. A fragment of a rowel spur (Fig. 14.7.6) discovered in 2007 is an early variant corresponding to type A, possibly type C, dated from the second half of the thirteenth to the first half of the fourteenth century (Kołodziejski 1985, 165–166; Hilczerówna 1956, 63 *et passim*). Apart from the rowel spur, this site also yielded a small iron buckle (Fig. 14.7.4), which I categorise as a spur fastener (Whitehead 1996, 29–30). The distinctive profiling of its frame corresponds to a style design characteristic in Western Europe in the period 1250–1305 (Fingerlin 1971, 218; Egan and Pritchard 2002, 22). A notable find is a silver *parvus*, i.e. a small penny of King Wenceslaus II struck in 1300–1305 (Fig. 14.7.1) (Hášková 1991, 24). An iron fire steel is less certain in terms of precise dating (Fig. 14.7.5). The most interesting find from Ciemna Cave is, however, a tinned copper mount with a maximum length of 3.9cm and three rivets for attachment (Fig. 14.7.2). The design, in *repoussé* and engraving, is presumably modelled on heraldic devices, but at present cannot be identified with any known coat-of-arms (Wojenka 2013, 256). The most likely timeframe for its deposition lies between the end of the thirteenth and the middle of the fourteenth century (Wojenka 2013, 256). Drawing on insights afforded by analogous finds, I have interpreted the mount from Ciemna Cave as an element of a knight's belt (Wojenka 2013, 247). This is supported by the discovery of another medieval belt fitting – an iron equal-armed fitting, about 3cm in length, with two characteristic lily terminals each with a rivet hole (Fig. 14.7.3). It is worth noting that Krabath (2001, 166) proposes that mounts with lily terminals date to the second half of the thirteenth century and the early fourteenth century. Unfortunately, the majority of the medieval artefacts from Ciemna Cave were found in disturbed contexts, intermixed with Roman and Neolithic material. The frequent occurrence of post-medieval pottery suggests that the cave strata were reworked relatively recently (Wojenka 2013, 230).

Finally, in terms of medieval finds from caves outside the Uplands, an iron bolthead and medieval pottery were found in the upper levels of Obłazowa Cave (Valde-Nowak 2003, 72–73, fig. 44), while 24 pottery sherds dating from the thirteenth to the mid-fourteenth century are known from Zbójecka Cave in Łagów (Hadamik 2013, 56–59, fig. 10). Not much can be said about the early and late medieval pottery sherds reported from Nad Stawem w

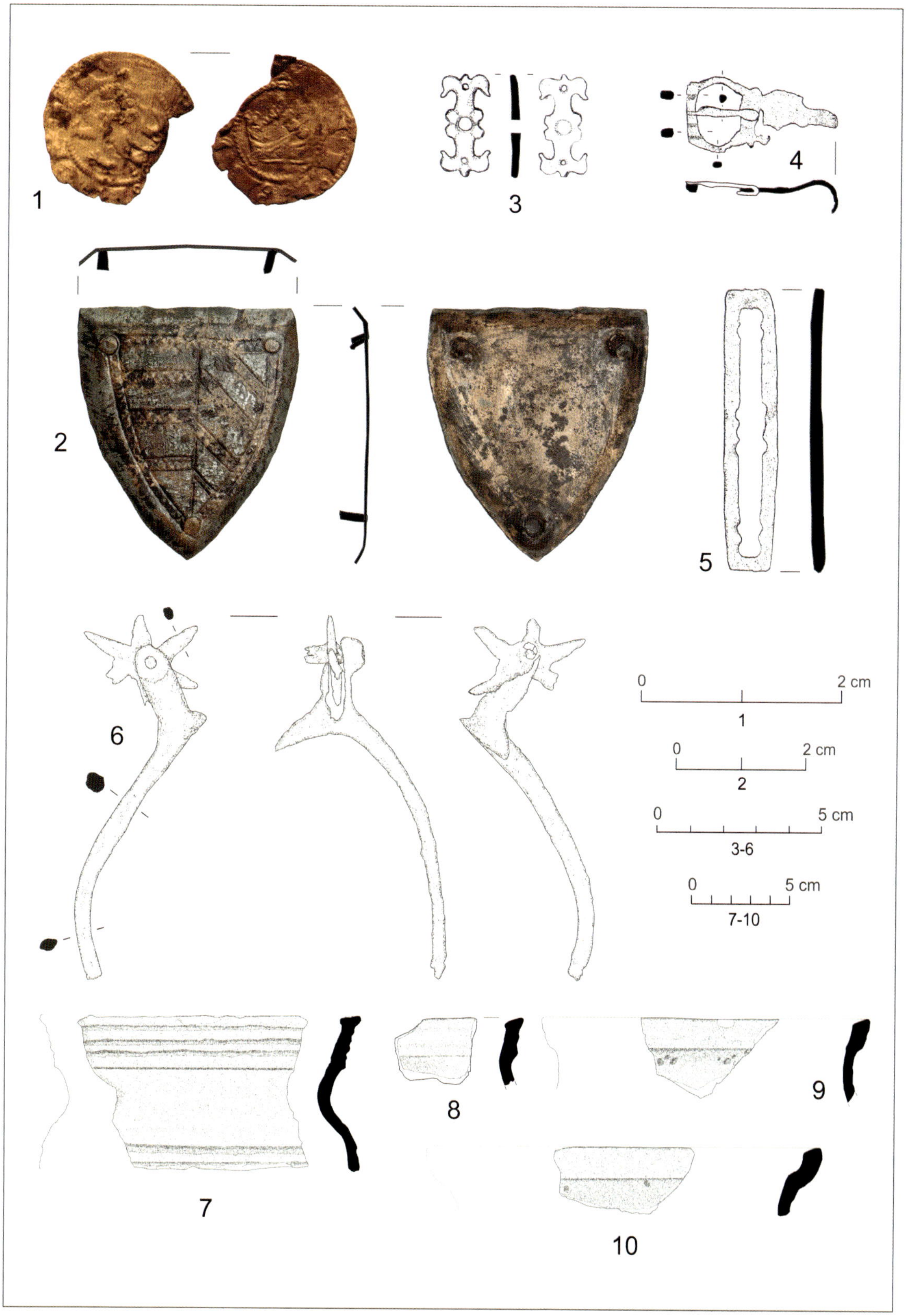


*Figure 14.7: Medieval assemblage from Ciemna Cave. 1. silver; 2. tinned copper; 3–6. iron; 7–10. clay. Photo: (1) M. Wojenka. (2) A. Susul. Drawing: (3–10) M. Wojenka.*

Gackach Cave in Leszcze (Informator Archeologiczny 1998, 31–32).

## The function of caves

The function of caves is a key issue all cave archaeologists engage with, and is often a difficult question to answer. The ideal situation, where the use of a specific cave is described in the written sources, is very rare. In Poland, this only exists for Smocza Jama Cave in Kraków, described in 1616 as part of an inn where cold beer was served (Firlet 1996, 43). With regard to the Middle Ages, the written records do not provide any information on Polish cave use, which means we must therefore turn to the archaeological record. Of course, correct interpretation of the surviving material culture in identifying function is frequently hampered when the archaeological context is ambiguous or lacking. The latter situation is prevalent given that many Polish caves were investigated in the nineteenth or early twentieth centuries by antiquarians without the benefit of modern scientific standards. Inevitably, this led to a loss of contextual information or at least what can be termed an 'impoverishment' of the information potential (Wojenka 2012a, 19).

Different models of cave usage have hitherto been defined in the literature, including occupation, storage, industry, ritual or funerary (Branigan and Dearne 1992, 4). I would argue that refuge should be added to this list, and is relevant to some Polish sites (see below). A further consideration is that a single cave can potentially provide information on a variety of different medieval activities. For instance, Okopy Wielka Dolna Cave in Ojców, where a silver hoard was deposited at the end of the eleventh century, also produced a large quantity of later medieval artefacts (Mycielska and Rook 1965). Due to a lack of evidence, the funerary use of caves during the Middle Ages can be omitted from consideration. There is also a notable lack of evidence for the ritual use of caves at this time, though we cannot exclude the possibility that some finds, coins in particular, could have been placed in caves as a form of ritual deposit. A similar absence of evidence exists with regard to the use of caves by hermits. The only religious usage I am aware of is Zawalona Cave in Mników, which the Camaldolese monks intended to convert into a chapel in the nineteenth century (Ossowski 1882, 33).

Permanent occupation of caves during the Middle Ages is not documented for the study area, though this does not mean that such usage did not exist. The lack of evidence may reflect the limitations of archaeology – not necessarily precise enough to identify year-round occupation. Significantly, in more recent times the use of caves as long-term working spaces, or as occupation sites for those living at a basic subsistence level, is recorded. For instance, Puchacza Cave in Ojców was intensively used by a blacksmith during the nineteenth century as indicated by large numbers of artefacts and a clay furnace (Czarnowski 1904b, 8). According to oral tradition, Dziadowa Skała Cave in Skarżyce was inhabited by beggars before World War II (Chmielewski 1958, 10). A similar situation is known in the Czech Republic where caves such as Pekárna and Kůlna are said to have been used by groups of migrating gypsies (Matoušek *et al.* 2005, 35; Branigan and Dearne 1992, 13).

Little can be said about the use of caves for storage in the medieval period. Caves in rural areas were potentially used for the storage of crops, fodder or perishable goods by inhabitants of adjacent villages. These sites are, however, difficult to identify, although some finds, pottery fragments in particular, can potentially reflect such activities. Considering the ethnographic evidence for storage – such as a cave at Sułoszowa in the Ojców area that was used as a barn prior to World War II (National Digital Archive, photo no. 1-U-6023; Czarnowski 1911b, 10, 51) or Jaskinia Zamieszkała in Prądnik Korzkiewski, which was used for storage (Ossowski 1884, 70) – similar usage could be argued for the Middle Ages. In my opinion, a storage function could be tentatively suggested for certain caves, particularly those located within the walls of strongholds or castles, such as Na Górze Słupsko rockshelter in Kostkowice, Biśnik Cave in Strzegowa, and Ostrężnicka Cave in Janów. The latter is easily accessible and is situated on a rock plateau surrounded by the enclosing wall of a late thirteenth- or early fourteenth-century castle (Kołodziejski 2004). Unfortunately, Ostrężnicka Cave has never been archaeologically investigated. Zamkowa Dolna Cave in Olsztyn, situated within the enclosing walls of the medieval Olstin/Holstain castle, served a different function: the cave is said to have been used as a smithy but no archaeological records were published to support this claim (Kopacz 1975, 71). The relationship between strongholds/castles and caves is poorly understood in Poland (Miśkiewicz 1964, 127; Nabiałek 2012, 267; Wojenka 2012a, 32), but is recognised in the Czech archaeological literature where the term 'cave castle' occurs (Fišera 2005).

Turning to industrial functions, although poorly published the aforementioned cave at Olsztyn is the best example (Kopacz and Skalski 1971; Kopacz 1975). However, a pincher found in Boczne w Ogrójcu rockshelter in Maszyce may indicate an industrial role for this site (Czarnowski 1914b, 46, fig. VII.O.5). Another type of 'industry' is represented in the remains of a counterfeiter's workshop at Żarska Cave. This site yielded copper or bronze plates with holes produced as a result of cutting out rogue coins. It is not possible to determine at present whether these plates are medieval or post-medieval in date. Counterfeiter's workshops in caves are known from medieval Slovakia and Czech Republic (Bárta 1960, 28; Matoušek *et al.* 2005, 35; Soják 2007, 63–64).

It is my belief that during the Middle Ages caves most often served as places for hiding and refuge. There are long traditions of such usage in Poland: even during World War II some caves in the Kraków-Częstochowa Uplands became places of mass refuge (Jędrzejowski 2007, 71–72). The big 'storage' vessels found near the fireplace in Żarska Cave (Fig. 14.6.1, 14.6.4, 14.6.11), and the pottery sherds from Łokietka Cave, represent typical 'rural' ceramic assemblages and may potentially reflect people who were seeking refuge in the caves during the Middle Ages. Alternately, a storage function is equally plausible for these two sites but they are not located in proximity to medieval villages.

The military equipment and riding gear, especially spurs, can hardly represent a single time horizon. Some caves may contain relics of warfare but, equally, they could have been visited by groups of robbers, hunters or poachers. Looking at the chronology of the artefacts, what appears to be significant is that there are no military objects dated to later than *c.* 1350. It is not only the spurs belong to the second half of the thirteenth to the first half of the fourteenth century, but probably also finds from Ciemna Cave: the 'heraldic' mount and the lily belt fitting. Also worth noting is the fact that both categories of object call to mind the world of knights and chivalry. The written sources do not record activities of armed groups in caves in the Kraków-Częstochowa Uplands. Nevertheless, a cave in a military context occurs in the oral tradition of how the Polish duke Władysław – the 'Elbow-high' (*Łokietek*) – found refuge in a cave near the village of Ojców (Fig. 14.8), possibly in the spring of 1306, as he struggled to wrest power from King Wenceslaus III in Krakow (Długopolski 2009, 80). The tale draws us back to the late thirteenth and early fourteenth centuries, a period of great political turbulence, when the area of Kraków acted as a background for the rivalry of some factions supporting Czech and some supporting Piast (Polish) rule over Poland. According to written sources of the time, while trying to take control over the Kraków area, Duke Władysław sought refuge in forests, marshes and uninhabited lands but no cave hideout was mentioned (Samsonowicz 2000, 81). Another

*Figure 14.8:* Łokietek at Ojców. *Wojciech Gerson, 1890. Oil on canvas.*

factor suggests the refuges of Duke Władysław were within the Ojców area. After 1354, Kazimierz III 'the Great' (a son of Elbow-high) built a castle called Ojców (*castrum Oczecz*) – a name said to be chosen to commemorate the wanderings of his father; in old Polish, the term *oczecz* means 'father' (Rymut 1967, 116).

According to some researchers, there could be a grain of truth in this old folktale (Rokosz 2003), while others have discarded it as a fabrication, and quite a late one at that (Samsonowicz 2000). However, the archaeological record from some caves in the region suggests we should not entirely dismiss the veracity of the legend (Kołodziejski 1997, 71; Wojenka 2012a, 33). Let us not forget that in terms of chronology, almost all the securely dated artefacts coincide with the period of Władysław's struggle to gain control over the Kraków region. In my opinion, the chivalric finds from caves plausibly confirm the credibility of the tale. In addition to the military objects (including the reliably dated mount with a lily terminal), an appropriate chronological marker for activity in the caves during this period of unrest is the Czech *parvus* of Wenceslaus II (although it is also possible that this coin was dropped after a longer circulation). To conclude, to establish the function of these caves in the Middle Ages, further fieldwork is required, ideally supported by contributions from other disciplines such as history or ethnography. There is no doubt, however, that the principal contribution to tackling this question will be archaeology.

## Acknowledgements

The above studies were supported by the National Science Center, Poland (grant decision No. UMO-2013/11/D/HS3/01877 awarded to M. Wojenka), which financed the excavations in the Żarska Cave in 2014. I am grateful to the same institution for financing the $^{14}$C-dating of human remains from the Żarska Cave (grant decision No. DEC-2011/01/B/ST10/06889 awarded to P. Wojtal). I take this opportunity to express my gratitude to P. Valde-Nowak and K. Sobczyk, the leaders of the project No. N N109 185240, financed by the National Science Center, for placing in my care the medieval assemblages from the Ciemna Cave.

## References

Alexandrowicz, S., Nadachowski, A., Rydlewski, J., Valde-Nowak, P. and Wołoszyn, B., 1985. Subfossil fauna from a cave in the Sobczański Gully (Pieniny Mts., Poland). *Folia Quaternaria* 56, 57–78.

Bárta, J., 1960. Zur Problematik der Höhlensiedlungen in der Slowakischen Karpaten. *Acta Archaeologica Carpathica* II, 5–39.

Bieroński, J., Burdukiewicz, J., Hercman, H., Socha, P., Stefaniak, K. and Nadachowski, A., 2009. Palaeogeographic, archaeological and palaeozoological studies in the Radochowska Cave.

*In*: K. Stefaniak, A. Tyc, and P. Socha, eds. *Karst of the Częstochowa Upland and of the Eastern Sudetes*. Sosnowiec-Wrocław: Faculty of Earth Sciences University of Silesia and Zoological Institute University of Wrocław, 455–475.

Branigan, K., and Dearne M., 1992. *Romano-British Cavemen. Cave Use in Roman Britain*. Oxford: Oxbow Books.

Chmielewski, W., 1958. Stanowisko paleolityczne w Dziadowej Skale koło Skarżyc w pow. zawierciańskim. *Prace i Materiały Muzeum Archeologicznego i Etnograficznego w Łodzi. Seria Archeologiczna* 3, 5–48.

Chmielewski, W., 1961. *Civilisation de Jerzmanowice*. Wrocław–Warszawa–Kraków: Polska Akademia Nauk.

Chmielewski, W., 1988. Ogólna charakterystyka jaskiń Doliny Sąspowskiej pod względem występowania w nich źródeł archeologicznych. *In*: W. Chmielewski, ed. *Jaskinie Doliny Sąspowskiej. Tło przyrodnicze osadnictwa pradziejowego*. Warszawa: Wydawnictwa Uniwersytetu Warszawskiego, 5–17.

Cyrek, K., 1994. Wyniki badań wykopaliskowych w schronisku skalnym Krucza Skała (stanowisko 1) w Kostkowicach, województwo częstochowskie, w 1991 roku. *Badania archeologiczne na Górnym Śląsku i Ziemiach Pogranicznych w latach 1991–1992*. Katowice: Centrum Dziedzictwa Kulturowego Górnego Śląska, 34–42.

Cyrek, K., 2002. Rekonstrukcja zasiedlenia Jaskini Biśnik. *In*: K. Cyrek, ed. *Jaskinia Biśnik. Rekonstrukcja zasiedlenia jaskini na tle zmian środowiska przyrodniczego*. Toruń: Uniwersytet Mikołaja Kopernika, 9–133.

Cyrek, K., 2007a. Jaskinie w polskich badaniach archeologicznych w latach 1939–1989. *In*: J. Lech, ed. *Pół wieku z dziejów archeologii polskiej: 1939–1989*. Warszawa: Polska Akademia Nauk, 251–264.

Cyrek, K., 2007b. Złodziejska Cave (Grota Lucyny). *In*: P. Socha, K. Stefaniak and A. Tyc, ed. *Karst and Cryokarst. 25th Speleological School. 8th GLACKIPR Symposium*. Sosnowiec-Wrocław: Department of Geomorphology, University of Silesia, Zoological Institute, University of Wrocław, 20–21.

Cyrek, K., 2009. Archaeological studies in caves of the Częstochowa Upland. *In*: K. Stefaniak, A. Tyc, and P. Socha, eds. *Karst of the Częstochowa Upland and of the Eastern Sudetes*. Sosnowiec-Wrocław: Faculty of Earth Sciences University of Silesia and Zoological Institute University of Wrocław, 145–160.

Czarnowski, S.J., 1898. Wykopalisko monet w Jaskini 'Okopy' Wielkiej nad Prądnikiem Ojcowskim. *Wiadomości Numizmatyczno-Archeologiczne* III, 446–454.

Czarnowski, S.J., 1902. Jaskinia Górna w Okopach na lewym brzegu Prądnika. *Pamiętnik Fizjograficzny* 17, 1–22.

Czarnowski, S.J., 1903. Czaszki jaskiniowe z okolic rzeki Prądnika. *Wszechświat* 22, 73–75.

Czarnowski, S.J., 1904a. Czaszka z jaskini Oborzysko Wielkie na lewym brzegu Prądnika pod Ojcowem. *Światowit* 5, 89–91.

Czarnowski, S.J., 1904b. Jaskinie i schroniska na Górze Smardzewskiej na lewym brzegu Prądnika pod Ojcowem. *Pamiętnik Fizyograficzny* 18, 3–24.

Czarnowski, S.J., 1909. Szczęka i żuchwy ludzkie z Jaskiń w okolicach Ojcowa. *Wszechświat* 28, 353–355.

Czarnowski, S.J., 1911a. Jaskinie i Schroniska w Kopcowej Górze. *Materiały. Antropologiczno – Archeologiczne i Etnograficzne* XII, 3–22.

Czarnowski, S.J., 1911b. *Jaskinie okolic Krakowa i Ojcowa i ich zabytki przeddziejowe*. Warszawa–Kraków: Wydawnictwo S.J. Czarnowskiego i sp.

Czarnowski, S.J., 1911c. Zabytki przedhistoryczne w okolicach Ojcowa i Miechowa, cz. 2. *Ziemia* II, No. 39, 633–635.

Czarnowski, S.J., 1914a. *Jaskinie i Schroniska na Górze Chełmowej*. Warszawa: Wydawnictwo S.J. Czarnowskiego i sp.

Czarnowski, S.J., 1914b. Jaskinie w skałach Ogrojca. *Pamiętnik Fizjograficzny* 22, 32–48.

Czarnowski, S.J., 1924. Jaskinie i Schroniska na Górze Koronnej na lewym brzegu Prądnika pod Ojcowem. *Prace i Materiały Antropologiczno-Archeologiczne i Etnograficzne* III, 3–26.

Czarnowski, S.J., 1926. Jaskinie Wąwozu Stodoliska na prawym brzegu Prądnika pod Ojcowem. *Przegląd Archeologiczny* III, 18–33.

Dąbrowska, E., 1962. Osadnictwo wczesnośredniowieczne na terenie powiatu krakowskiego. Zeszyty Naukowe Uniwersytetu Jagiellońskiego. *Prace Archeologiczne* 4, 7–132.

Dagnan-Ginter, A., Drobniewicz, B., Godawa, J., Miękina, B., Sobczyk, K. and Stworzewicz, E., 1992. Excavations in the Duża Cave at Mączna Skała near Cracow (southern Poland). *Folia Quaternaria* 63, 3–25.

Długopolski, E., 2009. *Władysław Łokietek na tle swoich czasów*. 2nd edn. Kraków: Universitas.

Egan, G., and Pritchard, R., 2002. *Dress Accessories c. 1150–c. 1450, Medieval Finds from Excavations in London*, 3. London: Museum of London.

Fingerlin, I., 1971. *Gürtel des hohen und späten Mittelalters*. Kunstwissenschaftliche Studien 46. Munich: Deutschen Kunstverlag.

Firlet, E., 1996. *Smocza Jama na Wawelu*. Kraków: Universitas.

Fišera, Z., 2005. *Jeskynní hrady středni Evropy*. Prague: Nakladatelství Libri.

Fraś, M., and Olszowski, J., 1971. Grottes récement découvertes à Tyniec au bord de la Vistula. *Acta Archaeologica Carpathica* XII, 73–78.

Gradziński, M., 2012. Nazewnictwo jaskiniowe – spojrzenie przyrodnika. *Prądnik. Prace i Materiały Muzeum im. Prof. Władysława Szafera* 22, 115–122.

Gradziński, M., and Szelerewicz, M., 2004. Jaskinie Wyżyny Krakowsko-Wieluńskiej – liczba i rozmieszczenie. *In*: J. Partyka, ed. *Zróżnicowanie i przemiany środowiska przyrodniczo-kulturowego Wyżyny Krakowsko-Częstochowskiej*, 1, Ojców: Ojcowski Park Narodowy, 69–82.

Grodzicki, J. 1991. Wprowadzenie. *In*: J. Grodzicki, ed. *Jaskinie Tatrzańskiego Parku Narodowego. Jaskinie Doliny Chochołowskiej i dolinek reglowych*. Warszawa: Polskie Towarzystwo Przyjaciół Nauk o Ziemi, 7–10.

Hadamik, C., 2013. *Kasztelania łagowska*. Warszawa: Towarzystwo Miłośników Historii.

Hášková, J., 1991. *Pražské groše (1300–1526)*. Prague: Národné Múzeum v Praze.

Hilczerówna, Z., 1956. *Ostrogi polskie z X–XIII wieku*. Poznań: Poznańskie Towarzystwo Przyjaciół Nauk. Komisja Archeologiczna.

Informator Archeologiczny, 1998. Leszcze, Jaskinia nad Stawem w Gackach gm. Pińczów, woj. kieleckie AZP/94-62, *Informator Archeologiczny. Badania. Rok 1994*, 31–32.

Jędrzejowski, T., 2007. *Czajowice dawniej i dziś. Zarys monografii*. Wielka Wieś: Gminny Ośrodek Kultury i Promocji w Wielkiej Wsi.

Jura, A., 1949. Siedziba łowców niedźwiedzia jaskiniowego w Grocie Magury w Tatrach. *Sprawozdanie z Czynności i Posiedzeń Polskiej Akademii Umiejętności* 50(9), 524–526.

Kołodziejski, S., 1985. Les éperons à molette du territoire de la Petite Pologne au Moyen Âge. *In*: A. Kokowski, ed. *Memoires Archeologiques*, Lublin: Uniwerystet Marii Curie-Skłodowskiej, 161–179.

Kołodziejski, S., 1997. XIII-wieczne budowle warowne w Dolinie Prądnika. *Teki Krakowskie* V, 71–80.

Kołodziejski, S., 2004. Zamek Ostrężnik w świetle dotychczasowych badań. *In*: J. Partyka, ed. *Zróżnicowanie i przemiany środowiska przyrodniczo-kulturowego Wyżyny Krakowsko-Częstochowskiej, 2 – Kultura*. Ojców: Ojcowski Park Narodowy, 19–24.

Kopacz, J., 1975. Stanowisko środkowopaleolityczne w Olsztynie, pow. Częstochowa. *Światowit* XXXIV, 71–80.

Kopacz, J., and Skalski, A., 1971. Nowe paleolityczne stanowisko jaskiniowe w Olsztynie, pow. Częstochowa. *Sprawozdania Archeologiczne* XXIII, 33–36.

Kowalski, K., 1951. *Jaskinie Polski*, I. Warszawa: Państwowe Muzeum Archeologiczne.

Kowalski, K., 1953. *Jaskinie Polski*, II. Warszawa: Państwowe Muzeum Archeologiczne.

Kowalski K., 1954. *Jaskinie Polski*, III. Warszawa: Państwowe Wydawnictwo Naukowe.

Kozłowski, J., 1972. Archaeological materials. Studies on Raj Cave near Kielce (Poland) and its deposits. *Folia Quaternaria* 41, 61–132.

Kozłowski, L., 1921. Stan i zadania badań nad epoką kamienną w Polsce. *Wiadomości Archeologiczne* VI, 23–46.

Krabath, S., 2001. *Die hoch- und spätmittelalterlichen Buntmetallfunde nördlich der Alpen. Eine archäologisch-kunsthistorische Untersuchung zu ihrer Herstellungstechnik, funktionalen und zeitlichen Bestimmung*. Internationale Archäologie 63, Vol. I, Text. Rahden/Westfalen: Verlag Marie Leidorf GmbH.

Krajcarz, M. *et al.*, 2014. Wyniki badań wykopaliskowych w Schronisku na Górze Słupsko w Kostkowicach oraz Jaskini Deszczowej w Kroczycach, województwo śląskie. *Badania archeologiczne na Górnym Śląsku i ziemiach pogranicznych w latach* 2011–2012, 22–29.

Krukowski, S., 1948. Paleolit. *In*: S. Krukowski, J. Kostrzewski, and R. Jakimowicz, eds. *Prehistoria ziem polskich*, Kraków: Polska Akademia Umiejętności, 1–117.

Lech, J., 2001. Archeologia Jury Ojcowskiej w zarysie. *In*: J. Lech and J. Partyka, eds. *Z archeologii Ukrainy i Jury Ojcowskiej*. Ojców: Ojcowski Park Narodowy, 127–182.

Lech, J., and Partyka, J., 2006. Początek polskiej prehistorii w Jurze Ojcowskiej. *In*: J. Lech and J. Partyka, eds. *Jura Ojcowska w pradziejach i początkach państwa polskiego*. Ojców: Ojcowski Park Narodowy, 55–83.

Liwoch, R., 2016. Groty strzał i bełtów/arrowheads. *In*: A. Tyniec, ed. *Chrzest 966. Oblicza Chrystianizacji/Baptism 966. Faces of Christianization*. Kraków: Archaeological Museum, 62–64.

Matoušek, V., Jenč, P., and Peša, V., 2005. *Jeskyně Čech, Moravy a Slezska s archeologickými nálezy*. Prague: Nakladatelství Libri.

Mączyńska, M., and Rook, E., 1972. Materiały z Jaskini Wierzchowskiej Górnej w zbiorach Muzeum Archeologicznego w Krakowie. *Materiały Archeologiczne* XIII, 113–150.

McNatt, L. 1996. Cave archaeology of Belize. *Journal of Cave and Karst Studies* 58(2), 81–99.

Mirosław-Grabowska, J., *et al.*, 2007. Studies on the deposits of the cave Jaskinia IV on Mt. Birów. *In*: P. Socha, K. Stefaniak, and A. Tyc, eds. *Karst and Cryokarst. 25th Speleological School. 8th GLACKIPR Symposium*. Sosnowiec-Wrocław: Department of Geomorphology, University of Silesia, Zoological Institute, University of Wrocław, 24–26.

Miśkiewicz, B., 1964. *Rozwój stałych punktów oporu w Polsce do połowy XV wieku*. Poznań: Uniwersytet im. Adama Mickiewicza w Poznaniu.

Muzolf, B., 1999. Problematyka badań archeologicznych Wyżyny Częstochowskiej w obszarze Jurajskich Parków Krajobrazowych województwa katowickiego, osiągnięcia i perspektywy. *In*: M. Broda, ed. *9. Sympozjum Jurajskie. Człowiek i środowisko naturalne Wyżyny Krakowsko-Wieluńskiej*. Dąbrowa Górnicza: Zarząd Zespołu Jurajskich Parków Krajobrazowych w Katowicach, 1–17.

Mycielska, R., and Rook, E., 1965. Materiały z Jaskini w Okopach Wielkiej, Dolnej, pow. Olkusz. *Materiały Archeologiczne* VI, 145–179.

Nabiałek, K., 2012. *Starostwo olsztyńskie od XIV do połowy XVII wieku*. Kraków: Towarzystwo Naukowe Societas Vistulana.

Olszyński, M., 1871. Wycieczka do grot ojcowskich. *Kłosy* XIII(337), 381–382.

Ossowski, G., 1880. Sprawozdanie z badań geologiczno-antropologicznych dokonanych w r. 1879 w jaskiniach okolic Krakowa. *Zbiór Wiadomości do Antropologii Krajowéj* IV, 35–56.

Ossowski, G., 1882. Trzecie sprawozdanie z badań antropologiczno-archeologicznych w jaskiniach okolic Krakowa, dokonanych w r. 1881. *Zbiór Wiadomości do Antropologii Krajowéj* VI, 28–51.

Ossowski, G., 1884. Sprawozdanie z badań paleo-etnologicznych w jaskiniach okolic Ojcowa dokonanych w r. 1883. *Zbiór Wiadomości do Antropologii Krajowéj* VIII, 61–86.

Ossowski, G., 1887. Sprawozdanie z badań paleoetnologicznych w jaskiniach okolic Ojcowa dokonanych w roku 1886. *Zbiór Wiadomości do Antropologii Krajowej* XI, 13–31.

Partyka, J., 1992. Ojców i archeologia w latach 1871–1924. *In*: J. Lech and J. Partyka, eds. *Prof. Stefan Krukowski (1890–1982). Działalność archeologiczna i jej znaczenie dla nauki polskiej*. Ojców: Ojcowski Park Narodowy, 71–86.

Reyman, J., 1966. Wczesnośredniowieczne skarby srebrne z Małopolski. *In*: M. Haisig, R. Kiersnowski, and J. Reyman eds. *Wczesnośredniowieczne skarby srebrne z Małopolski, Śląska, Warmii i Mazur*. Wrocław–Warszawa–Kraków: Zakład Narodowy im. Ossolińskich.

Reyman-Walczak, B., Ilisch, P., Malarczyk, D. and Nowakiewicz, T., 2013. Frühmittelalterliche Münzfunde aus Kleinpolen. *In*: M. Bogucki, P. Ilisch, and S. Suchodolski, eds. *Frühmittelalterliche Münzfunde aus Polen. Inventar IV, Kleinpolen/Schlesien*. Warszawa: Institut für Archäologie und Ethnologie der Polnischen Akademie der Wissenschaften, 7–222.

Rodzińska-Nowak, J., Nowak, M., and Poleski, J., 2002. Pottery and flint finds from the upper layers of the Lokietka Cave. *Préhistoire Européenne* 16–17(2000–2001), 317–333.

Roemer, F., 1884. *The Bone Caves of Ojcow in Poland*. London: Longmans, Green, and co.

Rokosz, M., 2003. Historyczne przesłanki ojcowskiego podania o Łokietku. *In*: Z. Woźniak and J. Gancarski, eds. *Polonia Minor Medii Aevi*. Kraków-Krosno: Polska Akademia Umiejętności w Krakowie, Muzeum Podkarpackie w Krośnie, 541–549.

Rook, E., 1963. Materiały z Jaskini Bębłowskiej Dolnej. *Materiały Archeologiczne* IV, 335–346.

Rook, E., 1964. Materiały z Jaskini Oborzysko Małe. *Materiały Archeologiczne* V, 193–210.

Rook, E., 1970a. Sprawozdanie z badań w Jaskini Nad Mosurem Starym, dużej w Grodzisku, pow. Olkusz. *Materiały Archeologiczne* XI, 271–274.

Rook, E., 1970b. Wyniki prac wykopaliskowych w jaskini nad Mosurem Starym, dużej w Grodzisku, pow. Olkusz, w latach 1967 i 1968. *Sprawozdania Archeologiczne* XXII, 57–65.

Rook, E., 1970c. Materiały z Jaskini Maszyckiej w zbiorach Muzeum Archeologicznego w Krakowie. *Materiały Archeologiczne* XI, 133–147.

Rook, E., 1980. Osadnictwo neolityczne w jaskiniach Wyżyny Krakowsko-Częstochowskiej. *Materiały Archeologiczne* XX, 5–130.

Rozmus, D., Szmoniewski, B., and Troncik, A., 2006. An Early Medieval assemblage of iron artifacts from 'Góra Słupsko' hillfort, site 2 at Kostkowice, Zawiercie district, Śląskie Voivodeship. *Acta Archaeologica Carpathica* XLI, 101–113.

Rymut, K., 1967. *Nazwy miejscowe północnej części dawnego województwa krakowskiego*. Wrocław–Warszawa–Kraków: Ossolineum.

Samsonowicz, H., 2000. Łokietek w grotach Ojcowa. *In*: F. Leśniak, ed. *Podróże po historii. Studia z dziejów kultury i polityki europejskiej ofiarowane profesorowi Stanisławowi Grzybowskiemu*. Kraków: Wydawnictwo Naukowe Akademii Pedagogicznej, 76–82.

Sawicki, L., 1949. Rozwój badań w zakresie prehistorii czwartorzędu w Polsce. *Sprawozdania Państwowego Muzeum Archeologicznego* 2(1–4), 13–30.

Sawicki, L., 1953. Stan badań nad wiekiem człowieka kopalnego. *Acta Geologica Polonica* 3, 171–189.

Sobczyk, K., and Sitlivy, V., 2001a. Badania wykopaliskowe w Jaskini Łokietka w latach 1998–2000. *In*: J. Partyka, ed. *Badania naukowe w południowej części Wyżyny Krakowsko-Częstochowskiej*. Ojców: Ojcowski Park Narodowy, 457–461.

Sobczyk, K., and Sitlivy, V., 2001b. Badania wykopaliskowe w Jaskini Łokietka w Ojcowskim Parku Narodowym w latach 1998–2000. *In*: J. Lech and J. Partyka, eds. *Z archeologii Ukrainy i Jury Ojcowskiej*. Ojców: Ojcowski Park Narodowy, 323–336.

Soják, M., 2007. *Osídlenie spišských jaskýň od praveku po novovek*. Nitra: Archeologický Ústav Slovenskej Akadémie Vied.

Stefaniak, K., and Bieroński, J., 2009. Caves and rock shelters of the Eastern Sudetes – catalogue of important speleological features. *In*: K. Stefaniak, A. Tyc, and P. Socha, eds. *Karst of the Częstochowa Upland and of the Eastern Sudetes*. Sosnowiec-Wrocław: Faculty of Earth Sciences University of Silesia and Zoological Institute University of Wrocław, 515–535.

Stefaniak, K., Socha P., Tyc A., Cyrek K. and Nadachowski A., 2009. Caves, rock shelters and palaeontological sites in quarries of the Częstochowa Upland – catalogue of important speleological features. *In*: K. Stefaniak, A. Tyc and P. Socha, eds. *Karst of the Częstochowa Upland and of the Eastern Sudetes*. Sosnowiec-Wrocław: Faculty of Earth Sciences University of Silesia and Zoological Institute University of Wrocław, 307–354.

Suchodolski, S., 1987. *Moneta możnowładcza i kościelna w Polsce wczesnośredniowiecznej*. Wrocław–Warszawa–Kraków–Gdańsk–Łódź: Zakład Narodowy im. Ossolińskich.

Świętosławski, W., 1997. *Archeologiczne ślady najazdów tatarskich na Europę środkową w XIII w.* Łódź: Instytut Archeologii i Etnologii Polskiej Akademii Nauk.

Valde-Nowak, P., 2003. Post-Pleistocene settlement. *In*: P. Valde-Nowak, A. Nadachowski, and T. Madeyska, ed. *Obłazowa Cave. Human Activity, Stratigraphy and Palaeoenvironment*, Kraków: Institute of Archaeology and Ethnology of Polish Academy of Sciences, 72–73.

Valde-Nowak, P., Alex, B., Ginter, B., Krajcarz, M., Madeyska, T., Miękina, B., Sobczyk, K., Stefański, D., Wojtal, P., Zając, M. and Zarzecka-Szubińska, K., 2014. Middle Palaeolithic sequences of the Ciemna Cave (Prądnik valley, Poland): The problem of synchronization. *Quaternary International* 326–327(2014), 125–145.

Whitehead, R., 1996. *Buckles 1250–1800*. Essex: Greenlight Publishing.

Wojenka, M., 2011. Problemy archeologii średniowiecza w jaskiniach Wyżyny Krakowsko-Częstochowskiej. *In*: M. Gradziński, J. Partyka, and J. Urban, eds. *Materiały 45. Sympozjum Speleologicznego*. Ojców: Sekcja Speleologiczna Polskiego Towarzystwa Przyrodników im. Kopernika, 105–106.

Wojenka, M., Wilczyński, J., and Sobieraj, D., 2011. Archaeological excavations in Żarska Cave (Żary, com. Krzeszowice, Krakow district) in 2011. *Recherches Archeologiques NS* 3, 143–156.

Wojenka, M., 2012a. Jaskinie Wyżyny Krakowsko-Częstochowskiej w średniowieczu. Wstęp do problematyki. *Prądnik. Prace i Materiały Muzeum im. Prof. Władysława Szafera* 22, 7–43.

Wojenka, M., 2012b. Zapomniane naczynie. Kilka uwag o pojemniku na skarb srebrny z jaskini Okopy Wielkiej, Dolnej w Ojcowie. *Notae Numismaticae* VII, 227–240.

Wojenka, M., 2013. The heraldic mount from Ciemna Cave at Ojców. From studies in the Medieval culture of chivalry. *Acta Archaeologica Carpathica* XLVIII, 227–263.

Zagórska-Telega, J., and Bochnak, T., 2001. Ein Depot mit frühmittelalterlichen axtförmigen Eisenbarren aus Kostkowice, Fst. 2, Gde. Kroczyce, Woiw. Śląskie. *Acta Archaeologica Carpathica* XXXVI, 39–47.

Zawisza, J., 1871. Ojcowska dolina i jéj okolice. *Biblioteka Warszawska* IV, 53–58.

Zawisza, J., 1874. Jaskinia Mamuta w Dolinie Wierzchowskiej. *Wiadomości Archeologiczne* II, 5–32.

Zawisza, J., 1876. Dalsze poszukiwania w Jaskini Mamuta. *Wiadomości Archeologiczne* III, 125–139.

Zawisza, J., 1882. Poszukiwania w Jaskini Mamuta. *Wiadomości Archeologiczne* IV, 1–30.

Zotz, L., 1939. *Die Altensteinzeit in Niederschlesien*. Leipzig: Kabitsch Verlag.

# Chapter 15

# Medieval cave sites in the Czech Republic

*Vladimír Peša*

*Caves as archaeological sites have been studied in the Czech Republic for more than 150 years, with the Bohemian Karst and Moravian Karst constituting the main areas of research. Since the 1990s, however, rockshelters and caves in Bohemian sandstone areas have also attracted attention. With few exceptions, there is little evidence for the medieval use of caves, as a result of which medieval finds are rarely mentioned in the literature. In the Czech Republic the medieval period is divided into the Early Middle Ages (500–1200), the High Middle Ages (1200–1300) and the Late Middle Ages (1300–1500). Early medieval caves are associated with hermits and with the initial phase of Christianity in the Czech territory. Rockshelters were used primarily for tar production from the High Middle Ages. During warfare in the fifteenth century, as well as in later periods, caves were utilised by local populations as refuges; and during peaceful times in the Late Middle Ages they functioned as hiding places for coin forgery practises. An exceptional site type in the Moravian Karst is the medieval fortress cave – the 'cave castle'.*

## Introduction

Academic study of caves in Bohemia and Moravia stretches back nearly 150 years, but the medieval era has yet to receive more comprehensive archaeological attention. Interest in caves as sites containing the remains of early human populations began in the second half of the nineteenth century and has continued in waves of research across different regions up to the present day. Until the middle of the twentieth century, cave investigations focused on the Palaeolithic. Other prehistoric periods and early historic periods were of marginal interest and often remain unpublished. The interpretation of medieval and early modern period finds was traditionally linked to the military use of the shelters. More recent studies have documented a significant difference in the nature of archaeological activities in caves during the Neolithic and the Bronze Age/Hallstatt versus the modern period subsequent to AD 1500. In prehistory, caves were typically associated with cult activities (Peša 2006a, 2011, 2013b), but during the modern period secular activities predominate (Peša 2013a). When assessing the role of caves in medieval society, we should ask whether cave usage at that time more closely reflects the prehistoric or modern situation. Was this the period when the human relationship to caves changed?

## History of cave excavations and cave regions

The highly varied geological nature of the Czech Republic led to the formation of caves in both karst geology (limestone, marble) and non-karst geology (sandstone, conglomerate, granite, basalt) (Fig. 15.1).

The country's main karst areas are located in Moravia: the Moravian Karst to the north of the Moravian metropolis of Brno, featuring the important (both from a touristic and historic perspective) Punkva Caves including the Macocha Abyss, and Sloup-Šošůvka Caves including the Palaeolithic Kůlna Cave. Small karst areas are also found in central Moravia (Konice, Javoříčko, Mladeč, Hranice karsts), to the north in Moravian Silesia (Štramberk, Jeseník) and in south Moravia (Pálava Ridge near Mikulov). Archaeological excavations in the Moravian Karst commenced in 1867 with the work of physician and founder of Moravian archaeology, Jindřich (Heinrich) Wankel; his investigations attracted other prominent antiquarians to karst research, including M. Kříž, J. Knies, K. J. Maška, J. Szombathy, R. Trampler (see Peša 2013a). These researchers expanded their studies into other karst regions in Moravia, and by the beginning of the twentieth century the majority of caves with Palaeolithic potential had been excavated, including upper historic

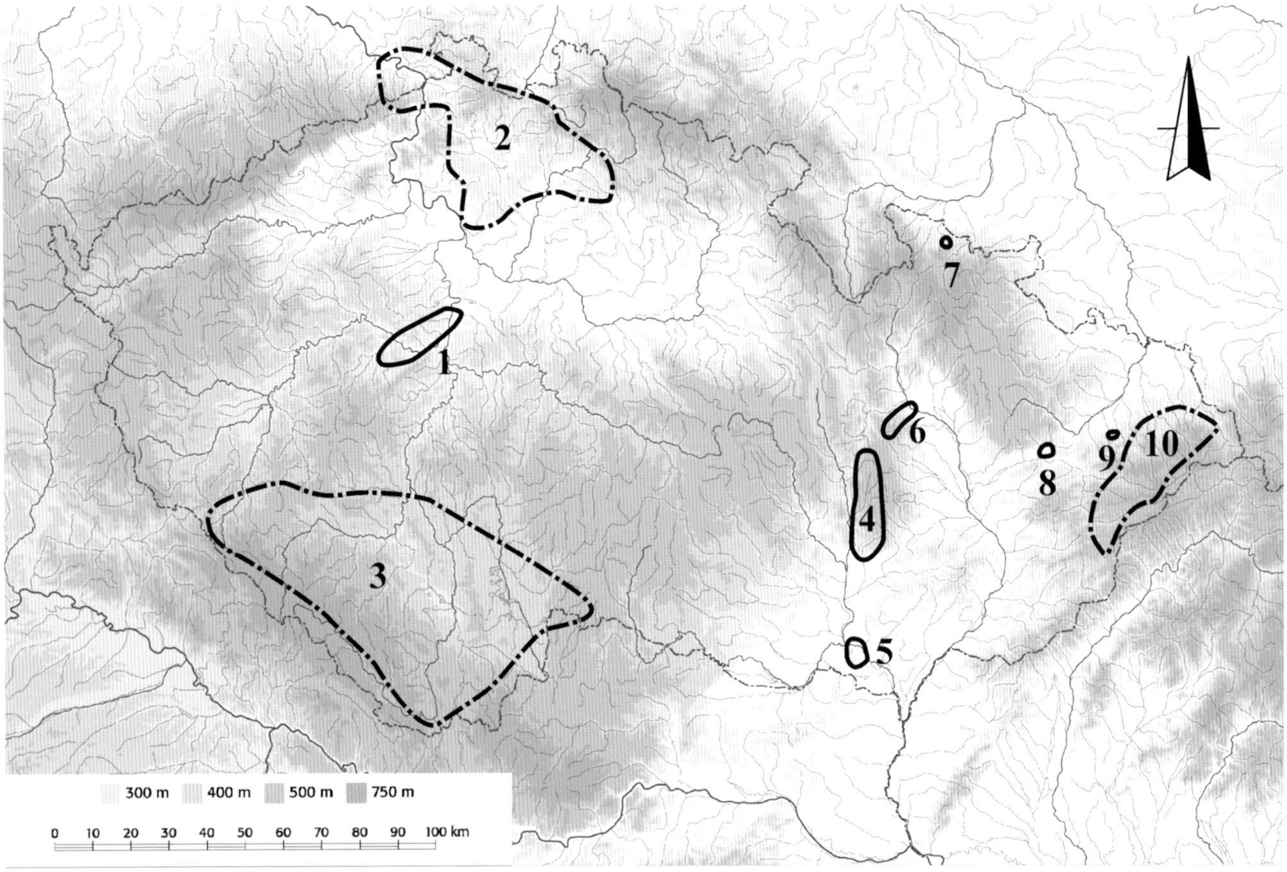


*Figure 15.1: The Czech Republic with the main cave regions: 1. Bohemian Karst, 2. sandstone areas of North Bohemia including Bohemian Paradise, 3. South Bohemia, 4. Moravian Karst, 5. South Moravia, 6. Karst of Javoříčko and Mladeč, 7. Na Špičáku Cave, 8. Karst of Hranice, 9. Karst of Štramberk, 10. Moravian-Silesian Beskydy Mountains: Map: V. Peša. Graphics: V. Novák).*

layers. Publications from that period frequently mention historical finds such as hearths, pottery sherds and metal artefacts, albeit without more precise dating. In the majority of cases, these finds did not become part of collections, which were mainly private at the time, but were discarded. As a result, the precise period of activities within the Middle Ages and the early modern periods as represented by these historic finds remains unknown.

The next great wave of Palaeolithic research at previously excavated caves in the Moravian Karst occurred after the Second World War (see Oliva 2013 for overview). Medieval, and some early modern, finds from these excavations were deposited in museums but received little analysis and have also been overlooked in relevant publications which focused on Palaeolithic material. Within this tradition, the excavations of historian and archaeologist Josef Skutil, which focused on post-Palaeolithic activities in caves, are an exception. The third wave of excavations, again aimed at investigating Palaeolithic and Mesolithic activities, were led by Jiří Svoboda in the 1980s and included most Moravian karst areas. This work produced concise but balanced information on all periods of activity encountered. Few excavations have so far been conducted in the twenty-first century, and are often rescue excavations, but testify to complex stratigraphic sequences in caves.

The only large and archaeologically interesting cave region in Bohemia is the Bohemian Karst south-west of Prague – both the karst region and the general size of caves here are substantially smaller than in the Moravian Karst. Cave excavations commenced in the first half of the nineteenth century in the Bohemian Karst and were initially focused on palaeontology concerns. The first wave of archaeological cave excavations took place at the end of the nineteenth century, and notably during the 1920s, by scholars such as J. Axamit, J. A. Jíra, F. C. Friedrich and J. Petrbok. Petrbok was the first Czech researcher to assess archaeological finds in relation to their environmental context – malacofauna in particular. In addition to larger caves, he also studied dozens of smaller caves that were typically deemed 'uninteresting' to archaeologists at that time, though they often produced remarkable archaeological finds. A series of cave excavations took place during the Second World War by researchers such as J. Petrbok and L. Zotz, while F. Prošek conducted a number of well-documented cave investigations during the 1950s (see Fridrich and Sklenář 1976 for an overview). In the 1980s and 1990s, as a result of a boom in speleology, many new sites were discovered, several of which were investigated by archaeologists including V. Matoušek and S. Vencl. Following this, a comprehensive processing and evaluation of all archaeological material from caves in the Bohemian Karst took place (summarised by Sklenář and Matoušek 1994). Modern excavations of previously investigated caves were not conducted, principally because sediments had been completely or largely removed from the majority of sites, or because sites had been destroyed by limestone quarrying in the twentieth century. Thanks to the later commencement of cave excavations in the Bohemian Karst, however, and the generally rigorous approach to investigations, many artefacts of historic date from these sites have been preserved in museum collections and have been published (Sklenář and Matoušek 1994; Peša and Slabina 1997).

The most important non-karst regions archaeologically are the sandstone areas of north and north-east Bohemia (the Bohemian Cretaceous Basin), which have been occupied from the Mesolithic up to the current day, though not continuously. Although cave research here was conducted intermittently prior to and following the Second World War, the main investigations began at the end of the 1970s, and especially in the 1990s, with the work of archaeologist Jiří Svoboda and his team of archaeologists and natural scientists. Excavations were focused on the Mesolithic period. More than 50 new sites were discovered during survey work, 26 of which were investigated in greater detail (Svoboda 2003). The sandstone region of Český ráj (Bohemian Paradise) in the central Jizera River Basin, between the towns of Mladá Boleslav, Turnov and Jičín, was investigated at the same time, from the 1990s (Matoušek *et al.* 2005; Jenč 2006). The main archaeological site type in this sandstone landscape is rockshelters, while larger 'true' caves are rare.

Other non-karst areas only feature small cavities in the form of shallow rockshelters, passages and crevices. A small number of finds are known from such sites, primarily from south and south-west Bohemia, thanks to field surveys conducted by Jiří Fröhlich (1998) over a twenty-year period. Similar sites in Moravia are rare, which is probably the result of a lack of field survey. Other potentially significant sites for later historic periods are the numerous detritus-crevice caves (crevices and clefts in the rock massive and also scree chambers) in the Moravian-Silesian Beskydy Mountains.

## Caves in the Early Middle Ages (500–1200)

The Early Middle Ages begin with the arrival of Slavs in the sixth century and include the creation of pre-state and early state formations (Samo's kingdom in the seventh century and the Great Moravian in the ninth century) and the integration of Moravia into the Bohemian principality under the Přemyslids in 1031. The first documented report on the baptism of an individual of nobility dates to 845, and the first christening of a Přemyslid prince (Bořivoj) occurred around the year 880. With the continuing Christianisation of Bohemian lands, the basic settlement network of farms, villages and central sites was gradually completed by the twelfth century, with churches in the Romanesque style and about 30 monasteries. The Bohemian principality became the Kingdom of Bohemia in 1198.

Archaeological finds from the Early Middle Ages occur in most of the main cave regions located centrally, or at least on the edge of, settled areas, and are represented primarily by occasional finds of pottery sherds (Fig. 15.2). In the Bohemian Karst, some of these caves are located on the edge of fortified settlements, for example, the now-destroyed Turské Maštale Cave and Bezinková Cave near the early castle of Tetín, and Ve vratech Cave in the area of the early castle of Kotýz near Koněprusy. Other sites are located in close proximity to settlement centres such as Nad Kačákem Cave near Hostim, Barrande Cave near Srbsko, Trojvchodová Cave near Prague-Jinonice, and the destroyed Prokopská Cave near Prague-Hlubočepy. The limited possibilities for dating the small number of pottery sherds make it difficult to determine a chronological relationship between the respective caves and castles (Sklenář and Matoušek 1994). Caves of all types and sizes were visited, from spacious caves (e.g. Na Průchodě Cave near Svatý Jan pod Skalou, and Nad Kačákem Cave) to small inconspicuous sites (e.g. Nová Cave near Srbsko, and Uzávěrová Cave near Korno). Another interesting site is the highest point in the Bohemian Karst – Bacín Hill (499m a.s.l.) – where crevices on the flat summit have produced finds of a ritual character dating to various prehistoric periods. A small quantity of medieval pottery is documented from the vicinity of the main sacrificial crevice (Matoušek 2001, 2005).

Despite the limited number of early medieval archaeological finds, there was one well-known reason for using caves in Czech lands during the Early Middle Ages – eremiticism, though this subject has yet to be studied in depth. A limited number of written sources indicate that eremiticism connected to caves, which originated in early Christianity, was popular in Bohemian lands and in neighbouring Slovakia, in the eleventh and twelfth centuries at the latest. In the thirteenth century, it became closely associated with monastic communities and solitary hermitages were replaced by monastic cells (Vlček *et al.* 1997; Sommer 1998; Lalkovič 2005).

According to folklore and historic accounts, the practice of retiring from society was pursued even earlier. In the ninth century, the hermit Ivan reputedly occupied a cave in a travertine mound (later called St Ivan's Cave – jeskyně Sv. Ivana), a site that was later incorporated into the monastery at Svatý Jan pod Skalou in the Bohemian Karst (Fig. 15.3).

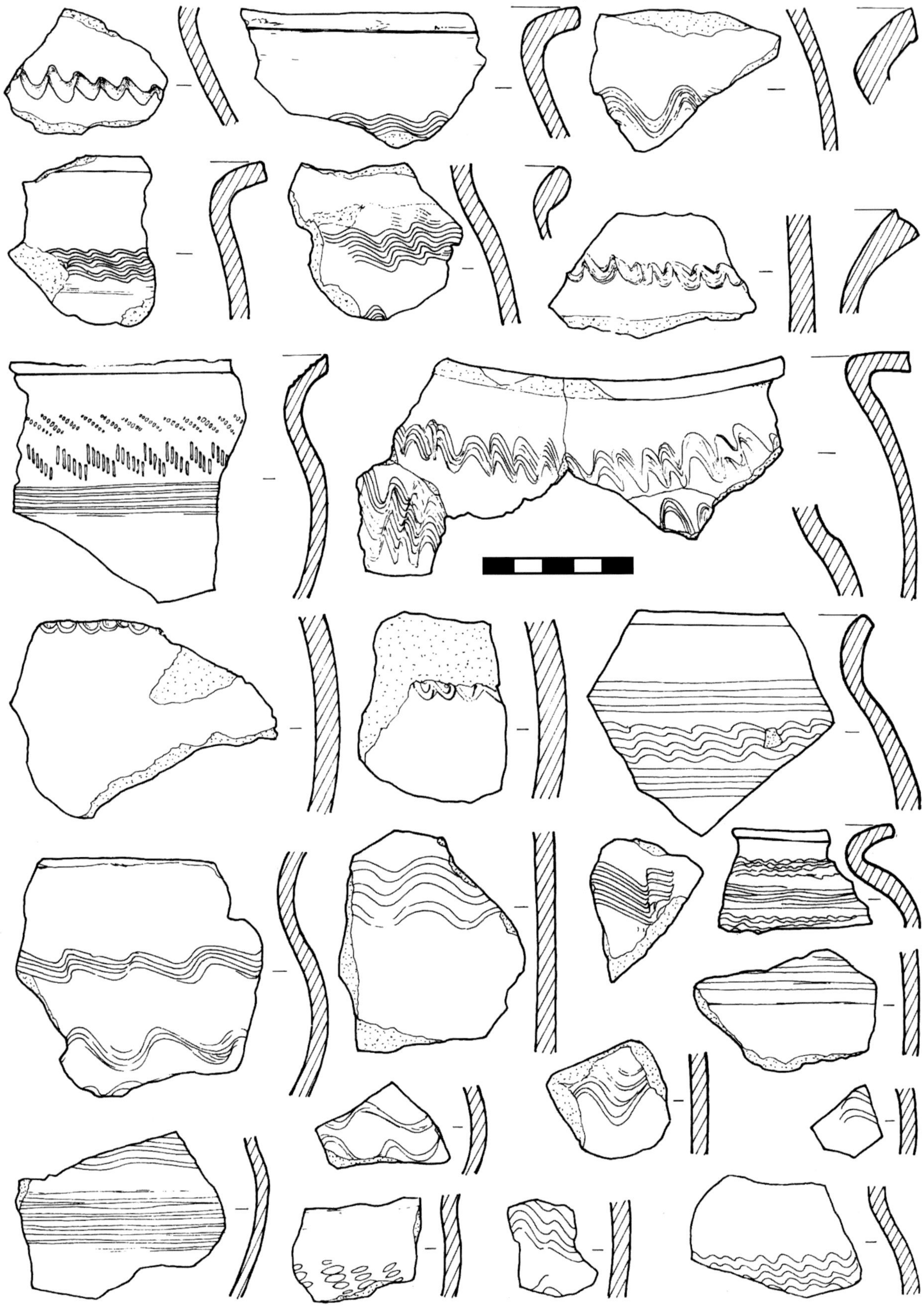

*Figure 15.2: Early medieval pottery from caves in the Bohemian Karst with typical decoration. After Sklenář and Matoušek 1994.*

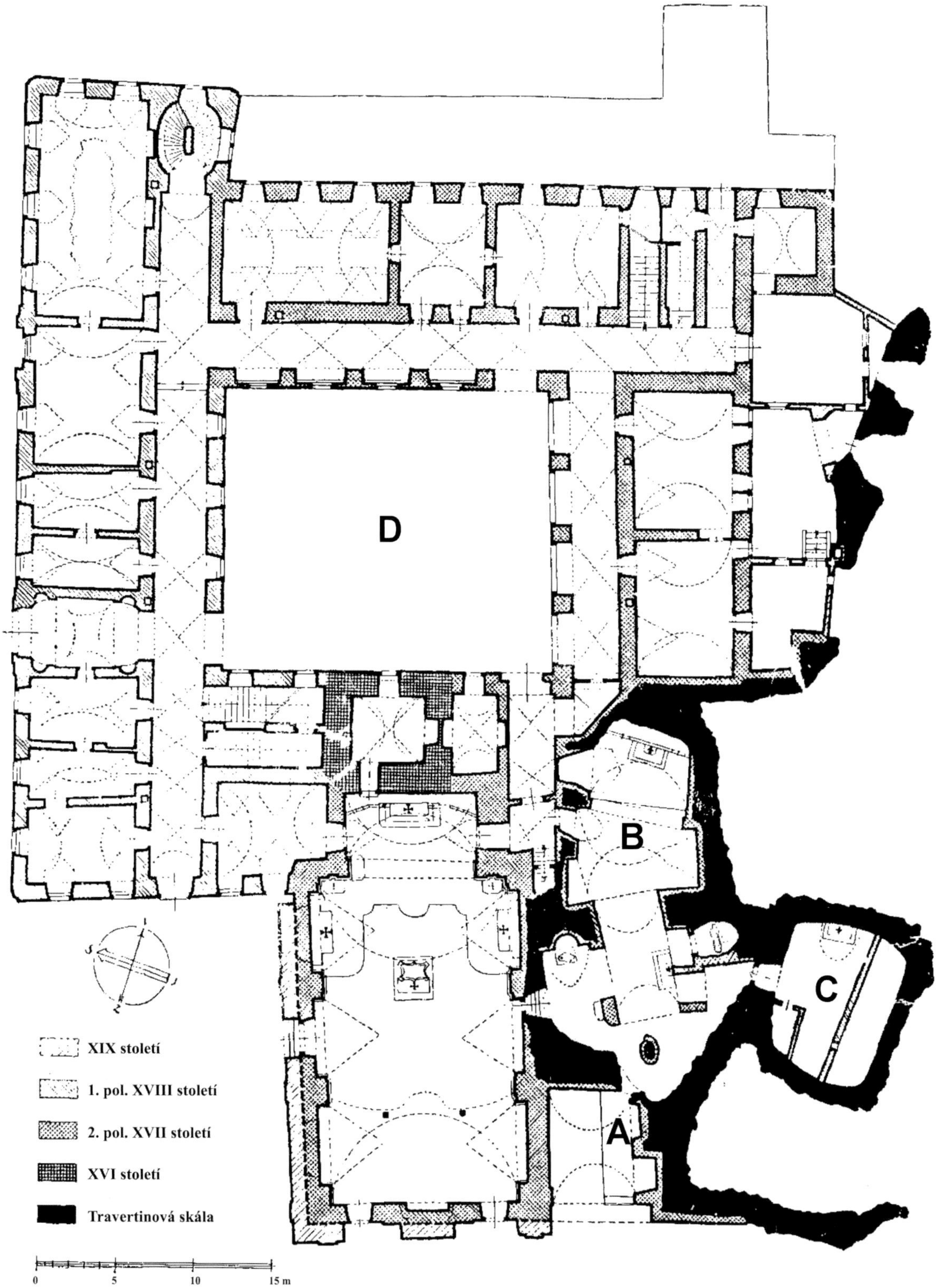


**Půdorys kláštera a kostela s jeskyněmi**

*Figure 15.3: St. Ivan's Cave in Svatý Jan pod Skalou, Bohemian Karst. The earliest cave hermitage in the territory of the Czech Republic, it was first mentioned in 1205 but according to tradition it was founded in the ninth century. The site, with a karst spring (A), acquired its present appearance after many modifications including a cave chapel (B) and a Baroque columbarium (C). The monastery (D) with today's Church of St John the Baptist (E) was reconstructed after 1650. After Kotrba 1944.*

This cave, which was significantly altered over the centuries, includes a karst water spring. Prokop Cave (Prokopská jeskyně), on the outskirts of Prague, was a well-known pilgrimage site named after the Bohemian St. Procopius. The site was destroyed by late nineteenth-century limestone quarrying but an early medieval coin (denarius) was found here (Sklenář and Matoušek 1994). The work of St. Procopius is clearly connected with the Sázava monastery that he founded, which also included a small cave that was expanded into a cruciform shape (Sommer 1998). In central Moravia near the town of Hranice, the hermit Jurik is linked in folklore to the small Jurik Cave (Jurikova jeskyně), similarly destroyed by quarrying (Fig. 15.4).

It is remarkable that these hermits were not poor ascetic monks, as might be expected according to early Christian sources. The legend of St Ivan references his friendship with the Bohemian Prince Bořivoj, ruler of the region at the end of the ninth century, who was said to have frequently visited the hermit. Although St Ivan is not documented in Bohemian literary sources, the cave chapel is noted as early as 1205, making this the earliest reference to a cave in today's Czech Republic (Kořán 1987). St Procopius was also a member of the social élite at the time and his contribution to Slavic liturgy had a major impact on cultural and political life in the Bohemian principality. The Moravian hermit Jurik (commemorated in 1169, died in 1209) was actively involved in the medieval colonisation of the region and organised the founding of villages in the vicinity of Hranice town (Hosák *et al.* 1969, 25–26). I believe that the *eremiticism* of these politically active men was primarily an expression of their spiritual journey, rather than any long-term occupation of particular caves – at least

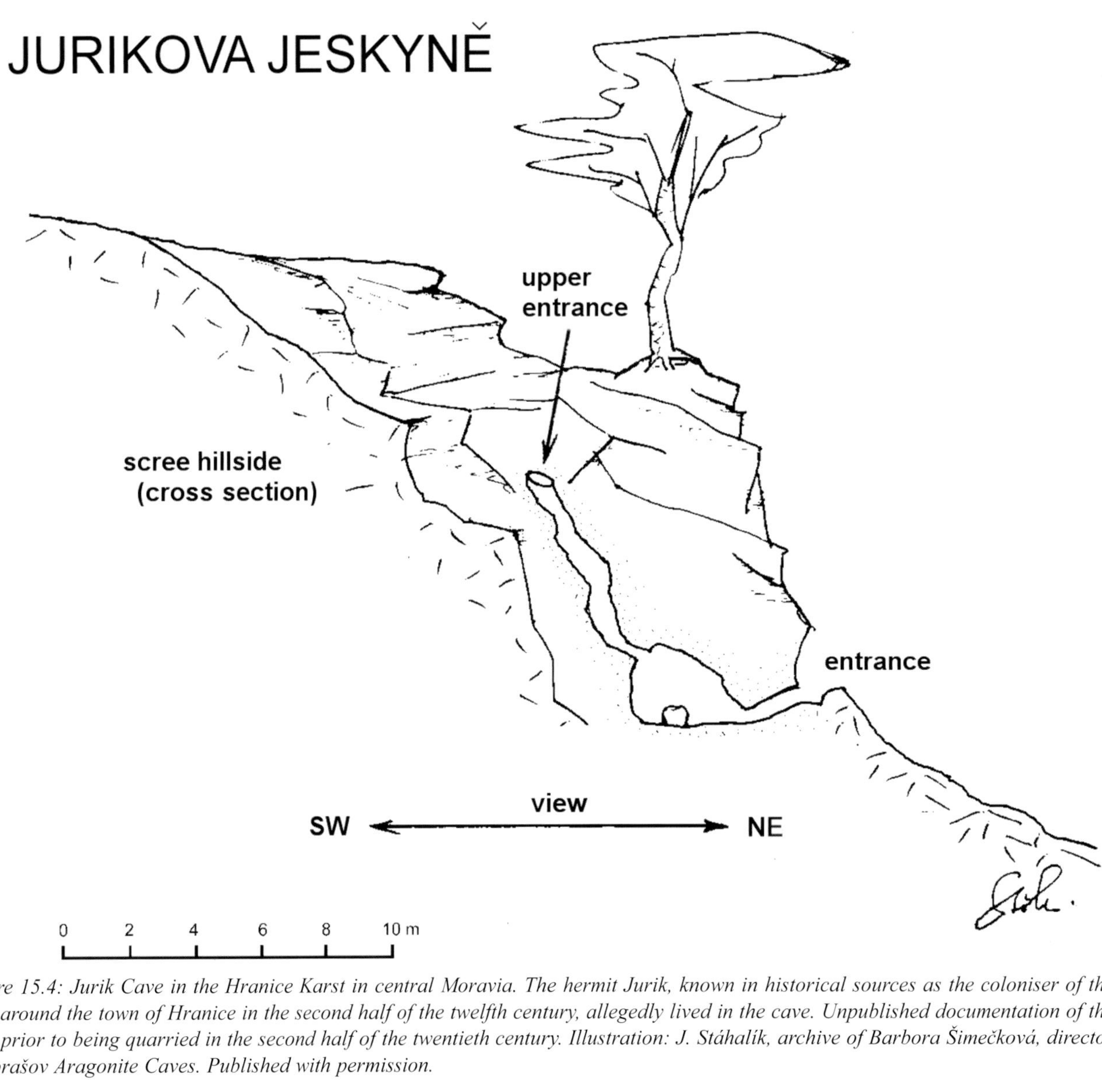


*Figure 15.4: Jurik Cave in the Hranice Karst in central Moravia. The hermit Jurik, known in historical sources as the coloniser of the area around the town of Hranice in the second half of the twelfth century, allegedly lived in the cave. Unpublished documentation of the cave prior to being quarried in the second half of the twentieth century. Illustration: J. Stáhalík, archive of Barbora Šimečková, director of Zbrašov Aragonite Caves. Published with permission.*

those attributed to them in later traditions. In this way, early medieval hermits differed from their eighteenth-century counterparts who came primarily from the poorer classes (Peša 2013a, 256). The only cave to have been subjected to archaeological study is that of St Procopius on the site of Sázava monastery, but all surviving finds relate to the later cult of Procopius in the High Middle Ages. It is uncertain if the site was ever home to a natural cave, as it was apparently refashioned into a cruciform-shaped space in the thirteenth or fourteenth century. Medieval pottery was limited to a basin in the floor that caught water dripping from the ceiling, thus documenting the use of a ready water supply. One interesting find is the capital of a Romanesque column that was carved into the shape of a mortar. This cold damp cave is associated with the ascetic monks of Sázava monastery, and is evidence of the cult of St. Procopius but not of the saint's actual life (Sommer 1998).

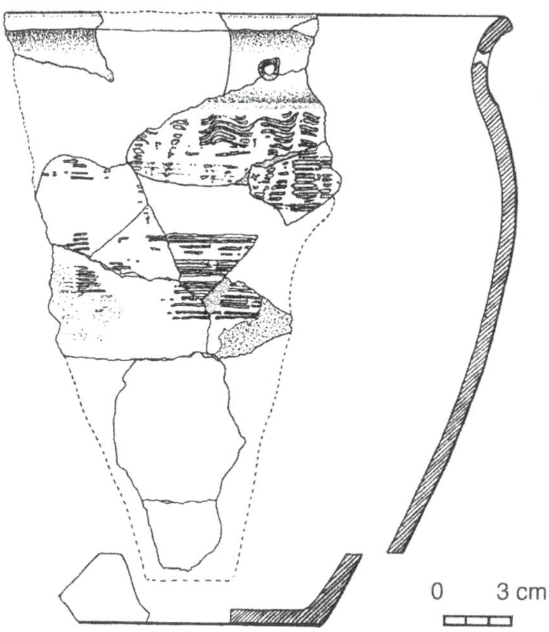


*Figure 15.5: The prominent sandstone Sokolka in Český ráj. A pot placed beneath the overhanging rock wall in the ninth century may have been an offering Photo: V. Peša. Illustration: P. Jenč.*

Early medieval finds have also been made in caves of the Moravian Karst and in the karst area of south Moravia. The most important cave in the Moravian Karst for this and other periods is Býčí skála ('Bull Rock Cave') near the village of Habrůvka, which is discussed in this volume by Martin Golec. Another important site is the spacious Pekárna Cave (a typical Palaeolithic site) near the village of Ochoz, where pottery sherds may have been associated with iron arrowheads and an earring from a late phase of the Early Middle Ages. These finds are difficult to interpret because of loss and a lack of contextual data. Supporting the use of small inconspicuous caves as hideaways, a small number of twelfth-century pottery sherds were found in Liščí díra ('Foxhole') Cave near Ochoz (Stuchlík 2002). Early medieval finds are also likely to have been retrieved from other caves whose assemblages have not yet been subject to modern analysis. A group of small caves with early medieval pottery is located in south Moravia at the edge of the town of Mikulov (Turold Hill and Křížový vrch Hill). Excavation reports from before the Second World War indicate that the pottery came from an ashy occupation layer with charcoal at both these sites. However, the main archaeological cave on Turold Hill was destroyed by quarrying activities (Jüttner 1930: Peša 2006a, 60–62). A noteworthy site in the Moravian-Silesian sandstone region is Ludmilina skála rockshelter near the village of Pulčín in the Beskydy Mountains: it has produced twelfth- or thirteenth-century pottery sherds from a possible occupation layer (Skutil 1961a).

From non-karst regions, early medieval finds appear in the sandstone of Český ráj (Bohemian Paradise) and in Bohemian-Saxon Switzerland (Elbe Sandstone region) on the border of Bohemia and Saxony. Pottery has also been recovered from two sites in Český ráj, located on the outskirts

*Figure 15.6: Bezděz in north Bohemia – the sandstone rockshelter known as Západní vyhlídka ('West Lookout'). The rockshelter was used in the thirteenth century as a workshop for processing tar and resin for the construction of the royal castle and town of Bezděz. Photo: V. Peša.*

and in proximity to the fortified settlement of Poráň – Poráň site no. 9 near Vesec/Jičín (Waldhauser 2004, 421–422) and Sprašová brána cave near Troskovice (Matoušek *et al.* 2005). Finds from caves in the Elbe Sandstone region in north Bohemia are most probably related to routes between the settlements of Děčín–Pirna/Dresden–Bautzen in the eleventh and twelfth centuries, particularly the route along the east bank of the Elbe River. These include Kipphornhöhle cave near Bad Schandau-Schmilka, Dolský mlýn and Šibeniční kámen rockshelters near Vysoká Lípa, and Ferdinandova soutěska rockshelter near Srbská Kamenice (Peša and Jenč 2007). These settlement regions were separated by kilometres of vast forested landscape, with an isolated hillfort and two rockshelters near Brtníky, which produced pottery (Pažourek and Velímský 1995). It remains unclear whether the beginnings of the economic exploitation of sandstone coincide with this period. Sokolka II rockshelter under an impressive sandstone cliff is an interesting site in Český ráj where part of a ninth-century vessel was discovered in isolation (Fig. 15.5). Other unusual finds come from the small Strážce valů Cave in the Prachovské skály sandstone rock complex in Český ráj: a two-part millstone, pottery sherds and an eleventh-century coin hoard contained in a vessel. Kudrnáčova pec Cave, also in Český ráj and near the village of Vesec in the Semily district, produced a bronze earring from the end of the Early Middle Ages or the beginning of the High Middle Ages (Matoušek *et al.* 2005).

## Caves in the High Middle Ages (1200–1300)

The High Middle Ages (1200–1300) saw the completion of the colonisation of outlying forested parts of the kingdom; the creation of royal towns; and the substantial strengthening of feudal aristocracy, which launched the mass construction of castles in the mid-thirteenth century. In this period, the landscape became densely settled, essentially similar to the present population density, including mountain regions where glassworks and hammers for processing iron ores were manufactured and the extraction of ore began. Human settlements thus came in closer proximity to caves. Church administration also strengthened substantially, with the construction of new early Gothic churches and the foundation of additional monasteries, thus concluding the formal Christianisation of the countryside. Notwithstanding, the chronicler Cosmas documented the widespread persistence of pagan ceremonies in rural areas in 1118–1125 (Cosmas of Prague 2009).

It is not clear from the archaeological data whether caves played a role in the comprehensive transformation of medieval society during the thirteenth century. Pottery finds from karst caves have not been precisely dated within the High or Late Middle Ages. It is necessary, therefore, to divert attention to the sandstone regions of north Bohemia where research only commenced in recent decades. In 1264, the Bohemian King Přemysl Otakar II began construction of Bezděz Castle near the town of Doksy (Česká Lípa district) and founded a town in the vicinity of an earlier village (Žemlička 1980). Two rockshelters in the adjacent forests produced finds of contemporaneous pottery, while tar and resin production was revealed at one of the sites – Západní vyhlídka ('West Lookout') rockshelter (unpublished excavation by V. Peša and J. Svoboda) (Fig. 15.6). It is probable that this tar production site was part of a complex of support facilities necessary for the construction of the castle and town. Evidence for the production of tar and related products is first documented in the thirteenth century by archaeological discoveries from the wooded and unsettled landscape of the Elbe Sandstones and the Bohemian Switzerland National Park, including Chatař rockshelter near Jetřichovice and Šibeniční kámen rockshelter near Vysoká Lípa (Fig. 15.7) (Peša and Jenč 2007). Local tradition of tar workshops located under rockshelters continued into the Late Middle Ages and the early modern period, and up to the early twentieth century (Fig. 15.8) (Peša and Jenč 2003, 2004, 2006; Belisová 2004). An isolated site, the shallow Portál Na Chodové Cave in Český ráj, revealed an occupation layer with a hearth, fragments of storage vessels and a whetstone (Fig. 15.9) (Jenč and Prostředník 1995; Jenč 2006). Based on current available information, it seems that during this period sandstone rockshelters became part of the economic support networks of villages (e.g. timber production, forest grazing) associated with colonisation in the High Middle Ages. Some may also have been used for refuge.

Other pottery finds from underground spaces represent human activities of uncertain nature. A small bowl placed in a crack above Na zabitým rockshelter near Kučeř in south Bohemia dates to the thirteenth century (Fröhlich 1997, 69), while four intact but empty vessels with two lids, dating to the second half of the fifteenth century, were found in the small Honzův klobouk Cave near Vesec in the Semily district of Český ráj (Klápště 1993). A similar example is documented from Dagmarka Cave near Ostrov in the Moravian Karst, where two pots and fragments of others were found along with stone cooking slabs (Skutil 1961b). The phenomenon of placing vessels in crevices, niches or simply on cave floors corresponds with human use of caves throughout the world in various historic periods (Peša 2007, 2008). These medieval vessels may represent some form of ritual activities, but alternately may represent the concealment of assets or valuables.

## Caves in the Late Middle Ages (1300–1500)

While the fourteenth century was marked by economic and cultural blossoming of Bohemian lands, especially during the reign of Emperor Charles IV, at the beginning of the fifteenth century society faced a deep crisis that culminated in the

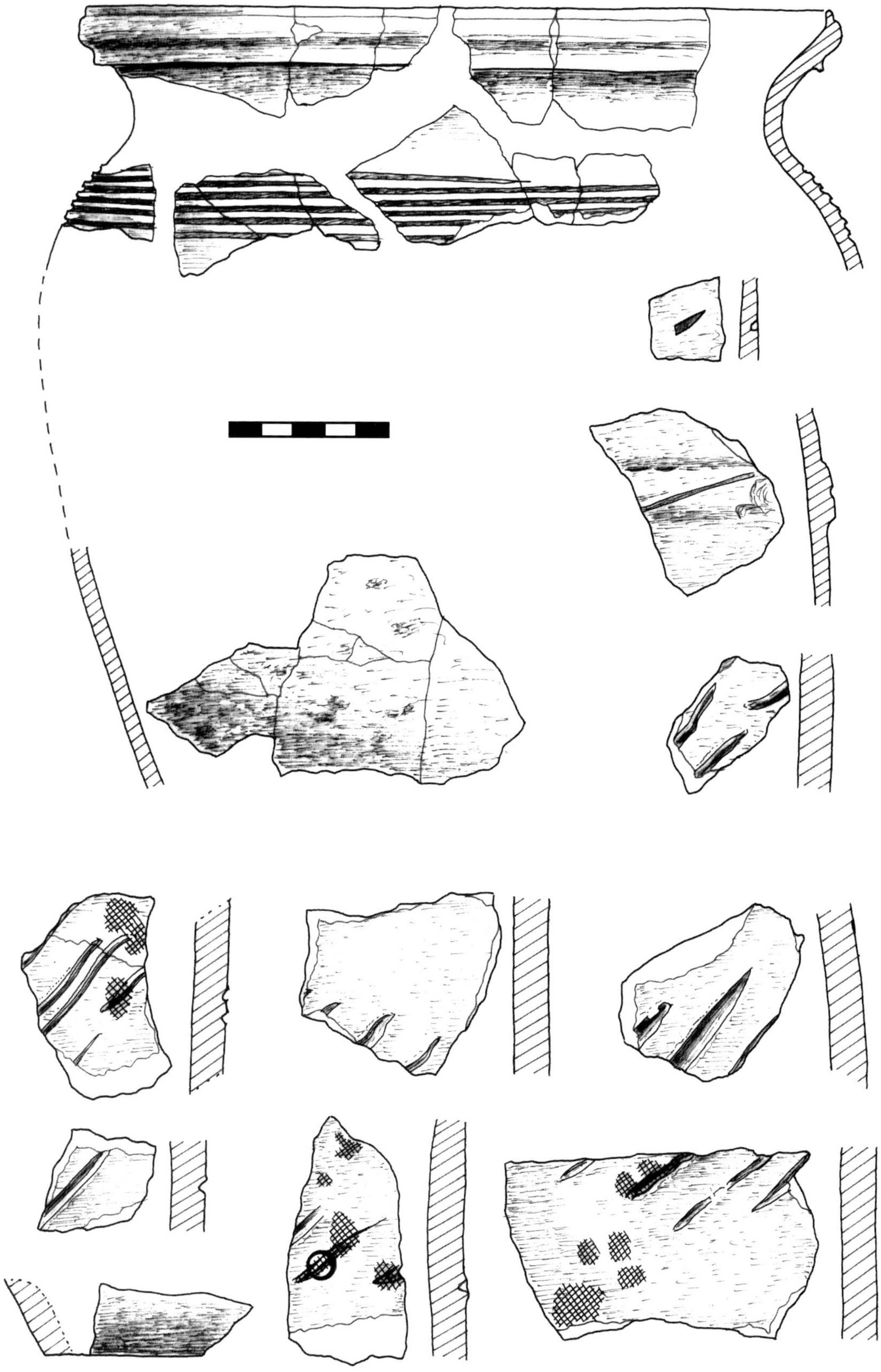

*Figure 15.7: Thirteenth-century pottery from Šibeniční kámen ('Gallows Stone') Rockshelter in Bohemian Switzerland (Elbe Sandstones). The smaller rockshelter was part of a tar production workshop. After Peša and Jenč 2007.*

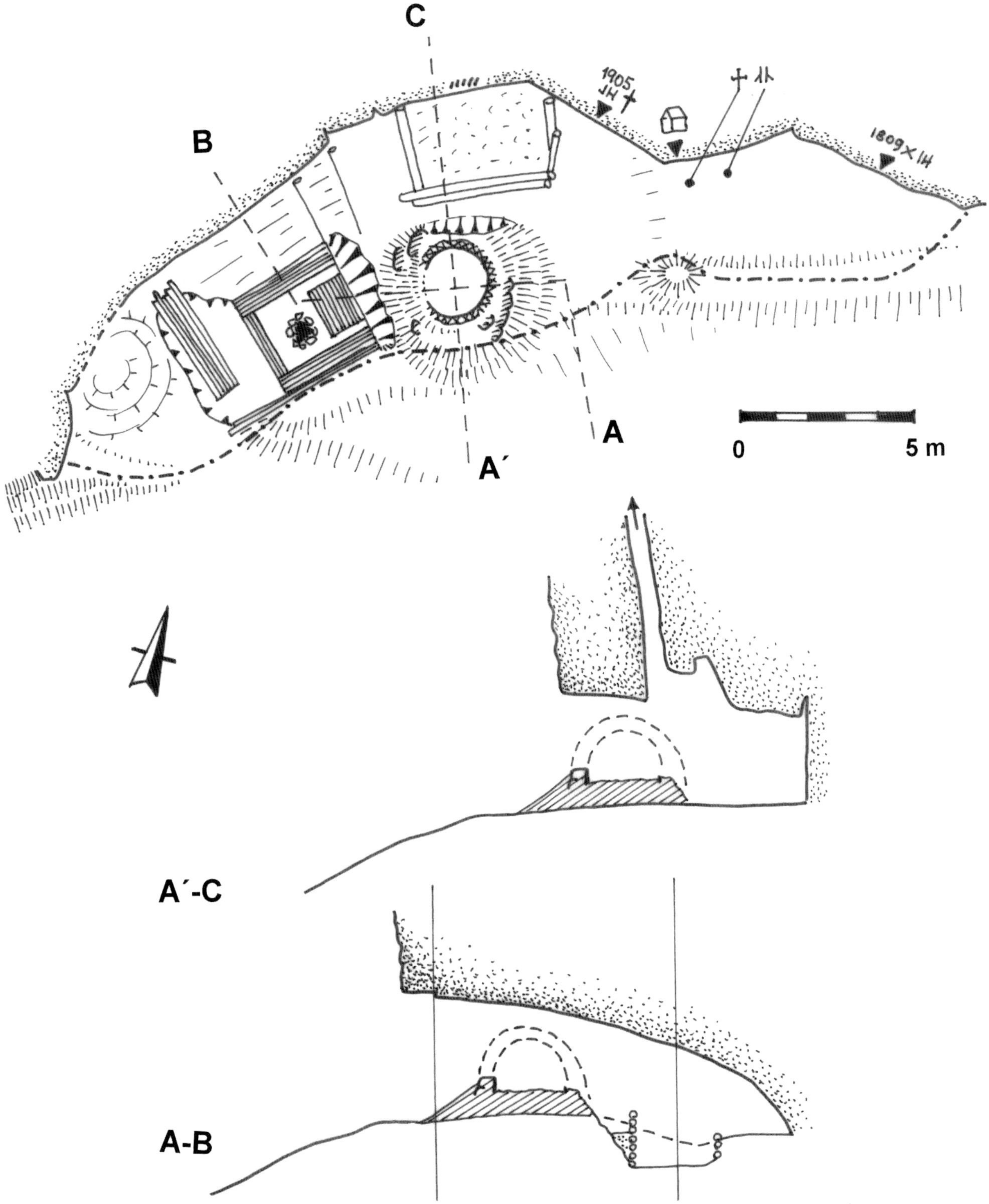


*Figure 15.8: Sample of a preserved tar oven in Červeňák Rockshelter in the Bohemian Swiss National Park. Although this oven is of early modern age, similar objects are also preserved in fragmented form from the late Middle Ages. After Peša and Jenč 2004.*

*Figure 15.9: Portál Cave in the western part of Český ráj with thirteenth-century finds. A refuge for local residents was situated in the adjacent enclosed rock space in front of Sklep ('Cellar') Cave between the second half of the fifteenth century and the beginning of the sixteenth century. Photo: V. Peša.*

*Figure 15.10: Rytířská ('Knight') Cave in the Moravian Karst – a 'cave castle'. Archaeological excavations at the entrance uncovered a medieval wall and arrowheads documenting an attack on this fortified cave. The modern retaining wall across the entrance approximately follows the line of the former medieval wall. Photo: V. Peša.*

*Figure 15.11: A forgery workshop in Mincovna ('Mint') Cave – today part of the visitor tour trail through Koněpruské Cave in the Bohemian Karst. The site represents the best-preserved coin forgery workshop in Central Europe and has been comprehensively investigated. The workshop was operated from 1450–1470 by a local aristocratic family whose rapid increase in wealth was registered in written sources. Photo: A. Komaško, Archive of the Cave Administration of the Czech Republic; published with permission.*

*Figure 15.12: Na Špičáku ('Prospector') Cave in Moravian Silesia with a gallery of inscriptions and symbols from the late Middle Ages to the beginning of the twentieth century. The alchemist symbols of gold (sun) and silver (moon) belong to the earliest horizon. The cave was discovered in the Middle Ages during limestone quarrying or mining for precious metals. It is open to public. Photo: V. Peša.*

'Hussite period', replete with military conflicts and religious disputes, followed by a complex political situation in the post-war economic depression. Interestingly, these events are reflected in the archaeological material from caves. The second half of the fifteenth century witnessed the revival of the Kingdom of Bohemia and the beginning of substantial economic activities by the aristocracy (e.g. fish farming, ore extraction, glassworking). The difficulty of accessing many castles that had survived the war period, along with their limited space, rendered these structures obsolete in the new social fabric of the emerging Renaissance, which quickly spread to Bohemian lands in the first half of the sixteenth century.

Inadequate publication and imprecise dating for pottery mean it is difficult to distinguish between fourteenth- and fifteenth-century material for most of the smaller archaeological assemblages. However, it is often possible to confidently assign a distinct horizon in a cave or rockshelter to the fifteenth century in association with specific political and/or economic events such as the Hussite Wars, the post-war depression and economic crisis, robberies, and local wars between nobles. In these cases, all evidence suggests primary use of sites as refuges for local residents, as was the case during the early modern period and the Second World War. One of the most prominent refuge sites is a pair of caves – Sklep and Portál na Chodové caves near Mužský in Český ráj (Fig. 15.9). The rock platform in front of these two caves produced a distinct Late Middle Ages assemblage, including a rare find of a bone comb with remains of human hair (Matoušek *et al.* 2005; Jenč 2006, 127, 147).

In karst and non-karst caves in Bohemia, finds are limited to a small number of pottery sherds and possible hearths within thin occupation layers, which are often difficult to distinguish from material from the early modern period or the earlier phases of the Middle Ages. A total of 25 sites are registered in Český ráj, approximately 20 rockshelters in Bohemian Switzerland, roughly 15 caves in the Bohemian Karst, and several other sites scattered about south Bohemia. The situation is also similar in the Moravian Karst where approximately 24 caves are recorded. Based on evidence from rockshelters in the Elbe Sandstones in North Bohemia, it can be assumed these sites continued to be used as war refuges as well as for economic activities located a distance from settlements – primarily tar production. Larger pottery sherds from the Pramenný (Spring) rockshelter near the village of Studený in the same area is probably related to use of a natural spring as water source. Another interesting rockshelter in this area is Dolský mlýn (Grundmühle) near Vysoká Lípa, the use of which probably began in the early thirteenth century. This site is located at a ford on the Kamenice River, and from the early modern period (perhaps even earlier) to the twentieth century it was a place where harvested timber was prepared for floating down the river (Peša 2013a, 254–255).

A remarkable site in the Czech Republic is Rytířská ('Knight') Cave near Lažánky in the Moravian Karst, which was fortified like the cave castles found in the Alps (Fig. 15.10). In 1960–1962, J. Skutil uncovered two phases of a stone wall in the spacious entrance chamber that closed off the cave. Finds date the wall to the fifteenth century, while five crossbow tips sunk into the wall document an attack on the cave, the historical context of which has not yet been established. Found behind the wall were the foundations of a structure, more than 1000 sherds of pottery, numerous iron artefacts (knives, weapons, nails, fishing hooks, slag), 33kg of animal bones, several bone artefacts, and cereals (Skutil 1961b; Jarošová 2002; Nývltová-Fišáková 2002). The nearby Hladomorna ('Dungeon') Cave in Holštejn is connected to a medieval castle in a different way – the cave is located in a cliff beneath the castle, and the natural entrance was walled up during the Middle Ages. The cave was entered through a vertical shaft, probably running from the grounds of Holštejn Castle. However, the assumed medieval age of the large number of human bones from Hladomorna Cave has not been scientifically established, as is also the case with the vast collection of pottery and other finds (Bednářová 1956). Sites with fewer finds include a bronze needle from the entrance to Kateřinská ('Catherine's') Cave and a horseshoe and knife from Švédův stůl ('Swede's Table') Cave near Ochoz, both of which are located in the Moravian Karst. Preserved in Pod hradem ('Below the Castle') Cave were three well-preserved medieval hearths, which in the case of more intensively used caves are usually scattered through the occupation layer as charcoal, burnt stones and fired clay. Visits to Pod hradem Cave may have been one-off occurrences.

The fifteenth century was marked by coin forgery. A lack of silver, even for official coins at the royal mints, led to copper substitutions – often obtained by recycling common copper vessels. Copper was used to mint small, lower quality coins that could easily be counterfeited. Historical reports indicate that forgery workshops were located in towns, castles and villages as well as in caves, including a number of cave sites in the Bohemian Karst, Český ráj and probably also the Moravian Karst. The most interesting site is the *in-situ* forgery workshop known as Mincovna ('Mint') in the upper part of the Koněpruské Cave system, which is now open to the public (Fig. 15.11). Artefacts from the entire coin production process were found on the cave floor and immediately beneath it, from remnants of copper vessels to large quantities of minting waste and blanks, and even unsuccessful silver plated coins. Unique finds include a wooden block used as an anvil, a crucible for melting metal, a stamp, and a set of coin weights. A hearth, traces of a furnace, pottery, animal bones and other items were also recovered. The workshop was perfectly hidden and the narrow entrance was completely filled in with sediment sometime around the beginning of the early modern period, thus preserving the archaeological remains. The operation of this workshop was linked to the Kořenský family from Terešov – members of the lower nobility involved in the engraving trade. According to historical sources, the family acquired wealth quickly during the fifteenth century, and coin production at the cave can be dated to 1450–1470 (Hejna and Radoměrský 1958). Coin blanks and ingots of metal related to coin forgery were also discovered at rockshelters in Bohemian Paradise such as Babí pec Cave near Loktuše (Matoušek *et al.* 2005, 72), Dr A. Nastoupilové rockshelter/U rybníka Věžák near Troskovice (Prostředník 2010), the now-destroyed Čertova díra ('Devil's Hole') karst cave near Štramberk in Moravian Silesia (Hejna and Radoměrský 1958, 522), possibly at Býčí skála ('Bull Rock') cave in the Moravian Karst (Peša 2006b) and in Slovak caves (Soják 2007).

The Late Middle Ages and early modern period up to the beginning of the Thirty Years War (1618–1648) was a period of increased prospection in all regions with the objective of sourcing precious metals or iron. The most extensively studied site is Na Špičáku Cave near Supíkovice in Moravian Silesia, because of a gallery of wall inscriptions and symbols, the oldest of which probably stretch back to the mid-fifteenth century. The earliest figures include symbols of the sun (gold in alchemy) and moon (silver) (Fig. 15.12), which are listed in the prospector's book edited around the end of the fifteenth century (Jenč *et al.* 2013). Another likely destination for prospectors was the Bohemian Karst with its caves close to residential Prague. Medieval and early modern period finds were made in Krápníková ('Stalactite') Cave near Hostim, the corridors of which were sometimes choked with sediment but were tunnelled through by prospectors, as was also the case in the older part of Koněpruské Caves (see Mincovna Cave above).

## Conclusion

It seems that the Early Middle Ages in Central Europe was a period of significant change in the role of caves. In some instances, a continuation of ritual associations continued from prehistory, but the practical utilisation of caves in the later historic periods became more pronounced. There is little information about the relationship between caves and early medieval castles despite their spatial connection. The phenomenon of eremitism is documented in the written sources and legends, but finds no supporting archaeological evidence. Christianity played a major role in turning attention away from people's relationship with nature and instead promoted the direct connection between individuals and the cosmic divinity via ecclesiastical structures rather than natural places in the landscape.

By the thirteenth century at the latest, caves appear to have been incorporated more into the profane, utilitarian landscape, especially rockshelters and smaller caves that were naturally well-lit. These sites offered refuge to people and equipment. Pastoralism can be assumed from the beginning of the early modern period, with deforestation of the countryside and the spread of grazing in upland and lowlands regions. Caves were used as refuges by local residents and their property, especially domestic animals such as horses and cattle. That caves served as war refuges can be assumed on the basis of Slovak parallels, perhaps as early as threats of Tatar raids into Moravia in 1241, though concrete evidence only becomes available in the fifteenth century. The exceptional case of Rytířská Cave in the Moravian Karst demonstrates the possibility that caves were fortified and subsequently seized in raids. During the period of currency devaluation and the subsequent economic crisis of the fifteenth century, caves served as hiding places for coin forgery workshops. Caves in wooded areas became part of the network of manufacturing workplaces, or their support facilities, for the production of tar, resin, wood charcoal and lime. In this period caves were probably a minor part of the economic landscape, a situation that continued through the early modern period when the majority of caves were not even named.

During the Middle Ages in Czech lands certain types of activities left only subtle or barely visible archaeological traces – both in terms of the composition and number of artefacts, and the contextual data – as was the case for hermitages, wartime refuges, or places for individuals to hide away from society for a variety of reasons. Occupation of these sites would likely have been short-term in nature – several days or a few weeks at most – and the majority of items taken to the site were again carried away when usage ended. Only activities that required the creation of particular material (e.g. facilities for the production of tar and resin) are more archaeologically visible.

Caves of the first Bohemian, Moravian and Slovak hermits fall into the transitional period of the Early Middle Ages when Christianity was expanding to the élites and the regular population. It is difficult to assess whether these early Central European hermits, who were socially important individuals of significant status, actually spent time in the caves later associated with them. Considering the historical tradition of these cave hermitages, however, it is possible that they did occupy the caves, even if briefly. Early Christianity could also have used caves as a symbol for *genius loci* i.e., places that important Christian saints visited on their spiritual journeys. This concept may well have been more important than the fact that a hermit physically inhabited a cave. The use of Central European caves as hermitages during the Early Middle Ages thus represents, in a slightly different manner, the last vestige of the lengthy prehistoric traditions that associated caves with ritual and cult.

## References


Bednářová, V., 1956. Z dějin hradu Holštejna. *Vlastivědný věstník moravský* 11, 113–133.

Belisová, N., 2004. Zpracování smoly v Českém Švýcarsku a Labských pískovcích. *Minulosti Českého Švýcarska* 2, 94–183.

Cosmas of Prague, 2009. *The Chronicle of the Czechs*. Transl. and intro. L. Wolverton. Washington D.C.: The Catholic University of America Press.

Fridrich, J., and Sklenář, K., 1976. *Die paläolithische und mesolithische Höhlenbesiedlung des Böhmischen Karstes*. Fontes Archaeologici Pragenses Vol. 16. Prague: National Museum.

Fröhlich, J., 1997. *Písecko v zrcadle archeologie*. Písek: Prácheňské muzeum.

Fröhlich, J., 1998. Archeologické nálezy z jeskyní a převisů v jižních Čechách. *Speleo* 27, 15–17.

Hejna, A., and Radoměrský, P., 1958. Penězokazecká dílna v jeskyni 'Mincovna' na Zlatém koni u Koněprus (Die Münzfälscherwerkstatt in der Höhle 'Mincovna' am 'Zlatý kůň' bei Koněprusy). *Památky archeologické* 49, 513–558.

Hosák, L., Indra, B., and Jašková, M., 1969. *Hranice – dějiny města, díl 1*. Hranice: Městský národní výbor.

Jarošová, L., 2002. Výzkumy Josefa Skutila v severní části Moravského krasu. *In*: J. Svoboda, ed. *Prehistorické jeskyně*. The Dolní Věstonice Studies Vol. 7. Brno: Institut of Archaeology, 255–287.

Jenč, P., 2006. Soupis speleoarcheologických lokalit Českého ráje – terénní průzkum a evidence nálezů v letech 1992–2003,

1. část. *In*: P. Jenč and L. Šoltysová, eds. *Pískovcový fenomén Českého ráje*. Turnov: ZO Křižánky & Správa CHKO Český ráj, 117–156.

Jenč, P., and Prostředník, J., 1995. Speleoarcheologický projekt Chodová. *Pojizerský sborník* 2, 44–54.

Jenč, P. *et al*., 2013. A gallery of Late Medieval and modern paintings and inscriptions in Na Špičáku cave, Silesia, Czech Republic. *In*: M. Filippi and P. Bosák, eds. *Proceedings of the 16th International Congress of Speleology* Vol. 1. Brno: Czech Speleological Society, 176–181.

Jüttner, K., 1930. Funde aus der Burgwallzeit im Bezirke Nikolsburg (Mähren). *Sudeta* 6, 76–78.

Klápště, J., 1993. Středověká keramika z Loktuše na Turnovsku. *Pojizerský sborník* 1, 58–62.

Kořán, I., 1987. Legenda a kult sv. Ivana. *Umění* 35, 219–239.

Kotrba, V.L., 1944. *Svatý Jan pod Skalou*. Poklady umění v Čechách a na Moravě LXII. Prague: Výtvarný odbor Umělecké Besedy.

Lalkovič, M., 2005. O možnom pobyte pustovníka Svorada v jaskyniach. *Slovenský kras* 43, 115–128.

Matoušek, V., 2001. Das urgeschichtliche Heiligtum auf dem Berg Bacín im Böhmischen Karst. *In*: M. Chytráček, J. Michálek, and K. Schmotz, eds. *Archäologische Arbeitsgemeinschaft Ostbayern/West- und Südböhmen* 10. Treffen 2000. Rahden/Westfalen: Verlag Marie Leidorf, 82–94.

Matoušek, V., 2005. *Bacín - brána podzemí. Archeologický výzkum pravěké skalní svatyně v Českém krasu*. Prague: Krigl.

Matoušek, V., Jenč, P., and Peša, V., 2005. *Jeskyně Čech, Moravy a Slezska s archeologickými nálezy*. Prague: Libri.

Nývltová-Fišáková, M., 2002. Nálezy pleistocénní a holocénní fauny z výzkumů Josefa Skutila v Moravském krasu. *In*: J. Svoboda, ed. *Prehistorické jeskyně*. The Dolní Věstonice Studies Vol. 7. Brno: Institut of Archaeology, 293–304.

Oliva, M., 2013. The Moravian Karst in the anthropological perspective. *In*: M. Filippi and P. Bosák, eds. *Proceedings of the 16th International Congress of Speleology*, Vol. 1. Brno: Czech Speleological Society, 18–21.

Pažourek, V., and Velímský, T., 1995. Nově zjištěné raně středověké nálezy z Labských pískovců - příspěvek k počátkům slovanského osídlení ve Šluknovském výběžku. *In*: J. Blažek and P. Meduna, eds. *Archeologické výzkumy v severozápadních Čechách v l. 1983–1992*. Most: Ústav archeologické památkové péče severozápadních Čech, 197–212.

Peša, V., 2006a: Využívání jeskyní v mladší době bronzové až halštatské ve vybraných oblastech střední Evropy (Höhlennutzung in der jüngeren Bronzezeit und Hallstattzeit in ausgewählten Gebieten Mitteleuropas). *Památky archeologické* XCVII, 47–132.

Peša, V., 2006b. Jižní boční síň a halštatské využívání Býčí skály v Moravském krasu. *Archeologické rozhledy* 58, 427–446.

Peša, V., 2007. Quer durch das Elbsandsteingebirge: Archäologie der Höhlen, Felsgebilde und Verkehrswege. *Śląskie Sprawozdania Archeologiczne* XLIX, 191–206.

Peša, V., 2008. Cult caves and settlement patterns in the rocky landscape of the Elbsandstone Mts. (Saxony/Bohemia). *In*: Centro Ricerche Carsiche 'Carlo Seppenhofer', ed. *Proceedings of the 10th International Symposium on Pseudokarst*. Gorizia: Federazione speleologica regionale del Friuli Venezia Giulia, 71–74.

Peša, V., 2011. Mensch und Höhle im Neolithikum. Thesis (PhD), University of Charles, Institute of Archaeology, Prague.

Peša, V., 2013a. Der neuzeitliche Mensch in der Höhle: Die Speläoanthropologie als archäologische Quelle. *Památky archeologické* 104, 231–316.

Peša, V., 2013b. Caves in the Neolithic and Early Aeneolithic periods from the Near East to Central Europe. *In*: M. Filippi and P. Bosák, eds. *Proceedings of the 16th International Congress of Speleology*, Vol. 1. Brno: Czech Speleological Society, 159–163.

Peša, V., and Jenč, P., 2003. Pravěké, středověké a novověké lokality Českého Švýcarska I. *Minulosti Českého Švýcarska* 1, 56–79.

Peša, V., and Jenč, P., 2004. Pravěké, středověké a novověké lokality Českého Švýcarska II. *Minulosti Českého Švýcarska* 2, 42–53.

Peša, V., and Jenč, P., 2006. Pravěké, středověké a novověké lokality Českého Švýcarska III. *Minulosti Českého Švýcarska* 3(2004), 89–104.

Peša, V., and Jenč, P., 2007. Pravěké a historické nálezy z převisů v okolí Vysoké Lípy. *Minulosti Českého Švýcarska* 4(2006), 48–56.

Peša, V., and Slabina, M., 1997. Nové datování keramiky z jeskyní Českého krasu. *Archeologie ve středních Čechách* 1, 205–212.

Prostředník, J., 2010. Troskovice, okr. Semily (No. 1324). *In*: D. Dreslerová, ed. *Výzkumy v Čechách 2007*. Prague: Archeologický ústav AV ČR: 313–314.

Sklenář, K., and Matoušek, V., 1994. *Die Höhlenbesiedlung des Böhmischen Karstes vom Neolithikum bis zum Mittelalter*. Fontes Archaeologici Pragenses Vol. 20. Prague: National Museum.

Skutil, J., 1961a. Z pravěku Pulčínských skal. *Zprávy Oblastního muzea jihovýchodní Moravy v Gottwaldově* 1961, 14–21.

Skutil, J., 1961b. Předběžná zpráva o výzkumu Verunčiny díry a některých jiných přilehlých jeskyní v Suchém žlebu v Mor. krasu. *Přehled výzkumů, Brno* 1960, 29–35, Tab. 4–14.

Soják, M., 2007. *Osídlenie spišských jaskýň od praveku po novovek*. Archaeologica Slovaca Monographiae, Studia T. 10. Nitra: Archeologický ústav SAV.

Sommer, P., 1998. Jeskyně svatého Prokopa v sázavském klášteře. Sázavsko 5, 34–47.

Stuchlík, S., 2002. Postpaleolitické osídlení jeskyně Kůlničky a Liščí jeskyně. *In*: J. Svoboda, ed. *Prehistorické jeskyně*. The Dolní Věstonice Studies Vol. 7. Brno: Institut of Archaeology, 173–175.

Svoboda, J. ed., 2003. *Mezolit severních Čech (Mesolithic of Northern Bohemia)*. The Dolní Věstonice Studies, Vol. 9. Brno: Institut of Archaeology.

Vlček, P., Sommer, P., and Foltýn, D., 1997. *Encyklopedie českých klášterů*. Prague: Libri.

Waldhauser, J., 2004. Varia archaeologica z Pojizeří a přilehlého území. *Archeologie ve středních Čechách* 8, 409–428.

Žemlička, J., 1980. Bezdězsko – 'královské území' Přemysla Otakara II. *Československý časopis historický* 28, 726–751.

# Chapter 16

# Bull Rock Cave (Býčí skála), Czech Republic, and its environs in the Middle Ages

*Martin Golec*

*The Moravian Karst is the largest karst region in the Czech Republic, covering an area of 92 sq. km and boasting approximately 1100 caves. Only five of these, included Bull Rock Cave, can be considered very large and have been frequently visited in the past. Bull Rock Cave is a multi-period site with evidence of multiple activities from the Palaeolithic through to the present day. Until now, the medieval phase (c. AD 800–1500) of activities has never been examined. The evidence includes pottery, an oven, a possible counterfeiter's workshop and inscribed art.*

## Introduction

Finds recovered during investigations in Bull Rock Cave (Býčí skála) between 1937 and 1943 shed light on our understanding of this Czech karst landscape in the Middle Ages. The ceramic assemblage indicates activities throughout the period, in the early (*c.* AD 800–1200) and High and late Middle Ages (*c.* AD 1200–1500). This article focuses on the role of this cave within the surrounding landscape, the people who used the site, and the artefacts they left behind. It offers a perspective on the social structures of those inhabiting the landscape outside the cave, which help address the question: Why did people go to the cave, and what did they do there?

Bull Rock Cave is located in the centre of the Drahany Highlands north of Brno (Fig. 16.1a), in the central part of the Moravian Karst, the largest karst region in the Czech Republic (Fig. 16.1b). There has been a long tradition of scientific research in this area, commencing at the end of the eighteenth century (Golec 2014). Research on the caves has gradually shifted from basic descriptions to matters related to both the natural sciences and the humanities. The earliest archaeological investigations were conducted by H. Wankel in 1867/1868 and revealed the first Palaeolithic cave site within the territory of the Austro-Hungarian monarchy, as well as evidence of later archaeological activities. Wankel's Hallstatt findings in the Entrance Hall of Bull Rock Cave in 1872 (Fig. 16.2 and Fig. 16.4) significantly influenced the formation and promotion of Moravian archaeology during the nineteenth century. This Hallstatt collection was discussed frequently in academic literature at the end of the nineteenth century and throughout the twentieth century, based on two of his publications (Wankel 1875, 1882). However, it was a further 113 years before the Hallstatt material from the cave was comprehensively examined (Parzinger *et al.* 1995).

During the nineteenth and twentieth centuries, cave research in today's Czech Republic was focused almost exclusively on the Palaeolithic (Svoboda 1999; Oliva 2005). This situation was analogous for Bull Rock Cave, with an overview of the research history outlined by Oliva (1995, 1996), but attention was rarely paid to the post-Palaeolithic archaeology of the site. There were some exceptions (e.g. Skutil 1970), but interpretation was negligible. In fact, post-Palaeolithic material from caves across the Moravian Karst has only recently been examined in any detail (Ondroušková 2011). Archaeological material discovered in Bull Rock Cave as a consequence of research conducted by the Moravian Museum in Brno from 1937–1943 is currently under analysis (Fig. 16.2 and Fig. 16.3–5). The medieval finds from that campaign are examined here.

A fundamental change in archaeological attitudes to cave research occurred as a consequence of the influence of Anglo-American processual archaeology. Though it appeared selectively from the 1980s in the cultural history

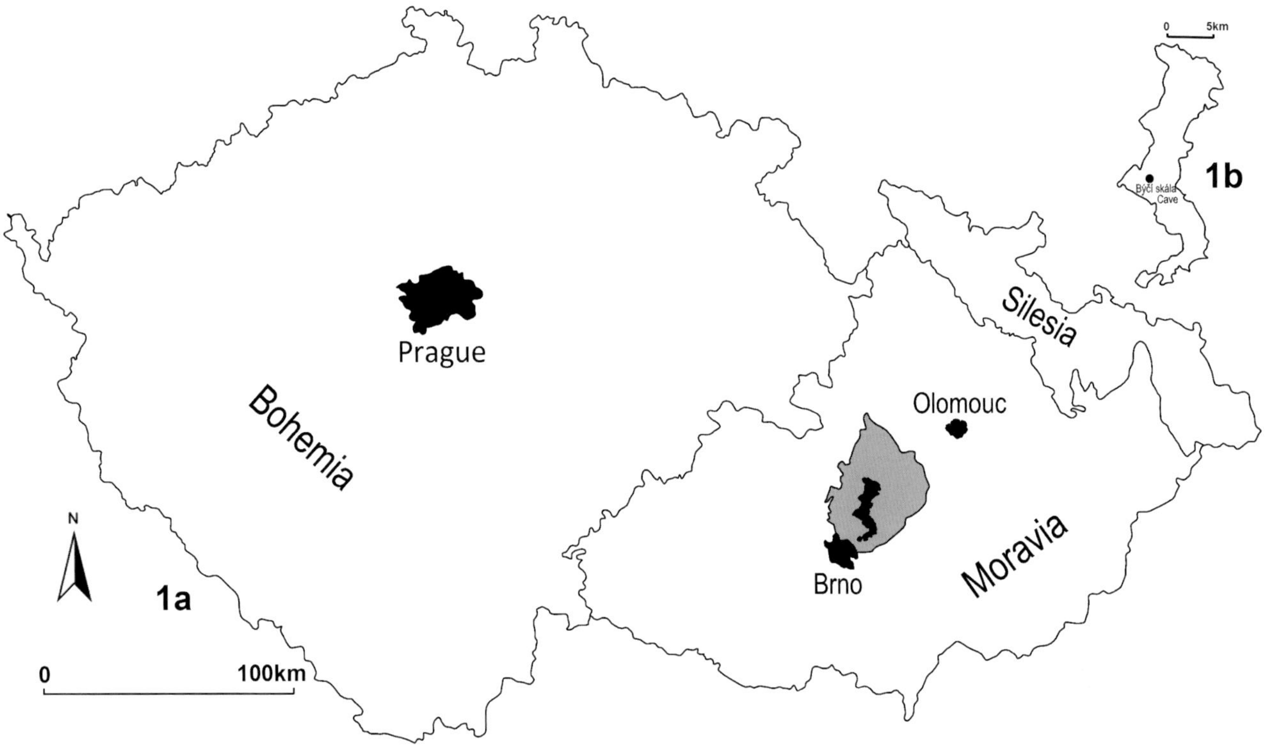


*Figure 16.1a: Map of the Czech Republic indicating the position of the Drahany Highlands in Moravia, north of Brno. Figure 16.1b: the location of Bull Rock Cave in the Moravian Karst.*

paradigm that dominated Czech archaeology (Matoušek 1987), the new approach did not fully assert itself until after the end of the Communist regime in 1989 (Dufková and Matoušek 1998; Matoušek 2005; Matoušek *et al.* 2005; Peša this volume). Caves started to be systematically investigated by scholars from the humanities, and not only by those from the natural sciences. The use of caves by people – not only in prehistory and in the Middle Ages, but also in recent periods – began to be explored. This approach was relatively new to Czech archaeology, arousing much distrust bordering on marginalisation amongst many traditional archaeologists who adhered to the cultural historical paradigm. The new cultural anthropological approach to caves was formed outside the Moravian Karst and subsequently applied to it (Matoušek *et al.* 2005). As regards Bull Rock Cave, Peša (2006) recently pointed out various possibilities for the use of individual parts of the cave by post-Palaeolithic archaeological cultures. However, the finds from 1937–1943 continued to escape attention.

## Overview of archaeological and historical activities

Bull Rock Cave (Fig. 16.6) in the Josefov-Křtiny valley represents an underground stream bed of the Jedovnice Creek and, in part also, a palaeo-resurgence cave of the stream. During high floods the palaeo-resurgence section, which is the main passage of the Old Bull Rock Cave, becomes a flooded stream bed and the cave entrance(s) an active karst spring. The cave consists of several sections individually named (from the entrance to the Serbian Siphon): Entrance Hall, Old Bull Rock Cave, New Bull Rock Cave, Broken-in Rock Cave, and Swim-through Rock Cave (Gregor 2015). Artefacts and human skeletal remains are known only from the Entrance Hall (Fig. 16.7) and the South Branch (Fig. 16.8).

The history of investigations at Bull Rock Cave stretches back 150 years. It is arguably the most studied archaeological site in the Czech Republic making it a perfect case-study for examining changes in theoretical paradigms, which illustrate how interpretations clearly reflect the decades when research was being conducted. Bull Rock Cave was initially examined at a time when an understanding of prehistory was first emerging, thanks to H. Wankel, as this had not previously existed in Central Europe. In Bull Rock Cave we can see the gradual process of changes in interpretative scientific paradigms from Romanticism through to cultural historicism and up to the present day.

A cave acts as a stable point in the landscape that can be repeatedly visited by people while, in contrast, artefacts are continually being deposited or perhaps also removed from caves. Because the reasons for visits change, we can speak about the various functions of caves in the human world. Through the study of artefacts and historical sources, it

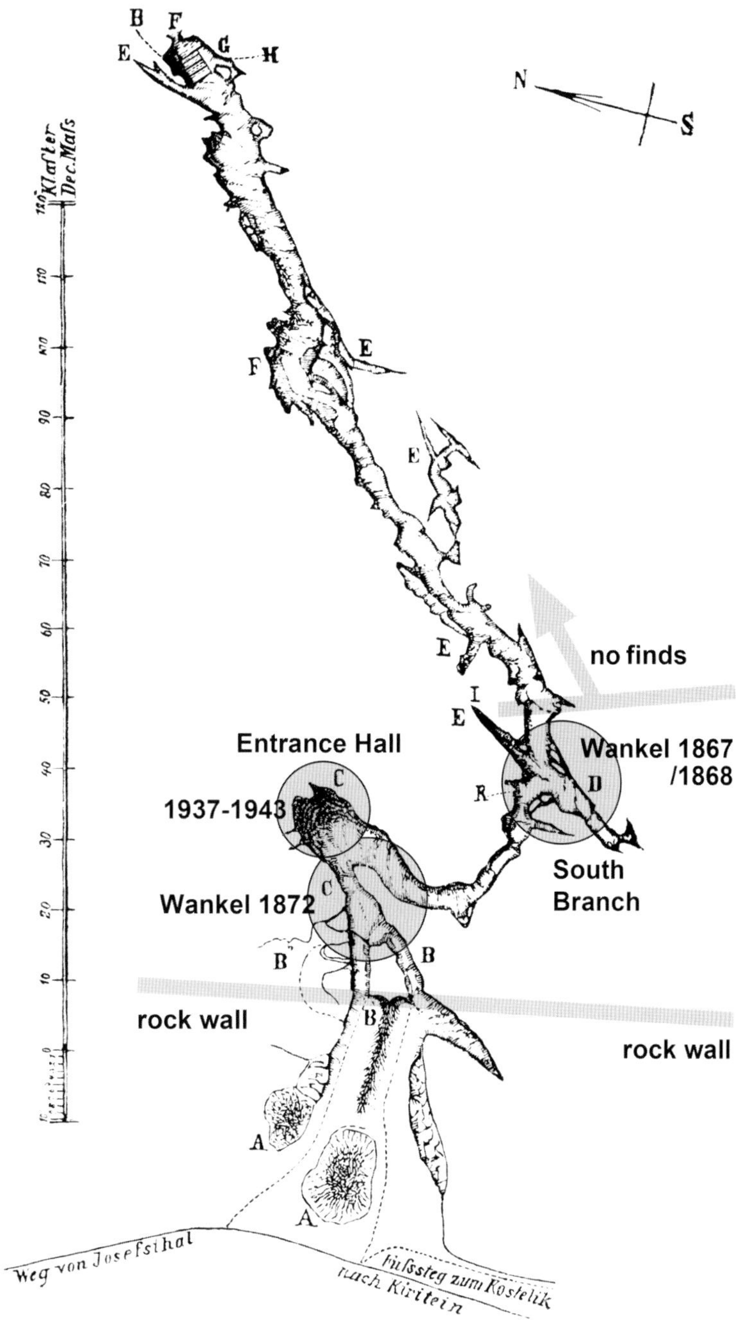


*Figure 16.2: Špaček's plan of Bull Rock Cave from 1871, with the medieval finds described by H. Wankel in the area of the Southern Branch in 1867 indicated. Other finds came from the Entrance Hall in 1937–1943.*

has gradually emerged that Bull Rock Cave was used by people from the Palaeolithic up to the present day. Nineteen particular periods are distinguished in the Moravian Karst, 16 of which are represented in the cave [*BR* signifies *Bull Rock*] (Oliva *et al.* 2015; Golec *et al.* 2017):

| | |
|---|---|
| BR I: | Palaeolithic |
| BR III: | Neolithic |
| BR IV: | Aeneolithic |
| BR V: | Bronze Age |
| BR VI: | Hallstatt |
| BR VII: | La Tène |
| BR VIII: | Roman |
| BR X: | Early and High Middle Ages |
| BR XI: | Late Middle Ages |
| BR XIII: | Baroque |

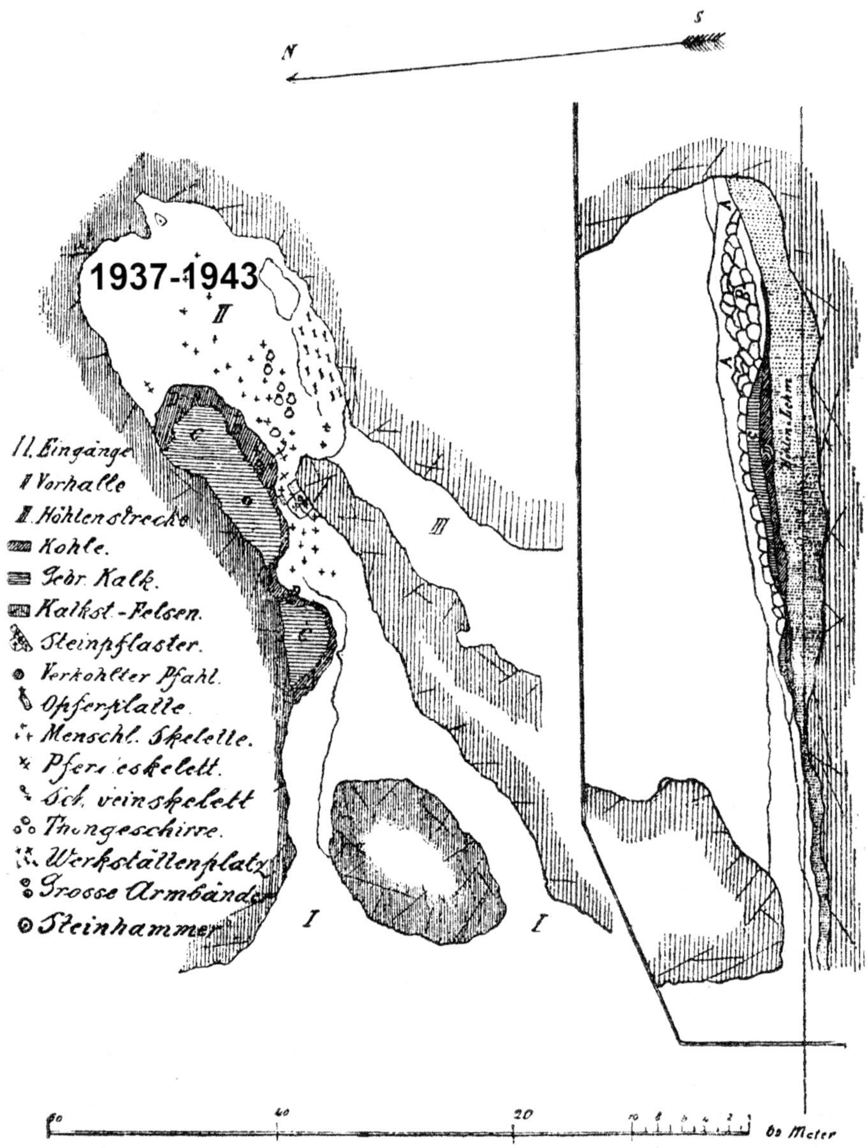


*Figure 16.3: Wankel's plan of the Entrance Hall of Bull Rock Cave in 1872 (after Wankel 1882) with the approximate location of the 1937–1943 investigation.*

| | |
|---|---|
| BR XIV: | Classicism, Romanticism |
| BR XV: | Austria-Hungary (1868–1918) |
| BR XVI: | Inter-war period (1918–1939) |
| BR XVII: | Second World War (1939–1945) |
| BR XVIII: | Post-WWII and socialism (1945–1989) |
| BR XIX: | Recent past (1989–present). |

Certain aspects of the use of Bull Rock Cave have been published; for example, the period 1796–1821 (BR XIV) when the cave was part of a Romantic Liechtenstein park of the English style (Golec 2014). Subsequently, the walls of Bull Rock Cave were densely covered in tourist graffiti (BR XIII–XVII) (Čermáková and Golec 2014). References to the cave gradually increase as we advance towards the present day. These were utilised by Peša (2013) for his discussion of 13 different functions caves and rockshelters in the Czech Republic during recent times:

1. Shelters during war
2. Shelters during the Counter-Reformation
3. Hideaways of highwaymen, gipsies, prosecuted or persecuted people
4. Shelters for lumberjacks, herdsmen and other economic usage
5. Investigations by prospectors and treasure hunters
6. Mining and production
7. Accidents, murders and suicides
8. Hermitages and places of pilgrimage

*Figure 16.4: Reconstruction of Wankel's 'Burial Hallstatt magnate'. Painting: L. Balák based on theme from M. Golec.*

9. Places of popular religious belief and superstition
10. Places for festivities and dance parties
11. Exploration and tourism
12. Shelters and factories during World War II
13. Resources for hikers

This chapter, however, is concerned with use of the cave during the Middle Ages (BR X–XI) and is part of a wider research project on the site. The medieval phase is important for two reasons. For the first time written sources are available: we are leaving the world of silent artefacts. Secondly, a fundamental change in settlement patterns occurred during the Middle Ages. We can *de facto* say that the Drahany Highlands were never continuously settled from the Neolithic to the beginning of the High/late Middle Ages (Oliva *et al.* 2015). Over this long period, the highlands served mainly as a 'visiting and transport' landscape for people from the surrounding plains (Figs. 16.9 and 10). A local iron working enclave from the early Middle Ages has been identified in the Drahany Highlands and a network of villages that emerged in the High Middle Ages form the basis of the present settled landscape. Several castles, two pilgrimage sites and a monastery also emerged. These changes had a fundamental impact on the human use of Bull Rock Cave. A set of smithy items from Bull Rock Cave (Parzinger *et al.* 1995) have been repeatedly suggested as medieval, but the set includes items for the production of bronze artefacts that are undoubtedly of Hallstatt origin. This important fact has been neglected in discussions so far.

The written sources from the Middle Ages do not document the functions Bull Rock Cave fulfilled, and thus it is useful to bear in mind the more recent ethnographic examples (Peša 2013). Since the set of 'affordances' a cave can offer are consistent through time due to their permanent and relatively unchanging geological structure, some forms of human exploitation are likely to be repeated. The dark and damp spaces of Bull Rock Cave are unsuitable for long-term occupation and the evidence instead points to repeated short-term stays. Where there is evidence of longer stays, this is usually a reflection of extreme situations such as war, or other exceptional circumstances.

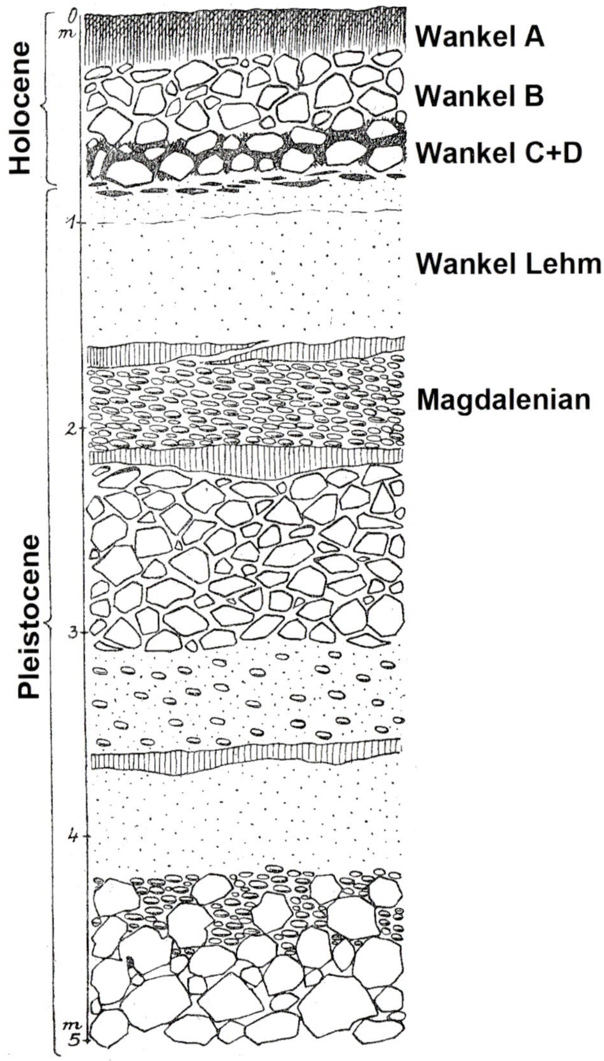


*Figure 16.5: The sediment profile in the Entrance Hall of Bull Rock Cave recorded in 1937–1943 (after Pelíšek 1949). It depicts Wankel's layers A–D and Lehm's from 1872. The medieval finds correspond to layers A or B.*

*Figure 16.6: Entrances to Bull Rock Cave. Photo: M. Golec.*

*Figure 16.7: The Entrance Hall of Bull Rock Cave. Photo: Š. Mátl.*

*Figure 16.8: The South Branch of Bull Rock Cave. Photo: Š. Mátl.*

## Bull Rock Cave in the Middle Ages

The hitherto unpublished artefact assemblage recovered from the Entrance Hall of Bull Rock Cave between 1937 and 1943 (Fig. 16.3), prior to the construction of a Nazi factory there, presents entirely new insights into the use of the cave. From 1942 it was known that the Entrance Hall was to become the location of the factory, which was constructed in 1944–1945. The investigations carried out by the Moravian Museum in Brno were never published, and the field documentation has not survived, only the artefacts. Museum notes record that the work was directed by German archaeologists H. Freising and K. Hucke in several stages, both before World War II and after it. Profiles of the cave sediments were published after the war (Fig. 16.5) (Pelíšek 1949). Objects from prehistoric times and those from the Middle Ages appear to have occurred approximately 50cm above Wankel's layers C and D, probably in the loamy layer A or perhaps in the rocky layer B (Fig. 16.5). The medieval artefacts from Bull Rock Cave comprise principally of pottery (Fig. 16.11) and can be divided into two basic periods: BR X (earlier part of the early Middle Ages, *c.* 800–1200) and BR XI (the High/Late Middle Ages, *c.* 1200–1500). The earliest historical reports contemporaneous with the artefacts from Bull Rock Cave

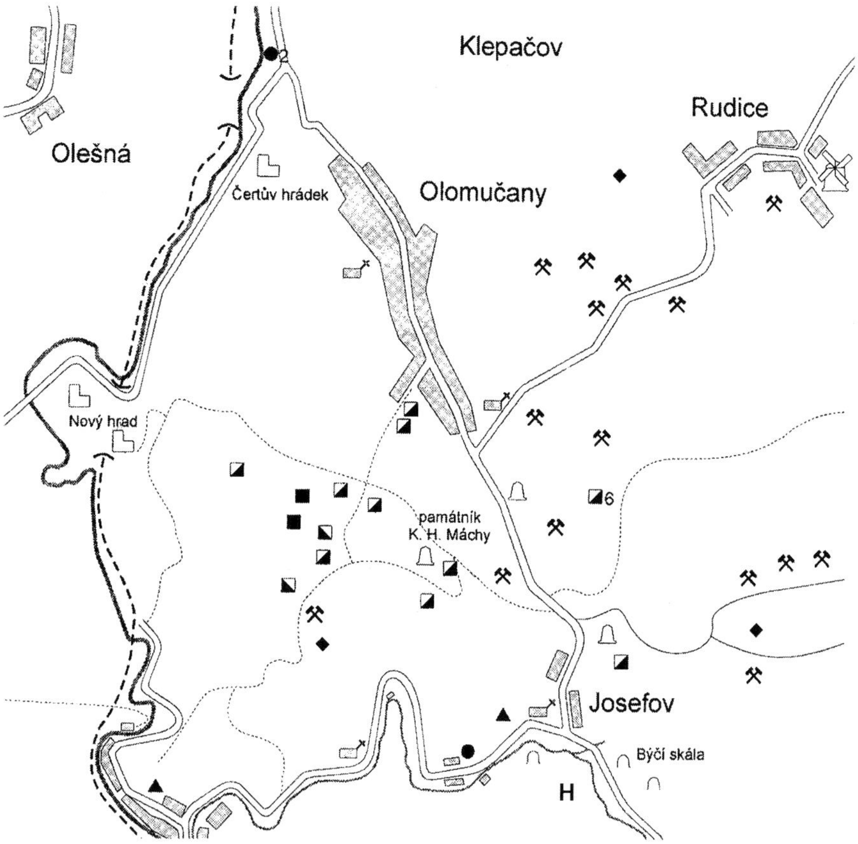


■ bloomeries from the end of 8th to the beginning of 9th centuries
◪ bloomeries from the 9th century
◩ bloomeries from the 10th and the 11th centuries
◆ bell-pit fields
▲ medieval ironworks
● ironworks from the 18th and the 19th centuries
⚒ places of iron mining
H hoard at Jidášova stěna Rock Wall from the 9th century

*Figure 16.9: Map of iron working near Bull Rock Cave in the early Middle Ages (after Souchopová* et al. *2011).*

relate to the Drahany Highlands region and the BR XI.2 period (Černý 1992). This comprises a reference to a castle called Nový hrad (New Castle), which was besieged by the invading Hungarian army in the winter of 1470 (Fig. 16.9).

### *BR X horizon (earlier part of the Early Middle Ages,* c. *800–1200)*

The Drahany Highlands is a landscape with rich evidence of human activities. The region has had a long tradition of iron working, mining, charcoal burning, lime burning, grease manufacturing, glass making, and potash and gunpowder manufacture. The industrial iron ore extraction of the eighteenth and nineteenth centuries undoubtedly had the greatest effect on the terrain, often obliterating earlier archaeological evidence. Local iron production stretches back to the early Middle Ages, from the eighth to the eleventh century based on dates from pottery and coins (Fig. 16.9). The principal research on the iron working agglomerations near Olomučany occurred in the 1970s and 1980s (Souchopová 1986, 1992, 1995; Pleiner 2000). Highly organised iron production in row furnaces was taking place at the end of the eighth century and particularly in the ninth century, during the Great Moravian polity. The organisation of ironworking changed from the second half of the tenth century and into the eleventh century. Industrial production disappeared. Now, individual furnaces were operated for a certain part of the year, probably during the winter when rural smiths did not have to work on their farms.

A fundamental technological change in iron production took place later, during the High Middle Ages, when water power was used. The smelting enclave in Olomučany was quite isolated in the centre of the Drahany Highlands,

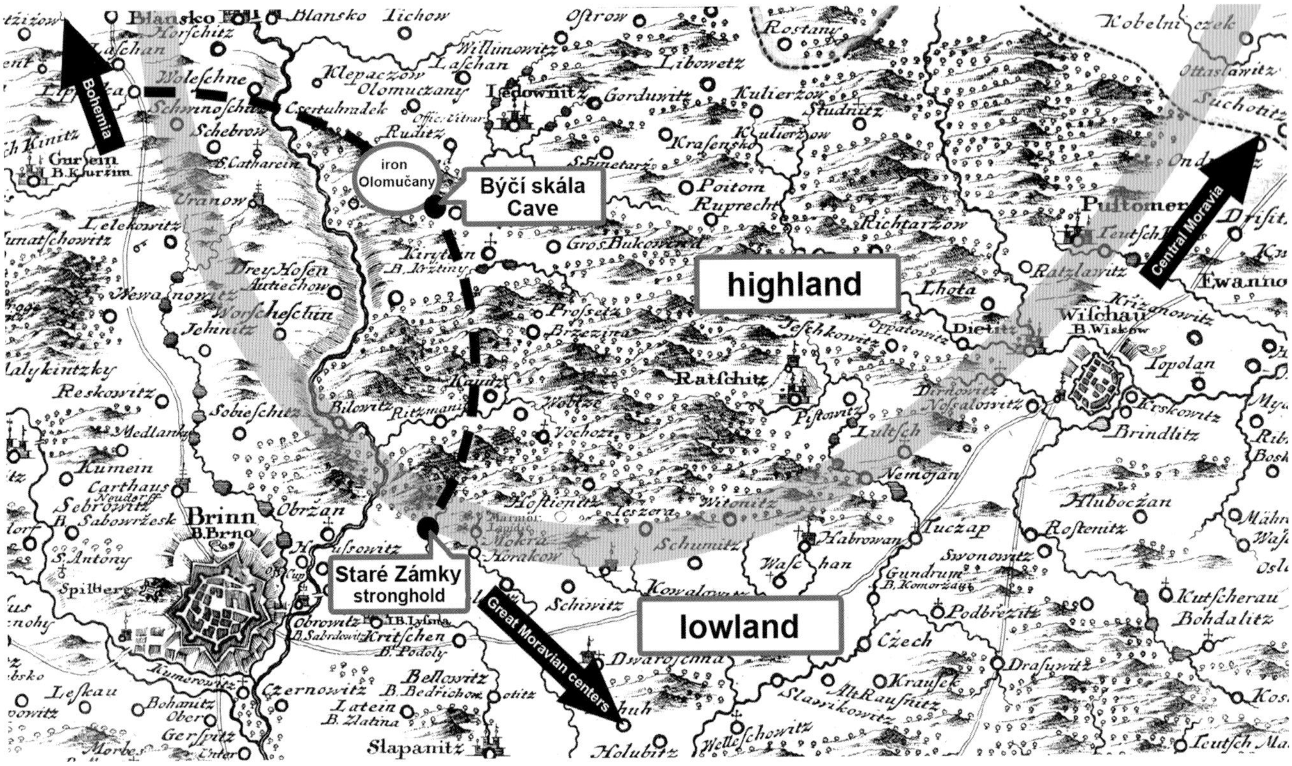


*Figure 16.10: Drahany Highlands on Müller's map of* c. *1750 (BR X.1–2).*

but essential social relationships with populations in the surrounding landscape can be presumed. The Staré Zámky (Old Castle) stronghold near Brno-Líšeň was situated on its outskirts, creating a social unit with the iron working agglomerations near Olomučany. The stronghold was also active from the ninth to the eleventh century and produced rich evidence of smithing (Lutovský 2001). Laser scanning revealed a hitherto unknown road network used in the Middle Ages between the iron agglomeration and the fortified centre of Staré Zámky (Martínek *et al.* 2014; Martínek 2015). This leads directly past Bull Rock Cave and near Judas Wall (Fig. 16.12). Two new places of pilgrimage, some 4 km and 7 km from Bull Rock Cave, were established in the High Middle Ages, at Vranov u Brna (Mihola 2010) and Křtiny, where a Premonstratensian nunnery of St. Norbert was established around 1200 (Kavička 2014). The routes to these pilgrimage places pass Nový hrad Castle and Bull Rock Cave (Fig. 16.13). Those travelling the roads may have used the cave for various purposes, including shelter and short-term occupation, as suggested by the hundreds of pottery sherds recovered from the Entrance Hall dating to two time horizons: BR X.1 (ninth century) (Fig. 16.11.1) and BR X.2 (tenth–twelfth century) (Fig. 16.11.2–11, Fig. 16.11.13–14). Early medieval pottery is seldom found in caves of the Moravian Karst, though High and late medieval ceramics are regularly recovered.

Another discovery illustrating that the early medieval landscape of the highlands was not void of human activities is a deposit of three iron items – an axe, knife/sickle and ploughshare (Fig. 16.13) – by the Jidášova stěna (the 'Judas Wall', a solitary block of rock with a number of very small caves on the surface) near Bull Rock Cave. These artefacts date to the ninth century, from the time of Great Moravia when the Olomučany agglomeration was probably working for its centres (Galuška 2006). A similar ninth-century *bradatice* (bearded axe) was found near Žitný (Rye) Cave, which is 4 km distant (Burkhardt 1950). Popular religious practices continued to take place during the early Middle Ages, and Christian criticism of the worship of 'pagan' gods in Bohemia is documented for the eleventh and twelfth centuries (Měřínský 2009). Apart from their functional importance, the symbolic meaning of the iron items may be important. The ploughshare relates to cultivation of the land, the knife/sickle represents harvest, and the axe is a weapon that sometimes served as an offering to the Slavic pre-Christian god Perun/Svantovít (Galuška 2006; Podborský 2006).

Early medieval people used artefacts to define their relationships to space, and caves were no exception. The pottery sherds from the Bull Rock Entrance Hall are possibly remnants of a temporary shelter. In contrast, the iron artefact deposit at the Judas Wall suggests different human interests. Here, people defined their relationship to spiritual forces in the form of an offering. Objects are regularly used in communication with the non-human spiritual world, determined by specific religious or cultural traditions. Some objects, such as iron items, can have a

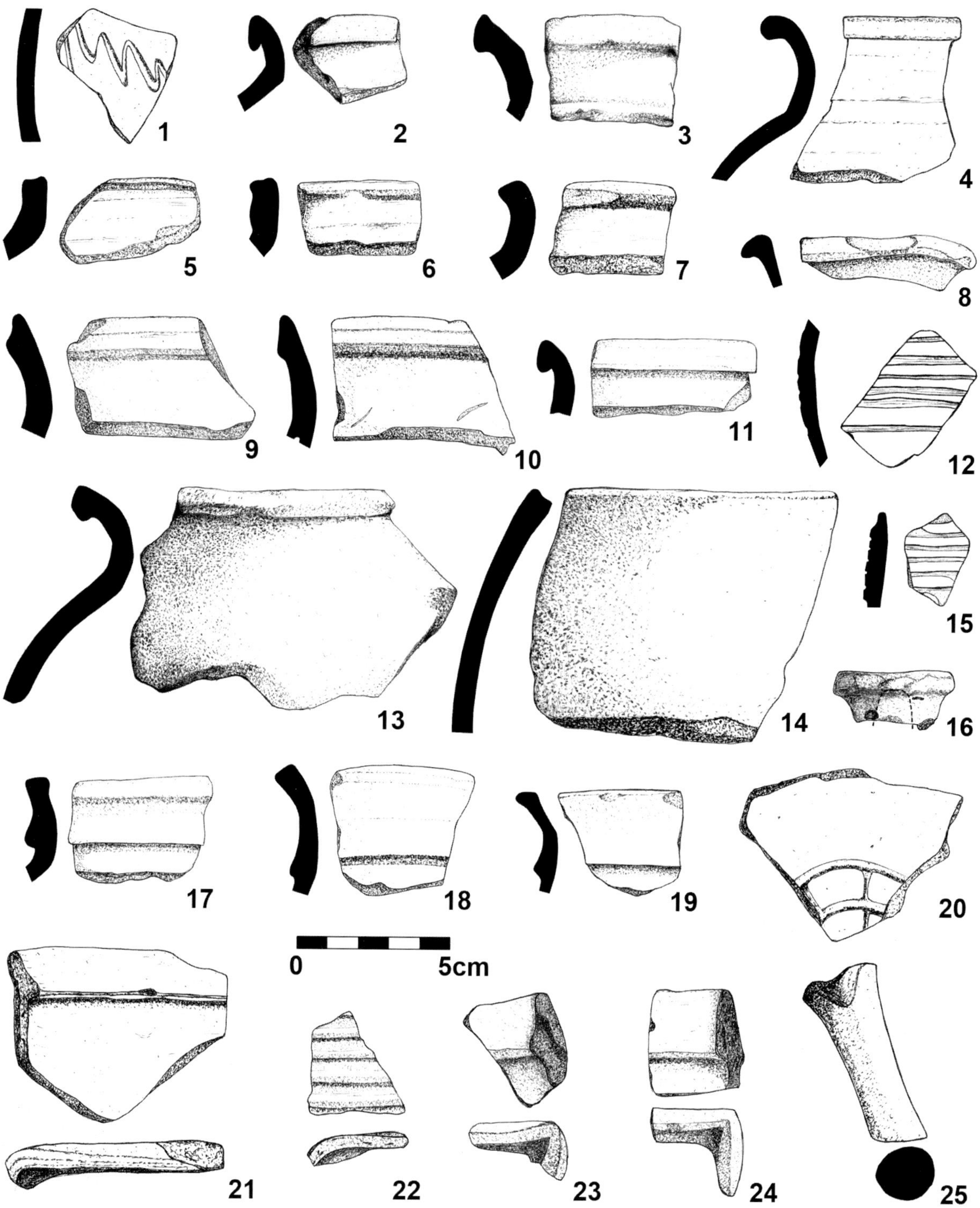


*Figure 16.11: Medieval ceramics from Bull Rock Cave. 1–7, 9–15, 17–19 (pots), 8 (bottle/bell-shaped lids), 16 (lid), 20 (mark on the bottom of a pot), 21–24 (cistern tiles), 25 (frying pan). BR X.1 (8:1, ninth century), BR X.2 (8:2–10, 8:13–14, tenth–twelfth century), BR XI.2 (8:11–12, 8:15–25, thirteenth–fifteenth century).*

higher value than other objects. That value becomes part of people's relationships with one another, and between people and a god or gods. The purpose of objects is also important. With swords, knives, axes, sickles or ploughshares people perform many of the main activities of life. In fact, these objects are always 'at hand' in the human struggle for life. An example of the importance of metal objects comes from ninth- and tenth-century Czech Republic. At this time hoards

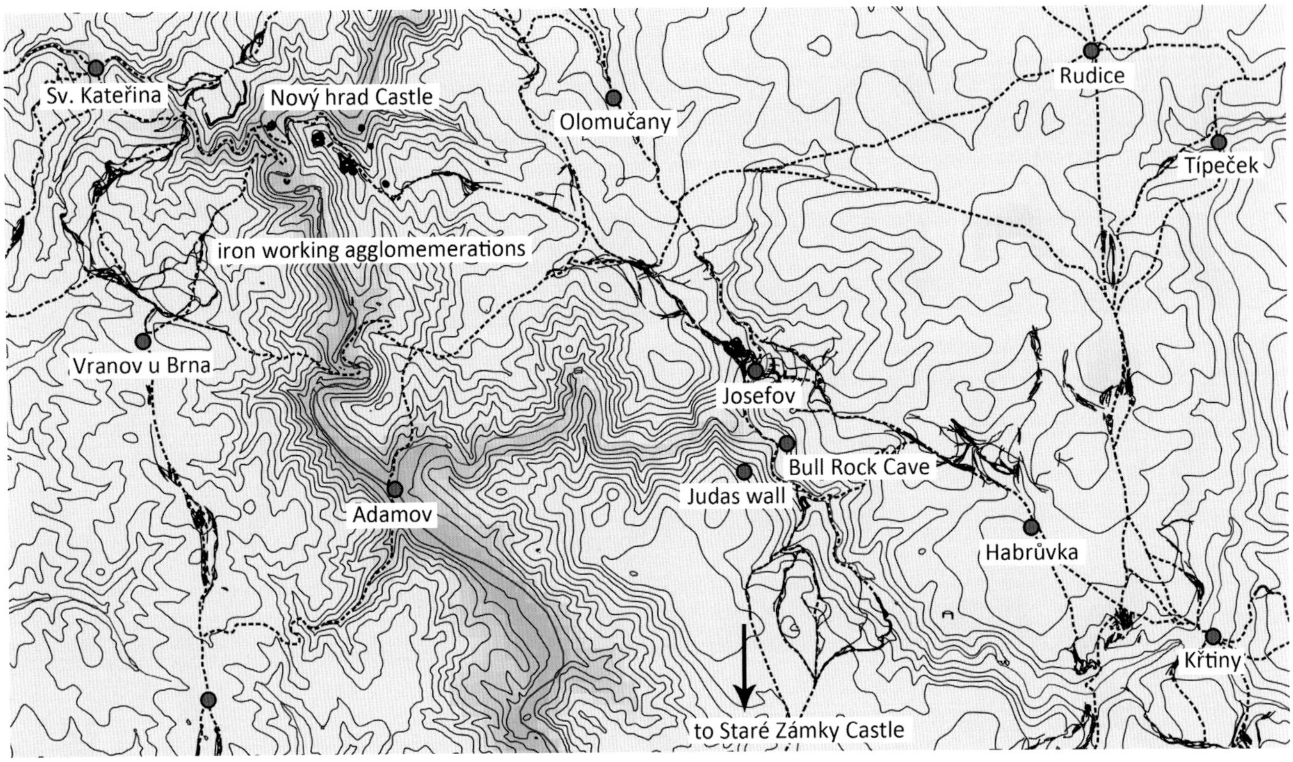


*Figure 16.12: A road from iron production centres to the stronghold of Staré Zámky in the Early Middle Ages leads around Bull Rock Cave and near the Judas Wall. Main road between the medieval pilgrimage sites of Vranov u Brna and Křtiny in the High and late Middle Ages also passes near Bull Rock Cave (after Martínek 2015).*

of metal objects were often buried, even creating a 'ritual mountain' of hundreds of iron objects at the stronghold of Klášťov, 15 km east of Zlín, where there is a 'devil's stone' and spring on the summit (Hlavica 2009; Profantová 2014).

## *BR XI horizon (High and Late Middle Ages, c. 1200–1500)*

During the High Middle Ages, a new network of villages was created in the Drahany Highlands, though many were subsequently gradually deserted (Černý 1992). The nobility were engaged there from the middle of the thirteenth century, in terms of colonisation and castle construction in this forested terrain (Plaček 2001). The new villages largely belonged to three owners who resided in the castles of Nový hrad, Blansek and Holštejn. Two new castles – Ronov and Čertův Hrádek (Devil's Castle) – were built several kilometres from Bull Rock Cave in the thirteenth century. Nový hrad (Figs. 16.9 and 16.12) established itself as a centre of power in the fourteenth century. Ceramics have also been recovered from the Entrance Hall of Bull Rock Cave dating to the period BR XI (Fig. 16.11.15–27 and Fig. 16.11.12). Documentary references to the cave may help in the interpretation of these finds (see below).

This unprecedented and most significant phase of settlement in the Drahany Highlands corresponds with numerous traces of human activities in Bull Rock Cave, attesting to various usages by different people. These are summarised below.

### *BR XI.1 drawing*

A drawing on the cave wall, executed with charcoal and resembling a deer, was $^{14}$C-dated to between 1265 and 1395 (Svoboda *et al.* 2005). It is situated near a Middle Aeneolithic drawing (BR IV) and eighteenth- and nineteenth-century visitor signatures (BR XIV) deep in the cave in the South Branch (Fig. 16.2) (Čermáková and Golec 2014). Various finds from post-Palaeolithic periods found here are now lost (Peša 2006).

### *BR XI.2 oven*

The nearby Nový hrad Castle was built before 1364 and owned by important Moravian nobles (Wankel 1882). During the so-called Bohemian–Hungarian War (Válka 1991), the invading Hungarian army besieged Nový hrad near Bull Rock in the winter of 1470 (Plaček 2001). The army reportedly held Nový hrad under siege for a full year, which had a drastic impact on the local inhabitants. In order to control supplies brought to the castle, the attackers built six smaller strongholds on the access roads; tiled ovens survive in three of these (Konečný and Merta 1976; 1980). Similar tiles were found in Bull Rock Cave (Fig. 16.11.21–24). One of the documentary sources (Kreps 1976) mentions that Althamr (*hamr* means 'iron production

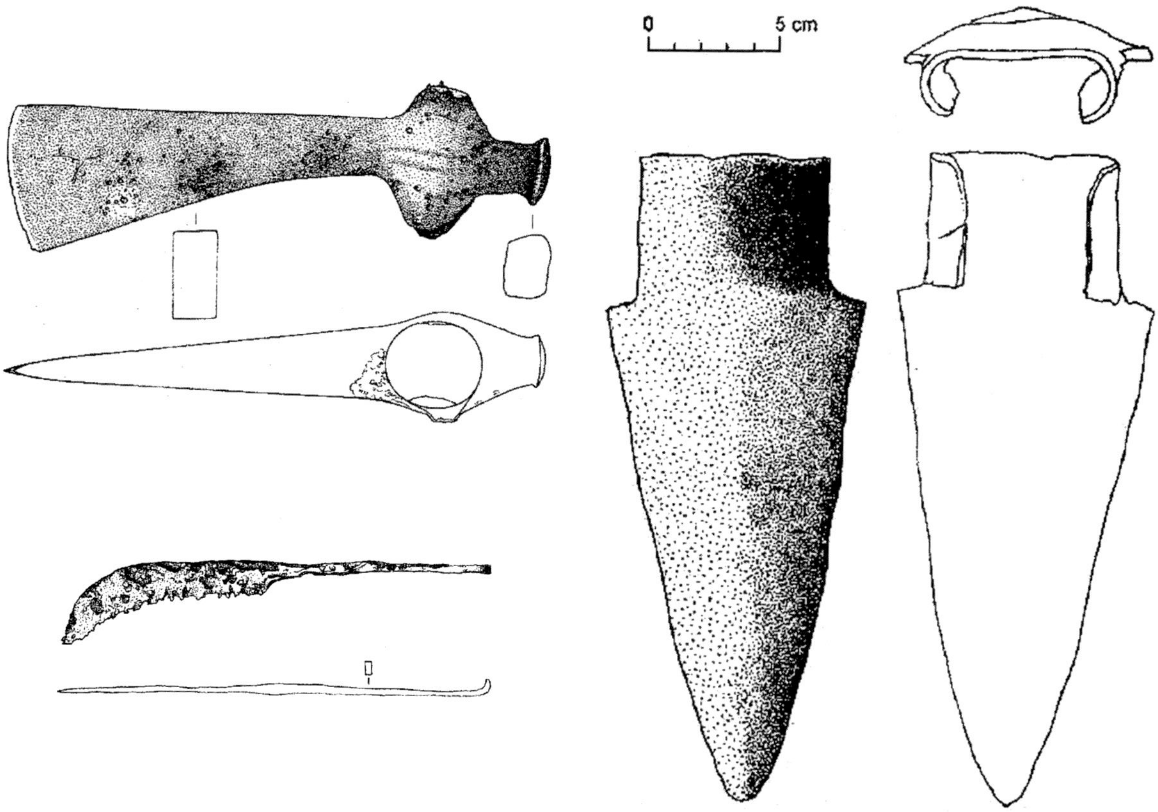


*Figure 16.13: Ninth-century deposit from the Judas Wall near Bull Rock Cave: axe, knife/sickle, ploughshare (after Galuška 2006).*

*Figure 16.14: Medieval deer drawing from Bull Rock Cave, $^{14}$C-dated to between AD 1265 and 1395.*

workshop'), 300 m from Bull Rock Cave, was destroyed. Mainly based on the recovery of tiles, I am of the opinion that the cave was used as a temporary shelter either by Hungarian soldiers or, more likely, by local inhabitants afflicted by the war in the winter of 1469–1470.

The Hussite and Czech–Hungarian wars in the fifteenth century fundamentally affected the Drahany Highlands. More than 40 villages in the Moravian Karst were deserted. The use of caves as temporary shelters and emergency abodes is plausible. Based on the presence of ceramics dated to this late period, Josef Skutil suggested that many caves, including Bull Rock Cave, were temporarily inhabited (Skutil 1970).

### *BR XI.3 possible counterfeiter's workshop*

Wankel's claim that plain, thin discoidal silver plates were found in the South Branch of Bull Rock Cave (Wankel 1870; 1882; Peša 2006) cannot be verified at present, but if correct, the plates probably represent the remnants of a counterfeiter's workshop. High and late medieval counterfeit workshops have been found in other caves in the Czech Republic: Koněprusy Caves in the Bohemian Karst, dating from the second half of the fifteenth century; Old Woman's Furnace (Babí pec) near Kozákov, Bohemian Paradise dating from the fifteenth century; and Devil's Hole (Čertova díra) near Štramberk (Matoušek *et al.* 2005). In the case of Koněprusy Cave, it is presumed that coins were forged there by the local nobility who owned the land in which the cave is located. Descriptions of robberies orchestrated by castle owners from the Drahany Highlands, including Nový hrad, are known from the fifteenth century. Nobles resorted to robbery in times of war (Bednářová 1958). A hypothesis that they may also have been involved in coin forgery inside Bull Rock Cave is plausible.

Matoušek suggested that if artefacts from a cave are of similar character to those from a regular settlement, they undoubtedly reflect the same function, i.e. use of a cave for habitation. However, if unusual items are found in a cave, their explanation must lead us in a different direction, i.e. atypical use of a cave (Matoušek and Peša 1998). From this perspective we can regard the drawing, oven and forgery workshop at Bull Rock Cave as atypical.

## Discussion and conclusions

Bull Rock Cave has been the subject of archaeological investigation since 1867, and was made famous by the discovery of Palaeolithic and Hallstatt material. The cave has been subject to interpretation many times during the last 150 years. Numerous post-Wankel cultural-historical publications presented varied opinions concerning what the cave had or had not been in prehistory. Since 2007, systematic research from a landscape archaeology and cultural anthropology perspective has provided new insights on the site. This cave can be considered a geologically stable, but socially unstable, variable system in the landscape. It was repeatedly, or more probably continually, visited from the Palaeolithic to the present day. This chapter, however, has focused on the identification of social structures and reasons for use of the cave during the Middle Ages.

The medieval material from Bull Rock Cave suggests its marginal position within the landscape; the main hub of human activities was elsewhere. The cave was probably only used for brief periods of time because of the natural restrictions of darkness and dampness. It probably also provided shelter during crises. The site presents an advantage in terms of military defence compared to shelter in open forested terrain. The relatively small entrances of the cave could have been easily blocked and defended. Large internal spaces offered the possibility of storing property, gathering together reserves of wood, stabling animals, and even constructing dwellings for a large group. Another advantage is the stable temperature of the cave, with year-round temperatures about 9°C in the Southern Branch and 3–15°C in the Entrance Hall, which must have been highly valued in winter months. Furthermore, water is easily available underground and the cave is easily accessible from a road in the valley. The combination of these characteristics is exceptional for the entire area. It can only be compared to Výpustek (Outlet) Cave where the inhabitants of Křtiny village sought refuge during the wars of 1645 and 1866 (Musil 2010). Fire is a necessity for subterranean dwelling. The oven in Bull Rock Cave suggests people lived there while also providing space for the illegal production of coins, an activity that risked severe punishment. We can state that the basic natural qualities of a cave present an important guideline for discussing its functions in the human world.

The social structures that relate to Bull Rock Cave are based on those populations living in closest proximity to the site (people from the uplands), and those from the regions around the Drahany Highlands (people from the lowlands). During the Early Middle Ages (BR X) and the High and Late Middle Ages (BR XI), an iron working centre was established at Olomučany not far from Bull Rock Cave. Archaeological evidence indicates the cave was visited at this time. In the High Middle Ages the landscape was systematically settled and colonised, which is reflected in the artefacts recovered from the cave. Apart from ordinary usage, exceptional activities have also been revealed: a drawing – a manifestation of the arts; an oven – settlement; a counterfeiter's workshop – illegal activity. Bull Rock Cave quite probably also functioned as a shelter in times of war and/or as shelters to highwaymen, and prosecuted and persecuted people. Research in the Drahany Highlands offers great potential. The presented article argues *against* selective archaeological focus on particular sites. We must presume that people inhibited the whole landscape.

## References


Bednářová, V., 1958. Osídlení Adamovska v letech 1200–1500. *Vlastivědné zprávy z Adamova a okolí* II(1), 3–9.

Burkhardt, R., 1950. Další prehistorický nález z Mor. krasu. Československý *kras* III, 292.

Čermáková, E. and Golec, M., 2014. Turistická kolonizace Moravského krasu na základě epigrafických památek Býčí skály. *Český lid* 101(2014), 459–482.

Černý, E., 1992. *Výsledky výzkumu zaniklých středověkých osad a jejich plužin*. Brno: Muzejní a vlastivědná společnost v Brně.

Dufková, M. and Matoušek, V., 1998. *Jeskyně a lidé*. Prague: Knižnice Dějin a současnosti, 7.

Galuška, L., 2006. Depot raně středověkých předmětů od Býčí skály v Moravském krasu. *In*: J. Zábojník, ed. *Aevum Medium. Zborník na počesť Jozefa Hošša*. Bratislava: Univerzita Komenského, 23–29.

Golec, M., 2014. Vranovsko-křtinský lichtensteinský areál. *Acta Musei Moraviae, Scientiae sociales* XCIX(2), 235–250.

Gregor, V.A., 2015. *The Moravian Karst. The Jedovnice Creek Cave System of the Rudice Plateau in the Moravian Karst – the Rudice Swallow Hole, Bull Rock and Bar Caves*. Available from: http://www.byciskala.cz [accessed 1 January 2017].

Golec, M., 2017. *The Phenomenon of the Býčí Skála Cave. Landscape, Cave and Mankind*. Archaeologica Olomucensia 1. Olomouc: Palack University Olomouc.

Hlavica, M., 2009. *Raně středověké kultovní aktivity na vrchu Klášťov a jejich odraz v archeologických pramenech a* ústní *lidové slovesnosti*. Thesis (BA), Institute of Archaeology and Museology, Masaryk University in Brno.

Kavička, K., 2014. *Poutní a farní chrám Páně jména Panny Marie ve Křtinách*. Brno: Kartuziánské nakladatelství Brno.

Konečný, L. and Merta, J., 1976. Zjišťovací průzkum středověkých fortifikací v okolí Nového hradu u Adamova. *Archaeologia historica* 1, 246–249.

Konečný, L. and Merta, J., 1980. Pokračování průzkumu středověkého opevnění kolem Nového hradu u Adamova. *Archaelogia historica* 5(80), 305–319.

Kreps, M., 1976. *Dějiny adamovských* železáren *a strojíren do roku 1905*. Brno: Blok.

Lutovský, M., 2001. *Encyklopedie slovanské archeologie v* Čechách, *na Moravě a ve Slezsku*. Prague: Libri.

Martínek, J., Létal, J.A., Miřijovský, J., Vích, D. and Kalábek, M., 2014. *Poznáváme historické cesty*. Brno: Centrum dopravního výzkumu.

Martínek, J., 2015. *Historické cesty* Čech, *Moravy a Slezska*. Available from: http://www.historicke-cesty.cz [accessed 1 January 2017].

Matoušek, V., 1987. *Postmezolitické nálezy v* Českém *krasu a využívání jeskyní v postmezolitickém vývoji ve střední Evropě*. PhD thesis, Archaeological Institute of the Czechoslovak Academy of Sciences in Prague.

Matoušek, V., 2005. *Bacín - brána podzemí. archeologický výzkum pravěké skalní svatyně v* Českém *krasu*. Prague: Krigl.

Matoušek, V., Jenč, P., and Peša, V., 2005. *Jeskyně Čech, Moravy a Slezska s archeologickými nálezy*. Prague: Libri.

Matoušek, V. and Peša, V., 1998. Keramické nálezy v jeskyních ve střední Evropě. Několik poznámek inspirovaných nálezy v jeskyních Českého krasu. *Archeologické rozhledy* L, 224–242.

Měřínský, Z., 2009. *České země od příchodu Slovanů po Velkou Moravu*. Prague: Libri.

Mihola, J., 2010. *Vranov u Brna. Mariánské poutní místo, paulánský klášter, hrobka Lichtenštejnů*. Vranov–Brna: Jiří Brauner – Kartuziánské nakladatelství Brno.

Musil, R., 2010. *Výpustek. Bájná jeskyně u Křtin. Její 400letá historie a význam*. Acta speleologica, 1/2010. Průhonice: Správa jeskyní Česke Republiky.

Oliva, M., 1995. Das Paläolitikum aus der Býčí skála. *Pravěk NŘ* 5, 25–38.

Oliva, M., 1996. Spodní paleolitická vrstva z Býčí skály. K poznání mýtotvorných procesů v naší speleoarcheologii. *Acta Musei Moraviae, Scientiae Sociales* LXXXI, 37–59.

Oliva, M., 2005. *Civilizace moravského paleolitu a mezolitu*. Brno: Moravské zemské muzeum.

Oliva, M., *et al*., 2015. *Býčí skála Cave: History and Prehistory. Studies in Anthropology, Palaeoethnology, Palaeontology and Quaternary Geology*, Vol. 39, N.S. 31, 2015. Brno: Moravské zemské muzeum.

Ondroušková, S., 2011. *Pravěk Moravského krasu*. Thesis (MA), Institute of Archaeology and Museology, Masaryk University Brno.

Parzinger, H., Nekvasil, J., and Barth, F.E., 1995. *Die Býčí skála-Höhle. Ein hallstattzeitlicher Höhlenopferplatz in Mähren*. Römisch-Germanische Forschungen 54. Mainz am Rhein: Verlag Philipp von Zabern.

Pelíšek, J., 1949. K charakteristice jeskynních sedimentů Býčí skály v Moravském krasu. *Československý kras* 2, 249–254.

Peša, V., 2006. Jižní boční síň a halštatské využívání Býčí skály v Moravském krasu. *Archeologické rozhledy* LVIII, 426–446.

Peša, V., 2013. Der neuzeitliche Mensch in der Höhle: Die Speläoanthropologie als archäologische Quelle. *Památky archeologické* 104, 231–316.

Plaček, M., 2001. *Ilustrovaná encyklopedie moravských hradů, hrádků a tvrzí*. Prague: Libri.

Pleiner, R., 2000. *Iron in Archaeology. The European Bloomery Smelters*. Prague: Archeologický ústav AV ČR.

Podborský, V., 2006. *Náboženství pravěkých Evropanů*. Brno: Ústav archeologie a muzeologie filozofické fakulty Masarykovy univerzity Brno.

Profantová, N., 2014. Raně středověký depot č. 11 z vrchu Klášťov, kat. Velké pole, okr. Zlín. *Pravěk NŘ* 22, 327–343.

Skutil, J., 1970. Pravěk a časná doba dějinná Moravského krasu. *In*: K. Absolon, ed. *Moravský kras* 2. Prague: Akademia, 315–329.

Souchopová, V., 1986. *Hutnictví* železa *v 8.–11. století na západní Moravě*. Studie Archeologického ústavu akademie věd České republiky 13/1. Brno: Academia Praha.

Souchopová, V., 1992. The main tendencies of development of West Slav iron metallurgy from its origin until the 11th century. *In*: *Medieval Europe 1992: Pre-Printed Papers Vol. 3 (Technology and Innovation)*. York: Society for Medieval Archaeology, 131–136.

Souchopová, V., 1995. *Počátky západoslovanského hutnictví železa ve světle pramenů z Moravy*. Studie Archeologického ústavu akademie věd České republiky 15/1. Brno: Academia Praha.

Souchopová, V., Merta, J., and Merta, O., 2011. Some aspects of the development of Great Moravian iron metallurgy. *In*: J. Hošek, H. Cleere, and Ľ. Mihok, eds. *The Archeometallurgy of Iron. Recent Developments in Archaeological and Scientific Research*. Prague: Archeologický ústav akademie věd České republiky, 73–86, 296–297.

Svoboda, J., 1999. *Čas lovců: dějiny paleolitu, zvláště na Moravě*. Brno: Archeologický ústav akademie věd České republiky.

Svoboda, J., van der Plicht, H., and Balák, I., 2005. Býčí skála: prvé datování skalních maleb. *Vesmír* 84, 574–575.

Válka, J., 1991. *Středověká Morava*. Brno: Muzejní a vlastivědná společnost v Brně.

Wankel, H., 1870. Der Menschenknochenfund in der Býčískálahöhle. *Mitteilungen der Antrthropologischen Gesellschaft in Wien* 1, 101–105.

Wankel, H., 1875. Die Höhle bei Býčí skála. *Tageblatt der 48. Versammlung deutscher Naturforscher und Aertze in Graz* 5, 169–175.

Wankel, H., 1882. *Bilder aus der Mährischen Schweiz und ihrer Vergangenheit*. Vienna: Adolf Holzhausen.

# Chapter 17

# The form and fabric of Late Antique and medieval cave use in Slovenia

*Agni Prijatelj*

*This chapter synthesises the available archaeological, historical and ethnographic data relating to a wide variety of human activities in 37 Slovenian caves and rockshelters between AD 300 and 1200. While some of the practices continued relatively unchanged from earlier periods, other types of cave use emerged. Most notably, underground places were appropriated by Roman, Christian and Slavic religious systems, resulting in a fascinatingly broad range of cave rituals with unparalleled diversity in their meanings, expression and mutual dynamics.*

## Introduction

The use of caves and rockshelters in Slovenia between *c.* AD 300 and 1200 (i.e. during Late Antiquity and the early and High Middle Ages) is currently attested by some 37 sites (see Appendix and Fig. 17.1), with archaeological evidence reflecting a wide variety of human activities. Some of the sites were used as temporary or more permanent shelters, pens, hideouts or dwellings, while others were utilised as convenient hideaways for hoards of various kinds. In addition, a significant number of sites were employed for distinct ritual and religious purposes, including burial rites, and for Roman, Christian and Slavic rituals. However, the numerous ways in which caves and rockshelters were used in Late Antiquity and the early and High Middle Ages have been almost totally overlooked within Slovenian archaeological discourse to date. Even though cave archaeology has a long history in Slovenia, stretching back 150 years, it has, until recently, been inextricably linked, almost exclusively, to the study of prehistoric periods (but see Prijatelj forthcoming). Caves and rockshelters have been surveyed, excavated and selectively published by prehistorians, and this has inevitably led to an unfavourable bias towards research on the Antique and medieval evidence (Prijatelj 2011).

This chapter, then, offers two things: firstly, a synthesis of the available archaeological, historical and folkloric material for Late Antiquity (*c.* AD 300–600) and the Early and High Middle Ages (*c.* AD 600–1200); and secondly, an overview and discussion of a broad range of cave rituals between *c.* AD 300 and 1200. In my writing, I employ a contextual approach by situating caves and rockshelters within the wider landscape, as well as within the socio-economic, political and religious settings of the Late Antique and medieval periods. The information on the relevant archaeological sites, discussed in depth in this chapter, has been collated by an extensive survey of Slovenian archaeological publications, and is summarily presented in the Appendix. There, sites have been classified according to the nature of the artefacts recovered, the built features preserved, and the dating of activities according to the primary reports. The numbers after the site names in the text are those assigned to the sites in the appendix and in Figure 17.1. The frequently occurring words '*podmol*/*spodmol*' and '*jama*' as components of site names are the Slovenian equivalents for 'rockshelter' and 'cave' respectively.

## From pens to fortresses: forms of habitation

In Late Antiquity and the Early and High Middle Ages, caves and rockshelters in Slovenia were regularly used as temporary pens and shelters for shepherds during annual cycles of herding. This practice, which was first recorded for the Middle Neolithic from *c.* 6500 cal BP onwards (Mlekuž 2010, 34), is arguably best documented in the Kras region

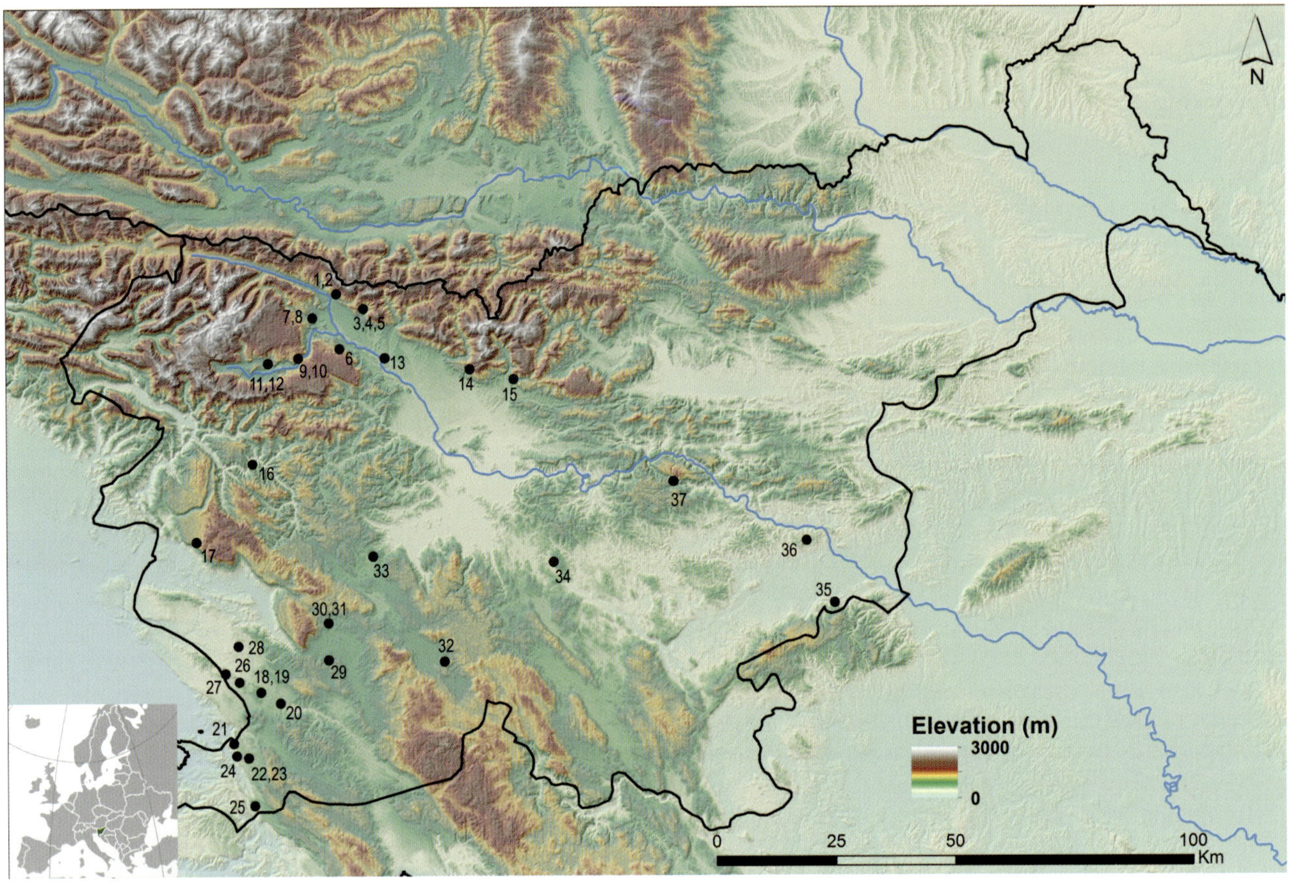


*Figure 17.1: Late Antique and early and high medieval cave and rockshelter sites in Slovenia.*

(south-west Slovenia). There, sites such as Mala Triglavca (18) (Leben 1988; Mlekuž *et al.* 2008), Podmol pri Kastelcu (22) (Turk *et al.* 1993) and Acijev spodmol (23) (Turk *et al.* 1992) exhibit long-term continuity of the practice, recorded within cultural layers from the Neolithic/Eneolithic up to and including Late Antiquity and the medieval period. As a result of repeat stabling activities, these sites contain thick stratigraphy with a distinct depositional structure in which dark organic-rich deposits alternate with greyish-white ashy lenses. Recent micromorphological analysis of sediment samples from Mala Triglavca (Prijatelj forthcoming) has confirmed a long-term practice of regular cleaning or sanitising of the interiors of rockshelters by burning dung layers, thus creating a sequence of horizontal ashy lenses within organic-rich deposits (Boschian and Montagnari-Kokelj 2000).

An insight into the lives of shepherds is offered by the domestic debris, which is frugal and of a utilitarian nature. It consists predominantly of bones of domestic animals, most commonly sheep and goats, and various types of coarse pottery, amphorae and tableware. In the very few instances where Late Antique and early medieval material has been analysed in the same rigorous fashion as prehistoric materials (e.g. Podmol pri Kastelcu [22]), it is clear that quantities of Late Antique and early medieval pottery are significantly smaller than assemblages of prehistoric pottery (Turk *et al.* 1993, 62). This could easily lead one to the conclusion that during Late Antiquity and the Middle Ages, the occupation of caves and rockshelters was perhaps shorter and less intense than in prehistory. Before one makes such a conjecture, however, it is important to bear in mind that the correlation between the quantity of recovered artefacts and the intensity of occupation is not always equivalent (Dowd 2015, 179).

What then, if anything, can be said about the duration of occupation of caves and rockshelters that were incorporated into pastoralist systems during the periods in question? Rather than being permanently occupied for several years, it is more likely that sites were used episodically during certain seasons but repeatedly over many years, decades or perhaps even centuries. More specifically, caves and rockshelters were probably embedded into the transhumance networks that are implied by several historic documents for the wider region of the eastern Adriatic. Among the oldest of these is a Roman inscription (CIL III 15053), carved into a rock at Lomska Duliba in the northern Velebit mountain range (Croatia), which has been dated to the first or second century AD (Šašel 1979). As a legal Roman decree, the inscription proclaims the right of the indigenous tribe of the Ortoplini to free access to the local spring within the territory of the neighbouring tribe of the Parentini. According to Šašel (1979, 355–357), it can be understood as the legal resolution, by the Romans, of a conflict between the two indigenous groups (*peregrini*) over their established transhumance practices in the karst landscape, since these placed considerable demands on the region's sparse water resources and led to fierce competition for them.

A number of medieval and early modern documents on the grazing rights and movement of flocks are also known. For instance, *Pactum Hlotharii I*, for the year AD 840 (MGH, *Capitularia Regum Francorum II*, no. 233), declared the rights of Aquileia and Grado settlers to graze their flocks on inland Friuli (north-east Italy), while other documents from the early medieval period describe the movement of flocks from Friuli to the Julian Alps (north-west Slovenia) (Novak 1970, 359). Some late medieval and early modern feudal documents, such as one *urbarium* for Postojna from the year 1498 and another for Kamnik castle from 1571, also identify distinct mountains and plateaus that were rented to shepherds for grazing on an annual basis (Kos 1954, 229; Cevc 1997). Recent archaeological surveys in the Slovenian Alps have also revealed traces of highland pastoralism from the Roman, Late Antique and medieval periods (e.g. Bremšak 2006; Cevc 2006, 117–121; Horvat 2006, 27–34; Malešič 2006).

It is possible, then, given the archaeological evidence and descriptions of routes and grazing areas found in the historic records, to discern two main types of transhumance networks in Slovenian lands and in the wider region of the eastern Adriatic during the periods in question. The first type consisted of paths and routes leading from the interior to the northern and eastern Adriatic coast; archaeological sites in the Kras region, including Mala Triglavca (18), Acijev spodmol (23) and Podmol pri Kastelcu (22), may fall into this group. The second type of route connected lowlands with highland pastures. It is quite likely that at least some of the caves and rockshelters located on the slopes of various mountains and plateaus were, like Lomska Duliba, embedded into pastoralist systems such as these (Bremšak 2006, 47; Malešič 2006). The archaeological assemblages from both transhumance site types are quite similar; they are distinguished simply by their location within the landscape.

Of course, some of the caves and rockshelters on mountains and plateaus may also, like those in hidden and hard-to-access locations, have been used as hideaways and refuges during times of significant political and social upheaval. Such sites most commonly comprise small- to medium-sized dry chambers that could shelter a few people. They often contain remains of hearths, where a fire would have warmed and illuminated the confined space, and also diverse habitation debris, regularly concentrated in the entrance areas of caves and rockshelters. That these sites were used as hideaways and refuges is suggested not only by the occurrence of valuables (coins and personal ornaments), along with weaponry, but also by structural alterations to the caves and rockshelters in question (see Appendix). Built features vary in their complexity, from a simple timber wall across the entrance of the cave at Lučka jama 2 (34) (Jamnik 2001), to thick stone walls fortifying the entrance of Osapska jama (24) (Guštin 2006). It is clear that these are defence walls as they completely block entrances and are much higher than the walls used to pen animals into a cave. Further, in some late medieval instances, the cave interior is remodelled into different levels or floors.

In the regions of Primorska (south-west Slovenia) and Gorenjska (north-west Slovenia), several caves and rockshelters were transformed into cave fortresses. While most of those were established in the fifteenth and sixteenth centuries during the time of the Turkish raids, the fortification of Osapska jama cave (24) (Fig. 17.2) is much older. This fortress was first referred to in a document dated to 1067 as part of the property of the Bishop of Freising (Guštin 2006, 102), and was, like the fortified towers along the routes connecting the Kvarner Gulf, the Istrian Peninsula and the city of Trieste (north-east Italy), initially used as a temporary outpost for controlling traffic and trade. However, in the late medieval and early modern periods (from the fifteenth century onwards) it became an interim refuge for local villagers and their animals during the Ottoman raids and various other lootings, including during the wars between the Habsburgs and the Venetian republic (Fister 1975; Guštin 2006).

*Figure 17.2: The remains of a fortification at Osapska jama cave. After Guštin 2006, 102.*

*Figure 17.3: Predjama cave castle. The entrance into Jama pod jamskim gradom cave can be seen in the bottom left. Photo: S. Sykora.*

Among the fortified caves, the Predjama cave system (30) in the region of Notranjska (south-central Slovenia) holds a unique position. In front of the gaping cave mouth, halfway up a 123 m high limestone cliff face beneath which the River Lokva disappears underground, a white castle protrudes from the grey rock face (Fig. 17.3). The existing four-storey structure is a Renaissance building (*c.* late sixteenth century), but the castle itself was originally Romanesque (twelfth century) (Reisp 1977; Stopar 2011; Bavdek and Čuk 2015). Given the comfortable dwelling conditions afforded by the cave, in addition to its dominating, defensive position within the surrounding landscape of rolling hills and dense woodland, its long history of cave use that spans the Eneolithic, Early and Late Bronze Age, Early Iron Age, Early and Late Antiquity, and medieval and modern periods is not surprising.

A series of archaeological excavations in 1922, 1932, 1941–1943, and 1951 yielded a wealth of finds within the second level of the Predjama cave system, known as Jama pod Jamskim gradom (31) (Fig. 17.3), which is located approximately 23 m below the castle (Korošec 1956, 1982). The stratigraphy in the entrance area of Jama cave, which functioned as horse stables during the medieval period, revealed intense and probably continuous habitation in Late Antiquity. Finds from the Late Antique layers, attributed to the late fourth and early fifth centuries, include a number of Roman coins, terra sigillata imitations, locally produced Early Christian oil lamps, three Germanic bone combs, belt buckles and an array of Roman armoury, including horse equipment and two Germanic bronze sheaths (Korošec 1982; Ciglenečki and Milavec 2009, 180). Significantly, no agricultural tools were found at the site, but skeletons recovered from the cave indicate that it was occasionally used for burial (see below). The specific structure of the archaeological assemblage, with many Roman weapons, the practically invulnerable position of the cave, and the prominent position of a cliff that could have been used as a lookout point for surveying the landscape and the road passing through Razdrto, have led researchers to the conclusion that Jama pod Jamskim (31) gradom functioned as a military fort. It has been suggested that during the late fourth and early fifth centuries, Roman soldiers, including Germanic *foederati* (as implied by the Germanic type of comb and sheath found at the site), were probably stationed at the cave in order to control a road leading from Emona to Tergeste and passing through Razdrto (Korošec 1982, 95; Ciglenečki and Milavec 2009, 179).

Selected case studies clearly show that the frequency, intensity, longevity and modes of habitation in caves and rockshelters during Late Antiquity and the early and High Middle Ages were far more varied and complex than has been commonly recognised. Whereas the majority of relevant studies (e.g. Leben 1969, 1975a; Ciglenečki 1997, 1999; Valič 1997) focus on the discussion of these sites primarily as refuges, they fail to acknowledge the crucial distinctions that exist between sites of this type. As has been mentioned above, some sites were used just once and/or for short periods, and consequently have only poorly developed anthropogenic stratigraphy with small quantities of habitation debris. Others, meanwhile, were re-used and therefore have produced larger archaeological assemblages; these also sometimes contain built features that enhance a site's natural defensive qualities. Furthermore, there are examples of sites that were used for various purposes other than hideaways; many caves and rockshelters, for instance, were re-used seasonally as shelters for shepherds and their flocks, either within interior-to-coast or lowland-to-highland transhumance networks. Lastly, a few others, such as Jama pod Jamskim gradom (31), were permanently occupied for longer periods of time. While having substantially different characteristics, all of the types of dwelling discussed here share an important feature: rather than being marginal places settled by individuals of low social standing or outcasts, caves and rockshelters were, by and large, strongly embedded in everyday life and the taskscapes of different social groups, including farmers, shepherds and even military troops.

## Buried in the dark: hoards and intentional depositions

Caves and rockshelters provided convenient hiding places for hoards of various kinds at times of social, economic and political instability. Specific places, such as on mountain and hill slopes, were chosen for their remoteness and distance from major roads. To know of their existence and location, one had to have an intimate knowledge of the landscape, probably acquired by walking and working in the uplands. Quite tellingly, all six documented Late Antique hoards from caves and rockshelters (see Appendix and Fig. 17.1) are located in the mountainous region of Gorenjska (north-west Slovenia). During the Roman period, this was a politically and strategically obscure part of the Slovenian lands that only gained importance during Late Antiquity with an increase in transport routes, defence systems and settlement (Valič 1997; Ciglenečki 1999; Bratož 2014).

Late Antique hoards from caves and rockshelters can be divided into two groups. The first group is comprised of mixed assemblages of artefacts found at the caves of Ajdovska jama (11) (Gabrovec 1975; Leben 1975a, 86), Ajdovska luknja (9) (Valič 1985), and Mali spodmol (10) near Ajdovska luknja (Valič 1985). These sites can probably be associated with local miners, metalworkers and smiths who sought, collected and smelted bog iron found on the nearby Pokljuka plateau (Ogrin 2006). At the Ajdovska jama site, for example, several bronze and two silver coins, dated to the fourth century, were buried together with crucibles (Gabrovec 1975). At Ajdovska luknja, on the other hand, the hoard consisted of an iron hatchet, two iron pickaxes, two iron hooks for a cooking cauldron (one with a chain attached), a smaller iron door for an oven, an iron knife, nails, several amorphous fragments of molten lead, and two bronze coins dated to the end of the fourth century (Fig. 17.4A). Remains of walls, burnt stones and Roman pottery were also discovered at the site (Valič 1985, 272). Another smaller hoard was discovered at the Mali spodmol site – a minor overhang formed in the same rock face, just a few metres below the larger Ajdovska luknja rockshelter. Intentionally deposited objects at Mali spodmol included three bronze bracelets, a bronze ring and a fragment of a bronze chain (Fig. 17.4B) which, given its fragmented state, might have been hidden with the intention of being re-melted and re-cast at a later date (Valič 1985, 272). These two sites appear to have been used intermittently by local craftsmen not only as hiding places for their belongings, but in the case of Ajdovska luknja, perhaps as a workshop or, more likely considering its size, as a temporary dwelling (M. Sagadin personal communication).

The second group of Late Antique hoards from caves and rockshelters consists of coins found at a nameless shelter at Dunaj (12) near Jereka (Valič 1958–1959; Prešeren 1991), Ciganska jama (13) (Leben 1975a, 88) and Jama pod Stiško vasjo (14) (Sagadin 2006). All of the recovered coins are bronze, with quantities varying from 29 at Ciganska jama to 42 at Dunaj near Jereka, and 69 at Jama pod Stiško vasjo. These are modest assemblages and can be considered small hoards (Miškec 2012, 380), contrasting starkly with other sites containing several thousand coins (e.g. Jeločnik 1973).

The quantity and denominations of the Late Antique coins from the aforementioned caves and rockshelters might imply that these hoards were modest personal savings hidden away during tumultuous times. Some distinct details relating to the archaeological context, however, hint at certain ritual elements in the deposition of the coins at one site in particular. At the Jama pod Stiško vasjo (14) site an enigmatic carving has been found where 69 coins were deposited (Sagadin 2006). The cave, which is rather narrow and short, is located within a steep and precipitous slope above Reka creek. It is only accessible through a narrow hole in the roof of the rockshelter beneath the cave. The great majority of the coins (dated from AD 330 to 457) were found at the rear of the cave in a small depression beneath the roof. The rock with carvings stands beside the crevice leading into the cave and is illuminated by light entering through a naturally formed window in the cave's western wall. According to Sagadin (2006, 53), two crosses are carved into the rock. Given that modern pottery fragments were found scattered in the uppermost layer in the cave, it is evident that the site was also frequented in post-medieval times and so a possibility that the carvings are of a later date than the hoard itself cannot be excluded. Regardless of whether the carving and the hoard are associated, the fact that some animal bones were found in the same depression as the coins may indicate that these were cult deposits. They might have been offered to a deity associated with the cave, similar to meat deposits of sacrificed animals.

In Late Antiquity, caverns in the region of Gorenjska became the temporary abodes of miners, smiths and metalworkers. Local craftsmen sought out and collected bog iron from the highlands and, on several occasions, utilised upland caves and rockshelters as interim dwellings and hiding places for their belongings. During Late Antiquity and the Middle Ages, such associations between caves and metalworkers were very common throughout Europe and have been documented for Britain (Branigan and Dearne 1992), Ireland (Dowd 2015), Norway (Barndon 2009) and the Czech Republic (Golec, this volume). In certain instances, this may indicate a perceived connection between the liminality of caves and rockshelters on the one hand, and the material transformations associated with metalworking on the other. The votive offerings of coin hoards or accumulations within caves and rockshelters are less well-known. The main reason for such a discrepancy is a general trend in interpreting coins as either on-site items, related to caves as temporary dwellings, or monetary hoards, associated with safe-keeping and caves as hiding places (e.g. Ciglenečki 1997; Valič 1997). However, the context and content of the archaeological assemblage at Jama pod Stiško vasjo (14) clearly illustrates that, in specific instances, coins (along with bones) might indicate ritual activities, even when unaccompanied by other typical Roman votive offerings.

## A deformed skull: no ordinary burial

Human bones have been found at four of the 37 Late Antique and early and high medieval cave and rockshelter sites in Slovenia (see Appendix, Fig. 17.1). None of these

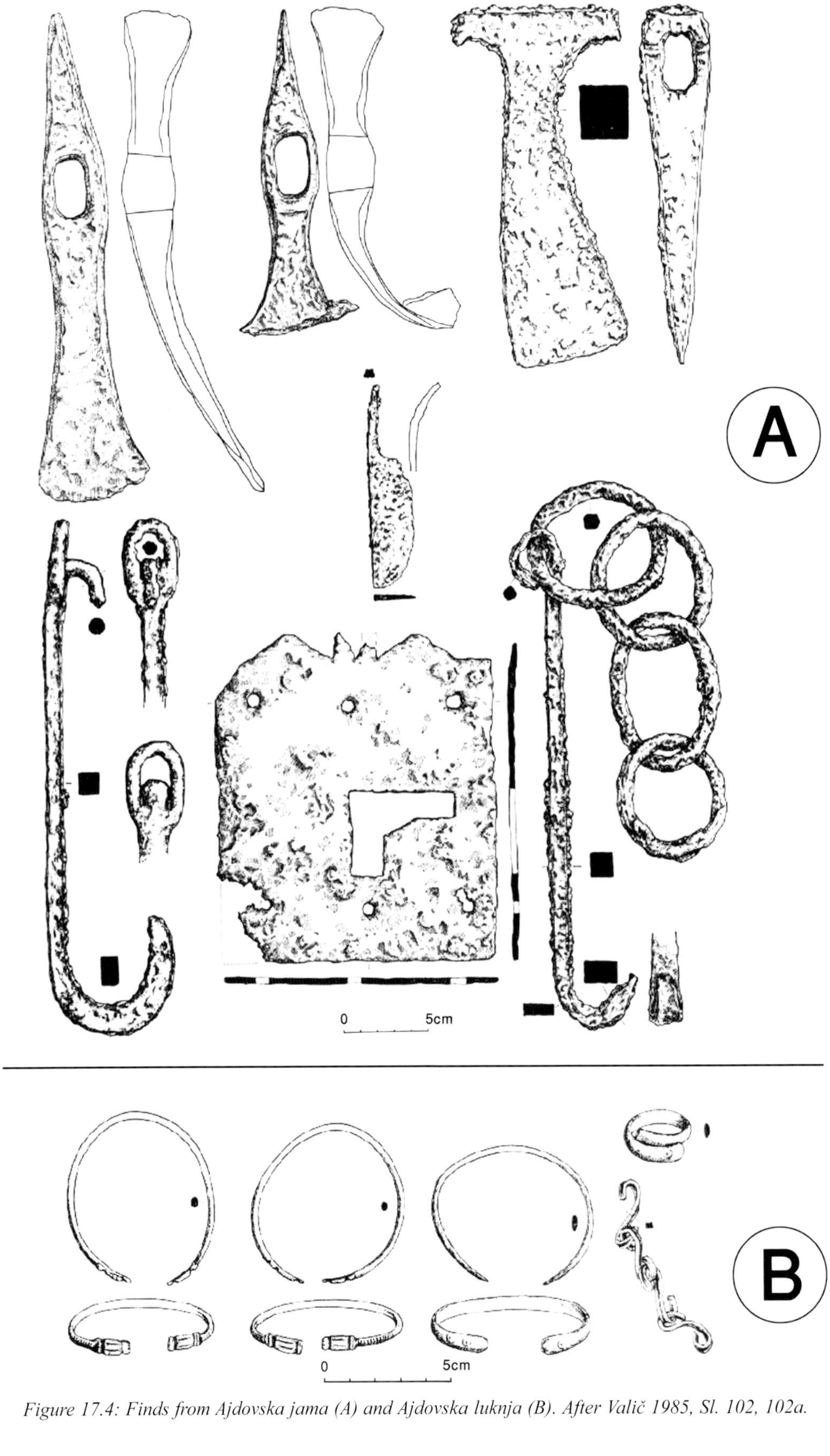


*Figure 17.4: Finds from Ajdovska jama (A) and Ajdovska luknja (B). After Valič 1985, Sl. 102, 102a.*

remains have been radiocarbon dated, and their depositional contexts vary significantly. Bones recovered from Acijev spodmol (23) (Turk *et al.* 1992, 34), for example, were concentrated inside the shelter against the wall, occurring at different depths in Holocene deposits. As Late Antique pottery has been found scattered through all the Holocene strata as deep as the Bronze Age layers (Turk *et al.* 1992, 31), it has been suggested that the bones became vertically dispersed by strong turbation processes, rather than being deposited at different times. While the possible diagenetic or anthropogenic processes that caused vertical displacement of the material were not addressed in the final report, Turk *et al.* (1992, 34) suggested that at least two adults were buried in Acijev spodmol rockshelter in Late Antiquity. This assumption was based on the location of the bones beneath an undisturbed Late Antique hearth (providing a *terminus ante quem* date for the human remains), and in close proximity to a fragment of a Late Antique brooch, which may have been part of the deceased's clothing.

The number of disarticulated human bones recovered at the Levakova jama site (35) (Guštin 1976) was even higher than at Acijev spodmol. The site was discovered in 1937 after heavy rains caused the cave to flood and water unblocked the entrance. The torrent exposed numerous human bone fragments and pottery sherds, causing a stir among local people who reported seeing cartloads of bones scattered around the opening after the flood. Later that year, Otto Auman, a local antiquarian, undertook excavations in the cave. In 1973 further discoveries were made in the cave by local speleologists, most notably a silver Roman ring with a gem, probably depicting Mars, and an artificially deformed human skull, reshaped during the life of the deceased by head binding (Guštin 1976; Slabe 1977).

Levakova jama was eventually systematically excavated in two archaeological campaigns in 1975 (Guštin 1976, 264–271). The Roman period finds, dating from the first to the fourth century, were recovered from the area in front of the cave and in the entrance chamber. Documented artefacts included bones of domestic and wild animals, numerous coins, pottery sherds, a quernstone fragment, a crossbow brooch and two glass beads. After the flooding and Auman's excavations, human bones lay scattered throughout the area. Their spatial distribution was uneven, but there was a higher concentration towards the rear of the cave. This might suggest that the area at the front served as a temporary shelter for everyday activities, while the area at the back, and perhaps one of the two passageways, may have been used for burial (Guštin 1976, 271). At least seven individuals – two adults and five children – were buried at Levakova jama during the Roman period (Guštin 1976, 270). Given reports on the number of bones recovered in 1937, it is likely that the original number of individuals was much higher. Rather than being used for four centuries, the cave probably became a burial place only in Late Antiquity when inhumation was newly established as the prevalent mode of burial (Guštin 1976, 271). The artificially deformed human skull (Fig. 17.5) indicates that the site was used for the deposition of human remains on at least one other occasion, during the fifth or sixth century, when Huns, Goths, Langobards and Alemans were passing through Slovenia. At that time, the custom of head binding – completely absent from the practices of the local Romanised population – was still retained by Barbaric groups such as Goths and Vandals and was also documented in some of the skeletons excavated at the cemeteries of Dravlje (Ljubljana) and Lajh (Kranj), and at Rifnik (Slabe 1977, 284–285).

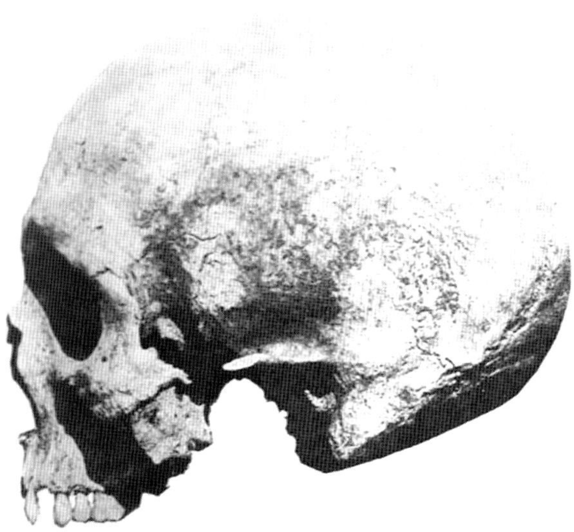

*Figure 17.5: Artificially deformed skull from Levakova jama, indicating the practice of head binding. After Guštin 1976, fig. 10.*

As at Levakova jama (35), excavations at Jama pod Jamskim gradom (31) yielded numerous human bones. Given that the majority of the research was carried out before the Second World War, with non-stratigraphic principles of excavation and inadequate recording methods, these remains are challenging to interpret (Korošec 1956, 4–11). Moreover, the site itself has a long and diverse history of use. Whilst permanently settled during the Late Antique period (see above), the cave was also used as a temporary shelter: first during the Eneolithic and Early Bronze Age, and then again in the Early Roman period and early medieval periods (Leben 1975h). Most of the human bones recorded from the site were disarticulated and described as belonging to children. Only a few were datable, including a child found with an Antique glass vessel, a cup, an awl and two rings (Korošec 1956, 17); and an Antique burial of a woman and child in the deeper part of the cave (Leben 1978, 14).

Korošec (1956, 16), who in 1951 re-examined the material excavated in 1922, 1932, 1941 and 1943 and the accompanying records, tentatively suggested that in addition to prehistoric and Antique burials, some of the recovered bones might be from the medieval period, given the depths at which the individuals were buried. The skeletons of two adults and two children of supposed medieval age were found without any items of personal jewellery, clothing appendages or pottery, and so the date cannot be confirmed without radiocarbon dating. Arguably the most intriguing of these four skeletons was buried within a layer of charred wheat 5cm thick. In contrast to Windischgraetz, who excavated the site, Korošec (1956, 16) argued that the wheat, rather than being part of the burial, represented remains from the earlier (medieval) phase of usage of the cave. As no drawings of the burial or its relationship with other anthropogenic deposits were ever published, it is difficult to interpret the inhumation further.

A correlation between local folklore and archaeological sites can provide an insight into possible reasons for the presence of human bones in caves and rockshelters in Late Antiquity and the Middle Ages. Like many of the aforementioned sites, Lučka jama 2 (34) – a 16 m deep rockshelter with two entrances, located in the region of Dolenjska (SE Slovenia) – was used as a temporary shelter in prehistory and in the late Antique, early medieval and late medieval periods (Jamnik 2001). Disarticulated human bones recovered from the uppermost late medieval layer have been determined as belonging to at least four individuals: an adult female and male, and two children aged 5–9 and 13–15. Osteological analysis of the bones has revealed that the older child died following trauma caused by a blow to the head, which left marks on the right temporal bone (Jamnik 2001, 72).

According to folklore from Luče village, local people hid in this cave during Turkish raids. After one of the villagers ran into the cave while troops were plundering the village, however, the hideaway was discovered and those sheltering in it were brutally murdered (Jamnik 2001, 68). Stories about Lučka jama 2 most likely embody a somewhat modified social memory of a particular violent event in the late medieval or early modern period, one that is supported by the archaeological record. It could be expected, given the tumultuous times, that some of the Late Antique and early medieval human bone assemblages represent refugees who met violent deaths, or perhaps others whose bodies were intentionally discarded underground after a conflict. If that were the case, one would expect to find complete skeletons or bones with some signs of trauma, and without a formal arrangement or accompanying gravegoods (Dowd 2015, 63–65). The case of the deformed skull discovered at Levakova jama cave (35) might be reconsidered in light of this theory, particularly given that no other cave burials for Huns, Goths, Langobards or Alemans have been identified in Slovenia.

Considering the available data, it is evident that cave and rockshelter burials were never a prevalent mode of burying the dead during Late Antiquity or the early and High Middle Ages. However, there are a few instances of caves being used for burying significant numbers of individuals, as at Levakova jama (35). This may imply either that the place had special significance for the identity of the local community or, more prosaically and more feasibly – in my opinion at least, that the location was utilised for burials in times of instability and unrest when access to normal burial grounds was limited.

## By the flickering oil lamp and humming stream: Late Antique Roman rituals

The cultic use of caves and rockshelters in Slovenian lands, as indicated by the archaeological record, remained a constant throughout the Roman period. Sometimes ritual usage continued from prehistory into Roman times, as in the case of the vertical shaft of Mušja jama (Leben 1990, 342–343; Frelih 1998; Šašel Kos 1999, 19–20). In such instances the pre-Roman deities associated with the underground were probably incorporated into the Roman pantheon as local gods and goddesses (Šašel Kos 1999, 2000; Matijašić 2013). Caves were also often used ritually for many consecutive generations. Both the Pod Gričo (15) (Knific 1995a) and Jama pod hribom Žičica rockshelters (2) (Knific 1995b), for example, acted as sanctuaries over several centuries.

Among the preserved finds, inscribed Roman stone monuments are an especially invaluable source, given that they indicate the breadth of cults and mysteries associated with caves and rockshelters. A votive inscription on a 30cm high stone plaque was, for example, found in a cave in the vicinity of Streliški vrh hill (Ins. It. X, 4, 350). Due to poor preservation, only a few letters of the inscription survive. This notwithstanding, it can be assumed that the cave is likely to have served as a ritual space for the inhabitants of the nearby military fort, *Ad Pirum* (Hrušica), on the Hrušica plateau – perhaps for a Mithras cult, given its popularity among soldiers.

One site that was, without doubt, used for the veneration of Mithras is the small cave of Zlodjev Graben in eastern Slovenia (Schmid 1945; Selem 1976, 8–9). The stone monuments found there include a Mithras cult relief and two votive aras dated to the third century AD (ILJug 335, 336; ILSl 56, 57). Upon the cave's discovery in 1918, it was revealed that at least part of the wall was overlaid with bricks. According to Walter Schmid (1945), who excavated the site, it is likely that timber was also used in the construction of a *speleum* (a private Mithraic shrine, evoking in its design the original cave in which Mithras was said to have slain a bull). In addition to larger architectural features and votive monuments, a number of small artefacts, including coins, pottery sherds and fragments of stone monuments and charcoal, were also discovered at the site.

A special group of inscriptions comprised of silver votive plaques in the form of palmettes or trees was found at the recently discovered cult sites of Pod Gričo (15) and Jama pod hribom Žičica (2). These sites were in use from the beginning of the second century AD up to and including the first part of the fifth century. Pod Gričo, near the village of Godič, is a small rockshelter in a marshy glen (Fig. 17.6A). During excavations between 1991 and 1998 the site yielded approximately 210 Roman coins dating from the second half of the first to the beginning of the fifth century AD, as well as significant quantities of fine pottery fragments, oil lamps, an iron knife, animal bones, and silver votive plaques (Miškec 2012, 380, Istenič 2015, 117–120). A path – 1.2 m wide and delineated by low stone walls – that led into the rockshelter was also excavated (Fig. 17.6B) (Knific 1995a).

Jama pod hribom Žičica, a cave located in the foothills of Stol mountain (Fig. 17.7A), yielded finds similar to those from Pod Gričo. Numerous finds were discovered in a burnt deposit but the original contexts did not survive as illegal excavations had disturbed most of the cave stratigraphy. Finds recovered by archaeologists during a rescue excavation in 1993 included 485 bronze coins dating from the beginning of the first to the end of the fourth century AD, silver votive plaques, fine pottery sherds and animal bones. While no built features were found, fragments of painted plaster indicate that the site probably also had some architectural features (Fig. 17.7B) (Knific 1995b; Miškec 2012, 380; Istenič 2015, 117–120).

*Figure 17.6: A. Pod Gričo rockshelter in a marshy glen (after Istenič 2015, fig. 139); B. archaeological excavations at the site (after Istenič 2015, fig. 140).*

*Figure 17.7: A. Jama pod hribom Žičica cave; B. selection of finds from Jama pod hribom Žičica cave. After Istenič 2015, figs. 141–142.*

The name of the venerated deity has not been preserved at either site, so any assumption naturally relies on parallels with similar sites and artefact assemblages. Šašel Kos (2000, 33) thus cites similarities with the cave sanctuary near Zillis (in the canton of Grisons, Switzerland), and cautiously posits that the two caves in Slovenia may well have been associated with one of the oriental cults. Istenič (2015, 117), on the other hand, compares the two caves with a confirmed *speleum* located in a rockshelter in the vicinity of Gradišče, near St Egyden in southern Austria. A cult vessel dedicated to Mithra, as well as an altar, a clay bull, a silver votive palmette, hundreds of animal bones and almost 300 coins (primarily from the fourth century AD), were discovered there (Gleirscher 2012). It is interesting to note that both of the Slovenian caves had running water: in the form of a spring emerging from inside Pod Gričo rockshelter, and in the form of an active siphon at Jama pod hribom Žičica (Knific 1995a, 1995b). These features may have played an important role in the selection of these specific sites for Mithraea given the importance of fresh water in some Mithraic rituals and, consequently, the frequent location of cult sites close to rivers and springs (Clauss 2000, 73).

Various other cult sites and inscriptions suggest that at least some of the caves dedicated to Mithras probably also served as cult places for other pre-Roman, Roman and oriental deities. The one on the votive ara from Emona in present-day Ljubljana (ILJug 302; CIMRM II 1463), for example, is dedicated to both Mithra and Silvanus (a local deity of the woods, at the time venerated under the name of his Roman counterpart) (Selem 1976, 10–11; Matijašić 2013, 65). Both gods were also worshipped in a *speleum* at Močići near Cavtat, Croatia (Selem 1976, 11). Within present day Slovenia there are other well-documented instances of temples dedicated to pre-Roman local gods in which dedications to oriental gods were subsequently asserted. On the bank of the Sava, for example, in the temple of the eponymous river god Savus and Celtic deity Adsalluta, a later inscription dedicated to Magna Mater was discovered (Šašel Kos 1999, 119–120). It is quite possible, then, that the ritual sites at the two rockshelters may have shared a similar history: initially ritual places of pre-Roman gods, they may eventually have been transformed into Roman cult places, perhaps associated with one of the oriental cults.

Between the third century and first half of the fifth century, therefore, a significant number of caves and rockshelters in Slovenian lands served as Roman cult sites (see Appendix, Fig. 17.1). Considering the evidence outlined here, it seems that underground places held a particular attraction for the followers of eastern cults, including the cult of Mithras. The latter has been unambiguously established at Zlodjev Graben (Schmid 1945; Selem 1976, 8–9) and in a *speleum* near Rožanec (Breščak 1984); it may also have been associated with Pod Gričo, Jama pod hribom Žičica (Knific 1995a, 1995b; Istenič 2015, 117–120), Bezen (Leben 1975b) and the cave close to Streliški vrh hill (Petru 1975). Adherents of the cult, always male and mainly soldiers, slaves and ex-slaves, would have gathered in the secrecy and darkness of the caves and rockshelters, which they illuminated with the flickering light of oil lamps. Initiation rites and other rituals would then have been performed, usually involving the use of fresh water (Selem 1976; Beard *et al.* 1998; Clauss 2000). As the finds at Pod Gričo and Jama pod hribom Žičica have shown, the preparation of food on an open fire, feasting, and perhaps the intentional destruction of ceramic and glass vessels, as well as offerings of coins and silver plaques to a god or gods, would all have played an important role at such gatherings (Istenič 2015, 117).

The two recently discovered cave sites of Pod Gričo (15) and Jama pod hribom Žičica (2) illustrate that far from disappearing, Roman cults were still practised well beyond AD 313. The fourth-century and early fifth-century coins from these two sites (Miškec 2012, 380; Istenič 2015, 117) imply that, unlike cult sites in Roman towns that were eventually destroyed or fell into disuse by the end of the fourth century AD (Selem 1976, 10; Beard *et al.* 1998, 387), cult places in caves and rockshelters survived for several more decades (Bratož 1990, 7–8). Christian intolerance of pagan rituals increased steadily throughout the fourth century AD, eventually reaching even these remote places. The cave sanctuary near Zillis in Switzerland, for example, was intentionally filled with rubble, possibly by early local Christians (Šašel Kos 2000, 33). Perhaps early Christians in Slovenia were also responsible for blocking the entrance to the Bezen cave with large stone slabs (Leben 1975b). In parallel with the growing influence of Christianity during Late Antiquity, therefore, the ritual use of caves and rockshelters decreased significantly. By the middle of the fifth century none of the Roman cult places discussed here were in use. As demonstrated in the next section, only a few were directly linked to Christian cult practices.

## A cross underground: early Christians and caves

The cult uses of caves and rockshelters decreased as Christianity gained official recognition and prominence from the fourth century onwards (see Appendix, Fig. 17.1). Whereas Roman cults were performed not only in towns and villages but also in various natural places (e.g. Šašel Kos 1999), the religious practices of early Christians in Slovenia were almost exclusively embedded in the cultural settings of towns, hillfort settlements, villages and monasteries (e.g. Bratož 1990, 2014; Knific and Sagadin 1991; Ciglenečki 1999). Evidence of Christian religious practice and eremitic use of caves and rockshelters in Slovenian lands during Late Antiquity and the early and High Middle Ages is sparse.

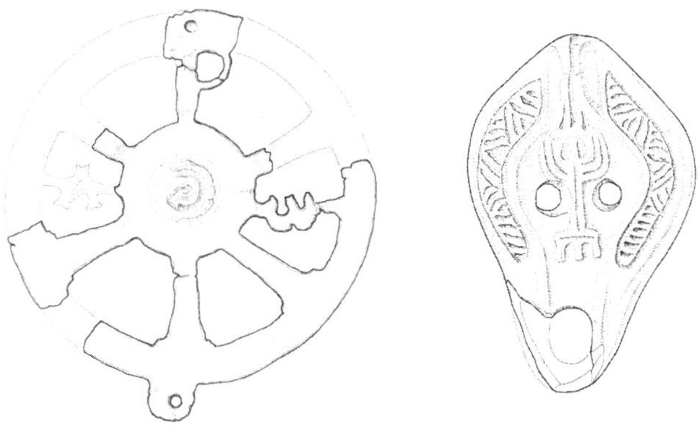

*Figure 17.8: Bronze sheet christogram and an Early Christian oil lamp (9.5 × 6.2 × 4.5cm) from Tominčeva jama cave. After Knific 1991, figs. 67–68.*

While we may reasonably assume that between 300 and 1200 the majority of people using caves and rockshelters as refuges, shelters and for hoarding identified as Christians, no Christian paraphernalia have been found at these sites – except at Jama pod Jamskim gradom (31) and Tominčeva jama (20), within the Škocjan cave complex.

At Tominčeva jama (Leben 1990, 332–338), a bronze sheet christogram and three early Christian oil lamps with images of menorah, St Paul the apostle, and a christogram were discovered (Fig. 17.8). It has been suggested that these finds may represent evidence of a small early Christian centre operating in the cave itself (Petru 1976, 40). Given that early Christian artefacts were discovered alongside Late Antique amphorae, terra sigillata, glass vessels, a brooch, nails, needles, knives, arrows, spearheads and javelins (Leben 1975i), it is evident that this cave also functioned, during the same period and perhaps at the same time as the early Christian centre, as a dwelling place and refuge. Similarly, the oil lamps with early Christian motifs discovered in the Late Antique layers at Jama pod Jamskim gradom (Leben 1975h) clearly indicate that those using the cave were Christians.

Archaeological and historical records documenting the presence of hermits occupying caves and rockshelters in Slovenian lands in Late Antiquity and the Early Middle Ages are even scarcer, in stark contrast to Ireland and Great Britain where the use of underground sites by early medieval monks as solitary retreats is well attested. At these sites, evidence such as rock-cut crosses inscribed on cave walls, ecclesiastical metalwork, habitation debris and contemporaneous hagiographic records survive (Dowd this volume; Ahronson this volume). In Slovenia, such eremitic practices were absent, though historical records attest to the involvement of Irish monks in the process of the Christianisation of Slavs in the Eastern Alps during the eighth century (e.g. Bratož 1990, 2014; Štih 2015). In fact, only one cave in Slovenia has been linked to a hermit: Sveta jama ('sacred cave') (21) is associated with St Servolo (Servulus) who is said to have been a Roman nobleman from Tergeste (Trieste, in Italy) in the third century AD. Legend has it that Servulus retreated to the solitude of Sveta jama cave for almost two years. On his return to his hometown, he converted the local population to Christianity and performed various miracles before dying a martyr in AD 284. Today, Sveta jama houses the only cave church in Slovenia. The original seventeenth-century marble altar, with an image of the saint to whom the church was dedicated, was intentionally destroyed in 1946. Up to the Second World War the cave was the destination of a large annual pilgrimage on 24 May, St Servolo's Day.

Pilgrimages to Sveta jama cave were chronicled in the seventeenth century by the Slovenian nobleman, historian and polymath Janez Vajkard Valvasor (1641–1693) in his book, *The Glory of the Duchy of Carniola* (1689). Valvasor, quite tellingly, also described a custom of annual blessings of potholes by local priests to prevent the destruction of crops by terrible thunderstorms emerging from these water sources (Valvasor 1984, 23, 44–45, 60, 93). Such beliefs clearly indicate that, over the course of centuries, caves were associated with demons or the devil himself. This common conviction is also reflected in some cave names, such as Hudičeva jama (Devil's cave) or Pekel (Hell). The Church purported to tame dark forces associated with the underground in a variety of ways. As seen in Valvasor's descriptions, potholes were regularly blessed; other caves were redeemed through their naming after a nearby church or saint (Gams 1979, 126, 129).

In Slovenian lands, then, only a small number of caves were claimed by Christians between 300 and 1200 AD. In the course of the fourth and fifth centuries, Christians began persecuting pagans and destroying Roman temples, initially in towns but later also in rural areas (Bratož 1990, 7–8; Beard *et al.* 1998, 364–388; Šašel Kos 2000, 33). The intentional blocking of the Bezen cave may represent an early Christian attempt to prevent pagan rituals; alternatively, the cave entrance may have been walled up for defensive purposes, perhaps even by practitioners of the cult themselves (S. Ciglenečki and A. Pleterski pers. comm.). Two carved crosses at Jama pod Stiško vasjo cave (14), meanwhile, may indicate that the cave, once used as a Roman cult place, was eventually appropriated by Christians (A. Pleterski pers. comm.). Caves were also redeemed from pagans by the performance of Christian services within them, as in the case of Tominčeva jama cave (20). At the same time, the equation of hell with Hades and the underworld as the abode of the dead had also commenced (Hauge 2013). This idea, which is expressed several times in the New Testament, may eventually have contributed to the formation of the popular belief that caves were inhabited by demons or the devil. From the early medieval period onwards, such beliefs may have been further stimulated by the practice of non-Christian rituals in caves and rockshelters, as discussed in the following section.

## Three-headed god and wild hags: cave rituals and early medieval popular religion

Early Slavs in the Eastern Alps and Pannonia became the first of all Slavic groups that were forced to adopt Christianity in the second half of the eighth century (Barford 2001; Štih 2015). Their early conversion, combined with the scarcity of concurrent written records on their beliefs, rituals and cults, renders any attempt to reconstruct their pre- and post-conversion belief systems difficult. Such challenges notwithstanding, it is clear that, like other traditional societies in early medieval Europe including Germans, Franks and Anglo-Saxons (e.g. Filotas 2005; Petts 2011), Slavs underwent a process of adaptation and acculturation into an alien religion. With the Church's rise, first to influence and then to power, the process led to the disappearance of many pre-Christian beliefs, superstitions, cults, offerings, rituals and magic, while many others were absorbed into early medieval popular religion and culture.

Sources for the study of early and high medieval non-Christian beliefs, mythology and rituals related to caves and rockshelters are not extensive, and are circumstantial at best. Whereas onomastics and toponymy hint at the association of distinct places with non-Christian gods, demons and spirits, folklore offers clues to distant myths and rituals, and archaeology provides material traces of various ritual acts. Ecclesiastical and secular documents such as pastoral literature, the liturgy, theological works, histories, chronicles, and biographies, however, are limited to diffuse, incomplete and frequently difficult-to-evaluate accounts on early and high medieval popular religion, none of which apparently refer directly to cave rituals (Bratož 1990, 2014).

Among historical sources, the three biographies of the German bishop Otto I of Bamberg (*c.* 1060–1139) by Ebbonis, Herbordus and Wolfger von Prüfening, offer detailed records of the pre-Christian beliefs and gods venerated by Western Slavs. In their accounts of the bishop's *vitae* that outline his missionary work in Pomerania on the shores of the Baltic Sea, Triglav (the 'three-headed') features as the Pomeranians' main god. He is described as having the biggest and most beautiful of the four temples in Szczecin/Stettin (Poland) dedicated to him (Szczepanik and Wadyl 2014, 6), taking the form of a golden idol (Trkanjec 2013, 9–10). As explained by the priests to the bishop, the three heads symbolised his ruling over the realms of heaven, earth and the underworld (Pleterski 2014, 105).

In areas populated by Slavs, Triglav's power over the realms of the sky and the underground has also been reflected in certain placenames. The names of the highest mountain in the Julian Alps (north-west Slovenia), a peak in Dinarides (Bosnia and Herzegovina), as well as two rockshelters in the region of Kras (south-west Slovenia), all derived from Triglav (Goss 2009, 39; Čok and Placer 2010; 371–373; Placer 2010, 319–320; Čok 2012, 22–23, 40). Furthermore, the latter rockshelters of Triglavca and Trhlovca were associated with fertility rites and divinations until quite recently. Fascinatingly, devotees from the neighbouring villages of Lokev and Prelože who performed rituals at these two sites provided descriptions of Triglav as the ruler of three realms similar to those given by Pomeranians in the twelfth century (Čok 2012, 21–24, 40–43; Pleterski 2014, 105–106).

According to ethnographic records, the fertility rite at Triglavca took place every autumn until the 1830s. It involved a nightly visit to a rockshelter by a group of five villagers from Prelože: namely, an elder who led the ceremony, and four young women. At the site, the group placed grains of wheat, rye and buckwheat in a small pool on top of a stalagmite column where water dripping from the stalactite above collected. According to local lore, the water dribbling from one and collecting in a pool on the other symbolised the union of man and woman (Fig. 17.9). The ritual act of the elder placing the grains into the pool was accompanied by incantations from the women asking for fertility. A few days later, the elder would return to the

*Figure 17.9: Dripstone and pool at Triglavca rockshelter – a site of fertility rituals until 1830. Photo: A. Prijatelj.*

rockshelter alone, by day, to collect the cereals that had sprouted in the meantime. On his way back to the village, he would secretly plant the young shoots in the devotees' ploughed and sown fields, once again uttering an incantation for abundant and fertile crops (Čok 2012, 21–22).

As late as 1970, the rockshelter of Trhlovca (19) – which is, significantly, also an archaeological site with attested use during the Neolithic, Eneolithic, Bronze Age, Iron Age, and the Roman and medieval periods (Leben 1988; Mlekuž 2010) – was associated with water divination. In early spring, water that had collected in a carved-out trough in a passage in the rockshelter was scooped up in a ceramic jug. This was then taken to an adjacent doline and, following the insertion of three hazel branches, placed in a small natural depression in a stone wall: an altar. One lunar month later, the altar was revisited and the hazel examined, as the number of branches with green shoots was understood to predict the quantity of summer rain and the abundance of crops. If none had germinated, further libations with water from Trhlovca were performed on the altar in order to reverse the dismal prospects (Čok 2012, 40–43).

In Slavic folktales, caves and rockshelters have also been associated with various spirits and supernatural beings, including *vile* (white wives or nymphs) and *babe* (hags). The earliest written source in which nymphs are mentioned is Procopius' *The Gothic War*, from the sixth century, which lists them among gods and spirits venerated by Slavs (Barford 2001, 193). A more detailed description can be found in numerous folktales recorded in the nineteenth and twentieth centuries in which *vile* were portrayed as beautiful, eternally young maidens with long hair, dressed in white, who taught people how to grow crops and herd cattle. They would also perform various chores for people, and present magic gifts when offered food and milk. In addition, they would foretell the future, particularly to newborns. Slavs believed that *vile* dwelt in natural places including trees, woods and mountain tops, close to springs, lakes and rivers, and in rockshelters and caves (Kropej 2008, 143–230; Kropej Telban 2012, 146–153).

Folktales describing *vile* dwelling underground often associate them with newborns. One tale from Pliskovica village in the region of Kras (south-west Slovenia), for example, tells of a cave under a nearby hill with an oak tree growing in front of its entrance. When a midwife visits the cave, the *vila* brings out a newborn. In a whisper, the second nymph confides the future to the baby before handing it to the midwife (Kocjan and Hadalin 1993, 57). Another cave associated with *vile* in the Kras region is Vilenica, named after the white wives themselves, and located close to Lokev village. Local people attributed mists issuing from the cave to white wives dancing within it (Čok 2012, 67). One of several tales tells of three *vile* dwelling in the cave and acting as fates. Eventually, the one who does the work of a midwife rebels; she is chastened by the other two by being expelled from the beautiful cave and forced to live alone in a small, dark rockshelter at the top of Kamni vrh hill where she is transformed into an evil *baba* (hag) (Čok 2012, 64).

When associated with caves and rockshelters, *babe* often represent an antipode to *vile*, especially in the folklore of western Slovenia (Josipović and Josif 1981; Hrobat 2010; Hrobat Virloget 2012; 2014; 2015; Kropej Telban 2012). If *vile* are eternally young, beautiful maidens who live in groups of three or more, *babe* are old, barren hags who often live alone underground. Whilst *vile* bring newborns into the world, *babe* eat children or enslave them. *Vile* and *babe*, then, embody two opposite female archetypes: while the former personify youth, fecundity and abundance, the latter embody old age, infertility, destruction and death. In folktales from regions of Idrijsko, Tolminsko and Kras, for example, *babe* dwelling in caves such as Šoket, Skruca, Zare, Babja jama, Divje Babe and Škocjan are portrayed as wild hags who have the ability to become snakes, lizards or bats, and are known to punish disobedient children, whom they kidnap and occasionally devour. Furthermore, they have the power to summon and unleash storms and hail showers when not appeased by food offerings (e.g. Medveščck 1992, 12; 2006, 251; Peršolja 2006, 25–36; Kropej Telban 2012, 49; Mihelič 2013, 71–72).

The interconnection of these two opposing forces – of fertility and abundance on the one hand, and barreness and death on the other – which occurs in and is experienced through nature's yearly cycle, is also reflected in the relationships between the supernatural beings that embody these forces (Pleterski 2014). The cyclical nature of birth and death, of growing and waning, was, for instance, expressed in a folktale about a rebellious *vila* from Vilenica cave, who was transformed into an evil *baba*, but after human intervention eventually became a *vila* again (Čok 2012, 64). The same idea is sometimes illustrated by the belief, as in the case of the *babe* from Zare cave near Grgarske Ravne village, that hags brought children into the world from their cave but also haunted them (Mihelič 2013, 71). Both of these examples point to the fact that supernatural beings associated with caves and rockshelters have a chthonic nature and are therefore associated with earth, fertility and abundance, as well as barrenness and death.

The chthonic character of venerated supernatural beings, as well as the caves and rockshelters themselves, influenced the nature of the rituals that were performed at these particular sites until recently – essentially rites focused principally on fertility, divination and healing magic (e.g. Medveščck 2006, 2015; Čok 2012; Hrobat Virloget 2015). For example, at Babja jama cave, near Gorenji Log village (north-west Slovenia), which was the most important site of popular religious practise in the area of Tolminsko until the construction of the railway in 1902, devotees appealed for fertile fields and luck in love. Women visited the cave in the hope of being able to conceive, and local people collected particular stones from inside and outside the cave, as well as different herbs believed to cure a variety of illnesses and ailments. While the exact nature of rites performed at the site remains unknown, informants revealed that rituals centred on the belief that a giant white snake dwelt in the cave (Medvešček 2006, 136–138; 2015, 67).

These and other recently published ethnographic accounts (e.g. Medvešček 2006, 2015, Čok 2012) have prompted several Slovenian archaeologists to enthusiastically declare them evidence for the continuity and existence of Slavic (and other) pre-Christian beliefs, religion and mythology right up to the early twentieth century (e.g. Odar 2012; Mihelič 2013; Hrobat Virloget 2014; 2015; Pleterski 2014; 2015a; 2015b). Yet such claims should be met with caution: the relationship between various types of data and early medieval and modern forms of popular religion needs to be critically examined and discussed; this is briefly attempted below.

Several historical documents testify that non-Christian beliefs and rites survived in Slovenia for a number of centuries. The second Freising manuscript, which was written as a sermon on sin and repentance during the second half of the tenth century, for example, warns against the major sin of pagan sacrifices at a time when Christianity had only recently been introduced among Slavs (Štih 2015, 18, 22). More than three centuries later, in 1331, a document issued by inquisitor Franciscus de Clugia recounts a march of priests, monks and volunteers in that year from Cividale del Friuli (north-east Italy) to nearby Kobarid (north-west Slovenia), where local people venerated a sacred tree and nearby spring. As part of the Church's violent intervention, the tree was cut down to its roots, the spring filled with stones, and the rituals consequently brought to an end (Juvančič 1984). Three centuries later, a preserved draft of a sermon by bishop Tomaž Hren from 1607 includes a brief note on the pagan gods Lada, Plejn and Poberin, which may still have been venerated by the local population at the time (Visočnik 2010). These documents indicate that non-Christian beliefs and religion either sprang up and re-emerged repeatedly throughout the centuries, or persisted unbroken among the local population. It is important to emphasise, however, that such long-term continuity goes hand in hand with change. This is clearly demonstrated by the well-documented history of Christianity and, more specifically, by vast and significant differences between its early medieval and modern forms (e.g. Bednarowski 2010, Madigan 2015). It may reasonably be expected that the same principle of continuity and change also applies to early medieval and modern forms of popular religion, especially since the principle of change within popular religion has also been ethnographically documented (Medvešček 2015, 235, 275, 441–442, 450, 468, 510).

The folklore under discussion, on rites and beliefs associated with caves and rockshelters is, therefore, first and foremost a record of popular religion as practised at the time when such accounts were recorded, and/or in the recent past. The association of certain sites with Slavic gods and supernatural beings may imply that such rituals had earlier origins, but given the lack of any relevant archaeological or historical records, the exact timing of their beginnings is hard to establish. At present, only tentative *post quem* dates – associated with the origins of nearby villages and their settlement history – are available for certain sites. Given that Lokev is first mentioned in the historical sources for the year 1234, and that the names of families from Prelože occur for the first time in an *urbarium* dated 1574 (Pleterski 2015a, 24–25), it is possible that the rites at Triglavca and Trhlovca – if they were indeed continuous on a long-term scale – originated as far back as the early modern period. Similarly, it is possible that rituals at Babja jama near Gorenji Log first took place some 500 years ago, as local lore records 14 consecutive elders in charge of major popular rites, including those occurring at the cave (Pleterski 2015b, 21).

In contrast to the rich ethnographic accounts of Slavic popular religious practises associated with caves and rockshelters, archaeological records on the same phenomenon remain distinctly sparse. Rather than a lack of appropriate archaeological research, the absence of data reflects, I believe, a central aspect of Slavic religion itself – namely the regular use of natural places as sacred sites without any significant modifications being made (Bradley 2000). The practice of venerating gods and spirits in holy groves, on mountains and hills, or in association with rocks, stones and water is well attested in several historical sources for Western Slavs including, for example, Thietmar's chronicle from the eleventh century and Helmold's *Chronica Slavorum* from the twelfth century (Szczepanik and Wadyl 2014, 5). The same principle is also well-documented in modern forms of popular religion (Medvešček 2006, 2015; Čok 2012). It is therefore not surprising that, so far, only one archaeological cave site – Japodska jama – has yielded material traces that have been interpreted by some archaeologists as associated with Slavic rituals (e.g. Hrobat Virloget 2014, 2015; Pleterski 2014, 317).

The cave of Japodska jama (near Ilirska Bistrica), where Slavic rites allegedly took place, has a collapsed roof, a spring emerging from the ground, and a dripstone with petroglyphs. A significant part of the dripstone, however, was cut away and stolen. Consequently, only some of the images were recorded making it difficult for archaeologists to interpret them. Those surviving consist of a stylised human figure, and a group of parallel lines, crosses, and stars, with the crosses and stars depicted several times within a circle. In addition, some of the petroglyphs are superimposed. Hrobat Virloget (2014) interprets the stylised figure as a horseman or archer that might be associated with the Slavic sky deity Perun, and the cross circles as his solar symbols (Fig. 17.10).

The claims that petroglyphs from Japodska jama are associated with Perun are debatable. Firstly, the petroglyphs have not been dated and, given the wide span of rock art, could have been executed anytime from prehistory onwards. Secondly, the human figure is not necessarily of the same date or time period as the other symbols, considering that there is a marked difference in the petroglyphs' execution: while the stylised figure is carved into the dripstone with deep, meticulous incisions (Fig. 17.10B), all other signs are much thinner and shallower (Fig. 17.10A). Finally, the interpretation of the carefully executed figure as a stylised horseman or archer is questionable. I believe the petroglyph in question bears a greater resemblance to an abstract sign rather than a human figure, and that it is perhaps a mason's or craftsman's mark (Fig. 17.10C) – a possibility that is also acknowledged (though not accepted) by Hrobat Virgolet (2014, 159). I applaud Hrobat Virgolet for bringing petroglyphs from Japodska jama cave to the wider attention of archaeologists. However, I also believe that in order to gain a greater understanding of the imagery, an unbiased, systematic and in-depth description of the motifs (i.e. their superimposition and juxtaposition, techniques of their execution), as well as an attempt at their absolute dating, are necessary.

To conclude: a combination of historical records and recently published ethnographic accounts has illuminated rich, diverse and long-term traditions of popular religious practice in Slovenia. However, rather than being static, non-Christian religion and beliefs have changed through time. Consequently, the ethnographic record reflects, first and foremost, popular religious rituals as practised nowadays or in the recent past. The association of certain sites with Slavic gods and supernatural beings, on the other hand, implies that at least some rites probably had earlier origins. A connection between caves and rockshelters and Slavic Triglav, *vile* and *babe*, reflects the chthonic character of these sites. It is therefore not surprising that various fertility rites and divinations, traditionally associated with these chthonic beings, are also documented in the folklore of sites such as Triglavca, Trhlovca and Babja jama near Gabrje. If indeed long-term, the rituals at these three locations may have originated as far back as the early modern period. In the context of Slavic popular religion, however, the use of natural places as sacred sites without significant modifications was a regular practice. Hence, archaeological traces of early and high medieval rituals in caves and rockshelters are almost completely absent.

The archaeological evidence from sites such as Poljšiška cerkev (7) (see Appendix, Map 1), on the other hand, does indeed testify to the use of caves and rockshelters during the early medieval period. Whilst the number of sites with traces of human presence during the early medieval period is significantly smaller in comparison to Late Antiquity, their presence nonetheless implies that early Slavs, once settled in their new homeland, imprinted their identity onto the landscape by using these particular places (Semple 2010). Considering the abundant analogies with earlier and later periods, it is clear that whenever people whose gods embodied nature's forces established relationships with caves and rockshelters, they used these not only for practical purposes, but also for the expression of beliefs and religious practice. This principle applied, for example, to the local population during the Roman and (early) modern period, and may also have held true for early Slavs. Circumstantial evidence in the form of archaeological data testifying to the use of caves during the early medieval period, toponymy associating caves and rockshelters with Slavic gods and supernatural beings, and ethnography documenting modern forms of popular religion, is strong enough to demonstrate that, as early as the medieval period, Slavs may have considered caves and rockshelters sacred places and performed distinct rituals there, most probably associated with chthonic aspects of their deities. In order to establish the exact time when such rites began, however, further interdisciplinary research is needed.

## Conclusion

This study on the use of caves and rockshelters in Slovenia between AD 300 and 1200 has explored ways in which successive generations selectively appropriated, inhabited, used, sacralised and transformed underground spaces. While some practices, such as the use of caves as pens, continued relatively unchanged from earlier periods, other types of cave usage diversified. Many of the sites that were employed as shelters and refuges, for example, had built features added, ranging from simple timber enclosures to thick stone walls. Eventually, some of these caves were even transformed into fortresses and, in one instance, a castle. This wide variety of shelters and refuges served a number of people for shorter or longer periods of time, including shepherds, farmers, metalworkers and even soldiers, who used them as temporary homes, pens, storage, working and hiding places, as well as defensible forts.

In historic periods, the importance of caves and rockshelters as burial places decreased. This trend may reflect the varied social mechanisms behind the practice of burying the dead through different periods. In prehistory, cave burials may have helped to establish and maintain identities, relationships, and boundaries between individuals in a group, with other communities, and between communities and their environment. During Late Antiquity and the early and High Middle Ages periods, these burials more often reflected sudden changes in social structures and patterns in times of instability and unrest when a community's access to the usual, open air burial ground was limited.

Between AD 300 and 1200, caves were appropriated by people adhering to three different religious systems: Roman,

*Figure 17.10: A. Petroglyphs from Japodska jama cave consisting of parallel lines, crosses, and stars. Crosses and stars vary in size between 4 and 8cm (photo: K. Hrobat Virloget). B. Petroglyph depicting an abstract sign, 13.3cm high (photo: K. Hrobat Virloget). C. Medieval mason's marks with elements comparable to B (after Žagar 2016).*

Christian and Slavic. Consequently, an unparalleled range of diverse ritual activities existed within this time span of 900 years. The multifaceted dimensions of rituals – motivation, formal variation and social significance – reflected the variety of ways that relationships between people and caves were established. Within the context of Roman religion, underground places held a particular attraction for the followers of eastern cults, especially the cult of Mithras. In the secrecy and dim light of caverns, groups of men (as Mithraism was an exclusively male cult), including soldiers, merchants, bureaucrats, ex-slaves and slaves, may have recited oaths and ritual formulas, shared meals and performed initiation rites or other distinct rituals that involved the use of fresh water. These dark and solitary places, hollowed out from rock, fulfilled the need of Mithras devotees for secrecy and exclusivity that were essential to their worship. Moreover, because *spelea* (temples constructed as replicas of Mithras' cave) were located in actual caves, they may have enhanced a devotee's personal relation to myths associated with the god, especially the story of the birth of Mithras from the rock and his slaying of the white bull in a cavern. By enabling structured ritual behaviour, caves could imbue even mundane actions, such as lighting torches and dining, with potent symbolic meanings. Located on the threshold between the wild and domesticated, the light and the dark, the transient and the immortal, caves may have, above all, reified core Mithraic ideas pertaining to the universal order and the gradual ascension of the soul of the Mithraic initiate.

The relationship between Christians and caves and rockshelters was more ambiguous. Caves that were associated with Roman gods like Mithras were seen as sites for pagan rituals and, therefore, were also suspected to be abodes of demons and, eventually, even the devil. As such, these places may have been avoided and sometimes even intentionally destroyed. On the other hand, Christians claimed a small number of caves for their own religious use. As legend has it, a hermit may have retreated to one such cave to come into closer communication with God. Two other caverns appear to have housed groups of refugees and offered a place to conduct religious services. The use of caves for services was probably a necessity for early Christians. Rather than being seen as spiritual centres, caves would have been perceived simply as convenient spaces for temporary dwellings, workplaces, refuges and hideaways. The main Christian religious practice was established and ultimately enmeshed in the cultural landscapes of towns, hillfort settlements, villages, churches and monasteries.

In contrast, the ritual topography of the Slavic religion included – similarly to earlier Roman ritual landscapes – places such as mountain peaks, hills, groves, water in its various forms, and caves. Gods and lesser spirits were intrinsic in nature. Those venerated at caves and rockshelters may also have been chthonic in character and would have embodied the forces of the earth, including fertility and abundance, growing and waning, barrenness and death. Rituals of supplication that addressed deities associated with caves would most likely have been concerned with fertility and good fortune. In addition, healing magic and divination may have been performed at these places. Most notably, prayers, vows and offerings that left no tangible material traces would have been designed to propitiate the forces of nature and would have, like other religions of pre-Christian peoples in Europe, reflected the cyclical concept of time.

Between 300 and 1200 AD, then, caves enabled the expression of a number of religious beliefs. Due to their unique physical and geographical properties, these places may have reified ideas of cyclical time, celestial order or the forces of nature. Often, caves were perceived in opposing terms, for example, associated with fertility or barrenness, life or death, *vile* or *babe*, Christ or the devil, as exclusively male places or sites visited by women too, as places of individual worship or communal rites. Regardless of these differences, observed within the context of Roman, Christian and Slavic religion, caves always provided spaces that were imbued with potent liminality where precise and repetitive ritual actions enhanced the group ethos of the devotees and heightened their sense of the mystical and the sublime.

## Acknowledgements

This article has benefited greatly from the generosity of many individuals and institutions. I am particularly grateful to the editors, Marion Dowd and Knut Andreas Bergsvik, who invited me to contribute to this volume and then encouraged and supported me through the lengthy gestation of this paper. Many colleagues have given generously of their time and expertise to read and comment on the paper. For providing constructive feedback, I would like to express my sincere gratitude to Dr Slavko Ciglenečki (Slovenian Academy of Sciences and Arts, Institute of Archaeology), Dr David Petts (Durham University, UK), Dr Andrej Pleterski (Slovenian Academy of Sciences and Arts, Institute of Archaeology), Dr Milan Sagadin (Institute for the Protection of the Cultural Heritage of Slovenia), Dr Sarah Semple (Durham University, UK), Dr Robin Skeates (Durham University, UK) and Dr Marjeta Šašel Kos (Slovenian Academy of Sciences and Arts, Institute of Archaeology). I am indebted to Lan Prijatelj for supplying me with copies of many Slovenian publications, and to Marco Nebbia for preparing a base map. Lastly, I would like to thank the following colleagues and institutions, all of whom very generously granted me permission to reproduce their photographs and illustrations: Stephanie Sykora (Fig. 17.3), Katja Hrobat Virgolet (Figs. 17.10A and 17.10B), Gorazd Žagar (Fig. 10C), The National Museum of Slovenia (Figs. 17.6, 17.7 and 17.8), The Institute for the Protection of the Cultural Heritage of Slovenia (Figs. 17.2 and 17.4), and ZRC Publishing House (Fig. 17.5).

## References

Adam, S., 2005a. Vitezi iz zavetišča (1). *Linhartovi listi* 4(15), 2–4.

Adam, S., 2005b. Vitezi iz zavetišča (2). *Linhartovi listi* 4(16), 1–4.

Barford, P.M., 2001. *The Early Slavs: Culture and Society in Early Medieval Eastern Europe*. London: British Museum Press.

Barndon, R., 2009. Caves and rockshelters – sacred crafts and smith's graves in a long-term perspective. *In*: I. Holm, K. Stene and E. Svensson, eds., *Liminal Landscapes. Beyond the Concepts of 'Marginality' and 'Periphery'*. OAS 11. Oslo: Unipub, 47–65.

Bavdek, A. and Čuk, A., eds., 2015. *Predjamski zaklad. The Predjama Treasure Cache*. Postojna: Zavod Znanje, javni zavod, Območna enota Notranjski muzej.

Beard, M., North, J. and Price, S., 1998. *Religions of Rome. Vol. 1: A History*. Cambridge: Cambridge University Press.

Bednarowski, M.F., 2010. Multiplicity and ambiguity. *In*: M.F. Bednarowski, ed. *Twentieth-Century Global Christianity: People's History of Christianity*. Minneapolis, MN: Fortress Press, 1–36.

Boschian, G. and Montagnari-Kokelj, E., 2000. Prehistoric shepherds and caves in the Trieste Karst (north-eastern Italy). *Geoarchaeology* 15(4), 331–371.

Bradley, R., 2000. *An Archaeology of Natural Places*. London: Routledge.

Branigan, K. and Dearne, M.J., eds., 1992. *Romano-British Cavemen. Cave Use in Roman Britain*. Oxford: Oxbow Books.

Bratož, R., 1990. *Vpliv oglejske cerkve na vzhodnoalpski in predalpski prostor od 4. do 8. Stoletja*. Ljubljana: Zveza zgodovinskih društev Slovenije.

Bratož, R., 2014. *Med Italijo in Ilirikom: slovenski prostor in njegovo sosedstvo v pozni antiki*. Ljubljana: Znanstvena založba Filozofske fakultete.

Bremšak, M., 2006. Odkrivanje arheoloških najdišč v slovenskem visokogorju. Entdeckung archäologischer Fundorte im slowenischen Hochgebirge. *In*: T. Cevc, ed. *Človek v Alpah: desetletje (1996–2006) raziskav o navzočnosti človeka v slovenskih Alpah*. Ljubljana: Založba ZRC, Znanstvenoraziskovalni center Slovenske akademije znanosti in umetnosti, 41–50.

Breščak, D., 1984. Rožanec. *Varstvo spomenikov* 26, 251–253.

Brodar, M., 1951. Poročilo o sondiranju v Zijalki pod Jamarskim vrhom. *Arheološki vestnik* 2, 204–206.

Brodar, M., 1985. Iskanje novih paleolitskih postaj v letih 1971–1982. *Arheološki vestnik* 36, 25–38.

Brodar, M., 1995. Končni paleolitik iz Poljšiške cerkve. *Arheološki vestnik* 46, 25–38.

Cevc, T., 1997. *Davne sledi človeka v Kamniških Alpah: arheološke najdbe v planinah (1995–1996)*. Ljubljana: ZRC SAZU.

Cevc, T., 2006. Arheološki dokazi o pašništvu v alpskem visokogorju: pogledi etnologa. Archäologische Beweise für die Sennwirtschaft im Alpinen Hochgebirge. Ansichten eines Ethnologen. *In*: T. Cevc, ed. *Človek v Alpah: desetletje (1996–2006) raziskav o navzočnosti človeka v slovenskih Alpah*. Ljubljana: Založba ZRC, ZRC SAZU, 113–124.

Ciglenečki, S., 1988. Borovak pri Podkumu. *Varstvo spomenikov* 30, 238.

Ciglenečki, S., 1997. Strukturiranost poznorimske poselitve Slovenije. *Arheološki vestnik* 48, 191–202.

Ciglenečki, S., 1999. Results and problems in the archaeology of Late Antiquity in Slovenia. *Arheološki vestnik* 50, 287–309.

Ciglenečki, S. and Milavec, T., 2009. The defence of north-eastern Italy in the first decennia of the 5th century. *Forum Iulii: annuario del Museo nazionale di Cividale del Friuli* 33, 175–187.

Ciglenečki, S. and Turk, I., 1986. Dobravlje, III, 11, Sežana. *Varstvo spomenikov* 28, 272.

CIL: *Corpus Inscriptionum Latinarum*, 1865-. Ed. Th. Mommsen *et al*. Berlin: Accademia Borussica.

CIMRM: *Corpus inscriptionum et monumentorum religionis mithriacae,* 2 vols. 1960 [1956], Pub. M.J. Vermaseren. The Hague: Martinus Nijhoff.

Clauss, M., 2000. *The Roman Cult of Mithras. The God and his Mysteries*. New York: Routledge.

Čok, B., 2012. *V siju mesečine: ustno izročilo Lokve, Prelož in bližnje okolice*. Ljubljana: Inštitut za arheologijo ZRC SAZU, Založba ZRC.

Čok, B. and Placer, L., 2010. Trhlovca = lokavska Triglavca. *Studia Mythologica Slavica* 13, 371–378.

Dirjec, J., Šercelj, A., and Turk, I., 1988. Rakitovec, 8, III, Sežana. *Varstvo spomenikov* 30, 209–210.

Dowd, M., 2015. *The Archaeology of Caves in Ireland*. Oxford: Oxbow Books.

Filotas, B., 2005. *Pagan Survivals, Superstitions and Popular Cultures in Early Medieval Pastoral Literature*. Toronto: Pontifical Institute of Medieval Studies.

Fister, P., 1975. *Arhitektura slovenskih protiturških taborov*. Ljubljana: Slovenska matica.

Frelih, M., 1987. *Jama pri rimskem zidu. Topografski zapisnik, 31.7.1987*. Ljubljana: ZRC SAZU, Inštitut za arheologijo.

Frelih, M., 1998. Škocjanske jame in mitični vhod v Hadovo kraljestvo. *Naše jame* 40, 81–108.

Gabrovec, S., 1975. Babna gora. *In*: S. Gabrovec, S. Jesse, P. Petru, J. Šašel and F. Truhlar, eds. *Arheološka najdišča Slovenije*. Ljubljana: Državna založba Slovenije, 167.

Gams, I., 1979. Bajeslovna izročila o jamah in vodah na Krasu. *Traditiones: zbornik Inštituta za slovensko narodopisje in Glasbenonarodopisnega inštituta ZRC SAZU* 5/6, 125–132.

Gleirscher, P., 2012. Abteilung für Ur- und Frühgeschichte. *Rudolfinum-Jahrbuch des Landesmuseums für Kärnten*, 2011, 15–22.

Goss, V. P., 2009. The three-header from Vaćani. *Starohrvatska prosvjeta. III. serija* 36, 36–54.

Guštin, B., 2006. Obrambna linija Kraškega roba. *In*: N. Gorenc, ed. *Gradovi, utrdbe in mestna obzidja: vodnik po spomenikih*. Ljubljana: Zavod za varstvo kulturne dediščine Slovenije, 98–116.

Guštin, M., 1976. Poročilo o izkopu kulturnih slojev v Levakovi jami. *Arheološki vestnik* 27, 260–282.

Guštin, M., 1977. Levakova jama pri Šutni. *Varstvo spomenikov* 21, 170–171.

Hauge, M.R., 2013. *The Biblical Tour of Hell*. London: Bloomsbury.

Horvat, J., 2006. Arheološki sledovi v slovenskem visokogorju. Archäologische Zeugnisse im slowenischen Alpengebiet. *In*: T. Cevc, ed. *Človek v Alpah: desetletje (1996–2006) raziskav o navzočnosti človeka v slovenskih Alpah*. Ljubljana: Založba ZRC, ZRC SAZU, 21–40.

Hrobat, K., 2010. *Ko Baba dvigne krilo: Prostor in čas v folklori Krasa*. Ljubljana: Znanstvena založba Filozofske fakultete.

Hrobat Virloget, K., 2012. Outlines of mythic characters in the villages of Lokev and Prelože in the context of Slavic mythology. *In*: B. Čok, ed. *V siju mesečine: ustno izročilo Lokve, Prelož in bližnje okolice*. Ljubljana: Inštitut za arheologijo ZRC SAZU, Založba ZRC, 173–182.

Hrobat Virloget, K., 2014. Petroglifi iz Jame v bližini Trnovskega studenca nad Ilirsko Bistrico na Snežniški planoti. *Studia Mythologica Slavica* 17, 155–172.

Hrobat Virloget, K., 2015. Caves as entrances to the world beyond, from where fertility is derived. The case of SW Slovenia. *Studia Mythologica Slavica* 18, 153–163.

Ins. It.: *Inscriptiones Italiae (Ins. It.)*, 1931-. Rome: Libreria dello Stato.

ILJug: *Inscriptiones Latinea quae in Iugoslavia inter annos MCMXL et MCMLX repertae et editae sunt*, 1963. Pub. A. Šašel and J. Šašel. Situla 5. Ljubljana.

ILSl: *Inscriptiones Latinae Sloveniae 1*, 1998. Pub. M. Lovenjak, Situla 37. Ljubljana.

Istenič, J., 2015. *Roman Stories from the Crossroads*. Ljubljana: Narodni muzej Slovenije.

Jamnik, P., 2001. 115. Luče – Lučka jama 2, Stari grad, Pri jamah. *Varstvo spomenikov. Poročila* 38, 67–72.

Jeločnik, A., 1973. *Čenturska zakladna najdba folisov Maksencija in tetrarhije*. Ljubljana: Narodni muzej.

Josipović, D. and Josif, J., 1981. Spodnja Lipnica. *Varstvo spomenikov* 23, 259–260.

Juvančič, I., 1984. Križarska vojska proti Kobaridcem 1331. *Zgodovinski časopis* 38(1–2), 49–55.

Knific, T., 1984. Arheološki zemljevid blejskega kota v zgodnjem srednjem veku. *Kronika* 32, 99–110.

Knific, T., 1995a. Godič – Pod Gričo. *Varstvo spomenikov* 36, 234–235.

Knific, T., 1995b. Moste – Jama pod hribom Žičica. *Varstvo spomenikov* 36, 236–238.

Knific, T. and Sagadin, M., eds., 1991. *Pismo brez pisave: arheologija o prvih stoletjih krščanstva na Slovenskem*. Ljubljana: Narodni muzej.

Kocjan, D. and Hadalin, J., 1993. *Bejži zlodej, baba gre: kraške štorije*. Kmečki glas: Kmečki glas.

Komelj, I., 1958. Begunje – Hudičev gradič. *Zavod za spomeniško varstvo LRS – spomeniška kartoteka*, Zap. XXXVI, 21.

Korošec, J., 1956. *Arheološke ostaline v Predjami*. Ljubljana: Slovenska akademija znanosti in umetnosti.

Korošec, P., 1982. Predjama konec 4. do sredine 5. stoletja. *Arheološki vestnik* 33, 84–114.

Kos, M., 1954. *Srednjeveški urbarji za Slovenijo III. Urbarji Slovenskega Primorja II*. Ljubljana: Akademija znanosti in umetnosti.

Kropej, M., 2008. *Od ajda do zlatoroga. Slovenska bajeslovna bitja*. Celovec; Ljubljana; Dunaj: Mohorjeva založba.

Kropej Telban, M., 2012. *Supernatural beings from Slovenian myth and folktales*. Ljubljana: Založba ZRC, Inštitut za slovensko narodopisje ZRC SAZU.

Leben, F., 1958–1959. Žegnana jama pri Orehku. *Varstvo spomenikov* 7, 287.

Leben, F., 1969. Arheološka podoba dolenjskih jam. *Naše jame* 11, 25–40.

Leben, F., 1975a. Arheološke jamske postaje na Gorenjskem. *Naše jame* 17, 85–99.

Leben, F., 1975b. Brestovica pri Komnu, Bezen nad Mohorini. *In*: S. Gabrovec, S. Jesse, P. Petru, J. Šašel and F. Truhlar, eds. *Arheološka najdišča Slovenije*. Ljubljana: DZS, 136.

Leben, F., 1975c. Nemška vas, Ajdovska jama pri Nemški vasi. *In*: S. Gabrovec, S. Jesse, P. Petru, J. Šašel and F. Truhlar, eds. *Arheološka najdišča Slovenije*. Ljubljana: DZS, 260.

Leben, F., 1975d. Orehek, Žegnana jama. *In*: S. Gabrovec, S. Jesse, P. Petru, J. Šašel and F. Truhlar, eds. *Arheološka najdišča Slovenije*. Ljubljana: DZS, 158.

Leben, F., 1975e. Osp, Grad pri Ospu. *In*: S. Gabrovec, S. Jesse, P. Petru, J. Šašel and F. Truhlar, eds. *Arheološka najdišča Slovenije*. Ljubljana: DZS, 142.

Leben, F., 1975f. Podbrezje, Ciganska jama. *In*: S. Gabrovec, S. Jesse, P. Petru, J. Šašel and F. Truhlar, eds. *Arheološka najdišča Slovenije*. Ljubljana: DZS, 172.

Leben, F., 1975g. Poljšica pri Gorjah, Poljšiška cerkev. *In*: S. Gabrovec, S. Jesse, P. Petru, J. Šašel and F. Truhlar, eds. *Arheološka najdišča Slovenije*. Ljubljana: DZS, 165.

Leben, F., 1975h. Predjama, Jama pod Jamskim gradom. *In*: S. Gabrovec, S. Jesse, P. Petru, J. Šašel and F. Truhlar, eds. *Arheološka najdišča Slovenije*. Ljubljana: DZS, 159.

Leben, F., 1975i. Škocjanske jame (Škocjan), Tominčeva jama. *In*: S. Gabrovec, S. Jesse, P. Petru, J. Šašel and F. Truhlar, eds. *Arheološka najdišča Slovenije*. Ljubljana: DZS, 132–133.

Leben, F., 1975j. Socerb, Jama pod Socerbskim gradom. *In*: S. Gabrovec, S. Jesse, P. Petru, J. Šašel and F. Truhlar, eds. *Arheološka najdišča Slovenije*. Ljubljana: DZS, 143.

Leben, F., 1975k. Šutna, Levakova jama. *In*: S. Gabrovec, S. Jesse, P. Petru, J. Šašel and F. Truhlar, eds. *Arheološka najdišča Slovenije*. Ljubljana: DZS, 256.

Leben, F., 1975l. Begunje na Gorenjskem, Zijalka pod Jamarskim vrhom. *In*: S. Gabrovec, S. Jesse, P. Petru, J. Šašel and F. Truhlar, eds. *Arheološka najdišča Slovenije*. Ljubljana: DZS, 162.

Leben, F., 1978. Osteološke in kultne najdbe prazgodovinskega človeka iz kraških jam Slovenije in mejnega ozemlja. *Arheološki vestnik* 29, 13–35.

Leben, F., 1988. Novoodkrite prazgodovinske plasti v jamah na Krasu. *Poročilo o raziskovanju paleolita, neolita in eneolita v sloveniji* 16, 65–76.

Leben, F., 1990. Arheološki ambient v porečju Reke in na Divaškem pragu. *In*: G. Cuscito, E. Halupca, and L. Foscan, eds. *Reka – Timav: podobe, zgodovina in ekologija kraške reke*. Ljubljana: Mladinska knjiga, 321–351.

Ložar, R., 1939. Staroslovansko in srednjeveško lončarstvo v Sloveniji. *Glasnik Muzejskega društva za Slovenijo* 20, 180–225.

Madigan, K., 2015. *Medieval Christianity. A New History*. New Haven, CT: Yale University Press.

Malešič, F., 2006. Naključno arheološko odkritje v Lepi glavi (1756m). Zufällige archäologische Entdeckung auf der Lepa glava (1765m). *In*: T. Cevc, ed. *Človek v Alpah: desetletje (1996–2006) raziskav o navzočnosti človeka v slovenskih Alpah*. Ljubljana: Založba ZRC, ZRC SAZU, 51–56.

Matijašić, R., 2013. Klasični kultovi, avtohtona vjerovanja i romanizacija. *In*: B. Kuntić-Makvić and I. Vilogorac Brčić, eds. *Znakovi i riječi. Signa et litterae. vol. IV: zbornik projekta 'Mythos – cultus – imagines deorum'*. Zagreb: FF Press, 61–70.

Medvešček, P., 1992. *Skrivnost in svetost kamna: zgodbe o čarnih predmetih in svetih znamenjih na Primorskem*. Trst: Založništvo tržaškega tiska.

Medvešček, P., 2006. *Let v lunino senco: pripovedi o starih verovanjih*. Nova Gorica: Taura.

Medvešček, P., 2015. *Iz nevidne strani neba: razkrite skrivnosti staroverstva*. Ljubljana: Založba ZRC, ZRC SAZU.

Meterc, J., 1982. Pregled rimskodobnih najdb na visokem Gorenjskem. *Numizmatični vestnik* 10, 299–305.

Meterc, J., 1992a. 230. Moste pri Žirovnici. *Varstvo spomenikov* 34, 257.

Meterc, J., 1992b. Begunje. Radovljica. Zijalka pod Jamarskim vrhom. *Varstvo spomenikov* 34, 193.

Meterc, J., 1993. Nove rimskodobne numizmatične najdbe s področja visoke Gorenjske. *Numizmatični vestnik* 21, 527–532.

MGH: *Monumentae Germaniae Historica, Capitularia Regum Francorum II/1–3*, 1890, 1893, 1897. Pub. A. Boretius and V. Krause. Hannover: Impensis Bibliopolii Hahniani.

Mihelič, M., 2013. Z lune na luno. Kamenodobni 'odmevi' v ustnem izročilu Zahodne Slovenije? *Arheo* 30, 67–98.

Miškec, A., 2012. Hoards of the Roman period in Slovenia from the 2nd century BC to the 2nd century AD. *Vjesnik Arheološkog muzeja u Zagrebu* 45(1), 379–393.

Mlekuž, D., 2010. Od voznih redov k vlakom: datiranje prehoda iz mezolitika v neolitik v kraških jamah. *Argo* 53(1), 34–40.

Mlekuž, D., Budja, M., Payton, R. and Bonsall, C., 2008. 'Mind the gap', Caves, radiocarbon sequences and the Mesolithic–Neolithic transition in Europe. Lessons from the Mala Triglavca rockshelter site. *Geoarchaeology* 23(3), 398–416.

Novak, V., 1970. Živinoreja. *In*: P. Blaznik, B. Grafenauer and S. Vilfan, eds. *Gospodarska in družbena zgodovina Slovencev.* Ljubljana: DZS, 343–395.

Odar, B., 2012. Potočka zijavka: Fertility rites in the Raining Cave. *Studia Mythologica Slavica* 15, 9–34.

Ogrin, M., 2006. Arheološke raziskave v Julijskih Alpah: Bohinj in Blejski kot. Archäologische Erforschungen der Julischen Alpen, Bohinj und Bleder Winkel. *In*: T. Cevc, ed. *Človek v Alpah: desetletje (1996–2006) raziskav o navzočnosti človeka v slovenskih Alpah*. Ljubljana: Založba ZRC, ZRC SAZU, 96–110.

Osole, F., 1977. Trhlovca pri Divači. *Varstvo spomenikov* 21, 173–175.

Peršolja, J., 2006. *Škocjanski kaplanci*. Škocjan: Turistično društvo.

Petru, S., 1975. Hrušica. *In*: S. Gabrovec, S. Jesse, P. Petru, J. Šašel and F. Truhlar, eds. *Arheološka najdišča Slovenije*. Ljubljana: DZS, 122.

Petru, P., 1976. *Zaton antike v Sloveniji*. Ljubljana: Narodni muzej.

Petts, D., 2011. *Pagan and Christian. Religious Change in Early Medieval Europe*. London: Bristol Classical Press.

Placer, L., 2010. Triglavca, kraj češčenja plodnosti. Poizkus etimologije Divače. *Studia Mythologica Slavica* 13, 313–323.

Pleterski, A., 2014. *Kulturni genom: prostor in njegovi ideogrami mitične zgodbe*. Ljubljana: Založba ZRC.

Pleterski, A., 2015a. Preplet 3 in 4, preloška Beli križ in Triglavca ter Zbruški idol. *In*: K. Hrobat Virloget and P. Kavrečič, eds. *Nesnovna krajina Krasa*. Koper: Založba Univerze na Primorskem, 21–33.

Pleterski, A., 2015b. Staroverstvo in pričevanja starovercev. *In*: P. Medvešček, ed. *Iz nevidne strani neba: razkrite skrivnosti staroverstva*. Ljubljana: Založba ZRC, ZRC SAZU, 15–33.

Prešeren, D., 1991. Keltske, rimske in kasnoantične najdbe na visokem Gorenjskem. *Jeseniški zbornik* 6, 113–134.

Prijatelj, A., 2011. History of cave archaeology in Slovenia. Politics, institutions, individuals, methods and theories. *Cave and Karst Science* 38(3), 137–143.

Prijatelj, A., forthcoming. Vibrant Places beneath the Surface. Caves and Rockshelters in the Kras Region, SW Slovenia. Thesis (PhD), Durham University.

Reisp, B., 1977. *Predjama*. Ljubljana: Zavod SR Slovenije za spomeniško varstvo.

Sagadin, M., 2006. 83. Grad pri Cerkljah – arheološko najdišče Jama pod Stiško vasjo. *Varstvo spomenikov. Poročila*, 39–41, 52–53.

Schmid, W., 1945. Das Mithrasheiligtum von Pohanca bei Rann an der Save. *Schild von Steier* 1, 10–17.

Selem, P., 1976. Mithrin kult u Panoniji. *Radovi zavoda za hrvatsku povijest* 8(1), 5–63.

Semple, S., 2010. In the Open Air. *In*: M. Carver, A. Sanmark, and S. Semple, eds. *Signals of Belief in Early England. Anglo-Saxon Paganism Revisited*. Oxford: Oxbow Books, 21–48.

Slabe, M., 1974. Levakova jama – Dol pri Šutni. *Varstvo spomenikov* 17–19(1), 200.

Slabe, M., 1977. Arheološke najdbe iz zbirke jamarskega kluba Kostanjevica na Krki. *Arheološki vestnik* 27, 283–288.

Stopar, I., 2011. *Predjamski grad.* Predjama: Predjamski grad.

Szczepanik, P. and Wadyl, S., 2014. A comparative analysis of early medieval north-west Slavonic and West Baltic sacred landscapes: an introduction to the problems. *Networks and Neighbours* 2(1), 1–19.

Šašel, J., 1979. Aditus ad aquam: k študiju pastirstva in transhumance na tleh Velebita in Julijskih Alp v antiki. *Traditiones: zbornik Inštituta za slovensko narodopisje in Glasbenonarodopisnega inštituta ZRC SAZU* 5/6, 353–360.

Šašel Kos, M., 1999. *Pre-Roman Divinities of the Eastern Alps and Adriatic.* Ljubljana: Narodni muzej Slovenije.

Šašel Kos, M., 2000. Sacred places and the epichoric gods in the southeastern Alpine area. *In*: C. Delplace, and F. Tassaux, eds. *Les cultes polythéistes dans l'Adriatique romaine.* Paris: Diffusion de Boccard, 27–46.

Štih, P., 2015. Ko je Cerkev začela govoriti slovansko. K ozadjem pokristjanjevanja v Karantaniji in Panoniji. *Zgodovinski časopis* 69, 8–40.

Trkanjec, L., 2013. Chthonic aspects of the Pomeranian deity Triglav and other tricephalic characters in Slavic mythology. *Studia Mythologica Slavica* 16, 9–25.

Turk, I., 1982. Begunje na Gorenjskem. *Varstvo spomenikov* 24, 183–184.

Turk, I., 1995. *Kevder v Vranjci. Poročilo o sondiranju, 4.5.1995.* Ljubljana: ZRC SAZU, Inštitut za arheologijo.

Turk, I., 1997. *Divje babe I. Arheološki kataster Slovenije.* [online]. Available from: http://arkas.zrc-sazu.si/index.php?kaj=viewNajdisce.poglej&id=010322.07 [accessed 24 June 2016].

Turk, I., Bavdek, A., Perko, V., Culiberg, M., Šercelj, A., Dirjec, J. and Pavlin, P., 1992. Acijev spodmol pri Petrinjah, Slovenija. *Poročilo o raziskovanju paleolita, neolita in eneolita v sloveniji* 20, 27–48.

Turk, I., Modrijan, Z., Prus, T., Culiberg, M., Šercelj, A., Perko, V., Dirjec, J. and Pavlin, P., 1993. Podmol pri Kastelcu – novo večplastno arheološko najdišče na Krasu, Slovenija. *Arheološki vestnik* 44, 45–96.

Turk, I. and Saksida, V., 1988. Sežana, 11, III, Sežana. *Varstvo spomenikov* 30, 265.

Turk, M., 2006. 248. Rijavci. *Varstvo spomenikov – poročila* 39–41, 168.

Valič, A., 1958–1959. Dunaj pri Jereki. *Varstvo spomenikov* 7, 330.

Valič, A., 1962–1964. Jama pri Begunjah, Radovljica. *Varstvo spomenikov* 9, 172.

Valič, A., 1966. Poljšiška cerkev pri Gorjah. *Varstvo spomenikov* 11, 132.

Valič, A., 1985. Ajdovska luknja pri Soteski v Bohinju, Radovljica. *Varstvo spomenikov* 27, 272–274.

Valič, A., 1997. Arheološki drobci vojaških prvin pozne rimske dobe na Gorenjskem. *Arheološki vestnik* 48, 261–268.

Valvasor, J.V., 1984. *Slava vojvodine Kranjske: izbrana poglavja.* Ljubljana: Mladinska knjiga.

Velušček, A., Dirjec, J., Turk, I. and Saksida, V., 1998. 271. Sežana. *Varstvo spomenikov – poročila* 37, 103.

Visočnik, J., 2010. Hrenova pridiga ob polaganju temeljnega kamna za kapucinski samostan v Ljubljani. *Studia Mythologica Slavica* 13, 59–74.

Žagar, G., 2016. *Kamnoseška znamenja* [online]. Available from: http://www.gradovi.net/kamnoseska_znamenja_seznam [accessed 24 June 2016].

## Appendix

| Map no. | Site | Locality | Site type | Cultural features | Period(s) of occupation* | Selected bibliography |
|---|---|---|---|---|---|---|
| 1 | Medvedova jama | Moste pri Žirovnici | Dwelling | Rhomboidal arrowhead, nail | LA?/EM? | Meterc 1992a |
| 2 | Jama pod hribom Žičica | Moste pri Žirovnici | Roman cult place | 485 bronze coins (1st to 4th century AD), silver votive plaques, fragments of painted plaster, fine pottery, animal bones | R-LA | Knific 1995b; Šašel Kos 2000; Miškec 2012; Istenič 2015 |
| 3 | Zijalka pod Jamarskim vrhom | Begunje na Gorenjskem | Dwelling | Eight Late Roman coins (238–387 AD); medieval cave fortress, (first mentioned in 1185 AD), spear, bridle, nails, medieval pottery, animal bones | LA, EM?, HM | Brodar 1951; Valič 1962–1964; Leben 1975a; 1975l; Meterc 1992b |
| 4 | Previs pod Jamarskim vrhom | Begunje na Gorenjskem | Dwelling | Late Antique pottery, animal bones, a hearth | LA, EM? | Turk 1982; Brodar 1985 |
| 5 | Hudičev gradič | Begunje na Gorenjskem | Dwelling | Three Late Roman coins (2nd–4th century AD); late medieval cave fortress (15th century AD) | LA, LM | Komelj 1958; Meterc 1993; Adam 2005a; 2005b |
| 6 | Častitljiva luknja | Spodnja Lipnica | Dwelling | Late Antique pottery; high medieval pottery | LA, HM | Josipović and Josif 1981 |
| 7 | Poljšiška cerkev | Poljšica pri Gorjah | Dwelling | Late Roman bronze coin (4th century AD); early medieval bronze ring (10/11th century AD), early medieval pottery | LA, EM | Valič 1966; Leben 1975a, 1975g; Meterc 1982; 1993; Knific 1984 |
| 8 | Tomažev cimer | Poljšica pri Gorjah | Dwelling | Early medieval pottery | EM | Brodar 1995 |
| 9 | Ajdovska luknja | Nomenj | Hoard; dwelling | Walls, two Late Roman bronze coins (end of 4th century AD), iron hatchet, two iron pickaxes, two iron hooks for a cooking cauldron, smaller iron door, iron knife, nails, molten lead, Late Antique pottery | LA | Valič 1985; 1997; Prešeren 1991 |
| 10 | Mali spodmol | Nomenj | Hoard | Three bronze bracelets, bronze ring, fragment of a bronze chain | LA | Valič 1985 |
| 11 | Ajdovska jama | Bitnje | Hoard | Bronze and silver coins (4st century AD), melting crucibles | LA | Gabrovec 1975; Leben 1975a; Valič 1985; 1997; Prešeren 1991 |
| 12 | Nameless shelter near Dunaj near Jereka | Jereka | Hoard/votive deposit? | 42 Late Roman coins (4th and 5th century AD) | LA | Valič 1958–1959; Prešeren 1991 |
| 13 | Ciganska jama | Gobovce | Hoard/votive deposit? | 29 Roman coins (134–395 AD) scattered in burnt sediment | LA | Leben 1975a; 1975f; Valič 1997 |
| 14 | Jama pod Stiško vasjo | Grad pri Cerkljah | Petroglyph, hoard/ votive deposit? | 69 Late Roman coins (330–457 AD), animal bones, rock with two incised crosses | LA | Sagadin 2006 |
| 15 | Pod Gričo | Godič | Roman cult place | 210 Roman coins (1st to 5th century AD), silver votive plaques, fine pottery, oil lamps, iron knife, animal bones, stone wall | R-LA | Knific 1995a; Šašel Kos 2000; Miškec 2012; Istenič 2015 |
| 16 | Divje Babe I | Reka | Dwelling | Late Antique pottery, animal bones | LA | Turk 1997 |
| 17 | Jama pri Pečini | Trnovo | Single find | Bone comb | LA | Turk 2006 |

(Contined on next page)

| Map no. | Site | Locality | Site type | Cultural features | Period(s) of occupation* | Selected bibliography |
|---|---|---|---|---|---|---|
| 18 | Mala Triglavca | Divača | Dwelling | Late Antique and medieval pottery, animal bones | LA, M | Leben 1988 |
| 19 | Trhlovca | Divača | Dwelling | Roman and medieval pottery, animal bones | R, M | Osole 1977; Leben 1988 |
| 20 | Tominčeva jama, Škocjanske jame | Škocjan | Dwelling; early Christian centre? | Late Antique amphorae, terra sigillata, glass vessels, fibula, knives, arrows, nails, needles, spearheads, javelins; oil lamps with Christian motifs, christogram; early medieval Slavic pottery, Merovingian bone combs | LA, EM | Leben 1975i, 1978, 1990; Petru 1976 |
| 21 | Sveta jama | Socerb | Single find; Early Modern cave church | Late Antique coin (4th century AD) | LA, EMO | Leben 1975j, 1978 |
| 22 | Podmol pri Kastelcu | Kastelec | Dwelling | Late Antique pottery, amphorae, animal bones, hearth; medieval pottery, pavement (stone slabs), animal bones | LA, M | Turk *et al.* 1993 |
| 23 | Acijev spodmol | Petrinje | Dwelling; burial | Late Antique pottery, bones of domestic animals; disarticulated bones of two individuals | LA | Turk *et al.* 1992 |
| 24 | Osapska jama | Osp | Dwelling | Four Roman coins (253–268 AD); cave fortress (first mentioned in 1067 AD) | R, HM, LM | Leben 1975e; Guštin 2006 |
| 25 | Jama pod Gabrkom | Rakitovec pri Hrastovljah | Dwelling | Late Roman pottery | LA | Dirjec *et al.* 1988 |
| 26 | Jama v Sežanski gmajni | Sežana | Dwelling | Late Antique pottery | LA | Turk and Saksida 1988 |
| 27 | Pečina pod Medvejkom | Sežana | Dwelling | Late Antique pottery | LA | Veluščelc *et al.* 1998 |
| 28 | Spodmol v Stršnicah | Dobravlje | Dwelling | Late Antique pottery | LA | Ciglenečki and Turk 1986 |
| 29 | Žegnana jama | Orehek | Dwelling | Roman and medieval pottery | R, M | Leben 1958–1959; 1975d |
| 30 | Predjamski grad | Predjama | Dwelling | Cave castle | HM, LM | Reisp 1977; Stopar 2011; Bavdek and Čuk 2015 |
| 31 | Jama pod Jamskim gradom | Predjama | Dwelling; burial | Roman coins (late 4th and early 5th century AD), Late Roman pottery, gems, three Germanic bone combs, belt buckles, armoury, Early Christian oil lamps; disarticulated bones of children, burial of woman and child; Ostrogothic silver coin (6th century AD), early medieval pottery | LA, EM? | Korošec 1956; Leben 1975h; Korošec 1982 |
| 32 | Kevder v Vranjci | Vranjca | Single find | Late Antique pottery fragment | LA | Turk 1995 |
| 33 | Jama pri rimskem zidu | Smrekovec | Dwelling | Late Antique pottery, glass bead | LA | Frelih 1987 |

| *Map no.* | *Site* | *Locality* | *Site type* | *Cultural features* | *Period(s) of occupation** | *Selected bibliography* |
|---|---|---|---|---|---|---|
| 34 | Lučka jama 2 | Luče | Dwelling; burial | Late Antique pottery; early medieval pottery, four bone awls; late medieval and early modern pottery, disarticulated bones of four individuals, animal bones, iron belt buckle, nail | LA, EM, LM, EMO | Jamnik 2001 |
| 35 | Levakova jama | Šutna | Dwelling; burial | Roman bronze and silver coins (1st–4th century AD), silver ring with engraved gem, Roman pottery, fibulae, two Late Antique glass beads, human bones; artificially deformed human skull | R, LA, EM | Guštin 1976; 1977; Slabe 1974; 1977; Leben 1975k |
| 36 | Ajdovska jama | Nemška vas | Dwelling | Late Antique pottery; medieval pottery, eight iron spearheads | LA, M | Ložar 1939; Leben 1975c |
| 37 | Mamula | Borovak | Dwelling | Roman coin, medieval pottery | LA, M | Ciglenečki 1988 |

*Note*: While most of the listed sites are multi-period, with the earliest occupation stretching back into prehistory, only periods of occupation relevant to this paper are listed in this table. Where period association or site type is not completely certain, a question mark has been inserted. Ritual sites discussed in the text are highlighted in light grey.

*Key to relevant periods of occupation: R: Roman period; LA: Late Antique period; EM: Early medieval period; HM: High medieval period; LM: Late medieval period; M: Medieval period; EMO: Early modern period.

# Chapter 18

# The triconchial medieval cave churches of Eski-Kermen (Crimea): recent results of investigations

*Nicolas V. Dneprovsky*

*This article presents the results of the investigation of three triconchial rock-cut churches (i.e. composed of a central hall expanded on three sides by semi-circular exedrae) situated on the southern slopes of the Eski-Kermen plateau. These are known as the 'Large Church', the 'Church of the Three Horsemen' and the 'Small Church'. In previous scholarship, the Large Church was considered a prototype for the Church of the Three Horsemen. There was no agreement amongst scholars as to the location of the* prothesis *zones in these churches. However, both have a small cave cell at the north-west side and my research indicates that these can be considered a* skevophylakion *– a special room for the ritual of preparation of the Eucharistic bread and wine – and thus these two churches can be attributed to the same period, between the tenth century AD and 1200. Analysis of the liturgical planning of the Church of the Three Horsemen, together with its mural and associated Greek inscription, suggests this fresco represents the former inhabitant of Eski-Kermen, and images of the Holy warriors were painted for the salvation of his soul. The third Small Church, considered a triconch by some researchers, is located near the city gate. In reality, however, it is of different form and was probably used not only as a church, but also as an observation point or guardroom for the monastery.*

## Introduction

As in other parts of the Christian world, dissemination of Christian ideas and rituals among the population of the Crimean Peninsula (known in various written sources as either 'Crimean Goths' or 'Greek Christians') led to the widespread construction of churches. Approximately 60 cave churches are located in the limestone cliffs of south-western Crimea. Almost all are artificial and only a few, such as the cave church of Tchelter-Koba, are likely to have originated from natural caves. These churches belonged primarily to monasteries (Inkerman, Tchelter-Koba, Tchelter-Marmara, Shuldan and two monasteries at Mangup-Kale), but parish churches of this type are also known (e.g. the church at Kil'se-Dere near Mangup-Kale). Most cave churches were devastated by various invaders, in particular the Tartars in the thirteenth and fourteenth centuries, and during the Turkish invasion of 1475. Thereafter, the cave churches were often used for alternative purposes. Almost no archaeological material has been recovered from these sites, which makes dating problematic. However, it is well-known that the evolution of Christian rituals was reflected in church plans and furnishings. The majority of Crimean rock-cut churches appear to be rather late and, based on liturgical planning, can be dated to the thirteenth and fourteenth centuries. The principal exception is the group of so-called triconchial cave churches at Eski-Kermen, which form the subject of this paper.

The plateau of Eski-Kermen (which means 'The Old Fortress') is situated in the south-western part of the Crimean Peninsula between Sevastopol and Bakhchisaray (Fig. 18.1). An imposing fortification was built on its summit by Byzantine engineers at the end of sixth century, and a city subsequently developed around it (Ajbabin 2013). From its foundation and up to the end of the thirteenth century, when the city was finally devastated by invaders, approximately 600 caves – used to serve a wide variety of purposes – were cut into the cliffs and rock outcrops in the valleys surrounding this medieval settlement. For a long

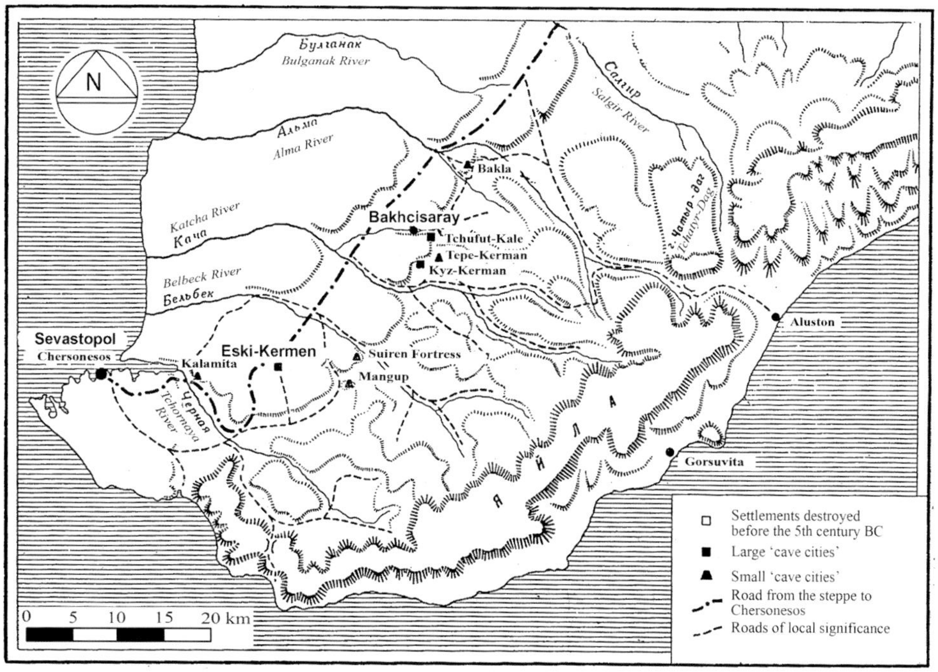


*Figure 18.1: Map of Eski-Kermen in Crimea. Modified from Veymarn 1958, 74.*

time Eski-Kermen was not only a settlement and fortress, but also a major religious centre. At least nine churches were constructed at different times around the three southern city gates and the access road leading to the settlement; four were typical church buildings, and five were cut out of the solid rock. Three of the rock-cut churches have traditionally been considered triconchs. This architectural term means a structure composed of a central hall or room expanded on three sides by semicircular *exedrae* (niches), each of which is usually covered by a semi-dome (conch). The original names of the three churches have been long forgotten, but nowadays are known as the 'Large Cave Church', the 'Church of the Three Horsemen' and the 'Small Cave Church'

## The Large Cave Church

The Large Cave Church is situated on a rock shelf at a height of about 2 m above the access road, before the first gate of Eski-Kermen. It is trefoil in plan though the western wall no longer survives. The central conch of the church was used as the apse. The altar and the sanctuary barrier are absent, but sockets in the rock floor reveal their original location (Mogarichev 1997, 41). A bench for the priests (*synthronon*) is located along the base of its eastern wall. In the centre of the *synthronon* is a recess in which the bishop's throne, probably wooden, was formerly installed (Dneprovskiy 2012b, 7–10). The side *exedrae* also have benches along the walls (Mogarichev 1997, 41; Dneprovskiy 2012b, 7–10), but there is no archaeological dating evidence for these features. There is also no designated place for the preliminary preparation of the Eucharistic bread and wine, in other words, the 'Liturgy of the Eucharist' or 'offertory' – called *proskomedia* or *prothesis* in the Orthodox Church. These two points are discussed further below.

## The Church of the Three Horsemen

The Church of the Three Horsemen is located at the early medieval cemetery of Eski-Kermen. It is carved into a huge boulder that had originally spalled off the cliff and rolled downslope. It is trefoil in plan, though slightly distorted because of the form of the rock. This church is famous because of its unusual shape and a mural depicting three holy martyrs in the form of riders. A small human figure can be seen behind the first martyr on the back of his horse. The second warrior is fighting a snake, while the third is riding at ease. Although the church and its mural have been studied in detail, several issues remain disputed. For example, as in the Large Cave Church, it was not clear how the offertory ritual could be performed there. Dating is also an issue, and the content of the fresco has also been debated. One of the primary goals of my research was to address these issues.

### *Liturgical planning*

The most significant obstacle in analysing the Church of the Three Horsemen from the point of view of ritual is the absence of a *prothesis* (Dneprovskiy and Shkurdoda 2010, 125). This Greek word denotes either the Liturgy of Preparation or the special table where this Preparation took place. Ernst (1929, 32) thought that a niche in the north-eastern wall of the altar apse was the *prothesis* (Fig. 18.2), but in reality, it could not function for such a purpose because of its high location and small size. In today's ceremony, the priest has to use the northern arch of the *templon* (this word, from the Greek τέμπλον meaning 'temple', denotes a barrier separating the nave from the sanctuary in Byzantine churches) for the offertory. This does not appear to have been the original intention of the church builders, however. Repnikov (1932, 108), Mogarichev (1997, 50) and Kharitonov (2004, 47) assumed that the niche carved into the southern wall could have been

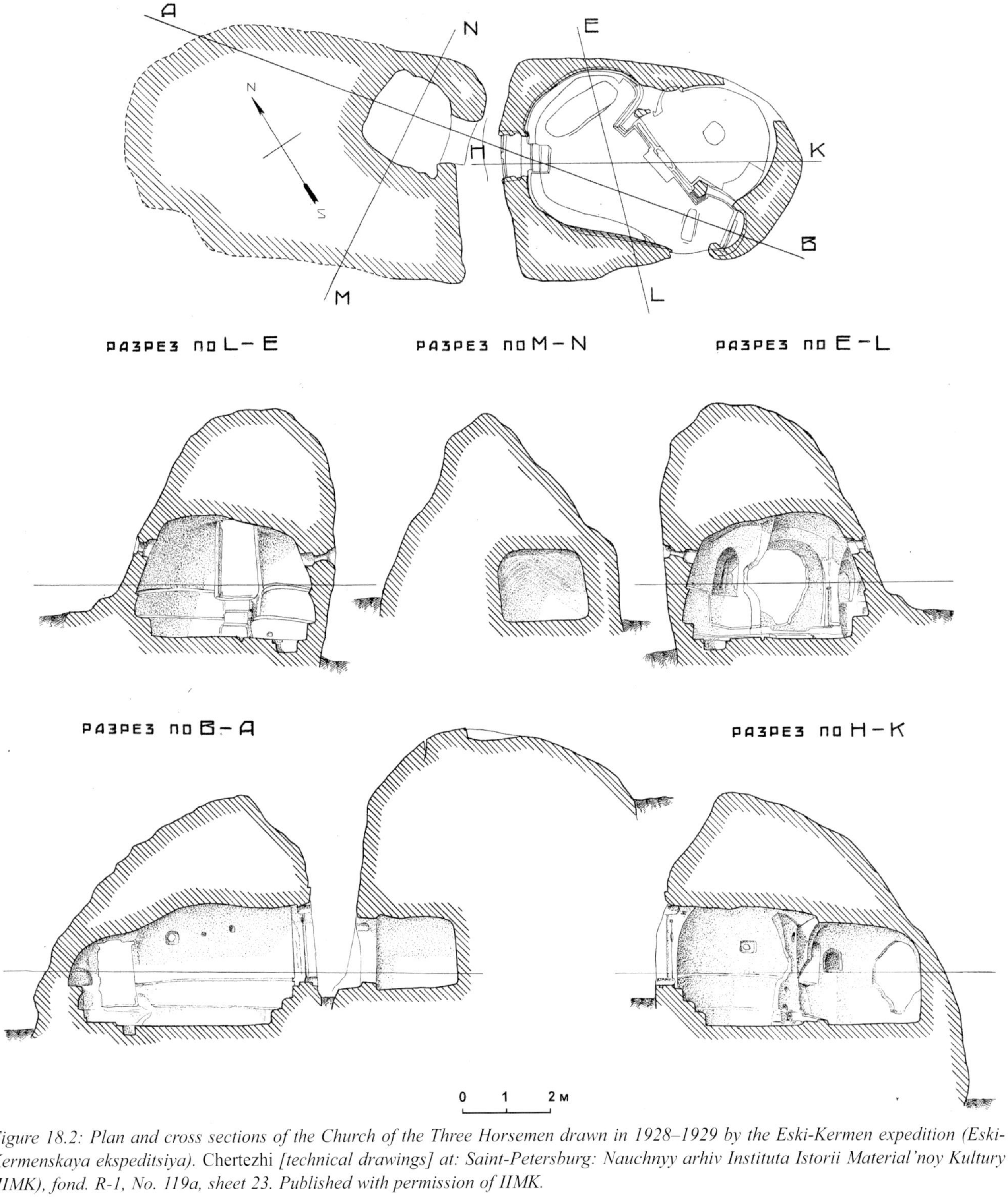


*Figure 18.2: Plan and cross sections of the Church of the Three Horsemen drawn in 1928–1929 by the Eski-Kermen expedition (Eski-Kermenskaya ekspeditsiya).* Chertezhi *[technical drawings] at: Saint-Petersburg: Nauchnyy arhiv Instituta Istorii Material'noy Kultury (IIMK), fond. R-1, No. 119a, sheet 23. Published with permission of IIMK.*

*Figure 18.3: Interior of the Cave of the Three Horsemen a), and the Large Cave Church b) Photo: N.V. Dneprovsky.*

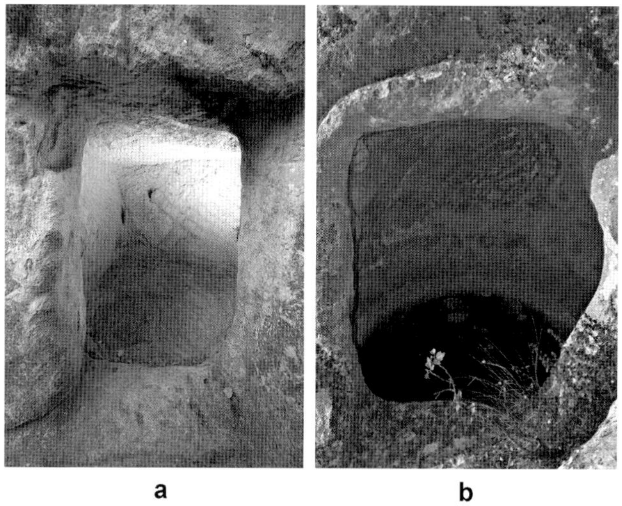


*Figure 18.4: The auxiliary caves to the north of the churches. Photo: N.V. Dneprovsky.*

used as the *prothesis*, but the real *prothesis* in Byzantine churches should be located to the north of the sanctuary. This location is strictly determined by the direction of the priest's movement with the Holy Gifts from the *prothesis* to the altar. Furthermore, the southern niche is located at the church entrance (Fig. 18.3a). It is hard to imagine the Preparation of the Holy Gifts taking place immediately in the path of parishioners coming into the church. Finally, the same type of niche exists in the Large Cave Church at Eski-Kermen (Fig. 18.3b). Repnikov (1935, 27) considered both this and the example in the Church of the Three Horsemen to be *prothesis* niches. However, in the Large Cave Church it is located too high on the wall and has a bench just beneath it and would thus be very difficult to use it as a *prothesis*. In sum, the southern niches in these two churches were carved for some other purpose.

Vinogradov *et al.* (2005, 74–75) classify the Three Horsemen as a church without a *prothesis* zone, and consequently believe it was rock-cut *before* the eighth century, because at that time the preliminary preparation of bread and wine took place outside the church. It is rather curious, however, that one of these same authors almost simultaneously formulated the completely opposite hypothesis: he assumed the existence of at least two or maybe even three places for the commission of oblation inside the same church (Gaydukov 2004, 170, 2006, 201). This inconsistency in opinion suggests that none of the authors were confident about the location of the *prothesis* inside the Church of the Three Horsemen.

There is also a direct reference in the literature concerning the place where the oblation should be performed in the early Byzantine period: not inside the sanctuary but in a special room at the left side of the temple (Dmitrievskiy 1993, 120). Babić also notes that the auxiliary building (*skevophylakion*) located to the north of the temple was a necessary element of the early Christian Palestinian church (Babić 1969, 72). Such a room is present in this instance – the artificial cave contiguous to the church (Figs. 18.2 and 18.4a) which has been cut out of the nearest boulder. The distance between its door and the north door of the church is less than a metre. The cross-sections clearly illustrate that the church and the northern cave were cut out as a single complex. The steps leading to the north door support the same argument because they had been intentionally left while cutting out the cave church. Consequently, the north door of the church had also been designed from the very beginning.

Repnikov (1932, 108) considered the adjacent cave to be a burial place, a view shared by Mogarichev (1997, 50) who added that it might also be a sacristy. Both interpretations were accepted by Kharitonov (2004, 52). Burial places, however, should have specific features to distinguish them from other caves, such as graves in the floor, special recesses (*loculae*) in the walls, or benches where corpses could be placed. If a cave was used as an ossuary it usually had a high threshold and particular grooves for positioning a stone slab to close the entrance. None of these burial features, however, are evident at this cave (Fig. 18.4a). On the other hand, its location and dimensions are ideal as a *skevophylakion*. A comparable cave without any signs of burial is similarly situated to the north of the Large Cave Church (Fig. 18.4b) and connected to it by means of a rock ledge (Fig. 18.5). This leads me to conclude that these two cave complexes have similar liturgical planning: each includes the church proper, the *skevophylakion*, and a means of connecting them. The existence of the *skevophylakia* near these two cave churches may, in turn, be the decisive factor in their dating. As Majeska (1998, 212) wrote in relation to the *skevophylakion* of St Sophia, 'the monographic studies of Thomas Mathews and Robert Taft leave no doubt that, at least in the pre-iconoclastic period, and quite possibly also later, this building … also served as the starting point for the "Great Entrance", the procession that brought the Eucharistic elements to the high altar of St. Sophia during the Divine Liturgy'. He also points out that this tradition lasted until at least 1200. It is quite likely, therefore, that the Large Cave Church and the Church of the Three Horsemen were cut before 1200. As to the date of their initial creation, Aybabin (1991) wrote that church building near the access road began at the end of ninth century, which may also apply to the Large Cave Church.

Aybabin (pers. comm.) discovered a burial vault immediately beneath the Church of the Three Horsemen that had been dug into the ground prior to the collapse of the massive boulder into which the church was later carved. Unfortunately, the vault was empty but a similar example located nearby probably originated in the eighth century. Taking into account the period when the cemetery was abandoned, and the fact that vaults of this type were generally used up to the tenth century, we can assume that the Church of the Three Horsemen was probably rock-cut between the tenth and the end of the twelfth centuries. The Large Cave Church and the Church of the Three Horsemen really can be attributed to the same period.

Repnikov's and Mogarichev's misinterpretation of the original use of the cave adjacent to the Three Horsemen led both to date this church to the thirteenth century. And, as the Liturgy of the Preparation occurred in the sanctuary at that time (and not in the *skevophylakion*), both scholars inevitably had to interpret the external room not as a *skevophylakion* but in some other way, for example, as a sacristy or burial place. Taking into consideration the esteemed reputation of these scholars, my next step was to clear up whether there were real reasons for their attempts to date the church to the thirteenth century, reasons mainly connected to the inscription under the fresco of the Three Horsemen. Consequently, I also had to re-investigate this inscription.

### *The inscription in the Church of the Three Horsemen*

References in the literature claim that as early as 1873, Grigorovich saw the date (or, rather, the first two digits of

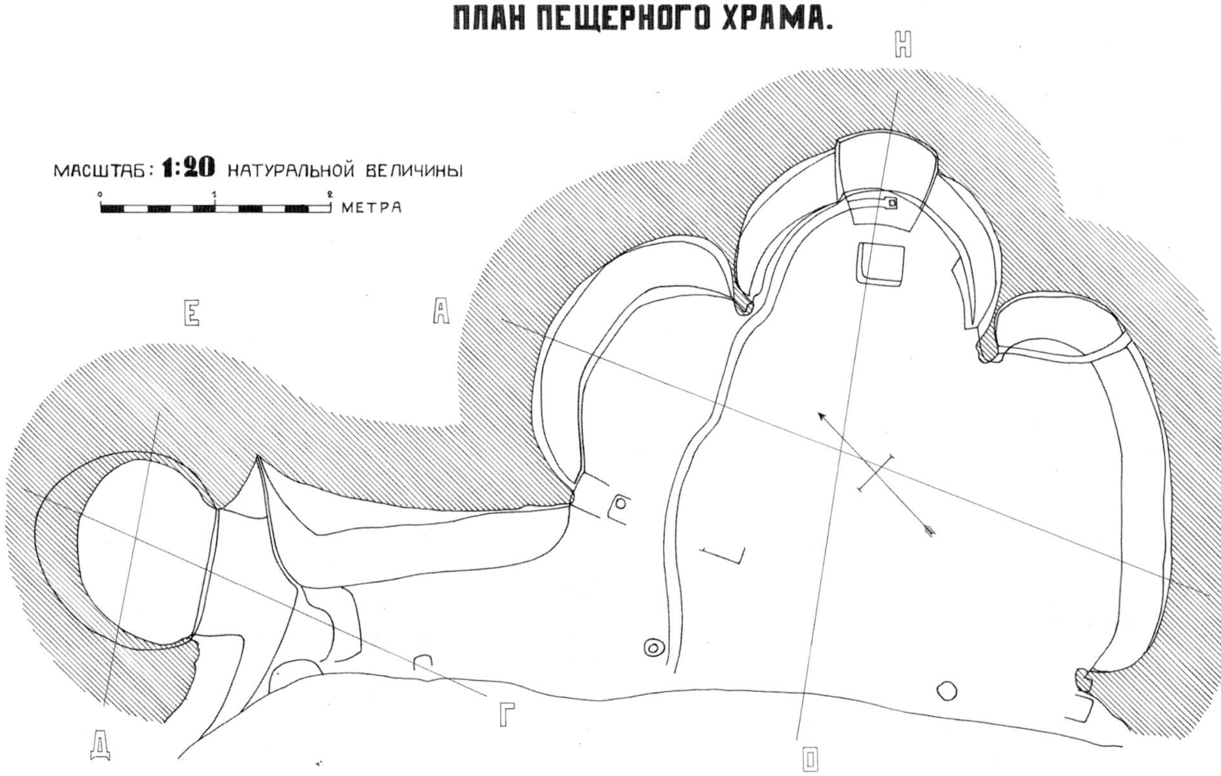


*Figure 18.5: Plan of the Large Cave Church drawn in 1928–1929 by the Eski-Kermen expedition (Eski-Kermenskaya ekspeditsiya).* Chertezhi *[technical drawings] at: Saint-Petersburg: Nauchnyy arhiv Instituta Istorii Material'noy Kultury (IIMK), fond R-1, No119a, sheet 13. Published with permission of IIMK.*

it) at the end of the Greek inscription beneath the fresco in the Church of the Three Horsemen. According to several scholars these remnants are still visible today (Rybakov 2003, 79; Gertsen and Makhneva-Chernets 2004, 124; Kharitonov 2005, 63–66). Considering that the debate about the foundation of these Crimean cave churches has been ongoing since the end of nineteenth century, such evidence is of paramount importance. Even though the complete text of this evidence should have been published prior to any attempts to analyse it, this has never happened.

A second curious fact is that Latyshev, who edited a book on Greek inscriptions, did not mention Grigorovich's 'discovery' or the lithograph made in the mid-nineteenth century for Count Uvarov (Uvarov 1851, fig. LIII) (Fig. 18.6a). To interpret the inscription, he instead used only the copy made by Kulakovsky (Latyshev 1896, tab. II, no. 43) (Fig. 18.6b):

> *…'†' Ελατομ[ήθησαν] κ(αὶ) ἀνιστορήθ[η]σαν … τοῦ Χ [ριστο]ῦ … ὑπ(ὲ)ρ ψυχι[κῆς σοτερια] ς κ(αὶ) ἀφέσε(ω)ς ἀμα[ρτιῶν].*
>
> … of Christ … were cut out and painted … for the sake of the salvation of the soul and the forgiveness of sins. (Latyshev 1896, 47–48)

Also relevant is that Latyshev never visited the Church of the Three Horsemen; he reconstructed the inscription according to purely philological considerations. In particular, two verbs in the inscription are joined by means of the conjunction 'and'. However, the ending of the first verb is absent in the original (*Ελατομ …*). As the preserved second verb (*ἀνιστορήθ[η]σαν*) means '*were* painted', Latyshev also reconstructed the first word as '*were* cut out'. The famous Crimean scholar Bert'e Delagard did not consider Kulakovsky's copy the best and sent his own copy to Latyshev. In the same letter, Bert'e Delagard wrote: 'Grigorovich tells about this inscription in "The Notes of Antiquarian", but still less than me and Yu. A. Kulakovsky' (Latyshev 1897, 152).

The next publication on the subject was by Ernst (1929). In his opinion, the inscription

> was published by Latyshev after a copy of Kulakovsky, though inaccurate, and was mentioned by V. I. Grigorovich (*The Notes of the Antiquarian*), yet quite corrupted … We read it so:
>
> *'ΕΛΑΤΟΜΙ[ΘΗ] ΚΑΙ ΑΝΙΣΤΟΡΗΘΗΣΑΝ Η ΑΓΙΟΙ ΤΟΥ ΧΡΙΣΤΟΥ ΜΑΡΤΥΡΕΣ ΥΠΕΡ ΨΥΧ[ΙΚΗΣ ΣΩΤ]ΗΡΙΑΣ ΚΑΙ ΑΦΕΣΕΟΣ ΑΜΑΡΤ[ΙΩΝ]'*
>
> [It was] cut out and the Holy Martyrs of Christ [were] painted for the salvation of the soul and the remission of sins….
>
> At the lost end of the inscription, probably, the name of the donor and the date had been indicated. (Ernst 1929, 32)

Firstly, Ernst confirmed that the inscription ending (including the date) was missing during his investigations; secondly, he was sure that the meaning of the inscription had been misunderstood by Grigorovich; thirdly, he was the first to recognise the word '*η αγιοι*' which had not been identified by Latyshev; and finally, unlike Latyshev, he took into consideration the church itself. Having not seen any sculptures there, he realised that the word 'carved' should be attributed to the church itself. Unfortunately, during Stalin's subsequent repression Ernst was put in prison and it was forbidden to even mention his name. But it was his translation (with minor changes according to Latyshev) that was inserted by Repnikov in his own article on the excavations at Eski-Kermen (Repnikov 1932). In the footnote to this translation, Repnikov wrote:

> V. I. Grigorovich (The Note of Antiquarian about his Trip to Kalka and Kalmius. Odessa, 1874, 12) saw the date at the end of this inscription: *ἔτους ςψ* … 67 … = 12. (Repnikov 1932, 108, footnote 1)

Thus, it is only in Repnikov's article that we hear for the first time of evidence for dating the fresco. Subsequent generations of researchers simply deferred to Repnikov. In particular, the aforementioned opinion was repeated again by Plontke-Lüning in her recent article (2013).

A new interpretation of the same inscription was suggested by Vinogradov:

> *+'Ελαθομή(θησαν) κ(αὶ) ἀνιστορήθ(η)σαν ἡ ἅγιοι τοῦ Χ(ριστο)ῦ τ(οῦτοι) ὑπ(ὲ)ρ ψυχι(κῆς) σο[τερ]ήας κ(αὶ) ἀφέσεως ἁμαρτ[ιῶν τοῦ δούλου τοῦ θ(εο)ῦ δεῖνος …, ἔτους] ςψ…*
>
> These saints of Christ were carved and painted, for spiri[tual salvation and forgiveness of sins of …] in the year 67… (Vinogradov 2004, 125)

Vinogradov again reconstructs *Ελατομή* as '*were* carved', which is rather strange because in the next paragraph he notes that this word should only be applied to the northern wall (Vinogradov 2004, 125). He also denies the presence of the word 'martyrs' in the inscription and he associates the dating, allegedly seen by Grigorovich, to the well-known text of the inscription.

In order to clarify this confusion, I decided to locate Grigorovich's original publication. To my surprise, Grigorovich simply wrote the following:

> Only in Tcherkess-Kermen in a cave temple I have succeeded to read the following note: …+*'Ελατοτομήθη καὶ ἀνιστρωρήθη ὁ πάνσεπτος οίκος ἔτους, ςψ.* (Grigorovich 1874, 15–16)

The content of this inscription differs greatly from the content of the inscriptions published by all aforementioned authors. I thus attempted to discover the earliest evidence for the actual content of the inscription in the Church

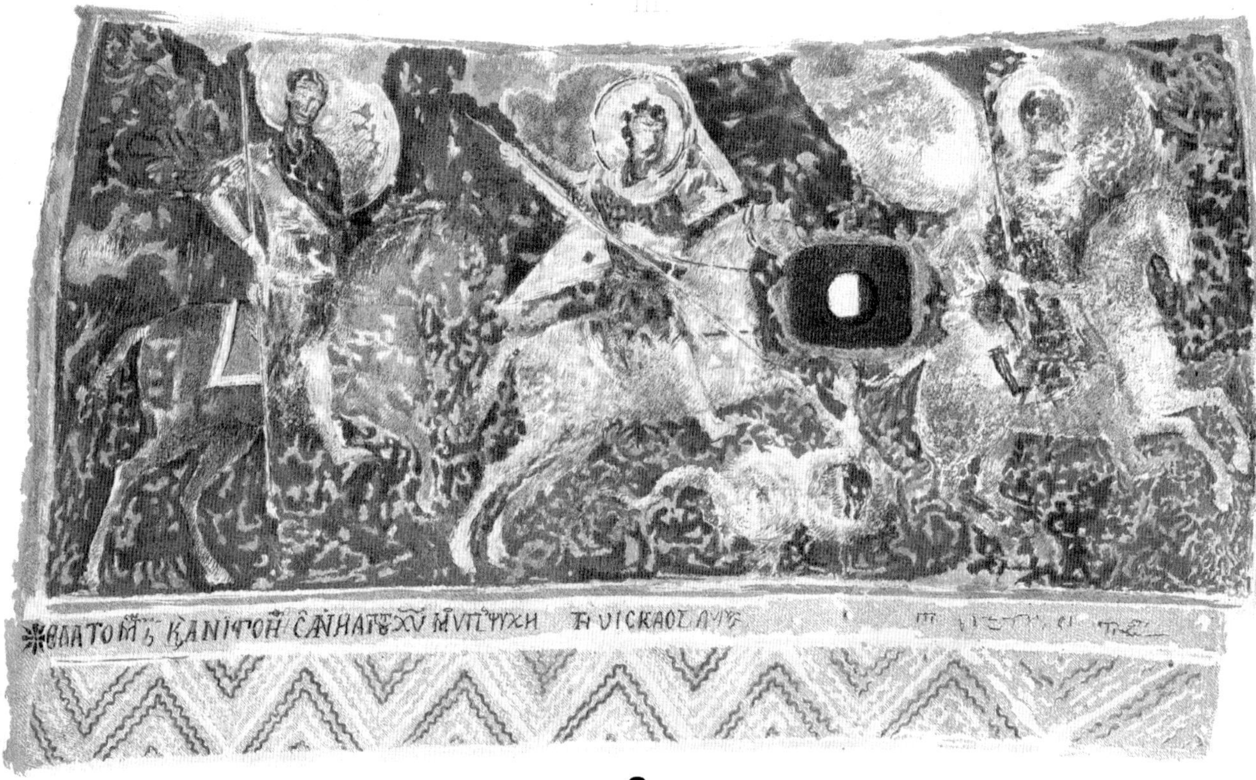

a

b

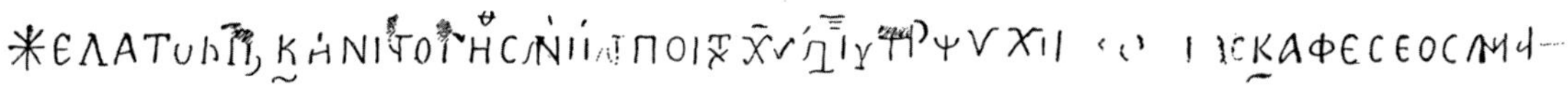

c

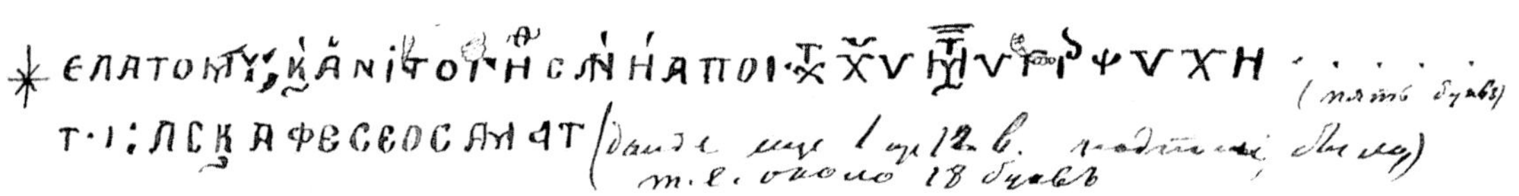

d

e

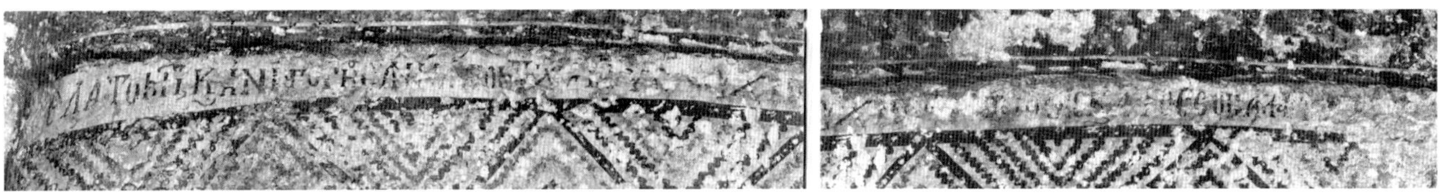

f

*Figure 18.6: Nineteenth-century copies of the inscription beneath the fresco in the Church of the Three Horsemen and photo taken in 1928–1929. Published with permission from IIMK, CMT and KRU BIKZ.*

of the Three Horsemen, and succeeded in finding three unpublished copies of this text. The first copy (Fig. 18.6c) was sent by Bert'e Delagard to Latyshev (Bert'e Delagard undated 1, d. 8641, sheet 4) who only used, however, a small group of characters from this copy. The second copy (Fig. 18.6d) is part of a draft also made by Bert'e Delagard (undated 2, d. 8770, sheet 48), while Strukov was the author of the third copy (Fig. 18.6e) (Strukov 1886, sheet 109). I also found an unpublished photo (Fig. 18.6f) taken about 1928–1929 (Veymarn undated, d. 10, sheet 237). All these images corroborate one another as well as Kulakovsky's record (Fig. 18.6b) and the lithography from Uvarov's album (Fig. 18.6a), but do not correlate with Grigorovich's text. None of these sources contain any dating evidence. Furthermore, Grigorovich's original text is shorter than that cited in all other copies despite their gaps.

I carried out further investigation of these copies together with Choref, who has extensive experience in the decryption of monograms and abbreviations found on Greek coins (Dneprovsky and Choref 2013). We discovered that Grigorovich's text contains spelling errors. Instead of the erroneous *ἐλατοτομήθη*, one should use the more accurate *ἐλατομήθη* (i.e. 'it was cut out'). The word *ἀνιστρωρήθη* should be replaced with *ἀνιστορήθη*, i.e. 'it was painted'. Considering the aforementioned details, we suggested the following: 'The all-venerable house [of God] had been cut out and painted in the year 67xx …'.

There are no obvious mistakes in the inscription beneath the Three Horsemen fresco. As for the content of the collected copies, it begins from the word *+'Ελατομή*. As mentioned, no traces of any relief could be found on the church walls, so it is reasonable to return to Ernst's reconstruction of this word, which undoubtedly bears a relation to the proper church or, at least, to its northern part. Consequently, we reconstructed it as *Ελατομή(θη)*. It should be noted that Vinogradov had substituted *θ* instead of *τ* in the first word (*+'Ελαθομή(θησαν)* without further comment (Vinogradov 2004, 125), although the latter option (*'Ελατομή*) is clearly visible in all copies. We also confirmed the existence of the words *ή ἅγιοι* ('Saints'), but we could not interpret any group of characters as the abbreviated word 'martyrs'. Taking into account the above considerations, we proposed that the inscription can be read as follows:

> *+'Ελατομ(ήθη) κ(αὶ) ἀνιστορήθ(η)σαν ή ἅγιοι τοῦ Χ(ριστο) ῦ τ(οῦτοι) ὑπ(ὲ)ρ ψυχικ(ῆς) σο[τερ]ήας κ(αὶ) ἀφέσεως ἁμαρτ[ιῶν τοῦ δούλου τοῦ θ(εο)ῦ δεῖνος ...].*
>
> [It was] cut out and the Saints of Christ [were] painted for the salvation of the soul and the remission of sins [of the servant of God …]. (Dneprovsky and Choref 2013, 190)

However, later I came to the conclusion that the badly damaged abbreviation after the word *Χ(ριστο)ῦ* could be read as 'MT' or 'MPT' (Fig. 18.6a–f), and contacted the contemporary Greek master of church mural painting, Panos Kontos, about this issue. In his opinion, this abbreviation almost undoubtedly means *ΜΑΡΤΥΡΕΣ*. He pointed out that Greek Christian believers still understand this word in its original meaning, i.e. 'the witnesses', and that the word *Ελατομήθη* is a specific term meaning 'cut from stone'. Therefore, Ernst was most probably correct and the inscription can be read as follows:

> *+'Ελατομ(ήθη) κ(αὶ) ἀνιστορήθ(η)σαν ή ἅγιοι τοῦ Χ(ριστο) ῦ μάρτυρες ὑπ(ὲ)ρ ψυχικ(ῆς) σο[τερ]ήας κ(αὶ) ἀφέσεως ἁμαρτ[ιῶν τοῦ δούλου τοῦ θ(εο)ῦ δεῖνος ...].*
>
> [It was] cut [from stone] and the holy witnesses of Christ [were] painted for the salvation of the soul and the remission of sins [of the servant of God …] (Dneprovskiy 2015, 42).

Only the first three words of this inscription can be considered the same as the first three words cited in Grigorovich's version, and only then after correcting errors in the latter. But there is still an essential difference between the remainder of the inscription and that in Grigorovich's book. Grigorovich refers to the establishment of a certain church, whose name and location was not mentioned, while the rest of the inscription in the church of the Three Horseman deals with the images created for the remission of the sins and for the salvation of the soul of an unknown person. Judging from the errors admitted in the first case, the inscriptions were made by different painters.

According to the rules of formal logic this means the following: until proven otherwise, we *must* assume that either the inscription published by Grigorovich and the inscription published by Latyshev are two different texts, similar only in their initial formulas, which means that Grigorovich saw his inscription not in the Church of the Three Horsemen, but in some other cave church; or he had indeed seen the inscription in the Three Horsemen, but the reproduction in his book is entirely incorrect. The date is an integral part of Grigorovich's text, but if the text was reproduced incorrectly then the dating cannot be trusted either. Furthermore, no indications of the date are present in any available copies of the inscription that were made between the middle and end of the nineteenth century. This means that the date must have been illegible during Grigorovich's visit. The first known copy of the inscription was made by Bieberstein at the end of the eighteenth century. It was published by Tunkina, though only in the electronic version of her article (2010, fig. 41) and not the printed one. Again, there is no evidence of dating. Consequently, there is every reason to believe that Vinogradov simply included the date published by Grigorovich into the main text published by Latyshev. It seems to me that such an artificial amalgamation of obviously different texts is quite unacceptable.

My research illustrates that, on the one hand, the inscription published by Grigorovich either does not relate to the Church of the Three Horsemen at all, or is misrepresented by the author to such a degree that it could by no means be considered evidence for dating. On the other hand, there is no evidence for dating in any of the available copies that are definitely related to the Church of the Three Horsemen. Consequently, the idea of attributing the inscription seen by Grigorovich to the Church of the Three Horsemen, and attempts to date the church in this way, are entirely unacceptable. This statement also applies to Repnikov's and Mogarichev's attempts to date the Church of the Three Horsemen to the thirteenth century. In contrast, I have no objection to dating this church based on its liturgical planning and Aybabin's archaeological dating of the surrounding vaults.

### *The fresco*

An understanding of the inscription encouraged me to examine the content of the fresco, which had also been interpreted in different ways. For example, Dombrovsky believed the three riders depicted St. George and two local warriors killed while fighting against invaders, and who were later canonised (Dombrovsky 1966, 40–41). Now, based on a fresh understanding of the inscription, it is obvious that his explanation is incorrect. The mural depicts several holy witnesses whose testimony should help a particular individual reach paradise. The next step was to investigate these witnesses and the individual. Ernst was inclined to believe that the three riders represent St George, St Theodore Teron and St Theodore Stratelates (Ernst 1929, 32; Volkonskaya 2003, 294, 2005, 224). Mal'gin and Mal'gina are of the same opinion (1993, 6). The most popular hypothesis was suggested by Bert'e Delagard who proposed that the fresco depicts just one saint – St George – who is presented in three different iconographical styles (Latyshev 1897, 152). Although we should bear in mind that the word *ἡ ἅγιοι* ('saints') in the inscription was not recognised at that time, this assumption, nevertheless, contradicts the rule of 'numerical identity' formulated by Florensky. This 'numerical identity' of the iconographical character is determined by 'the unity of style and manners, the identity or similarity of the facial features, shapes, some pieces of furniture, etc.' (Florenskiy 2000, 228–229). On the contrary, many details of the fresco (Fig. 18.7) deliberately emphasise the 'numerical difference' between the characters depicted (Volkonskaya 2003, 294; Dombrovskiy 1966, 35–36); and Dombrovskiy was critical of 'the theory of the triple St George' (Dombrovskiy 1966, 38–39).

This theory of the 'triple St George' is due to the presence of a small male figure on the rump of the right saint's horse, which has led the fresco to be interpreted as the 'miracle of St George with the youth'. It is unclear who the second rider fighting with a snake is, because both St Theodore Teron and St Theodore Stratelates are usually bearded but there are no bearded individuals in Dombrovskiy's reproduction. Mal'gin and Mal'gina (1993, 6) came to the conclusion that it is impossible to determine whether the figures were bearded or not because their faces were badly damaged. In contrast, Osaulenko (2008, 131) contested that he had found the remnants of a beard on the face of the middle rider. Korhmazyan suggested that the first rider depicts St Sargis with his son, but St Sargis 'was not recognised by the Orthodox Church as a saint' (Korhmazyan 2008, 44–45). Consequently, his image would not be painted in a Chalcedonite church.

The theory of the 'triple St George' was also supported by Ovchinnikova (1976) who discovered a late icon combining two different miracles of St George (i.e. the youth is sitting on the rump of the horse while the saint is fighting the snake) in one image. She attempted to correlate the three different images of the Eski-Kermen riders with the three images of St George, asserting that the same two miracles had simply not yet merged in the fresco (Ovchinnikova 1976, 231). The 'triple St George' theory is even mentioned in the modern *Orthodox Encyclopaedia* (*Pravoslavnaya entsiklopediya* 2005, 683), and a number of scholars consider it 'the most convincing' (Stepanenko 2003, 455; Kharitonov 2004, 125; Gaydukov 2011, 171). They believe that the word 'saints' in the inscription relates not to three different individuals, but to three different iconographical representations of the same saint. Grammatically, this explanation seems incredible; icons or mural paintings depicting serial images of a single saint are known, but no such image has the wording 'saints'.

Ovchinnikova's hypothesis is not at all convincing because the iconography of the 'double miracle' was known at least as early as the twelfth century (Reginskaya 2009, fig. 59), and in this iconographical style the 'numerical identity' of the same hagiographical character was achieved by combining two different miracles in one image. Dombrovsky believed that the 'boy' sitting behind the first rider was 'a mere page' (Dombrovsky 1966, 39, 106, endnote 32). He referred to Pokrovsky, who had attributed one of the icons of St George as 'St George with a page'. However, the 'double miracle of St George' can be seen in Pokrovsky's reproduction of this icon (Pokrovskiy 1916, 193, fig. 383) – it is clearly indicated by a wine vessel in the youth's hand. It is, therefore, also difficult to agree with Dombrovsky.

Mal'gin and Mal'gina (1993, 5) suggested that the human figure sitting behind the first saint could be identified not only as a boy, but also as an adult male whose height is diminished in relation to the first saint according to iconographic rules. I agree with their supposition, which contradicts the 'miracle of St George with the youth', because I have noticed a discrepancy between the traditional iconography of this miracle, Dombrovsky's drawing of the fresco, and his description of the image in his book (Dneprovskiy 2013a, 114). The tracing shows no vessel in the hand of the smaller rider, although his body is rotated and the hand is to the side exactly as on the icon depicting

a

b

*Figure 18.7: Tracing of the fresco in the Church of the Three Horsemen a) (Dombrovskij 1966, 40–41); and b) photo of the fresco taken in 1929. Adapted from Veymarn undated, d. 10, sheet 238. Published with permission of KRU BIKZ.*

the 'miracle with the youth' (Fig. 18.7a). At the same time, in his book he described this rider as holding onto the saint (Dombrovskiy 1966, 34-35). I carefully examined Uvarov's lithograph (Fig. 18.6a) and the photo of the mural taken in 1929 (Fig. 18.7b), which confirmed my belief that there is no reason to correlate the fourth rider with the young cupbearer from the 'miracle of St George'.

This led me to pay more attention to the role of the fourth rider in the overall meaning of the fresco, bearing in mind that the figurative system of murals cannot be understood without a holistic analysis of the sacred space in a church. This space, according to Orthodox doctrine, belongs to our world only in a physical sense. Symbolically, however, it belongs to the other world of 'eternal life' and, more importantly, it depicts this world in all its integrity. This symbolic space is represented both in the liturgical planning of the church and in its murals. The images in a church are usually painted according to an integral iconographic programme reflecting the purpose for which the church was built. In the Church of the Three Horsemen such a programme is absent, which means the missing elements of the programme must be substituted with appropriate elements of the liturgical arrangement. Therefore, I attempted to find such elements so that the theological content of fresco could be understood.

The main semantic centre of any church is the altar, which is also the main visual focus during the liturgy. The second visual focus in the Church of the Three Horsemen is, undoubtedly, the fresco. There are, therefore, two visual foci in this particular church. The centre of the entire composition, however, is the northern arch of the sanctuary and the image of the first rider with his smaller fellow traveller. Furthermore, the latter figure is precisely centred vertically, and there is a window in the wall nearby. In other words, the fourth character of the fresco unexpectedly becomes the visual 'centre of gravity' in the church interior. There is every reason to assume that he was also a semantic centre in the sacral space of the church. To fully appreciate the significance of this fact, it is worth remembering that 'true iconography is a mechanism of generating images' (Vaneyan 2010, 109).

Lazarev wrote that there is always a 'possibility to stretch the yarn from the birth of the new iconographical type to the real historical environment in which this type has been formed' (Lazarev 1953, 203). This means that to accurately understand the content of an image, its symbolic language should either be in accordance with everyday life, or should have a direct iconographical prototype. Further, the religious image must resonate with the unconscious of the viewer to activate his/her emotional response. It is necessary, therefore, to describe the entire architectural and iconographical composition of the Horsemen and to be aware, according to the rule of the Occam's razor, of any extravagant assumptions. Only after that can we try to assign a theological interpretation.

The saints are 'riding' in solemn procession towards the northern arch of the sanctuary. As there are different types of saints in the Orthodox Church, these saints almost undoubtedly are martyrs ('witnesses') according to their iconographic types (the probability of St. George's presence among them is discussed below). The sequence is headed by the rider with a male figure behind him. In other words, this co-rider is also leading the march. However, he does not seem to be an equal participant in this solemn procession, but rather a man being given assistance or even salvation. A snake tries to stand in the way of this procession and to attack the figure on the horse's rump, while the second rider drives away the snake with his spear. This action forces him to alter his formerly solemn pose. So, this part of the composition looks quite natural by itself. As for the first horseman with the smaller figure behind, he has the direct iconographical prototypes, including the 'miracle with the youth'. In this respect, it should be mentioned that, besides the well-known 'miracle of St George with the youth', Mal'gin and Mal'gina (1993, fig. 3) also published an icon of St Theodore Teron with a small human figure on the back of his horse. The pose of the second horseman is also typical of numerous images of St George, St Theodore and St Demetrius. The same can be said about the posture of the third rider. In sum, there are no details in the fresco that contradict Orthodox doctrine, which gives us every reason to believe that the theological content of the composition was in accordance with the same doctrine, and therefore was entirely 'readable' for the medieval believer, even if that is not the case nowadays.

Florensky wrote that the 'spatial core' of the church is described by its 'shells', i.e. elements such as the yard, the narthex, the naos, the sanctuary, the altar, the chalice, the Holy Mysteries, Christ, and the Father. The church is Jacob's ladder, leading us from the visible world to the invisible one; and the church sanctuary is heaven (Florenskiy 1995, 439). Taking into consideration both the triumphant poses of the riders, and the fact that the image of the first horseman literally rests against the northern arch of the sanctuary barrier (*templon*), we can assume that the fresco depicts the procession of the holy martyrs triumphantly entering the Kingdom of Heaven with the soul of the deceased, which was probably the donor of the church. They deliver this soul to the threshold of the throne of Christ (figuratively represented by the altar table), on which He himself dwells (figuratively represented by the holy gifts and the gospel). The presence of the fourth person symbolically means he is also worthy of entering paradise. Yet this procession stands at the threshold of the heavenly gates, figuratively represented by the arch of the sanctuary barrier, but not inside it. That is why the nimbus over the head of the fourth character is missing – but not because of age restrictions as Dombrovsky believed (1966, 41). It is only Christ who can permit the soul of the deceased to rest, 'in the settlements of His glory'.

Only the sins of the deceased man can obstruct his passage into the heavenly kingdom. Consequently, the question arises as to how this obstacle could be depicted. It is known that 'the icon sometimes portrays evil, but only an obvious, personified one' (Melik-Pashaev 2007, 111). It was the snake that caused the fall of human beings and their expulsion from paradise. According to Reginskaya, the Christian tradition firmly established 'the identification of the serpent with evil, the devil, Satan, who took only the shape of the serpent' (Reginskaya 2009, 30). In many archaic cultures, the serpent was also considered a symbol of the realm of the dead: 'the snake is a threshold in the transition from the "human world" into "inhuman" one … The "breaking" of the serpent is necessary for the ritual transition' (Reginskaya 2009, 92). In accordance with Christian belief, the transition from the 'human world' to the 'inhuman' one could only be achieved by means of prayer and confession. According to the Life of St George, he also defeated the serpent by means of prayer. With this in mind, we can assume that the central rider symbolically

*Figure 18.8: Image of St Demetreus (Strukov undated, sheet 4). Photo: V. Romushin.*

defeating the snake is really neutralizing the sins of the deceased by means of prayer. The first rider is depicted as the rescuer, because in the Middle Ages the idea of salvation could only be expressed through a limited set of images, i.e. the anchor, the ship or the saviour on a horse (as in the miracle of St George).

There appears to be direct confirmation of this assumption. Strukov's album, now stored in the Russian State Library (Strukov undated, sheet 4), contains an unfinished pencil drawing depicting an image of the holy rider (Fig. 18.8). The caption above the image states that the drawing is a reproduction of the icon that originated from St. George's monastery (Crimea). A second caption and the human figure under the horse's hooves indicate that the icon depicts St. Demetrius. There is also a small, long-bearded, male figure sitting on the rear of St. Demetrius' horse. He wears a monastic calotte, but without a halo around his head. Although this image seems quite late, we can make the following conclusions:

1. A type of holy warrior with a rider on his horse existed in the iconographical tradition of Crimean Greeks, and thus this iconographical style should not be associated exclusively with St. George. The icon of St Theodore Teron (Mal'gin and Mal'gina 1993, fig. 3) and the drawing of St. Demetrius in Strukov's archive are good examples of this tradition.
2. It is reasonable to assume that the male figure on the rump of St Demetrius' horse is a soul of one of the monks of St George's monastery, clearly depicted in old age despite his small size. Therefore, not only a youth but a man of any age could be depicted behind the saint warrior.
3. The content of this drawing is very similar to the Eski-Kermen fresco. It means that in the case of the latter, there is no need to identify the right horseman exclusively with the 'miracle of St George'.

As for the middle rider, it is worth noting that almost all scholars unanimously identify this rider as St George. As Osaulenko (2008, 131) contradicts this, however, I have tried to establish whether or not he is correct. Indeed, the remnants of a beard are clearly depicted on two small surviving fragments of the badly damaged rider's face. It is rather strange that no one other than Osaulenko ever noticed this detail. So, this image cannot depict St George: it is probably St Theodore Teron. If so, the concept of the 'triple George' is obviously false. In turn, the first rider can hardly be St Theodore Teron. He is, most likely, the namesake of the deceased man depicted behind him. Being his holy patron, the saint is obliged to defend him and pray for his soul. Perhaps minute analysis of the first rider's iconography will eventually provide his name and, therefore, that of his protégé. He is probably (though not necessarily) St George or, perhaps, St Demetrius. If so, the last (left) rider could be his counterpart (i.e. St Demetrius or St George). In any case, the visual and symbolical meanings of the fresco are in accordance with the inscription beneath the mural.

It is reasonable to assume that the rider behind the first saint is a deceased inhabitant of Eski-Kermen, whose name was not preserved at the end of the inscription. This rider is the protagonist of the mural, confirmed by his central position within the composition. Returning to the liturgical planning of the church, and taking into account that the northern wall with the mural surrounds the tomb cut into the floor of the northern compartment, we can assume that the fourth character of the fresco was buried in this tomb and not in a child's grave at the entrance as suggested by Dombrovsky (1966, 39). We can conclude, therefore, that this deceased inhabitant of Eski-Kermen was probably the donor of the church and was clearly of high social status. Analysis of his iconography can provide additional information about his status. Simultaneously with my investigations (Dneprovskiy 2013a), Plontke-Lüning also assumed the little rider was a historical person, i.e. 'the owner of the burial chapel' (Plontke-Lüning 2013, 268), though she did not reject the 'triple St George' theory. Plontke-Lüning tried to identify the rank of this 'lord of Eski-Kermen' based on the form of his hat, assuming that it was a *skiadion*. Unfortunately, as can be clearly seen (Fig. 18.7a), the rider's hat differs greatly from the *skiadion* shown on Plontke-Lüning's illustration (2013, 264, Abb. 6). It looks like a Greek *petassus*, although Italian hats of the same shape are also well-known.

In the course of my research, a comprehensive interpretation of the 'Three Horsemen' cave church has been carried out for the first time. I have succeeded in clarifying the liturgical planning of the church, the fresco's content and the content of the inscription beneath it. In sum, a separate *rock-cut* surface was specially prepared for the *fresco* that depicts *the holy martyrs ('witnesses') of Christ*. The first individual is a rider who is saving a man and delivering him to paradise, in other words, contributing to the *salvation of his soul*. The second saint neutralises the sins of this man, which are symbolically depicted in the form of snake; in other words, he contributes to the *remission of his sins*. The medieval painter not only had *visual* associations related to purely *theological* categories, that is, 'salvation' and the 'remission of sins', but he also succeeded in expressing them by means of a visual symbolic system and creating an appropriate sacred image. I have also tried to show that the visual content of the fresco is in accordance with the theological content of the inscription as well as with the liturgical planning of the church.

## The Small Cave Church

The 'Small Cave Church' is situated just off the access road before the third main city gate. It is more oblong in form, has an apse in the eastern wall, two stone 'couches', and an additional compartment at the south (Figs. 18.9 and 18.10a). Traditionally, scholars have considered this church to be the cemetery chapel (Mogarichev 1997, 42, Gaydukov 2006, 200). However, the nature of its southern compartment is still debatable. To Gaydukov (2006, 200) it was a 'mausoleum' but Mogarichev (1997, 42) considered it either a sacristy or a clerk's cell. To resolve this issue, I re-examined it (Dneprovskiy 2012a).

The interior of the compartment is quite simple, containing a 'couch', a window and a door. The stone threshold is broken but with an original height of no less than 0.7m, it is a rather extreme obstacle for a clergyman dressed in long robes and holding sacred vessels. The door itself was only 1m high, thus it is unlikely that this room was a sacristy or a clergyman's cell. Furthermore, a step 23cm high is located on the inner side of the compartment, but there is nothing similar on the outer side of the same threshold. It would seem this compartment was suited for convenient exiting but not for convenient entering. This is quite atypical for a cell or mausoleum. The window in this compartment is of equally unusual form and permits very little light. But it does provide one benefit: it acts as a kind of primitive 'periscope'. From inside, the window niche has a smooth surface and rounded forms, which are more comfortable for the head of an observer looking outwards. From outside, this window consists of a pronounced semi-cylindrical shape at right angles to the wall, which could potentially prevent a fired arrow from entering the room. From inside, the observer is

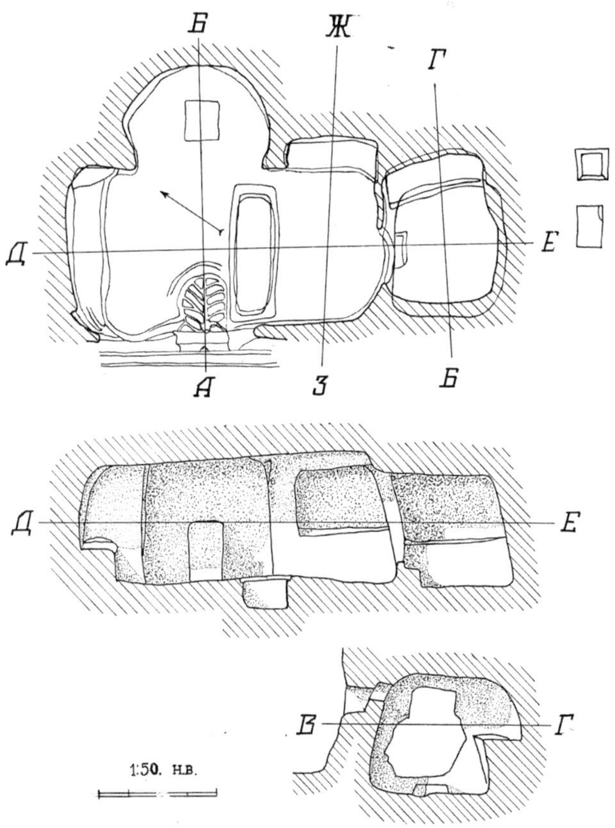


*Figure 18.9: Plan and sections of the Small Cave Church drawn by the Eski-Kermen expedition in 1928–1929 (Eski-Kermenskaya ekspeditsiya).* (Chertezhi *[technical drawings] at: Saint-Petersburg: Nauchnyy arhiv Instituta Istorii Material'noy Kultury (IIMK), fond R-1, No119a, sheet 22; Published with permission of IIMK.*

**a**

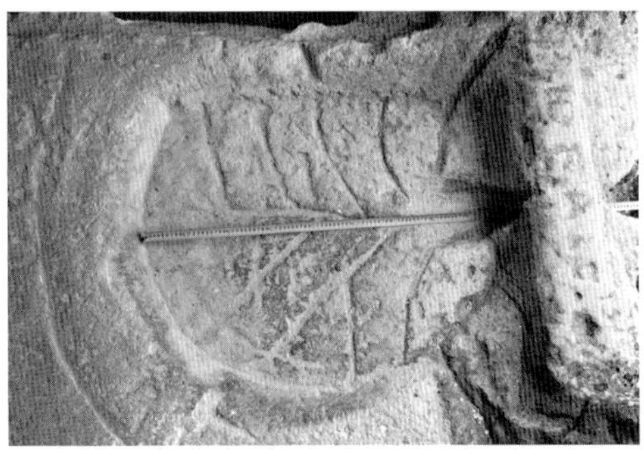

**b**

*Figure 18.10: Water drainage device at the threshold of the Small Cave Church. Photo: N.V. Dneprovsky.*

always facing west, though by adjusting the position of the head, he could watch the road regardless of the position of the sun, even at sunset. Thus, from a technical point of view, we can assume that this chamber was a well-designed observation post. The question thus arises as to whether the Small Cave Church at the city gates was simply a church or served a defensive function as well.

It is worth noting that the floor of the apse was more roughly cut than the floor of the naos. Perhaps the apse was carved into the wall of a pre-existing structure. However, this may also be the result of the fact that the sanctuary was slightly elevated above the naos floor, and thus the floor of the former could be covered with other material. Furthermore, the ceiling of the apse is slightly elevated relative to the ceiling of the naos, and looks like a flat dome. According to Bert'e Delagard (2012, 62), this feature is typical of Crimean cave churches, but such a flat dome is absent in the Large Cave Church.

The altar of the Small Cave Church was once a monolith cut from solid rock to the south of the centre of the apse: traces of it are evident on the apse floor. The basal dimensions are 0.55 × 0.6 m. There is also a unique drainage device at the threshold of the Small Cave Church (Fig. 18.10a). It consists of a horseshoe-shaped recess, at the bottom of which is a network of carved grooves that converge in a drainage hole (Fig. 18.10b). Repnikov believed this served to redirect rainwater flowing along the rock surface into the church (Repnikov 1932, 119–120; 1935, 36). Kharitonov agreed with this proposal (2004, 65; 2005, 72), but the suggestion requires more detailed analysis because such a technical resolution to this problem would seem rather strange. Initially, the church did not need such a device because the outer wall was undamaged and the door took its place. The most effective way of protecting the church from rain after the destruction of the wall would be by creating some kind of a roof over its entrance. In addition, a recess of this kind was unable to collect all the water during heavy rain. Nevertheless, it was carved with the utmost care and was likely intended for long term usage. We must therefore look for another explanation for this device.

Gus'kov suggested the drainage device functioned as a bath for washing feet, though admitting 'this procedure is rarely used in Christian churches' (Gus'kov 2007, 119). His contention is rather widespread amongst the tourist guides currently working at the site, many of whom are Crimean Tatars accustomed to removing their shoes when entering a mosque. Hence, this supposition combines Muslim and Orthodox rites because no similar practice is known in any other Orthodox church. Gaydukov suggested two different hypotheses. One idea is that this was a device for collecting water that flowed off during ablution of the deceased (Gaydukov and Dneprovskiy 2011, 21). The second suggestion is that it was a water drainage device hidden under the floor (Gaydukov 2006, 200), though the source of the water is not specified. Further, the slope of the floor around the recess would not allow water to flow into the recess. Mogarichev contented the device was a wine press (1994, 61; 1997, 42; 2005, 110; 2010, 138–139). However, the drainage hole of the device lies just 9cm above the road.

In order to establish the real purpose of the drainage device, we should note the following. Firstly, the grooves at the base are suitable for collecting water. Secondly, being almost equal to the doorway in width, it extends into the church for 0.8 m and is then contained within the elevated area. This device would have been ideal for collecting condensed water. However, what was the source of this water? I have previously argued that a cenobitic monastery had been founded around the city gates when they were in existence (Dneprovskiy 2011, 158–159). According to Studite rule, such monasteries should possess an inner and outer gate. Three gatekeepers were to be on constant watch at the inner gate, with pilgrims praying and waiting in the church until permitted to enter the monastery (Nikitenko 2005, 270–271). The Small Cave Church at the city gate was exceptionally well suited to accommodate this purpose. Indeed, as many as three gates originally led onto the road leading to Eski-Kermen. The outer gate was situated beneath the Large Cave Church while the Small Cave Church was cut out immediately in front of the second gate. The third gate formed the main entrance into the city and was also flanked by the church. The presence of three 'couches' in the Small Church, as well as a specially equipped room for observing the road, is convincing proof of my proposal. No trace of any heating device has ever been found in the building, meaning that the constant breathing of three men in a small unheated room would inevitably create condensation. The water collecting device may have been created to cope with this inconvenience. Cold air from the door produced condensation on the ceiling nearby, with droplets falling into the drainage device. This leads us to the conclusion that the construction of the Small Cave Church involved specialists skilled in both military and civil architecture. Their knowledge exceeded these limits, because the cave church also met the requirements of Studite rule and became a necessary ritual element of the cenobitic monastery located at the south end of the plateau.

## The problem of typology

Although several attempts have been made to create a typology of Crimean rock-cut churches (Bobrovskiy 2001; Vinogradov *et al.* 2005; Gaydukov and Dneprovskiy 2011), the small number of caves is insufficient for reliable statistical processing. It may be more useful to assign a particular church to a particular type based on function, as can be applied to the cave churches around the southern gates – including the Large, the Three Horsemen and the Small churches.

Gaydukov (2006, 197–198) believed that the Crimean triconch cave churches are of the same type as the 'Kruze' basilica (Chersonesos), the church in Hermopolis, the White Monastery and the four-apse memorial church in Chersonesos. I cannot agree with him, however. The detailed typology of triconch churches was proposed by Kurtović-Folić (1997, 479–481). According to this typology, we ought to classify the examples mentioned by Gaydukov as 'complex' triconchs (Kurtović-Folić 1997, 479, fig. 2, 480, fig. 3) because all have a narthex. The Eski-Kermen churches have no narthex and, therefore, should be classified as 'independent' triconchs (Kurtović-Folić 1997, 477, fig. 1). Even within this group I have found that while the liturgical planning of the Three Horsemen and the Large Church is quite similar, the architectural and the liturgical planning of the Large and Small churches exhibit the following differences (Dneprovsky 2013b):

1. The presence of a *synthronon* in the Large Church but not in the Small Church.
2. Evidence of a bishop's throne in the Large Church but not in the Small Church.
3. Burials in the Small Church but not in the Large Church. The latter two features indicate it is very unlikely these two churches were made for the same purpose, as the presence of the bishop's seat in a 'cemetery chapel' would be unusual.
4. The different forms of the eastern walls and conchs in the apses in the Large and Small churches.
5. The slot for the altar table in the Large Church and traces of a monolithic altar table in the Small Church.
6. The rough floor surface in the apse of the Small Church, suggesting it to be secondary to the floor of the main room.
7. The *skevophylakion* to the north of the Large Church and the asymmetrical arrangement of the altar table in the apse of the Small Church, suggesting the presence of the *prothesis* table just inside the apse of the latter.
9. The almost rectangular form of the Small Church flanked by the southern compartment, and the pure triconch form of the Large Church.

Though Mogarichev (1994, 61–63) suggested that the Small and Large churches were carved into the cliff almost simultaneously (and possibly even by the same group of workmen), the distinctive features specific to each church indicates they are not of the same type. The layout of the Small Church was presumably connected to the foundation of the monastery near the city gate. As the problem of typology is closely connected to the problem of dating, it seems more likely that an attempt was made to use the Large Church as a prototype for the Small Church. However, the latter did not have a *skevophylakion* but did have the additional compartment that was used as the observation post. So, a completely different structure was created as a result of this attempt. Mogarichev also argued that the Three Horsemen Church is secondary to the Large Church (Mogarichev 1997, 51). It is my opinion, however, that the resemblance of their liturgical planning does not support this contention. Rather, it is plausible that they were carved out at the same time.

## Conclusion

The recent investigations of the so-called triconchial cave churches located at Eski-Kermen revealed many common features both in the appearance and liturgical arrangement of the Large Cave Church and Church of the Three Horsemen (general layout; presence of *skevophylakia*; niche in south wall). Their dimensions are also almost equal. In fact, the only difference between them is the form of the priests' seats – a difference easily explained by the different ranks of clergymen. The remnants of a throne in the Large Cave Church proves the presence of a bishop's residence in south-western Crimea, while analysis of the inscription and fresco in the Church of the Three Horsemen proves its memorial character and reveals some features of burial rites at the site.

From a ritual point of view, the similarity between these churches, despite their differing function, may reflect the singularities of liturgical life quite typical for that particular place and time. In this context, the presence of *skevophyilakia* near these cave churches in conjunction with their triconchial form makes them truly unique in the Crimean Peninsula. There is evidence of performing the offertory ritual (committing the *prothesis*) in a special cave outside the church. These two churches appear to date to between the tenth century and 1200. We cannot be sure, however, that the third Small Church was founded at the same time. This too is another interesting example of combining ritual and practical usage, displaying highly skilled engineering. It may indicate the presence of cenobitic monastery around the city gates. The arrangement of the Small Church was probably connected to the foundation of this monastery whose ritual life was regulated by Studite rule. The Small Church was not only the monastic observation post, but accommodated pilgrims waiting to enter the monastery. This detailed investigation of the Eski-Kermen triconchial churches, therefore, demonstrates their importance in understanding the variety of Christian cave rituals in medieval Crimea.

## *Abbreviations*

CMT: Tsentral'nyy Muzey Tavridy
IIMK: Institut Istorii Material'noy Kultury
KRU BIKZ: Krymskoye Respublikanskoe uchrezhdeniye 'Bakhchisarayskiy Istoriko-kul'turnyy zapovednik

## References

Ajbabin, A.I., 2013. Die Mittelalterliche Siedlung auf dem Plateau Ėski-Kermen. *In*: S. Albrecht, F. Daim, and M. Herdick, eds.

*Hohensiedlungen im Bergland der Krim.* Mainz: Verlag des Römish-Germanishen Zentralmuzeums, 165–232.

Aybabin, A.I., 1991. Osnovnye etapy istorii gorodishtsha Eski-Kermen. *In*: A.I. Aybabin *et al.*, eds. Materialy po arheologii, istorii i etnografii Tavrii, vyp.2. Simferopol': Tavriya, 43–51.

Babić, G., 1969. *Les chapelles annexes des èglises Byzantines.* Paris: Klinksieck.

Bert'e Delagard, A.L., 2012. Ostatki drevnih sooruzheniy v okrestnostyah Sevastopolya i peshtchernye goroda Kryma. *In*: A.L. Bert'e Delagard, *Izbrannye trudy po istorii srednevekovogo Kryma.* Simferopol': Dolya, 7–153.

Bert'e Delagard, A.L., (undated 1). *Zametki k hristianskim nadpisyam iz Kryma (V.V.Latyshev).* Manuscript. *At*: Simferopol': Nauchnye fondy Tsentral'nogo Muzeya Tavridy (CMT), arhiv A.L. Bert'e-Delagarda, k. p. 22926, d. 8641.

Bert'e Delagard, A.L., (undated 2). *Chertezhi* (hand-made technical drawing). *At*: Simferopol': Nauchnye fondy Tsentral'nogo Muzeya Tavridy, arhiv A.L. Bert'e-Delagarda, k. p. 23055, d. 8770.

Bobrovskiy, T.A., 2001. Zametki o kul'tovoy skal'noy arhitekture Yugo-Zapadnogo Kryma. *In*: Yu.M. Mogarichev and I.N. Khrapunov, eds. *Bakhchisarayskiy istoriko-arkheologicheskiy sbornik* vyp. 2. Simferopol': Tavriya-Plyus, 256–278.

Dmitrievskiy, I., 1993. *Istoricheskoe, dogmaticheskoe i tainstvennoe iz"yasnenie Bozhestvennoy Liturgii.* Moscow: Izdatel'skiy otdel Moskovskogo Patriarkhata.

Dneprovskiy, N.V. and Shkurdoda, V.A., 2010. K voprosu o pervonachal'noy liturgicheskoy planirovke trikonhial'nyh peshtchernyh tserkvey Eski-Kermena. *Lavrs'kiy al'manah.* Vipusk 23. 124–143.

Dneprovskiy, N.V., 2011. Kultovyy kompleks u yuzhnyh vorot Eski-Kermena. *Materialy po arheologii i istorii antichnogo i srednevekovogo Kryma*, vyp. 3 [online], 148–184. Available from: http://maiask.ru/data/documents/MAIASK3-2011.pdf [accessed 4 October 2017].

Dneprovskiy, N.V., 2012a. K voprosu o naznachenii eski-kermenskogo 'peshtchernogo hrama u gorodskih vorot' *In*: V.I. Kuzishtchin, ed. *Prichernomor'e. Istoriya, politika, kultura.* Vypusk 8(3). Seriya A. Antichnost' i srednevekov'e. Izbrannye materialy IX Mezhdunarodnoy nauchnoy konferentsii 'Lazarevskie chteniya'. Sevastopol': Filial MGU, 81–98 [online]. Available from: http://old.sev.msu.ru/pdf/prich/prich-a-2012.pdf [accessed 4 October 2017].

Dneprovskiy, N.V., 2012b. K voprosu o pervonachal'nom vide sintrona 'Bol'shogo peshtchernogo hrama' na pod"ezdnoy doroge Eski-Kermena. *In*: K.K. Krayniy, ed. *Materiali Desyatoy Mizhnarodnoy naukovoy konferencii 'Tserkva – nauka – suspil'stvo: pitannya vzaemodiy'.* Kiev: Natsional'nyy Kievo-Pechers'kiy istoriko-kul'turnyy zapovednik, 7–10.

Dneprovskiy, N.V., 2013a. K voprosu o kanonicheskom smysle rospisi peshtchernogo hrama 'Tryoh vsadnikov'. *Materialy po arheologii i istorii antichnogo i srednevekovogo Kryma.* Sevastopol' – Tyumen', vyp. 5 [online], 108–138. Available from: http://maiask.ru/data/documents/MAIASK5-2013.pdf [accessed 4 October 2017].

Dneprovskiy, N.V., 2013b. K voprosu o tipologii peshtchernyh tserkvey na pod"ezdnoy doroge Eski-Kermena. *In*: K.K. Krayniy, ed. *Materiali Odinadtsatoy Mizhnarodnoy naukovoy konferencii 'Tserkva – nauka – suspil'stvo: pitannya vzaemodyy'.* Kiev: Natsional'nyy Kievo-Pechers'kiy istoriko-kul'turnyy zapovednik, 9–12.

Dneprovskiy, N.V. and Choref, M.M., 2013. K voprosu o mestonahozhdenii nadpisi, obnaruzhennoy V.I. Grigorovichem v okruge Tcherkes-Kermena. *Materialy po arheologii i istorii antichnogo i srednevekovogo Kryma.* Sevastopol'–Tyumen' vyp. 5 [online], 187–194. Available from: http://maiask.ru/data/documents/MAIASK5-2013.pdf [accessed 16 September 2014].

Dneprovskiy, N.V., 2015. "Svyatye Hristovy" ili "Svyatye svideteli Hristovy"? K prochteniyu odnoy abbreviatury is nadpisi v krymskom eski-kermenskom hrame "Tryoh Vsadnikov". In: Mihaylina, L.P. et al., eds. *Mogilyan'ski chitannya 2015. Sbornyk naukovyh prats.* Kyiv: Oleg Filyuk, 38–43.

Dombrovskiy, O.I., 1966. *Freski srednevekovogo Kryma.* Kiev: Naukova dumka.

Ernst, N.L., 1929. Eski-Kermen i peshtchernye goroda Kryma. *Izvestiya Tavricheskogo obshtchestva istorii, arheologii i etnografii* 3(60), 15–43.

Eski-Kermen expedition (Eski-Kermenskaya ekspeditsiya), 1928–1929. *Chertezhi.* Hand-made technical drawings. *At*: Saint-Petersburg: Nauchnyy arhiv Instituta Istorii Material'noy Kultury, fond R-I, No 119a.

Florenskiy, P., 1995. Ikonostas. *In*: *Svyashtchennik Pavel Florenskiy. Sobranie sochineniy v chetyryoh tomah* [Priest Pavel Florenskiy. Collected Works in Four Volumes] Tom 2. Moscow: Mysl', 419–526.

Florenskiy, P., 2000. Analiz prostranstvennosti <i vremeni> v hudozhestvenno-izobrazitel'nyh proizvedeniyah. *In*: *Svyashrchennik Pavel Florenskiy. Sobranie sochineniy. Stat'i i issledovaniya po istorii i filosofii iskusstva i arheologii* [Priest Pavel Florenskiy. Collected Works in Four Volumes]. Moscow: Mysl', 81–259.

Gaydukov, N.E., 2004. Liturgicheskie datirovki nekotoryh peshtchernyh hramov Tavriki. *In*: V.L. Myts, *et al.*, eds. *O drevnostyah Yuzhnogo berega Kryma i gor Tavricheskih.* Sbornik nauchnyh trudov (po materialam konferentsii v chest' 210-letiya so dnya rozhdeniya P.I.Keppena). Kiev: Stilos, 167–174.

Gaydukov, N.E., 2006. Sakral'noe prostranstvo i liturgicheskie ustroystva v doikonoborcheskih peshtchernyh hramah Yugo-Zapadnoy Tavriki. *In*: A.M. Lidov, ed. *Ierotopiya. Sozdanie sakral'nyh prostranstv v Vizantii i Drevney Rusi.* Moscow: Indrik, 186–207.

Gaydukov, N.E., 2011. Skrytaya relikviya: stolp-relikvariy pesctchernogo hrama 'Tryoh Vsadnikov' bliz gorodishtcha Eski-Kermen. *In*: A.A. Gun'ko, *et al.*, eds. *Speleologiya i spelestologiya.* Materialy mezhdunarodnoy nauchnoy zaochnoy konferentsii. Naberezhnye Chelny: NISPTR, 170–173.

Gaydukov, N.E. and Dneprovskiy, N.V., 2011. Tipologiya i struktura kompleksov, vklyuchayushtchih peshtchernye hramy yugo-zapadnoy Tavriki *In*: A. Pelin, ed. *Peshtchernye tserkvi i monastyri Vizantii i Rusi.* Materialy mezhdunarodnoy nauchno-prakticheskoy konferentsii. Saransk, 19–22.

Gertsen, A.G. and Makhneva-Chernets, O.A., 2004. *'Peshtchernye goroda' Kryma.* Simferopol': Tavriya-Plyus.

Grigorovich, V.I., 1874. *Zapiska antikvara o poezdke ego na Kalku i Kalmius, v Korsunskuyu zemlyu i na yuzhnye poberezh'ya Dnepra i Dnestra.* Odessa.

Gus'kov, A.A., 2007. *Atlas peshtchernyh gorodov Kryma. Puteshestvie k stroitelyam i obitatelyam peshtcher.* Khar'kov: Kursor.

Kharitonov, S.V., ed., 2004. *Drevniy gorod Eski-Kermen*. Saint-Petersburg: Filologicheskiy fakul'tet Sankt-Peterburgskogo gosudarstvennogo universiteta, 123–130.

Kharitonov, S.V., 2005. *'Peshtchernye goroda' Kryma*. Saint-Petersburg: SPD Brovkin A.V.

Korhmazyan, E.M., 2008. O freske 'Tryoh vsadnikov' v Eski-Kermene. *Issledovaniya po armenistike v Ukraine* vyp. 1. Simferopol: Feniks, 44–46.

Kurtović-Folić, N., 1997. Triconch – Its origin and place in the development of architectural forms. *'Facta Universitatis'. Series: Architecture and civil engineering* 1(4), 473–482.

Latyshev, V.V., 1896. *Sbornik grecheskih nadpisey hristianskih vremyon iz Yuzhnoy Rossii*. Saint-Petersburg: Tipografiya Imperatorskoy Akademii Nauk.

Latyshev, V.V., 1897. Zametki k hristianskim nadpisyam iz Kryma (Po soobshtcheniyam A. L. Bert'e-Delagarda). *Zapiski Odesskogo Obshtchestva Istorii I Drevnostey* 20, 149–162.

Lazarev, V.N., 1953. Novyy pamyatnik stankovoy zhivopisi XII veka i obraz Georgiya-voina v vizantiyskom i drevnerusskom iskusstve. *Vizantiyskiy Vremennik* 6, 186–222.

Majeska, G.P., 1998. Notes on the skeuophylakion of St. Sophia. *Vizantiyskiy Vremennik* 55, 212–215.

Mal'gin, A.V. and Mal'gina, M.R., 1993. K voprosu ob interpretacii freski 'Hrama tryoh vsadnikov' v Eski-Kermene (po materialam fonda A.L. Bert'e-Delagarda arhiva Krymskogo respublikanskogo kraevedcheskogo muzeya). *Izvestiya Krymskogo respublikanskogo kraevedcheskogo muzeya* 2, 4–7.

Melik-Pashaev, A.A., 2007. O duhovnyh osnovaniyah hudozhestvennogo tvorchestva. *In*: A. Kopirovskiy, *et al*., eds. *Tserkovnoe iskusstvo, ego vospriyatie i prepodavanie*. Materialy Vserossiyskoy konferentsii s uchastiem zarubezhnyh spetsialistov. Moskva, 11–12 maya 2006 g. Moscow: Svyato-Filaretovskiy pravoslavno-hristianskiy institut, 106–123.

Mogarichev, Yu. M., 1994. Peshtchernye tserkvi v rayone pod'ezdnoy dorogi Eski-kermena. *In*: Yu. M. Mogarichev, ed. *Problemy istorii i arheologii Kryma*. Simferopol': Tavriya, 57–67.

Mogarichev, Ju. M., 1997. *Peshtchernyye tserkvi Tavriki*. Simferopol': Tavriya.

Mogarichev, Yu. M., 2005. *'Peshtchernye goroda' v Krymu*. Simferopol': SONAT.

Mogarichev, Yu. M., 2010. *Krym. 'Peshtchernye goroda'*. Kiev: Vishtcha shkola – XXI.

Nikitenko, M.M., 2005. Simvoliko-funktsional'naya rol' nadvratnyh hramov drevnego Kieva. *Sugdeyskiy sbornik* vyp. 2, 265–275.

Osaulenko, E.N., 2008. Zbirayuchi mozaiku znov: serednyovichni freski Krymskoy Gotii. *Collegium* 24(2008), 127–147.

Ovchinnikova, E.G., 1976. Vnov' otkrytyy pamyatnik stankovoy zhivopisi iz sobraniya Gosudarstvennogo istoricheskogo muzeya.: *Vizantiyskiy Vremennik* 37, 228–234.

Plontke-Lüning, A., 2013. Ein Jerrn vom Ėski-Kermen? Überlegungen zum 'Dreireiter-Bild' in der Felskapelle am Südwesthang des Ėski-Kermen. *In*: S. Albrecht, F. Daim, and M. Herdick, eds. *Hohensiedlungen im Bergland der Krim*. Mainz: Verlag des Römish-Germanishen Zentralmuzeums, 251–269.

Pokrovskiy, N.V., 1916. *Tserkovnaya arheologiya v svyazi s istoriey hristianskogo iskusstva*. Petrograd.

*Pravoslavnaya entsiklopediya*, 2005. Tom 10. VTOROZAKONIE – GEORGIY. Moscow: CNC 'Pravoslavnaya entsiklopediya'.

Reginskaya, N.V., 2009. *Svyatoy Georgiy Pobedonosets – geroy-zmeeborets. Obraz svyatogo Georgiya Pobedonostsa v vizantiysko-slavyanskom iskusstve*. Saint-Petersburg: Peterburg – XXI vek.

Repnikov, N.I., 1932. Eski-Kermen v svete arheologicheskih razvedok 1928–1929 gg. *Izvestiya Gosudarstvennoy Akademii Material'noy Kultury* 12(1–8), 107–152.

Repnikov, N.I., 1935. Pod'emnaya doroga Eski-Kermena. *Izvestiya Gosudarstvennoy Akademii Material'noy Kultury* vyp. 117, 18–42.

Rybakov, B.A., ed., 2003. *Arheologiya. Krym, Severo-Vostochnoe Prichernomor'e i Zakavkaz'e v epohu srednevekov'ya, 2008*. Moscow: Nauka.

Stepanenko, V.P., 2003. K ikonografii freski hrama 'Tryoh vsadnikov' pod Eski-Kermenom. *In*: A.I. Aybabin *et al*., ed. *Materialy po arheologii, istorii I etnografii Tavrii* vyp. 10. Simferopol': KOIV NAN Ukrainy, 452–457.

Strukov, D.M., 1886. *Drevnie hristianskie pamyatniki Tavridy*. Hand-made water colour drawings. *At*: Saint-Petersburg: Nauchnyy arhiv Instituta Istorii Material'noy Kultury (IIMK), fond R-I, No. 339.

Strukov, D.M., (undated). *Risunki drevnih pamyatnikov hristianstva v Tavride*. Hand-made water colour drawings. *At*: Moscow: Otdel izoproduktsii Rossiyskoy Gosudarstvennoy Biblioteki, topograficheskiy shifr 105(5), 378.

Tunkina, I.V., 2010. Arheologo-epigraficheskiye issledovanya F. K. Marshala fon Bibershteyna d vostochnom Krymu i na Kavkaze v kontse XVIII v. Po neizdannym arhivnym documentam. *In*: I.S. Kamenetskiy and A.N. Sorokin, eds. *Chelovek i drevnosti*. Moscow: Grif i K, 588–610 [online version]. Available from: http://www.ranar.spb.ru/files/visual/Tunkina_PDF/Tunkina_Formozov.pdf [accessed 12 January 2017].

Uvarov, A.S., 1851. *Sobranie kart i risunkov k issledovaniyam o drevnostyah Juzhnoy Rossii i beregov Chyornogo morya*. Saint-Petersburg.

Vaneyan, S.S., 2010. *Arhitektura i ikonografiya. 'Telo simvola' v zerkale klassicheskoy metodologii*. Moscow: Progress-Traditsiya.

Veymarn, E.V., (undated). *Kladbishtshenskaya tserkov' 'Tryokh Vsadnikov'*. Manuscript. *At*: Bakhchisaray: Nauchnyy arhiv Krymskogo Respublikanskogo uchrezhdeniya 'Bakhchisarayskiy Istoriko-kul'turnyy zapovednik (KRU BIKZ),' fond 22, opis' 1, d. 10.

Veymarn, E.V., 1958. 'Peshtchernye goroda' Kryma v svete arheologicheskih issledovaniy 1954–1955 gg. *Sovetskaya arkheologiya* 1, 71–79.

Vinogradov, A.Yu., 2004. Svod grecheskih nadpisey Eski-Kermena I ego blizhayshey okrugi. *In*: S.V. Kharitonov, ed. *Drevniy gorod Eski-Kermen*. Saint-Petersburg: Filologicheskiy fakul'tet Sankt-Peterburgskogo gosudarstvennogo universiteta, 123–130.

Vinogradov, A.Yu., Gaydukov, N.E. and Zheltov, M.S., 2005. Peshtchernye hramy Tavriki: k probleme tipologii i hronologii. *Rossiyskaya arheologiya* 1, 72–80.

Volkonskaya, I.G., 2003. Freski peshtchernyh hramov Eski-Kermena i ego okrugi (Yugo-Zapadnyy Krym). *In*: L.S. Kertanova and A.K. Krylov, eds. *Russkaya kul'tura XVI veka – epoha mitropolita Makariya. Materialy 10 Rossiyskoy nauchnoy konferentsii, posvyashtchyonnoy Pamyati Svyatitelya Makariya* vyp. 10. Mozhaysk: Terra, 284–311.

Volkonskaya, I.G., 2005. Eski-kermenskie freski. Novye issledovaniya. *In*: V.L. Myts, *et al*., eds. *Tserkovnye drevnosti. Sbornik materialov III mezhdunarodnoy konferentsii 'Tserkovnaya arheologiya: liturgicheskoe ustroystvo hramov i voprosy istorii hristianskogo bogosluzheniya'*. Simferopol': Universum, 217–239.